STRUCTURES OF REFORM

The Mercedarian Order in the Spanish Golden Age

BY

BRUCE TAYLOR

BRILL
LEIDEN · BOSTON · KÖLN
2000

For this series Cultures, Beliefs and Traditions *manuscripts and manuscript proposals are invited by the editors and publishers. Please send these to Professor Esther Cohen, Department of History, Hebrew University, Jerusalem, Israel.*

This book is printed on acid-free paper.

Library of Congress Cataloging-in-Publication Data

Taylor, Bruce.
    Structures of reform : the Mercedarian Order in the Spanish Golden
Age / by Bruce Taylor.
        p. cm. — (Cultures, beliefs, and traditions, ISSN 1382–5364 ;
    v. 12)
        Includes bibliographical references and index.
        ISBN 9004118578 (cloth : alk. paper)
        1. Mercedarians—Spain—History.   2. Monasticism and religious
orders—Spain—History.   3. Church history—Middle Ages, 600-1500.
4. Spain—Church history.   I. Title.   II. Series.
BX3800.T39   2000
271'.45046—dc21   00–029791
                                                                CIP

Die Deutsche Bibliothek - CIP-Einheitsaufnahme

Taylor, Bruce:
Structures of reform : the mercedarian order in the Spanish golden age
/ by Bruce Taylor. – Leiden ; Boston ; Köln ; Brill, 2000
    (Cultures, beliefs and traditions ; Vol. 12)
    ISBN 90–04–11857–8

                            ISSN   1382–5364
                            ISBN   90 04 11857 8

PRINTED IN THE NETHERLANDS

For

Daniel and Alice Morgan

But let my due feet never fail
To walk the studious cloister's pale,
And love the high embowèd roof,
With antique pillars' massy proof,
And storied windows richly dight,
Casting a dim religious light.

MILTON, *Il Penseroso*, ll. 155–60.

CONTENTS

ACKNOWLEDGEMENTS

My first debt is to my supervisor at Oxford, Professor Sir John Elliott, for his patience and skill in guiding the completion of the thesis upon which this book is based. The idea for the present study was his, and I join the long list of scholars who have benefited from his insight and erudition in every aspect of my research.

The work of an indigent young scholar has been supported by generous grants from Exeter College, Oxford, and from scholarships awarded by the Spanish Foreign Ministry, the Instituto de Valencia de Don Juan of Madrid, the Institute of Historical Research of London and the Institut d'Estudis Catalans in Barcelona. I must also express my gratitude to the many friends — who will doubtless prefer to remain nameless — upon whose support I have relied in this respect, and to those whose encouragement and friendship have made my years of research at Oxford and elsewhere so memorable, especially Jodi Bilinkoff, Greg D'Elia, James Harris, Andrew Hegarty, Roger Highfield, Nikolas Jaspert, Alistair Malcolm, Roger Mettam, Ian Michael, Fr John O'Malley, Robert Oresko, David Parrott, Glyn Redworth, Rosalind Smith, Eric Southworth and Nick Clapton, Colin Thompson, Tony Thompson and Ron Truman. My particular thanks to my examiners, Ron Truman and Joe Bergin, for their invaluable suggestions and encouragement. It was my pleasure to co-host many of these at the First International Cañada Blanch Conference at Manchester University in December 1996, and let me record here the great debt I owe my friends in the Department of Spanish and Portuguese there for their *primus motus* and constant support: Nigel Griffin, Jeremy Lawrance and the late Gordon Kinder. I shall always cherish my year as a Cañada Blanch Research Fellow in Manchester, and my sadness at leaving academic life is made the more poignant by the fact that time and circumstance shall deny me the inestimable pleasure of all their company.

My sojourns in Spain between 1992 and 1996 were marked by the generosity for which its people are famous. I am much obliged to Mossèn Joan Bada of the Universitat de Barcelona, to Alberto Torra of the Archivo de la Corona de Aragón, to Sra. Doña Rosario Gotor de Ros for accommodating me in her beautiful home in Barcelona, to Henry Kamen for his advice and support, and to Xavier Gil and

Ignasi Fernández Terricabras for their boundless friendship and good company. My particular thanks to Don Gregorio de Andrés and the staff of the Instituto de Valencia de Don Juan for the welcome accorded me in Madrid, and to the Casa de Velázquez for allowing me to share its marvellous facilities.

To the Mercedarian Order itself I owe an immense debt of gratitude for the hospitality extended to me in both the Aragonese and Castilian provinces, and at the *curia general* in Rome. I am particularly grateful to the commendators and religious of the convents of Barcelona, El Puig, Valencia, Madrid and El Poio where every effort was made to assist me, and to the present chronicler of the Order, P.Fr. Luis Vázquez Fernández, for his constant help and encouragement. I am aware that the contents of this book may at times seem a poor return for their generosity; I hope, however, that they can understand that I have approached the subject on its merits, and reached my conclusions only after exhaustive study of surviving evidence.

Latterly I have enjoyed the benefit of affiliation to the Center for Medieval and Renaissance Studies at UCLA, to which, along with the University Research Library, I am glad to record my thanks.

I should also like to acknowledge the Real Academia de Bellas Artes de San Fernando of Madrid and particularly His Grace The Duke of Westminster OBE TD DL for kindly permitting me to reproduce the paintings which illustrate this book. The unfailing skill and courtesy of my editors at Brill and their staff have made the completion of this volume a wholly agreeable experience.

I cannot end without expressing my gratitude to my parents for their love and sacrifice, to Cynthia and Emma for all that they have given me, and to Peter Russell for the privilege of his friendship.

Bruce Taylor
Los Angeles, California
March 2000

NOTE ON TERMS AND NAMES

In preparing the pages that follow I have been confronted with the familiar problem of rendering the names of places and individuals of diverse locations and nationalities in a consistent yet intelligible form. With toponyms I have chosen to adopt the form by which the places in question are presently known on local maps: thus Mas-Saintes-Puelles in the Département de l'Ariège rather than the Mas de las Santas Puellas traditionally favoured by Mercedarian chroniclers in Castilian; and equally, of course, Lleida rather than Lérida. Where the Kingdom of Valencia is concerned I have decided to employ Castilian as against Valencian forms since this is the style most used in the documents consulted; thus, Orihuela rather than Oriola. Otherwise I have used accepted English translations except in the few instances where this seems archaic or needlessly confusing.

As for personal names, I have generally favoured the language of the owner while (where manuscript sources are concerned) leaving surnames in their original style, albeit with the addition of accents etc. where appropriate; thus Pere Joan de Tàrrega rather than Pedro Juan de Tar-rega. The exceptions to this are the names of Castilian and French monarchs, and of course the popes, where the usual English forms are employed. However, all passages transcribed from contemporaneous sources are given in their original orthography, except for the unravelling of contractions and the occasional use of punctuation for clarity's sake. The reader will also notice that I have chosen to give the titles and dignities borne by religious in the appropriate language; thus Fray (Castilian), Fra (Catalan, Italian) and Frey (French), and similarly M° (*Maestro*) and M^e (*Maestre, Maître*), etc. The variety of forms resulting from the use of this system seemed to me balanced by the value of the information imparted as to an individual's nationality and status; the reader will decide how effective this has been. Religious of more recent time are distinguished in bibliographical references with the use of 'P.Fr.' — 'Padre Fray'/'Pare Fra', etc. All other abbreviations will be found in the list which follows, or in the footnotes or index where relevant.

Where coinage is concerned, I have followed the guidelines laid down with admirable clarity in J.H. Elliott, *The Revolt of the Catalans: A Study in the Decline of Spain (1598–1640)* (Cambridge, 1963), pp. 553–5, to which readers are referred.

ABBREVIATIONS

Archives and Sections Thereof

ACA		Archivo de la Corona de Aragón
	CA	Consejo de Aragón
	LT	Lletres Trameses
	Mon.	Monacales de Hacienda
	Mss.Misc.	Manuscritos Miscelánea
	Mss.Varia	Manuscritos Varia
	RC	Registres de Cancilleria
ACPMC		Archivo de la Curia Provincial de la Merced de Castilla
ADH		Archives Départementales de l'Hérault
ADHG		Archives Départementales de Haute-Garonne
AGN		Archivo General de Navarra
AGS		Archivo General de Simancas
	Eº	Estado
	PR	Patronato Real
AHCB		Arxiu Històric de la Ciutat de Barcelona
	CC	Consell de Cent
		CCO	Cartes Comunes Originals
		Cons.	Consellers Mss.
		LDCC	Llibre de Deliberacions del Consell de Cent
		RLC	Registre de Lletres Closes
		RO	Registre d'Ordinacions
AHN		Archivo Histórico Nacional
AMAE		Archivo del Ministerio de Asuntos Exteriores
	SS	Santa Sede
APCC		Arxiu Provincial dels Caputxins de Catalunya.
APV		Archivo Privado, Valencia
ARM		Archivo del Reino de Mallorca
	AH	Arxiu Històric
ARV		Archivo del Reino de Valencia
ASV		Archivio Segretto Vaticano
	NS	Nunziatura di Spagna
	Inst.Misc.	Instrumenta Miscellanea
ASZ		Archivo Santiago Zabálburu
AUB		Arxiu de l'Universitat de Barcelona
BL		British Library
	Add.	Additional
BNM		Biblioteca Nacional, Madrid

Bod.L   Bodleian Library
BPC   Biblioteca Pública de Cádiz
BUV   Biblioteca de la Universidad de Valencia
IVDJ   Instituto de Valencia de Don Juan

Journals and Printed Sources

BOM   *Boletín de la Orden de la Merced*
BPCONSM   *Boletín de la Provincia de Castilla de la Orden de Nuestra
             Señora de la Merced*
CDEESS   Serrano, ed., *Correspondencia Diplomática entre España y
             la Santa Sede*
CODOLN   Fernández de Navarrete *et al.*, ed., *Colección de
             Documentos Inéditos para la Historia de España*
DHEE   Aldea *et al.*, ed., *Diccionario de Historia Eclesiástica
             de España*
Dietari   *Dietari del Antich Consell Barceloní*
HIE   García Villoslada, gral. ed., *Historia de la Iglesia en España*

Religious Orders

OCarm.   Ordo Carmelitarum (Carmelites)
OCD   Ordo Carmelitarum Discalceatorum (Discalced
             Carmelites)
OCist.   Ordo Cisterciensis (Cistercians)
OFM   Ordo Fratrum Minorum (Franciscans)
OFMCap.   Ordo Fratrum Minorum Capuccinorum (Capuchins)
OM   Ordo Minimorum (Minims)
OdeM   Ordo Sanctae Mariae de Mercede (Mercedarians)
OMD   Ordo Mercedis Discalceatorum (Discalced Mercedarians)
OP   Ordo Praedicatorum (Dominicans)
OSA   Ordo Sancti Augustini (Augustinians)
OSB   Ordo Sancti Benedicti (Benedictines)
OSH   Ordo Sancti Hieronymi (Jeronymites)
OSM   Ordo Servorum Mariae (Servites)
OSST   Ordo Sanctissimae Trinitatis (Trinitarians)
SI   Societas Iesu (Jesuits)

Others

carp.	carpeta
env.	envío
facs.	facsimile
Fr	Father
Fr.	Fray, Fra, Frey
M^o/M^e	Maestro/Maestre, Maître
leg.	legajo
lib.	libro, liber
P.	Padre, Pare
P^o/P^t/P^e	Presentado/Presentat/Présenté
Rvda.M.	Reverenda Madre
suppl.	supplement
unftd.	unfoliated

INTRODUCTION

Thence to the reading of the second part, in which we shall learn of calamity and shipwreck...[1]

In 1628 the Mercedarians of Seville commissioned the artist Francisco de Zurbarán to execute some twenty-two paintings for the vast convent rebuilt by the Order on its ancient site by the Guadalquivir. This commission, and those that followed it for the convent of Nuestra Señora de la Merced, have left us some of Zurbarán's greatest paintings. In retrospect, such patronage is especially significant since it provides tangible evidence that, after many vicissitudes, the Mercedarian Order was beginning to take its place as one of the principal Spanish religious institutions, and at last escape the crisis of identity that had brought it to the verge of destruction under Philip II.

The commission required Zurbarán, under the direction of the *comendador* (superior) of Seville, to execute a cycle of paintings illustrating the life of the thirteenth-century patriarch, Pedro Nolasco. The unprecedented importance given to Nolasco was no doubt owed to his imminent beatification, an event of immense significance to the Order and one that assured its continued development. Meanwhile, 150 miles away in Trujillo, Fray Gabriel Téllez, 'Tirso de Molina', one of the supreme playwrights of the age, languished in enforced exile from Madrid, obdurately maintaining his dramatical output despite the censure of Olivares' government. Both Zurbarán's commission and Tirso himself were, to varying degrees, products of the new Order that had weathered the tempest of reform and now looked forward to an age of success and prosperity unparalleled in its history. Had the Mercedarian Order, it seems fair to ask, finally reconciled its inherent contradictions and gloriously come of age?

To this, as shall become apparent, there is no simple answer. Though Zurbarán's commission reveals the confidence of his patrons, the artist's work also illustrates the bewildering tissue of

---

[1] Tirso de Molina (pseud. of Fray Gabriel Téllez), *Historia General de la Orden de Nuestra Señora de las Mercedes*, ed. P.Fr. Manuel Penedo Rey (2 vols., Madrid, 1973–4); II, p. 7.

truth, half-truth, confusion and deliberate misconception which, then as now, characterized the Mercedarians' perception of their order in the thirteenth century. After the establishment of a new regime during the reign of Philip II, the reformist brethren consolidated a version of the history of the primitive Order that accurately reflects their view of its place in late sixteenth- and seventeenth-century Spain. The numerous paintings executed by Zurbarán for the Mercedarians in the years after 1628 illustrate this admirably, but one canvas from the Nolasco cycle — the surrender of Seville to Ferdinand III of Castile in 1248 — seems particularly instructive. Nolasco, dressed in his numinous white robes, gestures in wonderment as the vanquished Axataf offers the keys of the city to Ferdinand, while behind the king an armoured Mercedarian knight, bearing the same Aragonese royal insignia as the Patriarch, leans on a staff and gazes out towards the viewer.

Of course, this was hardly the reality of the Order in 1248. The Mercedarian *centuria primera* was neither military as implied by the presence of the knight, nor clerical as Nolasco's flowing white habit would suggest. Such images were calculated to add a martial flavour to perceptions of the early Mercedarians and appeal to the militant religiosity of the age, while the aura of sanctity surrounding Nolasco suggested the spiritual depth enjoyed by the Order since its foundation. For contemporary Mercedarians, however, this canvas would also have conveyed a deeper meaning since it insinuates the triumph of adaptation that the Order, under the influence of the crown, had experienced within the span of their own lives. Fittingly, while Nolasco is the only figure to break the tension of Zurbarán's composition, it is Ferdinand who dominates the canvas, a tribute to the royal patronage long enjoyed by the Order and upon which its growth and success continued to depend. However, Zurbarán's art still succeeds in capturing for the informed observer the central and recurring theme of Mercedarian history: the often volatile dialogue between the clerical and lay elements in its make-up. It was this conflict that lay at the heart of the reform crisis, and this which, in their different ways, Mercedarian chroniclers felt themselves obliged to reconcile in the seventeenth century.

The basis of this renewed concern for the history of the institution lay in the late sixteenth century, when a new Mercedarian hierarchy, principally of the province of Castile, set itself the task of building the Order anew in the image of Catholic-Reformation Spain. If the new perception of the early Order has virtually no basis in fact then this surely reflects the experience of Philip II's reformers who, finding little that could stand as a primordial Mercedarian observance, felt able to restructure it largely unhindered by the past. The serious lack of detailed and reliable information for the early history of the Order they encountered represents a vacuum which Mercedarians of succeeding generations have been anxious to fill. The resulting apparatus reflects not only their appraisal of the past but also their vision of the contemporary institution and its role in society.

The early seventeenth century was in consequence a period of intense activity among learned Mercedarians. As Tirso wrote in 1638 in the introduction to his history of the Order: 'I have rummaged through documents ancient and modern, have read authors and chronicles both printed and in manuscript, have searched for references to archives and deposits…'.[2] Despite this claim, for all periods save his own Tirso's work smacks more of enlightened critique of other chroniclers' efforts than the result of years of patient research. Even so, it remains a testament to his genius, for in his *Historia* Tirso, alone among the Castilian chroniclers, looked back with nostalgia and not a little regret to an order that had changed greatly during the previous two or three generations — the old Order still perceptible at the time of his profession at Guadalajara in 1601. This awareness of profound change coloured Tirso's chronicle of the years around the turn of the seventeenth century that form the heart of this study. With some resignation he informs his readers that there is nothing which, once enfeebled, 'does not suffer the rigour of change, no matter what it be'.[3] But, for all the acuteness of his sense-impressions and the brilliance of his writing, Tirso fails to explain satisfactorily the causes of that change, the origin of those conflicts which make the Spanish Golden Age the great watershed in the history of the Mercedarian Order, as of the religious life generally.

---

[2] *Ibid.*, I, p. 1.
[3] *Ibid.*, II, p. 3.

Francisco de Zurbarán, *The Surrender of Seville* (1634).
By kind permission of His Grace The Duke of Westminster OBE TD DL.

CHAPTER ONE

CHANGE AND CONTINUITY:
THE ORDER FROM ITS ORIGINS TO 1467

Tell me, where is there a common rule of life so powerful as to bind
men together in unity and subjection to a primordial perfection [...]
not for months or years, but for centuries in one and the same being?[1]

I. *Reform and History*

In 1588 there appeared two works of surpassing importance to the
Mercedarian historiographical tradition and to the self-perception of
the Order.[2] In these historical *opuscula*, the author, Fray Francisco
Zumel, provincial of Castile, set out an interpretative framework for
the origins of the Order that, in many of its most salient details, has
yet to be questioned by Mercedarian scholarship. Although Zumel's
work was by no means completely original — he relies heavily on the
Speculum fratrum of the fifteenth-century Catalan general, Fra Nadal
Gaver — the circumstances and manner of its presentation were
wholly new and challenging.[3]

---

[1] Tirso, *Historia*, II, pp. 4–5.

[2] M° Fray Francisco Zumel, *De initio ac fundatione sacri Ordinis Beatae Mariae de Mercede Redemptionis Captivorum*, and *De Vitis Patrum et Magistrorum Generalium Ordinis Redemptorum Beatae Mariae de Mercede, Brevis Historia* (both Salamanca: Cornelius Bonardus, 1588, 4°). Both were first published along with the reform constitutions of 1588 (see *infra*, n. 4) and both drew on Gaver's *Speculum fratrum* (see ch. 2, n. 19). Another work reflecting the new interest in Nolasco and the 13th century is that of the Valencian reformer M° Fray Felipe de Guimerán, *Breve historia de la orden de nuestra Señora de la Merced de redempcion de cautivos* (Valencia: Herederos de Juan Navarro, 1591, 4°). The only general introduction to the history of the Order written in modern times is P.Fr. Guillermo Vázquez Núñez, *Manual de historia de la Orden de Nuestra Señora de la Merced* (2 vols., Toledo, 1931, & Madrid, 1936; vol. II fragmentary), complemented by the same author's *Mercedarios ilustres* [collected essays], ed. P.Fr. Ricardo Sanlés Martínez (Madrid, 1966), with useful appendices. Despite its shortcomings, P.Fr. Gumersindo Placer López, *Bibliografía mercedaria* (3 vols., Madrid, 1968–83) is an essential complement to the study of the Order.

[3] Zumel also drew on the other Mercedarian text of the 15th century, the *Opusculum tantum quinque* of the Aragonese Fray Pedro de Cijar (or Citjar, Sitjar); see ch. 2, n. 15. Selections from these and other texts are collected in P.Fr. Guillermo Vázquez Núñez, ed., *Monumenta ad historiam Ordinis de Mercede Reverendissimi Patris Natalis Gaver* (Toledo, 1928).

The fact that the *opuscula* were included, among other works, in the *editio princeps* of the Mercedarian reform constitutions compiled by Zumel himself is no mere coincidence.[4] This corpus of legislation, religious observance and history was the principal instrument of the new regime that emerged triumphant from the reform period of the late sixteenth century. It embodies not only a thorough restructuring of the institution, but also a conscious reappraisal of the Mercedarian past, at once reflecting and complementing the aspirations of the new Order that Zumel and his reforming generation had undertaken to rebuild.

One of the effects of the reform process to which the Order was submitted under Philip II (1556–98) was that it set into relief the serious deficiencies of an institution which had failed to meet the political and religious standards of late sixteenth-century Spain. Beyond the obvious problems of discipline and organization, Zumel and his companions evidently recognized that the heart of the Mercedarian crisis lay elsewhere, in the related questions of history and spirituality which had been so rudely exposed by the reform process. In particular, it had become obvious to the reformers that the Order had all but lost touch with its first century and with the observance of the patriarch Pere Nolasch — Pedro Nolasco — a figure about whom very little was and, indeed, is known for certain. Full realization of this appears to have come at a critical moment in the 1570s when royal reformers discovered the Order to have no satisfactory 'observance', either legislative or spiritual, to offer its religious in their hour of need.

Though commonly held to be the primordial legislation, the so-called Albertine constitutions of 1327 that governed the Order until 1574 were tainted by regional particularism and debased by being neither the work of Nolasch nor of his time. Meanwhile, the Marian devotion that had sustained the congregation for more than 300 years was no longer quite enough, and the spiritual apparatus of the Order, not to say the religious priorities of the age, demanded the individuality afforded by a canonized patriarch. Circumstances in the late sixteenth century were to convince the new Mercedarian hierarchy that, along with constitutional reform, the Order would have to develop a distinctive spirituality centred around Christ, the Virgin and Nolasch

---

[4] *Regula et Constitutiones Fratrum Sacri Ordinis Beatae Mariae de Mercede Redemptionis Captivorum* (Salamanca: Cornelius Bonardus, 1588, 4°).

himself, and set this into a proper historical context. Equally, the reformers were fully aware of the political realities of contemporary Spain that had awoken the Order from its slumber, and were eager to underline the royal patronage apparently enjoyed by Mercedarians since the earliest times. Only with this apparatus might the Order take its rightful place in the constellation of Spanish religious life and fulfil the true destiny for which they believed Nolasch had founded it.

Since the spiritual reform of the Mercedarian Order was informed by a recognition of the inherent problems thrown up by its disciplinary reform in the late sixteenth century, these are only different stages of the same general movement for change. In implying a partial suppression of the active lives traditionally enjoyed by many religious in favour of a more contemplative existence, the elaboration of a new Mercedarian iconography was therefore a correlative of this disciplinary reform. Not for the first time the thrust of Mercedarian reform was to be clericalizing, and the onus lay on the reformers of Zumel's generation, both legislatively and spiritually, to force a reconciliation between the conflicting lay and clerical elements in the Order's make-up — a task made no easier by the lay character of the *centuria primera* upon which Mercedarians had begun to fix their attention. In attempting this reconciliation the reformers had also to face a series of related spiritual and constitutional problems that drew them back to the anonymity and strife which characterizes the early history of the Order.

These questions must be addressed in due course, but it is important at this stage to emphasize that out of these inherent contradictions the reformers forged a new Order. They were not successful in all the fields of their activity, but, galvanized by the threat of suppression and a pervasive atmosphere of crisis, the reformers were obliged to confront many of the fundamental conflicts of Mercedarian life and in so doing provided the basis for the comparative unity and stability that would flower in the seventeenth century. In retrospect, Mercedarian Reform proved to be rather more than the movement for discipline and reorganization envisaged by its earliest champions, momentous as this was. In the context of the religious and political climate of the age, the full implications of reform went much deeper. On a conceptual level reform implied not only a crisis of history and spirituality, but also a crisis of identity. The diversity of interpretation to which reform lends itself — practical and spiritual, religious, social and political — is therefore manifest, and it is this that this study will be aiming to explore.

II. *The Vision of the Past*

By the mid sixteenth century, the unreformed Mercedarians appear
to have developed a curiously ambiguous view of the foundation of
their Order, the disjointed product of a disjointed history. It seems
that by the end of the fourteenth century the foundation legend set
down by Gaver in 1445 and later institutionalized, with suitable
embellishments, by Zumel in his *opuscula* had become established.
Tradition held that, on the night of 2nd August 1218, Pere Nolasch
experienced in Barcelona a revelation of the Virgin — Our Lady of
Mercy — instructing him to reconstitute the brotherhood for the ransom of Christian captives he had founded into an order of redemption with the assistence of the Aragonese crown. Nolasch immediately
made his way to the royal palace where he set his plans for the new
order before the youthful Jaume I and the king's Dominican confessor Ramon de Penyafort (Raymond of Pennafort), to both of whom
the Virgin had also appeared.[5] His proposals were favourably
received, and accordingly on 10th August the foundation ceremony
took place in the choir of Barcelona cathedral. In the presence of
Jaume, Penyafort, Bishop Berenguer de Palou and a great throng of
people, the Virgin was said to have descended and conferred upon
Nolasch and his companions the white habit of the Order.[6]

However, while Mercedarians in the 1560s, the eve of reform,
might have considered the thirteenth century to be the spiritual wellspring of the Order, it was the fourteenth that provided the origin of

---

[5] It should be noted that Jaume I (1208–76) was only ten years old in 1218 and
that the Catalan Ramon de Penyafort (*c*.1180–1275) did not join the Dominican
Order (of which he later became prior general) until 1221. There is no reliable evidence that Penyafort ever had anything to do with the Mercedarians.

[6] Recent Mercedarian historians have limited themselves to discussing aspects of
this narration of events rather than questioning its historical feasibility. The basic
introduction to the Order in the 13th century and the standard Mercedarian line on
the foundation remains P.Fr. Faustino D. Gazulla's unfinished *La Orden de Nuestra Señora de la Merced: Estudios historicocríticos (1218–1317)* (vol. I Barcelona, 1934; vols. I & II
collected and amended by P.Fr. Juan Devesa Blanco, Valencia, 1985). References to
this work are taken from the latter edition. Gazulla's untimely death in 1938 prevented him completing a work originally planned in three volumes. The third volume
would presumably have treated the period after the death of the Patriarch in *c*.1245.
The lacuna is partly covered in P.Fr. Joaquín Millán Rubio, 'Fray Pedro de Amer,
Maestre de la Merced (1271–1301): Treinta años de historia mercedaria' in *Estudios*,
29 (1973), pp. 3–63. For the latest statement on the 13th century by a Mercedarian,
see P.Fr. Juan Devesa Blanco, 'Los orígenes de la Orden de Nuestra Señora de la
Merced' in *Analecta Mercedaria*, 7 (1988), pp. 37–52, a highly tendentious article.

its existing structure, legislation and government, and particularly government from Barcelona. Throughout the reform period of the late sixteenth century the constitutions promulgated in 1327 continued to be referred to in official documents, quite erroneously, as the primordial legislation of the Order. The fact that this was patently known not to be the case is an indication, among other things, of the inscrutable quality of the *centuria primera* to contemporary Mercedarians, a period with which the Order seemed to retain little obvious connection. It fell to the reformers of Zumel's generation to employ every means at their disposal to tie the loose ends of Mercedarian history — lay and clerical, spiritual and constitutional — and square them with contemporary political and religious requirements. Luckily for them, it was a challenge they had both the resources and the will to confront.

By forcing the Order's conceptual horizons back to the early thirteenth century and reestablishing Nolasch as the patriarch, Zumel sought to emphasize that it was here and not in the fourteenth that the origins of the institution lay. In so doing, the new regime succeeded in shifting the historical focus away from the early fourteenth century when, in establishing the Mercedarian *ancien régime* at Barcelona, another band of reformers had consigned the *centuria primera* to virtual oblivion. However, it seems that any important documentation recovered by Zumel and his successors from the vacuum of the thirteenth century they either chose mostly to ignore or found more confusing than enlightening. Instead, working along lines already suggested by Gaver, Zumel and the chroniclers who followed him succeeded in moulding fact, tradition and aspiration into the extraordinary amalgam that is the Mercedarian thirteenth century. By the end of the seventeenth century, the Mercedarians had consolidated a foundation legend that married the divine, royal and military elements considered essential to the Order's make-up. The powers supposedly involved in the foundation of the Mercedarians — the Virgin, Jaume I and Nolasch himself — could be matched by few other institutions, and a new-found pride in the origins of the Order is expressed in the motto that emerges at this time — *Coelestis, Regalis, Militaris*.

The result is not only a testament to the perceptions and aspirations of Mercedarians from the late sixteenth century onwards with regard to their Order, both for its past and its present, but is also an indication of the historical and spiritual apparatus deemed essential for a contemporary religious institution. It was from this new iconographical reservoir, still growing in the 1620s, that Zurbarán drew in order to execute the various commissions entrusted him by the convent of Seville. Even if Zumel's sources for the life of the founder belong mostly to the fifteenth century at the earliest, it is to his generation — and the genre of the *crónica de la orden* whose great age this is — that we owe the expansion of the thirteenth century in the Mercedarian imagination and the achievement of Nolasch's elevation from cult-figure to saint in only forty years. He was beatified in 1628, in time to take his place in Bernini's great scheme for St Peter's Square in Rome.

To this historical and iconographical framework seventeenth-century Mercedarians added the spirituality that remains crucial to the Order to this day, and to which Tirso de Molina was a contributor both in his *autos sacramentales* and in his *Historia*. By the end of the century the Mercedarians had completed their transformation by becoming an officially mendicant order in 1690; the work of 'reclericalization' and of creating a Mercedarian 'observance' renewed in the late sixteenth century was now complete. However, the Mercedarian Order, whose inherent conflicts came to a head in the religious and political climate of Philip II's Spain, had a rather different origin and progress to that suggested in the work of Zumel and his successors. The Order that confronted its reformers in the 1560s retained, in the Crown of Aragon especially, all the aspects of a medieval institution — in structure, character and in outlook — despite the developments that had taken place within it in Castile. The survival of such characteristics owes much to the immutable nature of the redemption of captives, a highly specialized activity that Mercedarians continued to organize and conduct during and after the sixteenth century much as they had always done. Although the reformers may not have been fully aware of it, the conflicts and contradictions that rent the Order in their time were, like the redemption itself, of medieval origin.

III. *The Origins of the Mercedarian Order*

The Mercedarian Order grew out of the social and spiritual condition of the Crown of Aragon in the early thirteenth century.[7] In par-

---

[7] See James William Brodman, *Ransoming Captives in Crusader Spain: The Order of Merced on the Christian-Islamic Frontier* (Philadelphia, 1986; Catalan trans. Barcelona,

ticular, it was a product of the frontier society of the later *Reconquista* and the expansion of charitable activity from the twelfth century onwards. In undertaking the ransom of poor captives — the *pauperes Christi* — from Muslim bondage, Mercedarians were not only fulfilling a Christian obligation to assist the needy, but reflecting the charitable outlook of a society that now ascribed religious value to the mitigation of human suffering and equated poverty with sanctity. It was this awareness of social necessity that began to endow the mercantile origins of the redemption of captives with the quality of a religious vocation, and which provided the basis for the creation of fraternal organizations for their assistance.[8] During the twelfth century organized redemptionism, usually under episcopal auspices, had begun to institutionalize and regularize what had hitherto been a private endeavour. Outstripped by demand, diocesan redemptionism was gradually replaced by a number of new orders and confraternities that increasingly attracted the patronage of the crown. It was on these that Nolasch modelled his own institution.

The success of Nolasch's primitive brotherhood lay not only in its appeal to popular sentiment and the demand for its work, but in the powerful religious context for the redemption of captives that made this something more than a charitable initiative.[9] Behind the gradual transformation of a confraternity such as the early Mercedarians into an organized religious movement lay the recognition of this charism by the crown and the hierarchical Church, and a desire to harness its virtuous creative energy. For the crown the prospect of ransoming services offered by a new Aragonese religious institution no doubt proved attractive, especially given the demise of the military Order of Monjuich (Mountjoy), which had amalgamated with the ransom hospital of the Santo Redentor in Teruel in 1188 and was subsumed into

---

1990), to which I am glad to record my debt. An acute review article is Josep M. Salrach, 'Els orígens de l'Orde de la Mercè i el rescat de captius: Les Croades i l'exercici de la caritat a l'edat mitjana' in *Acta Medievalia*, 9 (1988), pp. 89–101. See also Fr Robert Ignatius Burns, *The Crusader Kingdom of Valencia: Reconstruction on a Thirteenth-Century Frontier* (2 vols., Cambridge, Mass., 1967); I, pp. 247–52, & Yves Dossat, 'Les Ordres de rachat, Les Mercédaires' in *Assistance et charité* [*Cahiers de Fanjeaux*, vol. XIII) (Toulouse, 1978), pp. 365–87.

[8] An alternative view of the coalescence of ransomers into confraternities is provided in Annie Cazenave, 'Les Origines catalanes de l'Ordre de la Merci pour la rédemption des captifs' in *Actes du 97ᵉ Congrès National des Sociétés Savantes (Section de philologie et d'histoire jusqu'a 1610; Nantes, 1972)* (Paris, 1979), pp. 277–86. This article is, however, factually wrong in a number of important respects.

[9] Brodman, *Ransoming Captives*, pp. 10–14.

the Order of the Temple eight years later. However, if the impulse behind the redemption of captives was charitable, then the scenario for this activity was war. The expansion of the Mercedarians is closely related to the conquering progress of Jaume I during his long reign (1213–76) and it is to this pattern of life — both urban and rural — that much of the surviving documentation of the thirteenth-century Order relates.

Stripped of legend, the circumstances surrounding the foundation of the Mercedarians and the origins of the Patriarch remain shrouded in an obscurity that centuries of Mercedarian scholarship have been unable to illuminate satisfactorily.[10] It seems likely that the new clerical regime which came to power in 1317 devoted much time and effort to suppressing all traces of the Patriarch and his primordial lay brotherhood, such of it as survived. In this they appear to have been very successful, and by the late fourteenth century the Order felt able to produce a number of forged foundation charters dated to 1218 — an attempt, perhaps, at associating the Mercedarians with the great mendicant orders of the age. This not only provides evidence for the elaboration of the new foundation story later set down by Gaver in 1445, but also reflects the oblivion into which the true origins of the Order had by now fallen.[11] The significance of this loss to future generations of the Order, and particularly that of the late sixteenth century, need hardly be mentioned. Although, as Brodman informs us, some 600 genuine charters survive from the Mercedarian *centuria primera*, these give up little information on the origins and nature of the early foundation, which remains as much the subject of conjecture now as in Zumel's day.[12]

Neither the tradition of a foundation in 1218 nor the supposed donation by Jaume I of the Hospital of Santa Eulàlia in that year has any genuine documentation to support it. The first reliable information we have of the Patriarch and his brotherhood is a bequest granted to Nolasch as 'trader for captives' in Mallorca in 1230.[13] To Brodman the absence of trustworthy documentation before this date sug-

---

    [10] *Ibid.*, pp. 15–16.
    [11] What may be the earliest surviving version of this story comes in a letter from Pere IV to Innocent VI in 1358, reproduced in Regina Sáinz de la Maza Lasoli, 'Los Mercedarios en la Corona de Aragón durante la segunda mitad del siglo XIV' in *Miscel.lània de textos medievals*, 4 (1988), pp. 221–99; 259–60.
    [12] Brodman, *Ransoming Captives*, x.
    [13] *Ibid.*, p. 15.

gests that the origins of the Order in fact lie in the late 1220s, and that its establishment is directly related to the military policy pursued by Jaume from this time on.[14] Nolasch's reputed presence on the expedition that captured Mallorca in 1229 would appear to set a pattern for his activity in later years; he seems to have made an impression here, and the Order became established in the aftermath of this conquest and those that followed it in both Aragon and Castile. It was therefore in war that Nolasch secured for the brotherhood some of its principal foundations.

On Nolasch himself and his companions there is virtually no reliable information. Tradition holds that Brother Pere Nolasch was born at Mas-Saintes-Puelles in the county of Toulouse, a Provençal like Jean de Mathe, the founder of the rival Trinitarians.[15] But, unlike Mathe, who established his order near Paris in 1196, Nolasch seems never to have abandoned the Mediterranean. His native region, if so it was, enjoyed close cultural, political, economic and linguistic ties with Catalonia, and it was to this mercantile and frontier society that he was drawn. Nolasch's supposed Occitan origins are backed up by early foundations at Perpignan and Narbonne and he may well have been a hospitaller in this region before moving to Barcelona as a redemptionist in the late 1220s.[16] Although traditionally put at 1180, Nolasch's date of birth is unknown, and that of his passing is also debated; Gaver gives 1249, but 1245 has recently been suggested.[17] Again, there is room only for conjecture, a reflection not only of the depredations of fourteenth-century reformers, but of the haphazard nature of an institution that remained strongly identified with the persona of the founder during his lifetime.

The first Mercedarian house for which we have reliable records was founded in Barcelona on a seafront site donated in 1232 by

---

[14] *Ibid.*, pp. 16 & 18, and summarized in *id.*, 'The Origins of the Mercedarian Order: A Reassessment' in *Studia Monastica*, 19 (1977), pp. 353–60.

[15] Unconvincingly challenged in Devesa Blanco, 'Los orígenes de la Orden de Nuestra Señora de la Merced', pp. 39–41, who maintains that Nolasch was born near Barcelona.

[16] Brodman, *Ransoming Captives*, p. 20. The house at Narbonne seems to have been founded by 1232 and that at Perpignan, established by 1235, appears to date from as early as 1227; see Carole Puig, 'La Merci de Perpignan et le rachat des captifs chrétiens au XIIIe siècle' in *Études roussillonnaises*, 14 (1995–6), pp. 31–8, esp. 32.

[17] See P.Fr. Juan Devesa Blanco, 'La verdadera fecha de la muerte de San Pedro Nolasco' in *Analecta Mercedaria*, 4 (1985), pp. 5–72, and Brodman, *Ransoming Captives*, p. 23.

Ramon de Plegamans — the commander of Jaume's fleet on the Mallorca expedition.[18] By 1234 a 'Hospital of Captives' dedicated to Santa Eulàlia, the patroness of the city, had been built here and was operating as an alms-house and hospice for freed captives with Nolasch as its commendator. Two more houses were established at this time in Palma de Mallorca (by 1232) and Girona (by 1234), with perhaps a third at Narbonne in Languedoc.[19] Over this tiny grouping dedicated, it seems, as much to the collection of alms and care of ransomed captives as to redemption itself, Nolasch now presided as *maioral* and *rector*, the first indication that he was beginning to draw on the usage of the military orders. These activities are reflected in the first names borne by the brotherhood — *elemosinarum captivorum* — 'the alms of captives', and later *Ordo Captivorum* — 'the Order of Captives'.[20]

The success of Nolasch's lay confraternity is confirmed by the appearance on 17th January 1235 of a bull — the short *Devotionis vestrae* of Gregory IX — recognizing its existence and conferring the Rule of St Augustine upon it.[21] Whether this was a natural development for Nolasch or the result of pressure on him to bring his institution formally into the fold of the Church remains unclear. Already in the early 1230s the amorphous lay brotherhood had begun to take on an institutional character, but even so no primitive constitutions have emerged either from this formative period or from later in the life of the Patriarch — an absence of great significance to the later Order. While the bull provides no indication of the existence of any primordial legislation, it does furnish the first official title of the brotherhood, derived from the mother house — 'The Brothers of the House of Santa Eulàlia of Barcelona' — and with this the formative phase of

---

[18] Brodman, *Ransoming Captives*, pp. 16 & 18.

[19] *Ibid.*, pp. 17 & 19. For brief historical *résumés* of the houses of the Order, see P.Fr. Guillermo Vázquez Núñez, *Breve reseña de los conventos de la Orden de la Merced* (Rome, 1932), serialized as 'Conventos de la Orden de la Merced' in *BOM*, 20 (1932), & 21 (1933). For notices of three hitherto unknown French houses of the 13th and 14th centuries — Le Vernet (1238), Milhau (?) and Fanjeaux (1324) — see Cazenave, 'Les Origines catalanes de l'Ordre de la Merci', pp. 285–6. Richard W. Emery, *The Friars in Medieval France: A Catalogue of French Mendicant Convents, 1200–1550* (New York, 1962), *passim*, lists only nine of the eighteen Mercedarian houses established in medieval France, though the author has fixed the foundation dates of some of these through archival research.

[20] For the development of the names of the Order, see Gazulla, *La Orden*, I, pp. 128–39.

[21] Brodman, *Ransoming Captives*, pp. 16–17.

Nolasch's association appears to be over.[22] The word *ordo* is frequently used to describe it from now on, but the brotherhood was emphatically lay in character, a condition enshrined in its first constitutions of 1272 and which would only begin to give way as the century drew to a close.

However, by the late 1230s the caritative ends to which the alms collected by the brethren were put — the ransom of captives — had led to a recognition of their disinterested service — *merced* — for others and in 1238 we find the first expression of this notion in the title of the Order — *Ordinis Mercedis Captivorum* — 'Order for/of the Service/Ransom of Captives'. This was not the first time that *merced* had been used in connection with the ransom of captives; by 1200 it was usual to describe this activity as a work of *merced* or *misericordia*, and those hospitals of the Order of Santiago whose rents were employed for ransoming purposes were already known as *casas de la merced*. However, in imbuing the concept of *merced* with a religious significance the brethren were crossing hitherto untrodden ground and, influenced perhaps by a desire for greater individuality, it is apparent that by the late 1240s *Nostra Senyora de la Mercè* — Our Lady of Mercy — had become established as the second patroness of the Order.

With a deeper appreciation of the Mercedarian *métier* and divine patronage came a commensurate spiritual development. To a sense of the physical *mercè/merced* (service) of ransom offered by the brethren, a spiritual dimension of *misericordia* (mercy or compassion) was added by association with Mary.[23] Upon these foundations the powerful Marian spirituality of the Order would develop, especially in the Crown of Aragon, and by the end of the century the Mercedarians had three shrines of varying importance dedicated to the Virgin at El Olivar (near Teruel), El Puig (near Valencia) and at Barcelona where construction began in 1249 on a church sited by the convent of Santa Eulàlia which became associated with Our Lady of Mercy in the 1270s.[24] The institution began to adopt the title of *Ordo*

---

[22] *Ibid.*, p. 17.

[23] By the 16th century both Catalan and Castilian had ceased to differentiate between the medieval *mercè/merced* and *misericordia*, in favour of the latter interpretation.

[24] For a history of the cult of Our Lady of Mercy in Barcelona, see P.Fr. Faustino D. Gazulla, *La Patrona de Barcelona y su santuario* (Barcelona, 1918). The Virgen de la Merced became patroness of the city in 1687 and her feast, 24th September, was placed on the Latin calendar in 1696.

Sancte Mariae Mercedis Captivorum in the 1240s, but even so it would be some time before the Virgin displaced Eulàlia completely in the hagiolatry of the Order. In the preamble to the 1272 constitutions, Fra Pere d'Amer referred in Limousin to an *ordo apellat de la Verge Maria de la Mercè de la Redempció dels catius de Sancta Eulàlia de Barchinona*, a curiously ambiguous title that reflects the spiritual condition of the contemporary Order. Indeed, there can be no doubt that Mercedarian spirituality remained in a state of becoming until at least the mid fourteenth century. Although the notion of 'redemption' had been foreshadowed before 1300, only thereafter did it begin to enter the religious framework of the Order. The sense that, in being ransomed from captivity, prisoners and brethren were partaking of an experience that was mutually redemptive for the first time added a christocentric element to a predominantly Marian institution. By the 1380s the name that the Order would be known by thereafter had become established: *Ordo Sancte Mariae Mercedis Redemptionis Captivorum* — Order of Our Lady of Mercy for the Redemption of Captives. It was for later generations to unite in the persona of the founder the compassion of the Virgin and the redemptive quality of Christ.

IV. *Growth and Development, 1235–72*

With Nolasch styling himself *minister*, after 1235 the Order entered a period of sustained expansion. Following Jaume into the Kingdom of Valencia, Nolasch began establishing convents and hospices for ransomed captives on the expanding frontier. Sarrión, on the Catalan-Valencian border, was the first of these in 1235, followed by Valencia in 1238, Tortosa in 1239 and the important shrine of El Puig in 1240. El Puig, lying before Valencia, had been the site in 1237 of an important battle after which, so legend has it, a Byzantine bas-relief of the Virgin and Child dating from Visigothic times was miraculously discovered buried under a bell — an incident recorded by Zurbarán in another painting from the Seville commission. The convent established on the site of this discovery was the first royal foundation of the Order and would continue to enjoy the patronage of the crown in the centuries to come. La Verge del Puig was made patroness of the Kingdom by Jaume I and remains in the custody of the Order in what has been one of its principal foundations. At the time of Nolasch's death in about 1245 the Order had expanded throughout the Crown of Aragon, with some sixteen foundations and a growing reputation for the ransoming activity that had dictated the nature and location of many of these.[25] The lay dominance of the primordial Order is reflected in the fact that of these houses only four had churches, none of which appear to have been staffed by permanent clergy.

In the generation following Nolasch's death (1245–71), the Order spread into the Kingdom of Castile and continued its rapid expansion in the Crown of Aragon and the Occitan, numbering over thirty houses in 1270.[26] Though the Mercedarians benefited from Ferdinand III's conquests in Andalusia with important foundations at Seville (1253) and Córdoba (by 1263), the brethren were late into the field in Castile proper. Here the Trinitarians and the Order of Santiago were already established as redemptionists and by 1263 the holdings of the Order north of the Guadiana amounted only to a little property in Cuenca. Another generation would pass before houses began to appear in Castile in numbers, and even then more as outposts for the collection of alms than as fully-fledged communities. Although outwardly dynamic, the years after the death of the Patriarch were nevertheless a period of internal upheaval, marked by scandal, nepotism and a succession of masters. The situation was restored under Pere d'Amer (1271–1301) by which time a clear administrative structure becomes discernible. In particular, the Order began enjoying the especial patronage of the Aragonese crown which, by the late fourteenth century, had developed into a relationship of great significance to later generations.[27]

Even so, it would be a mistake to expect the Brothers of Ransom to have benefited from the same degree of patronage as the great monastic and mendicant orders, and there is no indication that, beyond the usual *repartiment* or land distribution, Jaume I lavished any special favours on the Order during the conquest of the Kingdom of Valencia. The royal foundation of El Puig in 1240 was followed by another at Segorbe in 1248 — little enough for a monarch who, as it turned out, would not even remember the Order in his will.[28] How-

---

[25] Brodman, *Ransoming Captives*, pp. 18–23.

[26] *Ibid.*, pp. 27–31.

[27] See *id.*, 'The Mercedarian Order: The Problem of Royal Patronage during the Reign of James I' in *Jaime I y su época, X Congreso de Historia de la Corona de Aragón* (5 vols. in 2 tomes, Zaragoza, 1982), II, pp. 71–6.

ever, it was for their services as redemptors rather than as land man-
agers that the Brothers were chiefly known and equipped, and in this
domain Jaume rewarded them handsomely. By the early 1250s these
services on the frontier had begun to receive the recognition of a
crown eager for Christian settlement. In 1251 Jaume conferred upon
the Order its first and most important royal privilege — the *guidaticum*
or safe-conduct.[29] This amounted to a pledge of protection over the
property and personnel of the Order which was thereby made
exempt from custom tariffs — both on redeemed captives and on the
ransom itself. In token of this *guidaticum* the brethren were permitted
to wear the royal arms of Aragon under the white cross of Santa
Eulàlia, an insignia borne by the Order ever since.

   This was followed in 1255 by the extension to the Mercedarians of
a royal privilege giving all subjects the right to sell or donate a wide
variety of property to the religious orders. Finally, in a donation that
same year, the king referred to himself as the patron and founder of
the Order, a status confirmed by Jaume II (1291–1327) early the following century and which may well have added to the eclipse of
Nolasch at that time. This mantle of direct royal patronage enjoyed
by the Mercedarians from the thirteenth century onwards is a distinguishing feature of the Order, an honour shared only by the
Jeronymites among the religious congregations of the Peninsula. It
seems that, after a generation, the king had finally recognized in the
Order a homegrown institution whose principal vocation — the collection of alms for the ransom of captives — could be of service to the
crown. In Castile, meanwhile, the 'Orden de Santa Olalla de
Barcelona' was granted rights of alms collection by Sancho IV
(1285–95) in 1289, on the understanding that one third of all monies
gathered be devoted to the redemption of captives.[30]

V. *The First Mercedarian Observance*

By the time Pere d'Amer succeeded to the mastership in 1271 the
Order had adopted a recognizable system of government and organization. This system was consolidated in the statutes, composed of

---

[28] *Id., Ransoming Captives*, pp. 22–3 & 29–30.
[29] *Ibid.*, pp. 32–3.
[30] *Ibid.*, p. 34.

forty-nine chapters written in Limousin, that Amer promulgated at the chapter general of Barcelona in May 1272. The Amer constitutions represent both the first extant legislation of the Order and its own codification of the standard Augustinian Rule. As the master declared in the first article:

> We have visited all the houses in our order and have seen and collected the constitutions made by our predecessors and masters. Some we have completely abandoned; others we have amended; and others we have remade for the honour of God and of the Virgin Mary.[31]

Although these would be swept away in 1327, a number of the lay features enshrined in them, both of character and organization, would survive in a recognizable form into the sixteenth century. The Amer constitutions drew a range of features from the legislation and practice of the Orders of Santiago, the Hospital and the Temple that, from the late sixteenth century in particular, would allow Mercedarian chroniclers to depict the primeval Order as military.[32] Given the relative continuance of many important aspects of primordial Mercedarian life, it seems worthwhile now to attempt a description of the structure and observance of the medieval Order as it was beginning to take shape — the Order to which Zumel and his generation looked back at the end of the sixteenth century.

Rather than a military order, what the Amer constitutions actually reveal is a lay brotherhood reacting to a period of expansion and upheaval, and determined to correct past deficiencies with a careful winnowing of earlier legislation.[33] Its principal aims were to provide

---

[31] The earliest surviving MS is that in Gaver's *Speculum fratrum* of 1445. Apart from the possibility of their having appeared in an incunable of the *Speculum fratrum*, the 'Constitucions dels Pares antichs del Orde de la Verge Maria de la Mercé' were first published in *Recull de textes catalanes antichs*, vol. VI (Barcelona, 1907), ed. 'J.M.F.'. For critical editions, see P.Fr. Ramón Serratosa Queralt, 'Las constituciones primitivas de la Merced comparadas con la legislación militar religiosa: Estudio crítico, histórico y canónico' in *Estudios*, 12 (1956), pp. 413–583, & in P.Fr. Juan Devesa Blanco, 'Las primitivas constituciones de la Orden de la Merced o «Constituciones Americanas»: Códice del P. Nadal Gaver' in *Analecta Mercedaria*, 2 (1983), pp. 5–119. English translation in Brodman, *Ransoming Captives*, pp. 127–40, which is that used here; passage cited, p. 128.

[32] See in particular M° Fray Manuel Mariano Ribera, *Real Patronato de los Serenissimos Señores Reyes de España en la Real y Militar Orden de Nuestra Señora de la Merced, Redención de cautivos* (Barcelona: Raphaëlis Figueró, 1725), & *id., Centuria Primera de la Real, y Militar Instituto de la ínclita Religión de Nuestra Señora de la Merced Redempción de cautivos Christianos* (Barcelona: Raphaëlis Figueró, 1726). The tradition of the Order as military in origin appears to date from around 1500; see Vázquez Núñez, *Mercedarios ilustres*, p. 37.

[33] Brodman, *Ransoming Captives*, pp. 33–5.

stable government, legislate for the ransoming activity and punish the
serious infractions lately committed by the brethren. In particular,
Amer attempted to establish clear lines and limits of authority and
clarify the spiritual character and regimen of the Order. This desire
for consolidation in a more corporate and regulated structure was
mirrored by a number of caritative movements at this time, most
notably the Franciscans. While the constitutions may have saved the
Mercedarians from judgement by the Council of Lyon, which suppressed several congregations in 1274, Amer apparently failed to take
account of the degree to which the Order was still changing and
adapting. Fra Pere and those around him did not have the vision to
identify the course that the Order was embarked upon, and the
regime established at Barcelona in 1272 would not long outlast the
master. In particular, the constitutions had a number of serious pro-
cedural omissions that rendered them incapable of legislating for the
crises that lay ahead. The institutional and legislative insecurity
bequeathed to the Mercedarians by Nolasch would become clear early in the next century, just as it would be revealed again during the
sixteenth.

Driven by the upheavals that had shaken it since Nolasch's death,
the provisions laid down in 1272 indicate how far the Order had
moved from the Patriarch's informal personal leadership to a legislated system of government. The main forum of the Order was the
chapter general that met yearly at a place selected by the master, usually on the now defunct feast of Santa Cruz de Mayo (3rd May).[34] All
commendators and a brother from each house were convened but as
a rule only senior officers, local superiors and those on business
attended. The legislative process, including appointments, was conducted by the master and the prior — the senior clerical officer —
assisted by four diffinitors elected to represent the assembly. The
diffinitors — two clerics and two lay brethren — were drawn from
the senior commendators and, in the broadest sense, it was their duty
to check abuses of power by the master or prior in a mainly supervisory role. They also had the task of assessing penance and overseeing
punishment, and the equal division of the diffinitory between clerical
and lay members indicates the increased importance of ordained
brethren in the Order. The chapter as a whole would be required to

---

[34] *Ibid.*, pp. 57–9.

approve property transactions and ratify contractual obligations, as well as provide a forum for the voicing of complaints and the discussion of day to day administrative problems. However, now, as later, the most significant item commonly on its agenda was the annual ransoming expedition. It was here that the success of the previous redemption was assessed and its accounts made known, and here that alms were assembled and allocated, ransomers appointed and safe-conducts arranged for the next operation. The development of a provincial system from the fourteenth century onwards modified the scale, composition and frequency of the chapters, but the procedure and business carried out in them would follow a recognizable pattern into the sixteenth century and beyond.

The high office was that of the master — *maestre* — a title that only gained currency in the 1250s.[35] The election of the master took place at the chapter general with the holder enjoying life tenure. To him fell the responsibility of corporate representation before royal and ecclesiastical authority, as well as the negotiation of contracts and organizing the ransom of captives. No doubt as a result of recent abuses, the Amer constitutions attempted to curtail the overweening powers of the master and impose a collegial dimension on his authority. The master's jurisdiction over property, discipline, appointments and the collection of redemption monies, once absolute, were now subject to the scrutiny of the chapter general, including the prior. Even so, the master's temporal authority was not seriously challenged since he retained control over all other revenue, the supervision of the confraternities and his rights of pardon. The masters were itinerant, but towards the end of the century the office became associated with the house at Játiva, the income of which was given over to defray magisterial expenses in 1307, a practice mirrored in the Order of Santiago. The establishment of a clerical hegemony in the high office after 1317 did not prevent the barony of Algar (acquired in the late 1240s) near Arguines from being set aside later that century to meet the masters' personal expenses. In 1471 the thirteenth master Fra Nadal Gaver acquired the seigneurial rights of the barony, with which the generals of the Order henceforth styled themselves 'Lords of Algar and Escalés'. The barony carried with it the right to attend the *corts* of the Kingdom of Valencia in the nobiliary estate, a privi-

---

[35] *Ibid.*, pp. 43–8.

lege still exercised in the late sixteenth century when the sweeping
powers and lay characteristics of the high office were one of the chief
complaints levelled against the Mercedarians under Philip II.

During the thirteenth century, the master, as well as administering
the temporalities of the Order, was also, in theory at least, its religious superior. The yearly visitation of the Order conducted by him
in the company of his chaplain encompassed both temporal and spiritual matters. However, as the century wore on and the Order developed, the master's lay status increasingly undermined his spiritual
authority, and leadership in this field began to be shared with the
prior.[36] Beyond the administrative and disciplinary powers that the
prior shared with other prelates, as senior clerical officer he was
charged with admitting and supervising the ordained brethren of the
Order, and was entitled to conduct visitations and excommunicate in
his own right. The office apparently grew out of that of master's
chaplain and by 1272 had become the second dignity of the Order.
However, it continued to enjoy close ties with the high office and
remained in the gift of the master until the death of Amer in 1301.
The general stability of the Order under Amer no doubt owed much
to the cooperation of Fra Guillem d'Isona as prior, during whose long
tenure (1271–1302) the office gained in importance. However, after
Amer's death this relationship broke down and would only be
restored with the generalcy of the former prior Ramon Albert.
Though modified later, through the 1327 constitutions the nexus
between the priorship and the office of master general remained one
of the key features of the government of the Order until it was
reformed under Philip II.

Another of the lasting features of the Mercedarian institutional system was the office of commendator or superior, over whom the masters exercised direct control as the delegates of his authority.[37] Like
that of the master, the nature of the office was borrowed from the
practice of the military orders. As the Order expanded, so *comendadores* were appointed with local responsibility for a house or group
of properties and its *encomienda* (domain or commandery). Among the
duties of the commendator were the gathering of alms and legacies
and the patrimonial management upon which the income of the
Order depended. It was for him to remit the monies collected in his

---

[36] *Ibid.*, pp. 48–50.
[37] *Ibid.*, pp. 51–5.

domain (responsions) to the chapter general and to uphold the rights and position of the Order at local level — duties that changed little with the passage of time. Beyond this the commendator was responsible for local ransoming affairs, and above all for overseeing the spiritual life and welfare of his community and entry to it, but in major questions of discipline as much as of finance his independence was subordinated to higher authority. Even so, the appointment from around 1300 of commendators as preceptors with territorial jurisdiction foreshadows the establishment of provinces over the next two decades.[38]

The Amer constitutions required the consensus of master, prior and diffinitors in the chapter general for a commendator to be elected or removed, but despite the chapter's power of review in practice superiors remained under the direct supervision of the master. Office was invariably held for longer than the stipulated year (later extended to three), and individuals tended to move from commandery to commandery in local rotation; life tenure was a privilege occasionally granted to distinguished religious.[39] The commendators therefore represented the backbone of the Order, the essential link between hierarchy and rank and file. Fra Ramon Albert was to demonstrate in the early fourteenth century that successful government depended on the degree to which a prelate could muster the allegiance and cooperation of the commendators, as was still the case under Philip II. The Order was, as it remained until the sixteenth century, a relatively small institution, amounting to no more than 300 religious in 1317, at an average of four or five conventuals per house.[40] The picture, then, is of a widely but thinly spread organization, composed mostly of small communities many of which were little more than alms-collecting outposts. This is the predominant impression given by the Order as a whole until after 1500.

The majority of ordinary Mercedarians worked in patrimonial administration, staffing churches, preaching, collecting alms, caring for the sick and occasionally in the ransom of captives — tasks balanced by the more mundane chores associated with conventual life.

---

[38] For the formation of the provinces, see Appendix I.

[39] Brodman, *Ransoming Captives*, pp. 55–7.

[40] For a range of statistics, see *ibid.*, pp. 61–2. Hence, no doubt, the 16th-century adage discussed in P.Fr. Guillermo Vázquez Núñez, 'Comentando un refrán antiguo: «Los frailes de la Merced son pocos, mas hácenlo bien»' in *BPCONSM*, 22 (1984), no. 75, pp. 52–6. For later statistics, see Appendix III.

Those aspiring to enter the Order were first examined as to their eligibility; religious from other congregations were to be admitted only with the approval of the chapter general, while Trinitarians, or Mercedarians who had defected to that Order, were permanently barred.[41] Having been warned of the rigours of Mercedarian life, novices would be initiated into the Order and its mysteries on the second day of the chapter general, although in practice this seems usually to have taken place before commendators — a reflection of local recruitment. During the capitular ceremony novices placed their hands in those of the master and swore allegiance to him. This done, they went on to take the three vows of poverty, chastity and obedience and were then invested with the habit of the Order to the chanting of the *Veni creator Spiritus*.

The life awaiting the religious was, if hardly ascetic, not without rigour. Although there was no ban on corporate ownership of property, the Order exudes few signs of external wealth and those entering it were enjoined to renounce their worldly possessions *in imitatio Christi*.[42] However, while the Mercedarians may have been popularly associated with the mendicants, they reveal no clear affinity to the ideal of evangelical poverty. Above all, the 1272 constitutions provided for an Order that was active rather than contemplative in its vocation, that associated religious experience with caritative services to others rather than with personal asceticism, and so it would remain. As Brodman makes clear, the attraction of the *opera caritatis* was less to a way of life than to a specific work of charity open both to lay and clerical brethren.[43] The active vocation pursued by the lay brotherhood of the thirteenth century etched itself deeply and lastingly into the Mercedarian psyche. The image of the friars remained that of a hardy group of men for whom the travails of the body came more readily than the trials of the spirit. As the anonymous author of the *Lazarillo de Tormes* characterized him in about 1550, the Mercedarian was

> A sworn enemy of choir and of eating in convent, forever out and about, most gregarious and partial to worldly entanglements, so much

---

[41] Brodman, *Ransoming Captives*, pp. 62–8. On the reception and training of novices, see Antonio Vázquez Fernández, 'La formación en las diversas constituciones de la Orden' in *Analecta Mercedaria*, 2 (1983), pp. 317–62; esp. 318–21.

[42] Brodman, *Ransoming Captives*, p. 63.

[43] *Ibid.*, p. 69.

so that I think he wore out more shoes than the whole convent put together.[44]

It was the reality and persistence of this active life, centred around the work of redemption and enshrined in all its medieval legislation, that made the disciplinary reform of the Order such a challenge to royal and ecclesiastical authority in the sixteenth century.

VI. *The Redemption of Captives*

It is not until the late fifteenth and sixteenth centuries that enough material survives to record the *minutiae* of the redemption of captives, the principal work and *raison d'être* of the Mercedarian Order.[45] Although joint expeditions were not unknown (as in 1415, 1561–2 & 1627), from the fourteenth century onwards the business of ransoming captives developed into an exclusively provincial affair, with Castile, France, and the united Crown of Aragon organizing redemptions independently. The stuff of ransoming was of course the raising of money, and in this the Mercedarians acquired a number of important privileges. Not least of these was the ratification in 1366 by Pere IV (1336–87) of the Order's *privativa* or *exclusiva* (monopoly) over the collection of redemption alms — *limosna* — in the Crown of Aragon.[46] The granting of the *privativa*, confirmed periodically until the cessation of ransoming activity at the end of the eighteenth century, represents the single most important royal privilege in the history

---

[44] Anon., *Lazarillo de Tormes*, 1st pubd. Antwerp: ?, 1553; probably composed between *c.*1540 & *c.*1550. The original reads 'Gran enemigo del coro y de comer en el convento, perdido por andar fuera, amicísimo de negocios seglares y visitar: tanto, que pienso que rompía él más zapatos que todo el convento'; see Francisco Rico, ed. (Madrid, 1996), pp. 110–11. The brief tract from which this passage is drawn, *Cómo Lázaro se asentó con un fraile de la Merced, y de lo que le acaesció con él*, was suppressed in the expurgated edition of 1573.

[45] For a range of redemption books, see ACA, Mon., vols. 2691 & 2703, & BNM, mss. 2963, 3588 & 6569. Useful introductions can be found in P.Fr. Manuel Rodríguez Carrajo, 'La redención de cautivos. (Aspectos sociológicos)' in *La Orden de la Merced* [=*Estudios*] (Madrid, 1970); pp. 361–400, and *id.* & P.Fr. Bonifacio Porres, 'Redención de cautivos' in *DHEE*, suppl. I, pp. 625–42. For aspects of Mercedarian ransoming up to the 15th century, see Charles Verlinden, *L'Ésclavage dans l'Europe médiévale*, vol. I: *Péninsule ibérique, France* (Bruges, 1955), pp. 536–45, 608 & 610–11, and J.N. Hillgarth, *The Spanish Kingdoms, 1250–1516* (2 vols., Oxford, 1976–8), I, p. 149.

[46] See P.Fr. Joaquín Millán Rubio, *La Orden de Nuestra Señora de la Merced (1301–1400)* (Rome, 1992); pp. 302–4.

of the Order, since, in the Crown of Aragon at least, it ensured the primacy of the Mercedarians over the rival Trinitarians.[47]

Through this privilege, and others like it in Castile and elsewhere, the Order was permitted to engage lay *baciners* (lit. 'basineers') to beg for alms outside churches on specific days of the year. This, of course, reflected the Mercedarians' non-mendicant status, and was a source of extreme aggravation to other orders and the secular clergy who resented Mercedarian competition for alms. In view of this, in 1459 Juan II of Aragon (1458–79) permitted both *baciners* and friars to bear arms in defence of their *limosna*.[48] Once collected, the alms would be handed over to the commendator, who retained one third for the expenses of the Order and surrendered the rest at the following chapter provincial.[49] The chapter would see to the appointment of a pair of redemptors and, by the sixteenth century, of a *procurador de la redención* (procurator) whose duty it was to organize the finances and logistics of the ransoming expedition. It is here that the mercantile origins of religious redemptionism are most obviously reflected. The *procurador* was not only responsible for transferring the Order's specie to the port of embarkation — Barcelona, Valencia, Marseille or Seville in the case of Castile — but for the purchase of goods which could be sold at a profit on the Barbary Coast, the proceeds to go towards the ransoming fund.

Algiers, the corsairs' main base, was the most common destination for Spanish Mercedarians from the sixteenth century until the cessation of ransoming activity in 1779.[50] After a proportion of their funds had been deducted on arrival, the redemptors took up lodgings in the city and business began in earnest. By the 1580s the Castilian Mercedarians were spending an average of 25,000 ducats every three to four years, money that was increasingly American in origin. The ransom of an important captive might be a matter of 3000 ducats,

---

[47] The Mercedarian *privativa* in the Crown of Aragon was repeatedly challenged by the Trinitarians. For but one episode, in 1492–3, see Tarsicio de Azcona, *Isabel la Católica: Estudio crítico de su vida y su reinado*, 3rd edn. (Madrid, 1993), p. 771. For the Order's royal privileges in France and its disputes with the Trinitarians there from the 15th–17th centuries, see ADHG, 130H, nos. 12 & 37.

[48] See ACA, Mon., vol. 2660, ff. 48v–49v, dated Barcelona, 10th January 1459.

[49] The Mercedarian 'third' was conceded by Leo X in a bull of 28th July 1516. The Trinitarians had a similar privilege restricting them to a quarter of the alms collected.

[50] See Ellen G. Friedman, *Spanish Captives in North Africa in the Early Modern Age* (Madison, 1983), pp. 132–41.

though in such cases the individual's family would usually make significant contributions. The majority, however, were ransomed for much less, and the average cost of release seems to have been around 100 ducats per captive. Cervantes' ransom of 500 *escudos* in 1580 was more than five times the average sum.[51] In return for their freedom, captives were bound over to give a year and a day of service to the Order upon their safe return to the Peninsula. The procession of ransomed captives marching through town and country behind the banner of the Order was therefore a familiar sight in early modern Spain, though there was no shortage of ingrates who made off before their service was complete.[52]

Naturally, alms collection represented a significant source of income for the Order, particularly during much of the sixteenth century when ransoming operations became exceptional rather than the norm. The sale of indulgences for captives both inside and outside the Peninsula was another important source of revenue. Mercedarian *bulderos* (pardoners) were active both in northern France and England in the late fifteenth and early sixteenth centuries, as demonstrated by the survival of indulgences in the latter case.[53] However, Mercedarian income was not restricted to the ransoming sphere, and it was rents from property that constituted the most reliable source of revenue. The Order owned substantial property in Catalonia, the Balearics and Valencia, especially around Arguines, El Puig, Gandia and Valencia itself.[54] An eighteenth-century account book shows the priory of Barcelona to have had an extensive range of income-bearing properties in and around the city, as one would expect from a house enriched by a major shrine.[55] However, most revenues rested in the hands of senior officers rather than communities, and the gap between rich and poor in the Order remained very great. Legacies,

---

[51] *Ibid.*, p. 149.

[52] On the processions, see for example Hillgarth, *The Spanish Kingdoms*, I, p. 149 (1410 & 1412), ACA, Mss.Misc., vol. 49, pp. 149–50 (1589), & Pujades, *Dietari*, I, p. 371 (1604).

[53] For France, see Paul Deslandres, *L'Ordre des Trinitaires pour le rachat des captifs* (2 vols., Toulouse-Paris, 1903); I, pp. 361–2. Copies of indulgences printed in English survive in Bod.L., Arch. A b. 8 (4), (20*) & (20**), the first of *c.*1510, the latter two of 1532 signed by the Catalan general, Fra Benet Zafont.

[54] See James Casey, *The Kingdom of Valencia in the Seventeenth Century* (Cambridge, 1979), p. 108, ACA, Mon., vol. 2835 (Balearics) and AHN, Clero, carps. 3199–3207 (El Puig) & 3345–3354 (Valencia).

[55] ACA, Mon., vol. 2834.

donations, preaching, accompanying funeral cortèges and the singing
of masses supplemented conventual income, but by the reign of
Philip II many houses, especially in the Crown of Aragon, were
impoverished and their patrimony dissipated through fraud and
neglect.[56] Loss of documentation prevents us gauging the Castilian
economic situation to the same degree, but here American revenue
transformed the finances of the province from the late sixteenth century. By 1700 the Mercedarian Order was among the richest in
Spain.

Though voices were raised against institutionalized ransoming of
this sort in the seventeenth century, the act of redemption had a huge
religious and emotional appeal for Spaniards, one promoted assiduously by the Order. While there was of course a powerful spiritual
dimension to the redemption of captives, the practicalities of ransoming expeditions made these the preserve of men of rather exceptional
talents. The redemptors balanced a rock-like faith with the physical
and mental endurance to survive months and sometimes years of privation and maltreatment as they bargained for the ransom of captives. It was hard-headed, highly demanding work, unsuited for men
of a contemplative disposition and one which few Mercedarians ever
experienced, or probably ever wished to. Such reasons, and the wholly secular ambient of the captive market, prevented the act of
redemption being adopted as the Mercedarian 'observance' in the
sixteenth century, though, as will become apparent, the fourth vow
— redemption — dates from this time.[57]

The Order therefore preserved its active vocation, and mobility
and interaction with secular society remained key features of Mercedarian life into the early modern period. Reflecting the origins of
its *métier*, the Order always enjoyed closer ties with the mercantile
than the noble classes, whose patronage caused many of its houses to
be founded in the commercial quarters of towns, as in the case of
Barcelona and Valencia to name but two. Indeed, the lay tendency of
the religious was one of the main concerns of Philip's reformers and a
serious obstacle to their reduction into the ordered conventual life
that many had seen fit to abandon. The work of redemption there-

---

[56] Carlos M.N. Eire, *From Madrid to Purgatory: The Art and Conflict of Dying in Sixteenth-Century Spain* (Cambridge, 1995), pp. 129–30.
[57] For redemption as a quasi 'observance', see in AMAE, SS, leg. 34, f. 182r, a brief dated Rome, 5th November 1585.

fore afforded Mercedarians a marked sense of individuality and separateness with respect to other orders and the monastic vocation in general, even alongside the Trinitarians who did not enjoy the same Spanish pedigree. This perception Mercedarian reformers from Gaver onwards were anxious to dispel as the prevailing spiritual climate began to make increasingly stern demands on the religious orders.

VII. *Confraters,* Beatas *and Nuns*

Though established as a lay brotherhood, the affiliation of confraters from the mid thirteenth century for the first time brought laymen and women into the fold of the Order.[58] In return for the donation of money or property, individuals, married couples and families were admitted into the Order in the expectation of care in old age and the benefits of religious burial and spiritual remembrance in death. Initially, the reception of women was made conditional on their having sufficient means to support themselves in their own homes, but through the fourteenth century it is clear that both men and women affiliates and tertiaries were gathering into informal associations within the ambit of the Order.[59] In 1409 Beatriz of Castile, widow of John I (1379–90) and a Mercedarian tertiary, obtained approval from Benedict XIII for the foundation and constitutions of an enclosed community of Mercedarian nuns in Valladolid, though nothing had came of the project by the time of her death in 1440.[60] Even so, it is quite likely that a *beaterio* already existed at El Puig, which the Catholic Kings may have attempted to convert into a nunnery at the end of the century, though again without success.[61] By the early sixteenth century some of these lay associations had become formally constituted and were wearing the Mercedarian scapulary. The Mercedarian *germania* (confraternity) of Nostra Senyora de la Mercè in Valencia received its first statutes at

---

[58] See P.Fr. Guillermo Vázquez Núñez, 'Terciarios y cofrades de la Merced' in *BOM*, 5 (1917), pp. 66–71, & Brodman, *Ransoming Captives*, pp. 86–9.

[59] Brodman, *Ransoming Captives*, p. 133.

[60] See Vázquez Núñez, *Mercedarios ilustres*, pp. 671–4, esp. 673, & P.Fr. Manuel Rodríguez Carrajo, 'Ramas femeninas mercedarias' in *La Orden de la Merced* [=*Estudios*] (Madrid, 1970), pp. 329–56; 330–1.

[61] Vázquez Núñez, *Manual*, I, p. 405.

this time, and in 1509 we receive news of the earliest known *beaterio* in Castile, that of Guadalajara.[62] Other *beaterios* were founded in Murcia (1512), and Lorca (1515) in the diocese of Cartagena.[63] However, it was in the Basque country, and under the aegis of the house of Burceña, that the *beatas* took deepest root. The 'Beatas de la Orden de Nuestra Señora de la Merced' were established at Bilbao by 1514, though the community may date from as much as a century earlier.[64] A daughter house was founded at Deusto in 1538 and others followed at Lete (1539; refounded at Escoriaza 1578), Bérriz (*c.*1542) and Marquina (1548), etc. Over these houses the commendators of Burceña exercised powers usually accorded only to the provincial.

The Tridentine decrees, with their emphasis on the reduction of all female communities into cloistered congregations, had a marked impact on the Mercedarian *beaterios*. In 1577 the then general, Fray Francisco Maldonado, established a 'Congregación de Beatas Terceras' out of existing *beaterios* attached to the convents of El Puig and Orihuela, to which several other such foundations were added in Valencia.[65] A visitation of the ten Basque *beaterios* by Maldonado late in 1578 resulted the following January in their reduction into four houses, *viz.* Bilbao, Deusto, Marquina and Escoriaza.[66] The latter was in that year placed under strict cloister, but the first genuinely cloistered Mercedarian nunnery was that of La Asunción in Seville,

---

[62] See, respectively, Vázquez Núñez, 'Terciarios y cofrades', p. 68, & Rodríguez Carrajo, 'Ramas femeninas mercedarias', p. 331. The confraternity was approved and given new constitutions by archbishop Juan de Ribera in 1588; ARV, Clero, lib. 1720, p. 87. That of Palma de Majorca received its first statutes in 1516; see ARM, Clero, no. 4178.

[63] Rvda.M. Ángeles Fernández Martínez, 'Breve historia del Convento-Colegio de Madre de Dios de la Consolación [...] de la ciudad de Lorca, Provincia de Murcia' serialized in *BOM*, 12 (1924) & 13 (1925); see esp. 12 (1924), pp. 171–6.

[64] For the Basque *beaterios*, see Rodríguez Carrajo, 'Ramas femeninas mercedarias', pp. 332–4, 335–7 & 352, and three articles by P.Fr. Guillermo Vázquez Núñez, *viz.* 'El convento de Mercedarias de Bilbao' in *BOM*, 8 (1920), pp. 340–8, 'Los conventos de Mercedarias de Marquina y Escoriaza' in *BOM*, 18 (1930), pp. 12–26, and 'El convento de MM. Mercedarias de la Vera Cruz de Bérriz' in *BOM*, 18 (1930), pp. 210–13. It should be noted that the information provided by these authors conflicts in a number of important details, particularly as to foundation dates.

[65] On the El Puig *beaterio*, see APV, ms. Cavero, 'Varia', I, f. 119v–p.120 [*sic*], and ACA, Mon., vol. 2679, f. 147r; no professions were permitted here until 1583. Though refounded later, the Orihuela *beaterio* was in fact suppressed in 1582.

[66] See Vázquez Núñez, 'Los conventos de Mercedarias de Marquina y Escoriaza', p. 14, & Rodríguez Carrajo, 'Ramas femeninas mercedarias', p. 333. Another *beaterio* was founded in Huete in 1576; see BNM, ms. 2448, ff. 367r–368r.

founded by three noble women in 1566.[67] Through the mediation of their confessor and spiritual director, Mº Fray Antonio de Velasco, the women obtained permission from the archbishop and provincial of Castile for the establishment of a community in property which they themselves donated for this purpose. The house opened in August 1567 under the watchful eye of Velasco and nuns seconded from the Dominican convent of Santa María la Real, and was confirmed by Pius V in May 1568. The following decade an unsuccessful attempt was made to establish nunneries dedicated to the training of Indian girls in Peru, and the first Mercedarian *beaterio* in America had to wait until 1670.[68] However, the first Discalced nunnery at Lora del Río near Córdoba (1612) and later those of Fuentes and San José in Seville itself were opened with communities of nuns from La Asunción.[69] It was, moreover, from this tradition that Catherine McAuley founded her Sisters of Mercy in Dublin in 1827.[70]

VIII. *The Rise of the Clerics, 1272–1301*

Although the primordial lay brotherhood was uncloistered, the clericalized Order that grew out of the 1327 constitutions attempted to confine the religious to a more conventual existence, mitigated by the active lives that remained open to them. During the thirteenth century the regimen of prayer appears to have been neither long nor elaborate: while the clerical brethren chanted a version of the canonical hours, the lay members confined themselves to paternosters.[71] Efforts

---

[67] See Rodríguez Carrajo, 'Ramas femeninas mercedarias', pp. 334–5, & Vázquez Núñez, 'La Universidad de Salamanca', pp. 318–21. The founders were María Zapata de la Fuente, her daughter Beatriz de las Roelas and niece Francisca Saavedra Martel. The constitutions were approved by the provincial, Mº Fray Pedro Carrillo, in 1570 and first printed by Mº Fray Felipe de Guimerán in 1614. The community was eighteen strong in 1591. Despite Maldonado's efforts, the Basque *beaterios* did not become genuinely cloistered until 1621–5 and came near to being suppressed altogether in 1599; see *id.*, *Manual*, II, p. 117–8, Tirso, *Historia*, II, p. 232, & AHCB, ms. A-266, Antillón, *Memorias*, II, f. 98r–v.

[68] See Pérez, *Religiosos de la Merced*, pp. 209–10, & Vázquez Núñez, *Manual*, II, p. 39. The *beaterio*, opened in Lima in 1670, was enclosed as a Discalced nunnery in 1734; *id.*, *Mercedarios ilustres*, p. 724.

[69] Vázquez Núñez, *Manual*, II, p. 118, & *id.*, *Mercedarios ilustres*, pp. 677 & 700.

[70] See Roland Burke Savage, *Catherine McAuley: The First Sister of Mercy* (Dublin, 1955), & Rodríguez Carrajo, 'Ramas femeninas mercedarias', pp. 343–5.

[71] Brodman, *Ransoming Captives*, p. 67.

to change this after 1327 are consistent not only with the clericalization of the Order under Albert, but with the gradual broadening of
its spiritual base that took place from the early fourteenth century in
particular.

The thirteenth-century Mercedarians were by no means unique in
admitting both lay and clerical religious, a practice mirrored by many
orders of differing vocations.[72] All members were bound over to
observe the three vows and were therefore fully 'religious', partaking
of the same communal life, work and discipline. The main difference
lay in the ordination of clerics as subdeacons, deacons and priests, a
status that until 1317 barred them from most of the principal offices
in the Order, though neither the Rule of St Augustine nor the Amer
constitutions specifically required the master to be a layman. The
introduction of clerics into the Order is unclear, but seems to date
from the 1250s; by 1260 they had been united under the prior, and
emerged as a distinctive element thereafter. As several provisions in
the 1272 constitutions demonstrate, the clerics were growing both in
numbers and in influence, a consequence of the Order's continuing
acquisition of urban churches despite the resistance of the secular
clergy, and the liturgical demands made by patrons and confraters.
To the four churches and chapels possessed by the Order in 1245 a
further ten had been added by 1263, notably at Zaragoza, Seville and
Barcelona with more to follow.

In the growth of a clerical vocation the Mercedarians reflect a
deeper trend shared by other orders: the development in the clergy of
a caste mentality that appears to have manifested itself in a conscious
recruitment by the clerical minority of their own kind.[73] If this movement for clericalization reflects the aim of the hierarchical Church to
bring the gamut of popular spirituality under its control, then it is
also consistent with the diminished respect for the vocation of lay
brethren in the Church.[74] The gradual divorce between the spon-
taneity of lay religiosity and the control demanded by the clerical
hierarchy as experienced in the wider Church is therefore mirrored
in the internal affairs of the Mercedarian Order. The ensuing revolt
of the ordained brethren against their lay superiors indicates a new
assumption of superiority by the clerical estate, and an assertion of

---

[72] *Ibid.*, pp. 69–70.
[73] *Ibid.*, p. 70.
[74] *Ibid.*, p. 71.

the impropriety of lay control over persons in holy orders. This process, which unfolded in the early fourteenth century, represents the first clear expression of the underlying conflict between lay and clerical interest that would remain a constant feature of Mercedarian life.

IX. *Crisis and Mutation, 1301–17*

Though Amer had presided over a period of consolidation after years of strife, by the time of his death in 1301 the Order was incubating the seeds of further conflict and disunity. His tenure had seen a continued dispersion of the Order throughout the Iberian Peninsula, including Portugal, and Languedoc.[75] However, by 1317 the floodtide of Mercedarian expansion was over. Beyond the saturation of conquered and other territories with ecclesiastical foundations, the reasons for this gradual cessation lie in the religious and social upheavals of the age, and in an inevitable readjustment to the feudal and urban realities that asserted themselves after the fever of the later *Reconquista*. As the consequences of this readjustment began to affect the Mercedarian Order, so its ambiguities and latent institutional problems inexorably revealed themselves. Within a few years of Amer's death consolidation had given way to crisis.

In the closing years of the thirteenth century the priorship became associated with the house of Barcelona.[76] By 1296 Isona was installed there as both prior and commendator, and by the time of Amer's death in 1301 he had become the leader of a clerical faction within the Order. Though not the wealthiest Mercedarian foundation, Barcelona remained the most prestigious, and by the turn of the thirteenth century many — though not all — clerics had come to see the priory church with its shrine of Santa Maria de la Mercè as the spiri-

---

[75] *Ibid.*, pp. 35–7. Beja (founded by 1299) was the first of six Mercedarian houses in Portugal which, however, were all abandoned after 1350 with the onset of the plague. The Order's Portuguese patrimony was ceded to the Trinitarians in the late 14th century in return for recognition of the Mercedarian *privativa* over alms collection in the Crown of Aragon. Attempted foundations at Lisbon and Santarem in *c.*1599 came to nothing, but the Order had established a residence in the capital by 1662; see Vázquez Núñez, *Manual*, II, p. 61, & *id.*, 'Conventos de la Merced', pp. 390–1.

[76] Brodman, *Ransoming Captives*, p. 49.

tual home of the Order. It was here, therefore, that Isona and his
supporters began their campaign for a say in the Order's affairs commensurate with their increased importance within it. Their establishment in this urban environment therefore represents a decisive element in the ensuing struggle for power and a turning point in the history of the Order.

The rise of Barcelona at once epitomizes both the changing priorities and the gradual shift in focus that had characterized the Mercedarians under Amer. After the first wave of expansion in the generation following Nolasch's death, the Order began to add urban foundations and lucrative landed property in the heartlands of Castile and
Navarre to those that already existed on the Aragonese frontier: Burgos, Toledo and Valladolid (all by 1291), Guadalajara (1300) and
Pamplona (by 1299). There is no question of a withdrawal from the
frontier — the forum for its ransoming activity and the source of
much of the institution's wealth — but circumstances and the changing character of the Order impressed upon the clerical hierarchy in
particular the importance of an urban presence. As donations began
to fall away towards the end of the thirteenth century the Order
came increasingly to rely for its funds on preaching — both itinerant
and in its growing number of churches — and by extension on the
clerics who conducted this mainly urban-based activity and lent their
superior administrative talents to its organization.[77] Already by 1301
a lasting pattern for Mercedarian activity was therefore beginning to
establish itself. The Order was both urban and rural in character, at
home as much in the heartlands as on the frontiers of the Peninsula;
the continued dialogue, and occasional conflict, between these elements is a characteristic feature of Mercedarian life. Such developments indicate a newfound depth and range in the life of the Order
in response to the changing condition of society, and it now remained
for this maturity to be resolved, by attrition, into institutional reform.

Despite their preponderance at Barcelona by 1301, there was still
little to suggest that the clerics would shortly have a controlling interest in the affairs of the Order. Not all were of a reformist mentality,
and the lay brethren remained at the helm with the support of the
crown and the weight of tradition and legislation behind them.
Indeed, the bitterness and duration of the ensuing conflict reflects the

---

[77] *Ibid.*, p. 71.

vitality of the Mercedarian lay tradition over which the clerics had to enforce their own values. In this endeavour they were to enjoy only partial success, for the schism was resolved only with difficulty and, in the end, in compromise. As Philip II's visitors discovered towards the end of the sixteenth century, the events that filled the generation after Amer's death in 1301 did not extinguish the lay element in the Mercedarian psyche.

The tensions growing in the final years of Amer's tenure boiled over with the master's death. There is not space here to discuss the troubles that followed at any length. Suffice to say that disagreement over the election of Amer's successor, Fra Arnau d'Amer, caused the clerical faction to elect the Catalan Fra Ramon Albert anti-master of the Order at Barcelona in June 1302.[78] The matter was sent to Rome to await papal arbitration, and the Order recovered an air of normality despite the pervasive stench of acrimony. The lay organization was still running satisfactorily with much of the Order under its control when, in February 1308, Clement V declared in favour of Albert and, preparatory to further action, annulled both elections without addressing the legitimacy of either.[79] This was the first in a series of papal verdicts showing a strong clerical bias, despite the numerical inferiority of Albert's faction and the traditional role of lay brethren in the life of the Order. While the pretender Albert was subsequently appointed to the priorship of Barcelona — an office now accorded unassailable authority over the spiritual affairs of the Order — Amer was simply deposed and his fellow laic Fra Arnau Rossinyol raised to a diminished mastership. Further disputes culminated in episcopal arbitration in 1311 which granted the clerical brethren virtual autonomy within the Order, and gave Albert powers comparable with those of the master.[80] As a result the clerics were exempted both from the authority of the master and their commendators, and made responsible only to the prior and to local bishops, a judgement swiftly endorsed by Clement V.

Bereft of support, Rossinyol died in Valencia during the annual chapter general in May 1317, the last lay master of the Order.[81] Two months later the Order reconvened at Valencia at a chapter

---

[78] Millán Rubio, *La Orden*, pp. 3–13.
[79] *Ibid.*, pp. 33–8.
[80] *Ibid.*, pp. 65–78.
[81] *Ibid.*, pp. 105–29.

attended by nearly 200 religious — a substantial proportion of the brethren.[82] Despite Albert's entreaties, the seventy lay electors withdrew when the clerical faction refused to accept their demand that only laics be considered for the office of master. While the remaining religious elected Albert to the high office by an overwhelming majority, the lay brethren went on to appoint their own candidate, his fellow Catalan Fra Berenguer d'Hostalés. A double appeal to John XXII resulted early the following year in the annulment of Hostalés's election and, contrary to all legislation, in the confirmation of Albert as 'master general' with conjoined temporal and spiritual authority.

X. *A New Constitution, 1317–30*

Having consolidated his position, Albert set about perpetuating the clerical hold on the Order and forging the administrative structure that would govern it into the sixteenth century. His principal aim was to resolve the institutional crisis by creating a system that would allow the master to be elected and then to govern the Order more effectively and in greater stability than had been possible in the past. Albert recognized the need for a set of constitutions that would not only provide the Order with the balanced system of government that the Amer constitutions had so signally failed to deliver, but also legislate for a new religious identity.

The first elements of Albert's programme were passed at the important chapter general of Cuenca in Castile in May 1319 and then at the provincial session celebrated at Lleida the following year.[83] As Albert made clear at Cuenca, his immediate aims were the 'benefit, tranquility, peace and reform of the Order', and implicitly a restoration of its ransoming activity.[84] Taking the Dominican constitutions as a model, by 1327 Albert had expanded the body of emergency measures enforced in the early years of his generalate into a corpus of legislation that, in its vision and comprehensiveness, represents the first fully integrated codification of the life, devotion and

---

[82] For the *synodalia*, including both elections, see P.Fr. Guillermo Vázquez Núñez, ed., *Actas del Capítulo General de 1317...* (Rome, 1930).

[83] Millán Rubio, *La Orden*, pp. 137–40.

[84] Cited in *ibid.*, p. 143.

structure of the Order.[85] More than a collection and emendation of earlier statutes, the Albertine constitutions, with their particular character and notable omissions, amount to a manifesto of the clerical regime and a serious rupture with the past. It should be stated that no contemporaneous manuscript of the 'Constitutiones Fratrum Ordinis Sancte Mariae de Mercede Redemptionis Captivorum' survives, and neither is any papal confirmation known to have been granted.[86] The earliest extant copy — that contained in the *Speculum fratrum* of Fra Nadal Gaver of 1445 — has only come down to us with late fourteenth- and early fifteenth-century accretions.[87] However, the substance, if not necessarily the detail, of Albert's work appears largely unaltered.

From the outset the new constitutions were quite different in tone from those of 1272. Where Pere d'Amer had begun with a declaration of faith and a recognition of Nolasch's role in the foundation of the Order, Albert's prologue is an articulate argument for unity under a legislation that imparts no sense of debt, spiritual or other, to Nolasch and the lay brethren of the previous century.(8r–9r) Opening with a brief invocation and the statement: 'Here begin the constitutions of the friars of the Order of Our Lady of Mercy of the Redemption of Captives', the 1327 statutes have an air of independence and conscious newness that makes it easy to see how religious in the sixteenth century could portray them as the primordial legislation of the Order.(8r) The Albertine statutes certainly owe something to those of Amer, but, unlike 1272, the 1327 legislation was created as an end in itself and this is what makes it so radically dif-

---

[85] See P.Fr. Ernesto González Castro, 'Las constituciones del P. Raimundo Albert (1327), segundo texto constitucional de la Orden de la Merced: Presentación y análisis' in *Analecta Mercedaria*, 2 (1983), pp. 121–207, the most balanced approach yet to Mercedarian constitutional history.

[86] Any confirmation of the 1327 constitutions would, if publicized, of course compromise claims that this was in fact the primordial legislation of the Order.

[87] On the transmission of the text and its accretions, see González Castro, 'Las constituciones del P. Raimundo Albert', pp. 162–5 & 173–80 respectively. The earliest extant printing of the Albertine constitutions, with further additions, is that of the provincial of Castile, M° Fray Alonso de Zorita in the identically-titled *Speculum fratrum* of 1533; see ch. 2, n. 168. This version also survives in a 16th-century Castilian MS translation, BNM, ms. 2284, ff. 8r–75v, which is the one used here; references given in the text. There is a second 16th-century(?) Castilian translation in ACA, Mss.Misc., vol. 93, ff. 6v–55v. The last printing of the 1327 constitutions is that contained in the *Regula et Constitutiones* of the Castilian M° Fray Gaspar de Torres in 1565; see ch. 4, n. 20.

ferent in emphasis.[88] As Albert makes clear in the prologue, the
desired unity and discipline of the Order, both within its members
and in its being, rested on the observance of a set of 'customs' of
unspecified provenance.(8r) These customs, Albert continued, were
the better observed when set down as constitutions and imbued with
an inviolable authority, and his prologue concludes with a series of
injunctions making the alteration of these a matter requiring the
approval of two or even three chapters general.(8v–9r)

Nevertheless, the institutional provisions of 1327 would eventually
be overruled not only by expediency, but given the underlying awareness that many of Albert's 'customs' had long predated him, and that
their conversion into 'constitutions' was merely a façade for illegiti-
macy. However, legitimate or not, this should not obscure the thoroughness of a set of statutes that, for the first time, aimed to embrace
the lives of all religious and provide the Order with a measure for
every eventuality. Although Amer had identified problems and shortcomings, he had failed to legislate for them adequately; Albert, on the
other hand, not only succeeded in binding an important section of
the Order to his constitutions, but also hedged them about with a set
of provisions that made their eventual revocation under Philip II both
long and arduous.

XI. *The Albertine Observance*

The 1327 constitutions contain fifty-two chapters divided into two
equal sections or distinctions, these dealing firstly with the religious
observance and life of the Order, and secondly with its government.
The direct derivation of these from the Dominican constitutions, a
fact of extreme importance for the development of the Order, has
only recently begun to be recognized by Mercedarian historians.[89]
The reasons for this are not far to seek. From the time of his canonization in 1601 repeated claims that Ramon de Penyafort was not
only the legislator but the founder of the Order have caused Mer-

---

[88] For a discussion of the differences and similarities, see González Castro, 'Las
constituciones del P. Raimundo Albert', pp. 184–202.
[89] On the Dominican constitutions, see Fr Heinrich Denifle, 'Die Constitutionen
des Predigerordens' in *Archiv für Litteratur- und Kirchengeschichte des Mittelalters*, 5 (1889),
pp. 530–64, and for the text, G.K. Galbraith, ed., *The Constitution of the Dominican
Order, 1216–1360* (Manchester, 1925).

cedarians to minimize the Dominican role in its makeup.[90] However, there can be no denying the extent to which Mercedarian observance followed that of the Dominicans. As a provincial of Castile declared in 1570,

> As to its ceremonies, its statutes and constitutions, along with its ordinary, missal and breviary, as well as its methods of prayer and saying mass, this Order is much more akin to the Dominican Order than to any other; and failing the Order's own prayer books we employ those of the Dominicans [...] Accordingly, the Order has a statute to the effect that, if there be any dissent or disagreement in such matters, we must align ourselves with the customs of the Dominicans...[91]

And indeed, both as to structure and religious observance, the Dominican model represents an obvious choice for Albert, with its concessions to the active life and emphasis on a brief and succinct recitation of the divine office.

Appropriately enough given the clericalizing nature of Albert's reform, the first four chapters deal with the liturgy to be observed by an order founded, according to Albert in his prologue, 'for [the recitation of] the divine office and the redemption of Christian captives'.(8v) The role of liturgy is all the more significant in the Mercedarian observance given the apparent absence of communal meditation and examination of conscience until the late sixteenth century. Certainly, Albert's clericalization did not require the Mercedarians to embrace the *vita contemplativa*; along with the divine office, the reading in the refectory represented the main daily spiritual sustenance of the brethren.(10r–v;14r–15r) The friars were expected to receive communion every ten days and confess at least once every three months, this supplemented by periodic fasting.(13r–v) Where possible the religious were to be confessed or take communion from ordained brethren of the Order, but in the absence of these they might resort

---

[90] The tradition does not appear to date from much before 1599. The first Mercedarian chronicler openly to recognize the 1327 constitutions as being based on those of the Dominicans was M° Fray Damián Esteve, *Symbolo de la Concepción de María sellado en la caridad y Religión Mercedaria* (Madrid: Imprenta del Convento de la Merced, 1728), p. 286; see González Castro, 'Las constituciones del P. Raimundo Albert', pp. 122–4 & 145–7. It should be added that the Dominican constitutions upon which the 1327 legislation is based were prepared by Penyafort as prior general of the Order in 1239–41, though this cannot be ascribed to any involvement he may have had with the Mercedarians.

[91] IVDJ, env. 72, II, ff. 105r–106v. M° Fray Pedro Carrillo to the nuncio, Giambattista Castagna, undated but *c.*1570; f. 105v.

to a Dominican confessor or, failing this, a priest of another order or the secular clergy.

Based on the Dominican model, the Mercedarian breviary developed organically from the mid fourteenth century and by 1500 a variety of liturgies seem to have been in use, not all as prescribed by the Order.[92] In an attempt at uniformity, the Catalan general Fra Joan Urgell introduced the Order's first printed breviary and missal at the chapter general of Girona in 1506, though Dominican versions continued in use.[93] This appears to have provided the basis for successive Mercedarian breviaries, including those printed by generals Lorenzo de la Mata (1514?), Zafont and Sorell, though of these no copies are extant.[94] In 1533 the provincial of Castile, M° Fray Alonso de Zorita, had a complete ordinary printed at his own expense,[95] but the last Mercedarian breviary published before the introduction of the Roman liturgy in 1576 was that of the Catalan general Mc Fra Miquel Puig, who banned all previous ones at the chapter general of Barcelona in 1561.[96]

The Albertine constitutions went on to issue guidelines with regard to food, eating and the maintenance of silence, the care of the sick,

---

[92] See P.Fr. Guillermo Vázquez Núñez, 'La antigua liturgia mercedaria' in *BOM*, 22 (1934), pp. 12–20.

[93] *Breviarium secundum Morem Ordinis Fratrum Beatae Mariae de Mercede* (Venice: Lucantonio de Giunta, 1503). 400 were printed at a cost of 200 ducats; see Placer López, *Bibliografía mercedaria*, II, p. 973, & particularly José María Madurell Marimón & Jorge Rubió y Balaguer, *Documentos para la historia de la imprenta y librería en Barcelona (1474–1553)* (Barcelona, 1955), pp. 357–9; 374 & 391–2. For an apparently unfulfilled contract of 1506 arranged by Urgell for the printing of a Mercedarian missal, see *ibid.*, pp. 433–6 & 438–9.

[94] For details of the Lorenzo de la Mata (also called Llorens de la Mata) and Zafont printings, see Placer López, *Bibliografía mercedaria*, II, pp. 234 & 1059 respectively.

[95] *Ordinarium officii divini ex more fratrum ordinis beate Marie de Mercede redemptionis captivorum* (Valladolid: Nicolás Thierry, 1533). This was printed along with Zorita's *Speculum fratrum* and what appears to be the only surviving copy is bound together with this work: ACA, XXVI-4-3. See Placer López, *Bibliografía mercedaria*, II, pp. 1063–4.

[96] *Breviarium secundum ordinationem fratrum sacri ordinis beate Marie de Mercede redemptionis captivorum. Nunc recens fideliter emendatum* (Lyon: Pierre Fradin, 1560; distributed in Barcelona by Joan and Damià Bajes [i.e. Bages]). Puig had a missal printed simultaneously, the *Missale secundum consuetudinem sacrosanctae religionis...* (Lyon: as before). 1500 and 800 copies of these were printed respectively, the former at a cost of 12 Castilian *reales* per copy. See M° Fray José Linás, *Bullarium Cœlestis ac Regalis Ordinis Beatae Mariae Virginis de Mercede Redemptionis Captivorum* (Barcelona: Raphaëlis Figueró, 1696), pp. 159–60, Placer López, *Bibliografía mercedaria*, I, pp. 53–4, & II, pp. 560–1, & Madurell Marimón & Rubió y Balaguer, *Documentos para la historia de la imprenta*, p. 890. For Tirso's thoughts on the loss of the Mercedarian breviary, see *Historia*, II, p. 58.

tonsures and blood-letting (four times per year), beds and cloth-ing.(14r–17v) The Mercedarians wore Augustinian white, a reflection both of their Rule and the exigencies of ransoming activity in Muslim lands.(16r–v) The material was spun of rough wool and from at least the fifteenth century the design resembled that of the Friars Preach-ers. Zurbarán's paintings have left us a matchless record of the Mer-cedarian raiment.[97] The habit itself, tied at the waist by a long leather strap, lay under a scapulary that hung down to the friars' ankles and upon which, at breast height, the cloth shield insignia of the Order was fixed or suspended. Over this travelling religious wore a volumi-nous cloak tied at the neck and overlaid in its turn by the cape which covered the shoulders and reached down as far as the shield. To the cape an ample cowl was attached. No underclothing was permitted other than breeches, though in practice many religious wore vests against the coarseness of the habit, just as prelates took to using silk trappings to denote their rank. Friars wore ankle boots and tabards were permitted for those on horse or muleback. The outfit was there-fore somewhat elaborate, and reflects the active rather than contem-plative lives led by the religious. The first distinction concludes with statutes regarding the reception, training and profession of novices and *donados* or *hermanos legos* (lay brothers), the treatment of apostates and renegades, degrees of trangression and the discipline to be meted out in punishment, the modification of which lay at the discretion of the general alone.(17v–32v)[98]

Although he drew on many of its institutional features, Albert was anxious to enforce a more paternalistic and less representative system of government than that allowed for in the Dominican constitutions. To a degree at least, the government of greater consensus that had characterized the Order after 1272 now gave way to one centred on the persona of the general upon whom arbitrary powers were con-ferred. At Cuenca in 1319 a state of emergency granted Albert the authority to amend his new measures as he thought best.[99] This facul-ty was first employed at Lleida the following year where statutes were passed on behalf of all those who had yet to ratify them. The justifica-

---

[97] Compare with the guidelines for dress in the *Comentario* to M° Fray Gaspar de Torres' *Constitutiones*, ff. 27r–29r, reproduced in Vázquez Núñez, 'La Universidad de Salamanca', pp. 332–4.

[98] On the reception and training of novices, see Vázquez Fernández, 'La forma-ción en las diversas constituciones', pp. 322–7.

[99] Millán Rubio, *La Orden*, pp. 139–42.

tion for this increment in his powers was the urgent need for a resolution to the conflict of authority that had riven the Order over the previous twenty years. Even so, while the long-term survival of the institution may well be owed to Albert, the exalted powers accrued by the
high office during his tenure, and in particular its intimate association
with the priorate and the mother house at Barcelona, implied a loss
of flexibility that would in time have serious consequences for the
Order. Drawn up by a Catalan, the Albertine constitutions made little provision for the development of a power base beyond Catalonia,
and the future would inevitably bring conflict and division in the
Order along provincial lines. But at this juncture Albert's main concern was the extension of the general's authority and it was on this
principle that the restructuring of the Order took shape. The résumé
of Albert's institutional legislation that follows is particularly concerned to describe those institutional changes, both enshrined in
1327 and added later, that were observed by the Order in the sixteenth century and are relevant to its reform at this time.

XII. *The Structure of the Order*

The measures taken by Albert during his generalate reflect his own
experience gleaned from years of successful opposition to the lay hierarchy, which evidently gave him an unrivalled grasp of the politics of
the Order. In establishing a network of supporters among the commendators during his priorate, Albert had demonstrated a clear
understanding of the means by which the Order functioned and the
basis for power within it. His election in 1317 was marked by a spate
of political appointments to commanderies throughout the Order, a
right, shared with his vicar and the diffinitors, that constituted one of
the most significant powers at his disposal. However, Albert's experience as prior had also impressed upon him the influence wielded by
commendators at capitular level, and as general he now determined
to lessen this by marginalizing them to provincial fora that remained
fully accountable to the centre.

As early as 1319 Albert had identified the need for a partition of
the Order into five manageable provincial groups in preference to the
straggling arrangement then in force. These were to be Catalonia,
Aragon-Navarre, Valencia-Murcia, Provence-Mallorca, and finally
Castile with Portugal, a framework which survived in modified form

until the end of the sixteenth century.[100] In that year Albert introduced a system of annual chapters provincial presided over by the general or his vicar that were designed to embrace that local business, including commendatorial grievances, which had formerly choked the administration of the Order. For capitular purposes the five provinces were gathered in 1327 into two blocs, comprising, firstly, the three provinces of the Crown of Aragon including Provence, Murcia and Navarre, and secondly that of Castile with Portugal.

With regard to provincial government, Albert preserved the traditional system of the *comendador mayor* with lieutenants or vicars periodically appointed by the general to see to the smooth running of distant sectors of the Order. This system was employed continuously in Castile where the office first assumed the title of provincial in 1361, but it was only after 1467 that Castile was able to elect its own incumbent.[101] Valencia and Aragon-Navarre, which had had *comendadores mayores* and provincials periodically appointed by the generals since 1317 and 1375 respectively, followed suit in the sixteenth century.[102] The priors of Barcelona were *de facto* provincials of Catalonia. By 1467 the expansion of the province of Castile had made its administration the task of more than one prelate. Although the creation of a new province centred around Seville would have been fully justified, the Aragonese hierarchy balked at the prospect of an increased Castilian representation in the affairs of the Order. Nevertheless, in the interests of good government, Castile was divided into two administrative sectors, north and south of the Guadiana. While remaining under the jurisdiction of a single provincial, one of the sectors was entrusted to his appointed vicar, who, although enjoying full powers in his area, was obliged to cede authority to the provincial whenever he entered it. The creation of the province of Andalusia, observing the same geographical boundaries, had to wait until 1588. Provincials and, in the case of Castile, their vicars, enjoyed life tenure until the sixteenth century. At the chapter provincial of Guadalajara in 1539 the provincialate of Castile was reduced to six years, while those of Aragon and Valencia remained of life tenure

---

[100] *Ibid.*, p. 142, and particularly Appendix I for the Mercedarian provincial system as a whole.

[101] See P.Fr. Guillermo Vázquez Núñez, 'Los provinciales de la Merced de Castilla' in *BOM*, 11 (1923), pp. 111–17, & 12 (1924), pp. 133–8.

[102] See P.Fr. Amerio Sancho Blanco, *Provinciales de la Merced de Aragón* (Rome, 1933) & *id.*, *Provinciales de la Merced de Valencia* (Rome, 1933).

until 1574.[103] The provincials of France, who traditionally enjoyed close ties with the Catalan brethren, held office in perpetuity until the 1590s.

Reflecting the gradual fragmentation of the Order after the *Concordia* of 1467, from 1493 onwards routine business was conducted at chapters convened by each province. The chapter provincial lasted about three days and was normally attended by commendators or their representatives and religious of the host convent, though others might present themselves with the permission of the general, or the provincial in the case of Castile. The four-member diffinitory, which conducted the business of the chapter, was drawn from the assembled commendators at the start of proceedings under the scrutiny of the president. It was here that individuals were allocated to commanderies at the discretion of their superiors, who were in turn prohibited from removing them from office within a year of their appointment. By the sixteenth century, in line with the frequency with which chapters were convened, the commendator's tenure had been reduced to three years, though this rule was widely ignored and distinguished religious continued to be granted office in perpetuity. However, the main business of each chapter remained the collection of responsions (alms quotas) for the redemption of captives from the commendators and the organization of the next ransoming expedition.

Albert, for his part, recognized annual chapters general as a serious restraint on the authority of the master, and he therefore ruled that these were to sit only at three-year intervals or on the death of the general.[104] Without altering existing capitular procedure, Albert drastically curtailed the number of religious holding executive power in the chapters general, giving these an exclusivity they had previously never enjoyed. Attendance was limited to a diffinitory presided over by the general or his vicar which now consisted of two representatives elected by ballot from each of the chapters provincial, one of whom by the sixteenth century was the provincial himself.(46v–47v) It was, decreed Albert, the duty of the diffinitors to 'ordain, constitute, alter, add, diminish, laud, confirm, approve' legislation that was to be binding on the whole Order.(60v) Over their deliberations the president enjoyed the casting vote. Initially, for every three chapters general convened two were to be held in Catalonia with the third in

[103] Vázquez Núñez, *Manual*, I, pp. 449–50.
[104] Millán Rubio, *La Orden*, p. 142.

Castile, but this was not observed for long and as a rule chapters took place when and where the general chose. The separation of Castile from the rest of the Order in 1467 had the effect of lessening their significance, and it was only after 1574 that the chapter general resumed its role as the principal executive body of the entire Order.

With Albert's accession as general of the Order in 1317 the priorship of Barcelona resumed its former subordination to the high office. However, in recognition of the leading role it had played in the clericalizing of the Order, Albert installed the prior as the general's lieutenant and granted the office an exalted position in Mercedarian government.(45r–46v) The prior of Barcelona not only enjoyed the provincialcy of Catalonia, but, as superior of the mother house, perpetual and irrevocable office as well as the unique privilege of being elected by the community rather than nominated by the general. Yet, having confirmed the office in such powers, Albert was anxious that its incumbents should never again be able to compete with the masters general in the government of the Order as he had done during his own priorate. His solution was to ensure a complementary rather than competitive exercise of power with regard to the rest of the Order. The principal expression of this policy were the ordinances surrounding the electoral chapters general. Through these, and under the aegis of the mother house, Albert bound the offices of master and prior into the nucleus of the Mercedarian constitution.

As Albert made clear at Cuenca in 1319, one of the main reasons for implementing new legislation was 'to avoid the dangers, harm and scandal that can overcome the Order as the result of a long vacancy in the mastership'.[105] At Agramunt eight years later Fra Ramon went even further, declaring in the new constitutions his anxiety that, under interregum, 'the Order not be judged leaderless, monstrous or headless'.(40v) The vacancy had indeed shown itself to be the most delicate period in the life of the Order, and it is fitting that the elaborate provisions set down by Albert for this circumstance should lie at the heart of his constitutions. This legislation proved to be the most durable of Albert's measures: first set down at Lleida in 1320 and clarified in 1327, it survived unchanged into the late sixteenth century to have a major impact on the reform period.(36r–45r)

On the death or resignation of the general, the prior of Barcelona

---

[105] *Ibid.*, p. 137.

was to assume control of the Order as vicar general. He was required, within a stipulated period, to convene a chapter at the priory of Barcelona during which seven diffinitors general were to appoint a successor. The five provinces were each represented by an diffinitor, who was appointed for the sole purpose of fulfilling this duty.(47r–v) The remaining places in the electoral college were filled by the vicar general himself and, as his *socio* (companion), the ordained conventual of longest profession in the priory of Barcelona, so that three out of the seven electors were Catalans. Following mass at dawn on the appointed day, the seven electors were locked into a chamber where votes were cast until a majority decision had been reached.(60r–61v) Once the election had been made the brethren repaired to the priory church, or even the cathedral, and chanted the *Te Deum*. It was then incumbent upon the vicar general to publish the news to the rest of the Order and seek papal confirmation of the appointment, retaining supreme authority until such time as this were granted. The vicar general then resumed his office as prior of Barcelona.

The favoured status of Barcelona in this arrangement need hardly be emphasized. As the 1327 constitutions made clear, the priory was considered 'the head and foundation of all our Order', the basis of its spiritual and temporal authority and the accepted residence of the generals.(38r) By concentrating power at the centre Albert had hoped to put an end to the disunity of the Order and provide it with the focus that had been lacking. Unfortunately time would demonstrate that in solving one pernicious problem he had only laid the foundations of another. For here lies the central flaw in the Albertine constitutions that would colour the history of the Order for the next 250 years: in favouring the mother house above all others to such a degree, Albert legislated for a damaging particularism which, while it persisted, tied the fortunes of the Order to those of Barcelona. Although, as the constitutions made clear, the election was to be conducted 'without any violence', the opportunities for abuse and coercion that existed were soon exploited, and by the mid fifteenth century the priory of Barcelona had begun to exercise an onerous domination over the Order.(38r) Of the twenty-one generals who governed the Mercedarians from Albert to Fra Maties Papiol (1567–8), no less than fourteen were sons of the house of Barcelona, and, particularly in the sixteenth century, former priors as well. But while this legislation afforded Barcelona immense power, continued abuse undermined the status of the priory and the office of general with regard to the rest of the Order, and in the long term Albert's sucessors were to pay for this institutionalized particularism with conflict and division. The association of general, prior and Barcelona therefore lies at the heart of the Albertine constitutions, and the attempt by the reformers, from the 1560s onwards, to rend this triumvirate asunder would bring the Order to the verge of destruction.

XIII. *A Clericalized Order*

A natural corollary of Albert's measures was the clericalization of the Mercedarian hierarchy. In 1319, with the high office controlling both the spiritual and the temporal life of the Order, Albert restricted all electoral powers and senior offices, including that of master general, to ordained religious, thereby barring laics from the Mercedarian hierarchy.[106] The further injunction that lay brethren could no longer correct clerics reflects the virtual monopoly that these now had over the commanderies of the Order. A papal order of 1318 had protected lay superiors from being turned out of the commanderies that remained to them, obliging Albert to make a number of conciliatory gestures to individuals.[107] However, these were temporary measures and the diminished authority of the laics waned and died. This did not, however, signify the end of the lay presence in the Mercedarians, and *hermanos legos* — adult converts to the religious life — continued to play an essential role in the domestic life of the Order. Nor does the primacy of a clerical faction mean that all Mercedarians were ordained; it was the late sixteenth century before a majority of religious were in holy orders.

The period from the death of Pere d'Amer in 1301 to that of Ramon Albert in 1330 was therefore somewhat more than a process of clericalization, pitting as it did the progressive against the conservative elements in the Order. Albert's primary aim had been the restructuring of the Mercedarian institutional system, which he achieved by clericalizing the hierarchy of the Order. While it was consistent with the religious climate of the day, Albert's clericalization was carried out very much on Mercedarian terms and the result was

---

[106] *Ibid.*, p. 142.
[107] *Ibid.*, p. 137.

a compromise solution. The new *modus vivendi* retained many earlier characteristics within a restored framework; the lay power in the Order was expunged but the lay mentality ensconced within it lived on. Although Albert managed to secure for the clerics the right to conduct the ransom of captives that had previously been the preserve of lay brethren, the lay cast of mind that attracted Mercedarians to this activity persisted and the values of the primitive brotherhood remained etched indelibly into the psyche of the Order. The survival of these values into the sixteenth century provided another generation of reformers with a basis for distinguishing between what was acceptable and what was not in Mercedarian life against the religious and political standards of the age. Informed by a clericalizing rationale, the conflict that unfolded under Philip II therefore represents a further clash between the progressive and the conservative tendencies at the heart of the Order. Just as Amer's legislation had proved inadequate in the early fourteenth century, so Albert's, forced on the Mercedarians in a period of crisis, was by the sixteenth considered both inequitable and of doubtful legitimacy. It is this circumstance that, to a considerable degree, makes the crisis of reform under Philip II the unfinished business of the fourteenth century.

The early fourteenth century was therefore a period of 'reform', the principal aim of which had been clericalization within a transformed institutional framework, and thus was Albert's work perceived by later generations. Moral and disciplinary reform were discussed periodically in mid century, even provoking the formulation of plans at the chapter general of Barcelona in 1365 for a return to the 'primitive observance' of the Order.[108] But in practice only Albert's reform stood, and it was as an institutional rather than as a spiritual legislator that he was best remembered. As Gaver wrote in his *Speculum fratrum* of 1445, 'Albert […] did many good things in the Order; he reformed it and set out the constitutions we now have, in particular that notable statute regarding the election of the master general…'.[109] The comparable aims of the crown in tackling the reform of the Order in the sixteenth century reflects the underlying dialogue that existed with Albert's generation. The idea of Mercedarian Reform therefore implies a strong element of continuity that binds the Order

---

[108] Mᵒ Fray Alonso Remón, *Historia General de la Orden de Nuestra Señora de la Merced, Redempcion de Cautivos* (2 vols., Madrid: Luis Sánchez, 1618–33); I, f. 438r.

[109] Cited in Millán Rubio, *La Orden*, p. 106.

of Habsburg Spain with that of its *centuria primera* from Nolasch to Albert and beyond.

XIV. *Decline, Patronage and Survival, 1330–1429*

The years after Albert's death in 1330 would not deliver the unity and stability that he had called for in the preamble to the 1327 constitutions, and events would for some time overtake much of his legislation. Albert had, theoretically at least, strengthened the authority of the generals over the Order, but the crisis years of the early fourteenth century had caused lasting damage to the integrity and standing of the Mercedarian hierarchy. A tendency to preserve individual interests and prerogatives above those of the Order became the norm for superiors, who took to embezzling its funds and alienating its patrimony. For a time at least during the locust years the practice of redemption had diminished, and as the brethren became less worthy of respect so donations had fallen away, though this situation was not destined to last. On the other hand, while Albert had left the Order with a fully legislated system of government, the underlying cycle of dissent and insubordination that had set in after Nolasch's death would continue to assert itself periodically during the course of the fourteenth century and beyond. Moreover, the Mercedarian conflict had noticeably undermined the position of the congregation in the Church. In drawing upon the support of Clement V and John XXII during his priorate and then his generalate, Albert had been forced to surrender much of the independence of the Order to the papacy and to episcopal authority. In 1320 Albert was obliged to submit the Order to the authority of the bishop of Barcelona, and in 1341 the papacy arrogated to itself the power to appoint the generals.[110] This right, first exercised in 1345, was relinquished only after the death of the thirteenth master, Fra Nicolau Peris, in 1401, and it was Peris, too, who regained the Order a measure of independence from episcopal jurisdiction in 1399.[111] The effort to restore the Order's position, and the fierce opposition encountered by the brethren in their ransoming activities, gradually brought the Mercedarians back into the arms of the crown as the century unfolded.

---

[110] *Ibid.*, p. 223.
[111] Called Fray Nicolás Pérez by Mercedarian chroniclers. For the jurisdictional struggles following Peris' death, see Vázquez Núñez, *Manual*, I, pp. 283–8.

In 1331 Alfons IV (1327–36) began the extension of the priory church at Barcelona, leaving the house a number of endowments that prompted the construction during the 1330s of a large gothic convent on Plegamans' original site.[112] However, the status of the priory as both the spiritual and temporal home of the Order was by no means fully established. The shrine of El Puig in particular rivalled that of Barcelona both spiritually and as the burial place of the generals, including Albert, while its vicarship remained one of the most influential offices in the Order.[113] By this time the remote shrine of Nuestra Señora del Olivar near Teruel had also come to prominence, to be joined in 1335 by that of Bonaria in Cagliari on Sardinia. Together these would remain the focus of provincial spirituality in an Order increasingly fragmented and resistant to centralizing authority of the kind envisaged by Albert. The province of Castile-Portugal, already independent as to the redemption of captives, began to drift away from the general's authority, so that, enfeebled and lacking cohesion, the Mercedarians fell easy prey to the upheavals of the age. The onset of the plague in the late 1340s diminished both the personnel and the organization of the Order.[114] Provence and Castile-Portugal were worst affected with a total of six houses extinguished against only two founded in this period. In the Crown of Aragon another seven were destroyed or seriously damaged in the war against Castile (1356–75), though the province of Aragon-Navarre established an important house at Burceña near Bilbao in 1384. Impoverished by high mortality both among the religious and their alms-collecting coadjutors, the Mercedarians again faltered in their ransoming vocation and drifted into relaxation and lawlessness.

It is a measure of the state of the Order that in 1357 the general Frey Ponce de Barellis of Toulouse (1348–64) presented a ten-point plan to Clement VI for an amalgamation of the Mercedarians with the Trinitarians.[115] This Pere IV dismissed the following year as the work of a foreigner ignorant of the Order's historic relationship with the Aragonese royal house. The appointment of the Valencian Peris

---

[112] See Josefina Mutgé, 'Algunes notes sobre Alfons el Benigne i l'Orde de la Mercè de Barcelona' in *Anuario de Estudios Medievales*, 11 (1981), pp. 853–8.

[113] The short-lived Catalan general Fra Vicenç Riera (1344–5) referred to the institution as 'Ordo Beatae Mariae de Podio Valentie [= Puig de Valencia] Mercedis Captivorum'; Millán Rubio, *La Orden*, p. 225.

[114] *Ibid.*, pp. 255–6.

[115] *Ibid.*, p. 257.

as general in 1365 hastened the restoration of relations with the crown that the Order so desperately needed, faced as it was by widespread opposition and abuse of its alms-collecting rights by royal officials and elements of the secular and regular clergy. Mindful of the crown's traditional role both as founder and 'protector and conservator of the Order' and anxious for its good reputation, Pere made a policy of safeguarding Mercedarian property, rights and income, and expanding its privileges with respect to those of the mendicants.[116] To this Peris responded by placing the institution and its religious at the disposal of the crown. As patrons of the Order, the kings of Aragon were granted full legislative and convocatory powers over it, powers which, though exercised only rarely, coloured the process of reform under Philip II. The re-establishment of the Order into royal favour culminated in 1400 with the conferral in perpetuity of the chaplaincy of the palatine chapel of Santa Agueda in Barcelona, which remained in Mercedarian hands until the nineteenth century.[117]

The late fourteenth century therefore saw the development of a relationship of special importance to the later history of the Order, of mutual responsibility from both parties on a purely practical basis.[118] In return for royal patronage and protection from the opposition of local officials and both the secular and regular clergy to Mercedarian alms collection, the Order offered valuable ransoming and occasionally diplomatic services to the crown. Even so, there can be no doubt that the generalcy lost much of its power to control the commendators during Peris' tenure, and, as in other orders, restlessness and indiscipline continued to affect the Mercedarians at local level. In 1389 public denunciations were heard against the moral and spiritual decline of the brethren at the chapter general held in Barcelona that summer.[119] The high office provided little example in this matter, with Peris guilty of expropriating money from a number of houses. Under these circumstances the generals would have to be content

---

[116] The citation is in *ibid.*, p. 312. On Pere's attempts to expand Mercedarian privileges in 1373, see Vázquez Núñez, *Manual*, I, p. 257.

[117] See *ibid.*, pp. 280–2, & ACA, Mon., vols. 2673, 2730 & 2830.

[118] For a discussion of this, see James William Brodman, 'Ransomers or Royal Agents: The Mercedarians and the Aragonese Crown in the Fourteenth Century' in *Iberia and the Mediterranean World of the Middle Ages: Essays in Honor of Robert I. Burns S.J.*, vol. II, ed. P.E. Chevedden, D.J. Kagay, & P.G. Padilla (Leiden, 1996); pp. 239–51, an article prepared without reference to Millán Rubio, *La Orden*.

[119] Sáinz de la Maza Lasoli, 'Los Mercedarios', p. 240.

with exercising authority over an Order divided into fiefs controlled
by provincials and senior commendators, and whose discipline and
allegiance to the hierarchy varied from generation to generation.

XV. *Crisis and Division, 1429–67*

It was only a matter of time before local unrest was reflected in the
upper echelons of the Order. The election of the ambitious Fra
Antoni Dullan, prior of Barcelona, to the high office in 1429 marks
the beginning of a period of serious disturbance.[120] Thwarted in an
attempt to monopolize the leading offices, Dullan embarked on a dissolute rule that again brought the Order into the hands of the secular
clergy and exposed it to the flux of conciliar politics.[121] A wave of
opposition to Dullan centred in Castile succeeded in having him
overthrown at the Council of Basle in 1441, the first indication of the
influence now wielded by this province. In May of that year the bishop of Osma, Roberto de Moya, named Fray Pedro de Huete, commendator of Guadalajara, as general of the Order — the first Castilian to hold this office. Though the appointment was ratified by Euge-
nius IV, Huete was not accepted in the Crown of Aragon where the
prior of Barcelona, Fra Nadal Gaver, was declared general in January 1442 and later confirmed by Nicholas V. There followed a
decade during which neither claimant could obtain a consensus of
support even in his own province, while the Order languished in the
absurd situation of having two legitimate generals.

   The death of Huete in 1452 brought Gaver into uncontested command of the Order, but the events of recent years, the restored Catalan stranglehold on the generalcy and the scandalous abuse associated
with it had begun to rankle with the Castilian brethren.[122] The realiza-

---

[120] Despite the ample documentation that survives in ACA, APV, ADHG, ADH
and the Archives Départmentales de Gironde (Bordeaux), the 15th-century Order
has attracted very little attention from historians. The only secondary sources of any
note are Fr Conrad Eubel, *Die avignonesische Obedienz der Mendikanten-Orden, sowie der
Orden der Mercedarier und Trinitarier zur Zeit des grossen Schismus* (Paderborn, 1900), and
those of P.Fr. Guillermo Vázquez Núñez, *viz. Don Diego de Muros, Obispo de Tuy y de
Ciudad-Rodrigo de la Orden de la Merced (1405?–1492)* (Madrid, 1919), and the relevant
sections of *id., Manual*, vol. I, and *id.*, ed., *La Merced a mediados de los siglos XV y XVI:
Documentos inéditos y observaciones* (Rome, 1931).
[121] Vázquez Núñez, *Manual*, I, pp. 325–46.
[122] *Ibid.*, pp. 349–50.

tion that Castilians were effectively barred from competing fairly for the high office under the existing electoral system was enhanced by a taste for autonomy acquired during the Huete generalate. Castile would never be the same again. The province's recognition of Gaver's generalcy in 1452 was made conditional on the acceptance of four demands, first mooted by Huete, that represent the origin of Castilian independence. These conditions demonstrate that the Castilians were still prepared to participate in the existing system, but only on terms that reflected their growing importance in the Order. In the first place the province's representation at the electoral chapters general was to be increased from one to four, more even than Catalonia herself. Castilian chapters were to be presided over by the provincial as well as the general, whose entitlement to half the possessions of all deceased religious was seriously curtailed. Although Gaver's acceptance of these demands is an indication of the weakened condition of his office, the *status quo* remained unaffected. Substantial quantities of money from Castile continued to add to Gaver's personal income which at this time stood at around 450 florins per annum.[123]

By the end of the decade, however, Gaver was finding that the powers he had surrendered to the provincial M° Fray Macías de Monterrey (1452–64) in 1452 were making the maintenance of his authority increasingly difficult in Castile.[124] Within a few years Monterrey had begun, with the support of his province, to exercise an unprecedented degree of autonomy. Under these circumstances Gaver sought a renegotiation of the 1452 agreement, the fruit of which was a *concordia* signed with Monterrey at Toledo in 1459. This, however, came to nothing as Monterrey, sensing Gaver's weakness, decided to force the situation. In a blatant affront both to the general and to Catalan sensibilities, Monterrey began to move against those Castilian commendators who had given their loyalty to Gaver rather than to Huete during the 1440s. Having ignored repeated warnings, Monterrey was deposed by Gaver in December 1460 on the grounds that he had usurped the general's authority. But Gaver, who had become embroiled in the Catalan civil war, was in no position to assert his powers and again opted for a negotiated settlement.[125]

---

[123] *Ibid.*, p. 336.
[124] *Ibid.*, pp. 357–60.
[125] Though the Mercedarians were certainly active in this conflict, we have no details at present other than the sacking of the convent of Lleida in *c.*1464.

Gaver's appointment of M° Fray Diego de Muros as provincial of Castile in 1465 finally brought matters to a head.[126] In 1466 a certain Fray Pedro Payo Borrayo, conventual of Huete, appears to have trumped up a charge against Muros to the effect that he was planning to kidnap Gaver on his way to the chapter general of Toledo that year. This allegation Gaver seems to have swallowed whole, for he first appointed Borrayo his vicar general in Castile and then indignantly removed Muros from office at the chapter, excommunicating him and his supporters. Nonetheless, Gaver still granted the Castilians the right to elect their own provincial, which they proceeded to exercise. Within a few months, however, Muros appears to have extracted a confession from Borrayo that caused both him and the new provincial, P° Fray Hernando de Córdoba, to surrender their offices in Muros' favour. A chastened Gaver had no alternative but to restore Muros as provincial and convene another chapter, and it was against this absurd background that delegates gathered in September 1467 for the momentous chapter general of Guadalajara.[127]

Gaver was clearly in a weak position, and under these circumstances Muros succeeded first in advocating the autonomy of Castile as the only solution to the conflict that had smouldered for a generation, and then in dictating its terms. Gaver's recognition of the will of the Castilians for independence — for which later Catalans never forgave him — represents a turning point in the history of the Order. The so-called *Concordia* that resulted was essentially a pact of non-interference whereby the Castilians were exempted from the authority of the general in return for effectively surrendering their pretensions to the high office.[128] Under the terms of the agreement, the provincials of Castile were not only immune from the authority of the master, but exercised comparable powers over their religious, and were to give their obedience to the general on the understanding that the terms of the *Concordia* be observed inviolably. The generals, who were forbidden from intervening in the affairs of the province, were to receive an annual tribute — *vestuario* — of forty Castilian *doblas* in gold, payable in Valencia on the feast of St John the Baptist, along

---

[126] Vázquez Núñez, *Manual*, I, pp. 361–3.

[127] *Ibid.*, pp. 363–4. The *synodalia* are reproduced in *id.*, ed., *La Merced a mediados*, pp. 41–63.

[128] The term *Concordia* is not contemporaneous with the the the signing of this document, and is the invention of Castilian propagandists of the 16th century.

with the provincial's mule on the death of its owner. The Castilians retained the right to send two diffinitors to the chapters general, but their representation at the electoral meeting was reduced from four to the single voter provided for in the 1327 constitutions.

*

In a sense, the division of the Mercedarians in 1467 reflects similar schisms in other orders, though in this case the motivation was political rather than spiritual. The Castilians were destined to withdraw gradually from the life of the Order as a whole, so that time would not only divide the institution, but divide it against itself. For a century Castile and the provinces that remained loyal to the masters general were to follow widely divergent paths. In the Crown of Aragon the years after 1467 would bring eventual stagnation; for Castile the future held expansion into new fields and finally the assumption of power over the Order. By the 1630s Tirso de Molina could justifiably contemplate the history of his province over the previous 170 years as a reflection of the status of Castile herself in the affairs of the Peninsula. As he wrote in the *Historia* concerning the province of Castile,

> The truth is that, just as she lies in the heart of Spain, so she lies at the heart of all our Order, as much in her authority as in her size and in her learning, so that she is bettered by no other...[129]

The means by which the province of Castile began to acquire this exalted status is what now concerns us.

---

[129] Tirso, *Historia*, I, p. 395.

CHAPTER TWO

NEW FRONTIERS: THE RISE OF CASTILE (1467–1561)

The truth is that, just as she lies in the heart of Spain, so she lies at
the heart of all our Order, as much in her authority as in her size and
in her learning, so that she is bettered by no other...[1]

Although the chapter general of Guadalajara represents the beginning of a new phase in the history of the Order, it coincided with a
period of grave disruption in the Peninsula that was reflected in many
of the religious orders, not least the Mercedarians. Throughout the
Order the half-century following the *Concordia* of 1467 brought to a
culmination the undercurrent of lawlessness and insubordination that
had been developing since the fourteenth century. To these problems
the Order addressed itself somewhat diffidently and without direction
while, in Castile in particular, devoting much of its energies to expansion into old and new fields first in the Peninsula and then in the New
World. However, this period also saw the beginnings of what would
later become a cogent reform movement, one closely allied to the
development of an academic tradition in the Order. It is the formation of this movement, especially in Castile, that concerns us here.

I. *Conflict and Expansion*

The period remains unstudied, but it is apparent that in the eastern
provinces the Valencian general Fra Llorens Company (1474–9) and
his successor, Frey Antoine Maurel of Toulouse (1480–92),[2] had at
times considerable difficulty in maintaining their authority over those
sectors of the Order that remained to them. In the Crown of Aragon

---

[1] Tirso, *Historia*, I, p. 395.
[2] Called Fray Antonio Morell or Morelli by Spanish chroniclers. For a royal
decree condemning efforts to scupper Maurel's convocation of the chapter general of
Valencia in 1489, see Antonio de la Torre y del Cerro, ed., *Documentos sobre relaciones
internacionales de los Reyes Católicos* (6 vols., Barcelona, 1949–66); III, pp. 232–4.

the 1470s and '80s were punctuated by scandal both at local level and in the hierarchy of the Order, while the sub-province of Navarre mounted a campaign of disobedience to Company based, it seems, on the loss of the houses at Logroño and Burceña to Castile in 1467.[3] Refusing to pay their redemption responsions, the Navarrese brethren were brought to heel only with the threat of excommunication in 1478.

The principal Mercedarian foundations of the Crown of Aragon during the fifteenth century reflect the development of the Catalan seaborne empire. A house was established at Naples by Alfons V (1416–58) in 1442 and the important priory of Palermo followed in around 1463.[4] In France the first half of the century saw a marked expansion, with five new houses opened between 1400 and 1440, including those at Marseille (1418) and Bordeaux (by 1440).[5] This momentum, however, was not maintained. In the Crown of Aragon proper, Uncastillo (before 1443) was one of only three minor foundations in the centuries between the establishment of Tàrrega in Catalonia (1326) and the Colegio de San Pedro Nolasco at Valencia in 1630, eloquent testimony to the prolonged stagnation of the masters' patrimony.

From now on the survival of ransoming records allows us to gauge the condition of the Order in terms of the work of redemption. A joint Aragonese expedition mounted in 1475 to Algiers, Bougie and Bona returned with a meagre thirty-nine captives, and henceforth the provinces subject to the generals would lag further and further behind Castile in the principal vocation of the Order. Despite accusations of corruption and the adverse political situation in Castile, which prevented the celebration of a chapter general scheduled for Córdoba in 1477, the Castilian redemptors were able to ransom no less than 180 captives on the Barbary Coast that year.[6] Rivalling the rest of the Order in both houses and manpower, Castile began under its 'provincials general' to establish its independence from the masters and adopt a manifestly different character, though the province was

---

[3] Vázquez Núñez, *Manual*, I, p. 376.

[4] See *id.*, 'Conventos de la Orden', pp. 297–303. The erection of the Italian province would have to wait until 1606. Long after its foundation the convent of Santa Ana at Palermo remained the focus of intense episcopal and secular opposition to the collection of alms for the redemption of captives on the island.

[5] *Ibid.*, pp. 289–96.

[6] Tirso, *Historia*, I, p. 412.

for some time in a similar state of disorder to the Crown of Aragon.[7]
From 1471 the provincialcy was contested by the commendator of
Valladolid, Mº Fray Francisco de Mondragón, and Pº Fray Hernando de Córdoba whom Diego de Muros had apparently appointed as
his successor. This, however, appears to have been resolved by 1482.

After a slow start the expansion of the province of Castile quickened towards the end of the century.[8] The most significant development before 1467 was the refounding of the Order's house at Salamanca into the college of the Vera Cruz (c.1411), followed in the
1450s with convents at Cazorla, Toro (refounded) and elsewhere. In
the final decades of the fifteenth century a succession of gifted provincials opened the north-west of the Peninsula to the Order, culminating with the foundation of Santa Maria de Conxo outside Santiago
de Compostela in 1493. By this time, however, the Mercedarians had
been caught up in Castile's imperial destiny. The fall of Granada to
the Crown of Castile in 1492 was an event of particular significance
for the Mercedarians, for with it the last field for redemptive activity
within the Peninsula was extinguished. A string of houses followed in
Andalusia along with one at Oran on the Barbary Coast (1509), but
the frontiers that had always beckoned the Order were now elsewhere. Although Mercedarians had long been undertaking ransoming expeditions to North Africa, events now demanded a change of
perspective and it is therefore appropriate that at least one Castilian
friar accompanied Columbus on his second voyage to the Caribbean
in 1493.[9] From this moment the province was committed to an overseas enterprise to which it would devote much of its energy and from
which it would, years hence, derive great wealth. Time would
demonstrate the Castilian Mercedarians to be among the few Spanish religious congregations prepared to accept the challenge of expansion in the New World.

[7] On this see Vázquez Núñez, *Manual*, I, pp. 372–5, and the disordered notes of
the 17th-century Castilian chronicler Mº Fray Felipe Colombo in BNM, ms. 2684,
ff. 22r–25v.
[8] Vázquez Núñez, 'Conventos de la Orden', pp. 143–57.
[9] See Peter Martyr D'Anghera, *De Orbe Novo: The Eight Decades...*, trans. & ed. Francis Augustus MacNutt (2 vols., New York, 1912); I, p. 99. On Columbus and the
Mercedarians, see P.Fr. Guillermo Vázquez Núñez, *La Merced en Hispanoamérica*
(Madrid, 1968), pp. 23–31, esp. 27.

II. *Vocation and Self-Perception*

The rise of Castile to dominance in the Order owed much to the expansion of its horizons to America and the wealth it derived in return. However, by the end of the fifteenth century the Mercedarians had begun to establish a tradition of learning that would flower in the sixteenth and was to contribute greatly to the reformist mentality of the leading Castilian religious in particular. It is hardly surprising that an order endowed with a version of the Dominican constitutions should, to some degree at least, espouse the academic life, but here as in other ways the Mercedarians were late developers.

The growth of learning in the Order was a concomitant of the process of clericalization which it experienced from the end of the thirteenth century. Although the Order had established houses in a number of university towns — not least in Toulouse (by 1258), Montpellier (by 1263), and Salamanca (by 1317) — it is not until the 1330s that we receive indications of Mercedarian involvement in academic life. The Catalan general Fra Berenguer Cantull (1331–43) appears to have received the degree of master of theology in Paris in 1338 and Mercedarians began pursuing studies here from about this time.[10] In 1346 the reformist master Frey Dominique Sans (1345–8), a doctor of canon law at Paris and prominent in the university of Montpellier, stressed the importance of a theological and philosophical formation for the religious in their charitable vocation.[11] To this end, Sans is believed to have founded three *studia* at Montpellier, Girona and El Puig, though we have no further details on these. Nevertheless, if not customary, the taking of degrees was common from this time onwards and the Order maintained a moderate interest in academic life through the rest of the fourteenth century. The Valencian Fra Nicolau Peris appears to have held a chair in canon law at Montpellier before becoming general in 1365, which would make him the first Mercedarian professor, while Fra Francesc Olot became vice-rector of the university of Lleida in

---

[10] Millán Rubio, *La Orden*, p. 197.

[11] *Ibid.*, p. 239. Called Fray Domingo Serrano by Spanish chroniclers. See also Alexandre Charles Germain, *Histoire de la commune de Montpellier* (3 vols., Montpellier, 1851), III, pp. 272–3 & 325–6, & Vázquez Núñez, *Mercedarios ilustres*, pp. 54–8; the latter's suggestion that Sans was the first Mercedarian professor is unsubstantiated.

1383.[12] These developments culminated with the foundation of the
college of the Vera Cruz at Salamanca some fifteen years after the
establishment of the faculty of theology here in around 1396.[13]

During the generalate of the Castilian Mº Fray Pedro de Huete
(1441–52) religious with bachelor's degrees were, subject to the confirmation of the master, for the first time accorded special status and
thereafter learning began to assume real significance in the Order.[14]
By now a number of educated figures had begun to emerge, among
them Fray Pedro de Logroño, a graduate of the university of Paris
and eventually provincial of Castile (1482–90), and the Aragonese
Fray Pedro de Cijar (†1452), author of the propagandistic *Opusculum
tantum quinque*.[15] Like Gaver's contemporaneous *Speculum fratrum*, the
Opusculum represents a conscious attempt to portray the diversity and
equality of the Order with regard to other religious congregations, of
which the development of academic life was an important element.
As Gaver put it somewhat apologetically in the prologue to the
Speculum,

> We do all that other religious do, as well as freeing our neighbours
> from the infidel with alms gathered from the faithful. If other religious
> preach, then so do we; if others celebrate the divine office, then we do
> likewise; if others hear confessions, then we hear them also; if others
> praise God in chant and psalmody, we do the same; if other orders
> have men of learning, so have we many such among us, and as others
> have hands, tongues, feet and heads, so also have we. Thus, if the
> faithful give alms to these orders for such works and for their service to
> God, then likewise do they donate them to us — this quite apart from
> the exercise of that most excellent charity which our Lord and
> Redeemer Jesus Christ demonstrated toward us.[16]

---

[12] On Peris, called Fray Nicolás Pérez by Spanish chroniclers, see BUV, ms. 884,
pp. 45–64, 'Memorias de algunos varones illustres valencianos en santidad y letras',
undated but early 17th century; p. 58. On Olot, see Vázquez Núñez, *Manual*, I,
p. 258.

[13] Vázquez Núñez, *Manual*, I, p. 303.

[14] See P.Fr. Guillermo Vázquez Núñez, 'Los grados académicos entre los Mercedarios' in *BOM*, 19 (1931), pp. 283–7.

[15] *Opusculum tantum quinque [...] super conmutatione votorum in redemptionem captivorum*
(Zaragoza: ?, 1491; Barcelona: Pere Posa, 1491, 4°, and Paris: ?, 1506); see Placer
López, *Bibliografía mercedaria*, I, p. 346. There are selections from this text in Vázquez
Núñez, ed., *Monumenta ad historiam Ordinis*.

[16] From ACA, Mss.Varia, vol. II, ff. 1r–6r: 'Prohemium libri fundacionis ordinis
Beatae Mariae de mercede redempcionis captivorum'; passage cited f. 1r. Translated
versions of this passage are reproduced in Vázquez Núñez, *Manual*, I, pp. 353–4, &
id., 'Comentando un refrán antiguo', p. 54.

This desire for a diversity that would necessarily draw numbers of religious away from the Order's traditional vocation was not new. In 1327 Albert had declared the Order to have been established both for the redemption of captives and for divine worship; now in 1447 the queen of Aragon, María of Castile, could inform the pope that the Mercedarians had a double office: the redemption of Christian souls and the preservation of such souls through preaching and confession.[17] Finally, in 1457 the Castilian Logroño, then procurator general in Rome, sent a memorandum to the Borja pope Calixtus III, in which he declared the Mercedarian Order to be the most perfect after the Carthusians, a measure against the continual haemorrhaging of religious to other orders that was depriving it of personnel.[18]

The significance of the *Speculum fratrum*, composed by the Catalan general Fra Nadal Gaver in 1445, has never been fully recognized by Mercedarian historians. The actual title of the work — *Liber fundationis ordinis Beatae Mariae de Mercede redemptionis captivorum* — and the immense effort and expense that went into the manufacture of the master copy suggests that Gaver intended it to be a touchstone for the life and being of the Order. The vellum codex, which survives in the Archive of the Crown of Aragon, is, if nothing else, a masterpiece of fifteenth-century penmanship.[19] In it Gaver collected the medieval legislation of the Order: the Amer constitutions of 1272 and those of

[17] Vázquez Núñez, *Manual*, I, p. 354.

[18] See P.Fr. Guillermo Vázquez Núñez, ed., 'Memorial del Maestro Fray Pedro de Logroño a Calixto III' in *BOM*, 19 (1931), pp. 1–7; 7.

[19] There are three extant 15th-century MSS of the *Speculum fratrum ordinis beatissime virginis Marie de mercede redemptionis captivorum*, to use its full title. The master is in ACA, Mss.Varia, vol. II, a folio vol. in 196 ff. on vellum. There are later copies in the Bibliothèque Municipale de Toulouse, ms. 491 (1470), and the Bibliothèque Nationale, Paris, Numéro Acquisitions Latines: 1788. I have not seen the Paris and Toulouse codices, but the latter and the ACA volume both have later accretions. On this see Devesa Blanco, 'Las primitivas constituciones de la Orden de la Merced', pp. 14–23, & González Castro, 'Las constituciones del P. Raimundo Albert', pp. 181–4. There is a copy of 1644, less the 1272 constitutions, in ARV, Clero, lib. 1776, and the work has been published in part in Vázquez Núñez, ed., *Monumenta ad historiam Ordinis*. Despite Gaver's orders that it be preserved, the original MS in his own hand had disappeared by the mid 18th century; Devesa Blanco, 'Las primitivas constituciones', pp. 13–15.

The *Speculum* may have been published in Barcelona in 1468, which would make it the earliest book printed in Spain; see Ferran Soldevila, 'Un indici favorable a l'incunable Barceloní de 1468' in *Germinabit: Circular de la Unió Escolania de Montserrat*, 61 (April 1959), pp. 8–9; the 'indici' in question is in ACA, Mss.Misc., vol. 44, f. 5r. However, even if this were the case, no copy is extant nor appears to have been since at least the 17th century; see Placer López, *Bibliografía mercedaria*, II, p. 46.

Albert of 1327 are here, along with the Rule of St Augustine.[20] To
this he added a short biography of Nolasco together with an account
of the foundation and masters of the Order, the *Speculum fratrum*
itself.[21] Here, then, is the first official recognition of Nolasco's role in
the creation of the Order since the schism of 1317, and the first
attempt to evoke a sense of the primordial Mercedarian observance
since the Amer constitutions. Appropriately enough, Gaver goes on
to discuss the schisms — nine in all — that had shaken the Order
since 1301, and continued to do so in his own time and over his own
claim to the mastership.[22] There is a list of popes from Innocent III
(1198–1216) onwards, with their concessions to the Order where relevant, and notes on the priors of Barcelona.[23] The last item of importance, and the only one to address the issue of reform in any practical
sense, is a treatise on the procedure to be adopted by visitors in the
Order.[24] The impression, then, is of an order that now regarded itself
as mature enough to survey the course of its history and observance
after a long and painful gestation — an order that could look to the
future on the basis of a consolidation of the past.

The middle years of the fifteenth century therefore saw a new concern among leading Mercedarians for their place in religious society
and a conscious effort to change the image of the Order. The exemption from episcopal authority obtained by the Mercedarians from
Nicholas V in 1448 at a cost of 1000 florins is no doubt consistent
with this movement for expansion and diversity, a desire to share
some of the attributes of the mendicants while remaining dedicated
principally to the redemption of captives.[25] Thus, while other religious congregations were beginning to embrace spiritual renewal, the

---

[20] ACA, Mss.Varia, vol. II, ff. 44r–53v, 54r–110v & 120r–127r respectively. There
is also an 'Expositio' to the Rule of St Augustine: ff. 128r–173v.

[21] *Ibid.*, ff. 7r–14r & 14v–24v. There is a Castilian translation of the former in
ACA, Mss.Misc., vol. 93, ff. 56r–64v, dated *c.*1557.

[22] ACA, Mss.Varia, vol. II, ff. 177r–191v: 'Secuntur cismata seu divisiones que
fuerunt in ordine sacro de mercede captivorum'.

[23] *Ibid.*, ff. 27r–34v & 37r–42v respectively.

[24] *Ibid.*, ff. 111r–119r: 'Qualiter visitator quicunquae fuerit in visitacionibus pro-
cedere debet et forma quam servare tenetur in principio visitacionis et in tota
visitacione'.

[25] Vázquez Núñez, *Manual*, I, p. 346. The bull of exemption was itself granted
partly as a measure against apostasy, and in particular the tendency of delinquent
religious to seek the protection of bishops from their superiors. The dates of its expedition in Rome — 9th August 1448 — and presentation to the bishop of Barcelona
— 24th July 1449 — long remained feast days in the Mercedarian calendar.

Mercedarian hierarchy set about forging an image commensurate with its new independence within the Church, of which scholarship and learning was considered an indispensable attribute. Promoted from the 1460s by the Castilian M° Fray Diego de Muros as a measure against the palpable ignorance of most friars, it was only a matter of time before this new vocation received full constitutional recognition. In this climate the high offices of the province of Castile in particular began to fall into the hands of a select, learned minority, and increasing numbers of religious began to involve themselves in academic life and in other fields towards the end of the fifteenth century.

III. *New Men*

Fray Diego de Muros (†1492) is the great Mercedarian figure of the second half of the fifteenth century, and one of the very few members of the Order ever to move in the highest political circles.[26] Appointed royal preacher and chaplain to Henry IV of Castile (1454–74) in 1465, Muros was sent to Rome in 1469 to discuss the Turkish threat, and became bishop of the troubled Galician diocese of Tuy in 1471. The issues of royal patronage and clerical (including monastic) reform ranked highly in his second royal embassy to Rome in 1479, and there can be no doubt that Muros was among the more prominent reformist ecclesiastics during the reign of the Catholic Kings.[27] Among the Mercedarians, Muros' reformist mentality was reflected in the impulse he gave to academic life, and for some time it was here rather than in a movement for spiritual reform or 'observance' *per se* that the influence of religious change was felt in the Order. At Guadalajara in 1467 five scholarships were endowed for Castilian religious at Valladolid and Salamanca, while bachelors or licentiates in theology were granted a vote at the chapters provincial, a privilege

---

[26] See *id.*, *Don Diego de Muros*, and *id.*, *Mercedarios ilustres*, pp. 147–55, and also José Manuel Nieto Soria, *Iglesia y génesis del estado moderno en Castilla (1369–1480)* (Madrid, 1993), p. 450.

[27] On the embassies, see P.Fr. José García Oro, 'Conventualismo y observancia: La reforma de las órdenes religiosas en los siglos XV y XVI' in *HIE*, III(i), pp. 211–349; 270–1, and *id.*, *La reforma de los religiosos españoles en tiempo de los Reyes Católicos* (Valladolid, 1969), pp. 32, 34 & 52. Muros' undated instructions from the crown regarding the 1479 embassy are reproduced in *CODOIN*, VII, pp. 539–71.

later extended to graduates in canon law and the arts.[28] Following university norms, at Calatayud in 1475 the requirement for bachelors was set at four books (i.e. years) of *sententiae* (Peter Lombard) or (later) *scholastica* (Aquinas) at an approved *studium generale*, followed by a public defence at a chapter general or provincial.[29] Few went further than a bachelorship in theology since a doctorate was beyond the means of all but the wealthiest religious, but, as in the case of Muros, the title of *maestro* could be conferred on bachelors after long or distinguished service in the Order.[30] During the sixteenth century the Order began to confer its own title of *presentado* on bachelors, and from 1574 the degree of *maestro* was made conditional on the completion of a further three years of study.[31] In this year also the number of *maestros* and *presentados* per province was limited to twelve and twenty-four respectively as a measure against indiscriminate conferment, while their right to a vote in the election of the provincial was endorsed.

By the last decades of the fifteenth century the emphasis on learning was bringing forth a number of distinguished academics in the ranks of the Order. At the chapter general of Pamplona in 1487 the French master Frey Antoine Maurel styled himself professor of theology and dean of the university of Toulouse.[32] At Valencia two years later Maurel granted his countryman, M͟ Frey Sarransot de Dado, professor of theology at Bordeaux, command of the house there *ad vitam*.[33] Dado continued to teach from here until at least 1512, circumstances that underline the French focus of academic interest in the eastern provinces of the Order at this time. Although the mass of Mercedarians remained unlettered, books had clearly become highly prized among senior religious by the end of the fifteenth century. Inventories dating from the 1490s show several Aragonese superiors

---

[28] Vázquez Núñez, *Manual*, I, p. 364.

[29] *Ibid.*, p. 374. These requirements were reiterated almost without modification at the chapter provincial of Castile in 1569; see AGS, E°, leg. 151, no. 194, ff. 3r & 5v.

[30] The *magisterio* of Fray Francisco Zumel at Salamanca cost him around 4000 *reales*, though graduation was notoriously expensive here. Elsewhere it came much cheaper, and during the 17th century Mercedarians often graduated as *maestros* at the Dominican university of Ávila, later incorporating their degrees at Salamanca; Vázquez Núñez, *El Padre Francisco Zumel, general de la Merced y catedrático de Salamanca (1540–1607)* (Madrid, 1920), p. 15.

[31] ACA, Mon., vol. 4144, ff. 130v–131r.

[32] Vázquez Núñez, *Manual*, I, pp. 385–6.

[33] *Ibid.*, p. 388.

to have possessed substantial private libraries and humanistic tastes in literature.[34] At Pamplona and Zaragoza the commendators' *estudios* (studies) each contained over 100 titles, while the *librería* at Calatayud housed over forty, a collection maintained until at least 1519 before being dispersed later in the century. Finally, the important house of Nuestra Señora del Olivar boasted seventy titles in 1516, amassed in all likelihood by the general, the Aragonese Mº Fray Jaime Lorenzo de la Mata (1513–22).[35]

It is unfortunate that no such documentation exists for Castile because here especially a number of houses began to distinguish themselves in culture and learning from the middle years of the fifteenth century. Chief among these was that of Nuestra Señora de la Merced at Burceña near Bilbao. The house was founded in 1384 in the province of Aragon-Navarre for the ransom of Basque captives, seafarers in particular, by Count Fernán Pérez de Ayala and his son Pero López, Chancellor and chronicler of Castile.[36] Around the time of its transfer to the province of Castile in 1467, Burceña began to develop a tradition of learning that would give a string of distinguished men to the Order in the sixteenth century. Astride the main commercial route between Castile and Flanders, the community was well placed to tap into the current of religious ideas entering Spain from the Low Countries. The influence of Northern piety at Burceña may well be reflected in the cluster of *beaterios* that grew up around it in the first half of the sixteenth century.

For a time after 1500, it seems, interest in academic life was pro-

---

[34] ACA, Mon., vol. 2669: visitations in the Crown of Aragon, 1446–1539. References to larger booklists, including printed books ('estampat'): Pamplona — ff. 43v–44v (1494); Zaragoza — 52r–53v (1494); Calatayud — 64v–65r (1494), 133r–v (1511) & 137r (1519); El Olivar — 150r–151r (1516). Several of these inventories are complemented by supplementary lists. For a typical inventory of liturgical works, belonging in this case to the conventual church at Palma, see ARM, AH, leg. 4334, f. 53r, dated 14th May 1517. I am not aware that any such listing survives from the priory of Barcelona before the end of the 18th century: AUB, ms. 1500, 'Indice General de la Biblioteca del convento de la Merced de Barcelona'. However, the conventual library was recorded as having 424 books in 1579: ACA, Mon., vol. 2670, f. 402r. Remnants of this library can be found in ACA, BNM and the Biblioteca de Catalunya in Barcelona. An early-15th century MS copy of Ludolph of Saxony's *Vita Christi* from the priory survives in AUB, ms. 779.

[35] Also called Llorens de la Mata. See P.Fr. Joaquín Millán Rubio, 'El padre Jaime Lorenzo de La Mata y su convento de Santa María de El Olivar' in *Analecta Mercedaria*, 8 (1989), pp. 5–83.

[36] See A.E. Mañaricúa, *El convento mercedario de Burceña* (San Sebastián, 1956), and José de Arriaga, 'Los Mercedarios de Burceña' in *Estudios*, 11 (1955), pp. 121–4.

moted in the Crown of Aragon in a spirit of collaboration with the
rest of the Order. The first chapter general convened by the new
master, Mº Fray Jaime Lorenzo de la Mata, at Játiva in 1514 voted
subsidies to a number of students from the eastern provinces at the
universities of Paris, Zaragoza and Alcalá.[37] The following year Frey
Nicholas Barrère of Carcassonne established a college in Paris near
the Sorbonne on land donated to the Order by the Navarrese nobleman Alain d'Albret, comte de Dreux et de Gomis, which, however,
eked out a miserable existence until the following century.[38] Even so,
Mercedarian scholars in Paris were for the first time spared the cost
and inconvenience of having to seek accommodation in secular colleges or the houses of other orders. Progress towards the training of a
core of educated religious in the eastern provinces was boosted with
the election as general in 1522 of the Valencian Mᵉ Fra Benet Zafont,
a man of known Erasmian sympathies.[39] At his first chapter general
in Barcelona the following year, Zafont, in the presence of the Castilians, passed several ordinances regarding study and academic
degrees, dispatching a number of religious to Paris and extending to
doctors of canon law the privileges granted in 1467 to masters in theology.[40] These, along with masters of arts, were permitted extensive,
indeed excessive, privileges to absent themselves from communal and
devotional duties, to the detriment of conventual life. Although study
and the *stabilitas* required for it lay at the heart of the idea of monastic
reform, under these circumstances learning provided no direct conduit either to spiritual or disciplinary improvement. In Castile, however, steps were being taken towards the establishment of a powerful
academic tradition of lasting significance to the reform and being of
the Order.

---

[37] Vázquez Núñez, *Manual*, I, p. 410.

[38] *Ibid.*, pp. 416–17. For the Parisian Mercedarians during the 17th and 18th centuries, see Paul & Marie-Louise Biver, *Abbayes, monastères et couvents de Paris des origines à
la fin du XVIIIᵉ siècle* (Paris, 1970), pp. 243–51, & especially *Histoire de l'ordre sacré, royal
et militaire de Notre-Dame de la Mercy, Redemption des Captifs [...] composée par les reverends
Péres de la Mercy de la congregation de Paris* (Amiens: Guislain Le Bel, 1685).

[39] See P. José Luis González Novalín, 'La Inquisición española' in *HIE*, III(ii), pp.
107–268; 167, where he is referred to as 'Lafont'.

[40] For the *synodalia*, see ACA, Mon, vol. 2667, ff. 221r–237v, & AGN, Clero, vol.
402. See also Vázquez Núñez, *Manual*, I, pp. 429–30.

IV. *Castile: A Vocation Consolidated*

By the early sixteenth century the increasing vitality of the province of Castile in the academic field was becoming apparent. At Salamanca a collegial of the Vera Cruz, Fray Francisco Merino, became the first recorded Mercedarian professor in the university, being awarded the quadrennial chair of 'Partes de Santo Tomás' (Aquinas' *Summa*) in May 1509.[41] Already an unsuccessful candidate for the so-called 'texto viejo de Aristótil' chair in 1508, in 1513 Merino felt able to compete for the major 'Biblia' *cathedra* in theology, though without success. By 1518 he was commendator of Córdoba.

It was during this period, first under M° Fray Juan de Baena (*c.*1512–23) and then M° Fray Alonso de Zorita (1523–42), that the province of Castile set out to consolidate its presence at the heart of university life. At Salamanca the modest academic successes of recent years were capped in 1516 with the arrival from France of a religious destined to transform the intellectual life of the province of Castile. Anxious to reaffirm its intellectual primacy after the foundation of Alcalá, in about 1515 the university of Salamanca dispatched the theologian Antonio de Honcala (or Oncala) to Paris to find scholars to help restore its tarnished lustre. He returned with two highly regarded schoolmen in the traditions of Ockham and Scotus, Juan Martínez Silíceo, later professor of nominalist philosophy, archbishop of Toledo and tutor of Prince Philip, and the young Navarrese Mercedarian M͞e Frey Dominique de St-Jean Pied de Port (*c.*1494–1540), called Domingo de San Juan de Pie del Puerto in Spain.[42] San Juan had entered the Order at Montpellier, a house with a strong academic tradition, where he studied philosophy and theology before distinguishing himself as a nominalist bachelor at the university of Paris. A mathematician, astronomer and follower of John Mair at the Collège de Montaigue, San Juan was a leading figure in the introduction of

---

[41] Vázquez Núñez, *Manual*, I, p. 405, & *id.*, *Mercedarios ilustres*, pp. 169–73. For an important corrective to these remarks, see P.Fr. Vicente Múñoz Delgado, 'La Veracruz de Salamanca y sus dos primeros profesores de la universidad en la investigación de Guillermo Vázquez' in *BPCONSM*, 22 (1984), no. 75, pp. 27–42; esp. 33–5.

[42] Remón, *Historia*, II, ff. 174r–v & 176r–177r. See P.Fr. Vicente Muñoz Delgado, *La lógica nominalista en la Universidad de Salamanca (1510–1530)* (Madrid, 1964), pp. 135–42 & 277–310, & *id.*, 'La Veracruz de Salamanca', pp. 36–41 for the latest appraisal.

nominalist logic into Salamanca.[43] His first position in the university, as professor of nominalist philosophy, was followed in 1523 by the Aristotelian Vespers chair *Logica Magna* and later the office of vice-chancellor. As rector of the Vera Cruz San Juan brought Parisian humanistic teaching methods, the *modus parisiensis*, to bear in the training of the religious, and in doing so established the college as the main forcing ground of the Castilian hierarchy and, later, of reformist thinking in the province. Among San Juan's non-Mercedarian students was the noted Dominican theologian, Maestro Mancio de Corpus Christi (†1575), an involvement that places him at the heart of the Salmantine theological revival.

The developments in Salamanca were matched by the establishment of the college of La Concepción at the university of Alcalá in 1518. The interest taken by the chapter general of Játiva in Alcalá in 1514 has already been noted, and the early involvement of the Mercedarians in Cisneros' new humanist foundation is a significant indicator of the intellectual mood of an Order that had now begun to produce men of strong Erasmian sympathies.[44] Nevertheless, the foundation of the college was hedged around with a number of provisos that afforded it a peculiar character and served to arrest its development for some time. The donation by the rector and collegials of the *colegio mayor* of San Ildefonso of a property on perpetual lease was made conditional on the acceptance by the Mercedarian rector of the unsalaried office of university *juez apostólico conservador*.[45] Though appointed by the Order, the rector-*juez conservador* could nonetheless be summarily dismissed by the university in the event of any irregularity. The duties attached to it — disciplining seculars *in statu pupilari* and upholding locally the privileges and jurisdiction of the university — no doubt made for a rather burdensome post, but through it the

---

[43] See Muñoz Delgado, 'La Veracruz de Salamanca', pp. 37–9, and, for San Juan's nominalist writings, *id.*, 'La exposición sumulista de la doctrina silogística de Fr. Domingo de San Juan de Pie del Puerto († 1540)' in *Estudios*, 19 (1963), pp. 3–50.

[44] See P.Fr. Guillermo Vázquez Núñez, ed., 'Los Mercedarios en la universidad complutense' in *BOM*, 1 (1913), pp. 193–6 & 252–8; 2 (1914), pp. 317–22 & 413–19. See P.Fr. José García Oro, *La Universidad de Alcalá en la etapa fundacional (1458–1578)* (Santiago, 1992), pp. 103–4, 222–3 & esp. 242–4, which employs many of the same documents. For details of the college in 1569, particularly as to *limpieza de sangre*, see AGS, E°, leg. 151, no. 194, f. 2v.

[45] 'Proctor apostolic', equivalent to the office of *escolástico* at Salamanca. The construction of the college had begun some time before the 1518 agreement; García Oro, *La Universidad de Alcalá*, p. 243.

Order wielded some influence in local affairs.[46] The fact that San Ildefonso felt able to entrust the Order, in perpetuity, with an office requiring competence in both canon and civil law suggests that it had gained a reputation for producing friars qualified in these fields. Indeed, there is some evidence that Mercedarians were exercising the constituted office of *juez conservador* in the university before the 1518 contract, while religious habitually engaged in legal arbitration in this period.[47]

The principal end of the college, however, was the education of young religious in theology, canon and civil law and the arts to equip them for the new and challenging fields into which the Order was expanding. The original stipulations of 1518 provided for twelve Castilian collegials, including the rector-*juez conservador*, drawn from those houses with the means to provide for their religious: (in precedence) Burgos and Burceña; Toledo, Seville and Córdoba; and finally Cazorla.[48] The convents of Salamanca and Valladolid were of course expected to educate their own religious.[49] Other houses were permitted to present students with a licence from the provincial, which was in any case required by all for entrance into the university. However, affected by a lack of funds and other difficulties, it was some time before the Order was able to fill this number of places and partake fully in the academic life of the university. In the first of several amendments to the terms of the original donation in 1523, the chapter provincial of Castile at Segovia reduced the quota of students to six during such time as college rents remained insufficient to support any more.[50] However, while Castile was only required to provide for

---

[46] *Ibid.*

[47] Vázquez Núñez, ed., 'Los Mercedarios en la universidad complutense', pp. 196 & 252–3. For an interesting example of such arbitration, see P.Fr. Luis Vázquez Fernández, ed., 'Dos Mercedarios de Toledo [...] jueces defensores de los derechos de la viuda e hijos de Garcilaso de la Vega (1547)' in *BPCONSM*, 25 (1987), no. 89, pp. 23–41. For ordinances banning this in 1591, see BNM, ms. 2448, f. 355r.

[48] Vázquez Núñez, ed., 'Los Mercedarios en la universidad complutense', p. 254.

[49] Valladolid appears to have acquired full collegial status with the transfer of the conventual *studium* of theology from Segovia in 1594; BNM, ms. 2684, f. 27r. However, Mercedarians had attended and lectured in the university throughout the 16th century; for some remarks on this, see P.Fr. Vicente Muñoz Delgado, 'El convento de Valladolid y el apostolado mercedario' in *BPCONSM*, 16 (1978), no. 53, pp. 45–60; 48–9 & 53–8.

[50] Vázquez Núñez, ed., 'Los Mercedarios en la universidad complutense', pp. 256–8.

its own friars, the college was obliged to admit foreign brethren free
of charge, though these had still to be maintained by their native
provinces. Further, the Castilian precedence system was now done
away with. Would-be entrants were to be presented for consideration by their commendators at chapters provincial, with the selection of collegials entrusted to the provincial alone. Again, in line
with university curricula, the duration of a religious' residence at
Alcalá was established at three years of arts followed by four of theology for 'gramáticos', while those uninitiated in Latin undertook a
preliminary three years giving a total of seven or ten years of study
respectively.[51]

In 1539 three representatives from the province of Castile (San
Juan among them) were delegated to examine the 1518 contract
between La Concepción and San Ildefonso, with the aim of renegoti-
ating the terms of the donation and moderating the overbearing position of the university with respect to the college.[52] Eager to underline
the equality of his order with all others, the provincial of Castile Mº
Fray Alonso de Zorita instructed his delegates to ensure that the contract with the university placed the Mercedarians at no greater disadvantage than those signed with other *religiosos colegiales*.[53] Assisted no
doubt by the years of faithful service afforded the university by the
rector Fray Juan de Riaño (1518–45) as *juez conservador* and the
increased demand for places at La Concepción, the success of this
mission finally consolidated the foundation of the college. Anxious for
the upkeep of its buildings and for the college's financial independence, as well as its own income from matriculation fees, San Ildefonso replied by entailing the Mercedarians with a third house adjacent
to the existing property. The donation was made on the understanding that the Order spend 200,000 *maravedís* towards the erection of a
college building on the entire site over the following decade. The
number of permanent residents was now increased to ten with the
Order expected to provide for them from its own resources with
annual quotas of wheat and money, supplemented by contributions
from the friars' original houses.[54]

---

[51] *Ibid.*, p. 256.
[52] *Ibid.*, pp. 320–1, & García Oro, *La Universidad de Alcalá*, pp. 243–4.
[53] Vázquez Núñez, ed., 'Los Mercedarios en la universidad complutense', p. 319.
[54] *Ibid.*, p. 321. From 1593 the university began attempts to suppress the office of
juez conservador, which ended only in 1651; see García Oro, *La Universidad de Alcalá*, pp.
243–4 & ch. 8, n. 57.

The expansion of the Order into the universities early in the six-teenth century therefore consolidated the academic vocation towards which the province of Castile in particular had been moving for over a century. From the houses at Salamanca and Alcalá, as well as the convent-college of Valladolid, the province of Castile was to draw many of the men responsible for carrying out the transformation of the Order from the later sixteenth century, and making academic attainment the passport to authority within it.

V. *The Mercedarians and the Question of Reform*

Although expansion into academic life represented a significant broadening of Mercedarian intellectual horizons, it remained the pre-serve of only a minority of religious who had yet to impose them-selves or their mentality lastingly on the Order as a whole. However, the pursuit of learning could not in itself provide a solution to the serious problem of indiscipline with which the Mercedarians were becoming synonymous. While the superiors, in Castile particularly, presided over a notable expansion of the Order in a number of fields, they could only deplore the continued, and in the case of the Crown of Aragon, quickened moral and disciplinary degeneration of their religious from the late fifteenth century. Throughout the Order, the majority of friars and their superiors greeted the sixteenth century in, at best, agreeable conventual relaxation, and at worst in a state of gross intemperance. As in most other orders, the Mercedarian rank and file had emerged lawless and undisciplined from the internal and external upheavals of the fourteenth and fifteenth centuries, but in the Mercedarian case this situation was not mitigated by the appear-ance within the Order of an organized reformist movement until the reign of Philip II.

Given the peculiar circumstances of its foundation, development and active vocation, the Mercedarians had pursued a course rather different from that of other orders during the late medieval period. With no genuinely primitive constitutions or canonized patriarch and the reality of its lay origins obscured by the imposition of a clerical regime after 1317, the Order failed to share the yearnings of other institutions for the rigour of its primordial observance. By the end of the fourteenth century this unease had begun to produce observant congregations across the spectrum of Spanish religious life in reaction to the *Claustra*, as conventualism is known here.[55] In 1390 John I of Castile (1379–90) founded the abbey of San Benito in Valladolid, a future centre of Benedictine reform in Spain.[56] The Cistercian reform established itself under Fray Martín de Vargas at Montesión near Toledo in 1427 and at the ancient monastery of Valbuena near Valladolid three years later.[57] The foundation of the first Charterhouse in Castile, that of El Paular near Segovia in 1390, was followed by a string of others under Trastamaran patronage during the fifteenth century, the great age of Carthusian expansion in Spain.[58] The Franciscan Observance likewise took root in Spain around 1390, acquiring an official character after 1415 under Fray Pedro de Villacreces and Fray Pedro Regalado.[59] Franciscan influence was also felt in the development of the Dominican and Augustinian observant movements, founded by Fray Álvaro de Córdoba (Escalaceli, Córdoba, 1423) and Fray Juan de Alarcón (Villanubla, Valladolid, 1431) respectively.[60] Among the Trinitarians a reform movement took shape under Fray Alfonso de la Puebla in 1431, though this was not destined to last.[61] The inspiration for many of these reformed congregations came from Italy, and it is here that we must look for the origins of the Jeronymite Order: the institutional embodiment of the eremitical tradition in Spain.[62] Confined largely to the Peninsula, the Jeronymites developed with the arrival from Italy of Tomasuccio di Siena in company with a number of hermits. The Order was founded

---

[55] Useful summaries of this movement can be found in Hillgarth, *The Spanish Kingdoms*, II, pp. 101–6, & Ronald Cueto, 'On the Significance of the Reform of the Religious Orders in the Catholic Monarchy in the 15th, 16th and 17th Centuries: Teresa de Jesús, the Foundress, in Historical Perspective' in Margaret A. Rees, ed., *Teresa de Jesús and her World* (Leeds, 1981), pp. 19–50; 20–3.

[56] See Dom Ernesto Zaragoza Pascual, *Los generales de la congregación de San Benito de Valladolid* (6 vols., Santo Domingo de Silos, 1973–87); I, *passim*.

[57] See Cueto, 'On the Significance of the Reform', p. 22.

[58] See Ildefonso María Gómez y Gómez, 'La Cartuja en España' in *Studia Monastica*, 4 (1962), pp. 139–76.

[59] See P.Fr. Fidel de Lejarza & P.Fr. Ángel Uribe, eds., *Introducción a los orígenes de la observancia en España: Las reformas en los siglos XIV y XV [Archivo Ibero-americano]* (Madrid, 1958), *passim*, & *id.*, '¿Cuándo y dónde comenzó Villacreces su reforma?' in *Archivo ibero-americano*, 20 (1960), pp. 79–94.

[60] On the Dominicans, see P.Fr. Vicente Beltrán de Heredia, 'The Beginnings of Dominican Reform in Castile' in J.R.L. Highfield, ed., *Spain in the Fifteenth Century* (London, 1972), pp. 226–47; Álvaro de Córdoba is also known as Álvaro de Zamora. For the Augustinians, see Cueto, 'On the Significance of the Reform', pp. 22–3.

[61] Cueto, 'On the Significance of the Reform', p. 23.

[62] See J.R.L. Highfield, 'The Jeronimites in Spain, their Patrons and Success, 1373–1516' in *Journal of Ecclesiastical History*, 34 (1983), pp. 513–33.

through the coalescence of these and other eremitical groups in 1373 under the disaffected courtier Pedro Fernández Pecha as prior of the mother house of San Bartolomé de Lupiana near Guadalajara. Royal and noble patronage afforded the Jeronymites a spectacular growth, the Order numbering twenty-five monasteries by 1414.[63] Only the Premonstratensians, Carmelites, and Mercedarians remained outwardly unaffected by this period of spiritual ferment.

The wider monastic reform movement did not, however, leave the Mercedarians completely untouched. In 1407 the Catalan general Fra Antoni Caixal (1405–17) celebrated a chapter provincial in Valladolid at which a project for improved 'observance' was apparently laid before the brethren.[64] At Arguines seven years later Caixal approved the reform programme worked out by the commendator of Valladolid, Fray Juan de Granada, with the support of Doña Beatriz, the widow of John I, a Mercedarian tertiary and benefactress of the Order.[65] The programme, which was confirmed by Benedict XIII in October 1414, seems to have centred on the restoration of communal life, and its preservation through the election of commendators by the community. It is fitting that Valladolid, one of the great centres of monastic reform in late medieval Spain, should provide the backdrop for this initiative, but there is no evidence that it enjoyed any lasting success among the Mercedarians. In 1440 Queen María of Aragon, a notable patroness of monastic reform, responded to the major crisis that had beset the Order by offering the master Fra Antoni Dullan not only her mediation, but assistance in promoting that ecclesiastical commonplace, 'reformació e reparació aixi en lo capitol com en les membres', 'lo qual vehem esser molt necessari'.[66] It is not clear to what extent this 'reformació' was conceived as one of spiritual improvement, though the appearance of Fra Nadal Gaver's *Speculum fratrum* in 1445, including the Amer statutes of 1272, suggests that some religious at least were turning their thoughts to the earliest surviving Mercedarian observance. But for most Albert's reform represented the horizon of their spirituality.

Resisting sporadic calls from the crown and their superiors for reg-

---

[63] See *DHEE*, II, p. 1230.

[64] Vázquez Núñez, *Manual*, I, p. 294. Also called Caxal or Cajal.

[65] See *ibid.*, p. 296, & *id.*, *Mercedarios ilustres*, p. 673.

[66] ACA, Mon., vol. 2830, p. 52 (another copy p. 8). María of Aragon to Dullan, Valencia, 9th September 1440; 18th-century copies. For letters of similar tenor from Alfons V to Gaver, see *ibid.*, p. 40 (another copy p. 10), dated 19th June 1447, & another of that year, *ibid.*, pp. 65–9; 18th-century copies.

ular 'observance' and disciplinary 'reform', the Mercedarian rank
and file therefore pursued active lives within the parameters of Marian devotion and local religion. This circumstance, along with the
absence of a notable contemplative tradition, ensured that the Mercedarians would remain largely abstracted from the climate of spiritual anxiety that gathered over the Western Church from the late
fourteenth century. Reflecting the ebb and flow of popular piety, the
Order at large remained at the close of the Middle Ages in the same
mode of spiritual development that had characterized it since the
thirteenth century. As time would show, the problems inherent in the
Order could fit into no recognizable mould of reform, for, paradoxically, the medieval Mercedarians were a religious order with a rather
disordered vision of the religious life.

The lack of any strong reformist nucleus in the Order prevented its
featuring greatly in the programme of religious reform pursued with
energy, if with limited success, by the Catholic Kings from the
1470s.[67] Even so, the humanistic influences that contributed to the
establishment of the Order in the universities were also reflected in a
concern among superiors for moral and disciplinary improvement
from the late fifteenth century. There was no lasting movement for
change in this period, but were reform-minded individuals within the Order who, supported by the crown, attempted to extirpate the
most flagrant personal abuse and restore discipline. Although an
active ecclesiastical reformer in his native Galicia during the 1480s,
Diego de Muros apparently held reservations against wholesale
monastic reform and seems not to have involved himself in that of his
order.[68] Muros himself held the commandery of Guadalajara for
twenty-two years, and became abbot *in commendam* of the Cistercian
monasteries of San Clodio and El Sobrado in Galicia after his return
from Italy in 1469.[69] His attitude would be consistent with a process
that could only confront localized disciplinary problems and failed to
address the underlying conflicts of Mercedarian life. The solution to
these questions would rest with later generations of Aragonese and
particularly Castilian superiors, but while the activity of the turn of the

---

[67] See García Oro, *La reforma de los religiosos*, p. 31 *passim*.
[68] For Muros' reformist activities in Galicia as Bishop of Tuy, see especially P.Fr.
José García Oro, *Cisneros y la reforma del clero español en tiempo de los Reyes Católicos*
(Madrid, 1971), pp. 80–2, and *id.*, *La reforma de los religiosos*, p. 52.
[69] Vázquez Núñez, *Mercedarios ilustres*, p. 150.

fifteenth century enjoyed little practical success, it confirms the existence in the Order of a reformist mentality that would persist until the reign of Philip II provided a more fertile environment.

VI. *Spectres of Reform, 1485–1515*

We do not yet know under what circumstances the Mercedarians began to work with the crown towards disciplinary reform, but the first signs of activity in 1485 reveal the basic criterion of the Castilian superiors in this matter: to avail themselves of royal support and move against the engrained problem of contumacious and fugitive religious. In August of that year the crown ordered its *justicias* to provide the vicar provincial of Castile, Pº Fray Antonio de Valladolid, with all necessary assistance in returning vagrant religious to their houses.[70] Five years later Fray García, the commendator of Toledo, was granted the aid of the secular arm to bring a large number of refractory friars down from the Montes de Toledo where they had fled to avoid being submitted to regular discipline.[71] There are few details at present, but it appears that this concern for disciplinary reform was also reflected in the eastern provinces of the Order where Maurel struggled to assert his authority and curb continuing lawlessness among his religious. In 1493, as the Catholic Kings obtained briefs for the reform of the nunneries of the Crown of Aragon, the chapter general of Huesca voted to end all perpetual commanderies, though this was never rigorously enforced.[72]

After this time activity seems to have fallen away in both Castile and Aragon until early the following century, when the condition of the Order once again came to the attention of the crown. In 1501 Isabella petitioned the papacy for a bull placing the reform of the Mercedarians, Trinitarians, Carmelites and Premonstratensians under the Dominican Fray Diego de Deza, bishop of Palencia, and Fray Francisco Jiménez de Cisneros, the Franciscan archbishop of Toledo.[73] The

---

[70] García Oro, *La reforma de los religiosos*, p. 427.

[71] *Ibid.*, p. 441.

[72] Vázquez Núñez, *Manual*, I, p. 392.

[73] The petition, which refers particularly to the Trinitarians, is cited in P.Fr. Tarsicio de Azcona, *Isabel la Católica*, pp. 771–2. See also P.Fr. Otger Steggink, *La reforma del Carmelo español: La visita canónica del general Rubeo y su encuentro con Santa Teresa (1566–1567)*, 2nd edn. (Ávila, 1993), p. 18.

tenure of provincials and superiors was to be reduced to three years, and the religious required to live in community and embrace regular observance, though little seems to have come of this. Elsewhere, superiors again felt the need to reply to the challenge of unruly friars. In the Crown of Aragon the Catalan general Fra Joan Urgell (1492–1513) had recourse to Rome in 1505 when his right to visit the house at Palma was disputed by its commendator.[74] The matter was settled in Urgell's favour the following year, but the case indicates the continued obstacles to government in the provinces controlled by the generals. The steady erosion of the general's authority in the outlying areas of his patrimony was confirmed by the Catalan Fra Pere Aymerich, who, as Urgell's visitor in Sicily and Naples in around 1511, discovered the religious of Palermo to have elected their own prior and sold a large piece of conventual land to parochial authorities.[75] As the sixteenth century drew on and the high office became tied to the priory of Barcelona, successive generals were to find their ability to govern the Order outside Catalonia steadily reduced. The powers granted to Valencia and Aragon-Navarre from 1493 to convene their own chapters contributed to the development of strong provincial allegiances among the religious.[76] Accentuated by an unsavoury Barcelona particularism, the effect was to ensure the progressive fragmentation of the Order in the century after 1467.

In Castile a period of apparent passivity ended in 1508 with the election as provincial of M° Fray Jorge de Sevilla, who seems to have injected a new sense of urgency into the question of disciplinary reform. The renewal of the reform campaign is apparent in a royal letter of December 1510 instructing crown officials in Burceña to assist the vicar provincial of Castile, Fray Francisco de Campo, in his attempt to reduce a number of violent and insubordinate religious to obedience.[77] Some time before, Campo and an unnamed commendator of Burgos had been empowered at a chapter provincial (perhaps that of 1508) to 'visit and reform the houses and monasteries of the Order [in Castile] and the religious within them'.[78] The prob-

---

[74] Remón, *Historia*, II, ff. 99r–100v. It should be noted that Remón has greatly confused the names and succession of generals in this period.

[75] *Ibid.*, f. 102r–v.

[76] Vázquez Núñez, *Manual*, I, p. 393.

[77] See García Oro, *La reforma de los religiosos*, pp. 562–3. P. García has misread 'Luzena' for 'Burceña'.

[78] *Ibid.*, p. 562.

lem faced at Burceña by Campo and by the commendator, Fray Juan de Tapia, reflects the ease with which even the most noted houses could succumb to the violence that permeated the lower levels of Spanish religious life. The problem originated with a severe punishment for insubordination meted out by Campo to a certain Fray Juan de Axpurian during his visitation of the convent some time in November 1510. In retaliation, Axpurian secreted twenty armed men in the house who attacked and wounded the commendator as he formally prepared to pass sentence on him that night. Axpurian escaped, and Tapia and the remaining conventuals were forced to barricade themselves into the chapter house until dawn. The intervention of the royal *corregidor* (governor) later that day obliged Axpurian to relent and what proved to be but a temporary truce was imposed. The spectacle of religious drawing on local support in the face of a threat to the established pattern of their lives underlines the social implications of monastic reform. Though by no means unprecedented in this or in other congregations, for the Mercedarians such problems were but a taste of things to come.[79]

By 1512 the Castilians had translated the experience of several years' visitation into a programme of reform pursued with energy and royal support by the new provincial, M° Fray Juan de Baena. As the two visitors general of Castile informed the crown in February of that year, the delegates of a recent chapter had set down 'certain constitutions touching both on spiritual matters and on the temporal government and administration' of the province.[80] However, attempts at introducing disciplinary reform continued to be met with violent opposition. November found one of the visitors, Fray Juan de Soria, in Galicia attempting to depose the commendator of Conxo in the face of armed resistance. Three years later the efforts of M° Fray Martín de Samunde as 'visitor and reformer general' of Castile were coloured with the same violence and controversy. There were serious disturbances at the houses of Valladolid and Logroño, whose commendators refused to accept the authority of the hierarchy and the chapter provincial.[81] As ever, the result of disturbances in the Order

---

[79] For a Dominican example from the late 13th century, see Peter Linehan, *The Ladies of Zamora* (University Park, Pa., 1997), pp. 41–58.

[80] García Oro, *La reforma de los religiosos*, pp. 119–20.

[81] See P.Fr. José García Oro & María José Portela Silva, 'Felipe II y la reforma de las órdenes redentoras' in *Estudios*, 54 (1998), pp. 5–155; 9–10.

was a mass of fugitive religious. This situation is reflected at the chapter general of Játiva in 1514 where the new general, Fray Jaime Lorenzo de la Mata, reprimanded a number of Aragonese commendators for sheltering Castilian fugitives. The *synodalia* of a contemporary chapter provincial of Castile might well have contained similar injunctions.

VII. *Humanism, Heresy and Messianism*

The involvement in 1515 of Fray Martín de Samunde in the attempted reforms is particularly significant since, more so even than Muros, Samunde exemplifies the new men, trained in the universities and anxious for change, who had begun to appear in the Order and were to leave their mark indelibly upon it.[82] It was in this cast of mind, tempered in the Order's colleges and *studia*, that a generation of reformist Mercedarians took shape in the middle decades of the century.

We know very little about Samunde's early life. He was born at Baracaldo near Bilbao in the last quarter of the fifteenth century and professed at Burceña, probably in the 1490s. Soon after he transferred for reasons of study to the Franciscan house in Bilbao, an example of the intellectual exchange that routinely took place between religious orders.[83] However, he did not sever his ties with the Order, to which he returned with papal permission 'after many years' in the following century.[84] He reappears in 1515 having visited Rome and, as *maestro* in theology and commendator of Málaga, having established himself as the leading reformer in Castile. More than any other Mercedarian, Samunde therefore had occasion to grasp the implications of the ferocious attacks made against the mendicant orders in particular at the Fifth Lateran Council in 1512. He is also likely to have been involved both in the instalment of San Juan at Salamanca and in the foundation of the Order's college at Alcalá in 1518, which he helped to ratify as a diffinitor at Segovia in 1523.

---

[82] See Vázquez Núñez, *Mercedarios ilustres*, pp. 208–13, & P.Fr. Vicente Muñoz Delgado, 'El maestro Fray Martín de Samunde († ca. 1539) y su defensa de Erasmo en 1527' in *Revista española de teología*, 44 (1984), pp. 441–64.

[83] BNM, ms. 2448, f. 336r.

[84] Muñoz Delgado, 'Fray Martín de Samunde', p. 442.

The election of Mº Fray Alonso de Zorita as provincial in 1523 ensured the continued growth of academic life and the survival of reformist thought in Castile. Upon his election, Zorita conducted a visitation of the entire province finding the houses in a ruinous condition and the religious in need of a reform which he set out to codify.[85] Zorita's appointment of Samunde, the commendator of Burgos, as his vicar in Castile-León is an indication of the mentality that now prevailed among the provincial hierarchy. While Zorita established himself in Seville to oversee the province's expansion in America, Samunde remained in the north, the luminary and protector of the small circle of religious — perhaps a dozen individuals — who constituted the intellectual élite of the province of Castile. Samunde was clearly a humanist by inclination, but it is 1527 before the full spectrum of his allegiances becomes apparent. Taking advantage of the presence in Valladolid of senior religious at the *cortes*, the inquisitor general Alonso Manrique held a colloquy that summer to debate the orthodoxy of Erasmus. Although it was never concluded, this conference represents the apogee of Erasmian influence in Spain before attitudes hardened in the 1530s.[86]

In common with the other delegates, Samunde did not attend all the sessions of the *junta*, but the proceedings reveal him, along with the Benedictine Dom Alonso de Virués and the Franciscan Fray Gil López de Béjar, to have been the staunchest of Erasmus' supporters.[87] While recognizing Erasmus' occasional irreverence, Samunde defended both his superior philological skills and the freedom to investigate theological truths without actually defining them in terms of faith and the mysteries, a task only the Church itself could fulfil. He concluded that, rather than being guilty of error, Erasmus spoke 'non sine magna gravitate, maturitate et consilio' and, moreover, 'nihil periculo in fidem gignitur ibi'.[88] Samunde clearly saw in Erasmus' writing a welcome divergence from prevailing methods of scholastic exegesis, while at the same time underlining his debt to

---

[85] Remón, *Historia*, II, ff. 164r.

[86] See Marcel Bataillon, *Erasmo y España: Estudios sobre la historia espiritual del siglo XVI*, trans. Antonio Alatorre, 2nd Spanish edn. (Mexico City, 1966), pp. 226–78.

[87] For Samunde's contributions, see P.Fr. Vicente Beltrán de Heredia, ed., *Cartulario de la Universidad de Salamanca (1218–1600)* (6 vols., Salamanca, 1969–73), VI, pp. 105–11, with commentary in Muñoz Delgado, 'Fray Martín de Samunde', pp. 451–63.

[88] Cited in Muñoz Delgado, 'Fray Martín de Samunde', pp. 461 & 462 respectively.

Augustine and Peter Lombard, the authorities then favoured by the Mercedarian Order.

It is, of course, impossible to gauge how far Samunde's views reflect the thinking of his province, much less that of his Order. In Spain Erasmianism was espoused by individuals rather than institutions, particularly in the case of the religious orders whom Erasmus had so memorably excoriated in the *Enchiridion*: 'monachatus non est pietas'. Yet many of Erasmus' most committed followers were religious anxious for the change and renewal expressed so cogently in his writing. The humanist religious ideal of the union of *eruditio* and *pietas* was founded in the Augustinian idea of reform to which religious were themselves turning in an effort to raise standards in their congregations.[89] In this sense individuals were prepared to forgive Erasmus his ridiculing of the religious life out of respect for the values and method of evangelical humanism which many felt, through reform, to be the great goal and enterprise of their orders.[90] Moreover, it seems that leading Mercedarians, like many monastics, felt their Order to be excluded from the brunt of Erasmus' attacks against the mendicants by dint of its redemptive vocation. There is every indication that during the 1520s and early 1530s, in Castile especially, the Order imbued a small but important generation of intellectuals with Erasmian thinking. It is therefore no surprise that in 1570 the provincial, M° Fray Pedro Carrillo, dated the origins of the Castilian reform movement to this very period.[91]

Equally, it is no surprise to learn that from now on the province began to nurture a number of heterodox religious. One of these, M° Fray Rodrigo Guerrero, studied theology at La Concepción in the 1540s and was among the Protestants uncovered by the Inquisition of Seville in 1558.[92] Having fled to Milan, Flanders and then England — where he threatened to found a college for Spanish Protestants at

[89] See Stinger, *Humanism and the Church Fathers*, p. 226.

[90] For the idea of a monastic humanism, see Paul Oskar Kristeller, 'The Contribution of Religious Orders to Renaissance Thought and Learning' in *American Benedictine Review*, 21 (1970), pp. 1–55, esp. 15 & 18 — a brilliant article.

[91] IVDJ, env. 72, II, ff. 105r–106v. Carrillo to the nuncio, Giambattista Castagna, undated but 1570; f. 106r.

[92] See Vázquez Núñez, *Manual*, I, pp. 497–8, Ernst Schäfer, *Beiträge zur Geschichte des spanischen Protestantismus...* (3 vols., Gütersloh, 1902), I, pp. 332 & 336–7; II, pp. 56 & 273; III, pp. 72–3 & 119–21, & *Calendar of Letters and State Papers Relating to English Affairs, Preserved Principally in the Archives of Simancas*, vol. I, *Elizabeth, 1558–1567* (London, 1892), pp. 86–8 & 94.

Oxford — Guerrero was returned to Spain and sentenced to perpetual imprisonment by the Valladolid tribunal in 1561. Although given remission, he denounced himself to the Inquisition in 1569 and two years later was relaxed to the secular arm, accused of having 'taught heresy' to others. Neither Fray Rodrigo's fate nor the nature of his religious beliefs are known, but his case, and the few others for which details survive, indicate that the Mercedarians shared in this current of reform as much as any other.

The influence of Erasmus was not reflected so clearly in the Crown of Aragon but for a while the breath of reform was felt here also. During his tenure the Erasmian general Me Fra Benet Zafont (1522–35) reiterated the concern, first voiced by the fourteenth-century master Frey Dominique Sans in the tradition of Ramon Llull, that Mercedarian redemptors should be competent in theology.[93] Taking advantage of the Order's privileged access to Muslim lands, it was asserted that, beyond ransoming itself, the work of redemption should extend to conducting learned disputations with Muslim and Jewish theologians.[94] On these grounds Zafont ordained that all future redemptors be men of learning, and to this end appointed three provincial *lectores* in philosophy and theology to see that religious received a suitable education in schools and universities. This impulse had, of course, a propagandistic dimension, and in 1525 the three *lectores* passed through Rome obtaining papal confirmation of the privileges of the Order before embarking on a successful redemption to Tunis.[95]

Although there is no evidence that the practicalities of ransoming on the Barbary Coast ever permitted Mercedarians to engage in disputation, much less evangelization, the concern of the general for redefining the image of the Order's principal vocation in these terms,

---

[93] See Remón, *Historia*, II, f. 141r–v.

[94] The only suggestion that Zafont's call was being taken up comes with the appointment of M° Fray Pedro de Salazar of Burceña to the chair of Hebrew at Salamanca in 1542. Salazar was the leading light in the current of orientalist learning that flourished briefly among the Castilian Mercedarians at this time. In around 1545, however, Salazar was denied the *cátedra Trilingüe* — the chair of Hebrew, Chaldean and Arabic — in view his questionable command of the latter language, established during a visit to Granada with a university commission; see Vázquez Núñez, *Manual*, I, pp. 489–90.

[95] In 1516 the French and Aragonese provinces had, to great public acclaim, conducted the first recorded procession of ransomed captives in Rome; see Remón, *Historia*, II, f. 132r.

along with the impulse to study, reflects a humanistic mentality among elements of the French and Aragonese hierarchy. One of the *lectores*, Fray Jerónimo Pérez (or Peris), was the most distinguished Mercedarian scholar in the Crown of Aragon of the sixteenth century.[96] Born in Valencia in around 1485, Pérez entered the Order here and read theology at the university, appearing as a *maestro* in 1523. His first work, the *Monoctium*, was published in 1525 at the outset of his expedition to Italy and Tunis.[97] Upon his return from the Mediterranean in 1527, Pérez was elected first to the Vespers and then to the Prime chair of theology at Valencia, where he resided, eventually as commendator *ad vitam*, for the next twenty years.

The proselytic ideal of the redemptor-theologian certainly reflected the mentality of an age expressing its religious unease in messianic and apocalyptic spirituality. In 1509, the year of Cisneros' expedition against Oran, a number of Mercedarians from the house at Murcia, along with other friars, had dressed as soldiers and embarked for Africa fired with religious fervour, only to be recognized and returned to their convents.[98] Even so, the conquest of the *presidio* that year resulted in the foundation of a house as a forward ransoming base. In Castile itself the movement towards learning may well have been influenced by an urge for evangelization not only in North Africa but in the New World, a field in which the Aragonese were increasingly anxious to engage themselves.

VIII. *America: Establishment and Expansion, 1514–35*

Despite its early association with the Indies, nothing more is heard of the Order in America until over twenty years later.[99] The first Mer-

[96] See P.Fr. Vicente Muñoz Delgado, *Obras teológicas del P. Jerónimo Pérez († 1549), Mercedario* (Pontevedra, 1962), pp. 11–20, Vázquez Núñez, *Mercedarios ilustres*, pp. 214–21, & León Esteban Mateo, 'Catedráticos eclesiásticos de la universidad valenciana del siglo XVI' in *Repertorio de Historia de las Ciencias Eclesiásticas en España*, 6 (1977), pp. 349–439, esp. 403–4 & 432. Also Remón, *Historia*, II, ff. 186r–190v, & ACA, Mon., vol. 2681, f. 119r–v.

[97] Mº Fray Jerónimo Pérez, *Monoctium...* (Naples: Evangelistam Papiensem et eius Vxorem heredem, 1525).

[98] Vázquez Núñez, *Manual*, I, p. 408.

[99] For Mercedarian activity in the Indies, see P.Fr. Pedro Nolasco Pérez, *Historia de las misiones mercedarias en América* [=*Estudios*, 22] (Madrid, 1966) & *id.*, *Religiosos de la Merced que pasaron a la América española (1514–1777)...* (Seville, 1924), and P.Fr. Ricar-

cedarian house in the New World was founded at Santo Domingo in 1514, no doubt motivated as much with an eye to the acquisition of funds for the redemption of captives in North Africa as by missionary zeal.[100] In that year Fray Francisco de Bovadilla, the father of the Mercedarian missions, departed for Terra Firma with the notorious governor of Panama, Pedrarias Dávila. The presence of Bovadilla on this expedition, during which several houses were founded in Panama and Nicaragua, set the pattern for Mercedarian activity in America for over a century. The brethren excelled as military chaplains and most *adelantados* employed the services of Mercedarian friars, a fact which says much of the sort of men who found their way there in the early years.[101] The most notable of these chaplains was Fray Bartolomé de Olmedo (1485–1524), 'the first apostle of New Spain'.[102] Olmedo reached the Caribbean in 1516 and, after a period in Santo Domingo, moved on to Cuba where he joined Cortés' expedition to Mexico in 1519.[103] As Bernal Díaz's *Historia verdadera* relates, Olmedo played a significant role as negotiator between Cortés and Pánfilo de Narváez in early 1520 and survived the terrible retreat from Tenochtitlan later that year.[104]

---

do Sanlés Martínez, 'Trayectoria de la Merced en la conquista de América' in *La Orden de la Merced* [=*Estudios*, 47] (Madrid, 1970); pp. 49–82. P.Fr. Alfonso Morales Ramírez, *La Orden de la Merced en la evangelización de América, siglos XVI–XVII* (Bogotá, 1986) provides a résumé of earlier work. The best source for the impact of this expansion on the metropolitan Order, which is what I shall be concentrating on here, remains Vázquez Núñez, *Manual*, I, pp. 418 *passim* & 505–24, supplemented by P.Fr. Luis Vázquez Fernández, 'Cedulario mercedario en su relación con el Nuevo Mundo: 1518–1599' in *id.*, ed., *Presencia de la Merced en América* [=*Estudios*] (2 vols., Madrid, 1991); II, pp. 597–659. On the matter of redemption *limosna*, see P.Fr. Severo Aparicio, 'Los Mercedarios de América y la redención de cautivos, siglos XVI–XIX' in *Analecta Mercedaria*, 1 (1982), pp. 1–56.

[100] Vázquez Núñez, *Manual*, I, p. 419. For evidence of alms collection in Cuba in 1519, see Aldana, *Crónica de la Merced de México*, p. 45.

[101] The most infamous *conquistador* served by the brethren was Lope de Aguirre who led a revolt across New Granada as far as Trinidad in 1559–61. Aguirre, who despised missionaries, magistrates and lawyers, 'sólo toleraba a los Mercedarios'; cited in Marcel Bataillon, *El sentido del «Lazarillo de Tormes»* (Paris-Toulouse, 1954), p. 13.

[102] On Olmedo, see Fray Cristóbal de Aldana's apparently unfinished *Crónica de la Merced de México*, ed. Jorge Gurría Lacroix (Mexico City, 1953), a work composed towards the end of the 18th century. See also Robert Ricard, *The Spiritual Conquest of Mexico*, trans. Lesley Byrd Simpson (Berkeley, 1966), pp. 16–20.

[103] Vázquez Núñez, *Manual*, I, pp. 421–2.

[104] These Mercedarian connections caused the chronicler general of the Order, M° Fray Alonso Remón, to produce the first edition of the *Historia Verdadera de la Conquista de la Nueva España* (Madrid: Emprenta del Reyno, 1632). Remón's editorship did, however, result in Olmedo's role being magnified.

The Order continued to expand, and in 1522 an unnamed Mercedarian set out with Gil González Dávila from Panama on a journey that would extend the Mercedarian patrimony northwards through Nicaragua and into Chiapas.[105] Nevertheless, shortage of personnel and the need to confirm existing foundations sent Bovadilla back to Spain in 1524. Already in October 1518 the crown had extended to America the rights of alms collection enjoyed by the Order in Castile, the first in a series of privileges that consolidated the Mercedarian presence in the Indies.[106] Now, in 1526, the emperor provided a full endorsement of the Mercedarian missionary presence in the New World, confirming its houses and promising that land would be made available to the religious in all major new settlements.[107] Appointed vicar provincial by Zorita — the first sign of transoceanic organization — Bovadilla returned to the Indies in 1527, this time symbolically at the head of a party of twelve religious like his Franciscan and Dominican predecessors.[108] He was back for more in 1530 and 1534, but the rigours of missionary life were clearly not to every friar's taste, and the visits proved disappointing in this respect with a total of only eleven volunteers. Even so, it was some time before the inroads into Castile's human and financial resources were defrayed by the revenue that began to pour into provincial coffers from America in the late sixteenth century.

Meanwhile, Mercedarian expansion continued apace in the Indies until cut short in the early 1540s.[109] Missions were founded in Guatemala and Chiapas, and in 1534 two friars reached Quito with the *adelantado* Pedro de Alvarado, while others followed Sebastián de Benalcázar to Popayán. There were friars in Lima and Cuzco in 1535, and the Order had houses scattered throughout Peru by 1539. Two Mercedarians accompanied Diego de Almagro into Chile in 1535, while Zorita sent two more to the River Plate with Pedro de

---

[105] Vázquez Núñez, *Manual*, I, pp. 419–20.
[106] This document, 'Preuillegios imperiales e reales de la religion…', dated Ávila, 14th October 1518, is the first of three royal and papal privileges printed in an untitled chap-book by Zorita in the late 1520s. The complete chap-book, in 26 ff., survives as BNM, ms. 13,337, and with this first document only (ff. 1r–13v) in AHN, Clero, carp. 3520, no. 2. The document is reproduced in 'F.J.C.', ed., 'Notas y textos: Privilegios imperiales y reales de la religión…' in *Estudios*, 19 (1963), pp. 139–43. See also Vázquez Fernández, 'Cedulario mercedario', pp. 605–10.
[107] See Vázquez Fernández, 'Cedulario mercedario', p. 611.
[108] Vázquez Núñez, *Manual*, I, pp. 439–40.
[109] *Ibid.*, pp. 441–2.

Mendoza that year.[110] The murderous dispute that developed between the Pizarro and Almagro factions over possession of the city of Cuzco from 1537 halted further evangelization in the viceroyalty of Peru for the duration of the civil war.[111] But elsewhere also, the first period of Mercedarian expansion in America was drawing to a close.

IX. *The Order and America: Patronage and Jurisdiction*

Beyond its implications for expansion in America, the most significant element of the emperor's *cédula* (decree) of 1526 was the power it granted the provincials of Castile over the affairs of the Order in the Indies, to the exclusion of the master general. Naturally, this concession reflects the *Patronato Real* over the American Church that was vested in the Castilian crown in the first quarter of the sixteenth century. In 1508 Julius II had granted the Crown of Castile patronage over the Church in America with the bull *Universalis Ecclesiae Regiminis*, followed in 1522 by the *Exponi nobis* of Adrian VI which facilitated the dispatch of Castilian missionaries to the Indies and conceded further rights to the crown. By 1523 Zorita was therefore styling himself 'provincial of the Order in the Kingdoms of Castile, Granada, Portugal, and the Indies, Terra Firma and the Ocean Sea'.[112] However, measures taken by Castilian brethren through the 1520s to defend their expansion in the Indies reflect growing opposition in the Crown of Aragon to developments that were seen as both prejudicial to the rights of the general and counter to the *Concordia* of 1467. In particular, a royal *cédula* of May 1526 had required any brief ordering the transfer of Castile's American patrimony to another province to be ignored and referred immediately to the Council of the Indies.[113]

In the Crown of Aragon prevailing circumstances seem to have convinced the hierarchy that a renegotiation or revocation of the *Concordia*, now nearly sixty years old, was overdue. From Zorita's election as provincial in 1523 Zafont apparently conducted a dia-

---

[110] *Ibid.*, pp. 452–3.
[111] *Ibid.*, pp. 456–7.
[112] AHCB, ms. A-266, Antillón, *Memorias*, II, (loose f.).
[113] The *cédula*, dated Seville, 11th May 1526, is reproduced in Vázquez Núñez, *Manual*, I, pp. 436–7. See also Vázquez Fernández, 'Cedulario mercedario', p. 611.

logue with Castile through Fray Domingo de Clavería on a number
of jurisdictional and other issues, including rights of visitation and the
status of the Indies.[114] These negotiations ended in failure, and in
1530 Zafont began a *pleito* in Rome against the province of Castile.
Though the expansion of Castile to the Indies first under Fray Juan
de Baena and then under Zorita provided the immediate basis for the
dispute, Zafont saw the *Concordia* of 1467 as scandalously prejudicial
to his office and authority, and it was the revocation of this that took
Clavería and the future general Fra Miquel Puig to Rome in 1530.
Faced by the prospect of a long and costly solution to the dispute
through normal channels, Clavería, Puig and their Castilian counterpart, Fray Pedro de Miño, agreed to accept the arbitration of the
papal *auditor* Niccolò Piccolomini. After two years of negotiation Piccolomini drafted a *diffinitiva sententia* in favour of Castile.[115] Upholding
the terms of 1467, Zafont was prohibited from founding any houses
under his authority in Castile, whose affairs were to remain entirely
under the jurisdiction of the provincial. The transfer of the convents
of Murcia and Lorca from Valencia to Castile in 1467 was ratified,
while the Indies were established as a Castilian preserve. However, in
line with Aragonese rights of conquest in Africa, Castile was obliged
to surrender its outpost at Oran to the generals who would enjoy
exclusive jurisdiction over any new foundations on the Barbary
Coast. Finally, Castile was required to remit a further sixteen gold
doubloons annually to the forty agreed as tribute in 1467. This adjudication was a serious defeat for the generals, who had thereafter to
accept the unpalatable reality that, in absolute terms, the provincials
of Castile exercised greater authority than they themselves did.

It is not known whether the crown intervened in this matter, but
the negotiations must have been coloured by the awareness on both
sides of the favoured position of Castilian clergy in Spanish ecclesiastical affairs as a consequence of royal policy. Beyond its permutations
for the Mercedarians, this episode underlines the pressures exerted on
religious orders by the gradual development of a nationalist mentality
in the Castilian Church with regard to the rest of Spain and Europe.
The establishment of the *Patronato Real*, particularly after 1523, proved
to be a conditioning feature of the reform of the Spanish orders which

---

[114] See Remón, *Historia*, II, f. 153v.
[115] BNM, ms. 2906, ff. 5r–11v, a copy of the judgement, dated Rome, 19th June
1532.

under Philip II would for the first time be promoted from Castile in a truly centralizing spirit. The extension of reform from local or regional level to national level therefore represents a major development in the history of the religious orders over the course of the sixteenth century, at the cost of serious dislocation and reaction in the provinces.

X. *America: Crisis and Recovery after 1535*

Although the jurisdiction of the Castilian province over the Indies had been settled beyond all doubt, the activities of its religious in these parts was already raising serious concerns as to their ability to fulfil the high responsibility with which they had been entrusted. The first sign of trouble in the Indies comes in a royal *cédula* of 1531.[116] Addressed to the *audiencias* of New Spain and Hispaniola, it ordered all Mercedarians living without a licence from their vicar provincial to be rounded up and returned to Santo Domingo at the Order's expense. In 1533 an attempted foundation in Mexico City was for some reason blocked by the *provisor* (vicar general), and the brethren were obliged to abandon the city at the end of the year.[117] Scorned by the larger orders, the Mercedarians often found themselves marginalized to the most difficult terrain and the most intractable Indians.[118] Clearly, the skills that made the Mercedarians first into the field in many areas did not lend themselves readily to the delicate business of ministering to natives, and by the mid 1530s the brethren were beginning to acquire an unenviable reputation for violence and indiscipline. Such developments were evidently a source of concern to Zorita who in 1535 requested royal assistance in returning to Spain a number of religious guilty of 'dissolute and dishonest conduct worthy of punishment'.[119] In May 1537 Fray Pedro de Miño was given a licence to visit the Order's houses in Santo Domingo and Nicaragua, but, like the crown itself, the provincial was powerless to control the activities of his brethren further afield. In Peru, for instance, members of the Order seem mostly, though not exclusively, to have sided

---

[116] Vázquez Fernández, 'Cedulario mercedario', p. 612.

[117] Vázquez Núñez, *Manual*, I, p. 440.

[118] For an example of this in the western highlands of Guatemala, see Adriaan C. van Oss, *Catholic Colonialism: A Parish History of Guatemala, 1524–1821* (Cambridge, 1986), pp. 31–5, 43 & 48.

[119] Vázquez Fernández, 'Cedulario mercedario', p. 614.

with the colonists against the crown in the civil war that developed after 1537.[120]

By the early 1540s it is clear that leading figures in the American Church had come to regard the Order as unfit for missionary work. In New Spain the Mercedarians incurred the wrath of the formidable bishop of Chiapas, Fray Bartolomé de Las Casas, who described them as an unedifying spectacle and forced them out of his diocese.[121] Complaints were also voiced by the bishop of Guatemala, Francisco Marroquín, who in 1542 recommended that the brethren be withdrawn in view of their worldliness and poor example.[122] As the great missionary endeavour entered a period of sustained crisis, the Mercedarians' dubious status as mendicants, their religious and disciplinary shortcomings and general lack of organization all ran counter to the spirit of the *Leyes Nuevas* that finally appeared in 1543. In March of that year the Order was banned from making any further foundations in the Indies, while restrictions were placed on the dispatch and movement of personnel.[123] Supported by the new provincial, Fray Diego Enríquez, in December of that year the Council of the Indies appointed Fray Francisco de Cuevas vicar provincial and instructed him to reduce the Order's presence there to a mere five houses: Santo Domingo, Lima, Panama, León de Nicaragua and Cuzco.[124] The other fifteen were to be suppressed, their revenues applied to the surviving foundations and all unruly friars sent back to Spain. The intention of Enríquez and the crown appears to have been the establishment of a semi-independent province under Cuevas, for which purpose no less than thirty-four religious were selected to accompany him to the Indies. The crown looked to Rome for support, but Enríquez's death in 1544 came as a severe blow to the project.[125] The election of Fray Pedro de Oriona as his successor mobilized widespread opposition in Castile to any policy that might surrender the fruit of thirty years' labour, and though Cuevas reached the Indies in 1546 neither the suppressions nor the new province went ahead.[126]

---

[120] Vázquez Núñez, *Manual*, I, p. 458.

[121] *Ibid.*, p. 460.

[122] See Bataillon, *El sentido del «Lazarillo de Tormes»*, p. 13.

[123] Vázquez Núñez, *Manual*, I, p. 462, & Vázquez Fernández, 'Cedulario mercedario', p. 615.

[124] Vázquez Fernández, 'Cedulario mercedario', p. 616.

[125] *Ibid.*, p. 617.

[126] *Ibid.*, pp. 616–18. The Mercedarians were, however, dispossessed of houses and missions in Quito, Popayán and the diocese of Michoacán; see also Vázquez Núñez, *Manual*, I, p. 464.

Although the Castilians had successfully blocked this first attempt at separation, both practical considerations and the increasing independence of the American brethren dictated that this could not be delayed for very much longer. Meanwhile, the Order began a slow rehabilitation in the Indies under Fray Juan de Vargas, vicar provincial and commendator of Cuzco from 1547.[127] The ban on new houses and missions was gradually lifted, and measures were taken to end individual ownership of property in favour of the evangelical poverty advocated by the mendicants.[128] The turning point came with the appointment in 1555 of Fray Alonso de Losa as visitor and vicar provincial of Peru.[129] After a severe disagreement with Losa, all Mercedarian commendators south of Panama gathered at a rebel chapter in Cuzco in November 1556 and elected Vargas provincial of 'Perú y Tierra Firme y Popayán'.[130] Procurators were dispatched to Europe with instructions to obtain confirmation of this not only from the papacy, but from Puig in Barcelona.[131] It is not clear when they made their journey, but Puig seems to have given his support and the papacy apparently issued a brief in December 1560 confirming the establishment of the province.[132] However, the Castilians had received prior warning and were able to take precautions against this eventuality with royal support. A series of *cédulas* reiterated the 1526 decrees barring the annexation of Castile's American possessions by other provinces — implicitly those of the master general — and ordered all briefs in prejudice of this to be submitted to the Council of the Indies.[133] However, the need for a modified relationship with its American patrimony was recognized in Castile, and in 1561 Vargas and his companions were summoned to Spain for negotiations.[134]

What emerged in 1563 were four sub-provinces — Lima, Cuzco, Chile and Guatemala — each with its own provincial, but, like

---

[127] Vázquez Núñez, *Manual*, I, pp. 505–6. In 1559 Philip II issued a *cédula* confirming his father's endorsement of 1526 and permitting the Order to found new houses.

[128] Vázquez Fernández, 'Cedulario mercedario', pp. 619–20.

[129] Vázquez Núñez, *Manual*, I, p. 506.

[130] *Ibid.*, pp. 506–7, & *id.*, 'La erección de las provincias de América' in *BOM*, 21 (1933), pp. 125–36; 126–7.

[131] The procurators' *poder*, dated 12th November 1556, is reproduced in *id.*, 'La erección de las provincias de América', pp. 126–7.

[132] No copy of this brief, dated 30th December 1560, has been found, though it is reproduced in Remón, *Historia*, II, f. 151r.

[133] Vázquez Fernández, 'Cedulario mercedario', pp. 621–2.

[134] Vázquez Núñez, 'La erección de las provincias de América', pp. 128–9, and, for more of the background, *id.*, *Manual*, I, p. 511.

Castile, exempt from the authority of the general.[135] The province of
Castile retained rights to the alms collected in the Indies for the ransom of captives, and was to receive a total of 100 ducats annually in
vestuario.[136] Moreover, in token of their superior status, the Castilians
could maintain a visitor in the New World during every provincialate,
a position which for some time lent itself to scandalous abuse. Alienation of funds by visitors hampered the development of the missions
and caused the provinces to send a succession of religious to protest to
the crown in the early years.[137] However, these difficulties were eventually surmounted and by the 1590s the crown was regularly sending
Mercedarian missionaries to America under its own auspices.[138] From
the late sixteenth century the Mercedarians therefore built up a major
missionary presence in the Indies, which by 1770 numbered 1933 friars in 115 houses along with several hundred *reducciones*.[139] The effect
was not only a significant expansion of the Order, but a broadening of
the Mercedarian mind. Witness the *Historia general del Perú* completed
by the Basque missionary Fray Martín de Murúa in around 1613, and
the *convento máximo* erected by the Order in Quito from 1701, one of
the finest Baroque buildings in New World.[140]

Time would modify the connections between Castile and her
American daughters into a symbiotic relationship, but until creole
society reached full maturity in the seventeenth century the sub-
provinces remained dependent on the metropolis for personnel and
the formation of their élite. Parties of a dozen of more religious periodically embarked for the Indies, the loss of whom had had a marked
effect on the demography of the province of Castile by the turn of the

---

[135] *Id.*, *Manual*, I, p. 510. The foundation charter is reproduced in *id.*, 'Más sobre la
erección de las provincias de América' in *BOM*, 22 (1934), pp. 162–76; 168–72.

[136] The exclusive right of the province of Castile to American redemption *limosna*
was confirmed and extended to that of Andalusia in 1593; Tirso, *Historia*, II, pp.
188–89. The payment of *vestuario* was modified in 1574; see ch. 6, n. 133.

[137] See, for example, BL, Add., vol. 28,342, f. 388r, Fray Alonso Dávila (a prisoner
at Huete) to Philip II, 12th August 1581.

[138] Religious were sent to Guatemala at royal expense in the 1570s; see van Oss,
Catholic Colonialism, p. 34. Expeditions were also funded by the crown to Peru in 1588
and 1593, and to Tucumán in 1600; see Vázquez Núñez, *Manual*, II, pp. 48, 47 & 67
respectively.

[139] See Appendix III.

[140] On Murúa (or Morúa), see Vázquez Núñez, *Mercedarios ilustres*, pp. 327–34. The
Historia general del Perú was first published only this century: ed. Honorio H. Urteaga
& Carlos A. Romero (2 vols., Lima, 1922–5). The latest edition is by Manuel Balles-
teros Gaibrois (Madrid, 1987). The *convento máximo* was completed to the design of
José Jaime Ortiz in 1737.

sixteenth century.[141] But in other ways Castile's relationship with the Indies was fully reciprocal. Despite the foundation of Mercedarian *studia* in Lima (*c.*1580) and Mexico City (1594), the maintenance of the colleges at Salamanca and Alcalá owed much to the subsidies paid by American provinces for the education of their religious.[142] Indeed, the Order came to rely on America for the revenue upon which her growth, influence and prestige as the foremost ransoming agency in the Mediterranean depended. By the 1570s the province of Cuzco alone was sending 1300 ducats of *limosna* per year to Castile.[143] As one Castilian put it in 1684, 'the alms of which our work of redemption is made derive mostly from those sent from the Indies'.[144]

XI. *The Failure of Reform: The Crown of Aragon, 1526–61*

In the Crown of Aragon the late 1520s and early 1530s were marked by a renewed attempt at reform under Zafont, first independently and then under the auspices of the crown in conjunction with Castile. In 1526 the Andalusian-born Fray Juan Calvo conducted a visitation of the convents of Tarragona and Tortosa (at least) in the capacity of 'Reformator et visitator electus', but this campaign, which has left few traces in surviving documentation, does not appear to have had any lasting impact.[145] In 1531, at the petition of Charles V, the bull

---

[141] See Appendix III and, for some examples of this, Muñoz Delgado, 'El convento de Valladolid', p. 54.

[142] See Vázquez Núñez, *Manual*, II, p. 25, for the college in Lima, and Vázquez Fernández, 'Cedulario mercedario', p. 624, for that of Mexico City. During the 1550s negotiations had been conducted by M° Fray Gaspar de Torres with Salamanca-trained Mercedarians in America concerning the diversion of funds for the maintenance of the Vera Cruz; *ibid.*, p. 610.

[143] ACA, Mon., vol. 4144, f. 132r.

[144] Cited in Aparicio, 'Los Mercedarios de América', p. 2.

[145] ACA, Mon., vol. 2669. Two unnumbered 4° ff. inserted between ff. 163 & 164; inventories of Tarragona and Tortosa taken on 8th & 12th June 1526 respectively. See also M° Fray Juan de Antillón, *Epitome de los Generales de la Merced, c.*1640; originals in 3 MS vols. lost. Late 18th-century copies by the Valencian M° Fray Agustín Arqués y Jover of Part I, vols. i (1218–1474) & ii (1474–1574) survive in BPC, mss. 94-108 & 109. An earlier copy of I(ii) by Arqués y Jover is in APV, (no ref. no.), from which all references have been taken. Notes from a 'vol. iii' (i.e. part II, 1574–*c.*1625) by the 18th-century chronicler Fray José Nicolás Cavero survive in APV, (no ref. no.); see ch. 7, n. 174. However, Antillón's *Memorias Chronológicas* in AHMB, ms. A-266 covers the same period and may itself be Part II of the *Epitome*; see ch. 7, n. 29. APV, ms. Antillón, *Epitome*, I(ii), p. 1082 records that Zafont visited the province of Valencia in 1524.

Meditatio cordis nostri authorized a continuation of the Isabelline reform effort with regard to the Benedictines, Cistercians, Premonstratensians, Trinitarians and Mercedarians.[146] In the case of the latter two, the stated aim was to implant discipline in orders qualified as still 'unreformed'. The bull placed the reform in the hands of Cardinal Juan Pardo de Tavera, archbishop of Santiago and now *reformador general*, with the assistance of a prelate appointed by the crown and representatives of the orders concerned. The visitation campaign began a year later under the bishop of Badajoz, Jerónimo Suárez, who was soon reduced to arbitrating the mass of *pleitos* provoked by the confrontation of secular clergy and reformist religious with their unreformed brethren. We have few details concerning the progress of this effort in the Order except for a *cédula* of August 1533 addressed to the viceroys and all royal and ecclesiastical officials in the Crown of Aragon.[147] This enjoined in the usual terms that assistance be rendered to Zafont and his commissaries in their attempt to 'visit and reform the religious of their Order', so that in the Aragonese provinces 'they may freely correct those living out of observance and restore them to it according to [the rules of] God and their Order'. The following year Zafont, with Fra Vicenç Martí and Calvo as visitors provincial, conducted a visitation of Catalonia and Valencia.[148] Although this reform initiative bore few results in the Crown of Aragon, subsequent activity indicates that the pressing need to curb the most flagrant abuses had begun to be recognized.

The events of recent years evidently provoked both a hardening of attitudes against Castile in the Crown of Aragon and a new concern for reform among elements of the hierarchy. After Zafont's death in August 1535 a chapter general at Barcelona elected the prior, Fra Pere Sorell, to the high office in what, so far as the Castilian delegation was concerned, were thoroughly disreputable circumstances.[149] The following year Sorell's first chapter was convened at Zaragoza in the general's absence by his vicar, Fray Domingo de Clavería, without, the Castilians claimed, their being given sufficient notice to present themselves.[150] Even so, a frail Sorell bowed to internal pressure

[146] See García Oro, 'Conventualismo y observancia', pp. 295–7 and Steggink, *La reforma del Carmelo español*, 2nd edn., p. 26.
[147] BNM, ms. 2718, ff. 45r–46v, *cédula* of Charles V, Monzón, 31st August 1533.
[148] For the *acta*, see ACA, Mon., vol. 2669.
[149] Vázquez Núñez, *Manual*, I, p. 447.
[150] *Synodalia* in ACA, Mon., vol. 2667, ff. 238r–249v, 357r & 367r *passim*.

and a number of cosmetic institutional reforms were introduced at this chapter general. Change was felt, albeit temporarily, in two main areas, both of which reflect a growing provincial sentiment among Aragonese and Valencian religious in reaction to the Catalan and in particular *barcelonés* stranglehold over the generalcy. Although it was reversed in 1545, an adjustment to the provincial representation at the chapters general, first at Zaragoza and then at Valencia in 1544, reflects a gradual surrender of the general's authority over the Aragonese and Valencian hierarchy which the reformers were able to exploit in the 1570s.[151] Concern over gross peculation by the generals of the Order's funds, particularly tribute revenue from the loyal provinces and embezzlement of the redemption *limosna*, was reflected in a number of ordinances at Zaragoza. On Sorell's behalf Clavería replaced the system of tributes from the commanderies to the general with an annual payment of twenty-five *escudos* from each of the four subject provinces. Rather than being entrusted to the generals' care, ransom responsions were henceforth to be collected by specially appointed *depositarios* or *procuradores de la redención* who were to deposit these in the *taula* (municipal bank) of Barcelona. Again, however, the characteristic gap between legislation and practice asserted itself.

By this time the serious relaxation in which many of the religious communities of the Principality were living had once again come to the attention of the crown. In 1539 Charles V informed the new viceroy, Francisco de Borja, of 'the dissolution, evil practices and excess that reigns in some of the monasteries of friars and nuns of Barcelona and Catalonia'.[152] We cannot be sure that this comment extended to the Mercedarians, but in that year Clavería and Pérez, two of Zafont's three *lectores* of 1523, embarked on visitations of Catalonia and Valencia, the last recorded in these provinces until 1551. In 1547, as visitor general, Clavería organized what, so far as it is possible to tell, was the first visitation of Aragon and Navarre since 1518–19. With the exception of a few of the Catalan and Valencian houses for which visitation papers survive from 1551–2, no further convents appear to have been visited in the Crown of Aragon and Navarre until the major campaign of 1568–9. However, the nature of

---

[151] See Vázquez Núñez, *Manual*, I, pp. 448, 465 & 469. The *synodalia* of the chapter general of Valencia in 1544 are in ACA, Mon., vol. 2667, ff. 250r–256v.

[152] Cited in P. Joan Bada, *Situació religiosa de Barcelona en el segle XVI* (Barcelona, 1970), p. 130.

surviving visitation papers — inventories — indicates that the priority
was still the preservation of the Order's property before disciplinary
or spiritual reform.[153]

When it became apparent that Sorell was dying, the Catalans celebrated a chapter provincial at Montblanc in mid 1545 to ensure that
their diffinitors general were chosen and ready for the coming election.[154] Sorell expired in Barcelona in February the following year, to
be succeeded in May by the jurist M͡e Fra Miquel Puig, prior of
Barcelona. The Castilians were not represented, and the following
day M͡e Fra Joan de Mata became thirty-fifth prior of Barcelona, thus
ensuring Catalan dominance of the eastern provinces for another
generation.[155] Puig's first chapter general at Girona in May 1547
passed a number of ordinances in an attempt to promote moral and
disciplinary reform.[156] Measures were taken against 'fratres inobedi-
entes et rebelles', the most incorrigible of whom were to be gaoled in
the recently restored castle of Algar in Valencia, or at Toulouse if
French.[157] Concern to perpetuate earlier attempts at reform was
reflected in a confirmation of the *acta* of the chapters general of 1523,
1536 and 1544 and the decision to print these with suitable modifications, though this seems not to have been carried out.[158] Once again,
the Aragonese hierarchy had failed to address the major abuses without which reform could neither be lasting nor effective.

Puig celebrated a chapter general at Zaragoza in 1554, but few
ordinances were passed and the general, 'corralled', as the chronicler
Antillón puts it, in the priory of Barcelona, devoted the next few
years to protecting the Order's alms-collecting privileges both from
the secular clergy in Sicily and the *Cruzada* bull in the Peninsula.[159]
Meanwhile the general's entire Mediterranean patrimony drifted into

---

[153] For the *acta* of the visitations mentioned here, see ACA, Mon., vols. 2669
(1518–19), 2669 & 2670 (1539), 2670 (1547), 2668–2670 (1551–2) and 2668, 2670 &
2671 (1568–9). APV, ms. Antillón, *Epitome*, I(ii), p. 1319 claims that the life commendator of Zaragoza and provincial of Aragon-Navarre, Fray Agustín del Molinar,
was sent on a visitation of his province by Puig in 1556, though no documentation
survives from this.

[154] *Synodalia* in ACA, Mon., vol. 2667, ff. 257r–263v.

[155] APV, ms. Antillón, *Epitome*, I(ii), p. 1282; 'andavan estomagados de la elecion
[*sic*] passada'.

[156] *Synodalia* reproduced in Vázquez Núñez, ed., *La Merced a mediados*, pp. 73–89.

[157] *Ibid.*, pp. 78–9.

[158] *Ibid.*, p. 77.

[159] *Synodalia* in ACA, Mon., vol. 2667, ff. 278r–295v. This period is covered in
APV, ms. Antillón, *Epitome*, I(ii), pp. 1300–21.

chaos under his 'feeble and negligent' government.[160] The reception of sundry apostates and fugitives into the Italian houses earned the Order a rebuke from Paul IV in 1558, while the French convents languished on the eve of the Wars of Religion in the most abject poverty and decadence. Plague prevented the celebration of a chapter general at Barcelona in 1559, but, galvanized no doubt by preparations for the concluding phase of the Council of Trent, the reformist impulse of the bishop of Barcelona, Jaume Cassador (1546–61), and the awakening interest of the crown, Puig finally confronted the urgent question of reform at a chapter in May 1561.

Alarm bells were now ringing throughout the Crown of Aragon, and a well-attended chapter at Barcelona (including two Castilian diffinitors) passed numerous ordinances regarding reform that Puig later had printed.[161] Among a mass of disciplinary statutes of the kind that had appeared in chapters general throughout the century — regarding admission to the Order, fugitives, dress, ownership of property and abuse of redemption alms etc. — came the injunction

> that the Most Reverend Master General of the said Order choose two or three good, honest and learned religious to reform all the provinces of our Order, being Catalonia, Aragon and Navarre, Valencia and France, and the islands of the Mediterranean Sea. Which religious are to see to the correct and proper observance of each and every one of the statutes and measures passed by this chapter, and those whose observance has been enjoined at chapters general in times past, along with all the other constitutions of our Sacred Order according to the Rule of St Augustine under which we serve.[162]

Yet, for all this the delegates at Barcelona had manifestly failed to address the major institutional problems that afflicted the eastern provinces: commanderies held *ad vitam*, the overweening authority of the generals and the inequitable means by which they were elected. Neither is there any evidence that visitations were conducted until the crown addressed itself to the problem of reforming the Order at the end of the decade. By failing to implement even these basic measures, the Aragonese superiors had, unbeknownst to themselves, finally sur-

---

[160] APV, ms. Antillón, *Epitome*, I(ii), p. 1307.

[161] *Ibid.*, p. 1333. No copies are extant. The *acta* are in ACA, Mon., vol. 2667, ff. 295r–310v, while those touching on reform are translated into Castilian in APV, Antillón, ms. *Epitome*, I(ii), pp. 1333–45. For Puig's breviary published in 1560, see ch. 1, n. 96.

[162] Cited in APV, Antillón, ms. *Epitome*, I(ii), pp. 1343–4.

rendered the right to reform their own patrimony and were drawn unconsciously into the web of Philip II's religious policy.

XII. *Retrenchment and the Decline of Learning in the Crown of Aragon*

The belated attempts at reform in the Crown of Aragon from the 1530s and '40s onwards coincided with a modest intellectual flowering, the product of Zafont's patronage over the previous decade.[163] Even so, provisions for study among the Aragonese Mercedarians could not compare with the increasing academic capacity of Castile and inevitably it was to this province and to Paris that Aragonese intellectuals continued to be drawn. Among the duties of Aragonese and French procurators from 1536 onwards was the collection of contributions towards the maintenance in Paris of a scholar from each of the four loyal provinces, these to be chosen by a committee of five commendators in each case.[164] The increasing difficulty of dispatching Spanish religious to France after the royal decrees of 1557–9 meant that by 1561 provision was only being made for one of the four to study in Paris. The rest were expected to pursue their studies in Castile, a sign of the cultural ties that survived between sectors of the Mercedarian hierarchy despite provincial differences and royal injunctions.

During the 1530s and '40s the leading intellectual in the Crown of Aragon had been Mº Fray Jerónimo Pérez. A string of important offices, including those of visitor and then provincial of Valencia in 1539 and 1544–7 respectively, were followed in 1548 by the publication of introductory commentaries on Lombard and Aquinas which he dedicated to Francisco de Borja, duque de Gandía.[165] Pérez was an enthusiastic supporter of the early Company and the few details

---

[163] See Vázquez Núñez, *Manual*, I, pp. 447–9.

[164] *Ibid.*, p. 449 and *id.*, ed., *La Merced a mediados*, p. 78. At Girona in 1547 the provincial contribution per student was set at 20 *livres tournois* annually.

[165] Mº Fray Jerónimo Pérez, *Commentaria Expositio [...] super primam partem Summae S. Thomae Aquinatis, quantum ad ea quae concernunt primum librum Sententiarum* (Valencia: Typis Ioannis Mey Flandri, 1548); a copy survives in BUV, Z-7-59. The work, an introduction to Lombard on Thomist principles, begins with an interesting laudatory poem by Pérez's pupil Mᵉ Fra Pere Joan de Tàrrega. Of the second volume, *In Primum Secundae Divi Thomae Commentaria* (Valencia: same printer?, 1548) in which Pérez apparently attacked Cajetan, no copies are extant. For Pérez as a precursor of Molina, see Vázquez Núñez, *Mercedarios ilustres*, pp. 220–1.

we have regarding his academic life are from the Jesuits of Valencia who reported his competence as a Thomist to Ignatius in 1544. Upon his retirement after thirty years at the university he transferred to Gandía to assist in the establishment of Borja's new college there. 1549 saw him installed in a house on the campus instructing the seminarians in theology and philosophy, but his health soon failed and he died that winter. Pérez was succeeded at Gandía as 'liberalium artium magister' by his pupil and fellow recipient of the Spiritual Exercises, the future reformer M⁵ Fra Pere Joan de Tàrrega.[166]

The welcome extended by Pérez to the Jesuits in the Kingdom of Valencia — reflected in Castile by Fray Agustín de Revenga, the *converso* rector of La Concepción (1545–67)[167] — is an indication of the new mentality prevailing among elements of the Mercedarian élite. In the Crown of Aragon, however, this was not to last. Unlike Castile, the humanistic climate of the early sixteenth century failed to engrain itself lastingly in the Aragonese provinces and no significant academic centres were established here. Interest in the academic life, already meagre by Castilian standards, began to wane. This circumstance, together with the hardening of attitudes in the Crown of Aragon from the 1530s, ensured that few natural successors were found for the intelligentsia which began to disappear from the eastern provinces at this time. The senior Mercedarians of Zafont and Pérez' stamp, formed in the *studia humanitatis* of an earlier generation, were mostly, but not exclusively, replaced by religious more anxious to preserve the authority that remained to them than entertain a disruptive policy of reform. Some, like Fray Juan Calvo, reflect the changes brought about in the Crown of Aragon from the 1530s and '40s. Calvo, the reformer of 1526 and Zafont's companion in the visitations of 1534, presided as provincial of Valencia between 1547 and 1574 over a marked decline in moral and disciplinary standards in his territories. Threatened by the expansion of the province of Castile and confronted by an increasingly alien and unsympathetic government, the Aragonese hierarchy discarded the modest reformist ideals of the past and looked for security and retrenchment.

---

[166] See Esteban Mateo, 'Catedráticos eclesiásticos', pp. 410 & 437.
[167] On Revenga, see Vázquez Núñez, *Mercedarios ilustres*, pp. 266–9.

XIII. *The Castilian Reform Movement*

Lack of documentation prevents us gauging the mood of the Castilian
brethren to the same degree, but it is evident that under Zorita the
reformist movement of the early years of the century continued to
gather strength. In 1533 Zorita crowned the successful outcome of
the *pleito* with Zafont with the publication of his symbolic *Speculum
fratrum* in conscious rivalry with Gaver's identically titled work of a
century before.[168] The *Speculum fratrum* is at once the firmest statement
yet of Castilian independence and a declaration of the province's
reformist intentions. The work, embellished with Zorita's coat of
arms, was in six parts. Like Gaver, Zorita began with an account of
the foundation of the Order followed by the Rule of St Augustine.
Omitting the 1272 constitutions, Zorita then presented an edition of
the 1327 legislation. Though by no means unprecedented, Zorita's
version of the constitutions served not only to underline the absolute
autonomy of Castile, but also to remind all and sundry that its
provincial was effectively general of his vast patrimony in all but
name.[169]

The *Speculum*, then, captures Castile's sense of her separateness and
superiority with regard to the rest of the Order, feelings consolidated
in the decades to come. The achievement of independence from the
authority of the generals is celebrated by the inclusion of the *Bulla
concordiae* of 1467 and the recent *Sententia arbitraria* of 1532 as the fifth
and sixth items. However, perhaps the most significant element of
Zorita's *Speculum* was the fourth part, Gaver's short treatise addressed
to both superiors and friars on the conduct of visitations, the *Modus
servandus in visitatione*.[170] The inclusion of this treatise is especially
important since through it Zorita was attempting, like Gaver before
him, to embue the vigour and confidence of Castile with a sense of
reform and religious observance. The complete Mercedarian *Ordinarium* that he prepared and had printed simultaneously must be seen as
a contributary element to this new image.[171] Thus, though rooted in a

---

[168] Mº Fray Alonso de Zorita, *Speculum fratrum sacri ordinis sancte Maria de mercede redemptionis captivorum* (Valladolid: Nicolás Thierry, 1533). Copies survive in APV (no ref. no.),
and ACA, XXVI-4-3, this missing its first eight folios but including the *Ordinarium*. For
details of the contents, see Placer López, *Bibliografía mercedaria*, II, pp. 1062–3.

[169] A Castilian translation of the constitutions is in BNM, ms. 2284, ff. 8r–75v.

[170] For Gaver's treatise, the *Qualiter visitator*, see *supra*, n. 24.

[171] On Zorita's *Ordinarium officii divini*, see ch. 1, n. 95.

tradition that was Aragonese in origin, Zorita's *Speculum* was composed as a 'Castilian Observance' in deliberate contraposition to the observance of the general and his provinces as embodied in Gaver's *Speculum*. Already in 1526 the missionary Fray Francisco de Bovadilla had declared himself to be acting 'On behalf of the Provincial and friars of Our Lady Saint Mary of Mercy, for the redemption of captives, and of the order and observance of the Province of Castile'.[172]

More so than among the Aragonese brethren, circumstances during the 1530s and '40s confirmed the Castilian hierarchy in a gradual recognition that the basis of reform in the broadest sense lay in institutional change. Zorita's *Speculum* with its 'castilianized' constitutions had of course pointed the way, but the hardened religious outlook in the Peninsula clearly served to convince the hierarchy that action towards reform was long overdue. This realization was no doubt strengthened by the adverse fortunes of the Order in America during the 1530s and '40s; by an increasing awareness that standards would have to be raised if the province were to take its allotted place in the apostolic mission traced out by God for the Castilian Church.

It was during this period, therefore, that Castilians began to adopt the ideal of reform *tam in capite quam in membris*, the realization that moral and disciplinary reform could only succeed as part of a general spiritual and administrative reconstruction that touched every member of the province, and the hierarchy above all. The first serious attempt to circumscribe the powers of the hierarchy in the sixteenth century came at the chapter provincial of Guadalajara in 1539. In that year Zorita cut the duration of future provincialates from life tenure to six years, with no provincial permitted a second term of office until a further two had elapsed.[173] At Segovia in 1550 the chapter reserved the right of appointing a visitor if the provincial were either unable or unwilling to do so, and further reduced the provincialate to three years, renewable for a second term at the discretion of the following chapter.[174] Apart from the provincial hierarchy, the

---

[172] Vázquez Núñez, *Manual*, I, p. 436.

[173] A copy of the papal bull confirming the limitation of the provincialate to six years is in AGS, PR, 23-47, Rome, 16th March 1547.

[174] See Vázquez Núñez, *Manual*, I, p. 488. A copy of the bull confirming the principal decrees passed here is in AGS, PR, 23-48, Rome, 29th November 1553; see also Linás, *Bullarium*, pp. 141–4. This further reduction in tenure was reversed at Toledo in 1556, the *synodalia* of which (though not the *acta*) survive in a notarial copy dated 24th May 1556 in BNM, ms. 3530, ff. 2r–6v, reproduced in Vázquez Núñez,

privilege of voting at the chapter was limited to university graduates
in theology and commendators and *procuradores* of houses with ten or
more ordained religious. Although many of these measures enjoyed
only limited success, the Castilian hierarchy had begun to address
some of the major institutional obstacles to the reform of their
province. A broader and more rigorous definition of these would follow in the decades to come.

Beyond its expansion in the Indies, the key to the continued development of the province of Castile remained its commitment to the
growth of an academic vocation, and it was in this tradition that the
reformist brethren of the later sixteenth century were nurtured. The
leading reformist intellectual in the province of Castile in the middle
decades of the century was Mº Fray Gaspar de Torres (*c.*1510–84),
whose brother Baltasar was a noted Mercedarian contemplative.[175]
Born near Cazorla in Andalusia, Torres entered the Vera Cruz in the
1530s where he studied philosophy and theology under Fray Domingo de San Juan de Pie del Puerto. His first chair, a quadrennial *cátedra
menor* in philosophy, came in 1541, followed in 1548 by the 'Físicos'
chair (Aristotle's *Physics*). Finally, in 1549 he was appointed to the full
Logica Magna cathedra — once held by San Juan and over many
decades virtually a preserve of the Vera Cruz — before becoming a
maestro in theology. It was during Torres' long tenure as rector
(1545–68), therefore, that many of the reformist generation of the later sixteenth century were educated at the Vera Cruz.

Having established his academic position at Salamanca, Torres
turned his attention to the administrative affairs both of the university
and of his Order.[176] Torres was in the van of that group of Mercedarians who sought to raise the aspirations of the Order and replace the
idleness and abuse associated with conventual life with missionary
zeal and academic endeavour. Since greater discipline and higher
standards were now expected from religious in their chosen vocations, probity in the work of redemption emerged as a matter of para-
mount importance. In the years before and during his provincialate
(1559–65), Torres therefore attacked the negligence and dishonesty

ed., *La Merced a mediados*, pp. 92–5. Provincials' tenure was reduced at Torres' suggestion from six years to four at Toledo in 1565, being eventually fixed at three in 1569.
[175] See P.Fr. Guillermo Vázquez Núñez, 'La Universidad de Salamanca en los años
1548 a 1568: Biografia del Maestro Fray Gaspar de Torres...' in *BOM*, 12 (1924), pp.
228–47, & 13 (1925), pp. 272–80 & 317–35, & *id.*, *Mercedarios ilustres*, pp. 281–9.
[176] *Id.*, 'La Universidad de Salamanca', pp. 235–9.

of commendators in the collection of redemption alms, and this period is notable in Castile for several copious ransoming expeditions. In
once more making commendators responsible for the behaviour of
their friars, Torres echoes Albert's understanding of the role of superiors at the fulcrum of religious life.

Torres' reformist activities in the Order were complemented by his
administrative work in the university of Salamanca.[177] Already in
1547 Torres had become a university *diputado* (deputy) and three
years later he incorporated the college of the Vera Cruz fully into the
university. Reflecting his brethren's now traditional competence in
law, in 1550 Torres entered the *claustros*, the upper chamber or senate
of university government, becoming acting *maestrescuela* the following
year. Over the next few years he conducted a spirited defence of the
university against its royal visitor, Diego Enríquez, bishop of Coria,
particularly over the preservation of studies in the Classical and Biblical languages, fields in which the Vera Cruz had made its own contribution. However, Torres' main work at this time was in the preparation of the new university constitutions in which he took a leading
role. The constitutions, which appeared in 1561, contained the disciplinary regulations of the university and a new curriculum detailing
the principal texts in each subject. Copernicus was set for astronomy,
Hebrew and Greek were promoted and Peter Lombard replaced by
Aquinas as the main theological authority, a shift reflected in the
Mercedarian Order over the course of the sixteenth century. Finally,
a notable though futile attempt was made to raise theology to preem-
inence over canon and civil law in the academic life of the university.

Pressing business in both Order and university prevented Torres
attending the Council of Trent as the latter's representative, and neither did the Mercedarians send a delegate. However, Torres welcomed the publication of the Tridentine decrees, and these loomed
large in the reformulation of the Mercedarian constitutions to which
he brought his legislative skills to bear in 1565. As provincial of
Castile Torres was instrumental in shaping the crown's perception of
the Order after 1560, and he was rewarded with elevation to the episcopate in 1570.[178]

*

[177] *Ibid.*, pp. 239–44.
[178] *Ibid.*, p. 318.

In 1559 Puig sent three Navarrese religious to the chapter provincial of Castile at Toledo. It is not known what else they discussed with the provincial hierarchy, but the result of this embassy was a joint Aragonese-Castilian redemption to Algiers in 1561–2 which returned to El Grao in Valencia with a record 427 ransomed captives. This redemption represented a final show of unity as storm clouds gathered over the Order and its affairs entered the purview of the crown and the papacy. As Philip wrote to his ambassador in Rome in March of the following year,

> As you are aware, though the Order of Our Lady of Mercy is most holy, she no longer enjoys the purity and perfection to which she was accustomed in times past, which condition, it is clear, has come about through her not having observed the statutes and ordinances set down by her founding fathers...[179]

The Order, then, had been caught up in the political and religious concerns that shaped Post-Tridentine Spain.

---

[179] AMAE, SS, leg. 34, f. 1r–v, Philip II to Francisco de Vargas, Madrid, 12th March 1563. Another copy f. 7r–v. The 'statutes and ordinances' of the Order's founding fathers referred to here had of course been lost long before, if, that is, they ever existed as such.

CHAPTER THREE

REFORM AND GOVERNMENT

> *As the passage of time has shown, the religious observance in which the orders were instituted cannot be sustained [...] except through the prayers of their members and the watchfulness of princes and those who govern over them.*[1]

This chapter will attempt to set the reform of the Mercedarian Order into the context of the influences and conjunctures that were brought to bear on it from the 1560s onwards: the spiritual and legislative framework of the papacy as set down at Trent and later pursued by the nuncios; the political and religious concerns of Philip II, and the condition of the Crown of Aragon and of Catalonia in particular as an expression of the tensions and disparities characteristic of the dynastic union that was Habsburg Spain. Added to the peculiar condition of the Order as it had developed over the previous 350 years, the cumulative effect was to be greater than any single player in the ensuing drama could embrace. Coursing through this process is the perpetual question of *reform* itself, the historical element that unifies this movement without apparently defining it. What was the nature of reform in a Mercedarian context? How far was it shaped by external influences and by the history and internal dynamism of the Order itself? Ultimately, how might we begin to classify the idea and the reality of monastic reform under Philip II?

I. *The Mercedarians and the Crown*

The accession of Philip II in 1556 brought a new and highly personalized style of government to the Spanish kingdoms. The reign was characterized in almost all spheres of life by an unprecedented degree of royal intervention that aimed to condition people and institutions

---

[1] AGS, PR, 23-212. Untitled *memorial* by Cristóbal de Rojas y Sandoval, bishop of Córdoba, later archbishop of Seville, to Philip II, undated but *c.*1568–9; f. 1r.

of differing loyalties to a range of unifying religious and political concerns. In this the crown and its agents were only partially successful, for the endeavour precipitated a series of conflicts that illustrate both the limitations of royal authority and the awakening perceptions of individuals to their place in the *Monarquía Española*. Although, as we have seen, leading Mercedarians had made attempts at disciplinary and even institutional change, the process of reform to which the Order was subjected during the late sixteenth century was, more than had been the case during the reign of the Catholic Kings, conducted under the direct sponsorship of the crown. With the full involvement of the crown came the inevitable imposition of its political concerns onto the agenda, concerns that tied the reform of the Mercedarians and other orders to the social and political realities of contemporary Spain.

By 1561 the state of the Mercedarian Order appears to have come to Philip's attention. How had this happened? Although sectors of most religious orders had fallen into serious laxity at one time or another, the possible implications of this among the Aragonese Mercedarians in particular were especially disturbing to the crown. While the lamentable moral and disciplinary condition of the religious provided reason enough, certain institutional features peculiar to the Order made its reform a matter of the most pressing urgency in the light of social, political and religious developments both inside and outside Spain. Although at this stage Philip gives few signs in his correspondence of being aware of the condition of a somewhat obscure sector of Spanish ecclesiastical life, this seems to have been partly remedied during his journey to the Crown of Aragon to celebrate the *cortes* at Monzón in 1563–4. It was during this visit that the king appears to have formed opinions regarding the Order and its *milieu* which remained with him for the rest of his life.

Although by now accepted as having been established by Jaume I of Aragon in 1218, the Mercedarians, unlike the Jeronymites, the only other important order of Spanish foundation, showed little recognition of the authority of the crown whose patronage they continued to claim. As we have seen, the high officers of the Order resided in the Crown of Aragon where the king's writ did not run nearly so freely. Protected by the municipal and provincial privileges of Barcelona and the eastern kingdoms, and with the weight of tradition and legality behind it, the Aragonese hierarchy remained quite unaccountable to the government. To this circumstance was added the dispersion of the general's patrimony beyond the frontiers of the realm. With Languedoc overrun by Huguenots and banditry growing in the Crown of Aragon, the *cortes* of 1563–4 can only have served to confirm in Philip's mind the potential threat posed to the political and religious integrity of his kingdoms by the activities of several hundred dissolute religious living beyond the pale of royal jurisdiction. The obvious disparity between the condition and mentality of the Aragonese superiors and their Castilian counterparts that became apparent through the 1560s strengthened the king in his determination to alter the structure of the Order to Castile's benefit. It was with this foremost in his mind that Philip conducted his campaign to reform the Mercedarian Order.

From the standpoint of the crown the principal context of this process — the condition of the Crown of Aragon and Catalonia in particular — made the Mercedarian affair as much an exercise in the transfer of power as of 'reform' itself. The axis of this reform was therefore set by the unifying aims of the crown from the vantage point of Castile. Although new and unexpected circumstances would repeatedly colour and interfere with Philip's perspective, the process of Mercedarian reform continued to revolve around the king's religious and political agenda with regard to the Crown of Aragon in the context of the Spanish imperial system. It was in the eastern kingdoms, therefore, and particularly in Catalonia, that the root of the problem was seen to lie and here that the battle for reform, with its distinct and shifting interpretations, was to be waged.

II. *Catalonia: Government and Representation*

By the mid sixteenth century the Crown of Aragon had become marginalized within the composite structure of the Spanish monarchy.[2] Resistant to centralizing authority and largely excluded both by circumstance and design from participating in the wider Castilian empire, the Aragonese provinces maintained an increasingly zealous defence of their ancient privileges and exemptions with respect to the crown. Charles V had avoided antagonizing the traditional Aragonese

---

[2] See J.H. Elliott, *The Revolt of the Catalans: A Study in the Decline of Spain (1598–1640)* (Cambridge, 1963), pp. 3–113, & Ernest Belenguer Cebrià, *La Corona de Aragón en la época de Felipe II* (Valladolid, 1986).

institutions and advised his son to exercise caution when addressing
himself to the affairs of the Crown of Aragon, warning him to be

> very alert in this matter, since one may err in its government more eas-
> ily than in that of Castile, as much because the *fueros* (exemptions) and
> constitutions are what they are as because the people are no less pas-
> sionate than any other. Moreover, there are fewer means of discover-
> ing and punishing these passions, which they are wont to display more
> often and with firmer pretext than is usually the case.[3]

However, while Philip followed this advice to a considerable extent,
his accession brought a new perception of events and consequently a
new style of government to Spain. This approach provoked considerable opposition in the eastern provinces, especially in Aragon itself
and in Catalonia, the 'antechamber of Europe', which, in the defence
of its constitutional heritage, was to be every bit as passionate as the
Emperor had warned.

The Catalonia inherited by Philip II has been described as 'an
imperfect sovereign state, but a state nonetheless'.[4] The constitutional
order established during the reign of the Catholic Kings had weathered the foundation of the *Monarquía Española* and continued to function through the sixteenth century. Within this framework the Catalans had preserved their representative institutions along with a
regime of *furs* (exemptions) and privileges at odds with an increasingly
intrusive monarchy. Towards the end of the century the tenuous
association of quasi-statelet within a larger whole by which the Principality was tied to the crown began to give way as Catalans reacted
to assertions of royal authority with open resistance. The *furs*, the set
of checks and balances that had once codified a dynamic contractual
association between crown and institutions, gradually became the last
redoubt of a stultified legislative system. Faced by the reality of an
absentee sovereign, the Catalan institutions cast themselves in the
role of guardians of national interests and fell back on the defence of
their traditional rights and privileges and those of the Principality as a
whole. The wide-ranging influence still wielded by the *Generalitat* and
the *Consell de Cent* in particular enabled them to put up a spirited rear-
guard action to the incursions of royal policy, of which the reform of

---

[3] J.M. March, *Niñez y juventud de Felipe II* (2 vols., Madrid, 1941–2); II, p. 17.
[4] Cited, after Pedro de la Marca, in Núria Sales, *Els segles de la decadència: Segles
XVI–XVIII*, vol. IV (1989) of Pierre Vilar, gral. ed., *Història de Catalunya* (8 vols.,
1987–90), p. 99.

the Mercedarians is a significant example. Meanwhile, administrative difficulties and basic incomprehension limited Philip to what was often an unimaginative and unfocused policy of assimilation.[5]

In his absence, the king's *alter nos* in Catalonia, as in all the provinces of the empire except for Castile, was the viceroy.[6] The office, which in Catalonia was conjoined with that of captain-general, was the supreme expression of royal authority in the provinces apart from the king himself. Yet, despite the formidable power theoretically wielded by the viceroys, who were mostly Castilians, in practice this was greatly limited by the constitutional framework in which they were forced to govern, by the lack of a standing army, and by the condition of Catalonia herself. Under these circumstances the government of the Principality could be a frustrating task, as the impotent haranguings to which viceroys frequently subjected local officials bear witness.

As the summoning of the *corts* (estates) became increasingly infrequent over the course of the sixteenth century, so its standing committee — the *Diputació del General* or *Generalitat* — developed as the principal mouthpiece of Catalan national sentiment and the guardian of its most cherished customs and values.[7] The continual abuse by the crown and its officers of the rights and privileges of the *Generalitat* was therefore among the most resented aspects of royal government in Catalonia. 'In Catalonia,' so the ancient maxim ran, 'the lord king is obliged to adjudicate as disposed by the law', but the crown steadfastly refused to accept the *Generalitat's* constitutional jurisdiction in civil and criminal law in favour of the *Reial Audiència* (high court of appeals).[8] Granted a number of supervisory faculties by Charles V at the *corts* of 1553, the attempted expansion of royal authority under Philip II galvanized the *Generalitat* into a stalwart defence of the Constitutions, most notably in the crisis of 1568–70. And, like the *corts*, the *Generalitat* was concerned to influence royal policy on monastic reform throughout the Principality.

---

[5] Ferran Soldevila & Ferran Valls i Taberner, *Historia de Cataluña* (Madrid, 1982), p. 476.

[6] See Joan Reglà, *Els virreis de Catalunya* (Barcelona, 1956).

[7] See Soldevila & Valls i Taberner, *Historia de Cataluña*, p. 486. The six-member Catalan *Generalitat* was composed of two members from each estate who held office for three years.

[8] Cited in Sales, *Els segles de la decadència*, p. 100. The original reads: 'Lo senyor rey en Cathalunya es obligat judicar segons dispositio de dret'.

Of the Catalan institutions the most significant in the Mercedarian question was the municipal council of Barcelona, the *Consell de Cent*.[9] Although rivalry over precedence had long soured relations with the *Generalitat*, the steady erosion of their rights and sources of income at the hands of the crown served to bring the two institutions together in the late sixteenth century. This collaboration was nowhere clearer than in their opposition to the reform of the Catalan religious Order. The influence and respect in which the *Consell* was held, not only in the city but throughout the province, was based on three important aspects of its activity: its powers of mediation with the crown, as in the *excusado* crisis of 1569–70, its uncompromising patronage and defence of local institutions, and a reputation for upholding its own prerogatives by force if necessary.[10] The *consellers'* defence of the religious houses of both city and Principality against the threat of reform, of which the Mercedarian priory is the most notable example, typifies this stance. As an integral part of the religious and social life of the city, as well as being the mother house of the Order, it is not surprising that the priory of Barcelona should find its staunchest and most generous supporters in the *Consell de Cent*.

III. *Catalonia: Violence and Defiance*

Although the constitutional framework bequeathed to Catalonia by Ferdinand the Catholic after the Civil War of 1462–72 had managed to survive the development of the Spanish monarchy, the legal and economic structure he left proved quite unequal to the religious, social and political realities of the age. For if the Catalans had developed an increasingly disjointed relationship to the centre, then likewise urban Catalonia found itself ruptured from the countryside by the mid sixteenth century, a state of affairs which naturally presented serious problems to both secular and ecclesiastical authorities. The Catholic Reformation was principally an urban phenomenon and

---

[9] Soldevila & Valls i Taberner, *Historia de Cataluña*, pp. 487–9, & James Amelang, *Honored Citizens of Barcelona: Patrician Culture and Class Relations, 1490–1714* (Princeton, 1986), pp. 19 & 28–35. The day-to-day business of the *Consell de Cent* was conducted by a standing committee of five *consellers* appointed by insacculation for four-year terms until 1587 and yearly thereafter.

[10] On the crisis surrounding the *subsidio*, a tax on ecclesiastical income, see Bada, *Situació religiosa*, pp. 251–4.

since the political, cultural and to some extent religious life of Catalonia tended to focus on the capital, so in general terms Barcelona came to direct the progress of the reformist movement in the Principality.[11] However, in practice the Catalan countryside still enjoyed an almost complete autonomy from the centre, maintaining itself out of its own resources and quite beyond urban control. As the century drew on, so the ecclesiastical authorities of the city began to promote civic piety and ceremony and renew the process of religious reform with the aim of extending its spiritual influence throughout the province.

The uneasy relationship between rural and urban Catalonia during the late sixteenth century is typified in the experience of the Mercedarian priory of Barcelona, the urban centre of what was then, in the Crown of Aragon, largely a rural order. For nearly twenty years the affairs of the priory reflected the violence of the countryside as friars from throughout the Principality and beyond mustered to defend their way of life from outside interference. If this process was a reflection of the gradual development of Barcelona as the religious centre of Catalonia during the Post-Tridentine period, then it also signalled the painful transformation of the Mercedarians of the Crown of Aragon, and Catalonia in particular, from a predominantly rural order into a predominantly urban one.

The Mercedarians were not alone among the Catalan religious congregations in resisting the centralizing and unifying aims of the crown, or in being permeated by the mores of rural life: violence and banditry. However, it was the only order whose geographical expansion, condition and peculiar vocation — the ransom of Christian captives — associates it with the triangle of problems that afflicted Catalonia during the sixteenth century: the Huguenot threat from France, banditry in the Crown of Aragon and from over the Pyrenees, and the Muslim piracy of the wider Mediterranean sphere.

The sixteenth century saw a continued decline in Catalan trade and influence in the Mediterranean in the face of Castilian and Genoese competition and Muslim attack. The first serious Muslim incursion on the Catalan coast was made against Amposta and then Badalona in 1527 followed by an attack on the island of Menorca in

---

[11] Henry Kamen, *The Phoenix and the Flame: Catalonia and the Counter-Reformation* (New Haven, 1993), p. 171.

1535 when some 5000 people were either killed or captured.[12] The emphasis of Charles V on Italy and the Mediterranean for a time led Catalans to see their role as forging an African empire to counter-balance that carved out by the Castilians in America. This expectation was of course reflected in the agreement signed between the Castilian Mercedarians and the Catalan general, Zafont, in 1532. Barcelona provided the base for the attacks on Tunis and La Goleta in 1535 and Algiers in 1541 while the emperor revitalized the royal *drassanes* (shipyards) with commissions of galleys for the defence of his Mediterranean interests. However, the collapse of Spanish power on the Barbary Coast from the 1540s and the increase in piracy off the shores of the Principality soon disabused Catalans of this prospect. A succession of reverses culminating in the loss of Tripoli and the sacking of Ciutadella on Menorca in 1558 followed by the fall of the *plaza* (fortress) of Djerba in the Gulf of Sirte two years later put the Catalans and Valencians firmly on the defensive. The constant threat to coastal towns contributed to the siege mentality and war footing of the Catalan countryside; coastal *masies* (homesteads) and churches were fortified against both corsairs and oppressive landlords; armed confraternities and defence leagues were established in coastal towns. But as the dungeons and *baños* of the Barbary Coast filled with Christian captives, the Mercedarians of the Crown of Aragon slackened in their redemptive zeal so that one of the main accusations levelled against them in the late 1560s was negligence in this, their principal vocation.

Although clergymen and particularly canons had always been drawn into baronial feuding and disputes over ecclesiastical property, involvement in brigandage and acts of armed violence became common among the lower ranks of both the secular and the regular clergy during the second half of the sixteenth century.[13] Bellicose 'monjos giròvags' (vagabond monks) were common in Catalonia, and it is

---

[12] Josep M. Salrach & Eulàlia Duran, *Història dels Països Catalans: Dels orígens a 1714* (2 vols., Barcelona, 1981); II, pp. 429–30.

[13] The papacy issued bulls against bandit clergy in 1551 and 1572. On this see Bada, *Situació religiosa*, p. 255, and also Henry Kamen, 'Clerical Violence in a Catholic Society: The Hispanic World, 1450–1720' in W.J. Shiels, ed., *The Church and War* [*Studies in Church History*, vol. XX] (Oxford, 1983); pp. 201–16, & Jean-François Galinier-Pallerola, 'La Délinquance des ecclésiastiques catalans á l'époque moderne d'après les archives du tribunal du Bref' in *Annals du Midi*, 104 (1992), pp. 43–67, esp. 54–8 & 66–7.

clear that for many religious recourse to violence and banditry proved the only means of preserving a way of life threatened by royal intrusion and the reforming aims of a Church hierarchy increasingly staffed by aliens. As a Genoese commentator wrote after an ambush near Igualada in 1612, 'You must know that all these people round here are great thieves — even the friars, and particularly two of the Order of Saint Bernard...'.[14] The immunity from secular jurisdiction enjoyed by the clergy encouraged individuals and communities both to shelter bandits and participate in acts of violence. Just as the Benedictines of the Pyrenean monasteries of Ripoll and Sant Miquel de Cuixà, and the Canons Regular of Solsona and Sant Jaume de Calaf assisted bandits in attacks on royal troops billeted on them in the 1560s, so the Mercedarians of Barcelona resorted to incastellation and armed resistance to prevent the visitation of the priory in the years around 1580.[15] Yet, while many clergymen participated in acts of violence it is worth remembering that the Church itself became the target of attacks not only from Huguenot bandits but also from rapacious landlords.[16]

The violence of Catalan rural society was reflected in the almost universal presence of weapons. As early as 1517 royal laws had been passed sanctioning the bearing of arms for the purposes of defence against Muslim piracy and brigandage. However, as the century advanced and the short *pedrenyal per foc* (blunderbuss) became the favoured weapon of the *bandoler*, the government began legislating against the use of these. Despite passing restrictions of this sort, the authorities were anxious not to leave citizens defenceless against armed bandits and Huguenot heretics in the absence of an effective police force. But such fears were groundless since, as Fray Juan Álvaro, the Cistercian bishop of Solsona, declared in 1622, 'in this country everyone defends their jurisdiction with arms'.[17] In this the Mercedarians were no exception.

Popular banditry was greatly complicated by the problem of French immigration which added the tincture of religious dissidence to the escalating pattern of violence in Catalonia.[18] Heavy immigra-

---

[14] Cited in Elliott, *The Revolt of the Catalans*, p. 111.
[15] Ricardo García Cárcel, *Historia de Cataluña: Siglos XVI–XVII* (2 vols., Barcelona, 1985); II, p. 64.
[16] See Bada, *Situació religiosa*, p. 163.
[17] Cited in Kamen, *The Phoenix and the Flame*, p. 242.
[18] Sales, *Els segles de la decadència*, pp. 103–13.

tion into Catalonia began in the 1540s under the shadow of a Fran-
co-Turkish alliance against Spain and frequent border and coastal
incursions, a fact which no doubt contributed to the political and religious prejudices of Catalans against the *gavatx*, as the French were
known. As Calvinism spread throughout southern France to the
Pyrenees and Huguenots — the *lladres de Gascunya* ('Gascon thieves')
— joined the flow of immigrants into the Peninsula, animosity
between Frenchmen and Catalans turned to sectarian violence.

Naturally, this state of affairs placed the Mercedarians in a rather
delicate situation. One of the unique features of the Order was in
having dependent houses in France, rather than the other way round.
But what was the nature of the relationship between the French Mercedarians and their Catalan brethren? A number of French religious
were established in Catalonia during the sixteenth century, including
among the hierarchy, a reflection of the close ties that existed
between the two provinces which were amply borne out in the 1570s.
Though monopolized by the Catalans since the election of Fra Benet
Zafont in 1522, the French remained loyal to the generalcy and continued to send representatives to the electoral chapters. However, the
French religious necessarily enjoyed greater independence from the
authority of the general than the three Aragonese provinces, with visitations being conducted at the instance of the provincial who usually
resided at Toulouse. Although Philip no doubt remained concerned
at the possibility of fugitive and bandit Mercedarians turning to
heresy, events evidently settled any fears he may have harboured over
the confessional integrity of the Aragonese Mercedarians as a whole.
During the 1560s and '70s the Order's patrimony in southern France
was partly destroyed and its brethren scattered and murdered by the
Huguenots, and it was the end of the century before the Mercedarians had begun to reestablish themselves in these parts.[19]

---

[19] The following French houses were affected during the Wars of Religion: *Montpellier*, in trouble from 1547, was mostly demolished in October 1561 and abandoned
for *Carcassonne* in 1586, but restored the following century; *Béziers*, destroyed in 1562,
refounded on a different site in 1671; *Maleville*, burnt in 1563, refounded later;
Auterive in the county of Foix, threatened by the conversion of the Albret from 1548,
was eventually destroyed in 1570 but restored with assistance from Henry IV in
1598; *Avignon* had disappeared by the end of the 16th century. The principal French
house, *Toulouse*, was sacked in May 1562, but the community survived through the
efforts of its distinguished commendator, Mᶜ Fray Antoine de Tremollières, a member of the *parlement*; see Abbé Salvan, *Histoire générale de l'église de Toulouse* (4 vols.,
Toulouse, 1856–60); IV, p. 114. In 1585 Fray Fernando Suárez, Castilian procura-

While local authorities tended to protect the rights and security of immigrants, both Rome and the crown became increasingly concerned that the Huguenots filtering in over the border presented a serious threat to the religious security of Catalonia.[20] Fuelled by exaggerated reports from the Inquisition and with the Wars of Religion raging in France, by the late 1560s Philip had become convinced that Catalonia was on the verge of going over to Protestantism. Terrified by this prospect, during 1568 Philip ordered the viceroy Diego Hurtado de Mendoza to take a series of emergency measures. All Catalan frontier settlements were put on the alert, the 1559 ban on Castilians studying abroad was extended to the Crown of Aragon, censorship was gradually introduced (1568–73) and orders were sent to all Catalan bishops to ban French clergy from preaching.[21] Finally, Philip enjoined Mendoza to clamp down on the stream of armed 'Lutherans' entering Catalonia from France with the bandits, and to this end the viceroy travelled to the frontier in 1568 to marshal royal defences against an invasion that never materialized.[22]

The following year a serious conflict developed between the Inquisition and the *Generalitat* over the payment of the *excusado* or *fogatge* tax.[23] Attempts by the Holy Office to increase the Catalan contribution were resisted by the *Generalitat*, earning them a preposterous accusation of heresy by the Inquisitors. Harassed by the legion of problems afflicting the monarchy at that moment, Philip first ordered the *diputats* to apologize to the Inquisition, and then had them arrested in July 1569 when they refused to do so. Before long both Rome and the bishop, Guillem Cassador, had become embroiled in the affair, and with this the issues at stake began to shift to the more gen-

---

tor in Rome, described the French province as reduced to no more than 40 religious in four or five houses, and these often little more than a 'den of thieves'; AMAE, SS, leg. 34, f. 145r, Suárez to Martínez de Carnazedo, secretary of ambassador Olivares, undated but Rome, mid 1585. Main details from Vázquez Núñez, *Manual*, I, pp. 483–5 & *id.*, 'Conventos de la Orden', pp. 289–96. For *Montpellier*, see ADH, H50, nos. 25, 26 & 33; for *Béziers*, *ibid.*, no. 66; for *Carcassonne* and *Auterive*, *ibid.*, no. 51.

[20] Ferran Soldevila, *Història de Catalunya*, 2nd edn. (Barcelona, 1963), pp. 943–4.

[21] Though, as Kamen has recently demonstrated, these measures appear to have had little effect before the end of the century; see *The Phoenix and the Flame*, pp. 232 & 385–426.

[22] Hostilities were confined to border skirmishes, though Perpignan was briefly 'besieged' in 1571.

[23] Bada, *Situació religiosa*, pp. 243–9. Introduced in 1567 to help fund the wars in Flanders and against the Turks, the *excusado* consisted of a tithe of the most valuable piece of property in every parish.

eral question of ecclesiastical jurisdiction. Once the crisis had begun to blow over and the absurdity of the charges became apparent, Philip 'absolved' the *diputats*, who were released by Mendoza in March 1570. Ultimately, the Catalans, though certainly exposed to heresy, remained for the most part staunchly orthodox, choosing, like the Mercedarians, to express their dissatisfaction with royal authority by other means.

IV. *The Church and Religious Culture in Catalonia*

What was the religious condition of Catalonia in 1560, the eve of the Tridentine period?[24] In ecclesiastical terms, the bulk of the Principality of Catalonia lay within the boundaries of the archdiocese of Tarragona which did not observe political frontiers.[25] Apart from the archiepiscopal see itself, only four of Tarragona's six suffragan dioceses lay completely within Catalonia: Barcelona, Girona, Vic and Urgell. Of the other two, the diocese of Lleida strayed into Aragon while that of Tortosa lay mostly in the Kingdom of Valencia. Moreover, there were regions which, while politically Catalan, rested under French episcopal jurisdiction, a circumstance Philip was determined to remedy.[26] The Catalan counties of Rosselló and Cerdanya belonged to the French see of Elna which in turn constituted part of the archdiocese of Narbonne until transferred to that of Tarragona in 1573. The most celebrated case, the Pyrenean Vall d'Aran, lay in the diocese of Comminges and remained subject to the Toulouse tribunal of the Inquisition until it was annexed to the see of Urgell in 1568. Similarly, many of the 150 monastic and religious foundations belonging to nearly thirty orders and congregations of men and women in Catalonia lay under the nominal jurisdiction of French mother-houses, or, as in the Mercedarian case, had foreign houses subject to them. The Catalan Church did not, therefore, observe political frontiers then any more than it fits into convenient historical periodizations now.

---

[24] On this see P. Miquel Batllori, 'Temes i problemes de la història religiosa de Catalunya' in *Actes del Primer Congrés d'Història Moderna de Catalunya* [=*Pedralbes*] (2 vols., Barcelona, 1984); II, pp. 371–9.

[25] For a sumptuous treatment of this, see P. Joan Bada & Genís Samper, eds., *Catalonia Religiosa. Atlas històric: Dels orígens als nostres dies* (Barcelona, 1991).

[26] See Sales, *Els segles de la decadència*, pp. 45–6.

We have no accurate statistics for the clerical population of Catalonia, but numbers were proportionately rather higher here than in Castile — perhaps 2% (against 1.2%) which would translate into around 7000 individuals in 1553.[27] In that year the ecclesiastical estate amounted to 6% (i.e. *c.*2000) of the population of Barcelona, an extremely high proportion matched only by Toledo and Valladolid in Spain. As elsewhere, the Tridentine period saw a considerable rise in clerical numbers in Catalonia, but unusually the increase in male religious appears to have been greater than that of nuns. This circumstance no doubt reflects the movement by superiors to recruit religious for the defence of houses under the threat of reform and visitation, as was the case among the Mercedarians. The increasing pressure from Castile against which superiors were seeking to defend themselves was first felt at an ecclesiastical level in the provision to bishoprics. The crown's monopoly over episcopal appointments represented an important avenue for royal intervention, and throughout the Habsburg period only about 40% of incumbents were Catalans.

If this represents the basis of the ecclesiastical order, what was the religious and spiritual mood of the native Catalan clergy and their secular charges in the middle years of the sixteenth century? As Kamen has said, 'all the prelates recognised the crown as sovereign lord, but firmly within the framework of the constitutions of Catalonia and without compromising their own feudal lordship or their independence in a broad range of spheres'.[28] This was particularly true of the Mercedarian superiors, whose claims to be under royal patronage had long ceased to be reflected in practice. The allegiance of the brethren was to a way of life carved out within the means and tradition of the Order in the context of medieval Catalan Church and society. For them the reign of Philip II was to be a very rude awakening indeed. However, for other elements of the ecclesiastical hierarchy the reforming aims of the crown accorded with their own priorities, and consequently many of the crown's most loyal subjects were to be found here. At mid-century only 10 or 20% of Catalan benefices lay in the gift of the Church, with the rest in the hands of the nobility. The necessity of restoring these to the Church for the purposes of reform found ready support from prelates such as Jaume and Guillem Cassador at Barcelona who were eager to shake off the exactions of lay jurisdiction.

---

[27] See Bada, *Situació religiosa*, pp. 55–6.
[28] Kamen, *The Phoenix and the Flame*, p. 46.

As elsewhere in rural Europe, Catalan religion was deeply interwoven with the life of the community, rooted in local experience yet recognizing universal symbols.[29] Structured around a seasonal regime of work and leisure, individuals tended to view religious belief in communal terms rather than as a personal faith. The integration of both the sacred and the profane and emphasis on ritualized group religion rather than church religion translated into a markedly unsacramental approach to Christian worship, a situation the Tridentine decrees aimed to reverse. It is possible to identify four dimensions of local faith in Catalonia: the cult of a holy relic or image as a tangible object of religion; precise demarcation of the area in which worship took place; the invocation of specific properties relating to local conditions, and finally the exaltation of the social grouping most clearly identified with the image.[30] These characteristics are clearly reflected in Mercedarian worship. In seventeenth-century Rosselló, for instance, Nostra Senyora de la Mercè, patroness of Canet de la Costa, offered protection against sickness, plague, hail, war and general misfortune to a rural population, while another Mercedarian saint, Santa Maria de Cervelló (or Socós) became the patroness of a confraternity of Barcelona seafarers.[31]

Naturally, the attempt by the Tridentine clergy to alter this religious tradition met the same resolute opposition from Catalans as other interference had done throughout the sixteenth century. At the root of this resistance were those ordained and locally recruited priests and religious, the guardians of collective memory, language and culture, who represent a barometer of popular opinion both in towns and the countryside. Many of the *masies* had resident priests while religious houses were essential components of both the rural and urban landscape as landlord, employer and focus of the community. With the exception of literature, Catalan culture and religion proved highly resistant to foreign influence and a stubborn preference was maintained for native tradition. A generation would pass after the conclusion of Trent before the Tarragona rite and the breviaries observed by the Mercedarians were replaced by standardized Roman versions. As has been said, 'it remained difficult for the Counter Reformation to create any climate at all, since among those

[29] On this see *ibid.*, pp. 29–43, especially p. 30.
[30] *Ibid.*, pp. 140–1.
[31] *Ibid.*, p. 144.

who read books the known and traditional preferences continued to prevail', and neither was there any pre-existing means for exerting such leverage; 'At no time was it possible to bully the Catalans into accepting new ways', a statement that is amply borne out by the reform of the Mercedarians.[32]

The Tridentine Church remained committed to the vernacular at the level of popular culture, notwithstanding the linguistic barriers this presented to inquisitors and missionaries. While Catalan was spoken exclusively in most rural areas until the eighteenth century, it was gradually replaced by Castilian as the language of culture and relatively few books were printed in the vernacular after the early seventeenth century. Catalonia was flooded with Castilian literary, spiritual and theological works by 1550, a reflection of the decline of the native tradition in these fields and the progressive castilianization of Catalan intellectual life. By the end of the sixteenth century this situation had begun to provoke deep resentment among the broad spectrum of Catalans who had maintained their identity against the cultural erosion to which the Principality was slowly being subjected. The diarist Jeroni Pujades no doubt echoed the thoughts of many when he railed against the readiness of the crown 'to permit the destitution of our Catalans so that the Castilian dogs can devour the bread of our sons and drink the blood of our fathers'.[33] But, vituperation aside, what was the policy of the crown towards Catalonia?

V. *The Religious Policy of Philip II*

Until recently scholars have articulated the problems presented by the history of Catalonia during the reign of Philip II around the general thesis, first advanced by Braudel and later modified in the light of Spanish conditions by Reglà, of a *viraje* (shift, reorientation) of religious and imperial policy.[34] However, this view has recently been reassessed in favour of a so-called 'Catalan dynamic' extending beyond the familiar axis of relations between Barcelona and Madrid,

---

[32] *Ibid.*, pp. 356 & 436.

[33] The original, cited in Sales, *Els segles de la decadència*, p. 51, reads '...bonas causas perque el Reu consent a desterrar nostres pobles catalans y que vingan a menjar lo pa de nostres fills y beure la sang de nostres pares los cans de Castella'.

[34] Fernand Braudel, *Le Méditerranée et le monde méditerranéen à l'époque de Philippe II* (Paris, 1949) & Joan Reglà, *Felip II i Catalunya* (Barcelona, 1955).

of centralism and decentralization.[35] Alongside external influences and the policy of the crown, such a view would take greater account of social and economic conjunctures within the Principality itself, and in particular the capacity for radical resistance of Catalan institutions against royal authoritarianism, of which the Mercedarians are an example. The result is a fresh perspective on the history of Catalonia under Philip II to which this study hopes to contribute.

In line with this, Reglà's date for the supposed *viraje* of the crown towards a generalized policy of '*impermeabilitzaciò*' has been pushed back from the crisis of 1568 to the 1550s and even the 1540s. Thus, the catalogue of disasters that afflicted the monarchy in the late 1560s merely precipitated the inception in Catalonia of a general policy first developed during Philip's regency and already in various stages of implementation elsewhere in the Peninsula. In this light, the *viraje* appears as a gradual process that only unfolded in the fullest sense of Braudel's shift from the Mediterranean to the Atlantic after 1580. The timing and nature of the extension of this policy — if we can call it that — to Catalonia cannot therefore be attributed solely to the crises of 1568–70 or even to the conclusion of the Council of Trent in 1563, but to a range of issues both within and without the Principality and the Peninsula itself. Against this background, the unsettled condition of Catalonia along with wider geo-political considerations merely reaffirmed Philip's commitment to extend his authority to what had become a potentially volatile religious frontier. It was under these general circumstances, therefore, that the condition of the Mercedarian Order entered the purview of the crown and its reform became part of Philip's conjoined religious and political agenda. But what precisely was the king's policy?[36]

Informed by religious concerns, Philip's political criteria clearly enjoyed a strong element of continuity.[37] Ironically, however, these criteria were not readily translated into any concerted political pro-

---

[35] See Belenguer Cebrià, *La Corona de Aragón en la época de Felipe II*, p. 17, and now Ricardo García Cárcel, *Felipe II y Cataluña* (Valladolid, 1997), *passim*.

[36] On this see Ignasi Fernández Terricabras, *Philippe II et la Contre-Réforme* (Ph.D. thesis, Université de Toulouse-Le Mirail, 1999).

[37] Philip's political ethos is brought out in H.G. Koenigsberger, 'The Statecraft of Philip II' in *European Studies Review*, 1 (1971), pp. 1–21, while his religious policy is explored by John Lynch, 'Philip II and the Papacy' in *Transactions of the Royal Historical Society*, 5th Series, 11 (1961), pp. 23–42. A somewhat different interpretation is given in P. Ricardo García Villoslada, 'Felipe II y la Contrarreforma Católica' in *HIE*, III(ii), pp. 3–106.

gramme, at least until the 1580s. For though Philip was the heir to
the tradition of Ferdinand the Catholic and Charles V, the circumstances of his reign and his personal approach meant that neither in
policy nor in practice was he their direct successor. In 1539 the
emperor had enjoined the young Philip to 'live in love and fear of
God, our Creator, in observance of our holy and ancient religion,
and in union and obedience to the Roman Church and the Holy
Apostolic See and its commandments', followed in 1543 by the warning 'never to allow heresy to enter your kingdoms'.[38] But above all
Philip's personal ethos turned on a grim resignation towards the
ineluctability of God's will, the inscrutable nature of His ways. However, while the religious element in these principles was no doubt a
strong contributory factor, the king's decision-making was often driven by overtly political concerns, and informed by the belief that royal interests and those of religion were as one. In the climate of the
age, Philip justifiably regarded political and religious concerns as
indistinguishable, a conclusion that led him to conceive of the state
and the Church in similar terms. Philip, it has been claimed, held the
conviction that 'the person of the king should reflect the whole life of
the state, which, as a fully constituted political, spiritual and religious
structure, must by the same token reflect the community of the
realm'.[39] Under these circumstances the king's 'exalted view of his
office and of his duty to God for the just government of the subjects
entrusted to his care' translated into the growth of a near Erastian
domination over the Church by the Spanish crown, based on the
notion of absolute royal patronage.[40]

Philip's vision of his role as the ultimate arbiter of the religious and
political affairs of his kingdoms and subjects, including the clergy, was
enshrined in the royal *patronato* (patronage) over the Spanish Church.
The campaign by the crown to wrest ecclesiastical jurisdiction from
the papacy began in 1479, and a number of significant gains, notably
with regard to the Church in America, had already been made by the
time Adrian VI conceded the emperor the *Patronato Real* in 1523.[41] A

[38] The citations are from García Villoslada, 'Felipe II y la Contrarreforma Católica', p. 7, & March, *Niñez y juventud de Felipe II*, II, p. 13.

[39] Fidel García Cuéllar, 'Política de Felipe II en torno a la convocación de la tercera etapa del Concilio Tridentino' in *Hispania Sacra*, 16 (1963), pp. 25–60; 56.

[40] Koenigsberger, 'The Statecraft of Philip II', p. 5.

[41] The Mercedarian Fray Diego de Muros was a member of the embassy dispatched to Rome in 1479 to negotiate these and other matters.

succession of decrees in that year accorded the crown rights of presentation to bishoprics and control over provision to ecclesiastical benefices which confirmed its *de facto* headship over the Spanish Church. By the reign of Philip II the implications of the crown's *patronazgo* had been deepened by the concerns of imperial defence and religious integrity along with the king's personal ideology. Under the axiom *cuius regio eius religio* the crown had come to regard 'religious unity as the indispensable condition for political unity'.[42] Philip took the view that any circumstance that impinged upon these twin priorities was his personal concern, and that consequently it was incumbent upon him to take stern measures for the greater good of the monarchy. The king endeavoured to observe local laws and customs where possible, but there were circumstances in which he regarded his wider vision and overarching responsibility for the integrity of his kingdoms as justification for drastic action. In practical terms this outlook translated into an unprecedented level of intervention and state control. In the case of the Spanish Church it meant extending to the religious orders the royal patronage and influence already enjoyed by the crown over the episcopate. It was in this cast of mind, therefore, that Philip would declare in 1593, after thirty years of involvement with the Mercedarians, that 'the unruliness of this Order has been caused principally [...] by its superiors' desire to tyrannize [its members] and treat its affairs as if it were their own patrimony'.[43] The implementation of this implicitly reciprocal relationship, of obedience in return for patronage, was to be one of the guiding impulses of Philip's policy towards the Spanish Church and the Mercedarians in particular.

Yet, as Lynch says, 'the power of the crown had developed not simply in the interests of absolutism but also in the interests of reform', and on this subject Philip held equally strong convictions.[44] The king believed that the best defence against religious revolution lay in reform of the clergy and of the ecclesiastical institutions. However, at the beginning of his reign Philip retained the traditional Spanish mistrust of the papacy's ability to lead a general reform of the Church. Rome, Philip declared to Pius IV in 1562, 'is the last place that Christendom expects to find either the remedy for the ills and divisions that afflict

---

    [42] Lynch, 'Philip II and the Papacy', p. 32.
    [43] AMAE, SS, leg. 34, f. 53r, Philip II to Duque de Sessa, El Pardo, 13th November 1593.
    [44] Lynch, 'Philip II and the Papacy', p. 24.

religion, or the solution to the damage and disruption that has arisen as a result'.[45] However, it would take Philip twenty years to realize that, for all his power and *patronazgo*, the reform of the Spanish Church was impossible without the cooperation of the papacy.

Although Philip was fully aware of the need to reconvene the Council of Trent, he had very definite views on the form it should take. The king was adamant that any new convocation must continue the progress made in the first two sessions towards solving dogmatic and disciplinary problems and implanting reforms. Assurances from Pius and the threat of a French national assembly finally secured Philip's support, but he remained unhappy with the circumstances of the Council's opening and then its progress. The convocation had posed certain theological problems which, it seems, were never solved to Philip's satisfaction. Moreover, the abrupt conclusion of the Council in December 1563 with the hasty passage of a number of important decrees (including those concerning the reform of the religious orders) before the delegates scattered to the four winds convinced him that these should not be promulgated in Spain until they had been thoroughly vetted. Above all, Philip was mindful of the threat that unrestrained implementation of the Council's reforms would pose to the hard-won royal supremacy over the Spanish Church. As Kamen says, 'From the very beginning Philip made it plain that reform in Spain, though conforming to the principles of Trent, would be carried through as a clear act of state and on terms dictated by the state'.[46] As a result the provincial councils by which the Fathers of Trent had intended the decrees to be implemented took a rather different form in Spain from what the papacy had hoped.

The first of the six Spanish provincial councils opened at Tarragona in October 1564 under the archbishop, the Valencian Ferran de Loaces.[47] The readiness of the suffragans to gather in council reflects the relatively diligent tradition established by the province of Tarragona in this regard; the sessions of 1564–5 were the sixth to be convened in Tarragona since 1551, an enviable record given that none had been held anywhere else in Spain for forty-three years.[48] However, while

---

[45] Cited in García Cuéllar, 'Política de Felipe II', p. 20.

[46] Kamen, *The Phoenix and the Flame*, p. 54.

[47] *Ibid.*, pp. 56–7.

[48] *Ibid.*, pp. 77–9. Synodal activity, by contrast, was rather neglected in the province of Tarragona. Bishop Guillem Cassador's synod at Barcelona in 1566 appears to have been the first in living memory.

the council was of extreme importance to the Catholic Reformation in
Catalonia, as elsewhere in Spain it was but the centrepiece of a broader reform process conceived by Philip in three parts: diocesan, episcopal and monastic. The council was designed above all else to establish
the range of episcopal jurisdiction, so that although the authority of
the bishops over the religious orders was confirmed, the general question of their reform was not confronted. While still at Trent Guillem
Cassador had received the authority to visit all ecclesiastical institutions, including the orders, to reform religious officially exempt from
episcopal control if their superiors failed to do so, and to exercise jurisdiction over those *extra conventum degentes*.[49] However, while the reform
of the nuns was to a considerable extent committed to episcopal care,
Philip retained direct control over the affairs of all the regulars for the
time being. Thus, while at least twenty-three Catalan monastic foundations, including two of women, were represented at Tarragona,
only the reform of the nunneries appears to have been discussed in
any detail.[50] The friars, most of whom were to oppose Cassador at
every step, did not attend the council in any number, but bombarded
it with *memoriales*.[51] The Mercedarians, for their part, appear not to
have been represented at all.

The reform of the religious and monastic orders was, commensurate with their size, influence and condition, a pressing matter of state
to be conducted under the personal scrutiny of the king. Yet, how
might we classify the historical idea of reform which was already
being discussed with relation to the Mercedarians and other congregations in Spain and Rome?

VI. *The Idea and Practice of Reform*

Renovatio, restauratio, regeneratio, reformatio.[52] The notion of the history of
mankind as a sequence of new beginnings has long been an underlying assumption in historical interpretation, as reflected in the themes

---

[49] Bada, *Situació religiosa*, p. 166. The brief was issued on 17th July 1563.
[50] *Ibid.*, pp. 206–7.
[51] *Ibid.*, p. 195.
[52] The definitive work on the origins of the medieval concept of reform is Gerhart
B. Ladner, *The Idea of Reform: Its Impact on Christian Thought and Action in the Age of the
Fathers* (Cambridge, Mass., 1959). See also A.D. Wright, *The Counter-Reformation:
Catholic Europe and the Non-Christian World* (London, 1982), chs. 1 & 6.

of cyclical recurrence, of conversion and redemption, decline and fall, *corsi* and *ricorsi*, progress and evolution, challenge and response, rebirth, revolution and reform.[53] Linked with pagan belief, the notion of reform originated within the most basic tenets of Christianity, in the concept of sin and death conquered by divine redemption in a manner reflected by the unending pattern of life itself. Accordingly, the Christian idea of reform took shape around Pauline doctrine on the human person: the experience of man's newness in Christ was expressed in his personal reformation and renovation to the image-likeness of man to God — *ad imaginem et similtudinem Dei* — received by humanity in creation but tarnished through sin.[54] Thus, reform was not only the goal of all Christians, but an expression of perfect freedom. First classified by St Augustine, this notion attained its fullest realization in the phenomenon of coenobitic monasticism that had already begun to develop in the West under St Pachomius in late Antiquity, and which Augustine himself and later St Benedict transformed into one of humanity's most imposing designs for living.

Unlike eremitical life which had sought a complete withdrawal from the world, coenobitic monasticism aimed at the reform of the individual in a community that at once reflected and remained in complex spiritual dialogue with the life of Christian society. In Augustine's formulation, monasticism was not only service to God but also to the common good, and as such was among the highest manifestations of the Christian life and an example to all faithful people. The reformation of man in the image of God through collective contemplation by the monastic order was therefore analogous with the erection of the *civitas Dei* on earth. Under these circumstances religious were seen as the principal agents of reform in the world, and a reflection of the power of the Church in both the spiritual and the material order. Reform itself, then, along with the preservation of the spiritual integrity of the Christian polity, was the office and function of the religious.

The medieval interpretation of the concept of reform was therefore that of personal spiritual improvement for the greater good of Christianity, rather than the sense of repair of institutional or moral decay that it has since acquired. It was the twelfth century before the individual and monastic realizations of the idea of reform began to

---

[53] See Ladner, *The Idea of Reform*, pp. 1–5, esp. 1.
[54] *Ibid.*, p. 2.

expand into a programme for the reform first of the *Ecclesia*, and then
of all *Christianitas*.[55] By this time the monastic order, whose history
had been conceived of as a series of spiritual reforms, had itself
become the subject of reform rather than the driving force behind it.
Hence the gradual development of the notion of 'reform' as we
understand it today, but Augustine's interpretation of the idea of
monastic reform within the context of Christian society endured pow-
erfully. In 1576 Cristóbal de Rojas y Sandoval, archbishop of Seville,
voiced a recognizably Augustinian appreciation of the pivotal role of
religious in society. As he declared in a letter to the king,

> No matter is more important to the Church of God or the service of
> Your Majesty than the reformation of the ecclesiastical estate, and par-
> ticularly the monastic order, because the very foundation of the
> Church […] rests on the life of perfection professed by those who enter
> the orders […] And if these weaken through relaxation and neglect of
> their rule, what hope is there for the Church in these kingdoms except
> the travails we have seen befall others which, once full of sanctity and
> virtue, are now lost?[56]

Or, as Licenciado Juan Calvo de Padilla of the Council of State
informed him, the moral and institutional reform of the orders was
the more urgent 'because from them alone must issue the fire that is
to ignite the republic' in religious fervour.[57] Drawn out of the core of
Augustinian theology, the prevailing idea of reform therefore
accorded with Philip's renewed perception of himself as sovereign
lord over a Christian state.[58] The immediate reasons behind Philip's
sponsorship of the reform of the religious may well have been politically motivated, but there can be little doubt that he shared the
medieval appreciation of monastic life in its truest sense as a pillar of
the ordered Christian society, or, in Rojas' description of the orders,
as 'columns of the Church'.[59] As the king was at pains to underline
to Pius V in 1569 regarding his motives for sponsoring monastic
reform,

---

[55] *Ibid.*, pp. 4 & 423–4.
[56] IVDJ, env. 89, caja 125, no. 74, Seville, 12th December 1576, ff. 1v–2r. A similar view by the same commentator is expressed in AGS, PR, 23-212, f. 2r.
[57] ASZ, carp. 163, no. 29, 12th December 1574, f. 1r.
[58] See José Antonio Maravall, 'La oposición político-religiosa del siglo XVI: El
erasmismo tardío de Felipe de la Torre' in *id.*, *La oposición política bajo los Austrias*
(Barcelona, 1972), pp. 53–92, esp. 80–8.
[59] IVDJ, env. 89, caja 125, no. 74, f. 1v.

Let it be clearly understood that I have no human interest whatsoever at stake in this affair, but simply a desire that, through their life and example, the orders of my Kingdoms be such as to profit the people, serve God and greatly honour and uphold the Holy See, whence issued their rules and constitutions.[60]

Yet, if such was the ordained function and duty of the monastic order in Augustine's Christian society, how were individuals to reconcile the apparent contradiction of seeking the Kingdom of Heaven while at the same time working for the kingdom of this world? As Ladner puts it, the recurrent question informing the early monastic tradition lay in 'how far was it possible to seek at the same time the Kingdom of God, not of this world, and to strive for improvement of this world'.[61] How, in other words, were the religious to carry the idea of reform into practical effect? The answer, according to Augustine, lay in study and education.[62] At the heart of this concept was the acquisition of Christian learning — the *doctrina christiana* — through *recta eruditio* (spiritual improvement via study). The culmination of this process was the *mutatio vitae* (reform) of both the religious and his community, since, in acquiring the *doctrina christiana* the practicant was not only himself reformed, but thereby empowered to impart his learning to others and thus from generation to generation.

Beyond the crucial practical developments of St Benedict and Gregory the Great among others, there was one further aspect to be added to the Augustinian idea of monastic reform.[63] In attacking Augustine's theories on grace during the sixth century, the so-called Semi-Pelagians made a significant contribution to the debate on the relation of tradition and renovation to truth, or rather the means by which reform might be attained.[64] Questioning whether *mutatio vitae* could be the result of a physical process of study, the Semi-Pelagians confined this to the innermost precinct of faith while fixing on *eruditio* as the practical end of *doctrina christiana*, both in the sense of spiritual improvement in *imitatio Christi, and* in the active recall of a primitive

---

[60] AGS, E°, leg. 910, no. 134. Philip II to Juan de Zúñiga, El Escorial, 17th August 1569.

[61] Ladner, *The Idea of Reform*, p. 2.

[62] On this aspect, see Dom Jean Leclercq, *The Love of Learning and the Desire for God: A Study of Monastic Culture*, trans. Catharine Misrahi, 3rd English edn. (New York, 1982).

[63] Ladner, *The Idea of Reform*, pp. 403–24.

[64] *Ibid.*, p. 31.

perfection. As such, reform was not only a prospective movement of *instauratio in melius*, but also a retrospective process of *reparatio in pristinum*. Under these circumstances *doctrina christiana* was as essential a part of man's way back to God as of his spiritual development towards Him — the *imago Dei* as both beginning and end. Unlike other ideas of renewal or mutation, intentional repetition is essential to the concept of reform as religious experience, an element reflected in the related idea of the 'observance' of primordial discipline with the assistance of penance and correction. The concordant duality of past and future, of example and cynosure therefore lies at the heart of the concepts of reform and observance as expressions of the monastic life itself. Religious were by definition undergoing a process of perfection both against an established rule of life and towards a specific goal to the greater good of Christian society, and thus the idea of reform was transmitted to the religious mentality of Catholic Europe in the sixteenth century.

However, the passage of time confirmed a key feature of the concept of reform as we have described it: the difficulty of reconciling ideal and practice in the most immediate sense, in uniting the conditions and demands of the present with the pristine standards of the past. In the monastic ideal the reformed life implied a suspension of history in a pattern of constant renewal through repetition, 'the past as a reality homogeneously identifiable with the present'.[65] Under these circumstances, innovation in reform was not regarded as an abandonment of the monastic ideal so much as a conscious return to it, 'the necessity all creation has to return to its origin and the fount of its being'.[66] As Giles of Viterbo, prior general of the Augustinians, declared of his reform early in the sixteenth century,

> We are not innovators. We are simply trying, in accordance with the will of God, to bring back to life those ancient laws whose observance has lapsed.[67]

But the idea of reform had developed as an ordered design for living, not as a restorative tonic for a congregation lapsed into relaxation.

---

[65] See Fr John W. O'Malley, *Giles of Viterbo on Church and Reform: A Study in Renaissance Thought* (Leiden, 1968), pp. 101–10 & 182–3; citation p. 183.

[66] Cited, apropos of a verse from Virgil's Fourth Eclogue, in *ibid.*, p. 102: 'Magnus ab integro saeclorum nascitur ordo'.

[67] Cited in *ibid.*, p. 142. The original reads: 'Non enim nova facimus, sed leges patrum in ista patria extinctas, Deo ita jubente, suscitamus'.

The issue of the practical application of reform in the event of neglect, decay or misinterpretation had always been beset by an uncertainty that was greatly amplified with the appearance of the friars from the end of the twelfth century. The mendicant vocation of withdrawing from the secular world yet not leaving it posed a range of major dilemmas at the heart of the religious life and reformed living which, in the case of the Franciscan Order, proved utterly insoluble. More than ever, religious found it impossible to disengage the pattern of their spiritual lives from the reality of the world about them. Under such conditions the ambiguity between the *vita activa* and the *vita contemplativa*, between the vocational and administrative duties implied by the charism and functioning of an order and the spiritual and intellectual *opus* of the religious life itself, became more complex and more intractable than ever before. This ambiguity was nowhere more clearly felt than in the pursuit of academic learning in the schools and the *recta eruditio* of the cloister.

The issue of study therefore remained central to the question of monastic reform throughout the Middle Ages. The reform movement within the religious orders during the fifteenth century went hand in hand with a revival of scholarship, strongly influenced by humanism in the case of the monastics.[68] The mendicants largely adhered to scholasticism, but in many quarters opposition to the soulless speculation of the universities caused a marked reaction against study. In Castile the founder of the Franciscan Observance, the ascetic Fray Pedro de Villacreces (†1422), considered as relaxation

> any study of any subject which brings disturbance and disruption to the cloisters, except where it pertains to the divine office and to [the preparation of] breviaries, missals and other books necessary for the ministries of confession and preaching.[69]

---

[68] This was of course particularly the case in Italy. For an overview, see Denys Hay, *The Church in Italy in the Fifteenth Century* (Cambridge, 1977), pp. 91–109, & Barry Collett, *Italian Benedictine Scholars and The Reformation: The Congregation of Santa Giustina of Padua* (Oxford, 1985), pp. 1–27. For a particular example, see Noel L. Brann, *The Abbot Trithemius (1462–1516): The Renaissance of Monastic Humanism* (Leiden, 1981).

[69] Cited in Melquiades Andrés Martín, *Historia de la teología en España (1470–1570): Instituciones teológicas* (Rome, 1962), p. 105. The original reads: 'cualquier estudio de cualquiera esciencia que traiga estrépito y disturbio a los claustros, salvo solamente lo que pertenece al oficio divino, breviario y misal y libros necesarios para los ministerios de la confesión y predicación'. On the notion of '*docta ignorantia*' and the conflict of learning and spirituality in the Renaissance, see Denys Hay, 'Scholarship, Religion and the Church' in Keith G. Robbins, ed., *Religion and Humanism* [*Studies in Church History*, vol. XVIII] (Oxford, 1981), pp. 1–18.

However, the central importance of study to the idea and practice of reform was eventually recognized — though firmly in a conventual setting — and the first decades of the sixteenth century are marked in Castile and elsewhere by a withdrawal of the Franciscans from the universities into *studia sollemnia*.[70] The Dominican Observance, by contrast, placed a clear emphasis on study as the traditional vocation of the Order, and the reform of the Friars Preachers in Castile and the rest of the Peninsula was led by the great *studium generale* of San Esteban at Salamanca.[71]

Elsewhere programmes of monastic renewal were led by superiors whose perception of the significance of learning to reform was enhanced by the philology and exegesis of humanist scholarship. In Italy the attempted reform of the Camaldolese hermits by the general, Ambrogio Traversari (1431–9), was motivated by a desire to emulate the pristine fervour of early Greek and Latin monasticism by means of patristic scholarship.[72] It was Traversari's hope that the eloquence of patristic study would inspire his religious to the path of virtue and holiness, and to this end he established colleges at Siena and Fonte Buona in Tuscany in which the curriculum of the *studia humanitatis* formed the basis of the monks' training.[73] The renewed monastic interest in ancient authority is also reflected in the Benedictine congregation of Santa Giustina of Padua.[74] Recognized under its founder Ludovico Barbo in 1421, the congregation developed an important tradition of scholarship following his death in 1443 which culminated at the Council of Trent. Again, a reform centred on an *ad fontes* return to biblical and patristic authority stimulated interest in the humanist philological techniques that provided the means to a closer understanding of these texts.[75]

These concerns are also reflected in the reform ideal traced out for

---

[70] See Andrés Martín, *Historia de la teología en España*, pp. 91–134, esp. 109–10.

[71] *Ibid.*, pp. 135–60, & P.Fr. Vicente Beltrán de Heredia, *Historia de la reforma de la Provincia de España (1450–1550)* (Rome, 1939).

[72] See Charles L. Stinger, *Humanism and the Church Fathers: Ambrogio Traversari (1386–1439) and Christian Antiquity in the Italian Renaissance* (Albany, NY, 1977), pp. 169–85, esp. 180 & 182.

[73] *Ibid.*, p. 180. For a later advocate of patristic study, see Eugene F. Rice, 'The Humanist Idea of Christian Antiquity: Lefèvre d'Étaples and his Circle' in *Studies in the Renaissance*, 9 (1962), pp. 126–60.

[74] See Collett, *Italian Benedictine Scholars*, pp. 1–13. The incorporation of Montecassino in 1505 henceforth caused Santa Giustina to be known as the Cassinese congregation; *ibid.*, p. 5.

[75] *Ibid.*, pp. 12–13.

the Augustinians by Giles of Viterbo during his tenure as prior general (1507–18).[76] The basis of this reform lay in a return to the eremitical vocation that had characterized the early Order, and its realization once again turned on the restoration of 'sacred learning' as the conduit to mystical love for the person of the Redeemer.[77] Accordingly, the prior general went to great lengths to raise the standards of Augustinian *studia* and the degrees awarded by them, and to encourage young friars to participate in the intellectual life of the Order. However, like Traversari before him, Viterbo had founded his reform ideal on a wholly impractical basis and both failed to reach the ambitious objectives they had set their orders. In both cases the demands made on the religious were very severe: over-intellectual and over-affective on the one hand, unrealistic and unfeasible on the other.[78] In neither had the hierarchy founded the reform on a sufficient degree of institutional adjustment, and among the Augustinians the effect of Viterbo's measures was to accentuate the conflict of interest between the active and contemplative tendencies in the Order.[79] Even so, the humanistic cast of mind in which Traversari and Viterbo conceived their reforms and the range of their interests and connections are an important reminder of the contribution of monastic thought and learning to the Renaissance, and *vice versa*.[80] The monastic debt in epistemology was repaid in the humanist religious ideal of the union of *eruditio* and *pietas*, and in a common front against the worst excesses of scholastic intellectualism.[81] Such exchanges can also be detected in the congregation of Santa Giustina with its close ties to the university of Padua and the 'Catholic Evangelicals' or *spirituali*, with ecumenism through the multi-lingual study of the Fathers, with the conciliarist movement of the first half of the sixteenth century, and thence to the *sola scriptura* of Luther and the fringes of apocalyptic spirituality.[82] It also underlines the survival of

---

[76] O'Malley, *Giles of Viterbo*, pp. 139–60 & 168–9.

[77] *Ibid.*, p. 172.

[78] Stinger, *Humanism and the Church Fathers*, p. 182, & O'Malley, *Giles of Viterbo*, p. 159.

[79] Stinger, *Humanism and the Church Fathers*, p. 176, & O'Malley, *Giles of Viterbo*, p. 160.

[80] Kristeller, 'The Contribution of Religious Orders', pp. 21–2.

[81] See Stinger, *Humanism and the Church Fathers*, pp. 223–7, esp. 226, & Rice, 'The Humanist Idea of Christian Antiquity', pp. 126–32, 134 & 141.

[82] Collett, *Italian Benedictine Scholars*, pp. 4 & 11, & Stinger, *Humanism and the Church Fathers*, pp. 201–2 & 226.

Augustinian thought as a determining feature in the transition of religious culture from the medieval to the early modern age, to which the Mercedarians made their own contribution through Gaspar de Torres and his followers.[83]

The terms in which Viterbo, like Traversari, advocated the reform of his Order reflect not only a humanist's call for the recovery of the classical texts, but a wider vision of the reform of Christian life to the evangelical poverty of the early Church — 'to the ancient and original purity, light and splendour, a return to the sources...'.[84] But whatever the views of the hierarchy, the reform of the mass of their orders, as of the Mercedarians, turned on a more realistic assessment of the needs of each in the wider context of which they formed a part. It is in this theological, social and political context, in terms of both secular and ecclesiastical life, that Mercedarian Reform shall here be interpreted in all its complexity.

Despite the efforts of the previous 150 years, the monastic vocation at large therefore remained compromised by laxity and indiscipline to a degree that was unacceptable to the ecclesiastical and secular authorities of Catholic Europe in the mid sixteenth century. For many the religious life remained a byword for indiscipline and moral degeneration. The religious and political implications of the improvement of Christian society to which the Council of Trent directed itself demanded the reform of the orders as a matter of course. As the Fathers of Trent declared at the head of their monastic legislation, 'the Holy Synod is not ignorant how much splendour and utility accrue to the Church of God from monasteries piously instituted and rightly administered'.[85]

VII. *Trent and Monastic Reform*

The principal Tridentine legislation on the reform of the religious orders — *de regularibus et monialibus* — was entrusted to Carlo Bor-

---

[83] Collett, *Italian Benedictine Scholars*, pp. 19–20, & Wright, *The Counter-Reformation*, chs. 1 & 6.

[84] O'Malley, *Giles of Viterbo*, pp. 142–3; citation p. 142. The original reads: '...in veterem puritatem, in antiquam lucem, in nativum splendorem, atque in suos fontes...'.

[85] Cited in *The Canons and Decrees of the [...] Council of Trent*, trans. J. Waterworth, 2nd edn. (London, 1888), p. 237.

romeo and is contained in the third decree of the XXVth and final session of the Council in December 1563.[86] In only twenty-two short chapters, the decree, drafted as the Council was drawing to a close, gives every impression of being hastily put together and was by no means comprehensive. Ultimately, the nature and diversity of the religious life prevented the Council from laying down much more than the most basic principles of monastic reform, and the resulting decrees could not and did not legislate for each individual congregation. Although the constitutions of most of the religious orders had been submitted for the scrutiny of the delegates, there were to be some, including the Mercedarians, whose peculiar condition made literal enforcement of the main edicts quite impractical and whose specific problems were therefore not addressed.[87] Of the omissions, the absence of provisions for orders without a surviving primordial observance were among the most significant.

The basis of Tridentine monastic legislation lay in the observance of the ancient regular discipline of each congregation. To this end the Council enjoined

> that all Regulars, men as well as women, shall order and regulate their lives in accordance with the requirements of the rule they have professed; [...] that they shall faithfully observe whatsoever belongs to the perfection of their profession [...] as also all other vows and precepts that may be particular to any rule or order respectively appertaining to the essential character of each [...] For if those things which are the basis and the foundation of all regular discipline be not strictly preserved, the whole edifice must needs fall.[88]

However, the chapters following this general precept covered only a few of the matters in urgent need of reform, while the practicalities of implementing such legislation were barely addressed. Although the reform of the nuns was given fairly detailed treatment — particularly as to enclosure, the appointment of superiors, profession, confession, and the extent of episcopal jurisdiction over them — that of the monks and friars received scant attention by comparison. Legislation

---

[86] For the decrees, see *ibid.*, pp. 236–53. They are commented upon in Fr Hubert Jedin, 'Zur Vorgeschichte der Regularenreform Trid. Sess. XXV' in *Römische Quartalschrift*, 44 (1936), pp. 231–81, and in Steggink, *La reforma del Carmelo español*, 2nd edn., pp. 65–7.

[87] It is unclear whether any Mercedarian constitutions were in fact seen at Trent.

[88] *Canons and Decrees*, p. 237. I have made slight adaptations to this and the two succeeding citations for purposes of fluency.

was passed regarding the ownership of property by individuals, communities and orders as a whole; it was laid down that superiors should be elected by secret ballot and that where possible monasteries held *in commendam* were to be restored to the authority of the religious or congregation concerned. But there was little on monastic administration, on limiting the power of superiors or on visitation and censure. The critical issue of jurisdiction was avoided, and the emphasis on episcopal authority effectively limited reform efforts to the diocesan sphere rather than the wider territorial organization of the orders themselves. In short, many of the most serious problems and abuses were not directly addressed.

Ultimately, the Fathers of Trent had recognized that these matters could only be resolved in practice by the authorities, religious or otherwise, promoting their reform. The reformulation of the Mercedarian constitutions in the spirit and to an extent to the letter of the Tridentine decrees by M° Fray Gaspar de Torres in 1565 is a case in point.[89] As the decrees made clear, 'the present state of the times is so fraught with hindrances and difficulties that a remedy can neither be applied at once nor in common to all places'.[90] There can be no doubt that this realization, as much as anxiety to close the Council, governed the delegates' mostly superficial approach to the labyrinthine question of monastic reform, and most of their energies were devoted to legislating on issues that touched directly on episcopal jurisdiction, as in the case of the nuns.[91] The edict concluded with a further blanket injunction subjecting all orders without exception to the foregoing decrees, regardless of any existing privileges obtained in mitigation of them. Bishops and religious superiors were enjoined to execute this legislation immediately through their provincial councils and chapters general respectively. Finally, the Council exhorted and commanded

> all kings, princes, republics, and magistrates [...] to vouchsafe and to interpose, as often as requested, their help and authority in support of the aforesaid bishops, abbots, generals, and other superiors in the execution of the things comprised above; so that they may, without any hindrance, rightly execute the preceding matters to the praise of Almighty God.[92]

---

[89] See ch. 4, n. 20.

[90] *Canons and Decrees*, p. 251.

[91] The superficiality of the monastic legislation was severely criticised by an anonymous royal minister in a *memorial* to Philip II in 1566, AGS, PR, 23-225, ff. 5v–6r.

[92] *Canons and Decrees*, p. 253.

However, the Spanish crown viewed the matter in quite different terms. It was for the papacy to render assistance to the crown in the reform of the orders, not *vice versa*. After all, it was papal dispensation that had significantly contributed to the relaxation of the orders.[93] Moreover, it is apparent that while the papacy and the Tridentine delegates regarded monastic reform principally as an act of faith, Philip II viewed the matter above all as a question of obedience to royal authority. As in other matters, therefore, the issue of reform was to be assessed within the context of the *Patronato Real*, which, as Philip's ministers never ceased telling him, was completely at odds with the Tridentine decrees. As one wrote, 'For the orders to be reformed in accordance with the conciliar decrees Your Majesty would have to lose all his patronage over them, since without this the religious cannot follow the provisions laid down by the Council'.[94] To enforce Tridentine legislation without amendment therefore implied a surrender of *patronato*, and this Philip was not prepared to accept.

Although Trent had reiterated some of the fundamental precepts of monastic reform, the implementation of these and, indeed, the nature and course of the reform itself depended to a considerable degree on the priorities and circumstances of its sponsors. This state of affairs leads us to a basic conclusion regarding the practice of monastic reform: though the precepts and means by which an order might be reformed remain constant — spiritual improvement, regular observance, visitation, etc. — it was the principles and objectives of the individuals or institutions promoting it that gave a reform movement its defining character. In the case of several orders in late sixteenth-century Spain, these principles were to some considerable degree established by the crown in view of the perceived spiritual and disciplinary circumstances of each congregation, and in the context of local affairs and the religious and political conjuncture.[95]

---

[93] AGS, PR, 23-225, f. 6v.

[94] *Ibid.*, f. 7v.

[95] For some examples of this in France, see J.A. Bergin, 'The Crown, the Papacy and the Reform of the Old Orders in Early Seventeenth-Century France' in *Journal of Ecclesiastical History*, 33 (1982), pp. 234–55.

VIII. *Reform and the State*

The patronage of John I of Castile and María of Aragon apart, the tradition of active royal sponsorship of monastic reform had begun under the Catholic Kings.[96] Ferdinand and Isabella had inherited kingdoms whose social, political and ecclesiastical structures had been shaken to the core by decades of anarchy and civil war. Under these circumstances the crown considered moral and religious renewal to be an essential feature in its projected reconstruction of the state. It was therefore not only spiritually desirable but also politically expedient for the crown to promote the reform of both the secular and the regular clergy, to the end that the Church should surrender its temporal power in favour of a more earnest pursuit of its spiritual mission.

By the mid fifteenth century large sectors of most of the religious orders had fallen into serious indiscipline. This situation, as we have seen, was mitigated in many cases — though not all — by the development of congregations of regular observance within their ranks from the late fourteenth century. The orders, whose professed rules and constitutions theoretically bound their members in discipline and observance, therefore represented an attractive target for reform from early in the reign of the Catholic Kings. It was by promoting reformed congregations and through the laborious visitation and reduction of monasteries and provinces to regular observance that Ferdinand and Isabella expected, with the support of the papacy, to carry out a reform of Spanish religious life. However, this was to be long delayed and progress had been slow in all areas by the time the national assembly convened at Seville in 1478. The assembly recognized both the benefice system into which many of the orders had sunk and the range of privileges and exemptions enjoyed by religious as significant causes of monastic indiscipline. This realization prompted the crown to initiate a long diplomatic campaign in Rome towards obtaining the rights of patronage and presentation that

---

[96] For the reform of the religious orders under Ferdinand and Isabella see three works by P.Fr. José García Oro, the first two of which are strongly related in this matter: *La reforma de los religiosos, Cisneros y la reforma del clero español*, and 'Conventualismo y observancia', pp. 211–90. The wider theme of ecclesiastical reform is explored in P.Fr. Tarsicio de Azcona, *La elección y reforma del episcopado español en tiempo de los Reyes Católicos* (Madrid, 1960). For an excellent summary, see Hillgarth, *The Spanish Kingdoms*, II, pp. 394–410.

would pave the way for a general reform of Spanish religious life. Chief among its demands was a general concession in favour of episcopal intervention in monastic reform and the right of the crown to appoint bishops and religious in an executive capacity.[97] The papacy viewed these aims with considerable suspicion, but in 1493 the Borja pope Alexander VI conceded the Catholic Kings two bulls, including the *Quanta in Dei Ecclesia*, which, with later modifications, placed the reform of the orders in the hands of the crown. Bound up with the development of the *Patronato Real* over the Spanish Church, these rights provided the legislative basis for the reform initiative undertaken by Philip II.

The faculties contained therein permitted Ferdinand and Isabella to begin the first systematic attempt at reform under the auspices of the crown from the 1490s onwards. The details of this process are beyond the scope of the present study, but it is worthwhile considering for a moment the legacy of what was a largely state-led campaign in the context of monastic reform in early modern Spain. This matter has yet to be examined with the required objectivity, but it seems fair to say that, resolute as the endeavour was, the results were uneven and often proved to be of short duration. In some mendicant institutions such as the Dominicans and the Franciscans under Cisneros, large sectors of the orders were reformed through observant congregations which took the moral and spiritual high ground, and established a lasting momentum for renewal. In 1497, for instance, the Conventual houses of the Franciscan province of Castile were transferred *en bloc* to the Observance, with Cisneros assuming the title of provincial over all its brethren. Similarily, by 1504 the last of the Augustinians of Castile had been driven into the Observant congregation.[98] Elsewhere progress was much more limited, particularly beyond the borders of Castile itself. The triumph of the Observance in the Franciscan provinces of Santiago and Aragon had to wait until well into the sixteenth century, despite the repressive measures to which Ferdinand resorted in his kingdoms at the end of his reign.[99] Even among the Dominicans it was the 1520s before the Observance began to gain the upper hand in the Kingdom of

---

[97] Hillgarth, *The Spanish Kingdoms*, II, p. 401.

[98] See L. Álvarez, 'Contribución a la reforma religiosa en el reinado de los Reyes Católicos' in *Revista agustiniana de espiritualidad*, 5 (1964), pp. 145–212.

[99] Hillgarth, *The Spanish Kingdoms*, II, pp. 402 & 408.

Castile.[100] The Crown of Aragon followed a decade later on the heels of the assassination of its provincial and the prior of Valencia in 1534.[101]

In the monastic congregations, particularly in that of the Benedictines centred at Valladolid, reform had to be laboriously and often incompletely carved out house by house in the teeth of powerful ecclesiastical, nobiliary, and municipal opposition. By the close of the fifteenth century the great abbeys of Montserrat and Poblet stood as oases of dialogue and tranquillity amid the chaos of monastic life in Catalonia.[102] It was here and in Galicia that the brunt of the royal reform campaign against the monastics had fallen in the years after 1493, with the Benedictine and Cistercian nunneries singled out for special attention. Whatever hopes the crown may have entertained at the outset, the huge obstacles facing any such process soon became apparent. In Galicia the thirteen communities of Benedictine nuns were eventually reduced into a single convent in 1499, though only with the greatest difficulty.[103] In Catalonia, meanwhile, the Catholic Kings personally directed the reform effort from Barcelona, issuing twenty-four edicts of pitiless severity in November and December of 1493.[104] The effect of an inflexible and regalist programme was a flood of fugitives and a deep and lasting rupture with local authorities over the question of reform. In a codicil to her will in 1504 the Queen recognized the flaws in this initiative and the excesses of the reformers, most of whom had been Castilian nuns unsympathetic to the plight of their Catalan charges.[105] This sentiment was endorsed by Ferdinand in 1507, and where possible the crown henceforth favoured the services of reformed elements from the orders concerned. But in Barcelona especially the damage had been done, and monastic reform would show scant progress in the eastern kingdoms until the reign of Philip II.

---

[100] See P.Fr. Vicente Beltrán de Heredia, *Historia de la reforma de la Provincia de España (1450–1550)* (Rome, 1939), pp. 143–83.

[101] *Ibid.*, pp. 184–217, esp. 202.

[102] For Montserrat, which had joined the Benedictine Congregation of Valladolid in 1493 under abbot García Jiménez de Cisneros, see García Oro, *La reforma de los religiosos*, pp. 82–4. On Poblet, see Hillgarth, *The Spanish Kingdoms*, II, p. 102.

[103] See García Oro, *La reforma de los religiosos*, pp. 55–9, esp. 55. The convent in question was San Pelayo de Antealtares near Santiago.

[104] See *ibid.*, pp. 63–74, & P.Fr. Tarsicio de Azcona, 'Reforma de religiosas benedictinas y cistercienses de Cataluña en tiempo de los Reyes Católicos' in *Studia Monastica*, 9 (1967), pp. 75–166.

[105] Hillgarth, *The Spanish Kingdoms*, II, pp. 401 & 408.

The royal reform campaign generally enjoyed greater success in Castile, but even here the process was marked by failure in several critical areas. Despite resolute opposition from the chapter general at Cîteaux, the Spanish Cistercian congregation achieved the right to virtual independence from the mother house, but at the great nunnery of Las Huelgas outside Burgos a twenty-year struggle for reform ended in stalemate in 1515.[106] The Clares of Córdoba present a similar picture of frustrated hopes and expectations, while Cisneros saw to the dissolution of the reformed Congregation of Tordesillas after it had had the temerity to defy him.[107] The reign of the Catholic Kings had therefore seen significant progress in a number of areas, but a large proportion of the Spanish religious Order remained substantially untouched by the reform efforts of the past. With the accession of Charles V the ongoing campaign of former years lost the momentum and resolution upon which its effectiveness depended. As we have already seen, the renewal of the royal reform effort in the early 1530s was therefore doomed to ignominious failure. That this should be the case reflects not a lack of will so much as a failure of policy and organization. The prevailing outlook can be gleaned from Charles V's instructions to his new viceroy in Catalonia, Francisco de Borja, in June 1539:

> The dissolution, relaxation and excessive freedom prevalent in several monasteries of friars and nuns in Barcelona and Catalonia brings disservice to God, dishonour and disrepute to the city and the land, and infamy on religion. It is thus a heavy burden of conscience to allow this state of affairs to go on unchecked, and though reform is not now observed with its former rigour there is still every chance that, introduced little by little, the religious will deepen in their recollection and thus come in time to embrace the reformed life. Whenever you find the opportunity, you should therefore discuss these matters with any you think fit, including those on the Council [of Aragon], and inform us of the ways and means through which this might be executed, being sure always to follow the easiest and least scandalous path. Meanwhile, you should see that the religious live as rigorously as possible, and if you learn that they are transgressing, ensure that they are chastized and punished, either by their prelates and superiors, or by whatever means you can.[108]

---

[106] *Ibid.*, p. 402.

[107] *Ibid.*, pp. 402 & 409.

[108] ACA, RC, vol. 3899, ff. 150r–159r. Toledo, 26th June 1539. Titled 'Lo que vos el Illustre don francisco de Borja Marques de lombay nuestro Primo haveys de hazer en el principado de Cathaluña y condados de Rossellon y cerdaña con el cargo de nuestro lugarteniente general de que hos havemos provehido es lo siguiente'; passage cited f. 158r.

Even in Borja's hands the impact of this unfocused and ill-informed policy was negligible, and a year later the reform campaign was apparently reduced to one of subsidizing the poorest houses with money from royal coffers.[109]

Beyond the efforts of a few prelates and the establishment of new orders in the Peninsula, the monastic panorama towards mid-century is therefore largely one of consolidation, stasis, or decline. In 1525, for instance, an attempted reform of the Premonstratensian house of Retuerta in Castile ended in abject failure.[110] A decade later an initiative by the bishop of Burgos, Cardinal Íñigo López de Mendoza, to transform the leading monastery of La Vid near Burgos into the centrepiece of an exempt congregation met a similar fate, and a tortured destiny awaited the Premonstratensians under Philip II. Among the Friars Preachers of Castile, meanwhile, the Observance established itself as the sole viable expression of Dominican life in the spiritual and material order. Yet, in other congregations such as the Mercedarians the reformed life extended only to a handful of religious, and for these institutions the work of reform, in whatever form it was to take, remained to be done. The fact remains that not one of the orders subject to the reforming policy of the Catholic Kings or Charles V would escape the attentions of Philip II's reformers in some branch of their existence in some part of the Peninsula — especially the Crown of Aragon. Writing on the reform of both the Catalan and the Castilian monasteries in 1546, Francisco de Borja could justifiably lament 'the little fruit secured, either in the time of Queen Isabella, of blessed memory, or in our own time'.[111]

However, though the campaign failed to achieve many of its objectives, an important start had been made and the powers and experience acquired during the Isabelline reform were destined to influence the praxis and mentality of later generations of reformers. With Philip's accession, the reform of the religious orders once more became a priority of the crown. 'The King,' wrote Santa Teresa, 'is very well disposed to religious who are known to keep their Rule, and

---

[109] *Ibid.*, vol. 3900, ff. 24r–26r. Charles V to Borja, Madrid, 10th November 1540; f. 25r.

[110] Cueto, 'On the Significance of the Reform', p. 24.

[111] Cited in Kamen, *The Phoenix and the Flame*, p. 49. The letter was addressed to Ignatius of Loyola.

will always help them.'[112] But after years of neglect, the crown had much to learn regarding the conduct of monastic reform, not least that this matter simply could not be enforced under duress in the way of other policies; that orders were not institutions in the conventional sense, but a collectivity of individuals. Reform, above all, required time and patience. As an official declared to Philip in 1566 with regard to monastic reform in the Crown of Aragon,

> These monasteries of nuns, and some of those of the friars, were last reformed by [...] Queen Isabella, though it lasted as little as the others, from which Your Majesty can well understand the great difficulties involved in their reform, and how much care must be taken to ensure that theirs be not a three-day reformation, but one that is permanent.[113]

Yet, despite his strong personal association with the religious life and his high patronage of the Jeronymite Order, this approach only appears to have impressed itself on Philip towards the end of his reign. By 1586 he was urging the four reformers appointed to visit the Catalan Benedictines and Canons Regular to proceed 'with great gentleness and kindness', in marked contrast to the cavalier attitude adopted in the first years of the reform movement.[114] Time and bitter experience would show this to be among the most vexatious of issues, for Philip, like his predecessors, had to learn that the perspective of both the orders themselves and the papacy had to be taken into account, not just that of the crown.

As a living organism, the Church, with its mutable institutions and fallible members was by definition in perpetual need of reform and readjustment. Since spiritual reform, as we have seen, was the very essence of the religious life, it therefore represented, either in observance or in assimilation, a continuous process which authorities could hope neither to enforce nor precipitate. The spiritual reform of a relaxed order could only originate from within the congregation itself, and equally its extension throughout the institution was possible only through the efforts of a reformed or reform-minded congregation with some degree of independence from the unreformed majority. The crown or its agents could cajole, threaten and discipline; it could pro-

---

[112] Cited in *The Complete Works of St Teresa of Jesus*, trans. & ed. Edgar Allison Peers (3 vols, London, 1946); III, p. 142.

[113] AGS, PR, 23-225, f. 1v.

[114] Cited in Kamen, *The Phoenix and the Flame*, p. 71.

mote disciplinary, legislative and even institutional change, but ultimately it could not conjure the phenomenon of spiritual reform itself.
This, it seems, was also brought home to Philip only after repeated
failure, for there is one final axiom applying to unreformed religious
congregations: namely that, to be lasting, any voluntary spiritual
change must be founded on a degree of institutional and disciplinary
change. This model can surely be applied to all reformed religious
congregations, as much to the Dominican Observance of *c*.1423, as to
the Discalced Carmelites of 1562 or the Discalced Mercedarians of
1603, for if these are spiritual expressions of reform are they not by
foundation and definition institutional ones also? In our case, however, the fundamental question remains to be answered: to what extent
was the reform of the Mercedarians proper a spiritual reform?

Although, as we shall see, time would prove structural and disciplinary change to be sufficient for the purposes of the crown in the Mercedarian case, early attempts to impose both institutional and spiritual reform simultaneously reveal the blindness of the king and his ministers to the internal and external implications of monastic reform in
general. For though Philip retained a strong belief in the significance
of reform for the condition of *Christianitas*, this conviction was driven
by reason of state, by the apparent threat to the integrity of his kingdoms that the pollution of the religious life implied. As the king's
Franciscan confessor, Fray Bernardo de Fresneda, wrote during the
final session of the Council of Trent,

> The deviants of our Holy Faith first began their opposition to the
> Church by destroying these orders, which action they justified in view
> of the licentious and unrecollect living of the religious.[115]

It was in this frame of mind that Philip and his ministers embarked
on the reform of Spanish religious life.

IX. *The Opening of the Reform Campaign, 1561–7*

By the early 1560s the king had begun to formulate the priorities of a
general campaign for the reform of the Spanish orders.[116] Principal

---

[115] Cited in Stegginck, *La reforma del Carmelo español*, 2nd edn., p. 56.

[116] There is no in-depth study of the reform of the Spanish religious orders under
Philip II. Though primarily concerned with the Carmelites in the 1560s, by far the

among these was the final suppression of Conventualism, notably among the Dominicans and Franciscans of the Crown of Aragon and Navarre, and a severance of the ties between Peninsular religious and their foreign superiors. Both these aims were consistent with the king's basic objective of establishing an independent Spanish, or more properly Castilian, national Church. To Philip it was unacceptable that Spanish religious should be subject to generals resident in Rome or elsewhere who were not only heedless of their Peninsular subjects, but presided over congregations notoriously infiltrated by heretics. The uncovering of a large Lutheran cell at the leading Isidrite monastery of San Isidro del Campo outside Seville in 1557 had already given Philip an uncomfortable exposure to this phenomenon.[117] Accordingly, one of the first expressions of Philip's monastic policy was the cessation of Spanish Cistercian dependence, particularly in Navarre and the Crown of Aragon, on the abbot of Cîteaux and of the military order of Calatrava on the incumbent of Morimond, conceded by Pius IV in March 1561. The same policy was pursued by the Royal Council of Castile with respect to the Dominicans and Carmelites in particular, though rather less successfully.[118] But, as we shall see, this centralizing outlook was to have major implications for the reform of the Mercedarian Order, with its Spanish yet non-Castilian government.

That same March Philip began pressing in Rome for briefs towards a general reform of the Spanish orders.[119] Those in the frontier lands of the Peninsula were considered to be in particularly urgent need of reform. This process Philip optimistically hoped to initiate with papal sanction during the coming *cortes* at Monzón. Spurred on by the imminent reopening of the Council of Trent,

best introduction to the early policy is Steggink, *La reforma del Carmelo español*, 2nd edn., pp. 51–73, 221–6 & 305–7, but see also García Oro, 'Conventualismo y observancia', pp. 317–49, & *CDEESS*, IV, xxviii–l.

[117] See A. Gordon Kinder, *Casiodoro de Reina: Spanish Reformer of the Sixteenth Century* (London, 1975), pp. 10–16. The Isidrites or Hermits of St Jerome, a reformed branch of the Jeronymites, were founded in Andalusia by the general Fray Lope de Olmedo in 1424. By the 1560s the Order had seven monasteries in Spain and several more in Italy, where it was known as the Ordine di Santo Spirito. See Antonio Linage Conde, *El monacato en España e Hispanoamérica* (Salamanca, 1977), pp. 113–15, & L. Alcina, 'Fray Lope de Olmedo y su discutida obra monástica' in *Yermo*, 2 (1964), pp. 29–57.

[118] Steggink, *La reforma del Carmelo español*, 2nd edn., pp. 58–61.

[119] See *ibid.*, pp. 56–7, García Oro, 'Conventualismo y observancia', pp. 317–19, & *CDEESS*, IV, xix.

whose directives in this area he was anxious to influence, Philip dispatched copies of most of the monastic constitutions to Rome to assist the Council in its deliberations on this matter. By the end of 1561 he had presented his ambassador to the Holy See, Francisco de Vargas, with an ambitious programme for the reform of the regular clergy. Broadly speaking, all orders were to be reduced to observance by Castilian religious appointed by their generals in Rome, but along lines worked out in Castile and free from papal intervention. But apparently Philip had yet to grasp the fact that a number of orders, including the Carmelites, Trinitarians and Mercedarians, had little or no primitive 'observance' to be reduced to as such, and that, in consequence, other means of reform — whatever these might be — would have to be found. The episode illustrates the ignorance of Philip and his ministers not only as to the condition of the orders themselves and the diversity of their rules and constitutions but, above all, to the practicalities of monastic reform itself. Clearly, while the crown cherished its traditional leadership and patronage, changed circumstances and long neglect had reduced its competence in this field. To a Rome fearful of royal intervention and busy with its preparations for the Council, Philip's programme, incomplete and ill-conceived as it was, predictably fell on deaf ears. Concerted opposition from the generals in Rome and the expectation that a complete reform of the Church would be legislated for at Trent finally buried the initiative.[120]

However, it was not long before the king had prepared a second and more considered overture.[121] The period between 1563–4 that Philip spent travelling through the Crown of Aragon to celebrate the general and provincial *cortes* underlined the pressing need for monastic reform in the eastern kingdoms. The urgency of the situation was reflected in the highly charged petition he sent to Pius IV from Monzón in November 1563 calling for the reform of the orders.[122] Having underlined the serious moral decay into which Spanish religious life had fallen and the correspondingly urgent need for their improvement, Philip threatened, with perhaps a hint of desperation,

[120] Steggink, *La reforma del Carmelo español*, 2nd edn., pp. 61–2 & 72–3.

[121] *Ibid.*, pp. 62–5.

[122] Reproduced in Dom Luciano Serrano, *Pío IV y Felipe II: Primeros diez meses de la embajada de Don Luis de Requeséns en Roma* (Rome, 1891), pp. 70–84. See also Steggink, *La reforma del Carmelo español*, 2nd edn., pp. 62–5, & García Oro, 'Conventualismo y observancia', pp. 319–20.

to 'depopulate the aforementioned monasteries rather than allow them to continue living as they do' if action were not taken quickly.[123] The king went on to set out a far-reaching programme structured around a three-tier reform commission under the control of the crown. There were to be two executive levels, the upper of which was to consist of a number of royal and apostolic commissaries responsible for visiting and introducing new legislation. The commissaries, mostly bishops, were to be assisted by reformed nuns and religious from the orders concerned who were to perform an advisory role and then see to the execution of the ordained legislation. Philip projected wide canonical powers for the reformers, with rights to appoint observant superiors over reformed houses in triennial tenure; to transfer Conventual foundations to Observant control and suppress those incapable of maintaining a religious life; to prohibit the reception of novices in unreformed houses and impose strict enclosure on nunneries; and finally to suspend or revoke any constitutional privileges or appeals to Rome arising out of the reform.

The controlling influence in this matter was to be held by a small steering committee, the embryonic *Junta de Reforma* (Reform Committee), about which we still know relatively little.[124] Recalling a similar body established under the Catholic Kings, the *Junta* seems to have

---

[123] Cited in García Oro, 'Conventualismo y observancia', p. 320.

[124] See Steggink, *La reforma del Carmelo español*, 2nd edn., pp. 54–6. Not to be confused with Olivares' later *Junta de Reformación*, the *Junta de Reforma* was an adjunct of the Royal Council of Castile. Linda Martz, *Poverty and Welfare in Habsburg Spain: The Example of Toledo* (Cambridge, 1983), p. 71, underlines its involvement in resolving conflicts between secular and ecclesiastical jurisdiction (and, one presumes, between the secular and the regular clergy) provoked by the reform of certain monasteries. Three of the original members in 1561 were Fresneda (the King's confessor), Fernando de Valdés (inquisitor general and archbishop of Seville), the jurist Dr. Martín de Velasco (the notoriously anti-papal member of the Royal Council of Castile and the *Cámara Real*), along with Francisco de Eraso (secretary of the Royal Council), who joined in 1563. Later members were (from 1566) Diego de Espinosa, Cardinal Sigüenza (bishop of Sigüenza, president of the Royal Council and inquisitor general; d.1572), the Observant Franciscan Mº Fray Francisco Pacheco (the Queen's confessor), Licenciado Menchaca (member of the Royal Council and the *Cámara Real*) and Gabriel de Zayas (secretary of the Council of State). The *Junta* seems therefore to have been composed of three members and a secretary at any one time. It appears likely that much of the documentation regarding the reform of the religious orders of which AGS, PR, leg. 23 is composed emanated from this body. On Espinosa, see José Martínez Millán, 'En busca de la ortodoxia: El Inquisidor General Diego de Espinosa' in *id.*, ed., *La corte de Felipe II* (Madrid, 1994), pp. 189–228, esp. 201–7. Another influential figure in royal reform policy was Cristóbal de Rojas y Sandoval, successively bishop of Oviedo (1546–56), Badajoz (1556–62), and Córdoba (1562–71), and archbishop of Seville (1571–80); see *DHEE*, suppl. I, pp. 667–70.

been formed as early as May 1561, shortly after Philip began taking steps towards the reform of the orders.[125] The intended function of the *Junta*, which never appears to have been constituted on more than an *ad hoc* basis, was to plan and supervise the reform of each order through the appointment of commissaries with apostolic authority. It was at this stage to have been composed of the three metropolitans of the Crown of Aragon — Tarragona, Zaragoza and Valencia — where reform was obviously felt to be most needed, along with the archbishop of Santiago and the bishop of Cuenca, the Observant Franciscan Fray Bernardo de Fresneda, whose brain-child this and earlier projects had been.[126] Composed of men drawn from the king's religious inner circle, it was from this small committee that the ideologues of the reform movement under Philip II emerged.

The proposals were submitted to Pius IV in mid December 1563, only a few days after the concluding session of the Council of Trent had laid down its directives on monastic reform. These, as we have seen, had followed a notably moderate line, proposing disciplinary measures against Conventualism rather than the outright suppression advocated by Philip. The papacy was therefore in no mood to endorse the blatantly regalist programme being hawked about Rome by the new ambassador, Luis de Requeséns. After a few months the project was first shelved and then lost in a welter of other urgent Post-Tridentine business. But, as we shall see, the structure set out within it would provide the basis of reform organization in the years to come.

Despite this setback, Philip was determined to override conciliar legislation on monastic reform which, with the partial exception of that on the nuns, he rightly considered to be woefully inadequate. Already in December 1563 Requeséns had confirmed the king's worst fears when he informed him that 'the reforms carried out in this past session are in many respects useless and in other ways inexpedient'.[127] Mistrust of Rome, the tradition of royal leadership and

---

[125] On the Catholic Kings' circle of advisors on ecclesiastical reform, see Hillgarth, *The Spanish Kingdoms*, II, p. 407.

[126] On Fresneda, see P.Fr. José M. Pou i Marti, 'Fray Bernardo de Fresneda, confesor de Felipe II, obispo de Cuenca y Córdoba y arzobispo de Zaragoza' in *Archivo ibero-americano*, 33 (1930), pp. 582–603, *DHEE*, suppl. I, pp. 334–43, esp. 338, and an essay apparently written in ignorance of the latter, Henar Pizarro Llorente, 'El control de la conciencia regia: El confesor real Fray Bernardo de Fresneda' in José Martínez Millán, ed., *La corte de Felipe II* (Madrid, 1994). pp. 149–88, esp. 181–3.

[127] Cited in Steggink, *La reforma del Carmelo español*, 2nd edn., p. 112.

past experience in this field provoked a scathing reaction in Madrid. 'These reforms,' it was said of the Tridentine provisions, 'are completely ineffectual, having as they do no executors but the friars themselves.'[128] Religious, even generals, were apparently not considered capable of reforming their orders in a manner acceptable to the crown. Tension therefore mounted between Madrid and Rome through 1564 over the promulgation of the conciliar legislation in Spain, and this issue in particular. Rome replied accusing the ambitious Fresneda of goading the Spanish court into a blindly anti-Conventual stance, while Pius IV and his nephew Borromeo staunchly upheld the exempt status of the Tridentine decrees from royal intervention. Yet intervene is precisely what Philip felt himself obliged to do. Pacheco, Spain's cardinal protector in Rome, was no doubt voicing the king's intention of going his own way over the orders if necessary when he warned the papal curia to 'consider their actions very carefully in this matter', or the king 'might decide to purge his kingdoms of this pestilence himself'.[129]

Threats of this sort had their desired effect in Rome, and when it became clear that Philip was about to take unilateral action Pius IV responded by sending Ugo Buoncompagni, Cardinale di Santo Sixto and later Gregory XIII, at the head of a legation to Spain in July 1565.[130] Other members of the party were the new nuncio, Giambattista Castagna, and the Conventual Franciscan Fra Felice Peretti di Montalvo, later Sixtus V. Buoncompagni was granted faculties by Pius IV to find a solution to the problems presented by the reform of each order in consultation with the king — whether as to disciplinary reform, reduction to regular observance or outright suppression — as well as the other questions affecting papal relations with Spain: the Carranza case and the *Cruzada* bull.[131] The visit began in Catalonia where Buoncompagni and Peretti will no doubt have been appraised of the condition and prospects of the Aragonese religious Order, including the Mercedarians. October found the legation in Madrid where fruitful discussion regarding the orders, if not on other matters, continued until news reached the court in December of Pius IV's

---

[128] Cited in *ibid.*, p. 115.

[129] Cited in *ibid.*, p. 114. On Pacheco, see *DHEE*, suppl. I, pp. 567–71.

[130] On the improvement of relations, see Steggink, *La reforma del Carmelo español*, 2nd edn., pp. 115–17, & Dom Luciano Serrano, 'Un legado pontificio en la corte de Felipe II' in *Hispania: Revista española de historia*, 2 (1942), pp. 64–91.

[131] See Bada, *Situació religiosa*, p. 236.

death. With his commission effectively null and void, Buoncompagni immediately decamped and gratefully returned to Italy leaving a number of important agreements unratified.

Although the legation had failed to conclude its business, its very dispatch to Spain indicates a distinct change of heart in Rome with regard to monastic reform.[132] Above all, the papacy had ceased to be as monolithically Tridentine as it had been in the immediate aftermath of the Council, and henceforth the two sides would work towards broadly the same objectives. Already in August 1565 Pius IV had issued a brief ordering the reform of the Trinitarians to proceed as directed in Spain, while another placed the Italian congregation of the Isidrites under the authority of the Peninsular Jeronymite Order.[133] This was followed in September by the major bull *Militantis Ecclesiae* for the reform of the Spanish Franciscans, Augustinians, Benedictines, Carmelites and Premonstratensians. Issued no doubt on the strength of the good progress of Buoncompagni's legation, this document represents a half-way house between royal and Tridentine reform mentalities and as such is a significant moment in the history of the Spanish orders. As in other areas of religious policy, Spanish diplomacy had succeeded, though perhaps only temporarily, in obliging the papacy to address problems from the crown's own perspective. In this case the papacy had come to recognize that Tridentine provisions for monastic reform were indeed inadequate for the task in hand. Philip, on the other hand, dropped his demands for complete control over the reform process and agreed to take a more conservative approach. The bull provided for visitations by episcopal commissaries appointed with the approval of the orders concerned and accompanied by observant religious from reformed congregations, these acting under the supervision of bishops and archbishops with apostolic authority.[134] Further, the commissaries were given wide faculties to enforce observance of existing statutes and formulate new ones, to replace and punish personnel and impose a triennial generalate. Although the grave decadence of Conventual life in Spain was recognized, the threat of suppression was to be kept veiled until reform were proved to be impossible.

---

[132] Steggink, *La reforma del Carmelo español*, 2nd edn., pp. 118–19.

[133] *Ibid.*, p. 117.

[134] The burden, for such it was, of visitation and reform was borne by religious, many of them highly distinguished members of the Dominican, Franciscan, Jeronymite and Carthusian Orders.

The groundwork had therefore been laid, but a number of serious problems with regard to royal intervention as much in the provincial councils as in monastic reform itself remained to complicate relations with Rome. However, the imposition of the papal tiara on the ascetic Dominican Michele Ghislieri as Pius V represented a triumph for the Spanish reformist party, and with this came a gradual recognition in Rome that nothing could be done without the cooperation of the crown.[135] Thus, after much vacillation 'on these affairs which are his own vocation', the pope amplified the faculties of the *Militantis Ecclesiae* in the bull *Maxime cuperemus* of 2nd December 1566.[136] Ten days later Pius issued the bull that effectively sealed the fate of the Spanish Conventuals, and with this hurdle cleared the reform of the remaining congregations, including the Mercedarians, could now be initiated. The king underlined his priorities in February, and on 16th April 1567 three briefs titled *In prioribus* set out the procedure for the reform of the Carmelites, the Trinitarians and the Mercedarians, orders, we are informed, 'in which there is no distinction between Conventuals and Observants'.[137] On the same day the major brief *Superioribus mensibus* reiterated the suppression of the Conventuals and provided for the reform of the three 'unreformed orders' just mentioned along the lines of the *Militantis Ecclesiae*.[138] Finally, and most radically, the brief made provision for the incorporation of some of the smaller orders and congregations into a dominant or parent institution.[139] Armed with these seemingly broad faculties, the crown could now begin the work of reform.

---

[135] The general situation is brought out in *CDEESS*, I, pp. 338–40, Requeséns to Philip II, Rome, 18th November 1566.

[136] See *ibid.*, II, pp. 72–5, Requeséns to Philip II, Rome, 16th March 1567; p. 73.

[137] Cited in Stegginck, *La reforma del Carmelo español*, 2nd edn., p. 224; see *ibid.*, pp. 223–5, & BL, Add., vol. 28,404, ff. 168r–171r, Philip II to Requeséns, Madrid, 17th February 1567.

[138] Cited in part in *ibid.*, p. 224. Among the Franciscans the Conventuals were now finally suppressed in Spain, and the Order's houses in Navarre removed from the province of Aragon to those of Burgos and Cantabria in Castile with the assistance of a further brief of 18th August 1567; see Pizarro Llorente, 'El control de la conciencia regia', pp. 182–3.

[139] Namely, the absorbtion of the Franciscan Tertiaries into the Observance, and the Isidrites and Premonstratensians into the Jeronymites. Unlike the Isidrites, the Premonstratensians, it should be noted, bore little spiritual affinity to the Jeronymites and successfully resisted incorporation through a bitter campaign waged in Rome; see P. José Goñi Gaztambide, 'La reforma de los Premonstratenses españoles del siglo XVI' in *Hispania Sacra*, 13 (1960), pp. 5–96.

X. *The End of the Beginning*

Although the papacy had refused to grant the crown complete authority in this matter, the first stage of Philip II's model for the reform of the religious orders was now in place. What conclusions can be drawn as to the king's motivations at this early stage in the reform process?[140]

Certainly, all the evidence suggests that Philip had seriously under-estimated the size and complexity of the task which he and the *Junta de Reforma* had blithely undertaken. Warnings that by over-reaching itself in this matter the crown might lose control of the projected reform process altogether went unheeded.[141] Philip's eagerness to wrest the matter completely from the hands of the papacy now that the opportunity had presented itself led him to fall headlong into a labyrinthine campaign for the reform of many of Spain's several dozen congregations and 50,000 religious.[142] As yet unfamiliar with the diversity of the orders, Philip viewed the business of monastic reform in the same terms as the ordering of the monarchy within a set of established political and religious parameters. The crown laid great importance on a unifying reorganization of Spanish religious life, since, as Philip declared with regard to the Franciscans,

> It is not right that there should be such diversity of life in a single reli-
> gious order, because if certain religious desire to live more strictly than
> the observants, they have in their houses all the means for this that
> they could wish.[143]

The early part of the campaign was therefore marked by some extra-ordinarily insensitive attempts to mould orders into more manage-able geographical and institutional groupings. The fact that the Isidrites and the Alcantarine Franciscans followed more rigorous

---

[140] For some preliminary ideas on this, see Ignacio Fernández Terricabras, 'Un ejemplo de la política religiosa de Felipe II: El intento de reforma de las monjas de la Tercera Orden de San Francisco (1567–1571)' in *Primer Congreso Internacional del Monacato Femenino en España, Portugal y América (1492–1992)* (2 vols., León, 1993); II, pp. 159–71.

[141] For a cogent warning of the dangers and shortcomings of royal policy and the lack of information on the orders concerned, see the letter of Fray Francisco Pacheco, OFM, in AGS, PR, 23-227, ff. 21r–23v, undated but *c.*1566.

[142] For a range of statistics, see Felipe Ruiz Martín, 'Demografía religiosa' in *DHEE*, II, pp. 682–733, esp. 682–5 & 718–21, in conjunction with Annie Molinié-Bertrand, 'Le Clergé dans le royaume de Castille à la fin du XVIᵉ siècle: Approche cartografique' in *Revue d'histoire economique et sociale*, 51 (1973), pp. 5–53.

[143] Cited in Fernández Terricabras, 'Un ejemplo de la política religiosa', p. 167.

rules of life than the Jeronymites or Observant Franciscans into which they were incorporated was irrelevant.[144] Alteration of provincial boundaries and assimilation of lesser orders, often on economic grounds, was attempted with scant regard either to tradition or even the spiritual incongruity of such action. This attempt to restrict the proliferation of religious orders was a blatant contradiction not only of the establishment since the late fourteenth century of the reformed communities themselves, but also of those developing at that moment, notably Santa Teresa's Discalced Carmelites of 1562.

The *leitmotiv* of Philip's approach towards the religious was therefore obedience, not only through observance of what was termed the *instituto* of each order — a sense of the rule and constitutions as the essence of each — but obedience to the crown and its officers with their apostolic authority. As Philip declared regarding the nuns of the Franciscan Tertiaries,

> Having given their obedience, which is the hard part, they will relent little by little and, through prudence, gentleness and reasoning, will go on to obey the remaining ordinances.[145]

Similarly, the *Junta de Reforma* added that

> On this foundation [i.e. obedience] the nuns will be obliged to comply less obstinately with all else that is planned for their reformation.[146]

Yet such views hardly reflected either an understanding of the condition and spiritual *raison d'être* of the orders or, for that matter, the mores of human nature. If Philip had opted for an authoritarian reform model, it was because this appeared most compatible with his political priorities.[147] Believing that the life and values of the orders had been compromised through time and perverted by experience, the crown felt itself fully entitled to alter the character of these where this seemed appropriate in view of their unsatisfactory condition. It was this outlook that permitted Philip to tamper with the constitutions of religious orders, as in the case of the Mercedarians, and this also that reveals the political motivations which guided his approach to this matter.[148] Yet the disciplinary, geographical and legislative

---

[144] The Isidrites' standing had, however, been severely compromised by the uncovering of a Lutheran conventicle within its ranks in 1557; see *supra*, n. 117.

[145] Cited in Fernández Terricabras, 'Un ejemplo de la política religiosa', p. 168.

[146] Cited in *ibid.*, p. 167.

[147] *Ibid.*, p. 168.

[148] See Kamen, *The Phoenix and the Flame*, pp. 69–70.

reforms recognized by the crown by no means exhausted the cate-
gories into which this concept extended itself, or the degree to which
'reform' might be moulded by others or by other circumstances.

The relative ease with which first the Conventual Franciscans and
then the Isidrites were assimilated into their dominant bodies during
1567–8 served only to heighten Philip's misplaced confidence in his
reform programme. Only when the capacity for resistance and the
support enjoyed by other orders, both locally and in Rome, became
apparent did the naïvety of Philip's first model for monastic reform
stand revealed. No order demonstrated the limitations of this strategy
more comprehensively than the Mercedarians.

CHAPTER FOUR

AN ORDER TO BE REFORMED (1561–7)

I left him because of that and because of one or two other things I'd rather not mention.[1]

Although the Mercedarians were not singled out in Philip's opening campaign before the papacy in March 1561, the strong emphasis placed on the need for action in Navarre and the Crown of Aragon leaves no doubt that their condition had already come to his notice.[2] To Philip the sorry state of the orders in the border provinces rendered them especially vulnerable to the insidious heresy that had already tainted French monastic life, and which was now poised on the frontiers of his own kingdoms. As Philip instructed his ambassador in Rome in 1562 regarding contacts between the French and Spanish Cistercians,

> Ensure that all in Rome are aware both of the ruination of the Christian religion in France and the spread of the evil Lutheran sect in that kingdom, to the extent that some monasteries and orders have now become corrupted; a repetition of which could cause all conceivable damage in the Crown of Aragon, particularly if the Cistercians were to continue travelling to Cîteaux as was formerly the case.[3]

The threat of heresy was therefore intimately joined in his mind with the indiscipline and unruliness ('soltura y libertad')[4] of those who might harbour it, and it was to the reform of such individuals and the institutions responsible for them that Philip now addressed himself.

---

[1] Anon., *Lazarillo de Tormes*. The original, referring to a Mercedarian friar, reads 'Y por esto y por otras cosillas que no digo, salí dél'; see Francisco Rico, ed. (Madrid, 1996), p. 111. For Fray Juan de Burgos, a possible prototype of Lazarillo's friar, see Tirso, *Historia*, I, cclxxxix & pp. 389–90.

[2] For the first mention of the Mercedarians, see Steggink, *La reforma del Carmelo español*, 2nd edn., p. 63, citing a letter of 13th March 1561 from Philip to Rome seeking a 'comision general' for the reform of all the orders, both those with observant congregations, 'y de todas las otras aunque sean de San Juan [i.e. Knights Hospitaller] o de la Trinidad o de la Merced'.

[3] *CDEESS*, IV, xxx. Philip's accompanying letter to Pius IV is reproduced in Joan Reglà Campistol, *Estudios sobre los moriscos*, 3rd edn. (Barcelona, 1974), p. 203.

[4] Cited by Philip with respect to a large proportion of the Italian clergy in 1572; see Reglà Campistol, *Estudios sobre los moriscos*, 3rd edn., p. 204.

I. *Royal Overtures, 1561–3*

Ironically, as Philip prepared his preliminary ideas on the reform of the religious orders, delegates from throughout the Mercedarian Order, including Castile, were preparing to attend the reformist chapter general at Barcelona summoned for Pentecost 1561 by the master, the Catalan Mᵉ Fra Miquel Puig. The imminent resumption of the Council of Trent with the reform of the religious orders high on its agenda had no doubt galvanized Puig into addressing the question of reform, but the measures passed at this chapter were to yield few concrete results and the Order sent no delegate to Italy. Puig's secretary, Mᵉ Fra Maties Papiol, was appointed temporary vicar general and sent to visit and reform the houses at Zaragoza and Valencia, though little seems to have come of this.[5] The principal practical result of the chapter was the joint Castilian-Aragonese redemption which set off for Algiers that summer on what was to be the greatest ransoming expedition yet undertaken by the Order.[6] But if Puig and the Aragonese hierarchy, aware no doubt of the interest being taken in them by the crown, had expected a long overdue redemption to allay the king's fears and demonstrate to the world the reformed state of their Order, then they were quite mistaken.

Moves to reconvene the Council had also served to focus Philip's attention on the question of monastic reform which, in the case of the Crown of Aragon, he optimistically hoped to enforce at the coming *cortes* of Monzón. Though Philip's ill-conceived proposals of March 1561 were, as we have seen, quickly discarded in Rome, the king redoubled his efforts and began to reformulate his plans on the basis of a somewhat clearer understanding of the peculiarities of each congregation. The information to which Philip now began to gain access derived no doubt from contacts established by the *Junta de Reforma* with reformed religious, most of them Castilians, in the orders concerned. In this the Mercedarians were clearly no exception, and by March 1563 Philip was ready to draft the first extant plan for the reform of the Order.

---

[5] On this see AGN, Clero, vol. 402, and Vázquez Núñez, *Mercedarios ilustres*, pp. 262–3. Regrettably, none of the substantial MS vols. I have consulted in AGN have been foliated.

[6] In November 1562 the five redemptors, two Aragonese and three Castilians, disembarked at El Grao in Valencia having disbursed over 40,000 *escudos* for a record 427 captives. The documentation is in ACA, Mon., vol. 2691, ff. 73r–132v.

The three documents which comprise this initiative set the tone for Philip's involvement with the Mercedarians over the next thirty years.[7] Addressing Francisco de Vargas, his ambassador in Rome, Philip put the unhappy condition of the Order down to non-observance of its primordial legislation — whatever he understood this to be — and in familiar style went on to express his desire that Pius IV should 'by his own hand restore the Order to its ancient condition'.[8] However, as Philip made clear both here and in an accompanying letter to Pius himself, papal involvement in the affair was to be restricted to issuing the brief committing its execution to him alone. In a passage that captures Philip's enduring perception of the reform of the Mercedarians within the wider political conjuncture, the king declared his need of such endorsement

> so that I, by dint of His Holiness' commission, may appoint suitable individuals to address themselves with diligence to the reform of the said Mercedarian Order, placing its affairs and its houses in the requisite harmony in accordance with its ancient and laudable statutes and whatever, given the state of things and the situation of the moment, might be considered most agreeable to the service of our Lord God and the good of the said Order, which is the sole and principal end which has moved me to obtain this...[9]

The papacy was therefore expected to grant the king absolute powers to execute the reform of the Order, which was to be carried out where possible in conformity with its constitutions, but otherwise as best suited the interests of the crown. Although circumstances would eventually oblige Philip to abandon his basic aim of sole and unhindered direction of the reform of this and other orders, his opinion that the affairs and implicitly the character of each should be surrendered to reason of state remained constant. It was this inflexible and indeed unrealistic outlook that was to turn monastic reform, so complex in itself, into such an intractable problem for the crown.

---

[7] The documents, dated Madrid, 12th March 1563, are in AMAE, SS, leg. 34. They are: (i) Philip to Vargas, f. 1r–v (copies f. 7r–v, & AGS, E°, leg. 897, no. 39); (ii) an accompanying (though undated) *memorial*, ff. 3r–4v: 'Lo que en nombre de su Magestad se ha de supplicar a nuestro muy sancto Padre Pio iiij para la reformaçion de la Orden de nuestra señora de la merçed como especial patron della es lo siguiente' (copies f. 2r–v, & AGS, E°, leg. 897, no. 40); & (iii) Philip to Pius IV, f. 5r (copy f. 6r).

[8] *Ibid.*, f. 1r.

[9] *Ibid.*

If this first corpus of documentation provides a foretaste of Philip's mentality with regard to the Mercedarians in the years to come, then likewise the practical changes laid out within it represent a foundation for the institutional reform of the Order. Arranged in nine short paragraphs, the *memorial* began by enjoining observance of the vows and constitutions of the Order, the only reference in it to spiritual reform. Turning immediately to institutional change, the *memorial* accepted that the office of general should remain perpetual, but provided for an equal representation of all provinces (with three votes each) at the electoral chapter general which was to be held alternately in Castile and the Crown of Aragon. The provincial and diffinitors were to be elected by commendators and graduates in theology, a reflection of the general concern to promote study as central to the monastic vocation. The offices of provincial and vicar provincial were to be limited to six years, a reform recently adopted in Castile. Moreover, the provincial was required to give account of his actions to the chapter at the end of his tenure, a measure against the corruption to which the high offices of the Order traditionally lent themselves. But in all other respects the *Concordia* of 1467 was to be observed, particularly with regard to the autonomy of the provincials of Castile from the masters general.

Although they were not brought into effect, these proposals had touched on many of the crucial issues over which the battle for Mercedarian reform was to be fought. Reflecting the strong Castilian bias of those involved in its preparation, the *memorial* captures the determination of this province, after nearly a century of independence from the authority of the generals, to acquire what was felt to be a rightful share in the government of a unified congregation. The establishment that same year of four sub-provinces in the Indies under the aegis of Castile now promised to remove the numerical disadvantage traditionally suffered by the Castilians in the election of the master. Further, the idea of alternating *loci* for the elections insinuated the introduction of Castilian and Aragonese generals governing in rotation. Yet, in so doing the Castilians were threatening what for Catalans was the most cherished and fundamental element of the Albertine constitutions: the unquestioned right of the house of Barcelona to host the election of the masters general and the role of the prior in its convocation. It was upon this privilege that the Catalans would make their last bitter stand against the reformers twenty years later.

Nevertheless, the reform proposals, short though they are, show little recognition of the major structural and disciplinary problems afflicting the Order. In confirming the perpetuity of the office of general and ignoring the widespread embezzlement of *limosna* (alms) collected for the redemption of captives, this document ignored two issues at the heart of the Order's institutional and moral decline. The Castilian hierarchy, whose views are most clearly reflected in the *memorial*, seem as yet more concerned to promote the interests of their province with regard to the generalcy than address the desperate condition in which much of the Order found itself. The underlying tone of change predicated on provincial ambition was clearly at odds with the Tridentine emphasis on the restoration of primordial legislation, both in spiritual and institutional matters. Under these circumstances Philip's first initiative in Rome for the reform of the Mercedarian Order foundered without trace.

The issue of the transfer of power was therefore early established as central to Mercedarian reform, but the Castilian hierarchy would have to learn, as it eventually did, that this could only be effected as part of a state-led campaign for the moral and structural improvement of the Order as a whole. With neither a reformed congregation nor a fully committed hierarchy, the Mercedarians had effectively surrendered the right to reform themselves in the eyes of the crown. Moreover, this reform was, as Philip declared at the outset, to be conducted by the crown in a manner reflecting the king's status 'as patron of the said Order'.[10] Philip's projected reform therefore implied not only a transfer of the focus of authority from Catalonia to Castile, but also from the Mercedarian élite to the crown: a recognition of the monarch as the ultimate arbiter of its affairs. However, the 1563 documentation contained one further element of crucial importance to the nature of Mercedarian reform. Although Philip had referred to the 'ancient and laudable statutes' of the Order, in implying that its reform might also be governed by a different scale of values — 'whatever, given the state of things and the situation of the moment, might be considered most advisable' — the crown revealed its readiness to alter rather than merely enforce existing constitutions according to its own priorities.[11] In this respect the new reformist climate found most — though not all — Mercedarians quite unprepared.

---

[10] *Ibid.*, f. 4r.
[11] Both citations *ibid.*, f. 1r.

Even as the Council of Trent prepared to deliberate the question of monastic reform in November 1563, Philip was turning his attention once more to the vexatious state of the Spanish orders. Several months in the eastern provinces had confirmed to him the serious condition of the orders in these parts, not least the Mercedarians, while the *cortes* of Monzón was itself demanding a general reform of the Aragonese religious Order.[12] Galvanized by the failure of earlier initiatives, the urgent reform petition dispatched by the king from Monzón on 15th November to his ambassador in Rome, Luis de Requeséns, was his most cogent statement yet on monastic reform.[13] But, as we have seen, Philip's approach betrayed a palpable *naïveté* both with regard to the issues at stake and the condition of the orders themselves. Arriving in Rome just days after the drafting of the monastic decrees in the XXVth and final Tridentine session, Philip's incongruous plans received a predictably poor hearing. Within a few weeks the king had begun to address the wider implications of Trent itself and the Mercedarian question, obscured by other urgent business, temporarily slipped off the royal agenda.

II. *Reform and* Mudanza

Although the Mercedarians now receded from the king's political horizons, there can be no doubt that concern for reform continued to grow within the Order itself, particularly in the province of Castile. Among the Castilian brethren this concern was informed by a growing conviction that their superior moral and material condition gave them an unquestioned right to lead the reform of the Order as a whole. The *memorial* of March 1563 had referred obliquely to the need for 'the reform of those provinces that are not reformed, so that the whole Order observes what it professes'.[14] The underlying assumption is that Castile and her four subject provinces in the Indies are more reformed than any other. But on what grounds might Castile claim this for herself, and the leading role in the reform of the Order that went with it? Indeed, what type and degree of reform was the Castilian hierarchy in search of? For if the prospect of reform had

---

[12] *CDEESS*, IV, xxxii.
[13] Reproduced in Serrano, *Pío IV y Felipe II*, p. 70.
[14] AMAE, SS, leg. 34, f. 4r.

been received diffidently in the Crown of Aragon, in Castile it was the cause of much confusion and disagreement.

As discussed elsewhere, the leading reformist figure in Castile at this time was the Andalusian M° Fray Gaspar de Torres (c.1510–84). It was under Torres, as rector of the college of the Vera Cruz (1545–68) and as provincial (1559–65), that the handful of men destined to lead the reform of the Order were nurtured during the 1550s and '60s. According to Remón, Torres was summoned by Philip II to Madrid not long after the court had settled there in 1561 in order to provide theological advice on 'certain *consultas* and *juntas de conciencia* regarding these kingdoms'.[15] It is probable that he had been called in to inform the *Junta de Reforma* on the state of his Order, and if this is so then the likelihood is that the 1563 *memorial* was prepared on the basis of his suggestions.[16] Whatever the case may be, by 1564 the Castilian hierarchy, and Torres in particular, had become aware both of the interest being taken by Philip in the affairs of the Order and of the royal patronage he was beginning to exercise over it.

Anxious to remain abreast of royal policy and with the court apparently settled in Madrid, the province of Castile took the momentous step of establishing a house here in 1564.[17] The Castilians obtained archiepiscopal authorization to found in August of that year, and by October nine friars were installed in a group of houses on the now-disappeared Calle del Barrio Nuevo.[18] Local opposition from the parish clergy of San Justo was brushed aside, and the province slowly began constructing what would become one of the major religious houses of Madrid and the greatest in the Order. Although the convent was founded without direct patronage, its inau-

---

[15] Remón, *Historia*, II, f. 203v. It should be noted that Torres had in April 1560 obtained a royal *cédula* assisting him in the reform of the province; see García Oro & Portela Silva, 'Felipe II y la reforma de las órdenes redentoras', p. 10.

[16] It is, however, unlikely that Torres himself was the author of the *memorial*, as suggested in Vázquez Núñez, I, *Manual*, p. 496.

[17] See Elías Gómez Domínguez, *Primer convento mercedario en Madrid: Monasterio de Tirso de Molina* (Madrid, 1986), pp. 22–36. The Order had failed to take up an offer by the city to found a house in 1503. See also Jerónimo de Quintana, *La muy antigua, noble y coronada villa de Madrid. Historia de su antigüedad, nobleza y grandeza* (Madrid: Imprenta del Reyno, 1629), ff. 410r–421v.

[18] This number had grown to 37 by c.1575; for a list of conventuals, see IVDJ, env. 72, II, f. 137r–v. The community reached a maximum of 128 religious in 1664–6, much the largest in the Order; see Gómez Domínguez, *Primer convento*, p. 70. Until its demolition in 1835 the convent of Nuestra Señora de los Remedios occupied the site of what is now Plaza Tirso de Molina, formerly Plaza del Progreso.

guration in October 1564 seems to have been an event of some moment. The foundation stone was apparently laid by Philip's eldest son, the ill-fated Don Carlos, in the presence of members of the royal family and the nobility, while the ceremony was officiated by the royal confessor and bishop of Cuenca, Fray Bernardo de Fresneda, the leading light in the *Junta de Reforma*.[19] The Castilians had established themselves at court at a crucial moment in the history of the Order, for in doing so they ensured their capacity to influence the decision-making both of the crown and the nuncios in the coming reform period. Moreover, by founding here the Castilians had effectively mounted the first challenge to the status of the priory of Barcelona as the principal convent of the Order.

Though Torres was unable to attend the final sitting of the Council of Trent, he was clearly alive to the significance of its decrees for his Order in the reformist climate of Philippine Spain. Mindful no doubt of the disruption that external interference in the affairs of the Order would bring, Torres addressed himself like Zorita and Gaver before him to the task of providing the Mercedarians with a means to their own reform. Within two years of the closure of the Council he had produced a 'corrected' version of the 1327 constitutions, amending their picturesque Latin and incorporating elements of Lateran and Tridentine legislation.[20] However, the seminal importance of Torres' volume lay in the extended commentary in Castilian on the constitutions that he appended to them, to which task he applied the classical learning of a humanist scholar. The result was nothing less than a practical and intellectual framework for the internal reform of the Order. The volume, it must be stated at the outset, was never endorsed by the province of Castile for which it was principally written, but Torres' influential approach to the problems facing the

---

[19] See Gómez Domínguez, *Primer convento*, p. 35. Don Carlos' recovery from illness in 1562 had been marked in Salamanca by a procession of thanksgiving at which Torres preached the sermon; see Vázquez Núñez, 'La Universidad de Salamanca', p. 272.

[20] M° Fray Gaspar de Torres, *Regula et Constitutiones sacri ordinis beatae Mariae de mercedis redemptionis captivorum* (Salamanca: Mathius Gastius, 1565, 4°). This volume contains (i) a brief account of the foundation of the Order, the *Initium ordinis beatae Mariae de Mercede. De initio ac fundatione sacri ordinis...* (ff. 1r–3v); (ii) the Rule of St Augustine (ff. 3v–10r); and (iii) the 1327 constitutions (ff. 10r–64v). Bound into the same volume is (iv) a commentary on these in Castilian, the *Comentario en lengua vulgar [a] las Constituciones y ordinario de la Religion...* (ff. 1r–161r). References are henceforth given in the text.

Order and the changing attitudes that are reflected in his work repay close scrutiny.

Influenced no doubt by the *Spiritual Exercises*, by Fray Luis de Granada's *Guía de pecadores* and by other devotional works of this kind, Torres presented his *Comentario* as a manual for the spiritual reform of the brethren at conventual level. As he declared with regard to its preparation,

> I have tried only to fulfil some of the duties that accrue to my office, which is that of initiating novices and beginners in their duties, and advising them on the paths they tread.(150v)

To this end Torres adopted a number of rhetorical devices to put his point across. While discussing friars' behaviour under visitation, and especially the duty of fraternal correction, Torres therefore slips from the third into the first person, so that readers would find themselves expounding their own responsibilities rather than being simply lectured on them.(141v–142v) Passages such as these reflect the degree of intellectual control that Tridentine reformers of Torres' stamp deemed it necessary to exercise over their charges. As he declared, 'No one can afford to navigate this age without a pilot to guide him'.(27r) The effect was an invaluable standard against which Torres' successors could measure their own reform methods and legislation.

The *Comentario* set out Torres' vision of an order, united and reformed both spiritually and institutionally, in which each and every friar would contribute to the achievement and maintenance of its restored condition. However, the work also reflects the author's awareness of a task yet to be accomplished, and the commentary is therefore rooted in a basic assumption of the idea of reform: that the Order, its members and, in this case, its statutes as well, were by definition ripe for change and perfection. This recognition represents a highly significant development in the reform mentality of the Castilian élite.

To Torres, the renewal of the Order depended on the united observance of its constitutions, particularly where the divine office was concerned, 'for the decline and dissolution of an order can readily be attributed to neglect in this matter'.(24v) But this could be no passive observance, for, as Torres continued, 'we cannot rely for our salvation on the ceremonies of our forefathers [...] unless we observe them in essence'.(25v) Yet, like many reformers at this moment, Torres recognized the fundamental necessity of institutional adjustment for spiritual and disciplinary reform to be lasting. Moreover, he firmly believed that the basis of reform lay in the imposition of a strict and cogent hierarchical structure on an Order with no clear chain of command. It was, he said, the duty of the provincial to 'enforce the constitutions, rule and ceremonies to the end that the houses observe these and so extirpate abuses'.(147r) The Order, or at least the province, was to be made to worship and behave as one in observance of its rule and constitutions. But few men were capable of bearing the burden of such high responsibility, and since the leadership of the reform of the Order would rest mainly on the offices of visitor and provincial these were presented as encompassing all others.[21] It was imperative, therefore, to set out a precise definition of the role and requisite qualities of the Mercedarian hierarchy as the principal agent of reform and, by extension, the duty of obedience owed it by the rest of the Order. As Torres declared on the basis of the most impeccable classical authority,

> It is not the same (says Aristotle) to be a good man and a good citizen. Likewise, it is not the same to be a good friar and a good commendator, any more than one might consider this sufficient [qualification] to make a good provincial. Those who hold the supreme responsibility of governing the republic (says Plato) should be the finest and wisest men in it [...] And thus only the finest are to hold the supreme government [of the Order].(144r)

Torres therefore conceived of the Order in humanistic terms as a hierarchical republic in which every religious had his place and his duty. The general was to be elected for life by the provincials, who were in turn to be elected for a period of four (rather than six) years by the commendators and graduates of each province. The commendators were to be appointed for a limited term by the provincial hierarchy, rather than elected in conventual chapters, 'for we have already seen in other parts and ourselves witnessed what can happen in such cases'.(147r) It is clear, therefore, that Torres was aiming to minimize the constraints that had traditionally hampered the commendator's authority over conventual life, and turn him into the instrument of a centralizing reformist élite.

In reaching this conclusion the author had touched on a problem

---

[21] *Ibid.*, ch. 13, 'Del oficio del visitador' (ff. 134v–143v), & ch. 14, 'Del oficio e instrucion del Provincial' (ff. 143v–150v).

of critical importance to the reform of the Mercedarians. Torres was acutely aware that the spiritual and disciplinary life of the Order was ultimately dependent on the state of its constituent houses. The reform of the Order would therefore turn on the axis of relations between the hierarchy and the commendators; on the degree to which its conventual life could be brought under the authority of the provincial hierarchy and then reconciled to its reformist mentality. The implementation of religious and disciplinary reform could not, as had effectively been the case in the past, be left solely to the commendators, but rather to a cadre of men with the necessary spiritual and intellectual formation to carry it through. It was the prevailing disparity between the mentality of the Mercedarian rank and file — the 'vulgo ignorante' (147v) — and that of the new élite which was to reform it that Torres' *Comentario* was therefore attempting to address.

Eager to underline the compliant place of commendators with regard to the provincial hierarchy in his reform ideal, Torres counselled that 'it is important in the formulation of laws to ensure that as little as possible be left to the judgement and volition of the commendator'.(149r) This does not mean that he failed to recognize the role of the commendators at the fulcrum of Mercedarian life, only that he considered it their duty to act in accordance with the constitutions and on the provincial's initiative rather than their own. The four qualities that Torres considered most desirable in commendators — that they be authoritative in disciplining their charges, God-fearing, truthful and not greedy — reflect the critical importance of their participation in his projected reform of conventual life.(149v–150r) For the thrust of Torres' reform lay, via institutional and legislative change, in the enforcement of regular discipline and the fostering of spiritual observance at conventual level — responsibilities that commendators had in the past shown themselves unable or unwilling to fulfil.

The success of this system therefore rested on the establishment of a clear chain of command hitherto unfamiliar to the Order. It was the commendator's duty to forsake his traditional independence from hierarchical authority, to obey and then to guide and govern through discipline and by example. However, the process of reform did not end here. In perceiving the Order as a pseudo-republic, Torres viewed authority as reciprocal and therefore acknowledged the important role of commendators as the provincial's lieutenants within a consultative system of government:

> Because he is only one man, the provincial has need of ministers and
> prelates to assist him [...] It is the commendators who are to assist the
> provincial, and the whole being of the Order [therefore] turns on the
> appointment of suitable superiors.(149r)

Ensuring the dispassionate appointment of suitable commendators
was thus among the provincial's most important duties. But if commendators were worthy of advising the provincial it was because,
through study, they had acquired the mentality of the Order's
reformist cadre. In this Torres was not only setting down a goal for
the future, but warning his contemporaries to continue making provision for an educated élite as he himself had done. As he said,

> The provincial can only ensure his being surrounded by people to
> assist him so long as he never ceases to send able religious to study at
> the colleges or provide them with their needs. For without wisdom
> nothing can be ruled or governed, as God in His infinite wisdom has
> taught us.(150r)

Naturally, this system was also designed to regulate the unbridled
exercise of authority to which the Mercedarian hierarchy had
shown itself to be prone. However, while Torres was anxious to
curb such excesses, he was equally concerned to strike a balance of
power that would give prelates sufficient authority at the moment it
was most needed. Drawing once again on Aristotle, Torres declared
that 'if [a prelate] has no authority to effect changes — *mudar* — he
cannot be obeyed, while if all change none shall retain the authority
to govern as required'.(146v) The concept of *mudanza* (change, alteration) reiterates a fundamental element in the reform mentality of
the Castilian Mercedarians. Distinct from the patristic idea of *reformatio* with its clear spiritual content, *mudanza* imparts the notion of
an institutional or constitutional change as distinct from a purely
spiritual or composite one. Thus, while Torres declared it to be 'the
duty of the provincial not to permit official changes to our rule [of
St Augustine] under any circumstances'(147v), he took a rather
more flexible line with regard to the constitutions of the Order.
Having claimed that 'the constitutions should be revered given their
antiquity and inviolable given their sanctity'(148r), Torres significantly added that

> we cannot deny the necessity, as Aristotle himself admits and as reason
> demonstrates, of changing laws in instances of clear benefit or of grave
> need. Changing circumstances oblige the altering of laws.(148v)

Thus, as the 1563 reform documents had implied, the Mercedarian constitutions could be modified if circumstances required it. Yet on what grounds could Torres and the crown justify this derogation of the guiding statutes and, by extension, the 'observance' of the Order? What legislative problems might this bring with it?

III. *Legend and Reality*

The answer draws us back to the obscure primordial history of the Mercedarian Order and to the overlapping traditions and claims that continued to be made for it. As we have seen, the earliest extant Mercedarian constitutions were those of Fra Pere d'Amer of 1272, dating from well after both the foundation of the Order (before 1230) and the death of the Patriarch (*c.*1245). The schism that transformed Nolasch's lay brotherhood into a religious order early the following century was enshrined in the Albertine constitutions of 1327 which were based on the Dominican model. Along with the Amer statutes, the 1327 constitutions reached the sixteenth century via Gaver's *Speculum fratrum*, compiled in around 1445. There are no extant copies of the Albertine constitutions predating this work, much less any manuscript of the statutes as Albert left them, and every indication that these had been altered from the late fourteenth century. As the Valencian M꞉ Fra Pere Joan de Tàrrega declared in around 1573, there were many clauses in the constitutions 'that our predecessors ordained for their own purposes', and which now ran 'counter to the good practice enjoyed by successful orders, and it is necessary that these be remedied'.[22] The two Castilian versions of the constitu-

---

[22] IVDJ, env. 72, II, ff. 256r–267v, (4°), f. 265v (the original draft in Tàrrega's own hand is at ff. 323r–329v). Anonymous, undated and untitled *memorial*, but by Tàrrega, commendator and vicar provincial of Valencia, to Castagna *c.*1571–2. The document has been misbound, and the folio numbers given here correspond to their order in the MS vol. rather than that in which they were written. References to this document are henceforth given in the text.

The main sources for the Mercedarian Crown of Aragon in the years leading up to 1574 are Tàrrega's six lengthy *memoriales* in env. 72, II, of which this is the earliest. The remaining five, also undated and anonymous, though with titles, all date from 1573–4. They are: (b) ff. 26r–33r (a later version is ff. 247r–255r); (c) ff. 224r–236v; (d) ff. 440r–443v; (e) ff. 446r–452v; (f) ff. 482r–491r.

I am grateful to Dr. Xavier Gil of the Universitat de Barcelona and Mr Andrew Hegarty of Merton College, Oxford for drawing this extremely significant collection of papers to my attention.

tions, those of Zorita (1533) and Torres himself (1565), were therefore not exceptional in containing alterations.[23] The repeated emendations to which they had been subjected, the accretions of successive chapters general and the notorious disregard of many of the most fundamental precepts had served to tarnish the image and the validity of the Mercedarian statutes. This quite apart from the fact that they were patently not the pristine legislation the Order claimed them to be, as the survival of the 1272 Amer constitutions bore witness.

There can be no doubt whatsoever that Torres, and indeed any informed Mercedarian, was fully aware of the complex and deeply unsatisfactory constitutional history of the Order, for the total absence of genuinely primordial legislation was matched by the inequitable character of the existing statutes. What Mercedarians considered the essence of their religious life was inextricably bound up with the institutionalized domination of the priory of Barcelona, and the energies of a generation of reformers from Torres onwards would be devoted to resolving the contradictions presented by this. The time had not yet come when, with a canonized patriarch and a set of reformed constitutions, the Order could set aside all earlier legislation and look back with pride and confidence to a *centuria primera* replete with saints and miracles. Meanwhile, the Mercedarians were obliged to make do with several vague and inconsistent versions of the nature of the primeval institution which are a reminder of the immense pressures placed on the Order during the reform period. And of these versions none is so vague and inconsistent as that put forward by Torres himself in his *Comentario*.[24]

Having opened with the same words as the Amer constitutions, Torres declared the Order to have came into being in Barcelona in 1218 after the Virgin Mary had appeared to King Jaume I in a vision.(1r,5v)[25] During the foundation ceremony in the cathedral, the Mercedarian habit was imposed on Nolasch by bishop Berenguer,

---

[23] For details of the alterations contained in these editions with respect to the 1445 codex, see González Castro, 'Las constituciones del P. Raimundo Albert', pp. 124–6. On the reception and training of novices, see Vázquez Fernández, 'La formación en las diversas constituciones', pp. 327–8 & 331–5.

[24] See, in the *Constitutiones*, the *Initium Ordinis*... (ff. 1r–3v), and especially in the *Comentario*, ch. 4: 'De la institucion de la orden' (ff. 7r–9r), & ch. 5: 'Del recogimiento de la orden en su fundacion' (ff. 9v–13r). References are henceforth given in the text.

[25] The citation, translated from the Limousin into Latin, is unattributed.

while Jaume conferred his royal arms on the fledgling institution.(7r–v) Although he is referred to as 'el primero frayle', Nolasch is given little more than a walk-on part in the foundation, and it is evidently the king who is the central figure in the establishment of the Mercedarians.(3r,7v–8r,9v) However, if, as Torres makes clear, Jaume was the founder of the Order, the misleading implication is that his confessor, Fra Ramon de Penyafort, was its first legislator.(8v) It is because Penyafort was a Dominican, we are cryptically informed, that 'the constitutions, ceremonies and liturgy of the Order are the same as those of the Friars Preachers'. It was he who in 1228 petitioned the papacy for the confirmation of the Order, which was supposedly granted in 1230 along with the Rule of St Augustine (actually in 1235).(9r–v)[26]

But though Nolasch is marginalized in the foundation story, he emerges as symbolic of the conjoined vocations of the Order, lay and clerical, active and contemplative, each leavened by the other.(10r) Anxious to generate a sense of the primordial Mercedarian observance, Torres, following Albert, declares the Order to have been founded for the celebration of the divine office and the redemption of captives.[27] So that the pursuit of one vocation was not disrupted by the other, the Order was divided, 'like Martha and Mary', into laymen and clerics, 'action and contemplation as sisters'.[28] To reconcile these two extremes, Torres has Nolasch retreating, like St Francis, from the cares of the world into recollection in 1232.(10r) The author then moves on to the life and organization of the early Order in a passage clearly drawn from the Amer statutes, but when he returns to institutional history the inconsistencies in his account pile up alarmingly.(10r–v) We are first informed that the primitive statutes of the Order were composed in Catalan, and then that Amer, who became general in 1271, gathered and redrafted all the early legislation 'into the constitutions we now have'.(10r,11v) Yet before long Torres is discussing the confirmation in 1317 (actually sometime after 1327) of the Albertine constitutions 'which we now observe'.(13r)

However aberrant Torres' reasoning, his views were widely shared.

---

[26] The year given — 1228 — is interesting since, as we have seen, it is a highly plausible date for the Order's foundation. For another example of this, see IVDJ, env. 72, II, f. 72r.

[27] Torres, *Initium*, f. 1r, *Constitutiones*, f. 10v & *Comentario*, f. 10r.

[28] *Id.*, *Comentario*, f. 10r.

In a *súplica* (appeal) addressed to Pius V in 1568, the Aragonese hierarchy provided a brief account of the foundation of their Order which
closely resembles that given by Torres in his *Comentario*.[29] But though
the Aragonese follow Torres almost to the letter, more than a hint of
political expediency can be detected in the omission of the Dominican
Penyafort from the tableau, it being his order that was currently visiting the Mercedarians. On the other hand, the religious were anxious
to point out that the Order had always been obedient to the pope,
while resting under the protection of the crown. A third version, submitted to the crown by a non-Mercedarian at almost the same time,
provides a somewhat more specific, if no more accurate account of the
historical and institutional background of the Order.[30] Once again,
the Order is declared to have been founded by Jaume I in Barcelona,
though no foundation date is given and neither is there any mention
of Nolasch.[31] However, its constitutions 'which in effect are almost the
same as those of the Dominicans', were set down by Penyafort in
Catalan before being put into Latin.[32] Small wonder that the Mercedarians have had to fend off persistent claims from the Dominicans
to be the founders of their Order.[33] Yet it was upon such specious and
apocryphal versions of events that Mercedarians had to rely in order
to explain away the legislative discrepancies which, after more than
three centuries, had come to represent such a serious threat to the
integrity of the Order.[34]

---

[29] AGN, Clero, vol. 402. Undated, but Barcelona, 20th or 21st January 1568.

[30] IVDJ, env. 72, II, ff. 72r–74v (4°). Anonymous, undated *memorial* written
between mid 1568 and mid 1569.

[31] *Ibid.*, f. 72r.

[32] *Ibid.*, f. 72r–v.

[33] See, for instance, P.Fr. Faustino D. Gazulla, *Refutación de un libro titulado «San
Raimundo de Peñafort, fundador de la Orden de la Merced»* (Barcelona, 1920). The book in
question, whose author Gazulla never mentions, is by P.Fr. Enrique Vacas Galindo
(Rome, 1919). A balanced discussion of the historiography is provided in González
Castro, 'Las constituciones del P. Raimundo Albert', pp. 134–5 & 142–8; see also ch.
1, n. 90.

[34] Elements of all three accounts are contained in Carrillo's version of the foundation as relayed to the nuncio, Giambattista Castagna, in *c.*1570. IVDJ, env. 72, II, ff.
105r–106v; f. 105v. For a rare insight into the survival of these dilemmas into the
20th century, see González Castro, 'Las constituciones del P. Raimundo Albert', p.
144, n. 39, citing from a letter from the historian P.Fr. Guillermo Vázquez Núñez to
P.Fr. Ramón Serratosa Queralt, Madrid, 3rd July 1934.

IV. *The Mercedarian Constitution in Crisis*

Such accounts could hardly be expected to stand up to close scrutiny, and indeed by 1567 the legislative origins of the Mercedarians had become a matter of extreme interest to the crown. As with the other orders, Philip was adamant that the basis for Mercedarian reform should lie in the observance of its primordial rule and constitutions. The uncovering of these was therefore one of the principal tasks he assigned to those entrusted with the 'three unreformed orders' as they were known — the Mercedarians, Carmelites and Trinitarians — in 1567. As Philip reminded the Catalan bishops of the contents of an earlier *memorial*,

> Among other things you were instructed, as an absolute priority, to read and study the rules and institutions belonging to each of these three orders, to the letter of which you are to attempt to reduce them. Moreover, you were required to examine the said rules very closely, extract anything of importance from them, and then compare your findings with the state and life of the Order as it is at present. You were to take very careful note of any instance where the life of the religious differs or has deviated from their primordial institution, indicating the means by which they might be restored to observance. Further, you were to uncover any bulls and briefs in the possession of the orders (since our reform briefs give ample powers to bring these to light), noting where these deviate from the rule and marking out any that you think might profitably be abrogated by His Holiness. Similarly, you were to see where the constitutions and statutes now in use differ from the said rules, or militate against good government and the observance of the rule and profession of the orders, as well as the means by which the prelates are elected, for on this hangs much of the execution and ultimate completion of this reformation.[35]

Thus did Philip conceive the means and in some sense the end of monastic reform, but how did Mercedarians interpret this term and the peculiar difficulties associated with it? As Mᵒ Fray Pedro Carrillo suggested to the king early in 1569,

> Though reform means to reduce an order to its primordial institution, this should not be seen as requiring the Order to be restored to the situation when, as in the very beginning, it had two types of people: lay commendators and clerical friars. Rather, reform should be under-

---

[35] ACA, RC, vol. 4352, ff. 118v–121r. Philip II to Catalan bishops, Madrid, 14th June 1568, ff. 119r–v. In this section Philip is restating the contents of a *memorial* dated 30th November 1567.

stood as the exercise by the religious of the two ends for which this Order was founded: the divine office on the one hand, and the redemption of captives on the other.[36]

Unlike Torres, Carrillo saw little connection between the primordial order and that of his own time, and the twin vocations underlined by him as a theoretical basis for the Mercedarian 'observance' date in fact from the 1327 constitutions. The adaptation of accepted canons for Mercedarian purposes was again in evidence at the chapter provincial of Guadalajara in June of that year. Thus, the chapter interpreted the Tridentine decrees on monastic reform as requiring

> the orders to be reduced to the strictness of the ancient and Regular discipline and perfection they once practised, that their professed observance be in conformity with this, and that the prelates of these orders attempt by all means possible to persuade their subjects to live and remain in this condition.[37]

In this sense, observance was construed as a distillation of the most ancient rules, customs and values of the Order rather than what, in the Mercedarian case at least, would be a futile and undesirable attempt to recover a past that had been irretrievably lost. Like Torres before them, the Castilians at Guadalajara therefore made a clear distinction between the rule, customs and religious observance of the Order, and the institutional provisions for its government; ultimately, between what they wished to preserve of the Order's past and what they did not. Thus, the *Concordia* of 1467, they declared, militated neither against 'any constitution of the primordial statutes, nor the ancient and regular perfection and discipline of the said Order'.[38] It was through such expedients that the Castilians began to establish a canonical and conceptual outline for their reform, and thereby impart to it a distinctively Mercedarian character.

The unique problems presented by the Mercedarian case therefore defied the formulaic and often simplistic approach to reform adopted

---

[36] Cited in Vázquez Núñez, ed., *La Merced a mediados*, (doc.ii), pp. 105–6. The document reproduced (pp. 103–11) is AGS, PR, 23-51(i), an undated *memorial* to Philip II by M° Fray Pedro Carrillo, commendator of Toledo. Internal evidence indicates that the *memorial* was prepared in early 1569 (not 1568 as Vázquez Núñez suggests). References to this document (ii) are henceforth given in the text. An apparently earlier draft is in IVDJ, env. 72, II, ff. 152v–157v. Carrillo, twice provincial of Castile (1569–72 & 1582–5), was a central figure in the reform of the Order.

[37] AGS, PR, 23-53(xxv), an unsigned *memorial*, undated but early June 1569; f. 1r.

[38] *Ibid.*: '...ni a costituçion alguna de la primera instituçion ni la antigua y regular perfection y disciplina de la dicha Ordem...'. The point is reiterated further down.

by a bureaucracy obsessed with discipline and uniformity. Above all, the king had yet to grasp that it was the very absence of primordial constitutions in the Mercedarian case that had helped to thwart attempts at its reform in the past, and stood as one of the main obstacles to reform now. And it was ignorance of the major constitutional shortcomings of the Order that in 1567 caused Philip to change his stance of 1563 and declare that its projected reform would imply

> no alteration of the Order, only that it observe the same Rule and constitutions with which it was instituted by the Apostolic see in its earliest days.[39]

However, once the unfortunate legislative situation inherited by the Mercedarians had became apparent to the authorities — as it evidently had by the early 1570s — Philip felt able to break his promise and abrogate the existing constitutions as he had first implied in 1563.[40] Nevertheless, until they had been replaced, the fiction that the Albertine statutes actually dated from the foundation of the Order continued to be publicly endorsed. The very real possibility that the Order might at a stroke be denuded of the entire legislative basis for its privileges, and indeed its very existence, was clearly one that the authorities were careful to avoid. For though the 1327 constitutions were unacceptable to the crown in their structural provisions, the decrees on the life of the Order represented the only cogent Mercedarian 'observance' to which the religious could be reduced. As it turned out, the legislators of the reformed constitutions of 1588 drew heavily on the abrogated Albertine statutes in a manner reflecting the common perception of their primordial status, and in such a way as to imbue the new decrees with an essential element of continuity. By this time, moreover, the Mercedarians had begun to construct the elaborate spiritual and historical framework of the *centuria primera* to which the reformed legislation of 1588 was presented as the natural corollary. Within this vast new schemata the statutes of 1272 and 1327 were marginalized by the chronicles that began to appear from the end of the sixteenth century as mere details in the institutional

---

[39] IVDJ, env. 91, no. 500(i), f. 2v. Philip II to Diego Hurtado de Mendoza, viceroy of Catalonia, Madrid, 7th September 1567.

[40] The nuncio Castagna at least seems to have become aware of this situation by 1569. See ASV, NS, vol. 4, ff. 67r–69v, Castagna to Alessandrino, Madrid, 15th March 1569; f. 69v.

development of the Order.[41] God, it seemed to Mercedarians in the early seventeenth century, had conferred upon *their* generation the task of fulfilling the providential mission traced out for the Order four centuries earlier.

But in the 1560s the Mercedarian constitutional framework was looking increasingly inadequate. In the absolute terms laid down by Trent, the Order had no genuinely primordial legislation against which it could be reformed. Further, the inescapable implication of remarks in Philip's letter to Vargas in 1563 and in Torres' 1565 *Comentario* on the status of the constitutions was that these could be abrogated should the need arise. To members of the Mercedarian élite, as to the king himself, 'changing circumstances' had indeed made both constitutional and institutional *mudanza* highly desirable, but it remained to decide by what means and to what degree this was to be carried out. Neither the Castilian brethren nor the crown had yet seriously addressed the practicalities of reuniting the Order under the authority of the master general after nearly a century of independence. Torres' tacit recognition in the *Comentario* of the powerful regional distinctions that had coloured Mercedarian history reflects the particularist mentality of the brethren, whose allegiances did not readily cross provincial frontiers. The Mercedarians might gather once more under the authority of the master general, but in practice reform and provincial government was still considered largely a matter for the provinces themselves. The prospect of interference from a general not of the province was, as it had always been, deeply unpalatable to all concerned. The *Concordia* of 1467 had not only granted the Castilians independence from the authority of the master, but underlined certain irreconcilable provincial differences which events in the late sixteenth and early seventeenth century merely confirmed. The unity of which Torres spoke was destined to be one of institutional and to a degree spiritual and disciplinary observance, never of mind, outlook or temper.

In June 1565 the chapter provincial was celebrated at Toledo to elect Torres' successor.[42] But if Torres had hoped that the electors

---

[41] For examples of the summary treatment of these, see Tirso, *Historia*, I, pp. 152–3 & 250 respectively.

[42] Two notarial documents survive for this chapter provincial in AGS, PR, 23-53, (xvii) & (xviii). The former, dated 25th January 1566, is a declaration of Peñaranda's election, while the latter, dated 17th March 1569, is the capitular oath of obedience to him.

might endorse his new version of the constitutions along with its *Comentario* then he was to be disappointed. The Castilian brethren clearly wanted a more vigorous statement of their province's right to the government of the Order than Torres had allowed, while his outspoken remarks in the *Comentario* against ignorance and indiscipline were poorly received by members of the provincial hierarchy. In his desire to promote internal reform, Torres had made the error of lauding both the perpetuity of the generalate and the role of Barcelona as the spiritual and administrative wellspring of the Order.(10r,10v,13r) Rather than the observance of the past, Castilians wanted an expression of change for the future. Besides, the appearance of a second private version of the Mercedarian constitutions in thirty years was an uncomfortable reminder of the highly questionable status of the Order's corpus of legislation. The remarks on the 1565 edition by Carrillo, one of Torres' reformist successors, reflect the extreme anxiety felt by Mercedarians for the status of their legislation in the present climate:

> When I refer to constitutions, I mean those that are both ancient and approved by the Order [...] and not those written and printed by Mº Fray Gaspar de Torres [...] for although these are most learned and worthy of their author, they are not constitutions at all — though they have been so styled — nor have they been accepted or declared to be such [...] for neither a provincial nor a general, even with the agreement of their chapters, has the authority to make constitutions...(ii,104)

Carrillo, as we shall see, was adamant that the constitutions themselves should be tampered with no further. However, this was not intended to rule out modification of these through capitular ordinances, as he himself demonstrated as provincial a few years later. But despite this basic disagreement, Torres' work, and particularly the *Comentario*, had made a deep impression on Carrillo and the Castilian reformist community as a whole, on 'those who live in the new manner'.[43] Thus, in criticizing the *Constitutiones*, we find Carrillo employing the same language of political theory that Torres' *Comentario* brought into the mainstream of the Order's thinking: '...it is therefore obvious that, in communities, republics and orders, things made by individuals without authority are *ipso facto* odious and abhorrent...'.(ii,104) But though he rejected Torres' *Constitutiones* out of

---

[43] *Ibid.* (ii), p. 104; '...los que viven al estilo nuevo...'.

hand, Carrillo deemed the *Comentario* worthy of a place in the cell of
every friar 'for the instruction of the religious and, in some respects,
for the clarification of the *other* constitutions'.[44]

Torres' work was therefore rejected at Toledo, but one of his institutional provisions — that the tenure of the provincials be reduced
from six years to four — was passed on the understanding that the
crown had petitioned the papacy for a general bull to this effect.
Unfortunately, the bull was later withdrawn, much to the annoyance
of the new incumbent, Mº Fray Juan de Peñaranda, who considered
Torres to have cheated him out of two years of office.[45] The ensuing
rumpus drove Torres out of the Order, but his volume continued to
be widely read in Castile and elsewhere. Above all, the highly significant profession formula set out within it became standard in the
Order. By 1570 novices in Segovia were taking a fourth vow both to
redeem captives and stand surety for those whose faith was in danger:
...*et in sarracenorum potestate in pignus si necesse fuerit ad Redemptionem Christi
fidelium detentus manebo.*[46] It is therefore fitting that the reformed
statutes of 1588 prepared by Torres' famous pupil, Mº Fray Francisco Zumel, should be deeply influenced by his work of a generation
before. The new reformist tendency of the province of Castile had
made its first lasting statement.

V. *Castile on the Eve of Reform*

Yet much remained to be done. In the same *memorial* and in the others he wrote on the question of reform in 1568–9, Carrillo — who

---

[44] *Ibid.* My italics.

[45] It should be stated that the tenure of the American provincials remained of four
years until 1574.

[46] Though the Order had long been understood to have a fourth vow to redeem
and to stand hostage, this, with the exception of a nun's profession at Bérriz in 1542,
appears to be its first formulaic expression; see P.Fr. Joaquín Millán Rubio, 'El voto
Mercedario de dar la vida por los cautivos cristianos' in *Studia Silensia*, 1 (1975), pp.
113–41, & Vázquez Fernández, 'La formación en las diversas constituciones' pp.
329–31 & 334. For the Segovia vow, see AHN, Clero, vol. 13,410, f. 1r, dated 1st
January 1570. Huete had followed suit by 1572 and Zaragoza by 1577; see, respectively, *ibid.*, vol. 3320, f. 95r, & ACA, Mss.Misc., vol. 49, pp. 81–2. In Barcelona the
first such professions, which date from November or December 1572, restricted
themselves to the act of redemption itself: *et transmigrationem maris ad sarracenos causa
christianos redimendi*; ACA, Mon., vol. 2710, though the folio in question, no. 85, is
now missing.

succeeded Torres as the crown's man of confidence — set out a Castilian interpretation of the problems of the Order and the means by which they might be addressed. Above all, he was concerned to impress on the government the distinct character of Castile with regard to the rest of the Order. 'The province of Castile alone,' he declared, 'is much finer and greater than all the others put together, given the number and distinction of the houses of which it is composed', quite apart from the four sub-provinces it had established in America.[47] The province was certainly in need of reform, but its condition could not be compared with that of the Crown of Aragon. As he made clear,

> It is highly desirable that this province of Castile should be completely reformed and brought up to standard, but equally so that its affairs should not be mixed with those of Aragon, Catalonia and Valencia. (ii,103)

If, as seemed obvious, Castile was to provide the basis for the reform of the Order, then she required treatment different from that to be meted out to other provinces. The policy regarding Castile must therefore be based on the consolidation of existing gains if she were one day to undertake the reform of her sister provinces. Her acquisition of this status, Carrillo suggested,

> will not be as difficult as some believe, for much progress has already been made along this path […] quite apart from the fact that her religious are for the most part gentle and tractable, and the other provinces therefore need only be reduced to the style of this one. (ii,103)

However, though these remarks were based on an element of truth, Carrillo had presented an image of the condition of his province that is not reflected in the rest of his work. Indeed, in many respects Castile was in as ruinous a state as the Crown of Aragon.

As had been the case throughout the Order for some time, the redemptive vocation had broken down under gross peculation from commendators and prelates alike. The Castilians had conducted no ransoming expedition since the joint effort with the Aragonese in 1561–2. Carrillo laid the blame squarely on a succession of provin-

---

[47] Cited in Vázquez Núñez, ed., *La Merced a mediados*, (doc.i), p. 100. The document reproduced (pp. 100–3) is AGS, PR, 23-51(ii), an untitled *memorial* to Philip II by Mº Fray Pedro Carrillo, undated but written in the spring of 1568. References to this document (i) are henceforth given in the text.

cials, and the long tradition of embezzling redemption *limosna* (alms) that went with it.[48] The provincials, he declared, had not addressed the matter with the required diligence, for they had neither constrained commendators to gather and surrender *limosna*, nor had they put this to good use when it was collected.[49] The fruit of decades of alms collection had fallen into an unrecorded 'abyss' that, Carrillo warned the crown, it would be pointless to try to recover.(ii,106) The province, he lamented, had no idea how to draw up accounts of the *limosna* collected or even whom to approach for such information. Many of the religious implicated were dead, while others had no means of paying up even if they wanted to, such was the impoverishment of the Order. The only solution, Carrillo concluded, was to wipe the slate clean, open a new redemption book based on the monies submitted since 1565, and issue a general pardon for all past misdemeanours. Even so, chief among Carrillo's suggestions for the restoration of this, the Order's principal vocation, was his recommendation that ex-provincials should have their accounts subjected to the scrutiny of senior religious or the crown itself.(ii,107)

This situation was emblematic of the gross abuse to which the office of provincial, along with the other high posts of the Order, had traditionally lent itself, and which Carrillo was now determined to address. Along with all other religious, provincials had to be made accountable for their actions to the Order at large. As Carrillo reported,

> provincials are wont to commit outrages against individuals, against houses and against the province itself without there being any hope of redress. This is possible because the outgoing provincial remains a superior and controls the chapter, appointing and dismissing as he pleases, while keeping the provincial-elect cornered until he has received confirmation from the general.[50]

Even the then provincial, Peñaranda, the most reticent of commentators, agreed with Carrillo on the need for the formation of a committee to investigate the probity of the outgoing regime.[51] Moreover,

---

[48] It should be stated that Torres' provincialate (1559–65) appears to be an exception in this regard.

[49] AGS, PR, 23-49. Anonymous report in Carrillo's hand, undated but 1569. An apparently earlier draft is IVDJ, env. 72, II, ff. 149r–152r.

[50] AGS, PR, 23-49, f. 2r.

[51] *Ibid.*, 23-50(i), undated *memorial* of M° Fray Juan de Peñaranda to the crown, probably written in 1568–9. A shorter version with alterations is *ibid.*, 23-50(ii).

provincials gave a poor example to their charges in the private own-ership of property, one of the most noxious abuses afflicting the reli-gious life at large.[52] Incumbents were in the habit of appropriating goods and money belonging to deceased commendators to the detri-ment of their houses, one of the many sources of revenue available to them during their tenure. Prelates and commendators usually owned private land from which they could reap large incomes, along with the valuables — vestments, books, bedding, mules and the like — that were carried from house to house and circulated among the hier-archy. There can be no doubt that many senior Castilian Mercedari-ans were used to handling substantial quantities of lucre, particularly those with experience of America or 'those nurtured when there was plenty of money' in the Order, as Carrillo noted ruefully.[53] However, precious little of this seems to have been applied to the Order itself which, through fraud, neglect and over-recruitment had lately been reduced to near penury.

The sector that suffered most from this state of affairs was the growing Castilian rank and file. As commendators, following the example of their superiors, took to appropriating the revenue of their houses, so the lot of the brethren for whom they were spiritually and personally responsible began to decline. Friars were ill-housed, ill-clothed and ill-fed, while many suffered neglect in times of sickness. Commendators, said Carrillo, now surrendered for the expenses of the convent as a whole the money formerly provided just for mainte-nance of the friars.(ii,108) The practice of allowing priests to divide among themselves the earnings they received from the saying of masses provoked deep resentment among the lower brethren, who were left to make do as best they could. Under these circumstances friars were often driven to find alternative means of supplementing their pitiful allowances. The relative wealth of superiors therefore contrasted sharply with the grinding poverty suffered by the mass of this as of other orders. Although Carrillo accepted the essential rigour of conventual life, he also made clear that the welfare of the religious was a commendator's principal domestic responsibility. As he reminded visitors and provincials, the erection of conventual build-ings by commendators was invariably founded on the hunger and neglect of the brethren.(ii,109)

---

[52] *Ibid.*, 23-49, f. 3r.
[53] *Ibid.*

To the differences in mentality between reformist and conservative brethren, as well as those between the hierarchy and the commendators that Torres had identified, were therefore added tensions
between the haves and have-nots of conventual life. The inevitable
consequence of this situation was a deep rupture in the social composition of the Order, as much in Castile as in the Crown of Aragon.
It was this circumstance that, in its varying manifestations, lay at the
heart of the moral and disciplinary decline of this order as of so
many others, and presented the greatest single obstacle to its reform.
Like Torres before him, Carrillo recognized that the basis of this
decline rested on the increasingly disjointed and stratified pattern of
Mercedarian life. In Castile, disagreement among the provincial
hierarchy meant that time and again important capitular ordinances
went unobserved by the brethren at large. The enforcement of discipline and indeed the whole legislative process itself had been deval-
ued by the abuses of provincials and the regularity with which they
set about revoking the ordinances of their predecessors. 'Because of
this,' Carrillo noted, 'there is neither the discipline nor the reformation in this Order that laws and statutes have been passed to bring
about.'[54]

But even when it agreed on statutes in chapter, the provincial hierarchy had few effective means of enforcing them at conventual level.
Centralizing authority was held in contempt by commendators and
friars who recognized both the impotence and the inconsistency of
capitular ordinances. As one observer declared,

> There have been provincials who, in chapter or during visitations,
> have laid down precepts as to what should be observed. But once they
> leave office the friars return to their old ways, because laws are of little
> use if there is no one to execute them. And although problems might
> be remedied and well provided for in Castile at one moment, this situ-
> ation never lasts because it is against the will of almost all religious.
> The reformation of this Order has this particular difficulty: that friars
> who do what they are ordered are nowhere to be found…[55]

Harsh though this judgement may be, it accurately identifies the signal failure of the hierarchy to bridge the gap between its own mental-

---

[54] *Ibid.*, 23-49, f. 2v.
[55] IVDJ, env. 72, II, ff. 73v–74r. The same general point is made regarding the
Aragonese brethren by the Dominican M° Fray Pedro de Salamanca to Ormaneto,
ibid., ff. 82r–83r, Valencia, 2nd November 1575; f. 82r.

ity and that of the rank and file. Local power rested in the hands of commendators who controlled conventual funds and might spend decades ensconced in a single house. Aping the abuses of the hierarchy, commendators were often in a poor position to enforce ordinances on their religious, who were in turn disinclined to bring abuses to the attention of the authorities. As Carrillo declared of the rank and file,

> the religious are generally docile and submissive people who with a little discipline will do as they are ordered, and if they are not more reformed than they are then the blame lies with their superiors. (ii.107)

To the nameless majority of Mercedarians for whom the religious life was a more mundane exercise, the promulgation of reform decrees was therefore received with complete inertia. Such were the obstacles that confronted Carrillo and his like. on the eve of the reform of the Order.

However, these problems did not prevent a massive recruitment of religious in Castile which began in the middle decades of the sixteenth century and continued among all the orders for 200 years, often in defiance of the wider demographic conjuncture. There are no figures for the period immediately preceding the reform of the Order, but it seems that between 1553 and c.1576 the province of Castile grew from approximately 330 religious in thirty-four houses to no less than 828 members in thirty-five houses, not counting its American dependencies.[56] The development of the Order in the Indies naturally stimulated the expansion of its presence in Andalusia, often with men from Castile. Already in 1569 Carrillo, a native of La Rioja, was complaining of a constant drain of religious from Castile to the South — religious who were then loath to return because, as he noted, 'they find Andalusia a land more to their taste'.(ii,110) A less acceptable side of Mercedarian mobility was the habit of delinquent religious taking refuge in neighbouring provinces of the Order or elsewhere to escape the wrath of their superiors. This, the bane of the Order, Tàrrega and later Tirso blamed on the divisions imposed by the *Concordia* of 1467, and it is clear that through

---

[56] See Appendix III. The 1553 figures are based on those given in Vázquez Núñez, ed., *La Merced a mediados*, pp. 95–7. For the 1576 figures, see IVDJ, env. 72, II, ff. 139r & 140r. The new foundation was that of Madrid in 1564, and the house at Badajoz, not included in either estimate, is added here.

such channels the generals continued to wield some influence in Castilian affairs.[57]

Recruitment on the scale experienced in Castile in the second half of the century became a severe burden on the financial resources of the province. In mid-century habits were being conferred indiscriminately on large numbers of impoverished men who often came to the Order without a dowry. The inevitable effect, as Carrillo saw it, was that 'houses never prosper and expenditure is forever rising'.(ii,109) At the important convent of Huete, we are told, recruitment had been such that the resources of four similar houses would not be sufficient to support the brethren. Neither were those being recruited likely to be any adornment to the province. As Carrillo lamented, 'the truth is that these are not people whose intellect, wealth or other attributes are liable to provoke envy at having them'.(ii,110) 'The Order,' he said, 'is full of ignoramuses, who in some places are not taught at all, and where they are taught it is only at great cost and effort to the Order.'(ii,109) The solution to these problems, Carrillo maintained, lay in the implementation of higher standards for the recruitment of novices, including denying entry to any without the approval of the provincial himself. Ordinances to this effect had been issued many times in the past, only to be waived by provincials or disregarded by those commendators who recognized the opportunities for exploiting the novices in their care. Meanwhile, groaned Carrillo, 'it is apparent that the numbers and ignorance of the friars continues to grow at the expense of conventual finances'.(ii,109)

Ignorance was of particular concern to Carrillo, a leading member of that generation of Castilian religious for whom study was an essential element in the reform of the Order and the basis for advancement within it.[58] He was appalled at the restrictions that Peñaranda had seen fit to place on the electoral rights of graduates at chapters provincial. Under such circumstances, Carrillo warned, the election of provincials would be left mostly to the commendators, 'of whom half are so ignorant as never to have studied theology, which is a source of great shame and disgrace'.(ii,110) Although the province of

---

[57] See *ibid.*, ff. 482r–491r; Tàrrega to the nuncio, Niccolò Ormaneto, undated but Madrid, shortly before August 1573, f. 489r, and Tirso, *Historia*, II, p. 11. On the influence of the generals, see Vázquez Núñez, ed., *La Merced a mediados*, (doc.i), pp. 100–1 (or AGS, PR, 23-51(ii), f. 1r).

[58] For a 17th-century assessment of Carrillo's role in promoting the academic life of the Order during his first provincialate (1569–72), see BNM, ms. 2684, f. 37r.

Castile had gone to great lengths to establish a core of educated men in its ranks, neither here nor elsewhere had learning yet established itself as the essential qualification for promotion in the Order. Moreover, it appears that, in their anxiety to improve their image, the Castilians had been conferring the degrees of *presentado* and *maestro* on religious without due rigour.[59]

Carrillo has left a highly critical picture of Castilian conventual life on the eve of the reform of the Order, though no doubt it is one that reflects his own reformist agenda. Nevertheless, the Order continued to exercise a powerful attraction for young Castilians during the middle decades of the sixteenth century, partly no doubt for the very pattern of life which Carrillo and his like were determined to stamp out. It is impossible to assess the reasons behind an individual's entry into the Mercedarian Order. The spiritual and vocational impetus was of course present, but there can be no doubt that many recognized in the Order those opportunities for sustenance, contentment, profit or advancement unavailable to them — for whatever reason — in other congregations and walks of life. For, in its own way, the Mercedarian province of Castile, like the Kingdom itself, had entered the most dynamic period of its history. It was on the basis of the great and as yet untapped spiritual, human and financial potential of their province that the Castilian élite now felt able to challenge for the leadership of the Order. As Carrillo indicated,

> we have lost count of the years that have passed since the general was not a Catalan, which circumstance [...] is perhaps one of the principal reasons why it has become imperative to attempt the reform [of the Order].(i,100)

Against this design the Aragonese hierarchy had the weight of legality and tradition behind it, though this the Castilians were determined to reverse.

VI. *The Crown of Aragon on the Eve of Reform*

Regrettable though the problems of the province of Castile were, they do not bear comparison with those of the Crown of Aragon. To the reformers, the condition of the brethren in these parts and the

---

[59] AGS, PR, 23-212. Untitled *memorial* by Cristóbal de Rojas y Sandoval, bishop of Córdoba, to Philip II, undated but 1568–9, f. 5r–v.

malaise that had settled over the Order as a whole was a reflection of
the utter dissolution into which the Mercedarian high office had fall-
en. As Carrillo made clear,

> Although it is true that many other things are necessary to achieve the
> desired condition, the principal and most important matter is that of
> the general as head [of the Order].(i,100)[60]

Echoing the traditional ideal of *reformatio tam in capite quam in membris,*
Carrillo added that

> if the Order is to be reformed, then it is essential that the head be
> included along with the rest of the Order; because unless the head be
> reformed, the members will not be properly reformed either.(i,101)

To Carrillo, one of the central problems was the life tenure of the
generalcy and the sense of complete unaccountability this imparted
to the incumbents. As he declared,

> the office of general is perpetual, and recognizes neither superior
> authority nor the restrictions against excess to which other offices are
> subject. This circumstance causes generals to concern themselves
> rather less with the common good of the Order than would be the case
> if they were obliged to pay respect or render account to a body, or if
> their office were temporary.(i,100)

Moreover, the masters general had grown accustomed to living in the
lap of luxury. Most resided in an extensive suite of rooms in the priory of Barcelona, where they were attended by a host of secular servants. In respect of the Lordship of Algar and the authority they
enjoyed over the conjoined spiritual and temporal traditions in the
Order, the masters had adopted the title of *senyor,* much to the disgust
of the reformers. The generals, Tirso lamented, had become secularized to such a degree that

> they behaved like bishops or titled nobility, enjoying sumptuous cells
> and journeys upon which money was expended superfluously, calling
> themselves Barons, Lords of vassals and attending royal palaces rather
> than to their observant obligations.[61]

As one commentator put it, 'vive el general poco religiosamente'; one
finds it hard to disagree.[62]

---

[60] This view is shared by Philip II in a letter to Zúñiga, AMAE, SS, leg. 34, ff.
8r–9v, Madrid, 19th August 1568; f. 8v.
[61] Tirso, *Historia,* I, p. 466.
[62] IVDJ, env. 72, II, f. 73r.

As we have already seen, the abuse of the office of general was nothing new in the Order. The schism of 1317 had originated in Barcelona and it is not surprising that the priory should eventually acquire a dominant role in Mercedarian affairs. By the early fifteenth century this domination had become institutionalized to the extent that the office of general developed into a virtual perquisite of the priory of Barcelona. Of the fifteen generals who held office in the 170 years before the reform of the Order, no less than eleven were sons or former priors of Barcelona. However, in recent times this succession had been prolonged not only as a result of the inequitable provisions in the constitutions, but because of the coercion and violence increasingly inflicted on electors by the conventuals of Barcelona. The Castilians had long suffered duress at the chapters general, but by the 1530s this was being meted out to the electors of neighbouring provinces as well. At the chapter general of 1535 the Valencian electors Fray Jerónimo Pérez and Fra Vicent Murta apparently had to flee the priory for their lives after refusing to cast their votes as demanded.(263r)

Such circumstances no doubt reflected the frustration felt by Catalans after the adverse judgement of the *Concordia* with Castile in 1532, but the result was a gradual souring of relations between Catalonia and the provinces that remained under the thrall of the masters general. A particular source of resentment in the Aragonese provinces was the generals' habit of claiming inheritance to the effects — *espolio* — of deceased commendators. Through this 'gran tyrania' the priory of Barcelona enriched itself in books, vestments and money at the expense of its subject houses.(263v) Like other offices, the vacant commandery was then sold in perpetuity to the highest bidder or filled through a client network. For it became the aim of the prior of Barcelona to secure, through bribery and coercion, the votes of the electors general on the death of the master, and on this, and the election of the prior himself, Mercedarian politics in the Crown of Aragon now turned.

In these unfavourable conditions provincial government and conventual discipline had almost completely collapsed, a fate shared by many congregations in these parts. Few chapters provincial had been held or visitations conducted in the decades preceding the reform of the Order. Conventual account books were almost non-existent, and friars openly cohabited with women and engaged in trade like seculars. Many of the brethren owned swords, pistols or blunderbusses which, as one might expect, they found it necessary to bear on their travels. The lack of care extended to the lesser brethren both in sickness and in health had caused many to desert the Order. As a result the Mercedarian population of the Crown of Aragon remained static while that of Castile was multiplying. In the early 1570s the provinces of Catalonia, Valencia and Aragon-Navarre retained a total of around 300 religious, unchanged from 1547.[63]

As in Castile, the first casualty of relaxation in discipline had been the work of redemption.(260r–262v) After the successful joint expedition to Algiers in 1561–2, the general Me Fra Miquel Puig obtained permission to preach a bull of redemption through the Crown of Aragon in 1563. Over the next few years this netted Puig a total of 7500 *lliures* in the Kingdom of Valencia alone, and he died leaving 'thousands of ducats' of redemption *limosna* — monies destined never to be applied to the ends for which they had been given.(265v) Realizing that funds were being misappropriated, bishops began to ban Mercedarian *baciners* (secular alms collectors) from parish churches and refuse licences to preach the redemption in their dioceses.(261r) Moreover, the business of preaching had been left to ignorant and dissolute religious who were polluting the name of the Order through town and country. The office of redemptor, among those sold by the general to the highest bidder, was coveted as an opportunity for mercantile profit. Constant friction between Mercedarians and commissaries of the *Cruzada* tax reflect growing anger in official circles at misuse of alms and collecting privileges as the Muslim offensive broke against the Spanish coast.[64] There can be no doubt that, in the eyes of many, it was this gross neglect of the Order's principal vocation that called most insistently for its reform.

As the Order fell into a sharp decline in the Crown of Aragon, the incipient academic movement of the first half of the sixteenth century came to an end. The passage of years had hardened attitudes among many of the leading Aragonese Mercedarians against the reformist values traditionally espoused by learned members of the Order.

---

[63] Figures from *ibid.*, ff. 34r–36r, untitled summary by the Dominican M° Fray Guillermo Montaña, commissary apostolic of the Order in the Crown of Aragon; undated but *c.*1573. These figures do not include the houses of Perpignan (province of Catalonia) and Oran (Valencia). That at Palma de Mallorca still belonged to the French province; see Appendix III.

[64] See, for example, *ibid.*, f. 270r–v. Pedro Joan de San Cilia & Antonio Torrella to Francisco de Soto Salazar, bishop of Segorbe, Mallorca, 7th June 1574.

Among these was Me Fra Pere Joan de Tàrrega, a protégé of Fray Jerónimo Pérez whom he succeeded both as a professor at the Jesuit college-university at Gandía and as commendator of Valencia. Until his death in 1575 Tàrrega was the leading reformist figure in the Crown of Aragon and a sworn enemy of the Barcelona régime, against which he penned a succession of damning *memoriales*. Although there can be no doubt that Tàrrega's mostly anonymous work was informed by considerable personal animus, his sense of outrage at the decline of intellectual standards among his Aragonese brethren comes through sincerely enough. As he said, 'it is the greatest pity in the world to see that the majority of the brethren of the Crown of Aragon are barely able to read or count or conduct ceremonies as friars should'.(266v) This situation, he continued, had been brought about through complete neglect of the noviciate, while many of the Aragonese hierarchy were shamefully ignorant of Latin. There were, he lamented, very few 'frares Theolechs' in the Crown of Aragon, and the educated few had suffered persecution and abuse at the hands of their unlettered brethren.(266v) The hierarchy, he implied, were afraid of the example educated men might give to others. This circumstance no doubt explained the failure of the Aragonese to set up colleges for the study of grammar, logic and theology, as had been repeatedly ordained in past chapters general and 'as is the case in our monasteries in Castile'.(256r) As Tàrrega made clear, in the Crown of Aragon the Order had ceased to make any provision for the education of its religious.

VII. *On the Threshold*

It is perhaps not going too far to say that the religious life of the Mercedarian Order had completely broken down throughout much of its range. But although many were convinced of the desperate need for the situation to be remedied, there were few obvious means of bringing this about. For in seeking to address the condition of their Order, Mercedarians found themselves confronted by many of the dilemmas inherent in monastic reform. The reform of a religious order required the supreme effort of reinterpreting and indeed reconciling its spiritual and institutional past in terms of the perceived requirements of the present and the future. Such endeavours were infallibly shaped by the environment and the criteria that had made reform itself imperative, and the Mercedarian case was no exception. Thus, although Carrillo claimed that 'reform means reduction to the primordial institution'(ii.105), bare practicalities dictated that the Order could not simply be reformed to the letter of its constitutions. But how might it be reformed in such a way as to preserve the *spirit* of these, without extinguishing what was seen as the essence of Mercedarian 'observance'? It was this problem that troubled the Castilian brethren in particular on the eve of the reform.

All reformist Mercedarians were agreed that, ultimately, the root of the ills of the Order lay in the constitutions. As Carrillo thundered,

> Of course, the origin of all these problems is the tyranny and duress inflicted [on the Order] by the constitutions, which were wrought by Catalans from that house of Barcelona. Rather than monastic govern-ment, their intention appears to have been that of establishing lordship and dominion [over the Order] in the manner of the generals and commendators of military orders.(i,101)

Moreover, not only was the institutionalized domination of the gener-als 'notoriously obstructive of reform'(i,101), but circumstances had changed in Castile's favour since the offending constitutions had been formulated. As he declared, 'when these particular constitutions were set down there was not the greatness in the province of Castile and those of the Indies that there now is'.(i,101) For, in practice, Carrillo — like the crown — perceived reform in institutional terms, and it was his aim that Castile's superior condition should be reflected in a greater say in the affairs of the Order as a whole. However, his con-cern for the status of the constitutions caused him to recommend that where possible this be brought about within the existing legal frame-work, rather than through the formulation of yet more statutes:

> It is preferable that there be no mounting up of statutes, ordinances, laws and rigours beyond those we already have in our constitutions, and that these be limited and moderated so that they may be more easily borne.(ii,103)

Tàrrega, however, was much less restrained. For him the Albertine constitutions were ripe for abrogation:

> There are many in our Order who labour under a certain delusion, namely that nothing in the constitutions can be touched; but the con-stitutions themselves say that new constitutions can be made in chap-ter, and indeed the ordinances of the last two or three chapters general all enjoy such status.(265r)

Unfortunately for Carrillo, it was Tàrrega's outlook that was to be adopted by the authorities leading the reform of the Order, and not his own. For in delivering the matter to the crown, Carrillo and his like had surrendered the few claims to direct the reform of their Order that remained to them.

CHAPTER FIVE

THE PATH TO REFORM (1567–70)

*Since the religious of this Order do not outwardly display their unease,
I suspect that they bear it in their spirits. This, it seems to me, would
cease if they understood just what was required of them.*[1]

With the conceptual framework for the reform of the Order in place
it remained for this to be translated into a workable scheme.
Although few documents have survived to shed light on the progress
of events within the Order itself during the mid 1560s, it is clear that
the impact of the Tridentine decrees was felt as keenly in the Crown
of Aragon as it had been in Castile, albeit in rather different ways.[2]
There is only circumstantial evidence, but it seems that the Catalan
general, Me Fra Miquel Puig, recognized in the decrees on monastic
reform set out in session **XXV** the revocation of the *Concordia* of
1467.[3] On this basis Puig apparently decided to steal a march on the
Castilians, whom he no doubt suspected of manipulating royal
reform policy to their own ends, and himself play the new climate of
reform to the advantage of the generalcy. It is not clear exactly when
Puig began this process, but he was represented in Rome by *procuradores* (procurators) from at least July 1565 and the matter was
apparently still being debated here in 1567.[4] After arranging the dispatch to Rome and Madrid of a succession of *memoriales* on the unreformed condition of Castile, Puig, we are told, asked the crown to
endorse his petition to visit the province.[5] Unlikely as it seems, he

---

[1] AGS, E°, leg. 150, no. 59. Gaspar de Zúñiga y Avellaneda, archbishop of Santiago, to Philip II, Santiago, 14th October 1568.

[2] Regrettably, the section in Antillón's highly informative ms. *Epitome*, vol. I(ii) covering the period July(?) 1561 to September 1567 had been lost by the time Arqués y
Jover made the APV & BPC copies in the late 18th century.

[3] *Ibid.*, pp. 1358 & 1414. The crucial chapter in the *Decretum de regularibus et monialibus* is no. 22: 'The Decrees touching the Reformation of Regulars shall be carried
into execution at once by all'; *Canons and Decrees*, p. 252.

[4] AGN, Clero, vol. 416. Fra Thomàs Serralta to Puig, Rome, 29th July and 17th
August 1565.

[5] Remón, *Historia*, II, ff. 278r–279r. No such *memoriales* appear to have survived.

may have been successful in this for, according to Remón, early in 1567 Philip wrote to Pius V and the cardinal protector of Spain, Francisco Pacheco, asking that a bull empowering Puig to visit the whole order be conceded.[6] Whatever the case may be, no such bull was ever issued, nor is it likely that it would have been given much consideration in the prevailing circumstances.

I. *The Campaign Opens, 1567–8*

On 16th April 1567, as we have seen, the general briefs *Superioribus mensibus* and *In prioribus* entrusted the reform of the Mercedarians to the bishops, with the assistance of two Dominican visitors in each diocese. Along with the Carmelites and the Trinitarians, the Mercedarians were to be reduced, as a summary of the main brief put it, 'to the true observance of their orders, in accordance with each of their constitutions'.[7] However, the aims of the campaign were in practice rather conservative. As Philip declared in a letter of *instrucción* to the bishops,

> There must be no movement [of friars] from one order to another, nor changes either to the Rule, Constitutions, or structure of the orders. Rather, it must be the principal aim [of the visitation] that all these things be preserved as hitherto, removing only those abuses, excesses and disturbances that exist and have existed in the orders concerned.[8]

It took some months of covert organization before the briefs were put into effect. We have few details of their implementation among the Castilian Mercedarians, but it appears that Philip intended the reform of the three orders to begin simultaneously and proceed along the same lines throughout his kingdoms.[9] Not long after the brief was

---

[6] *Ibid.*, ff. 286r *et seq.* Antillón also alludes to this; see APV, ms. *Epitome*, I(ii), p. 1358 *et seq.* Provincial rivalry has caused the significance of this affair to be greatly exaggerated by Mercedarian chroniclers.

[7] *CDEESS*, II, pp. 72–5, Requeséns to Philip II, Rome, 16th March 1567, where the three orders, along with the Canons Regular of St Augustine, are referred to as 'without observant religious'; p. 72.

[8] Cited in Steggink, *La reforma del Carmelo español*, 2nd edn., p. 306. This document, dated 30th August 1567, was printed in Madrid; a copy survives in the Bibliothèque Publique et Universitaire de Genève, Collection Edouard Favre, vol. 82, ff. 5r–6v.

[9] See AGS, PR, 23-85, ff. 5v–6r, Philip II to Fray Juan de Salinas, Dominican provincial of Castile, Madrid, 14th July 1567, in which Salinas is summoned to court to discuss the appointment of Castilian commissaries.

issued Puig was summoned to Madrid to discuss the reform of his Order, but he justifiably pleaded age and infirmity and never appeared.[10] However, the crown had already begun to move, and the suppression of the Benedictine priory of Sant Pau del Camp in Barcelona the previous year and the imposition by force of the Observant rule on the Conventual Franciscans in May 1567 had provided a foretaste of things to come.[11] Having petitioned the papacy to allow Catalan religious in general no recourse to Rome, in August Philip turned his attention to the situation of the three orders in the Crown of Aragon.[12] The reform process opened with the dispatch of the general *instrucción* to the Catalan bishops, followed on 6th and 7th September by the mass of documentation upon which the coming reform campaign would be based.[13] Surviving records have left a clear impression not only of the gruelling and repetitive administrative process that underlay the reform of religious orders under state sponsorship, but of the serious shortage of basic information that attended these first initiatives.

The viceroys lay at the hub of the process. On 6th September Philip wrote to his lieutenant in Catalonia, Diego Hurtado de Mendoza, informing him of his plans for the reform of the three orders and enjoining him to support the bishops and Dominicans who were to carry it out on a diocesan basis.[14] The entire preliminary documentation relating to the Catalan religious was to be sent to the chancery in Barcelona for Mendoza to distribute as instructed by the crown. From the most complex memoranda addressed to the bishops to the plethora of letters to local officials commanding support for the 'reformaçion' of the houses in their midst, all was to pass through the viceroy's hands before being allocated at the appointed time. The brief itself was a matter of the utmost secrecy, whose contents could

---

[10] IVDJ, env. 91, no. 500(i), f. 2r. Philip II to Diego Hurtado de Mendoza, viceroy of Catalonia, Madrid, 7th September 1567. The validity of Puig's excuse was apparently verified by the bishop of Barcelona, Guillem Cassador, and Mendoza himself.

[11] For the general situation see Bada, *Situació religiosa*, pp. 235–40, esp. 239.

[12] *CDEESS*, IV, xxxv.

[13] The *instrucción* covering the reform of the Mercedarians does not appear to have survived, but one of its final clauses outlining the ultimate objectives of the visitation is cited in ASZ, carp. 165, no. 137, untitled and anonymous *parecer* to the crown prepared by a Castilian Mercedarian in *c*.1571; f. 2r.

[14] Copies of fourteen letters, contingency or otherwise, are in ACA, RC, vol. 4351, ff. 201r–216r, dated Madrid, 6th & 7th September 1567.

only be divulged piecemeal for fear of warning local authorities or other congregations of the crown's designs.[15]

Apart from the viceroy, the leading players in the campaign were bishop Cassador of Barcelona and the Dominican provincial of the Crown of Aragon, Fray Juan Ladrón. On 6th September Philip informed Ladrón that every Catalan bishop had been instructed to send him lists of the houses to be reformed in his diocese.[16] In accordance with the briefs, the provincial was then required to appoint two of his religious as reformers of the houses involved in each diocese. Both secrecy and haste were deemed essential, so that those delegated could meet the bishops to whom they were responsible before embarking on their missions punctually and without warning on the start date: Sunday, 5th October 1567.[17] Bishops were requested to conduct visitations personally where possible, and always in the company of the Dominicans, though the episcopal presence was in practice delegated.[18] Requests for compliance and assistance were prepared for the religious communities themselves,[19] for the *justicias* (judges) and *jurados* (parish representatives) of towns and cities in or near where they were to be found, and for the *diputats* in the case of Catalonia.[20]

However, for all his organization, Philip had from the outset to admit his ignorance as to the exact number of houses involved in each diocese, though the crown seems to have reached a provisional figure of around fifty-six for the three orders in the Tarraconensian province as a whole.[21] As ever, one of the greatest obstacles to the crown's reform initiatives was the difficulty of obtaining even the most basic information on local conditions. It is therefore inevitable

---

[15] IVDJ, env. 91, no. 500(i), f. 2r, & no. 502, f. 2r. The latter is from Philip II to the Catalan bishops, Madrid, 6th September 1567.

[16] ASZ, carp. 163, no. 2. Madrid, 6th September 1567.

[17] Those appointed for the diocese of Barcelona were Fray Lorenzo López, prior of Barcelona, the Castilian Fray Pedro de Salamanca, rector of his order's *studium generale* in Valencia, and, most significantly, the then prior of Puigcerdà, Fray Guillermo Montaña, who here began a long and momentous association with the Order. For details of all three, see P.Fr. Laureano Torres, 'Pedro de Salamanca, O.P., reformador de la Merced' in *Estudios*, 38 (1982), pp. 85–96.

[18] AGN, Clero, vol. 402. Undated brief (but 1567) addressed to bishop Guillem Cassador for the reform of the Mercedarians.

[19] ASZ, carp. 163, no. 8. Madrid, 7th September 1567.

[20] *Ibid.*, no. 7. Madrid, 6th September 1567.

[21] IVDJ, env. 91, nos. 502, f. 2r, & 500(i), f. 1v respectively. Some houses were indeed forgotten by the authorities and had to be provided for later.

that the crown regarded these first visitations as an exercise in reconnaissance and intelligence-gathering as much as of actual reform. In November Philip felt obliged to write to Mendoza asking him to submit precise details of those Catalan houses as yet 'unreformed' with a view to dealing with them quickly.[22] Yet within a few weeks he had sent what must have been a huge questionnaire to the Catalan bishops requesting detailed information on the rules, constitutions life and property of the orders concerned.[23] As Philip pointed out to the bishops, their presence on the spot permitted them to discuss and evaluate affairs with much greater facility than the policy-makers in Madrid.[24] However, when Philip returned to this matter in June 1568 he had yet to receive a single one of the reports demanded the previous November. Nothing could alter the fact that monastic reform in rural Spain was, and remained, a leap in the dark.

The visitation of the Catalan Mercedarians reflects this general picture. Among the letters drafted by the crown in early September was one addressed to Puig in Barcelona, confiding in his support and stressing that Pius V (rather than Philip himself) had made provision for the 'visitation and reform of the monasteries of your Order'.[25] Philip placed Puig under the authority of the viceroy from whom he was to receive this letter shortly before the all-important date, 5th October 1567. With his characteristic eye for detail, Philip intended that, in the presence of bishop Guillem Cassador, Mendoza should convey to Puig the king's hope for the successful outcome of the reform of the Order, the more so 'since it was founded by our predecessors, the Most Serene Kings of Aragon'.[26] However, there are few details of the progress of the campaign. Having visited the priory of Barcelona, Cassador entrusted the visitation of the Mercedarian houses in the diocese to the prior himself, Mᵉ Fra Maties Papiol,

---

[22] ASZ, carp. 163, no. 9. Madrid, 22nd November 1567.

[23] The contents of this questionnaire, dated 30th November 1567, are summarized in ACA, RC, vol. 4352, ff. 118v–121r. Philip II to Catalan bishops, Madrid, 14th June 1568.

[24] *Ibid.*, f. 120v.

[25] ASZ, carp. 163, no. 4. Madrid, 7th September 1567. This was apparently followed on 8th September by letters to the Barcelona community and to the prior himself, Mᶜ Fra Maties Papiol, to all commendators in the Crown of Aragon and to the Order at large. Reported in IVDJ, env. 72, II, f. 492r.

[26] IVDJ, env. 91, no. 500(i), f. 2v.

thereby defeating the object of the exercise.[27] This seems to be typical
of the mismanagement and general lack of interest that characterized
the reform campaign in Catalonia at least, while the transfer of archbishop Ferran de Loaces from the see of Tarragona to that of Valencia in April 1567 deprived it of a motivating figure. Among the areas
in which Philip found his bishops wanting in June 1568 was their failure to report on the projected suppression of several minor Mercedarian houses in rural Catalonia.[28] His inordinate concern to real-
locate their piteously small rents reflects the generally confused
impression still held by the crown of the Aragonese Mercedarians.
The battle to reform the Order would be fought principally in its
major urban houses — particularly Barcelona — not in its crumbling
and virtually deserted rural patrimony. In this sense the visitation
campaign also reflects the wholly unrealistic approach to monastic
reform under which the crown was still labouring.

We have no information at all regarding the progress of reform in
the province of Aragon-Navarre, where Fernando de Aragón, archbishop of Zaragoza, seems not to have been involved. In the province
of Valencia, visitations were begun with Dominican assistance under
the new archbishop, Ferran de Loaces, though very little had been
achieved by the time of his death in February 1568.[29] However, from
1569 the reform of that province was taken up by his great successor,
Patriarch Juan de Ribera.

Details of the implementation of the briefs are very scarce for Castile,
where the same arrangement of joint visitation by episcopal delegates
and Dominicans was adopted.[30] Peñaranda's visitations of New Castile
and Andalusia during mid 1567, along with those of his secretary, Pº
Fray Francisco Maldonado, through Old Castile and León, appear to
have formed the prelude to this campaign.[31] There are very few notices
of official reform activity in 1567, and all we can say with certainty is
that the houses at Soria and Raíces (Asturias) were visited by the bishops

---

[27] See Vázquez Núñez, *Mercedarios ilustres*, pp. 257 & 263, and for Papiol in general
ibid., pp. 255–8. For evidence of Cassador's involvement, see ASZ, carp. 165, no.
136, an unsigned letter in support of Papiol written to Philip II. Undated but
Barcelona, *c*.April 1568.

[28] ACA, RC, vol. 4352, f. 120r–v.

[29] IVDJ, env. 72, II, ff. 224r–236v. Mᶜ Fra Pere Joan de Tàrrega, probably to the
nuncio, Niccolò Ormaneto, undated but Madrid, late 1573; f. 226r.

[30] See, however, AGS, PR, 104 (i) & (ii); this reference is owed to García Oro &
Portela Silva, 'Felipe II y la reforma de las órdenes redentoras', p. 10.

[31] See Vázquez Núñez, *Mercedarios ilustres*, p. 310.

of Osma and Oviedo respectively before the end of the year.[32] Nothing further is heard until June 1568, on which more in due course.

II. *Reaction and Evasion in Catalonia, 1567–8*

The reform initiative had hardly begun before it was overtaken by a succession of important developments within the Order itself. No doubt sensing that a storm was about to break over his provinces, the ailing Puig summoned a chapter general at Barcelona for 21st September 1567, two weeks before the start of the royal reform campaign.[33] Letters of convocation were sent out as usual and all provinces were represented except for Castile. Informed of the convocation by the viceroy, Philip decided not to make a stand against it, declaring that 'those who will gather there are not so important as to be able greatly to impede the reformation'.[34] The years to come would reveal this to be a gross miscalculation on his part.

The ordinances passed at the chapter — titled 'Acts and New Constitutions, along with a Confirmation of Old Constitutions' — were indeed a mixture of old and new.[35] There was a strong element of continuity with the previous chapter general of 1561 and, now as then, Puig attempted to impart a sense of his leadership and example in the reform of the Order. However, unlike 1561, this leadership was now implicitly extended to cover the province of Castile:

> We order, desire and command that all the provinces and each individual house in this Order be visited yearly by a person or persons approved by the Most Reverend Lord General...[36]

---

[32] AGS, E°, leg. 161, no. 120. There may well have been activity in the archdiocese of Burgos and the diocese of Salamanca also; see ff. 3r, 5r & 7r–v.

[33] Given Puig's infirmity the chapter appears to have been presided over by the Catalan diffinitor Fra Cristòfor Balla, who was accorded the general's faculties. See IVDJ, env. 72, II, f. 343r, Barcelona, 21st September 1567.

[34] ACA, RC, vol. 4351, f. 216r–v. Philip II to Mendoza, Zarzuela, 19th September 1567.

[35] The *synodalia* in Latin are in ACA, Mon., vol. 2667, ff. 311r–337v. As in 1561, the *acta* were printed, though no copies appear to have survived. A rather different set of *acta* are reproduced in Castilian in APV, Antillón, ms. *Epitome*, I(ii), pp. 1351–7, which may reflect the printed version.

[36] Cited in APV, Antillón, ms. *Epitome*, I(ii), p. 1355. It should be made clear that this citation does not appear in the *acta* in ACA, Mon., vol. 2667. What does appear, however, is the same general reform ordinance as that set out in the 1561 *acta*, which makes no mention of Castile.

The responsibility for reform was placed squarely on the provincials, but characteristically the delegates seem to have perceived their duties as extending little further than moving troublesome religious from one house to another, 'so that all unsavoury suspicions be brought to an end'.[37] Not for the first time, a chapter had approached the business of reform with greater concern for the Order's image than for lasting internal improvement. Although several of the problems later identified in Tàrrega's *memoriales* were addressed — conventual finances, friars' pittances and fugitives — the Aragonese had again neither provided sure means for their improvement nor confronted the serious social and institutional problems that underlay them. Even so, it is clear from later visitations that the ordinances passed at this chapter made at least some impact in the Crown of Aragon.

However, while the delegates at Barcelona were no doubt concerned to pass improving ordinances, the reason behind Puig's convocation of the chapter was to prepare his territories for the long reform campaign that must shortly be unleashed against them. To this end the chapter made several hard-headed provisions for the trials that lay ahead. Recognizing the strong regional identity that had lately asserted itself among the Mercedarians of the Crown of Aragon, Puig granted its component provinces the right of appointing a *procurador* empowered to represent the interests of each before secular and ecclesiastical authority. Over these Puig placed a single *procurador general* vested with some of the general's most significant powers to act in emergencies. Aware that the office of general would be one of the first targets of the reformers, Puig granted the *procurador general* the freedom — should the need arise — of mortgaging the Order's property to fund those 'lawsuits now being contested, those shortly to be brought, and those expected to be held in the Order'.[38] As in the past, the aim was, through litigation, to shipwreck the reform process on the tangled reef of monastic privilege. The first incumbent was the Catalan Fra Pere Castelló, prior of Sant Ramon Nonat.[39]

In Castile, meanwhile, Peñaranda summoned the provincial hier-

---

[37] Cited in *ibid.*, p. 1356.
[38] *Ibid.*, p. 1358.
[39] Castelló's *poder* as *procurador* granting him the faculty to defend the Order before all tribunals is reproduced in *ibid.*, pp. 1358–9.

archy to Seville for consultation.[40] As a result of discussions held here, on 18th October Maldonado was instructed to proceed to Rome as *procurador* in order to represent his province before the papacy. It is not clear what the exact nature of Maldonado's mission to Rome was, but the Catalans came to believe that he had been dispatched expressly to put an end to the life tenure of the generalcy.[41] He received his authority in Salamanca on 4th November and set out towards Catalonia three days later. Reaching Barcelona at the end of the month, he discovered that Puig had died on the 22nd at the age of nearly seventy. Maldonado momentarily considered postponing his journey to await further instructions, but letters from Peñaranda reporting the Castilian cause to be completely undefended in Rome decided him. Having written to Peñaranda he embarked for Italy bearing dispatches for the Spanish ambassador, Luis de Requeséns, and for Francisco Pacheco, Cardenal de la Santa Cruz. If the Aragonese had hitherto enjoyed an advantage over the Castilians, it was one they now lost, for here was a window of opportunity that Maldonado seems to have been determined to exploit. For the surrender of the Order's affairs to higher authority that followed, the Catalans, justifiably or not, never forgave him.

The unusual haste with which the Catalans went about preparing themselves for the chapter general that would elect Puig's successor indicates the pressure they felt themselves to be under. Within three days of Puig's death, Papiol, the prior of Barcelona and now vicar general, had dispatched letters of convocation for a chapter to be held at the priory on 20th January 1568. Determined to ensure his own election to the high office, Papiol headed for Valencia where a chapter had been convened to appoint the electors general.[42] Presiding over it, Papiol managed by coercion to secure the appointment of those whose votes he could count on in the coming election. However, he did so only at the cost of alienating much of the Valencian hierarchy once and for all, the long-term consequences of which were to be very serious indeed for the Catalan cause.

In Castile, both Peñaranda and Carrillo, the vicar provincial, were

---

[40] On this episode, see Remón, *Historia*, II, ff. 286v–288r, who claims to base his information on original documents in his possession.

[41] APV, Antillón, ms. *Epitome*, I(ii), p. 1360.

[42] The exact date of this chapter is not known — it may in fact have taken place before Puig's death — and the *acta* appear not to have survived. The present details are from one of Tàrrega's *memoriales*, IVDJ, env. 72, II, f. 265r.

to claim that they had never been officially convened to the chapter general, which, they declared, was consequently illegal *ab initio*. However, from the perspective of the 1630s, Antillón presents a rather different picture of the circumstances leading up to the chapter, one that reflects the bitter memories still evoked by this period among Aragonese of his generation.[43] According to him, on Puig's death Papiol immediately dispatched his secretary and nephew, Fra Sebastiá Bertrán, to Madrid bearing letters of convocation for the province of Castile and missives for the nuncio. Reaching Madrid on 9th December, Bertrán presented himself at court where he was arrested on the orders of the president of the Royal Council of Castile, Cardinal Diego de Espinosa, and detained in the Mercedarian convent there. If the crown had been prepared to permit Puig to celebrate a chapter largely unhindered in September, it was certainly not going to allow Papiol to preside over the election of another perpetual Catalan general now. Informed of Puig's death by Maldonado and counselled by Carrillo and others in Madrid, Philip had, it appears, already taken steps in Rome to prevent the celebration of the chapter general and impose a reforming interregnum on the Order. But, as Antillón maintained, until Philip's diplomacy and Maldonado's machinations bore their expected fruit in Rome, the celebration of the chapter general had to be obstructed by all means possible.[44]

Although the Castilians failed to keep Bertrán within the convent, he was still bound over by Espinosa to remain in Madrid, and was thus unable to deliver the convocation officially to Peñaranda, then in Andalusia. From here he protested against this blatant obstruction while keeping Papiol abreast of developments. As a result news of his arrest became common knowledge in Barcelona where a serious conflict between the crown and the *diputats* was coming to a head. In a letter cited by Antillón, Bertrán warned that Espinosa had written to Barcelona ordering Papiol not to proceed with the electoral chapter, but that this should be ignored as mere subornation.[45] Quite the con-

---

[43] APV, Antillón, ms. *Epitome*, I(ii), pp. 1360–8.

[44] *Ibid.*, pp. 1364–5. It was probably at this moment that Philip sent a *memorial* to the Catalan bishops ordering them not to conclude the visitation of the Order, but to continue this and their reports to the crown until further instructions had been sent; reported in ACA, RC, vol. 4352, f. 119v.

[45] APV, Antillón, ms. *Epitome*, I(ii), pp. 1365–7. Madrid, 12th December 1567. This letter was sent to Rome as evidence of the Castilians' behaviour in January 1568; see AGN, Clero, vol. 402.

trary, it was essential that the election and its confirmation take place as soon as possible, for, as he reported, the Castilians were daily taunting him 'as if they were already certain of it, that there will never again be a general from Catalonia, nor of the [Aragonese] provinces either'.[46] But, Bertrán reminded Papiol, against these slings and arrows the Catalans enjoyed 'a most excellent defence, which is our Constitutions'. Relying on these and on existing privileges, Bertrán was sure that, with expert advice, the brethren could resist all the assaults of their enemies. But, as time would show, in this the Catalans also were guilty of misplaced confidence.

As delegates began to gather in Barcelona for the chapter, so the crown and the Castilians took direct steps to nullify its proceedings. On 21st December, the day after the statutory month's notice required for convocation had elapsed, Peñaranda wrote to Papiol from Seville declaring that, contrary to the constitutions, he had not been officially summoned and that the chapter could not therefore take place.[47] With a keen sense of timing, Peñaranda hired a messenger to take his letter to Barcelona, where it was delivered to the priory on 17th January 1568, only three days before the chapter was due to begin. On the 20th Papiol replied to Peñaranda denouncing him for a fraud and condemning his province's treatment of Bertrán.[48] Admonitory letters from the crown were brushed aside and the chapter addressed itself to the business of appointing a successor to Puig.

Once again, all the provinces of the Order were represented at Barcelona except for Castile. Among the five Catalan electors was the sub-prior of Barcelona, Mᵉ Fra Bernat Duran; the Aragonese delegation was led by the reformist provincial Fray Miguel Dicastillo who had been educated in Castile, while the French were headed by the provincial and commendator of Carcassonne, Frey Pierre Penchenat. Having discussed the Castilians' non-attendance, the delegates celebrated high mass in the priory church before repairing to the capitular chamber for the election. Under the supervision of two scrutineers, the vicar general Mᵉ Fra Maties Papiol was unanimously elected to the high office. The chapter then went on to prepare a sheaf of

---

[46] APV, Antillón, ms. *Epitome*, I(ii), p. 1367.

[47] AGN, Clero, vol. 402, in Latin, dated 21st December 1567. Castilian translation in *ibid.*, vol. 416. Also in APV, Antillón, ms. *Epitome*, I(ii), pp. 1369–71.

[48] APV, Antillón, ms. *Epitome*, I(ii), pp. 1372–4. See AGN, Clero, vol. 402, for a letter in Latin, dating perhaps from March or April 1568, protesting at the behaviour of Peñaranda and his fellow elector, M° Fray Pedro Carrillo.

documents with which the commendator of Mallorca, Fra Jeroni Antich, was dispatched to Rome as *procurador* to obtain Papiol's confirmation.[49] Having negotiated this Antich was to work towards obtaining a full papal endorsement of the Order's privileges and exemptions — notably that from the authority of the ordinary clergy — and then recruit the services of a cardinal as protector of the Order.[50] In order to fund his activities in Rome Antich was allegedly provided with monies intended for the redemption of captives submitted at the previous chapter general.[51]

III. *The Catalans Stifled*

In Rome, meanwhile, the efforts of Maldonado and the new ambassador, Juan de Zúñiga, were rewarded on 19th January, the day before the chapter sat, with the dispatch of a brief suspending the election of any general and prohibiting the convocation of further chapters until the apostolic visitations had been completed.[52] In

---

[49] See a *memorial* by the Catalan Mᶜ Fra Jaume Grauset to nuncio Ormaneto, IVDJ, env. 72, II, ff. 80r–81r. Undated, but late 1574; f. 80r. Joseph Amfós, a Girona clergyman resident in Rome, was also made *procurador*. The documents — seven of them — dating from 20th and 21st January 1568, are listed in *ibid.*, pp. 1384 and in AGN, Clero, vol. 402, which also contains Antich's general instructions (there is a second set of these in the same vol.). Five of the documents, as well as a number of draft copies, are in vol. 402, of which one — the *acta* of Papiol's election, dated Barcelona, 20th January 1568 — is reproduced in Vázquez Núñez, *Mercedarios ilustres*, pp. 259–61. Another copy of the *acta* is in APV, Antillón, ms. *Epitome*, I(ii), pp. 1378–84.

[50] The Catalans appear to have wanted Cardinal Alessandrino, Pius V's nephew, for their protector, but none had this responsibility until Íñigo Dávalos, Cardinal of Aragon, was appointed by Gregory XIII in 1572, holding the appointment until his death in 1600; see Vázquez Núñez, *Mercedarios ilustres*, p. 265, & *id.*, *Manual*, II, p. 30. He was succeeded from *c.*1606–35 by Antonio Zapata y Cisneros, Cardenal de la Santa Cruz; Tirso, *Historia*, II, p. 291. The first recorded protector of the Order dates from the age of conciliar politics: Carlos de Urriés, Cardinale di San Giorgio, accepted the post in *c.*1409 and held it until his death in 1420. He was succeeded in 1422 by Pedro de Fonseca, Cardinale di Sant Angelo and bishop of Sigüenza, who died that same year and was not replaced until 1446; see Vázquez Núñez, *Manual*, I, pp. 292–3 & 320. Vice-protectors were occasionally appointed, as during Zapata's tenure.

[51] ASZ, carp. 165, no. 137. An untitled and anonymous *parecer* to the crown, prepared by a Castilian Mercedarian. Undated, but early 1569; f. 1r–v.

[52] The brief is reproduced in APV, Antillón, ms. *Epitome*, I(ii), pp. 1387–91. Maldonado's negotiations may have been assisted by the fact that he was a *pariente* (relative) of Cardinal Pacheco's family in Salamanca. See also Remón, *Historia*, II, f. 287v.

accordance with the constitutions, Papiol was to remain as vicar general for the duration of the vacancy. Moreover, in entrusting the reform of the Order solely to the nuncio, the archbishop of Tarragona (Loaces) and to bishops Cassador of Barcelona and Fresneda of Cuenca — the head of the *Junta de Reforma* — the brief seems to have recognized that Mercedarian affairs could not be addressed simply within the framework of diocesan visitation or together with the affairs of two other orders. The crown, it appears, had finally realized that monastic reform had to reflect the geography and peculiarities of the orders concerned rather than that of the dioceses in which they lay.

The brief was received by Cardinal Espinosa in Madrid from where it was relayed to Barcelona, reaching Cassador in mid March. Having accepted his amended reform commission, on 26th March Cassador informed Papiol that his election as general had been suspended.[53] After ten days' deliberation Papiol prepared the first of several letters to Pius V protesting against this decision.[54] The chapter general, he declared, had been convened with almost two months' notice and the election itself was conducted by secret ballot in accordance with the Council of Trent.[55] Although at first rejecting charges that he had been disobedient in proceeding with the election, Papiol later admitted that he had indeed ignored direct orders from the crown to abandon the chapter.[56] However, it was to the papal mandate rather than that of the crown that Papiol expressly pledged allegiance and, arguing that the brief had been issued without the knowledge of the chapter, he implored Pius to confirm his election in the interests of reform. The following day an official appeal against the suspension was made by Fra Pere Castelló, the *procurador general*, which, along with Papiol's letter, was conveyed to Rome by the *procurador* of Aragon, Fray Jorge del Olivar.[57] These were backed up by a

---

[53] For copies of the commission, dated Barcelona, 20th March 1568, see APV, Antillón, ms. *Epitome*, I(ii), pp. 1391–5, & AGN, Clero, vol. 402.

[54] AGN, Clero, vol. 402, Papiol to Pius V, Barcelona, 5th April 1568; the document is also reproduced in APV, Antillón, ms. *Epitome*, I(ii), pp. 1397–9.

[55] Papiol specifically mentions Trent sess. XXV, I, iii, no. 6, 'On the manner of choosing religious superiors'; *Canons and Decrees*, p. 241.

[56] AGN, Clero, vol. 402, Antich to Pius V, undated, but *c*.May 1568. A copy was sent to Pius' confessor, Lucatello. This document is also copied in APV, Antillón, ms. *Epitome*, I(ii), pp. 1401–3 and is reproduced in part in Vázquez Núñez, *Mercedarios ilustres*, pp. 261–4.

[57] AGN, Clero, vol. 402, Barcelona, 6th April 1568.

letter to the crown underlining the support for Papiol of the *Consell de Cent,* and another from the *Generalitat* asking Philip to favour Papiol's confirmation in Rome.[58] The involvement of the *diputats,* while not surprising, is especially significant given the tense atmosphere prevailing between Barcelona and Madrid at this time.

Although no replies from the papacy to these and other *súplicas* appear to have survived, we do have a brief summary of Pius' reaction to Papiol's appeals furnished by the papal confessor, Lucatello.[59] Irritated with the whole affair, on 13th May Pius apparently ordered it transferred to Madrid for resolution there.[60] Until news from Spain arrived requesting otherwise, the pope was unwilling to confirm Papiol's election. Letters had in any case been sent to Philip and the nuncio, Giambattista Castagna (later Urban VII), ordering the visitation to proceed as directed in the January brief. As things were, only once this had been completed might the election be ratified and, indeed, letters arrived from Spain soon after making it plain that no such confirmation could be given.[61]

As Antich continued his struggle in Rome, Papiol decided to leave Barcelona for Aragon accompanied by Bertrán — now returned from Madrid — and another nephew, Fra Bernat Papiol.[62] The reason for his departure is unclear — he may have intended to conduct a visitation — but he never returned to Catalonia. After a short illness he died at the convent of San Lázaro in Zaragoza on 28th July 1568. Bernat Papiol and Bertrán hastened back to Barcelona in disguise where they secretly broke the news to the sub-prior, Fra Bernat Duran, on 31st July.[63] Having suborned the conventuals of Barcelona, Duran, in clear defiance of established convocation procedure, called a chapter which elected him prior the following day. He immediately had himself confirmed by the conventual of longest profession, Fra Lluís Valls, who in turn relinquished the office of vicar general in Duran's favour. Groomed by Papiol as his successor,

---

[58] See ASZ, carp. 165, no. 136. Anonymous and undated, but *c.*April 1568. See also a similar letter, ACA, LT, vol. 785, ff. 114v–115r. *Generalitat* to Philip II, Barcelona, 7th July 1568.

[59] An excerpt of a note, probably written by Antich, is reproduced in Vázquez Núñez, *Mercedarios ilustres,* p. 264.

[60] APV, Antillón, ms. *Epitome,* I(ii), p. 1401.

[61] *Ibid.,* p. 1404. See *CODOIN,* VII, pp. 529–38, Philip II to Zúñiga, Aranjuéz, 14th May 1568, reporting the execution of the January brief; p. 537.

[62] IVDJ, env. 72, II, f. 224r.

[63] ASZ, carp. 165, no. 137, f. 1v.

Duran's election at the age of thirty-nine makes him perhaps the youngest religious ever to hold these conjoined offices.[64]

However, the highly irregular circumstances under which the election had been celebrated did not go uncontested in Catalonia. Duran had made no attempt to convene those sons of the priory of Barcelona who resided in the provinces, while the validity of his confirmation by Valls was open to question. Among those most aggrieved was Mᵉ Fra Climent Ginebrosa who made a series of protests to the reformers, the bishop of Barcelona (Guillem Cassador) and the Dominican prior Fray Lorenzo López.[65] Before long Duran had imprisoned Ginebrosa in the priory, with Cassador and López powerless to stop him. One night Duran had his charge bound and gagged, hauled down to the harbour and bundled onto a waiting ship for transportation 'overseas', perhaps to Mallorca or even Oran. However, this time the reformers caught wind of what was happening and Ginebrosa was rescued off the ship by López the following morning. Having sheltered in the Dominican convent for a few days, Ginebrosa agreed to return to his commandery. No sooner had he left Barcelona than Duran moved against him decisively, and he was eventually confined to the house at Palma de Mallorca.[66] The episode provides a foretaste of the ruthlessness with which the Barcelona hierarchy would pursue their ambitions, and defend the status of the priory as the fount of their authority.

Immediately after his election Duran had instructed Antich to prepare a new petition to the effect that, the office of general having fallen vacant, the January brief was therefore annulled and the Order permitted to elect a new master.[67] This was backed by a furious letter from the *Generalitat* to Madrid accusing the king of deliberately blocking Papiol's confirmation, and demanding that he now sanction the election of a new general.[68] However, it is a measure of how desperate the Catalans were that they attempted to make their petition to

---

[64] ACA, Mon., vol. 2710, f. 28r. Copy of Duran's profession dated 24th February 1549, stating his age as 20.

[65] IVDJ, env. 72, II, ff. 224v–225r.

[66] *Ibid.*, f. 225r–v.

[67] AGN, Clero, vol. 416. Letter to Antich, undated but probably Barcelona, 1st August 1568. There are two copies of this in vol. 416.

[68] ACA, LT, vol. 785, f. 125r–v. Dated Barcelona, 8th August 1568. Among the appeals to the crown to allow the election of a new general is one from the *procurador general* of Castile; see AGS, PR, 23-50(v), report of a letter of Fray Felipe Tavira to Cardinal Espinosa, undated but August 1568.

Rome more attractive with a number of half concessions. In return for permission to hold an election the Catalans would ensure both its celebration within the three months stipulated by the constitutions, and the participation of all provinces as demanded by Trent 'as is always the case' — an arrant lie.

On the basis of these instructions, Antich prepared a *súplica* which he submitted to Pius V on 4th September.[69] Receiving no reply, he anxiously resubmitted it a week later, this time with the endorsement of Cardinal Colonna. But now he had to contend with both Maldonado and the intervention of the crown. Determined to avoid the delays that had followed the death of Puig, the king wrote to Zúñiga within a few weeks of Papiol's death requesting the dispatch of another brief prohibiting the celebration of any chapter until the visitations were completed.[70] However, the pope was now anxious for results from the visitation itself and increasingly concerned at the degree of secular intervention in monastic affairs.[71] Pius therefore declined Philip's request, and announced that no further decisions would be taken on the future of the Order until the visitations had been completed and progress made towards its reform through existing provisions.[72] In line with this, on 15th September he transmitted a noncommittal reply to Antich through Colonna.[73] The intercession of Cardinal Alessandrino came to nothing and Antich, sensing that his mission was over, returned to Barcelona shortly after.

But though the opportunity now presented itself, the crown failed to assert its authority over the Aragonese brethren in the matter of reform. For a few crucial months in late 1568 the Mercedarian issue disappeared off the royal agenda as the monarchy entered a period of crisis. The death of Queen Isabella and Don Carlos, deteriorating relations with France and England, the revolt of the Alpujarras and the *Generalitat* affair in Catalonia in mid 1569 temporarily banished the question of monastic reform from the king's mind. Under these cir-

---

[69] AGN, Clero, vol. 402. There are three copies of this document in vol. 402, which is also reproduced in APV, Antillón, ms. *Epitome*, I(ii), pp. 1406–7. The second submission was dated Rome, 12th September 1568.

[70] AMAE, SS, leg. 34, ff. 8r–9v. Madrid, 19th August 1568.

[71] AGS, E°, leg. 910, no. 58. Juan de Zúñiga to Philip, Rome, 10th January 1569; f. 2r.

[72] Despite this, on 24th February 1569 Zúñiga reported to Philip that Pius was willing to concede the Catalans a licence to elect a general. AGS, E°, leg. 911, no. 21, f. 1r; another copy at no. 22.

[73] APV, Antillón, ms. *Epitome*, I(ii), p. 1408.

cumstances the Catalans, led by the energetic and resourceful Duran, changed tack and began to regain the initiative in Mercedarian affairs in the Crown of Aragon. Confirmed as vicar general like Papiol before him, Duran now set out to demonstrate by action what words and experience had failed to convey: that the Barcelona régime was genuinely committed to the reform of the Order.[74] Unable to convene chapters, the hierarchy turned to visitation both for the purposes of reform and as the only sure means of communicating directly with the mass of the religious at this most sensitive time.

IV. *Visitation and Repression in the Crown of Aragon, 1568–9*

As surviving documents show, the form taken by a visitation reflects the priorities of those conducting it.[75] Although the enforcement of discipline was clearly an important consideration, the encouragement of lasting 'reform' was far from being the sole or even the most significant element on Duran's agenda. As in the past, the Catalan hierarchy took the opportunity to assert its authority over the brethren, to replace uncompliant superiors with more amenable ones and gauge the state of the Order's finances. Moreover, in the light of recent developments, Duran was no doubt anxious to test the water of provincial loyalty in the event of a chapter general, to appraise commendators of the prevailing situation, and prepare the mass of religious for the trials that lay ahead, even to the extent of providing them with weapons.[76] Above all, it was Duran's priority to make him-

---

[74] See IVDJ, env. 72, II, f. 455r for Duran's letter to Castagna dated Barcelona, 7th October 1568 asking for confirmation as vicar general of the Order.

[75] The transcript of a full visitation consisted firstly of interrogations of the religious as to the spiritual and disciplinary state of the community, with their signed depositions appended. This was accompanied by an inventory of the contents of the house along with an examination of its accounts and the yield of its lands. Finally, a set of ordinances was laid down by the visitor which reflected both his impression of the condition of the house and those directives issued by higher authority for the improvement of the Order. However, this process required much time and effort, particularly in larger convents, and it was only partially implemented in the Crown of Aragon at this time; see ACA, Mon., vols. 2668 & 2670–2671. A classic example is that described in the *Hodoeporicon* of the Camaldolese general Ambrogio Traversari, a diary of his visitation of the Order in Italy between 1431–4; ed. Vittorio Tamburini & Eugenio Garin (Florence, 1985).

[76] ACA, Mon., vol. 2670, f. 329v. In 1569 the commendator of the Valencian house of Arguines, Fra Jerònim Marí, claimed he had been sold an *arcabuset* (arquebus) by visiting Catalans carrying a stock of such weapons — presumably in 1568.

self known to the brethren as vicar general of the Order during the vacancy. Such concerns are reflected in the visitation transactions that have come down to us.

The campaign apparently opened with a tour of Catalonia in late summer 1568 while the royal visitation was still being carried out, but few documents have survived from it.[77] However, that winter Duran embarked on a major visitation of the province of Aragon-Navarre accompanied by his *procurador*, Fra Jeroni Antich.[78] Leaving Barcelona on muleback on 17th November, the visitors travelled across Catalonia and reached Uncastillo in north-western Aragon on 28th November.[79] Here as elsewhere the visitation consisted of an inventory, a review of conventual accounts and finally the drafting of brief ordinances for the 'correction' and 'reformation' of the Order. These covered a range of familiar issues, from prohibitions on playing cards and dice to instituting a proper procedure for depositing conventual funds. Although entries claim Duran to have received the verbal depositions of the religious, there is no trace of these in the documentation and it is questionable whether sufficient time was always allowed for him to take them properly. The visitors crossed into Navarre on 29th November and a week later Duran removed the commendator of Pamplona from office, apparently for refusing to accept him as vicar general.[80] By mid December the visitors were in western Aragon visiting the convents south of the Ebro. At Calatayud, not far from the Castilian border, Duran inflicted a similar punishment on the commendator, Mº Fray Pedro López de Cárdenas, replacing him with the vicar provincial of Aragon, Fray Francisco de Salazar.[81] The violent removal of Cárdenas, a noted preacher, by a party of religious 'armed like bandits' led by Fray Pedro Alegría provoked much local opposition in Calatayud.[82] As for ordinances, Duran required the brethren to

---

[77] *Ibid.*, ff. 195r–197r & 192r–194r, visitations of Vic by Fra Jaume Cisterer, 20th August and 18th September 1568 respectively.

[78] The *acta* of the 1568–9 visitation of Aragon-Navarre are in ACA, Mon., vol. 2668, ff. 294r–314v, & vol. 2671, ff. 1r–68v. The latter contains the ordinances of the thirteen houses visited, the former the inventory and accounts of six of these.

[79] APV, Antillón, ms. *Epitome*, I(ii), p. 1408 and ACA, Mon., vol. 2671, ff. 1r–3v.

[80] ASZ, carp. 165, no. 137, f. 1v.

[81] APV, Antillón, ms. *Epitome*, I(ii), pp. 1411–12. For the visitation *acta*, see ACA, Mon., vol. 2671, ff. 28r–30v, 19th December 1568. See also ASZ, carp. 165, no. 137, f. 1v.

[82] This action, apparently carried out with the support of the *justiciar* of Aragon, caused the *justicia* and *jurados* (judges) of Calatayud to issue a protest to Pius,

cease wearing linen underclothing, and to inflict six days' penance on any Castilian fugitive arriving at the convent so attired, before sending him back to his province in disgrace.[83]

On 26th December the visitors reached Zaragoza, where the commendator and provincial Fray Miguel Dicastillo suffered the same fate as his fellows at Pamplona and Calatayud, being replaced by Fray Pedro de Ángulo.[84] In less than a month, therefore, Duran had deprived the three principal superiors of Aragon-Navarre of their commanderies. There can be no doubt that, coupled with events in Valencia a year earlier, the high-handed attitude of the Catalan hierarchy had begun to erode the allegiance traditionally given it by its subject provinces.[85] Having installed a commendator upon whose support he could rely, Duran moved on to the remote house of El Olivar in the diocese of Teruel before passing through Upper Aragon. The visitation ended at Barbastro on 4th February 1569. A month later in Barcelona Duran confidently informed Philip that

> I have visited and reformed all our houses in the Province of Aragon and Navarre to the letter of our holy constitutions, which fact Your Majesty can corroborate with the bishops of these provinces...[86]

But just how 'reformed' these houses actually were is of course a matter for conjecture. The visitation had evidently been driven by aims other than reform itself, and it is clear that, like previous vicars general, Duran was ensuring the provincial vote at the electoral chapter he no doubt felt was coming. He did so, however, at the expense of the long-term support of the Aragonese for the Catalan regime. Anxious to strengthen his position, Duran invited the commendator of Carcassonne and provincial of France, Frey Pierre Penchenat, to Barcelona to obtain the support of his province for a favourable outcome to any future election.[87] News of such close ties with the French

---

Castagna and the king, who wrote to Cassador in Barcelona regarding this. See IVDJ, env. 72, II, ff. 225v–226r; citation f. 225v. An explanatory letter from Duran to Philip, dated Barcelona, 12th March 1569, is reproduced in APV, Antillón, ms. *Epitome*, I(ii), pp. 1412–13. Cárdenas headed for Madrid where he died that year having made formal protests to Philip and Castagna.

[83] ACA, Mon., vol. 2671, f. 30v. This injunction was repeated at El Puig the following year for *any* Castilian fugitive; see *ibid.*, vol. 2670, f. 343r.
[84] IVDJ, env. 72, II, f. 80r.
[85] ASZ, carp. 165, no. 137, f. 1v.
[86] APV, Antillón, ms. *Epitome*, I(ii), pp. 1412–13.
[87] ASZ, carp. 165, no. 137, f. 1v.

brethren, transmitted to the crown in early 1569, must have been particularly unwelcome at a time when Philip believed Catalonia to be on the verge of succumbing to Huguenot heresy.

With the pace of events quickening throughout the Order, it is hardly surprising that within a few months of Duran's return to Barcelona in February 1569 Mercedarian superiors were abroad again throughout the Crown of Aragon. On 5th July the Andalusian-born provincial of Valencia, Mº Fray Juan Calvo, was at Sarrión in the north of the Kingdom.[88] At that moment Fra Jeroni Antich, now visitor general, was beginning a journey that would take him through the entire Crown of Aragon over the next five months. In the company of Duran's secretary Fra Sebastiá Bertrán, Antich opened his visitation at Barbastro on 6th July.[89] Following a route similar to that he had taken with Duran less than a year earlier, Antich made a rapid tour through the province of Aragon-Navarre, rarely staying longer than a day or two in each house and reinforcing the vicar general's earlier ordinances.

Five weeks and fifteen houses later Antich and Bertrán crossed into Valencia, reaching Sarrión on 16th August and then the capital itself a week after.[90] However, whereas the royal reform effort had faltered in Catalonia and was virtually non-existent in Aragon, in Valencia it had been energetically resumed under Patriarch Ribera and the Augustinian bishop of Segorbe, Fray Juan de Muñatones. Visitations of at least two Mercedarian houses — Valencia and the major shrine of El Puig, a few miles to the north of the city — had already been conducted by the time Antich and Bertrán reached the province.[91] Although the transcripts of Ribera's visitation have not appeared, the experience of El Puig in particular clearly brought home to him the scandalous condition into which much of the province had fallen.[92] At Valencia he responded by appointing the reformist commendator,

---

[88] ACA, Mon., vol. 2670, ff. 269r–275v.

[89] *Ibid.*, vol. 2671, ff. 119r–125v. Antich and Bertrán's visitation of Aragon-Navarre is contained in this volume. In *ibid.*, vol. 2670, f. 356r we learn that Antich's *poder* as visitor general was granted him by Duran in Barcelona on 28th June 1569.

[90] The visitation of the province of Valencia is contained in ACA, Mon., vol. 2670. For that of Sarrión see *ibid.*, vol. 2671, f. 161v, and for Valencia, visited between 22nd & 28th August 1569, see *ibid.*, vol. 2670, ff. 281r–289v. The house had 26 conventuals.

[91] For further details on this see IVDJ, env. 72, II, f. 257v. There is also news of episcopal visitations of the houses at Játiva (*ibid.*, f. 256r) and Arguines (f. 266r).

[92] *Ibid.*, f. 226r.

Me Fra Pere Joan de Tàrrega, to the office of vicar provincial, and passed a number of basic ordinances.[93]

The Order's own visitation was therefore conditioned by Ribera's recent activity. The Catalans already suspected Tàrrega of favouring the Reform and now set out to cook his goose in the usual manner: through a sustained campaign of persecution and public defamation. Joined by the provincial, Calvo, and the commendator of El Puig, Fra Vicent Murta, Antich and Bertrán therefore conducted an especially rigorous investigation of the house. Despite generally favourable reports by the conventuals on their commendator, the visitors claimed to have found his administration of the house to be seriously wanting. Stressing adherence to the edicts of the Council of Trent and the constitutions of the Order, here as elsewhere the visitors issued a number of decrees drawn both from Tridentine principles and the ordinances passed at the chapter general of Barcelona in 1567.[94] Strict observance of the divine office and the feast days of the Order was enjoined, while the Rule of St Augustine and constitutions were to be read out weekly in the refectory.[95] Though Tàrrega retained his office, he was threatened with removal if these were not implemented.

While Tàrrega was clearly far from blameless, the visitors' attitude was driven by deep personal animus towards an individual who was regarded as having taken sides with the archbishop against his own brethren. Equally, there can be no doubt that this contempt was fully reciprocated. Tàrrega was exasperated with the continued abuse by Catalans of the office of general, and the domination of Barcelona over the provinces that accompanied it. The successor at Valencia of M° Fray Jerónimo Pérez, Tàrrega was particularly angry at the general decline of intellectual standards in the Crown of Aragon. Given the status of the house of Barcelona and the responsibilities of the prior, it was essential, he declared, that the incumbent be both lettered and of sufficient experience, 'y no ydiota ni joven' — a clear reference to Duran.[96] Tàrrega's emphasis on academic attainment reflects the concerns of the Castilian reformers, and his own attempts at

---

[93] *Ibid.*

[94] ACA, Mon., vol. 2670, ff. 288v–289v.

[95] *Ibid.*, f. 288v. This ordinance appears to have mirrored that passed by Ribera at Valencia. See IVDJ, env. 72, II, f. 226r.

[96] IVDJ, env. 72, II, f. 264v; 'and neither illiterate nor young'.

reform were based on Castilian practice to a considerable extent. Despite his Catalan name, Tàrrega would become the bitterest enemy of Barcelona in the Crown of Aragon, and make Valencia a centre of opposition to the *ancien régime* in these provinces.

Having completed the visitation of Valencia in late August, Antich and Bertrán moved on to cover the four houses in the south of the province. By the time they began to retrace their steps to Valencia, the disruption they were causing had come to the attention both of Ribera and the viceroy, the conde de Benavente. In September Ribera issued a diocesan decree prohibiting the transfer of any religious belonging to the three orders from their houses, backed up by a demand that none of his reform provisions were to be interfered with.[97] Informed that Antich and Bertrán were carrying weapons, the viceroy had them disarmed and severely reprimanded.[98] However, this did not prevent them conducting the visitation of El Puig which began on 4th October.[99] The situation Antich and Bertrán claimed to have uncovered at Valencia in August pales in comparison with what they encountered here. The visitors' findings endorse Ribera's original assessment of the house. During the thirty-five years of Calvo's residence here as rector (twenty-two as provincial), conventual life had drifted into a cycle of corruption, insubordination and immorality against the background of simmering tension with the local community.[100] The visitation reveals some engaging characters — particularly Fray Miguel Ángel Bruxola, who boasted of having carnal knowledge of every woman in El Puig and regularly entertained girls in his cell with renditions on a viola — but the overriding impression is of a complete breakdown of authority, of a failure of leadership that lay at the heart of the decline of the Order.[101]

Completing the visitation of Valencia's eight houses here on 9th October, Antich passed into Catalonia and early November found

---

[97] The former is reported in *ibid.*, ff. 421r–422r, Ribera to Tàrrega and conventuals of Valencia, Valencia, 22nd September 1570 [*sic*], f. 421r, and the latter in *ibid.*, f. 226v.

[98] *Ibid.*, f. 226v.

[99] ACA, Mon., vol. 2670, ff. 321r–343v. The house had at least seventeen conventuals. See also IVDJ, env. 72, II, f. 256v.

[100] For evidence of similar tensions in 1386, see Brodman, 'Ransomers or Royal Agents', p. 245.

[101] ACA, Mon., vol. 2670, ff. 323v & 324r. Bruxola's character and mores did not, however, prevent him becoming president of Valencia and later commendator of Calatayud.

him at Vic in the company of Duran.[102] The campaign ended at Agramunt in north-western Catalonia on 15th December 1569, five months after it had started.[103] The impact on religious of two or, in the case of Vic, three visitations in the space of less than a year after what may have been decades of inactivity is to be imagined. It was under such circumstances that the mass of Mercedarians began to awaken to the new religious and political climate in which Order found itself.

V. *Division and Uncertainty in Castile, 1568–9*

While official involvement in Mercedarian reform seems to have been temporarily curtailed in the Crown of Aragon towards the end of 1568, in Castile visitations continued in accordance with the briefs until March of the following year. The assumption to be drawn from the few documents that survive for this period is that most if not all of the Mercedarian province of Castile was visited by reformers under royal and apostolic authority. Although the visitation was not uneventful, the reformers were on the whole received without opposition. In July 1568 the Dominican prior of Murcia, Fray Martín de Santis, was visiting the Mercedarian and Trinitarian convents of that diocese.[104] There are reports of visitations of Mercedarian houses in the archdiocese of Toledo — including Madrid and Alcalá in mid 1568, and Toledo itself some time later — and of the convents at Seville, Jerez de la Frontera and Badajoz.[105]

---

[102] *Ibid.*, ff. 231r–232v & 345r–348r, dated 8th November 1569. Either the surviving documentation for the visitation of the province of Catalonia in vol. 2670 is incomplete (as seems likely), or it failed to include all the southern houses along with those at Tàrrega and Berga to the north. Only seven of the fifteen houses were included, though the priory of Barcelona was by tradition effectively exempted from visitation by officers of the Order.

[103] *Ibid.*, ff. 365r–367v.

[104] AGS, PR, 23-69, & 23-68. Santis to Philip II, Murcia, 2nd July 1568, with an accompanying *memorial* (23-68). For news of a scandal involving a Cordovan Mercedarian, see AGS, E°, leg. 150, no. 42, Cristóbal de Rojas y Sandoval, bishop of Córdoba, to Philip II, Córdoba, 8th July 1568.

[105] Regarding the archdiocese of Toledo, see AGS, E°, leg. 150, no. 63, Gómez Tello Girón (governor of the archdiocese in Carranza's stead) to Philip II, Toledo, 27th August 1568. The house at Madrid was at this moment being visited by Licenciado Muñoz with Dominican assistance (f. 1r). Toledo was visited by Dr. Jerónimo Manrique de Lara, visitor general of the archdiocese, probably in early 1569; see IVDJ, env. 72, II, f. 76r–v, Carrillo to Castagna, undated but Córdoba, 1570. For

However, only the visitation of Santa María de Conxo outside Santiago de Compostela by the archbishop Gaspar de Zúñiga y Avellaneda, his Dominican assistants, and Peñaranda himself, is well documented.[106] The lamentable condition of the house and the air of 'general permissiveness' that pervaded it almost brought about the removal of the commendator and professor at the university of Santiago, M° Fray Cristóbal de Soto.[107] Though Soto was allowed to remain in office, Zúñiga, no doubt on the basis of some experience of the Order, remained concerned at the disturbing restlessness he detected in the Mercedarian psyche. As he declared to Philip,

> Since the religious of this Order do not outwardly display their unease, I suspect that they bear it in their spirits. This, it seems to me, would cease if they understood just what was required of them.[108]

The remark is perceptive since, in the few months that it had been in force, the Mercedarian reform process had provoked distrust and above all incomprehension both among the religious and the authorities responsible for implementing it. And indeed, many of the crucial questions remained unanswered: by what standards were the religious to be reformed and to what criteria, by extension, were the reformers themselves to operate? As time would reveal, neither the religious nor the crown and its ministers had grasped the full implications of the process in which they had become involved. Before the wider reform campaign was much more than a year old it had become apparent to the crown that a serious reappraisal was necessary if it were to maintain its momentum and achieve its desired end.

The onset of the reform process was not therefore greeted by Mercedarians in a spirit of unity. Quite the contrary, the Order was divid-

---

Badajoz, where the commendator was controversially removed by the diocesan visitor Dr. Coderes, see AGS, E°, leg. 149, no. 174, anonymous Mercedarian *procurador general*, perhaps Fray Benito Carrillo, to Bishop of Badajoz, undated but late 1568 or early 1569. Another troubled visitation was that of Jerez, where Mercedarians claimed that the visitors, including the Dominican M° Fray Antonino de León, had abused their authority and needlessly brought ridicule and dishonour on the house; see IVDJ, env. 72, II, ff. 113r–114v, anonymous *memorial*, undated but late 1568 or early 1569.

[106] There are four documents on the visitation of this house written by archbishop Zúñiga to Philip II in AGS, E°, leg. 151, no. 192, & leg. 150, nos. 59–61, dated 15th August to 14th October, when the visitation was declared complete.

[107] *Ibid.*, leg. 150, no. 61, f. 1v. Conxo, 2nd September 1568; '…la permision General que en algunas cosas que se hallaron…'. The house had ten conventuals.

[108] *Ibid.*, no. 59. Santiago, 14th October 1568.

ed against itself as never before. Religious of all persuasions were both
confused and in disagreement as to the nature and direction of a movement that clearly lay beyond the full control of the Order. Above all,
insecurity bred a widespread concern to defend established patterns of
life now felt to be under serious threat. Recent developments were
everywhere making individuals consider the nature of their allegiances
and assess their place within the Order. Rather than binding religious
to a notion of the Order as a single entity, the prospect of reform therefore served to strengthen and define existing loyalties to a tendency,
province, house, or to a leading individual. Ultimately, the effect was to
confirm the traditional fragmentation of the Order. Beyond the ancient
feud between Castile and the Crown of Aragon, it is evident that both
Valencian and Aragonese brethren had already begun to question the
hegemony of the priory of Barcelona over the eastern provinces. In
Castile, disagreement over the nature of the reform precipitated a division of the hierarchy into two opposing factions. Throughout the
Order, therefore, reform was implemented against the background of
an ongoing network of disputes and allegiances that inevitably shaped
its progress. In this sense at least, reform represents no more and no
less than the history of a *querelle des moines*, the struggle of one or more
interpretations of reform against another.

Even as Fray Gaspar de Torres was preparing his edition of the
constitutions in 1565, it is clear that a serious rift had begun to develop among the Castilian hierarchy over the question of reform. The
immediate cause of this conflict lay in the circumstances of Peñaranda's election as provincial at Toledo in 1565. As we have seen, under
Torres' influence Peñaranda had been elected for a term of four
years rather than the usual six, on the understanding that the crown
was about to enforce this duration of tenure on all comparable religious offices. When no such modification was introduced, Peñaranda's chagrin at being deprived of two years of office was heightened
by more deep-seated reservations as to the aims and conduct of the
reform to which the Order was being subjected by the crown. The
result was a conflict which represents an important watershed in the
history of the province, and the Order at large.

Although the question of Peñaranda's tenure arose soon after his
election, it was 1567 before the first signs of a split in the Castilian
hierarchy regarding the reform process itself become apparent. In
that year Peñaranda had underlined his determination to extend his
term of office from four to six years by refusing to convene the obliga-

tory mid-term chapter scheduled for the summer of that year.[109] This action alienated much of the reformist hierarchy of Castile, which now coalesced around the vicar provincial, Mº Fray Pedro Carrillo. However, it was the sudden enactment of the papal briefs in October 1567 that made the issue of reform the main bone of contention. Such public and unprecedented interference by the crown in the affairs of the Order was highly disturbing to those Castilian religious, Peñaranda among them, who favoured a more measured and above all internal process of reform. Thus, while Carrillo established himself as the crown's leading informant on Mercedarian affairs, Peñaranda began a campaign of sullen opposition to the Reform and its supporters in the province of Castile. By the time Carrillo had composed the first of his *memoriales* to Philip II in the spring of 1568, the rift was hardening into open conflict.[110]

Torres was the first casualty. Disagreeing with Carrillo, who did not share his ideas on reform, and despised by Peñaranda given his collaboration with the crown, Torres was isolated by the changing structure of Mercedarian politics. Easy prey for his enemies, the former provincial was subjected to a campaign of petty defamation by elements of the Castilian hierarchy and virtually hounded out of the Order.[111] The offer in 1569 of the post of auxiliary bishop of Seville no doubt provided a welcome opportunity to escape the *mêlée* of Mercedarian affairs once and for all. The wider Castilian situation becomes clear in a letter dating from August 1568 concerning the visitation of Mercedarian houses in the archdiocese of Toledo written by the governor in Carranza's absence, Gómez Tello Girón.[112] It is apparent that Peñaranda had recently removed Fray Benito Carrillo — Pedro's brother — from the office of *procurador general* of Castile, replacing him with one of his own supporters, Fray Felipe Tavira. According to Tello, Benito Carrillo's dismissal had been due to his having given the crown 'important information about the reformation of this Order', a disposition he therefore shared with his brother.[113] Carrillo was promptly

[109] AGS, PR, 23-49, f. 4r; also in IVDJ, env. 72, II, f. 152r.

[110] AGS, PR, 23-51(ii), reproduced in Vázquez Núñez, ed., *La Merced a mediados*, (doc.i), pp. 100–3.

[111] IVDJ, env. 72, II, ff. 482r–491r. *Memorial* from Tàrrega to the nuncio, Niccolò Ormaneto, undated but written in Madrid shortly before August 1573; f. 482r.

[112] AGS, Eº, leg. 150, no. 63. Gómez Tello Girón to Philip II, Toledo, 27th August 1568.

[113] *Ibid.*, f. 1r.

reinstated, but the episode demonstrates the degree of hostility being generated by Peñaranda against those cooperating with the crown and against the reform itself. Indeed, as Tello makes clear, Peñaranda was attempting to wreck the whole visitation campaign through appeal in Rome.

At some point in mid 1568 Peñaranda had presented his secretary in Rome, Pº Fray Francisco Maldonado, with the task of obtaining the suspension both of the apostolic visitations and the forthcoming chapter provincial, and of arranging for the visitors' transactions to be sent to Rome.[114] The only detailed information to survive on this matter is contained in a letter sent by Maldonado to Peñaranda that fell into Pedro Carrillo's hands in June 1569.[115] According to Maldonado — still battling against the Catalan *procuradores* and a host of other religious with their own axes to grind — Pius V had responded sympathetically to his entreaties regarding the visitation, but remained non-committal. The pope, as we have seen, was dissatisfied with the progress of the visitations, but had yet to decide on how best to deal with the matter.[116] While not unhopeful, Maldonado, like his Aragonese counterparts, was acutely aware of the difficulties of negotiating in Rome and of the number, duplicity and selfishness of the enemies ranged against him.[117]

However, in seeking to end the entire visitation, Peñaranda was clearly at one with the Aragonese brethren, and it was to them that Maldonado suggested he should turn for support.[118] Thus, he urged Peñaranda 'always to consult with the fathers of these other provinces [i.e. of the Crown of Aragon], since in agreement lies

---

[114] Vázquez Núñez, *Manual*, I, pp. 530–1. In a *memorial* of early 1569 — see either AGS, 23-51(i), ff. 5r–v, or Vázquez Núñez, ed., *La Merced a mediados*, (doc.ii), p. 110 — Carrillo suggests that Peñaranda, suspecting that the province's degree-holders were unsympathetic to him, had obtained a brief in Rome that would have prevented most of them from voting in the forthcoming chapter. Further, he is claimed to have unfairly refused to confirm three or four new degrees until the chapter itself. These claims, however, are unsubstantiated.

[115] AGS, PR, 23-53(xxiii), Rome, 9th May 1569. Carrillo reports having obtained it in an addendum to a letter to Gabriel de Zayas, *ibid.*, (xx), Guadalajara, 9th June 1569, f. 2r.

[116] *Ibid.*, (xxiii), f. 1r

[117] *Ibid.*, f. 1v.

[118] *Ibid.*, ff. 1v & 2r. Maldonado reports having been in agreement on this matter with an unnamed Valencian friar in Rome (possibly Alegría) secretly attempting to have himself appointed 'pro hac vice general' (f. 1v). For more on Mercedarian *procuradores* in Rome at this time, see AGS, Eº, leg. 911, no. 21, Zúñiga to Philip II, Rome, 15th March 1569. Another copy is *ibid.*, no.22.

greater dispatch and better results'.[119] Extreme as they are, Maldonado's remarks reflect the view of many Mercedarians at this time. For them, the interference to which the Order was being subjected was a consequence of the bitter and public schism that had divided it since 1467. Although any sort of agreement between the Catalans and the Castilians was in the present climate extremely unlikely, it is clear that many religious, even in Castile, were now yearning for the strength that the Order's lost unity might bring. For many, therefore, the reform of the Mercedarians must have reunification under a single general as its principal aim, albeit on terms that reflected the changed status of its component provinces.[120] There can be no doubt that Peñaranda and Maldonado harboured deep and sincere misgivings regarding the process to which their order was being subjected, particularly given the draconian action being planned and enacted against a number of orders and congregations, ranging from amalgamation to outright suppression. To them, as to other friars of conservative leanings, the collaboration of the reformist party in the designs of the crown threatened both province and Order with severe damage, if not outright destruction. As Maldonado declared,

> let us hope to God that, for their greater confusion, the very blindness of those who would destroy us prevents them sustaining the double-dealing necessary to achieve their ends.[121]

Far from being the simple duel between Castile and Catalonia in which it has hitherto been characterized, the reform of the Mercedarians represents a tangle of conflicts to which the Order alone could provide no lasting solution.

The interception of Maldonado's letter, as a summary written on it would suggest, was both damaging to Peñaranda's reputation and a revelation of the internal politics of the Order.[122] For, indeed, the complexities of reforming the Mercedarians were already becoming apparent to the crown. As Gómez Tello Girón had commiserated with Philip some months earlier,

---

[119] AGS, PR, 23-53(xxiii), f. 2r.

[120] IVDJ, env. 72, II, f. 135r–v. Fray Pedro de Velasco *et al.* to Zayas(?), undated but Madrid, *c.*February 1572; f. 135v.

[121] AGS, PR, 23-53(xxiii), f. 2r.

[122] *Ibid.*, f. 2v. For further comment on this letter, see AGS, PR, 23-53(xx), f. 2r (addendum).

> Your Majesty has every reason to be tired out with the visitations of
> these religious, and to take a dim view of their squabbling, for, to be
> sure, their enmities and rancour are borne with such passion as to
> make it impossible for them to live with a clear conscience.[123]

Set against the backdrop of the visitation of the Order and the question of Peñaranda's tenure, the conflict between the reformist and
conservative parties in Castile reflects a number of important problems common to monastic reform in general. In its widest sense,
reform requires those implementing it to balance the demands of the
present with the traditions of the past and hopes for the future.
Although underlying circumstances were of course quite different in
each case, to a greater or lesser degree the reform of every Spanish
congregation under Philip II reflected the traditional conflict between
those who envisioned change along existing lines, and those who perceived it in terms of a past and future ideal. This is usually, though not
always accurately, characterized as a conflict between Conventualism
and Observance. At the very moment that Maldonado was writing to
Peñaranda from Rome in May 1569, Franciscan Conventualism was
being expunged from Spain after more than 350 years.[124] Conventualism — whether Dominican or Franciscan — has traditionally been
excoriated as both obscurantist and unsightly, as the *bête noir* of Peninsular religious life. Yet, whatever the case may be, Conventualism —
adherence to a mitigated interpretation of the religious life — represented an important and lasting current in Spanish monasticism that is
echoed in the Mercedarian Order. The Mercedarians had no conventual branch *per se*, any more than they had an observant one, but the
Order as a whole took an overridingly pragmatic approach to the
monastic vocation that recalls Conventualism. It was to this tradition
that Peñaranda and his supporters gave their allegiance against the
ostensibly reformist movement embodied by Carrillo. However, even
Carrillo's reformism was conditioned by his Order's pragmatic assessment of its vocation as one of action. As he declared to Castagna, .

> The religious life is not about speculation but about execution, for in
> execution one encounters obstacles that are not apparent in mere spec-
> ulation...[125]

---

[123] AGS, E°, leg. 150, no. 63, f. 1r.
[124] See P.Fr. José García Oro, *Francisco de Asís en la España medieval* (Santiago de
Compostela, 1988), pp. 519–39.
[125] IVDJ, env. 72, II, ff. 105r–106v. Undated, but 1570; f. 106r.

For the Mercedarians, it is clear, religious observance was above all expressed in the endeavour of an active apostolate.

Only one *memorial* from Peñaranda to the crown is extant, compared to the half dozen or so by Carrillo that survive from this period, but these documents and the actions of their authors reflect the differences in their approach to the prospect of reform. Peñaranda, obviously unhappy at the degree of external interference being visited upon the Order and aware that his own record was under close scrutiny, is guarded with his information and refrains from making any accusations. These attitudes are reflected in the titles of their memoranda: while Carrillo gives details of 'what is most important for the reformation of the Order', Peñaranda merely discloses what he feels 'is in need of remedy' for its good government.[126] Although Peñaranda supported the reform of the generalate, he rightly recognized that intervention here would go hand in hand with interference in the Castilian provincialate also. His policy therefore appears to have been one of attempting to block dangerous innovation and above all maintaining the *status quo* within the province of Castile itself. While Carrillo was also anxious that immoderate action be avoided, he was equally determined to underline the desperate need for an assertion of authority over the Order.[127] As he said, no doubt with some exaggeration,

> neither the provincials nor any other senior officers in our Order have the means or the ability to obtain or pass ordinances for its greater good, even in their own provinces, because those adversely affected have recourse to the general with gifts or through other avenues. The general then carries out what is asked of him by whatever means he thinks fit.[128]

---

[126] The citations are taken from the titles of two *memoriales* (both of them *c.*1568–9), respectively AGS, PR, 23-49 (also IVDJ, env. 72, II, ff. 149r–152r), and AGS, PR, 23-50(i) (also 23-50(ii) — substantially the same document); the respective titles are 'Memorial de las cosas que pareçe que son mas inportantes para la reformacion de la orden de nuestra señora de la merced de Redencion de Cautivos en la provincia de Castilla', and 'Lo que a mi frai Juan de peñaranda provincial de la orden de nuestra señora de las mercedes me pareçe ay neçesidad de que se Remedie para el buen govierno desta Sagrada Religion es lo siguiente'.

[127] AGS, PR, 23-51(ii), reproduced in Vázquez Núñez, ed., *La Merced a mediados*, (doc.i), pp. 100–3; f. 1r or p. 100.

[128] *Ibid.*, f. 1r, or pp. 100–1.

The inference to be drawn is that this *impasse* could only be broken through royal intervention, without which there could be no hope of lasting change in the Order.[129] The eventual effect of this beneficent involvement would be the unification of the Order under a general elected by *all* its component provinces.[130] Moreover, as Carrillo's *memoriales* make increasingly clear, it was only by placing the Order under the direct patronage of the crown that any improvement could be brought about. As Carrillo, mindful no doubt of his prospects for personal advancement, declared to Philip at a particularly unctuous moment,

> It must be pointed out that, because this holy order belongs so entirely and so exclusively to Your Majesty's royal crown, those of us who aspire to its improvement and its reformation want nothing other than to place ourselves in your royal hands so that, through your most holy zeal, you may impart order to our reformation as something pertaining to your crown and royal patrimony. We therefore have no intention of taking the matter of the visitations to Rome, nor do we wish to take advantage of the apostolic see except where this would be to the service of Your Majesty, since we understand that all of Your Majesty's ordinances shall be passed under His [i.e. the pope's] holy obedience. Moreover, we suspect that, because of this, some have sought to delay what they should have looked to encourage. While other orders might think it right to make separate arrangements [i.e. with the papacy], this does not befit our Order, for, as I have said, we are but the creatures and property of the royal crown, and so confide that, as things belonging to Your Majesty, all help and favour shall be granted us.[131]

Though Carrillo sang a different tune in letters to the nuncio, with this declaration he was effectively surrendering his Order up to the will of the crown as the ultimate master of its destiny. In doing so Carrillo also placed himself at the head of a reformist and regalist party within the Castilian province that regarded Philip's personal patronage as the only means to its improvement. This approach, of course, would have been vigorously opposed by Peñaranda. As his attempt to draw the issue of the visitation away from Madrid and back to Rome indicates, Peñaranda, like other religious superiors, was anxious to restore the balance between papal and royal jurisdiction over his Order. By following Carrillo's unashamedly regalist pol-

---

[129] *Ibid.*, ff. 2r–v, or pp. 102–3.
[130] *Ibid.*, ff. 2r, or p. 102.
[131] AGS, PR, 23-53(xix), f. 2r–v. Undated, but probably Toledo, 13th May 1569.

icy, the Order could well close the few avenues to obtaining redress in Rome from royal interference that remained to it. Like the Catalans, Peñaranda therefore looked to the papacy rather than to the crown as the fountainhead of authority for the Mercedarians. As he concluded in his surviving *memorial* to the crown,

> All these suggestions have been sent to the royal court, along with others that also treat of the reformation, and it goes without saying that requests for their confirmation should be made to His Holiness, to the end that they be inviolably observed.[132]

Peñaranda was therefore voicing the concerns of a conservative and papalist tendency in the province of Castile, one determined to prevent the Order falling entirely under the sway of the crown. However, this attitude ran contrary to developments in the relationship between the crown, the Church and the papacy in Spain during the 1560s. After the conclusion of the Council of Trent, the impetus for religious reform had been skilfully harnessed by Philip to the persona and interests of the crown above those of the papacy, a circumstance that would have far-reaching effects for the orders in the years to come. As Carrillo observed to Philip in May 1569, implicitly, reform now carried with it the authority of the crown.[133]

VI. *The Chapter Provincial of Guadalajara, 1569*

As the date appointed for the chapter provincial of Castile drew closer — Trinity Sunday 1569 — and it became apparent that Peñaranda had no intention of bringing his term to a close, so religious became increasingly concerned for the future of the province. Matters had not been helped by the behaviour of the crown, which first upheld Peñaranda's claims to a six-year tenure, only to reverse this decision on the advice of the royal canonist, Dr. Velasco. The general situation emerges in a letter written in early March to Cardinal Espinosa by an anonymous Mercedarian *procurador*.[134] While obviously a supporter of Peñaranda, prevailing circumstances obliged the *procurador* to beg the crown to assert itself in this matter,

---

[132] *Ibid.*, 23-50(ii).

[133] *Ibid.*, 23-53(xix), f. 2r.

[134] AGS, Eº, leg. 149, nos. 133 & 133 dentro. Undated and anonymous, but probably written by Fray Felipe de Tavira.

otherwise the province will be left leaderless and without a shepherd to
watch over it, a situation which would bring about its utter ruin since
each religious would do whatever took his fancy…[135]

As Carrillo reiterated several weeks later, the forthcoming chapter
presented a clear opportunity for the king to stamp his personal
authority on the affairs of the Castilian Mercedarians once and for
all.[136] Accordingly, in mid May the crown convened the chapter
provincial for 4th June 1569 at Guadalajara, and appointed the visitor general of the archdiocese of Toledo, Dr. Jerónimo Manrique de
Lara, to preside over it.[137] Manrique's function, as Carrillo later put
it, was 'to ensure that matters proceed juridically, to spare the
province the overbearing tyranny that has affected other orders, and
to make the necessary arrangements for the reformation to take
effect'.[138] The nomination of a president is of course consistent with
Philip's policy towards the Spanish provincial councils which met
after the conclusion of Trent, almost all of which were supervised by
a royal delegate. It was by such means that the crown went about
asserting its presence within the institutional and legislative framework of the Spanish Church, and the orders in particular.

However, from the beginning the chapter provincial of Castile presented a number of serious juridical difficulties that had to be surmounted. The problem centred around Peñaranda's refusal to preside over the chapter, thereby depriving the new incumbent of the
immediate confirmation traditionally given by the ex-provincial.[139] In
these exceptional circumstances, the Castilians were obliged to turn
to the vicar general, Fra Bernat Duran. The *Concordia* of 1467 had
required provincials-elect of Castile, as a mere formality, to seek the

---

[135] *Ibid.*, no. 133, f. 1r. More emphatic support for Peñaranda is given in an undated and anonymous letter, AGS, PR, 23-50(iv), asking the crown to let him serve out
his six-year tenure.

[136] AGS, PR, 23-53(xix), f. 2r, and what is probably its covering letter addressed to
Gabriel de Zayas, *ibid.*, (xvi), Toledo, 13th May 1569. It was Zayas who, as principal
secretary of the Council of State and of the *Junta de Reforma* in Madrid, coordinated
Mercedarian affairs between Castile and Catalonia over the following weeks.

[137] The canonist Manrique was a royal councillor, commissary and *juez apostólico* of
the archdiocese of Toledo, later becoming bishop of Cartagena (1583) and Ávila
(1590). Manrique had visited the Mercedarian house of Toledo earlier that year; see
supra, n. 105.

[138] IVDJ, env. 72, II, ff. 86r–87v, Carrillo to Castagna, Guadalajara, 16th June
1569, f. 86r.

[139] In the event M° Fray Juan de Móstoles, commendator of Segovia, was delegated as acting president under Manrique's overall control.

endorsement of the general or his vicar before taking office. On this occasion, however, the confirmation would rest entirely in the hands of the vicar general in Barcelona. Given the climate prevailing between Castile and Catalonia, Duran was unlikely to approve the election as Puig had done in 1565. Aware of the impending difficulties, Carrillo, as vicar provincial, presented a *memorial* to the royal secretary Gabriel de Zayas in May 1569 outlining a procedure by which the new provincial might be confirmed and the chapter thereby enabled to complete its business.[140] Rather than leave the confirmation to Duran himself, the vicar general was to be asked by the crown to empower one or two Castilian religious present at the chapter to confirm the provincial-elect in his name. A letter to this effect was hastily prepared by Zayas and dispatched to Duran even as the Castilian delegates were gathering at Guadalajara.[141] Fresh from his successful visitation of the Crown of Aragon, Duran was in pugnacious mood and in no mind to make concessions to the Castilians. He therefore refused to accede to the crown's requests and himself went on the offensive.[142] Taking up a theme first mooted by Puig in 1565, Duran declared the *Concordiae* of 1467 and 1532 to have been invalidated by the Tridentine decrees.[143] Under these circumstances, the Castilians could neither celebrate the chapter nor elect a new provincial without his direct authority, while Castilian affairs now reverted to the control of Barcelona. This position, as the viceroy informed Philip, was backed up by a *parecer* prepared, no doubt with the assistance of the *Consell de Cent*, by a committee of nine canonists and theologians.[144] However, this was not all. Exercising the powers supposedly vested in him by the papacy and the constitutions, Duran took it upon himself to appoint Carrillo as vicar provincial, with authority to govern Castile in his name until such time as a new general were

---

[140] AGS, E°, leg. 149, no. 141, undated but probably Toledo, 13th May 1569.

[141] AGN, Clero, vol. 402, Aranjuez, 26th May 1569. Copied in APV, ms. Antillón, *Epitome*, I(ii), pp. 1415–16.

[142] AGS, PR, 23-53(vii), Duran to Philip II, Barcelona, 1st May 1569. Other copies in AGN, Clero, vol. 416 & APV, ms. Antillón, *Epitome*, I(ii), pp. 1417–19.

[143] The basis of Duran's claims lie in Trent sess. XXV, I, iii, ch. 22, 'Praedicta de Reformatione Regularium nulla Mora Interposita Observentur'; *Canons and Decrees*, p. 252.

[144] AGS, PR, 23-53(ii), Diego Hurtado de Mendoza, Príncipe de Melito to Philip II, Barcelona, 2nd June 1569. The *parecer* has not survived, but its nine authors are listed by Mendoza. They include senior representatives of six orders in Catalonia, two canons of Barcelona (Guerau Vilana, who here began a long association with the Order, and Lluís Joan Vileta), and the diocesan vicar general, Jerònim Manegat.

elected.[145] Although Duran could hardly have chosen a more amenable figure as far as the crown was concerned, his pretensions were taken as a serious threat to Castile's cherished provincial independence, and to its prospects for reform.[146]

In Guadalajara, meanwhile, the chapter opened in the convent of San Antolín on Saturday 4th June under Manrique's presidency and in an atmosphere of considerable tension. Having done all he could to prevent the chapter taking place, Peñaranda presented himself on the opening day apparently determined to disrupt the proceedings.[147] When it became known that he was preparing a vehement protest to the king against the celebration of the chapter in the name of the whole province, he and others were flung out of the convent by Manrique and set off towards Madrid. In reply, thirty-one of the forty-eight delegates, headed by Carrillo, prepared a document denouncing Peñaranda's protest as 'falsa y siniestra' and as the work of two or three religious determined to obstruct the progress of the chapter.[148] Although this petition shows Carrillo to have had a strong basis of support, he was clearly some way from carrying the whole province, and at least four major houses, including Madrid, did not send representatives to Guadalajara. Surprisingly, given Peñaranda's attempts to prevent graduates from voting in the chapter,[149] only ten out of the eighteen *presentados* joined Carrillo in condemning him, but there can be little doubt that other factors influenced their decision-making. Nevertheless, on Trinity Sunday, 5th June, to the tolling of the conventual bell, Carrillo was comfortably elected 'provincial of Castile, Portugal, Andalusia, the Indies and Terra Firma', evidently with Manrique's assistance.[150] The following day Peñaranda, smarting at the indignities heaped upon him, arrived at the Escorial and made a

---

[145] AGS, PR, 23-53(vii), f. 1r–v. Carrillo's *poder* as vicar provincial, dated Barcelona, 2nd June 1569, is in AGS, PR, 23-52(i). For other copies see AGN, Clero, vol. 402 & APV, ms. Antillón, *Epitome*, I(ii), pp. 1419–21.

[146] See AGS, PR, 23-53(iv), Philip II to Manrique, El Escorial, 6th June 1569, f. 1v, & (viii), Manrique to Philip II, Guadalajara, 9th June 1569, f. 1r. A copy is *ibid.*, (vi).

[147] *Ibid.*, f. 1r–v.

[148] AGS, PR, 23-53(xxii) for the original. Dated Guadalajara, 4th June 1569; f. 2r & 2v. There is a copy in *ibid.*, (xxiv).

[149] On this see AGS, PR, 23-49, f. 4r & *ibid.*, 23-51(i), reproduced in Vázquez Núñez, ed., *La Merced a mediados*, (doc.ii), pp. 103–11; f. 5r–v or p. 110.

[150] The *acta* of the election, dated 6th June 1569, are in AGN, Clero, vol. 416. Another copy in APV, ms. Antillón, *Epitome*, I(ii), pp. 1425–8. The Order, it should be noted, had possessed no houses in Portugal since the later 14th century.

formal protest to the king.[151] In it he denounced both Manrique's blatant favouritism of Carrillo and his unwarranted intervention in provincial affairs beside the actual election. However, Philip refused to alter Manrique's commission, advising him only to proceed within legal bounds and avoid causing offence.[152] Peñaranda he ordered back to Madrid.

The election of the king's favoured candidate was an important victory for the crown, but the problem remained of obtaining his confirmation. On Monday 6th June, the day of Peñaranda's visit, news reached the Escorial of Duran's refusal to comply with Philip's requests regarding the confirmation, and his appointment of Carrillo as vicar provincial instead. This was clearly a setback, but the election as provincial of Duran's own choice as governor of Castile strengthened the possibility that he might grant the confirmation without further ado, and it was with this in mind that Philip transferred the matter to Manrique.[153]

In Guadalajara, Manrique immediately delegated a five-member committee to reply to the Barcelona *junta* and present a case for Carrillo's confirmation. By 9th June the committee — composed of the Franciscan provincial of Castile, two senior Dominicans along with Carrillo and Mº Fray Cristóbal de Soto — had concluded its deliberations, though not without difficulty.[154] The *Concordia*, they cryptically declared, had not been nullified by the Council of Trent, since it militated neither against its decrees, nor against 'the ancient and regular life and perfection practised [by the religious], nor their primordial constitutions'.[155] In instances where the *Concordia* had failed to legislate, as in this case, the right to convene the chapter and the validity of the election could be assured through strict observance of Conciliar rulings.[156] But the fact is that the ambiguity of the Tridentine decrees on monastic reform, coupled with the utter confusion into

---

[151] Reported in AGS, PR, 23-53(v) — an addendum to *ibid.*, (iv) — Philip II to Manrique, El Escorial, 6th June 1569, f. 1r–v. For Dr. Velasco's comments on this to Zayas, see *ibid.*, (xiv), El Escorial, 7th June 1569.

[152] *Ibid.*, (v).

[153] *Ibid.*, (iv). See Dr. Velasco's comments on this to Zayas, *ibid.*, (xiii), El Escorial, 7th June 1569, in which he is clearly still unaware of Carrillo's election.

[154] *Ibid.*, (xxv), an undated, unsigned copy. Details of the authors are given in *ibid.*, (viii), f. 1r; apart from the Mercedarians, only the Dominican procurator general of Castile, Fray Juan de Segovia, is named. See also *ibid.*, (xx), f. 1v.

[155] *Ibid.*, (xxv), f. 1r.

[156] *Ibid.*, f. 1v.

which the Mercedarian constitution had fallen, made it virtually impossible for a cogent judgement to be reached on this question. Indeed, it was upon this very ambiguity and confusion that both Barcelona and Guadalajara were relying to support their claims. The Guadalajara *letrados* described Duran's obstacles to making the confirmation as 'not very legitimate', but the same might well have been said of the Castilian reply.[157]

Although the Castilians had now drawn up their refutation of the Barcelona *parecer*, the question remained of presenting it and obtaining Duran's confirmation. To this end, the crown prepared documents empowering four citizens of Barcelona to put the case for confirming Carrillo before Duran on Castile's behalf.[158] It was left to the viceroy to select the most suitable go-between, who was to be provided with twelve doubloons in gold to pay the tribute traditionally rendered by Castile on this occasion. The negotiator was instructed to inform Duran that if he did not confirm Carrillo within thirty days the matter would devolve to the papacy.[159] However, this measure never had to be resorted to, for among the documents dispatched to Barcelona from the Escorial was a highly conciliatory letter from Philip to Duran.[160] Although recognizing the difficulties of the case, the king emphasized that prospects for future dialogue and the interests of the Order as a whole would be best served by Carrillo's confirmation. Heeding the voice of reason, on 16th June Duran drafted a letter confirming Carrillo as provincial, though under protest.[161] As Duran later declared to Philip, he would have confirmed Carrillo immediately had it not seemed to him a contravention of the Tridentine decrees.[162]

---

[157] *Ibid.*, f. 2r.

[158] The *letrados'* suggestions to the crown on this are in *ibid.*, (xxvi). Undated but probably Guadalajara, 9th June 1569. Among those appointed was an inquisitor, Rodrigo de Mendoza, and a Catalan Mercedarian, Fra Pere Pau Lleó who later became an important figure in the defence of the priory.

[159] *Ibid.*, (xx), f. 1r–v.

[160] *Ibid.*, (iii[a]), Philip II to Príncipe de Melito, El Escorial, 11th June 1569. See also *ibid.*, (xv), Dr. Velasco to Zayas, same place and date. For Philip's letter to Duran, see *ibid.*, (iii[b]), same place and date. Other copies in AGN, Clero, vol. 416 and APV, ms. Antillón, *Epitome*, I(ii), pp. 1428–30.

[161] Duran's letter of confirmation, in Latin, is in AGS, PR, 23-52(ii), while another copy is in APV, ms. Antillón, *Epitome*, I(ii), pp. 1431–3. A similar letter to the papacy of the same date is in AGN, Clero, vol. 402.

[162] AGS, E°, leg. 333, (unftd.), dated Barcelona, 17th June 1569. Other copies in AGN, Clero, vol. 416 and APV, ms. Antillón, *Epitome*, I(ii), pp. 1430–1.

Duran's letter of confirmation reached Guadalajara on 22nd June, ten days after the chapter had concluded its main business. The final days of the chapter had gone some way towards establishing Carrillo's authority in the province, and, for now at least, to destroying Peñaranda's reputation. On 9th June Carrillo informed Zayas of the discovery in Madrid of Maldonado's highly sensitive letter to Peñaranda, revealing the lengths to which he had been prepared to go to obstruct the Reform.[163] After his election on 5th June Carrillo had written an emollient letter to the ex-provincial assuring him of his safety, but now he was determined that Peñaranda and his cohorts should face the full rigour of the law.[164] Peñaranda and another religious were immediately arrested and Carrillo headed for Madrid once the chapter proper had ended on 12th June. Zayas and Manrique, judging a conciliatory approach to be the surest means of enhancing Carrillo's authority, urged leniency and discretion.[165] The provincial was eventually brought round to this point of view, but the problem remained of what to do with Peñaranda, who, not surprisingly, had placed himself under the nuncio's protection.[166] Carrillo agreed to receive Peñaranda back into the fold, but, as he made clear to Castagna, the province was not about to suffer any further disruption at the hands of a thwarted prelate.[167] As Carrillo reminded him, 'it is we who are responsible for the reformation, which will be to no effect if we permit religious the unbridled freedom to disrupt individuals and communities'. If Peñaranda were to return to the Order, then Castagna would have to stand surety for his good conduct. Clemency therefore prevailed. Carrillo had already offered the crown a free hand in the provision to commanderies, and, at Zayas' instigation no doubt, Peñaranda was eventually granted that of Guadalajara itself.[168] Zayas was urged to impress upon the religious in question the benign treatment they had received at Carrillo's hands, to render him their obedience, 'and to ask

---

[163] The letter in question is AGS, PR, 23-53(xxiii); for Carrillo's comments, see *ibid.*, (xx), f. 2r.

[164] See *ibid.*, (xxi), Carrillo to Zayas, Guadalajara, 10th June 1569. Regarding Carrillo's letter to Peñaranda, see *ibid.*, (xi), Manrique to Zayas, same place and date, f. 1v; a condensed version is *ibid.*, (xii).

[165] *Ibid.*, (x), Manrique to Zayas, Guadalajara, 11th June 1569.

[166] IVDJ, env. 72, II, ff. 86r–87v, Carrillo to Castagna, Guadalajara, 16th June 1569.

[167] *Ibid.*, 86v.

[168] For Carrillo's offer to the crown, see AGS, PR, 23-53(xx), f. 1v. See also IVDJ, env. 72, II, f. 135r–v.

for no more than they have been granted, for they surely do not deserve it'.[169] His words, however, would not be heeded long.

Nevertheless, Carrillo was determined to enforce now what he had been suggesting for some time, namely that Maldonado should be recalled from Rome.[170] Anxious to prevent any further damage, the chapter immediately revoked Maldonado's commission as *procurador general*, and on 16th June he was ordered to return to Spain as his presence in Rome was now 'neither suitable nor necessary'.[171] Maldonado was no doubt tarred by his association with Peñaranda, but he had served his province well against the Catalans and it was this that would endure in the minds of Mercedarians in the years to come.[172]

VII. *An Agenda for Reform*

The *acta* of the chapter provincial of Guadalajara have not come down to us as such, but a highly detailed account of the ordinances passed there has survived.[173] Although these are the earliest extant ordinances from a Castilian chapter provincial, we can be fairly certain that they were of an unprecedented thoroughness. In forty-one chapters, Carrillo, who was clearly their principal architect, laid out a basic agenda for the internal reform of the province over the next few years. The results closely reflect the contents of his first three extant *memoriales* to the crown of 1568–9.[174] The chapter immediately recognized private ownership of property by the religious as one of the main obstacles to reformed life, 'the great moth of the Order' as Carrillo characterized it elsewhere.[175] The routine ownership by friars of money, goods and even land had to be curbed if reform were to be seriously contemplated. As the decrees opened,

---

[169] AGS, PR, 23-53(x).

[170] *Ibid.*, (i), reproduced in Vázquez Núñez, ed., *La Merced a mediados*, (doc.ii), pp. 103–11; f. 5v or p. 111.

[171] See AGS, PR, 23-53(xx), f. 2r. The recall is in AMAE, SS, leg. 34, ff. 123r–124v, Guadalajara, 16th June 1569. See also AGS, PR, 23-53(xi), f. 1r–v.

[172] The chapter made him commendator of Málaga. See Vázquez Núñez, *Mercedarios ilustres*, p. 311.

[173] AGS, E°, leg. 151, no. 194. Undated but June 1569. References to this document are henceforth given in brackets in the text.

[174] See ch. 4, nn. 36 & 47.

[175] IVDJ, env. 72, II, f. 86r; 'la mayor polilla de la religion'.

> It is extremely important for the reformation of this Holy Order that the vow of poverty be entirely and diligently kept, for on its observance depends that of the remaining vows, as well as the harmony and order that is essential among religious.(1r)

In token of this, the delegates were forced to make a public declaration of the private property they had brought with them, ranging from books and clothing, through mules and silverware, up to the slave which a commendator was obliged to part with for ninety ducats, the proceeds going to his house.(1r–v) Not for the first time, we learn, a chapter provincial had ordered a deposit box with three keys to be installed in each convent, and a procedure laid down to keep account of the money consigned to it.(4r) As much a place to hold the monies permitted to the brethren, the conventual deposit was designed to safeguard the alms for the redemption of captives that had been dissipated in the past; only 1300 ducats of *limosna* was presently available, and a mere sixty had been surrendered at the chapter.(1v–2r) Commendators were particularly required to find and display in their houses copies of the redemption bull granted the Order by Leo X in 1516 detailing the means by which alms were to be collected and distributed.(1v) This alone is a measure of the neglect into which the ransoming vocation had fallen.

If the Castilian hierarchy were concerned for the financial mores of the Order, then they were equally preoccupied with the quality of those being recruited into it. In accordance with a papal brief banning religious from leaving one congregation for another, the chapter instructed commendators to eject from the Order all those who had joined it apostate in recent years.(4v–5r) For, as the chapter declared, 'it is not right that this Order should be the refuge of such people'. Commendators were warned against receiving fugitives from any part of the Order, while the chapter begged the crown to dissuade Duran from harbouring Castilians fleeing the wrath of their superiors.(3v,6r) Even so, this was one area in which, outwardly at least, elements of the Castilian hierarchy were in agreement with their Aragonese counterparts.[176]

---

[176] Compare with the ordinances passed on this matter by the chapter general of Barcelona in 1567 and by Duran during his visitation of Aragon-Navarre in 1568–9.

[177] The first Mercedarian *estatuto de limpieza de sangre* appears to have been passed by the Valencian general Fra Llorens Company at the chapter general of Valencia in 1478; Vázquez Núñez, *Manual*, I, p. 479. The ordinance, reiterated by Maurel in 1480 and 1489, and by Zafont in 1523, barred *conversos* and *moriscos* from entering

However, taken all round, the Mercedarians were not especially discriminating where recruitment was concerned. Those receiving the habit were to be no younger than fifteen, and with either a basic knowledge of Latin or, as the ordinances bluntly put it, 'a dowry large enough to make good and remedy their ignorance'.(4r) *Converso* or *morisco* blood appears to have been a bar to entry only when the genealogical taint was notorious, though even this was not rigorously enforced.[177] In this the Order's standards were somewhat below those of other institutions, as problems between the college of La Concepción at Alcalá and the *colegio mayor* of San Ildefonso indicate.(2v)[178] In 1564 or 1565 Pius IV was forced to issue two secret briefs ordering none to be admitted to the Vera Cruz or La Concepción without having been examined as to their *limpieza de sangre*.[179] These both Torres and Peñaranda refused to promulgate, and it was left to Carrillo to enact them during his provincialate.[180] This would appear to support allegations that a former provincial (probably Torres or Peñaranda, perhaps both) was himself of New Christian blood.[181] On

---

the Order but otherwise made only unprofessed novices liable to expulsion from it on these grounds; see APV, Antillón, ms. *Epítome*, I(ii), p. 1337, & Vázquez Núñez, *Manual*, I, p. 388. In 1561 Puig extended the ban on New Christians to indians; *ibid.*, p. 479.

[178] The dispute would seem to have centred on the long-serving rector of La Concepción, Fray Agustín de Revenga, who held office from 1545–67 and died two years later; Vázquez Núñez, *Mercedarios ilustres*, p. 266. The fact that the province chose not to wait until the next chapter (1569) before replacing him is significant, particularly since the two college rectorships were supposedly of life tenure. Revenga was succeeded by Pº Fray Francisco Zumel who gained his first chair at Salamanca in 1570 and was himself investigated as to his *limpieza de sangre* in 1574; see *id.*, *El Padre Francisco Zumel*, pp. 3 & 10–11. Problems over *limpieza* continued at Alcalá until the mid 17th century; see ch. 8, n. 57.

[179] *Id.*, *Manual*, I, p. 500. These requirements were reiterated with respect to prospective Andalusian collegials at the chapter general of Zaragoza in 1587; *ibid.*, II, p. 44.

[180] *Ibid.*, I, pp. 500–1.

[181] On this see IVDJ, env. 72, II, f. 133r–v, Fray Pedro Galindo, rector of Alcalá, to Castagna, undated but probably 1572, in which Galindo further claims the province to be full of descendants of *conversos* attempting to have one of their number elected provincial. The main allegation would appear to have been shared by Carrillo as well; see Vázquez Núñez, ed., *La Merced a mediados*, (doc.i), p. 103 & AGS, PR, 23-49, f. 4r. The evidence suggests that the Order provided a relatively safe haven for *conversos* until at least the early 1570s, and it was not until the early 17th century that concerted efforts were made to reverse this; see Vázquez Núñez, *Manual*, II, p. 96. There appears to have been no serious vetting of entrants on racial grounds until the late 1580s; see ARV, Clero, lib. 1305, Receptions and professions at Valencia, 1576–1631, esp. ff. 125v–126r. In the late 1590s the *procurador general* in Rome, Mº Fray Bernardo de Vargas, admitted to Clement VIII that lay brothers were allowed into the Order without any investigation as to their purity of blood; see Serratosa Queralt, 'La leyenda del sacerdocio de San Pedro Nolasco', p. 72.

the other hand, the brethren would welcome any individual 'so qualified as to honour the Order with his presence',[182] for public honour
and a raising of standards — moral, disciplinary and intellectual —
was what leading Mercedarians were particularly anxious to
achieve.(4r)[183]

While the hierarchy no doubt regarded the fulfilment of religious
standards as a central part in this process, Mercedarian reform was
not at this stage conceived in terms of spiritual rigour. Religious in
larger houses were expected to keep the seven canonical hours, but
communities with under ten friars were exempted from matins, and
preachers (who increasingly were graduates also) from prime, nones
and compline as well.(3r,3v)[184] Contrary to what the constitutions
ordained, the chapter dispensed the brethren from the ban on eating
meat on Mondays (while preserving that for Wednesdays), and fixed
pre-Christmas fasting at one month rather than the statutory two.(3v)
For, as the ordinances implied, the Order quite simply could not
afford to immobilize its religious from money-earning activity by
enforcing a strict ascetic regime upon them.(3v) As Carrillo had
admitted to the crown earlier that year,

---

[182] The most interesting case of this in the 16th century was the Valencian physi-
cian M° Fray Gregorio de Arciso (also known as Arcisio, Ascisio or Narciso Gregorio, or, in Catalan, Narcisi Gregori). A late convert to the religious life, Arciso studied in Paris under Jacques Dubois (Jacobus Silvius) and held chairs at Valencia
before joining the Order in *c.*1546. He spent the 1550s at the Vera Cruz in Salamanca, gaining chairs in arts and natural philosophy while conducting a lucrative med-
ical practice. Arciso returned to Valencia as commendador of El Puig in 1559 but
died in Madrid in 1561, a testament to the opportunities and independence open to
wealthy and learned members of the Order. His principal work was the *Dialectica
Aristotelis, Boethio Severino interprete, cum argumentis Politiani, ac in calce novis Scholiis* (Salamanca: Andrés de Portonares, 1554; 2nd edn. Alcalá: Brócar, 1556 etc.). See BUV,
ms. 884, p. 56, Vázquez Núñez, *Mercedarios ilustres*, pp. 233-7 & 238-41, & Esteban
Mateo, 'Catedráticos eclesiásticos', pp. 364–5.
[183] The province's concern for its image is reflected in AGS, E°, leg. 149, no. 174,
anonymous Mercedarian *procurador general* to Bishop of Badajoz, undated but probably late 1568 or early 1569, and in IVDJ, env. 72, II, ff. 113r–114v, an anonymous,
undated but contemporaneous document concerning the visitation of Jerez de la
Frontera. In the former case the author described the removal of the commendator
by the diocesan reformer as 'a public scandal in which the Order is losing much of its
former prestige'. Regarding Jerez, the author accused the visitors of 'causing great
injury and offence to this monastery to the prejudice of its honour' and status within
the town (f. 113r); see *supra*, n. 105.
[184] Regulations on this were less stringent in the Crown of Aragon. From 1571
houses with less than sixteen religious were exempted from singing matins; see IVDJ,
env. 72, II, f. 238v.

> Human nature is not as strong and healthy as once it was [...] and the
> Order has little temporal wealth and is of few means, which is the fibre
> and nourishment by which the severe rigours of other wealthier orders
> are sustained.[185]

Asceticism, then, was paradoxically a luxury beyond the purse of the
Order, and this must be seen as an important bench-mark in the
study of the religious orders at this time.[186]

It is only in a contemporaneous *memorial* that the full importance of
spiritual reform comes through. Discussing the necessary qualities of
those entrusted with conventual office, the author concludes that
holders should be of 'sufficient character, religion, zeal and Christianity to reduce things to the primordial institution of the Order, and
enact that which most piously has been ordained'.[187] On such men
the 'recollection, organization and religion' of the Order depended.
Although it is still not clear quite what 'things' are being referred to,
it was evidently at conventual rather than capitular level that spiritual
reform had to be implanted.

As the chapter dispersed to the four winds, its business finally concluded, Carrillo therefore embarked on a major visitation of Castile.
Again, absence of documentation prevents us following his progress
through the province as has been possible for the Crown of Aragon,
but it is clear that his trail, which began in La Mancha, led him eventually to Andalusia. While it is still much to be regretted, the overall
loss of papers has been greatly mitigated by the survival of the visitation book of Huete in the diocese of Cuenca which, appropriately
enough, commences in 1569.[188] Carrillo reached the house on 13th

---

[185] AGS, PR, 23-51(i), reproduced in Vázquez Núñez, ed., *La Merced a mediados*, (doc.ii), pp. 103–11; reference f. 1r or p. 103.

[186] The importance of funding reform and reformers is reiterated by the Dominican M° Fray Pedro de Salamanca in a letter to Ormaneto, IVDJ, env. 72, II, ff.
82r–83r, Valencia, 2nd November 1575; f. 82r & 82v. Salamanca reports that the
crown had provided 3000 ducats for the reform of the Augustinians of the Crown of
Aragon, along with an annual sum of 300 *escudos* for the visitor's expenses.

[187] AGS, E°, leg. 149, no. 169. Anonymous *memorial*, undated but written between
June and August 1569; citations f. 1r. The offices are those of commendator, vicar,
porter, sacristan and novice master.

[188] AHN, Clero, vol. 3320. The only other house known to have been visited by
Carrillo in 1569 is that of Jerez de la Frontera; see ACPMC, ms. 720, *Varia*, f. 199r.
The visitation seems to have lasted into 1570, for the provincial was at Córdoba in
the earlier part of that year and was again visiting Guadalajara in early December;
see, respectively, IVDJ, env. 72, II, f. 76r–v, Carrillo to Castagna, undated but 1570,
and BNM, ms. 2684, f. 119r.

July and remained there a week, passing ordinances that reflect the aspirations of the chapter provincial.[189] Again, much emphasis was placed on putting an end to the ownership of money and property, particularly that appropriated from the Order itself. As Carrillo declared, 'the alienation by commendators of property and goods belonging to the convents has caused severe damage to the Order'.(8r) In order to combat this, Carrillo insisted that records be maintained of the full range of conventual activities: masses, donations, house documentation, property, rents, and ordinary accounts, all of which were to be preserved under lock and key in the deposit box. With a community of fourteen, the house was expected to observe all the canonical hours, but, as Carrillo declared, these were to be kept 'neither to excess nor for too long'.(7r) However, from September until New Year the commendator was strictly enjoined to arrange daily readings of *casos de conciencia* (cases of conscience) to the professed brethren.(7v) Immediate provision was to be made for the novices, with the appointment of a novice master and the allocation of a room specially for them.(8v–9r) On a more mundane level, Carrillo ordered all religious to be provided with their own beds, while the commendator was given a month to bar all windows giving onto the street.(7r)

The tenor and the content of many of the ordinances passed at Guadalajara and then at Huete have much in common with those laid down at the chapters general of Barcelona in 1561 and 1567. But, unlike the Crown of Aragon, the province of Castile had not only begun to define the objectives of its reform, but also establish the means of bringing them about. However, given the condition of the Order and the position of Castile within it, the enactment of this reform remained tied to the patronage, authority and organization of the crown. Concerned for the future, many — though by no means all — Castilian Mercedarians began to recognize in the crown the only sure means of guaranteeing their stability. From the royal perspective, recent events had presented a unique opportunity that Philip had been careful to exploit to the full.[190] Manrique's reports to the king on the progress of the chapter are nothing if not over-opti-

---

[189] AHN, Clero, vol. 3320, ff. 3r–9v. References from this volume henceforth given in the text. It should be noted that f. 6, which contained the beginning of the ordinances, has been removed from this volume within the last 70 years. For a summary of some of this folio's contents, see Vázquez Núñez, 'La Universidad de Salamanca en los años 1548 a 1568', p. 237.

[190] See in particular AGS, PR, 23-53(iv), f. 1v.

mistic, but this cannot obscure the gradual change of heart taking place in the province:

> The chapter has been very eager to fulfil its duties both to Our Lord and to Your Majesty, and the religious have begun to disabuse themselves [of their suspicions], all recognizing the service and favour that Your Majesty has done them. Those who once disagreed with the Reformation now desire it, aware that, through the offices of Your Majesty, they will derive much benefit.[191]

It was with the assurance of this royal patronage that the Castilian reformers braced themselves for the trials and challenges that lay ahead.

VIII. *The Orders, the Crown, and the Papacy, 1567–9*

By early 1569 the royal visitation of the three so-called 'unreformed' orders, including the Mercedarians, was dragging slowly towards completion. Although few visitation documents have survived, it is clear that prolonged contact with the orders concerned and cooperation with leading religious had afforded the crown a rather better grasp of the distinctive features of each. Already by the end of 1568 it had become apparent to the crown that, for a range of geographical, practical and jurisdictional reasons, the reform provisions of April 1567 were no longer satisfactory. With the benefit of over a year's experience behind him, Philip now began to petition Rome for a new set of briefs that would allow the crown to build on the foundations that had been laid. As the Mercedarian case demonstrates, although some progress had been made towards institutional change, the crown had yet to observe any success in the moral and spiritual elements of its reform agenda. Indeed, Philip was evidently still toying with the idea of suppressing the Mercedarians, and incorporating them and others into the Dominican Order along lines already traced out for the Isidrites and the Premonstratensians.[192] But if Philip had expected Pius V, a former general of the Domini-

---

[191] AGS, PR, 23-53(viii), f. 1v.

[192] See AGS, E°, leg. 910, no. 58. Juan de Zúñiga to Philip II, Rome, 10th January 1569, f. 2r. See also AGS, PR, 23-225, an untitled *memorial* of 1566 by a royal minister recommending the gradual extinction of any unruly order by preventing it receiving novices; ff. 8r–9r. The author intended the revenues of suppressed houses to be applied to the foundation of seminaries.

cans, to agree to this, then he was soon to be disabused. The pope and his principal advisor on clerical reform, the future nuncio Nic-colò Ormaneto, took the state of the orders extremely seriously — inordinately seriously as far as Zúñiga was concerned.[193] 'The reform of the religious orders is one of the pope's principal aims for his pontificate', the ambassador reported, and his zeal in this out-stripped even that of the king himself.[194] Thus, as both Zúñiga and the pro-Aragonese Cardinal Alessandrino made clear, Rome had no intention of sanctioning the suppression of any independent Spanish order, however ruinous its condition or unruly its members.[195] The orders were going to be reformed, and this could only be brought about 'con carità e con spirito' on the part of the crown, not through brazen self-interest.[196]

However, both parties were equally dissatisfied at the laggardly progress of the visitations of the three orders. While Alessandrino complained from Rome at the delay in their completion, Philip emphatically declared that nothing of use could be achieved until a new brief were forthcoming.[197] This view was accepted by Pius, who by the end of February 1569 was looking forward to the arrival of the visitation *acta* in Rome with a view to making further arrange-ments.[198] By mid March Castagna, by now in possession of the *acta* — about a hundred of them — was mulling over the original briefs of 1567, while Philip began to set out his requirements for the future of

---

[193] Ormaneto's appointment as Gregory XIII's first nuncio to Spain in 1572 no doubt owed much to his familiarity with the reform of the orders there. A close asso-ciate of Cardinal Borromeo in Milan, where he was appointed vicar general in 1564, Ormaneto had been trained under the reformist bishop Gian Mateo Giberti of Verona (1495–1543) and accompanied Cardinal Reginald Pole to England in 1554; see John M. Headley & John B. Tomaro, eds., *San Carlo Borromeo: Catholic Reform and Ecclesiastical Politics in the Second Half of the Sixteenth Century* (Washington, D.C., 1988), pp. 69, 80, 120 & 202.

[194] AGS, E°, leg. 911, no. 37, Zúñiga to Philip, Rome, 11th May 1569, f. 3r. Another copy is *ibid.*, no. 38.

[195] *Ibid.*, leg. 910, no. 58, f. 2r, and *CDEESS*, II, pp. 450–1. Alessandrino to Castagna, Rome, 28th August 1568.

[196] *CDEESS*, II, p. 450.

[197] ASV, NS, vol. 6(ii), f. 373r; Alessandrino to Castagna, Rome, 21st January 1569. Another copy is f. 374r. Already in May 1568 Philip had reported that a *relación* of the visitation of the three orders was in the course of preparation for the pope, though this can hardly have been the case; *CODOIN*, VII, p. 537. On the new brief, see AGS, E°, leg. 910, no. 85; Philip to Zúñiga, Madrid, 12th January 1569, f. 1v.

[198] AGS, E°, leg. 911, no. 21. Zúñiga to Philip, Rome, 24th February 1569, f. 1r; another copy *ibid.*, no. 22.

the three orders in consultation with the nuncio.[199] In the first place,
Philip underlined the need for separate provisions for Castile and the
Crown of Aragon. As demonstrated in the Mercedarian case, though
the crown had been able to thwart the Aragonese hierarchy in Rome,
local conditions had prevented any progress being made towards
actual reform in the eastern kingdoms. Secondly, though Philip now
recognized the importance of religious orders being visited by religious themselves, he still regarded reform as essentially incumbent on
the bishops, whose important executive and supervisory role in this
matter he wished to preserve. Expecting these provisions to be quickly accepted in Rome, Philip kept the visitations open so that momentum would not be lost.

However, while the curia agreed with many of Philip's proposals,
Pius remained concerned at the degree of secular and episcopal intervention that was being inflicted on the orders as a whole.[200] The
reform campaigns of recent years had raised a storm of protest in
Rome from religious superiors, and the matter threatened to founder
on the familiar rock of monastic and papal jurisdiction. Rome was
particularly angry at the obstruction encountered by the Carmelite
general, Fra Giambattista Rossi (called Rubeo in Spain), from the
Royal Council of Castile during his momentous visitation of the
Peninsula in 1566–7. Royal tribunals, the papacy noted, were con-
stantly infringing ecclesiastical jurisdiction. As Alessandrino declared
to Castagna, the crown should adopt a less authoritarian and more
consultative approach to these matters.[201] Moreover, Pius was concerned that the presidency of chapters general and provincial —
where the reform ordinances would be promulgated — should not be
given to prelates or laymen under royal appointment. The news that
Manrique had presided over the chapter provincial of Guadalajara in
June at the behest of the crown naturally added fuel to these argu-
ments.[202] For Pius was adamant above all else that the religious
orders should be visited and reformed by their own kind, not by lay-

---

[199] Regarding the *acta*, see AGS, PR, 23-208, f. 1r; anonymous and undated, but
1568 or 1569, & ASV, NS, vol. 4, ff. 67v–69v, Castagna to Alessandrino, Madrid,
15th March 1569; f. 69r. AGS, E°, leg. 910, nos. 91–93, Philip to Zúñiga, Madrid,
12th March 1569, f. 3r–v. Other copies *ibid.*, nos. 92–93.

[200] AGS, E°, leg. 911, no. 37, f. 2v.

[201] *CDEESS*, III, pp. 138–9, Rome, 6th September 1569.

[202] *Ibid.*, p. 138. It should be said, however, that the papacy was clearly not aware
of the exceptional circumstances surrounding the convocation of this chapter.

men or the secular clergy. The pope was especially annoyed at the greed of certain Catalan and Aragonese bishops who he felt had abused their powers of reform over the Franciscan Conventuals in these parts.[203] The bishops, he believed, were too poorly informed on the life and 'rules' of the orders concerned, and had too many responsibilities governing their own dioceses to give this matter the attention it deserved.[204] The vexations associated with episcopal visitation are vividly characterized by Carrillo as 'getting up in the middle of the night to surrender one's will to that of the bishop'.[205] As he made clear, 'the miseries, indigence, travails, infirmities, journeys, dispensations, rigours and such like' of religious life should only be picked over by religious themselves.

Philip, however, was equally determined that the issue should be settled to the satisfaction of the crown, and that as much of the decision-making be left to Madrid as possible. In this too he evidently had Castagna's support since, much to Pius' fury, the visitation *acta* had still not been remitted to Rome in May, purportedly 'so as to provide information on a wide range of issues'.[206] But the pope was not about to suffer this procrastination, and Castagna duly relinquished the *acta* on strict orders from Rome.[207] After much thought and wide consultation with religious, Pius decided to issue briefs entrusting the Dominican visitors first with the duty of presiding over the chapters, and then with the task of visiting and reforming the three orders — to the exclusion of the ordinary clergy.[208] However, any reform provisions that did not comprehend the bishops were quite useless as far as Philip was concerned. As he wrote to Zúñiga with undisguised irritation,

> Ensure that he [i.e. the pope] understand that, however good and holy the ordinances drawn up for the reformation [of the orders] may be, they will (for a time at least) be of no consequence unless the bishops

---

[203] See *ibid.*, IV, xxxvii–xxxviii. Bishops had apparently attempted to suppress and amalgamate Conventual houses with Benedictine ones.

[204] *Ibid.*, III, pp. 201–3. Alessandrino to Castagna, Rome, 16th December 1569; p. 201.

[205] IVDJ, env. 72, II, ff. 105r–106v. Carrillo to Castagna, undated but 1570; f. 106r.

[206] AGS, PR, 23-53(xxiii). Maldonado to Peñaranda, Rome, 9th May 1569, f. 1r–v; 1r.

[207] AGS, Eº, leg. 910, no. 134. Philip to Zúñiga, El Escorial, 17th August 1569, f. 2v. Another copy is *ibid.*, no. 135.

[208] *Ibid.*, leg. 911, no. 61. Zúñiga to Philip, Rome, 1st July 1569, f. 1r.

have the authority to ensure their observance. For long experience has shown that, when friars are themselves the executors, the ordinances are either soon forgotten or dissipated through indulgence, remission and dissimulation, with the friars returning to their old ways. This, however, would not happen if the friars knew that they were to be supervised in their observance of these ordinances by the bishops, something His Holiness (having been a religious himself so many years) should understand better than I, and recognize the more readily as what is for the best.[209]

However, the pope stood his ground and refused point-blank to commit the reform of the orders to the ordinary clergy. Philip, whose impatience now turned to frustration, tried to play for time, but Pius had been moved by the complaints of religious in Rome and, as Zúñiga reported, ultimately took 'a friar's view of this affair'.[210] Plans were finalized, and Pius sent instructions to the Dominican general, Cardinal Fra Vincenzo Giustiniani, then in Spain for the celebration of his Order's chapter general, to appoint provincial visitors for each of the three congregations. In late August Zúñiga informed Philip that briefs to this effect were ready, having been 'written and rewritten by Ormaneto ten or twelve times'.[211]

The brief, again called *Superioribus mensibus*, represents one of the most significant documents in Mercedarian history.[212] The reform of the Order was placed in the hands of two Dominican commissaries apostolic, M° Fray Guillermo Montaña, prior of Girona, with responsibility for the Crown of Aragon, and the Extremaduran M° Fray Felipe de Meneses, rector of the college of San Gregorio in Valladolid, for Castile. The appointments are an interesting combination of experience of the Order and immense spiritual and pastoral erudition. Montaña, along with his fellow Dominican M° Fray Pedro de Salamanca, had been appointed visitor apostolic of the three orders in the diocese of Barcelona in October 1567, and was no doubt familiar with the state of the Order in general and the Crown

---

[209] *Ibid.*, leg. 910, no. 128. Philip to Zúñiga, Madrid, 13th July 1569, f. 3r. This passage echoes the feelings of the crown in 1563 towards the Tridentine provisions for monastic reform, which were condemned as placing too much reliance on the reforming efforts of religious themselves.

[210] *Ibid.*, leg. 910, no. 134, f. 2v, and *ibid.*, leg. 911, nos. 77 & 78. Zúñiga to Philip, Rome, 11th & 12th August 1569 respectively, f. 1r & 1v (citation).

[211] *Ibid.*, leg. 911, no. 80. Rome, 25th August 1569, f. 1r.

[212] The original, on vellum, survives in IVDJ, env. 72, II, f. 223. Dated Rome, 20th August 1569. There are later copies in ACA, Mon., vol. 2830, pp. 251–4, & AGN, Clero, vol. 402.

of Aragon in particular. Meneses, meanwhile, was among the most distinguished Spanish religious of the age, an important spiritual writer in the illuminist tradition who was deeply committed to the reform of society.[213] His *Luz del alma christiana* published in 1554 was among the most popular manuals of reformed piety in contemporary Spain.[214] Widely travelled in the Peninsula, Meneses was among those who, from the 1550s onwards, brought home to the authorities the massive ignorance of Christian doctrine in which large sectors of Spanish society lived. As he wrote in his manual, 'experience has shown that there are Indies in Spain, and that in the very heart of Castile there are mountains, in this case of ignorance'.[215] Such were the men entrusted with the reform of the Order.

The brief granted the commissaries full executive and legislative powers to reduce the Order to 'regular observance'. They were made responsible to none but the nuncio and ultimately the papacy itself, while the support of all clergy and lay persons was enjoined. All Mercedarian officials were placed under the direct authority of the commissaries, who were to mete out punishments as laid down in the constitutions and pass ordinances in accordance with the Tridentine decrees. The commissaries were intended to build on earlier progress and were required to consult the *acta* of the episcopal visitations. Although the commissaries were expected to confer and draft major ordinances together, the visitations themselves would be conducted independently. The briefs for the three orders were followed on 30th August by a letter from Pius to Philip requesting his support in their execution.[216] In October came a further brief reiterating the limitations imposed by Trent on religious transferring from order to order.[217] This was followed by yet another in January 1570 withdrawing the commission of 1567 from the bishops and ordering the new arrangements to be brought to the attention of the congregations concerned.[218] This last measure would surely not have been passed

---

[213] See Bataillon, *Erasmo y España*, 2nd Spanish edn., pp. 541–5 & 778, & Kamen, *The Phoenix and the Flame*, pp. 87–8.

[214] *Luz del alma christiana contra la ceguedad y ignorancia en lo que pertenesce a la fe y ley de Dios* (Valladolid: Francisco Fernandez de Cordoba, 1554).

[215] Cited in Kamen, *The Phoenix and the Flame*, p. 88.

[216] AGS, PR, 23-179.

[217] See García Oro, 'Conventualismo y observancia' in *HIE*, III(i), p. 325. Dated 13th October 1569.

[218] The brief *Dudum per nostras*, dated 31st January 1570, is reproduced in APV, Antillón, ms. *Epitome*, I(ii), pp. 1439–41. See ASV, NS, vol. 6(i), ff. 238r–239r,

had the papacy realized how long the new campaign would take to organize. As it was, the lengthy lacuna between the two visitations was to have serious consequences for the Mercedarians.

Pius' provisions were not of course received without opposition. From Rome Zúñiga questioned whether the Dominicans would be able to bear the burden of reform and visitation without the assistance of the secular clergy.[219] By April 1570 the Royal Council of Castile was again putting up considerable resistance to the reform of the three orders by friars under papal appointment.[220] Rome yielded only to the extent of permitting the Dominican reformers to be nominated by the crown, but in the event the existing appointments were ratified. Yet despite the papacy's show of independence, little could be done without the direct support of the crown, and by ignoring Philip's own reasons for sponsoring monastic reform Pius had founded his plans on a somewhat unrealistic basis. The business of visiting and reforming the Mercedarians would inevitably draw the commissaries into the web of royal organization, particularly the *Junta de Reforma* with its distinctly episcopal outlook. The curia had to learn that nothing could be done without the crown, just as Philip had eventually to accept the reality that, in this matter, he was helpless without the continued support of the papacy.

Alessandrino to Castagna, Rome, 31st January 1570, f. 238r, and *ibid.*, vol. 13, ff. 118r–v & 124r–126v. Castagna to Cardinal Rusticucci, Madrid, 31st January & 8th March 1570 respectively.

[219] AGS, E°, leg. 911, no. 116. Zúñiga to Philip, Rome, 31st October 1569, f. 1r. Another copy is *ibid.*, no. 117.

[220] *CDEESS*, III, pp. 321–4. Alessandrino to Castagna, Rome, 29th April 1570, p. 323.

CHAPTER SIX

THE PROGRESS OF REFORM (1570–5)

…but Our Lord is powerful and the cause is His.[1]

The circumstances behind the enactment of the reform briefs are not entirely clear, but by the end of 1570 the visitors had formally accepted their commissions and set to work in both Castile and the Crown of Aragon. What is clear, however, is that hostility to the visitations from outside the Order was mirrored by opposition within it. While the implementation of the briefs was still at a planning stage, news reached Carrillo from Rome that a *relación* had been sent to the pope, probably from the Crown of Aragon, declaring the Dominicans to have neither the authority nor the means to conduct the reform of the Order.[2] Although Carrillo evidently found the prospect of visitation by another order as distasteful as any of his brethren, he was aware how fortunate the Mercedarians had been to be entrusted once again to Dominican reformers, who shared both their rule and constitutions.[3] In this sense, the lot of the Order was, outwardly at least, rather more bearable than that of the Carmelites or the Trinitarians, who had less in common with the Friars Preachers. Determined that this advantage not be lost, Carrillo went to great lengths to underline the conformity of the two orders. Far from being unsuited, reform by Dominicans held the prospect of even greater compatibility between institutions that already observed similar lifestyles.[4] Indeed, as he declared,

> Our monasteries could very well be regulated and placed in conformity with those of the Order of St Dominic, though not with the most opulent of these, but rather those of medium size which resemble our own as to income, alms, numbers of religious and buildings.[5]

---

[1] IVDJ, env. 72, II, f. 306r–v. Mº Fray Juan Izquierdo (OP) to Montaña, Tortosa, 29th June 1572.

[2] *Ibid.*, ff. 105r–106v. Carrillo to Castagna, undated but 1570; f. 105r.

[3] Already in 1567 the establishment of the Mercedarian nuns in Seville had been effected with Dominican assistance.

[4] IVDJ, env. 72, II, f. 105r.

[5] *Ibid.*, f. 106r.

Carrillo would no doubt have moderated his language had he known how earnestly the crown had considered reducing the three orders into that of St Dominic.[6] Nevertheless, his attitude reflects the aspirations of leading Castilian Mercedarians since at least the early sixteenth century to reform the Order to Dominican standards, to which the development of academic and missionary vocations bears witness.

I. *The Apostolic Visitation of Castile, 1570–2*

Satisfied though he was with Meneses' appointment, Carrillo was anxious that he should not conduct the visitation of Castile without his own participation in an intermediary capacity. Writing from Córdoba, Carrillo asked for permission to consult with Meneses in Valladolid before setting forth with him on the visitation.[7] The campaign, he advised, no doubt on the basis of several months' visiting Andalusia, should begin in Castile itself — 'because matters there are in a better state of readiness' — and preferably at his former commandery of Toledo.[8] These suggestions Castagna and Meneses appear to have accepted, in principle at least. While preparations continued in Castile, Carrillo concluded his business in Andalusia by appointing religious to 'visit and reform' the four provinces in the Indies before travelling north to meet Meneses in the second half of 1570.[9]

Once again, lack of documents prevents us following the progress of the visitation. Although work had started by early October, no fur-

---

[6] For an indication of this, see in the 'Advertimientos' of M° Fray Francisco Pacheco (OFM) in AGS, PR, 10-23, f. 227r, undated but 1567.

[7] IVDJ, env. 72, II, f. 76r–v. Carrillo to Castagna, undated but Córdoba, 1570; f. 76r.

[8] *Ibid.*, f. 76r & 76v.

[9] *Ibid.*, f. 76v. These appointments, as Carrillo reminded Castagna, he made under royal licence rather than under apostolic authority. The main appointment was P° Fray Diego de Ángulo as visitor general of Peru, where he was elected provincial of Lima in 1574; see Vázquez Núñez, *Manual*, I, p. 540, Muñoz Delgado, 'El convento de Valladolid', p. 54, & Vázquez Fernández, 'Cedulario mercedario', pp. 625–6. The others were P° Fray Alonso Sánchez for Guatemala and Fray Mateo García for Santo Domingo in 1570, and M° Fray Antonio Osorio to Chile in 1571; Pérez, *Religiosos de la Merced*, pp. 106–8, 58–9, & 268 respectively. The Castilians had already dispatched a 'reformer' to the Indies in 1566; Vázquez Fernández, 'Cedulario mercedario', p. 624. Fray Juan de Valencia followed as visitor of Peru and Chile in 1567; Pérez, *Religiosos de la Merced*, p. 207.

ther news survives from Castile until letters from Meneses to
Castagna in June and July 1571.[10] However, the contents of these are
sufficient to give us an impression of the conduct of the visitation. It is
clear that Meneses had agreed to allow Carrillo to travel ahead of
him, preparing the way for the visitation proper, and actually to be
present himself — generous treatment indeed, as Meneses later recognized.[11] The campaign began in autumn 1570 in the archdiocese
of Toledo, probably at the convent of Toledo itself.[12] The visitation
book of Huete records Carrillo's fleeting presence in December, and
though there is no news here of his visit, Meneses is sure to have followed.[13] In this way the visitors toiled across New Castile, taking in
the houses at Madrid, Alcalá, Cuenca and Guadalajara apart from
those mentioned.[14] In the new year they covered the Order's five
convents in north-eastern Castile: Almazán, Soria, Burgos, Logroño
and finally Burceña on the Bay of Biscay, along with the handful of
beaterios attached to this house.[15]

So far as it is possible to tell, the apostolic visitations were a notable
success. As Meneses informed Castagna,

> The visitation has passed off as one would expect, with the religious
> accepting the ordinances willingly and, I understand, executing them
> as well. In several houses I discovered that observance of some things
> had started because religious had heard that they were being imple-
> mented by me.[16]

All the same, it is clear that by July 1571 Carrillo's participation had
become a nuisance to Meneses, who now forbade him from making
any further visitations on his own.[17] According to Fray Felipe, Carrillo had begun to obstruct his work by forewarning the religious of his
intentions and goading them into appealing against the ordinances.
The disruption caused by Carrillo was in sharp contrast to the attitude of religious at large who had welcomed the commissary and,

---

[10] ASV, NS, vol. 4, ff. 158v–159r, Castagna to Rusticucci, Madrid, 9th October
1570, f. 158v. See also IVDJ, env. 72, II, f. 308r, Castagna to Meneses, Madrid, 27th
September 1570, informing him of his commission.
[11] IVDJ, env. 72, II, f. 99r–v. Meneses to Castagna, Segovia, 10th July 1571.
Meneses was by now prior of the Santa Cruz in Segovia.
[12] *Ibid.*, f. 103r. Meneses to Castagna, Segovia, 20th June 1571.
[13] AHN, Clero, vol. 3320, f. 10r–v. Huete, 6th–8th December 1570.
[14] IVDJ, env. 72, II, f. 103r.
[15] *Ibid.*
[16] *Ibid.*
[17] *Ibid.*, f. 99r.

thought Meneses, shown more sense than their provincial. However, this was by no means the only reason for Meneses' curtailment of Carrillo's powers. Thanks to him, communities were being overwhelmed by repeated visitation, at least three times a year and in some cases three times in eight months. Unlike the provincial, who appealed to Castagna against this decision, Meneses seems to have recognized that the mass of religious, unfamiliar with this degree of scrutiny, were struggling to come to terms with the pace of change in the Order.[18]

For many, indeed, the pace of change was too quick, and Carrillo's brand of reform too rigorous. Again, lack of documentation prevents us following events closely, but it seems that Meneses' restraint of Carrillo was above all a reflection of the growing unrest in Castile against his behaviour as provincial, and even the legitimacy of his election.[19] Feelings were still running high in the wake of the chapter provincial of Guadalajara, and Carrillo's visitations had proved too much for many frustrated members of Peñaranda's party, who now gathered in open resistance.[20] Manrique's presidency of the chapter was condemned, the Guadalajara *junta*'s conclusions rebutted, and the election of Carrillo, implicitly a creature of the crown, declared null and void.[21] It was alleged of Carrillo himself that he had misspent provincial funds, including redemption *limosna*, imprisoned religious without justification and driven others into hiding.[22] Yet this opposition was apparently still underpinned by the conviction among Peñaranda's supporters that the *Concordia* of 1467 — the cause of all the Order's ills — had been annulled by the Tridentine decrees, and that the affairs of the province were consequently matters for the vicar general and the papacy, not the crown, its agents and officials.[23]

In order to settle these questions, Meneses convened the provin-

---

[18] *Ibid.*

[19] AGS, PR, 23-50(iii). Anonymous *memorial*, undated but September 1571.

[20] IVDJ, env. 72, II, f. 135r–v. Fray Pedro de Velasco *et al.* to Zayas(?), undated but Madrid, *c*.February 1572; f. 135r. Another signatory to this document was Fray Felipe Tavira, Peñaranda's ex-procurator general, while those endorsing it included Peñaranda himself and the commendator of Seville, Mº Fray Alonso Muñoz. Opposition to Carrillo may also have been founded in his efforts to enforce the briefs of Pius IV against New Christians at the colleges of Salamanca and Alcalá; see Vázquez Núñez, *Manual*, I, pp. 500–1 & ch. 5, nn. 178, 179 & 181.

[21] AGS, PR, 23-50(iii).

[22] IVDJ, env. 72, II, f. 135r.

[23] *Ibid.*, f. 135v.

cial hierarchy to a chapter in Segovia for 20th September 1571, promising that all questions would be addressed. This, however, immediately raised the hackles of the crown. Ministers were concerned that, by agreeing to review the plans set out with such elaborate care at Guadalajara, Meneses was not only exceeding his commission but impugning royal authority as well. Moreover, the crown was increasingly unhappy at the degree of independence shown by Fray Felipe during a visitation that seemed to bear little sense of continuity with that which had preceded it in 1567–9. Above all, underlying fears of an alliance between the orders and their religious visitors against royal interference was now threatening to become reality. However, here the matter ended, for no sooner had the religious begun to assemble in Segovia than Meneses died with only four houses left to be visited.[24] Taking advantage of this situation, Carrillo ordered the religious to his powerbase at Toledo where he proceeded to bully them into submission, threatening severe penalties against any who presented themselves at court. He then resumed his visitation and November found him back at Huete, where Fray Antonio Martínez, a member of Peñaranda's party, was no longer commendator.[25] Carrillo found conventual accounts to have been seriously neglected and both capitular and visitation ordinances generally ignored.[26] If the situation at Huete is anything to go by, the province was bordering on chaos, but here at least matters had improved by the time of his return in April the following year.[27]

With Meneses dead and the province divided into two warring factions, the appointment of a new commissary was an urgent priority, the more so since an electoral chapter was due to begin at Toledo on 4th May 1572.[28] Appeals were made to Philip to commit the matter to the papacy, and it was duly transferred to Castagna who made a thoroughly regalist appointment. The Dominican M° Fray Hernando del Castillo, prior of Nuestra Señora de Atocha in Madrid and the Inquisition's leading theological consultant, was of an altogether dif-

---

[24] *Ibid.*, f. 135r.

[25] AHN, Clero, vol. 3320, ff. 10v–11v. Huete, 25th November–2nd December 1571.

[26] *Ibid.*, f. 11v.

[27] *Ibid.*, f. 12r–v. Huete, 4th April 1572.

[28] IVDJ, env. 72, II, f. 101r. Anonymous *memorial*, perhaps to Castagna's secretary, undated but early 1572. See also *ibid.*, f. 135r–v.

ferent stamp to Meneses.[29] Unlike Fray Felipe, Castillo was at the centre of royal administration. As a member of Philip's religious inner circle he was among those charged with providing the king with theological justification on matters that weighed on his conscience. A staunch supporter of Santa Teresa, Castillo had in 1569 been sent to visit the Augustinians of Barcelona, and the following year was expressly appointed by Philip to witness the secret execution of Baron de Montigny at Simancas.[30] It is therefore a measure of the importance Philip accorded the reform of the Mercedarians that he released one of his most trusted ministers to ensure its successful outcome. Castillo's appointment, which seems at this stage to have been only a temporary measure, could not be made before the chapter was due to sit in Toledo, and it finally opened under his presidency in July 1572.[31]

The task with which Castillo was entrusted was especially delicate, for there can be no doubt that the province was undergoing a crisis that centered on the nature and meaning of the reform being implemented there. The extent to which Castillo's was a fence-mending exercise is reflected in the capitular ordinances, the only part of the Toledo *synodalia* to have survived.[32] As he declared, the intention behind his appointment had been to ensure that

> the chapter be celebrated for the peace and tranquility of the province and its religious, and to put an end to the differences and conflicts that had either arisen or were anticipated.(96v)

These conflicts, Castillo continued, owed as much to the circumstances of the chapter provincial of Guadalajara in 1569 as to the events of Carrillo's tenure and the accusations levelled against him and others. Having heard the depositions of all those involved, Castil-

---

[29] See *DHEE*, suppl. I, pp. 118–19, & John Lynch, *Spain, 1516–1598: From Nation State to World Empire* (Oxford, 1991), p. 259. Castillo's last act before being seconded to the Mercedarian reform was his condemnation of the doctrine of the Augustinian exegete Fray Alonso Gudiel in June 1572; see *ibid.*, p. 359, & Maurice Boyd, *Cardinal Quiroga, Inquisitor General of Spain* (Dubuque, Iowa, 1954), pp. 66–72 & 92.

[30] See Edgar Allison Peers, *Handbook to the Life and Times of St Teresa and St John of the Cross* (London, 1954), p. 135, & Bada, *Situació religiosa*, pp. 238–9.

[31] Castillo's appointment, extending only to Castile, was finally ratified by Gregory XIII on 2nd June 1573. This document is reproduced in Remón, *Historia*, II, f. 279Ar–v (foliation extremely confused in this part of the volume).

[32] IVDJ, env. 72, II, ff. 88r–97v (4°); dated 29th July 1572. References to this document are henceforth given in the text.

lo decided to lay the issue to rest with a general amnesty, backed by a declaration from the religious that all accusations would be dropped and perpetual silence imposed.(96v–97r) The drafting of a scurrilous *memorial* against Carrillo not long after indicates that the conflict was far from over, but the issue seems to have subsided, if not disappeared, with the election as provincial of a neutral figure, Mº Fray Juan de Covarrubias, the commendator of Burgos.[33]

Nevertheless, the troubles of Carrillo's provincialate did not go unmarked in the ordinances. Severe penalties were to be imposed on any religious bringing papal injunctions against the common good of the Order or without the sanction of a chapter, since 'such activities have been the cause of much disturbance and confusion, and have greatly prejudiced the peace' of the province.(92v) Similar punishments were to be meted out against any friar appearing at court without the express permission of the provincial, while the procurator and the commendator of Madrid were to be informed of any matter being pursued there.(93r) Ordinances were again passed regarding fugitive religious, and the numbers of *maestros* and *presentados* were limited to twelve and thirty respectively, 'given that over-generous facilities for graduation are the cause of many problems'.(95r)[34] Provisions for the establishment of three- or five-member conventual councils in all houses reflect the first significant attempt to curb the traditional independence of the commendator.(89v) The quality of those being recruited was still a cause for concern, and the chapter felt the need to order that 'henceforth none be received as novices with notable physical defects — which in law render men unfit for the altar — nor those who are mad, nor imbeciles, nor epileptics'.(90r) Though no mention of it is made here, by the end of 1573 at least two provincial noviciates had been established at Toledo and Olmedo to remedy this.[35] Further, a total of 3000 ducats of redemption *limosna* had been deposited at Toledo by the end of Carrillo's provincialate, more than double the figure for 1569.[36] Although much had still to be done, this

---

[33] *Ibid.*, ff. 117r–119v. Anonymous and undated but *c.*1572–4.

[34] This quota was reduced to twelve and 24 respectively in 1574. The poor standard required by the Mercedarians and the Trinitarians for graduating their members was identified by Cristóbal de Rojas y Sandoval, bishop of Córdoba, in a *memorial* to the crown, AGS, PR, 23-212, f. 5r–v; undated, but *c.*1568–9.

[35] IVDJ, env. 72, II, ff. 482r–491r. Tàrrega to the nuncio, Niccolò Ormaneto, undated but Madrid, shortly before August 1573; f. 490v.

[36] *Ibid.*, f. 485r.

sum bears tribute to the energy Carrillo had devoted to the restoration of this most fundamental vocation.

However, this was not all. Meneses' special contribution to the
spiritual reform of the province of Castile was recognized in the following statement:

> As for prayer, recollection, silence and cloister, the father provincial is
> to see that all convents observe the ordinances left by [...] the visitor
> general in the houses he visited by order of His Holiness.(94v)

Although the substance of these ordinances is not revealed, it is likely
that Meneses made close reference to the relevant sections of the constitutions, in which Mercedarian observance mirrors that of the
Dominicans. The emphasis on spiritual reform is reflected in the
ordinances passed during Covarrubias' only visit to Huete in June
1573.[37] Having issued several pointers as to the celebration of the
divine office, the provincial ordered two periods of a quarter of an
hour to be set aside each day for mental prayer, the first after matins
and the second after nones or compline, depending on the sea-
son.(13v–14r) As laid down at Toledo the previous year, the commendator was to read one of the *casos de conciencia* to the assembled
religious every day, while licenced conventuals were to begin hearing
the confessions of their brethren.(14r)

The death of Fray Felipe had therefore deprived the Castilian
brethren of a sympathetic reformer who had unerringly found the
pulse of the Order.[38] It is a great pity that virtually nothing else
survives to document the fortunes of the province under the more
pragmatic leadership of Castillo, the king's choice as commissary
apostolic.[39]

---

[37] AHN, Clero, vol. 3320, ff. 13r–15v. Huete, 10th–14th June 1573. References
are given in the text. Covarrubias is reported by Remón as having visited Madrid
immediately after the conclusion of the chapter; *Historia*, II, f. 265v.

[38] Meneses was by no means universally popular; witness an anonymous letter to
Ormaneto of *c*.1576–7, IVDJ, env. 72, II, f. 115r.

[39] The lack of details in part reflects the largely trouble-free nature of Castillo's visitations. In June 1574 Ormaneto declared the commissary to be satisfied with all
houses in Castile but one; see ASV, NS, vol. 8, ff. 239r–240v, Ormaneto to Cardinale di Como, Gregory XIII's secretary of state, Rome, 8th June 1574; f. 239v.
Castillo is reported by all the chroniclers to have visited Valladolid in the company of
the bishop of Palencia. A particularly fanciful account of this episode is provided in
Tirso, *Historia*, II, pp. 17–19.

II. *Revenge in Valencia, 1569–70*

Although Montaña, like Meneses, began his work in October 1570, the renewal of his contacts with the Order must be seen in the context of the aggressive policy directed by Duran against reformist brethren from 1569 onwards, particularly in Valencia. During the months that elapsed between the return of Antich and Bertrán from their visitation of Valencia in October 1569 and the moment when Montaña finally took up his commission a year later, Duran did everything in his power to annihilate the small circle of reformist and anti-Catalan brethren that had gathered round Mᵉ Fra Pere Joan de Tàrrega at Valencia. The survival of this group owes much to the determination of Tàrrega himself, and to the support of Patriarch Ribera of Valencia, bishop Muñatones of Segorbe and the Dominican Fray Lorenzo López, who in the autumn of 1569 exchanged the priorship of Barcelona for that of Valencia.

By the end of 1569 the vicar general had clearly identified Tàrrega as the main instigator of a campaign of resistance to his authority under the aegis of the Valencian episcopate.[40] Spurred on no doubt by news of a second apostolic campaign, he determined to snuff out the incipient reform movement by undermining the basis of the vicar provincial's support: his reputation as a reformer of the convent of Valencia. According to Tàrrega, in late 1569 Duran ordered Mᵒ Fray Asencio Lagarria to Valencia with virtual immunity from his authority as commendator in a blatant attempt to disrupt his efforts at reform.[41] Lagarria was quickly ordered out by Ribera and López, but much disruption had been caused by the time he departed for Barcelona. Student conventuals at Valencia were soon protesting to Duran at the sudden imposition of a regime originally drawn up for the Castilian colleges at Salamanca and Alcalá.(227v) That Tàrrega favoured reformed Castilian practice is apparent from his appointment as novice master of the Castilian Fray Miguel de Argote, who introduced the new regime with Ribera's support.(230r–v) It is not clear how much assistance Tàrrega received from the Castilians, but he was an admirer of both Carrillo and Torres, and the new regime

---

[40] An undated letter in Fra Sebastiá Bertrán's hand to Ormaneto denouncing Tàrrega's activities during the period 1569–72 is in IVDJ, env. 72, II, ff. 499r–500r.

[41] *Ibid.*, ff. 224r–236v. Tàrrega, probably to Ormaneto, undated but Madrid, late 1573; f. 227r–v. References to this document are henceforth given in the text.

may well have been based on that set out in the *Comentario* to the 1565 constitutions. In reply, Duran ordered the traditional observance to be restored and permitted a group of roving Mercedarians from Játiva under Fra Vicent Murta to interfere in conventual affairs at will.(227v–228r) After several months of this Ribera ordered Tàrrega to obey no further orders from the vicar general or any other superior without his consent.(228v)

Infuriated by this development, and by episcopal restrictions on Mercedarian rent and alms collection, Duran resorted to violence where threats and coercion had failed.[42] The events that followed reveal the fragility of the incipient reform and the readiness of the Catalans and their supporters to take the law into their own hands. It reveals also the powerlessness of the authorities in the face of concerted action. In the spring of 1570 Duran dispatched Fra Pere Castelló and Fray Pedro Alegría to Valencia with orders to arrest Tàrrega and bring him back to Barcelona. The operation resembles the removal of Mº Fray Pedro López de Cárdenas from Calatayud in December 1568. Accompanied by Murta and others, these two entered the convent with an *alguacil* (constable) to make the arrest — neither the first nor the last time that the hierarchy would rely on a network of secular sympathizers to achieve its ends. According to Tàrrega, only swift action from Ribera and viceroy Benavente prevented him falling into Duran's clutches. Ordered by Ribera to leave Tàrrega alone, the Catalans turned instead on the hapless commendator of Arguines, Fra Jerònim Marí, who was suspected of supplying information on the Order to Muñatones, bishop of Segorbe.(229r) Defying orders to the contrary, Alegría fell on the convent one night at the head of a party of seculars armed with arquebuses, captured Marí and dragged him off to Barcelona. Unfortunately for Fra Jerònim, the bishop, his protector, died soon after and he was destined to suffer a long incarceration in the priory.

Ribera protested to the crown against these outrages, but circumstances were turning against him. In March or April 1570 news came through that Pius had revoked the apostolic commissions of 1567,

---

[42] The Catalans had been banned from collecting the generals' traditional rents in the archdiocese of Valencia since Puig's death in 1567, although this was lifted in late 1570 after Duran appealed to Rome. Similar bans existed in the diocese of Segorbe, which denied Barcelona the revenues of the barony of Algar and the house of Arguines; see *ibid.*, f. 266r, and for the generals' annual rent in the kingdom at this time, f. 309r. For restrictions on the Order's *baciners*, see *ibid.*, f. 261r.

curtailing bishops' powers and leaving the reform process in dangerous limbo.(229v) Taking advantage of this, Duran travelled to Tortosa, not far from the Valencian border, and summoned his supporters from throughout the Crown of Aragon to a chapter. Among those
who gathered there were many of the leading opponents of the
Reform in the Crown of Aragon: Calvo, Alegría and Murta from
Valencia; Ángulo from Aragon and Castelló from Catalonia. Having
annulled most of the measures passed by Tàrrega and Ribera, the
vicar general crossed the Ebro and made his way to Valencia.(230r)
Mustering a band of supporters, Duran descended upon the convent,
restored the traditional observance of choir and ordered Argote back
to Castile.(230v) The result, Tàrrega lamented, was utter chaos, 'with
some singing one way, and others singing another, so that, rather
than a house of religion, it became one of confusion'.(230r) Thereafter Duran and his cohorts rampaged through the province with
impunity, removing those favourable to the Reform 'with great
harassment and duress', and replacing them with their own supporters.[43] By September 1570 the vicar general had turned his attention
back to Valencia itself, and seemed on the point of unseating Tàrrega
when Ribera reiterated his decree of the previous year ordering
Duran's commands to be ignored.[44] When it was learnt that Duran
had ordered Fray Pedro Alegría to visit the house at Valencia, the
archbishop instructed Tàrrega to arrest him on arrival and await further instructions. There are no details of the outcome of this episode,
but the eventual enactment by Montaña of his commission late in
1570 must have come as a great relief to the embattled reform party
in Valencia.

III. *A Reconnaissance of the Crown of Aragon, 1570–1*

Although Montaña probably knew of his appointment long before,
he reports receiving the brief only on 31st October 1570.[45] On 20th
December he presented his commission to Duran in Barcelona, and

[43] *Ibid.*, ff. 421r–422r. Ribera to Tàrrega and conventuals of Valencia, Valencia,
22nd September 1570; f. 421r.
[44] *Ibid.*, f. 423r. As before, Valencia, 26th September 1570.
[45] *Ibid.*, f. 282r–v. Montaña to Ormaneto(?), undated but probably Madrid 1574;
f. 282r.

the following day opened his visitation campaign at the priory itself.[46] Over the next few months Montaña visited thirty-five of the thirty-eight foundations in the Peninsular Crown of Aragon on what was essentially a voyage of reconnaissance. The result of this and of subsequent tours is a unique record of the character and condition of the Order in the eastern kingdoms.[47] Surviving documents reflect his interest in the state of religious worship and observance at each house, in the living arrangements of the friars and the condition of conventual buidings, in provisions for study and the training of novices, and in the income of a commandery in relation to the number of religious residing within it.[48]

The transactions of Montaña's visitations also reveal the extent to which the religious life in general had disintegrated in the Crown of Aragon. Throughout the entire territory there were provisions for only one conventual (as against personal) library — that of Barcelona — which he found dirty and emptied of its contents.(34r) The only satisfactory noviciate was that recently established by Tàrrega at Valencia.(35Br) Infirmaries and hospices existed only in the very largest convents, while dorters and chapter houses were completely absent in Mercedarian architecture. The typical Mercedarian house in the Crown of Aragon — that at Lleida for instance — was a somewhat anonymous building, often outside the city walls, centred around a small cloister adjacent to a modest church and belfry.[49] Many had been allowed to fall into ruin. Montaña particularly lamented the dilapidated condition of several cloisters, a distinguishing feature of monastic architecture and a metaphor for the religious life itself. Despite the concession of a papal indulgence for its reconstruction, the house at Pamplona had never fully recovered from the damage sustained during the siege of the city in 1521, while at El Puig, as we have seen, decay in the

---

[46] *Ibid.*, f. 319r–v. Montaña to Ormaneto(?), undated but Madrid 1574; f. 319v.

[47] Montaña's general report to Ormaneto is in *ibid.*, ff. 34r–40r (there are two f. 35s), untitled and undated but 1573–4. References to this document are henceforth given in brackets in the text.

[48] Montaña's interests reflect the views put forward in an important *memorial* by Cristóbal de Rojas y Sandoval, bishop of Córdoba, to Philip II, which may be taken as a statement of royal policy on the reform of the religious orders: AGS, PR, 23-212, undated but 1568–9.

[49] See Richard L. Kagan, *Spanish Cities of the Golden Age: The Views of Anton van den Wyngaerde* (Berkeley, 1989). The house at Lleida is particularly well illustrated in the foreground of Van den Wyngaerde's view of the city executed in 1563; p. 156.

fabric of the convent reflected that in the morals of its inmates.[50] (35Br,35Bv)

Montaña was above all struck by the overtly secular atmosphere of Mercedarian life in these parts, 'to which the perdition of the Order and its religious is principally due'.(36v) Apart from their luxuriously appointed rooms in the priory, the generals occupied an adjoining house resembling that of any gentleman in the city.(34r) Here they gave lavish banquets, ate off silver and were waited on by a host of secular servants. In their callous treatment of the brethren and undemanding approach to the religious vocation, the generals, Montaña concluded, behaved 'more like lords than friars'.(37r) Their lofty bearing was aped by many commendators, who, much to Montaña's irritation, insisted on being addressed as 'vuestra merced'.(37v) Elsewhere, the commissary discovered some convents to be virtually indistinguishable from secular dwellings.(35Av) In Valencia the house at Arguines seemed to Montaña like a labourer's cottage, while that of San Ginés resembled a watchtower 'better suited to seculars than to friars'.(35Bv,36r) The Mercedarians have, with a few notable exceptions, never been sophisticated builders. Even so, it must be borne in mind that monastic buildings on whatever scale reflect the circumstances of an order's presence in a given place. The main occupation of the four conventuals of Arguines was therefore the harvesting of grapes and the production of wine upon which part of the general's income depended. San Ginés, on the other hand, was in a desolate spot in southern Valencia at constant risk from *morisco* attack. Apart from some land suitable for growing wheat, its four religious were apparently forced to rely on hunting for their sustenance.

However, it was in the laxity of religious observance that the secularized atmosphere of Mercedarian life in the Crown of Aragon was most apparent. The divine office was usually attenuated, and sometimes barely observed at all. At San Ginés, we are told, the conventuals hold mass and sing the canonical hours 'only when they feel like it'.(36r) In many houses visited by Montaña the form of worship was that of popular devotion rather than the hierarchical observance one might expect from a religious order. At least a dozen houses did not have the sacrament, while at San Ginés the altar was in one of the friars' cells. Though all convents were under an advocation — most

---

[50] On the printing of the indulgence, granted by Adrian VI in 1522, see Madurell Marimón & Rubió y Balaguer, *Documentos para la historia*, pp. 640–2.

often Our Lady of Mercy — by no means all had a cult, and the Order's four main shrines in the Peninsular Crown of Aragon had yet to establish a widespread following.[51] These were Nostra Senyora de la Mercè in Barcelona, to which the confraternity of the *escudellers* (potters) was attached; Sant Ramon Nonat not far from Lleida, supposedly containing the relics of the thirteenth- or fourteenth-century Mercedarian cardinal; Santa Maria del Puig with its Byzantine relief of the Virgin and Child served by a confraternity; and Nuestra Señora del Olivar in southern Aragon.[52] With the exception of El Olivar none was recognized as a place of spiritual recollection for the religious themselves.

Because, as we have seen, communities were considered to require a certain level of income to sustain a reformed religious life, it was one of Montaña's priorities to assess both the finances of the houses and the number of religious in them. Montaña records a total of nearly 300 religious in the thirty-eight convents of the mainland Crown of Aragon, an average of less than eight per house. As a general rule, the crown had laid down that religious houses should have no less than thirteen friars, and that forty *escudos* per annum was required 'para mantenerles honestamente'.(40r) A total annual income of 520 *escudos* in rent or in kind would therefore be needed to maintain such a community. However, as in many other areas of monastic policy, such figures were based on the income and needs of the very largest orders, and bear no relation to the state of smaller institutions. With a declared net income of only 3500 ducats per annum in the Crown of Aragon — only a quarter of the requisite figure — the royal provisions were, as Montaña admitted, beyond the means of all but the wealthiest houses.[53] Barely twelve houses could in any sense support the religious residing within them and though official criteria were outwardly observed, allowances seem to have been made in the Mercedarian case.[54] There was, however, a huge disparity between rich and poor convents in the Crown of Aragon. El Puig

---

[51] The other shrine was that of Nostra Signora di Bonaria in Cagliari on Sardinia.

[52] See Millán Rubio, 'El padre Jaime Lorenzo de La Mata', *passim*.

[53] Montaña's estimate for the total net income of the Crown of Aragon is in IVDJ, env. 72, II, f. 319r.

[54] See *ibid.*, f. 319r, & f. 220r–v, Montaña's estimates of the number of religious each house in the Peninsular Crown of Aragon could support. Undated but *c.*1573. The totals range from 220 to 250 religious in 37 houses. Two houses appear not to have been visited: Palma de Mallorca and Oran.

with sixteen religious collected rents of over 1100 Valencian *lliures* per annum; the house at Uncastillo, on the other hand, provided its four conventuals with a pitiable thirteen Aragonese *sueldos*.(35Bv,35Br) In Catalonia and Aragon — though much less so in Valencia — the lands of many smaller convents appear to have been absorbed into the great provincial concerns at Zaragoza, Girona, and Barcelona in particular, whose declared income of 600 *escudos* per year was almost certainly but a fraction of the true figure.(39v) Wealth in the Crown of Aragon, along with power, was concentrated in the hands of a few privileged individuals. The master general and the provincials of Aragon and Valencia, the prior of Barcelona and the vicar of El Puig all received a substantial income as a matter of course. That said, high office was by no means the only indicator of wealth. Montaña discovered the *indiano* commendator of Orihuela, Fray Francisco de Zaragoza — a fugitive from Castile — to have amassed a fortune of 2000 *pesos* in the New World, and it was this colonial lucre that allowed him to bribe Duran for the privilege of living out of convent.(35Bv)[55]

Montaña had therefore encountered a congregation in spiritual, material and disciplinary prostration: ill-governed, uneducated and utterly unaccountable — the 'Indies' of Meneses' *Luz del alma christiana*. Yet given what we know of the past of the Order, it is hardly surprising that the Mercedarians failed to reflect either the standards of mendicant Observance or the renewed perception of religious in society by which Montaña measured them. But it was to these standards nonetheless that he, like Meneses and then Castillo, intended to tie the Mercedarian Reform.

IV. *A Reform Programme for the Crown of Aragon, 1571*

Having completed his opening visitation in the spring of 1571, Montaña, like Meneses in Castile, convened the three Aragonese provinces to a chapter at Zaragoza for September of that year.[56] We have no

---

[55] See also *ibid.*, f. 231r.

[56] The *acta* are in ACA, Mon., vol. 2667, ff. 338r–355v. Dated Zaragoza, 8th–9th September 1571. The date of convocation is not known, but it seems to have been May 1571. The chapter has an unusual status in that, although called a 'chapter provincial' (f. 338r), the presence of three provinces affords it the character of a general congregation.

indication of how or where he spent the intervening months, or of the atmosphere in the eastern provinces during this time. There is news only of a summer visitation in Aragon by the provincial, Fray Miguel Dicastillo.[57] Although Montaña was present at the chapter, he seemed content merely to observe the Order's legislative and capitular procedure at close quarters, and made no attempt to interfere with the provisions laid down there. Proceedings were therefore controlled by Duran, who filled the diffinitory with three key supporters: Lagarria for Valencia, Ángulo for Aragon and Calvo (the provincial of Valencia) representing Catalonia. No details survive of provision to commanderies, but it is clear that Duran made every effort both to favour his supporters in this, and to prepare the ground for his election in any future chapter general.[58] Duran had the opportunity of making a lasting contribution to the reform of the Order, but it was one he signally failed to grasp. As Montaña declared of the chapter some years later, 'I saw neither charity nor zeal for the service of God, neither repair nor improvement of this benighted Order, but concern only for personal interest and worldly affairs'.[59]

The ordinances laid down on the second day of the chapter were mostly a repetition of those passed at Barcelona in 1561 and 1567.[60] The now familiar injunctions on the reception of novices, purity of blood, the care of religious, dress, conventual accounts and the treatment of Castilian fugitives were reiterated, often word for word. So too were the ordinances, first passed in 1567, demanding that the Order be visited each year, and that provincials 'scrutinize every friar [...] and reform their convents', transferring religious from house to house as they saw fit.[61] Only in the collection of redemption *limosna* was there a serious attempt at reform with the enforcement of the system of conventual quotas or responsions introduced by Sorell in 1536. The provincial *procuradores de la redención* were to gather the responsions between the feasts of St John the Baptist and St Luke (24th June and 18th October), and deposit them in the *taula* of

---

[57] *Ibid.*, vol. 2668, ff. 298r, 299v & 306v. The inventories of 1568 were supplemented by Dicastillo at Tudela (10th July), Tarazona and Daroca. Details of a visitation of Zaragoza on 24th–27th July, probably by Dicastillo, are in IVDJ, env. 72, II, f. 290r–v.

[58] IVDJ, env. 72, II, f. 236r.

[59] *Ibid.*, f. 38r.

[60] ACA, Mon., vol. 2667, ff. 343r–346r.

[61] *Ibid.*, ff. 345v & 346r.

Barcelona ready for disposal by the chapter general.[62] This *limosna*, the ordinances pointedly declared, was to be devoted solely to the 'act of the Holy Redemption'. The urgency of the situation is reflected in the fact that only 22% — 280 Catalan *lliures* — of the total responsion debt of 1231 *lliures* was paid off at the chapter, taking the total deposited in Barcelona to a mere 1844 *lliures* — sufficient for no more than a dozen captives.[63] In Aragon, however, a total of 2200 *libras* of redemption *limosna* was on deposit in the *tabla* of Zaragoza by July 1571.[64] Although an important start had been made, at an average ransom of 100 ducats per captive the Crown of Aragon was still some way from mustering sufficient *limosna* to carry out a serious redemption expedition. But despite these measures, nothing had been done to remedy the central problem: that of the generalcy itself. Once again, the hierarchy had looked to the repair of the Order's ancient vocation as a means of staving off the inevitable. For Montaña, as eventually for Castillo, the prevailing situation could not be ignored for very much longer.

The chapter over, Montaña retired to the Dominican priory of Valencia to draw up his first reform ordinances, no doubt in consultation with Tàrrega. What emerged in November 1571 was by no means wholly original, for Montaña, unlike Meneses, harboured a strong sense of continuity both with recent reform efforts and with the legislative past of the institution.[65] The ordinances, which confine themselves to the life of the Order rather than its institutional structure, are based on the Rule of St Augustine, the constitutions and the Tridentine decrees. It was upon observance of these, and of the three vows, that reform was to be founded.(238r) The ordinances had been prepared, so the ancient formula ran, 'that the religious may see in them, as in a mirror, where they are failing in their duty and so mend their ways'.(492r) That said, Montaña was from the beginning anxious to place the reform process in broader compass. Twice daily the

---

[62] *Ibid.*, f. 344v.

[63] *Ibid.*, ff. 341r–342v, 347v & 353r. Of the outstanding debt of 951 *lliures*, 435 was owed by Catalonia, 303 by Aragon and 213 by Valencia.

[64] IVDJ, env. 72, II, f. 290v. This balance is dated 27th July, and 2100 *libras* of the total had been deposited by the convent of Zaragoza itself.

[65] There are two near-identical copies of this document in *ibid.*: ff. 238r–242v, and the more complete ff. 492r–496v. Neither has a title as such, though the latter is addressed to Duran; both are dated Valencia, 8th November 1571. Citations are taken from the former document, except in the case of the introductory paragraph which is present only in the latter.

religious were to pray not only for God's favour in the reform of their
Order and the Church, but also for the extirpation of heresy, the success of the Holy League and the maintenance of peace among
Catholic princes.(238r) Henceforth, Mercedarians were to consider
their reform as being at one with the wider revival of Catholic *Christianitas*.

Montaña's primary concern here was the reform of conventual life
and the restoration of the Order's twin vocations: the divine office and
the redemption of captives.(238v) In the matter of redemption, the
religious were to uphold the bull granted for this purpose by Leo X in
1516, particularly as to the collection and disposal of *limosna*. The
observance of the three monastic vows, and especially that of poverty,
Montaña considered central to the achievement and maintenance of
reform.(239r) Equally, private ownership of property was recognized
as a particular bane of the religious life. The usual injunctions were
passed regarding the reception of novices, care for the sick — 'that no
friar's health or life be wasted through meanness and dearth' — and
the establishment of a proper system for depositing conventual
funds.(239r,240r–241r) Searches were to be instituted to recover lost
conventual documentation, most likely the deeds of properties alienated from the Order through long neglect.(240r) Finally, students were
to be favoured in all ways possible, though, as Montaña lamented,
many had abandoned their studies given the freedom with which
licences to preach and hear confession had been issued.(242r,241v)

However, what set Montaña's ordinances apart were the special
provisions he laid out for their enactment. Within eight days of the
ordinances being read out to the friars, the commendator was to hold
a chapter to discuss their implementation, and to appoint individuals
to a range of offices.(240r,242r) A sensible budget for conventual
expenditure was then to be worked out, and the results transmitted to
the provincial.(239v) Within a month the commendator was required
to make a full inspection of the house and take an inventory of its
contents.(239r–v) Underpinning the whole process was a relentless
observance of the rule and constitutions of the Order, of past decrees
and the ordinances themselves, which were to be copied and read out
to the religious over and over again.(238r) Punishments were to be
meted out in accordance with the constitutions by specially appointed
visitors provincial.(242v,241v) Organization, implementation, repetition and correction: thus did Montaña conceive the progress of
reform.

It is not clear whether Montaña communicated directly with his counterparts in Castile, but many of his provisions for conventual reform were mirrored in the ordinances passed by Castillo at Toledo in 1572, especially as to redemption alms and the divine office. However, while there is nothing to suggest that Castillo and Montaña met to discuss the future of the Order before 1573 or '74, it is important not to lose sight of the relevance of their independent visitations for the institution as a whole. For Montaña in particular, the office of commissary apostolic in the Crown of Aragon, with its privileged access to the priory of Barcelona, carried certain responsibilities of great significance for the spiritual reform and self-perception of the Order as a whole.

V. *The Quest for Mercedarian Observance*

As in Castile, spiritual improvement, while not yet the pivot of Mercedarian reform, was beginning to play its essential part in the renewal of individuals and coenobia in the levantine provinces. It fell to Montaña to create a situation whereby the brethren could be instructed in a truly religious life so that spiritual observance might fulfil its role in the Mercedarian vocation. For the problem, as Montaña saw it, was not one of conscious or even official relaxation so much as the acquisition of bad habits through long neglect — what he called 'the engrained slackness and poor example inherited from prelates past' — itself an eloquent comment on the nature of Mercedarian Reform.[66] Thus, as the survival of an interrogation questionnaire used at Barcelona in 1572 confirms, Montaña gave great importance to a religious observance founded upon study and the proper celebration of the divine office.[67] Upon this the spiritual renewal of the Order and the untarnishing of its public image would ultimately depend. As a start, Montaña ordered the religious to observe periods of silence each day, attend a weekly chapter of faults, and, like their Castilian brethren, begin to hear *casos de conciencia* on a regular basis.(240v–241r,242r) But above all, the Mercedarians were

---

[66] *Ibid.*, f. 319r, & f. 320r, an undated letter from Montaña written in late 1574 or early 1575.

[67] AGN, Clero, vol. 402. This copy is dated 23rd July 1573. Regrettably, the friars' answers to this questionnaire have not survived.

to be guided in their 'observance' by a higher example, that of the Patriarch himself, whose life and work was to be the very touchstone of their reform. For though he remains anonymous, it was evidently to Pere Nolasch that Montaña was referring. The commissary therefore desired all prelates

> to assist and favour this holy work [of reform] with words and examples in imitation of that high master [...] to the end that, through his good example and wise counsel [...] they may instruct their sons and subjects as the eagle instructs his young in flight. This so that, through desire and the accomplishment of these works, they may fulfil this holy reformation...(242v)

As part of his commission Montaña had searched, probably through the remains of the priory archive of Barcelona, for the most ancient legislation of the Order. All the indications are that the conventuals buried the bulk of the archive in a charnel-house under the priory church to keep it from investigation.[68] However, they could hardly have kept Gaver's *Speculum fratrum* from him, and it was no doubt here that Montaña found the 1272 constitutions, the source to which all prelates were to turn for traces of the Patri-

---

[68] See M° Fray Juan de Antillón's fragmentary *Chronologicon Generalicio del Orden de Nuestra Señora de la Merced y Redemptores* in a draft copy of 1636, ACA, Mss.Misc., vol. 103, f. 4r–v (for an earlier draft of this work — ACA, Mss.Misc., vol. 39 — see ch. 7, n. 136). The effects of perhaps 20 or 25 years underground are to be imagined, and Antillón notes that much had been destroyed by the time the documents were unearthed, probably in the 1590s. He also reports that a substantial amount of documentation was transferred from the Crown of Aragon to Madrid early in the 17th century as source material for the histories of the Order then being written; the Barcelona archive was, however, clearly less affected by this than those of other regional centres; see *ibid.*, ff. 2Ar–v & 5v–6r. An indication as to when the priory archive might have been hidden is provided in ACA, Mon., vol. 2679, f. 139v, in which the Valencian M° Fray Felipe de Guimerán declares having witnessed the opening of the sarcophagus of the third master of the Order, Fra Bernat de Sant Roman, in 1573. Another 13th-century figure, Fra Bernat de Corbera, was disinterred in 1574; see Vázquez Núñez, *Manual*, I, p. 539, and, for more on this question, ch. 7, n. 171. Nevertheless, the archive survives in ACA as one of the great monastic holdings of Spain; see Alberto Torra Pérez, 'Los antiguos archivos de los conventos de Trinitarios y Mercedarios de Barcelona' in *Memoria Ecclesiae*, 11 (1997), pp. 337–53. Further evidence of tampering in the priory church comes in 1570, when the hair, clothing and shoes of the image of *Nostra Senyora de la Mercè* were gilded over and the *camisoncillo* painted red. The community was severely admonished for this by the general, Fray Francisco de Torres, in 1574, who ordered the image to be left undisturbed and dressed only in white vestments; see P. Miguel Saló, *La imagen de Nuestra Señora de la Merced: Algunas noticias acerca de su origen y belleza artística* (Barcelona, 1881), pp. 10–11.

arch's example.[69] Though Torres had discussed Amer's access to primitive statutes in his 1565 edition of the constitutions, his version of the legislative history of the Order is hedged round with such masterful sophistry as to be quite unintelligible.[70] Montaña must therefore be credited as the first reformer openly to accept the significance of 1272 for the future of the Order, regardless of the effect on the current constitutions. By underlining the need for the brethren to be reformed in conscious imitation of the first and greatest of their forefathers, Montaña had broken ground of incalculable importance for Mercedarian spirituality and begun to push the legislative horizons of the Order back from 1327 into Pere Nolasch's *centuria primera*. Before long Montaña was conjuring up a sense of some forgotten observance, referring to 'the needs of this Order and its having fallen from the condition in which those its saints and founders created and left it...'.[71] Of course, Montaña could not give tangible form to this example since, as we have established, virtually nothing survived to document the life and deeds of the founder and his followers, and centuries of relaxation had done the rest. As Tirso admitted, 'the regular perfection of our founders was gradually reintroduced [...] though for the most part only the faintest traces of these remained, when, that is, they had not been forgotten altogether'.[72] But even so, the scale of Montaña's realization makes this nothing less than a halfway house between the Mercedarian *ancien régime* and the new Order that rose in the late sixteenth and early seventeenth centuries.[73]

---

[69] In 1582 Gaver's *Speculum fratrum* was referred to by Catalans as 'lo llibre de la fundacio de dit orde'. See AGN, Clero, vol. 416, an anonymous and undated *memorial* entitled 'Instructions pera la executio del breu apostolich dirigit al Reuerendissimo de Girona', i.e. bishop Dom Benet Tocco.

[70] Torres, *Regula et Constitutiones*, f. 11v.

[71] See also IVDJ, env. 72, II, f. 372r (4°). Montaña to Philip II, undated but 1574.

[72] Tirso, *Historia*, II, p. 27.

[73] Evidence for the increased status of Nolasch is provided by the Catalans themselves in 1578, when he is described as 'Sant Pere Nolasch' in the *Consell de Cent*'s instructions to Fray Luis de Dusayel (Fra Lluís Durall?), its ambassador to Philip II. Nolasco was not in fact beatified until 50 years later, and was canonized only in 1664. Cited in ACA, Mon., leg. 293, (unftd.), an early-17th century discussion of the alleged foundation charter of the Order, of which only the first 2 ff. survives.

VI. *Rejection in the Crown of Aragon, 1571–3*

Once again, there is little direct news of the reception of Montaña's ordinances in the Crown of Aragon, though several of his visitors provincial, including Tàrrega, were on hand to supervise their implementation.[74] In Catalonia at least, Montaña intended the circulation of the ordinances to be left to the religious themselves.(242v) Upon receiving the ordinances, the commendator was to read them out to his community, sign and date the originals, have them copied and then sent on to the next house in a pre-arranged itinerary. Montaña, meanwhile, remained in Valencia until April 1572 when he began a second tour of the Crown of Aragon, during which he revisited twenty of its most important houses.[75]

Much to his chagrin, Montaña soon discovered that virtually nothing in his ordinances was being observed. Only at Valencia were things progressing at all satisfactorily.[76] In Catalonia, meanwhile, the ordinances were ignored by Duran, who had turned to an increasingly effective campaign of obstruction.[77] Perhaps through his own fault, Montaña's powers of visitation in the priory of Barcelona were now limited by an agreement with the *Consell de Cent* preventing him passing sentences of excommunication.[78] Lacking adequate support, Montaña felt unable to mete out punishment to the mass of religious who were contravening his orders. With Meneses recently dead in Castile and little scope for falling back on episcopal authority, the inherent weakness of Pius' policy of reform by religious alone now became apparent. Montaña found himself in the classic position of a reformer unable either to move the majority or galvanize the few who were genuinely sympathetic to change. As Tàrrega put it, Montaña quite simply discovered 'neither friars to assist him in his reform, nor any willing to keep its precepts'.[79] Ultimately, there was little he could do with a congregation that had no concerted desire to reform itself. The

---

[74] For an account of this journey, see IVDJ, env. 72, II, ff. 351r–354v. Tàrrega to Montaña, Valencia, 22nd February 1572.

[75] *Ibid.*, f. 38r.

[76] *Ibid.*, f. 231v. It should be noted that this is Tàrrega's interpretation of events, though his views are borne out elsewhere.

[77] For Duran's shortcomings according to Tàrrega, see *ibid.*, ff. 232r–233v.

[78] AGN, Clero, vol. 402. *Consellers* to M° Fray Francisco Maldonado, Barcelona, 27th January 1576.

[79] IVDJ, env. 72, II, ff. 436r–437r. Tàrrega to Ormaneto, undated but Madrid, late 1573; f. 436v.

events of the next few months would serve only to confirm the depth of opposition to the process he had set before the Aragonese brethren.

The turning point came with the death of Pius V in May 1572, and the subsequent recall of Castagna. Once news of this reached the Crown of Aragon in June, Montaña's position rapidly deteriorated. The diminished scope for royal involvement in this affair was no doubt partly responsible. As Tàrrega maintained, the death of the pope led the religious to believe that the reform was over, since they reckoned the king unlikely to pursue the matter with the zeal he had shown in previous years.[80] However, the immediate origins of the crisis that developed in the aftermath of Pius' death can be traced to the previous September, if not before. In what appears a misguided attempt at appeasement, Montaña had given a prominent member of Duran's party, Fray Pedro Alegría, a commission to visit southern and western Aragon.[81] The nature of the commission is unclear, but Alegría, Duran's main agent in Valencia during 1570, seems to have taken the opportunity to pursue a vindictive agenda of his own.[82] By the time he had returned to his commandery at Tortosa in May 1572, severe disruption had been caused at Daroca, Calatayud and Teruel, where Alegría fell foul of the duke of Segorbe and the Inquisition amid allegations that he was counterfeiting coinage.[83]

Once news of Pius' death had reached him in June 1572, Alegría's contempt for authority turned to open defiance. Urged on no doubt by Duran, Alegría declared Montaña's commission rescinded and his authority forfeit to that of the vicar general and the provincials.[84] As in the spring of 1570, when the episcopal commissions had been withdrawn, the Catalan party now turned against Tàrrega and lost no time in striking the first blow. Travelling to Barcelona at Mon-

---

[80] *Ibid.*, f. 436r.

[81] *Ibid.*, f. 355r. Alegría to Montaña, Teruel, 24th September 1571. Alegría would appear to have been among the visitors provincial appointed by Montaña at the Zaragoza chapter.

[82] *Ibid.*, f. 360r–v. Alegría to Montaña, Tortosa, 8th May 1572.

[83] For a short biography of Alegría, see *ibid.*, f. 427r–v, Tàrrega to Ormaneto, undated but Madrid, 1573.

[84] *Ibid.*, ff. 306r–v & 278r. Mᵒ Fray Juan Izquierdo (OP) to Montaña, Tortosa, 29th & 30th June 1572 respectively. Montaña positioned Izquierdo as an informer in sensitive areas, including San Lázaro at Zaragoza (where he appears as a conventual in July 1571; see *ibid.*, f. 290r), and the Dominican house at Tortosa with its strategic position near the Valencian border. The conclusion of Izquierdo's first letter (*ibid.*, f. 306r–v) provides a rare insight into the cooperation that existed between reformist brethren.

taña's behest, Tàrrega lodged at Tortosa in a *mesón* (inn) where on
29th June Alegría had him arrested by the *sotsveguer* ('sub-vicar', sher-
rif) and placed in a secular gaol. Though letters from Montaña and
appeals to the bishop from one of the commissary's lieutenants, the
Dominican M° Fray Juan Izquierdo, soon secured Tàrrega's release,
matters were rapidly getting out of control.[85] It is a measure of Alegría's truculence that he gathered a party of armed men outside the
bishop's palace for a second — though abortive — attempt at detain-
ing Tàrrega before fleeing to Calatayud.[86]

As the commissary's authority collapsed in the latter half of 1572,
Duran once again focused his attention on Valencia.[87] Montaña
could only look on impotently as the vicar general began to dismantle
his work of eighteen months, and the Reform degenerated into a petty cycle of allegation and counter-allegation.[88] Ridiculed and tor-
mented by a stream of accusations, Montaña had left for Madrid by
the end of the year. Within a short time of his departure the conventuals of Valencia had rebelled against the vicar and novice master
installed by Montaña, forcing them to return to Castile.[89] At length
Duran saw to the replacement of almost every conventual officer, culminating in that of Tàrrega himself in the spring of 1573.[90] The circumstances of his removal are not clear, but on 26th April Duran
made an inventory of the house witnessed by the new president, M°
Fray Miguel de Bruxola, the viola player of El Puig.[91] Days later a
heart-broken Tàrrega was in Madrid protesting that Duran had confiscated both his vestments and his private library, the fruit of over
thirty years' collecting.[92] But even as he set to work on the succession
of damning *memoriales* he drafted against Duran's regime, Tàrrega
must have sensed that it would be many years before the reformist

---

[85] *Ibid.*, f. 310r. Fray Martín de Córdoba y Mendoza (OP), bishop of Tortosa, to
Montaña, Tortosa, 2nd July 1572. Izquierdo himself became bishop of Tortosa in
1574.

[86] *Ibid.*, f. 280r. Izquierdo to Montaña, Tortosa, 3rd July 1572.

[87] *Ibid.*, f. 278r.

[88] On the allegations, see *ibid.*, ff. 17r–20v, anonymous and undated *memorial*. Tàrrega had to defend himself against accusations of chicanery; see *ibid.*, f. 417r, Valencia, 10th September 1572.

[89] *Ibid.*, f. 233v.

[90] *Ibid.*, f. 234r.

[91] For the *acta*, see ACA, Mon., vol. 2670, ff. 371r–384v.

[92] Reported in IVDJ, env. 72, II, f. 304r, Ormaneto to Montaña, Madrid, 30th
April 1573. See also *ibid.*, ff. 430r–431r, an undated and anonymous letter written to
Ormaneto from Madrid demanding restitution.

party regained its tenuous foothold in the eastern provinces. As Montaña himself admitted, his attempt to implant reform had been a complete failure.[93]

With his hands free, Duran began to reconsolidate his position and work towards the fufilment of his own aims. In October 1573, for instance, he was elected administrator of the ecclesiastical estate in the Valencian *Generalitat*.[94] Even before Tàrrega had been driven out of Valencia in April of that year, the vicar general had dispatched his religious on a number of important missions. Late in 1572 Fray Pedro Alegría and Fray Asencio Lagarria were sent to Rome to put an end to the reform campaign, and obtain permission to convene the chapter general that must surely elect Duran to the high office.[95] Aware that Philip would never agree to this, Duran sent a conventual of Girona, Fra Benet Camps, to the court of Charles IX of France hoping to find support for the revocation of the January 1568 brief.[96]

Naturally, such diplomacy cost money, and both in Rome and Paris, Tàrrega reported, Duran's pretensions were being backed by funds originally collected for the redemption of captives. Since 1570 Duran had been aware that the authorities were preparing to demand that he account for the 30,000 ducats of *limosna* collected by the generals since 1555.[97] Anxious to conceal the gross misuse to which ransoming funds had lately been put, Duran began to obstruct the collection of conventual accounts by the reformers and petition Philip for a licence to mount an expedition to Algiers.[98] Repeated refusals to grant this caused Duran to send the commendator of Zaragoza, Fray Pedro de Ángulo, to Madrid in December 1573,

---

[93] *Ibid.*, f. 317r. Montaña to ?, undated but Madrid, 1574.

[94] AGN, Clero, vol. 402. Íñigo López de Mendoza, marqués de Mondejar, viceroy of Valencia, to Duran, Valencia, 14th October 1573. Other copies in *ibid.*, vol. 416, & APV, Antillón, ms. *Epitome*, I(ii), pp. 1456–7.

[95] IVDJ, env. 72, II, f. 427v.

[96] *Ibid.*, f. 436v.

[97] *Ibid.*, f. 436r.

[98] For details of a gagging order placed by Duran and Calvo on the conventuals of Elche, see *ibid.*, f. 284r–v, undated but *c*.1572. An undated copy in 4° of one of Duran's petitions to the king is *ibid.*, f. 50r–v, in which he declares the Crown of Aragon to have gathered 8000 ducats of redemption *limosna*; f. 50v. Another petition of 13th October 1572 to Cardinal-archbishop Gaspar de Cervantes of Tarragona and bishops Martín Martínez del Villar of Barcelona and Dom Benet Tocco of Girona is in M° Fray José Linás, *Bullarium Cœlestis ac Regalis Ordinis Beatae Mariae Virginis de Mercede Redemptionis Captivorum* (Barcelona: Raphaëlis Figueró, 1696), pp. 153–4. The need for a redemption was the more urgent after the reconquest of Tunis by Euldj Ali in 1570 and the taking of thousands of captives.

before travelling there himself in the new year.[99] But, as he soon discovered, Philip had as little intention of relenting on this question as
he had in that of the chapter general. Despite the undeniable importance of this matter, it is hard to believe that Duran would have ven-
tured out from his Catalan fastness had he not been aware that something of much greater moment was afoot. And indeed, though Montaña had retired defeated from the Crown of Aragon, his passing had
marked the end only of the first, exploratory stage of his commission.

VII. *The Task in Hand*

Though Montaña returned to the Crown of Aragon during 1573, his
sojourn was not destined to be a long one and in January of the following year Ormaneto ordered him back to Madrid to discuss the
appointment of a new general, 'and all else touching on the religious
life of this Order'.[100] On 31st January 1574 Montaña declared his visitation officially closed and hastened to Madrid carrying all his papers
with him.[101] Though Ormaneto evidently wished the affairs of the
Aragonese provinces to receive special attention, he reminded Montaña that, together with Castillo, he would be responsible for map-
ping out the future of Mercedarian Reform as a whole. Apart from a
few preliminary documents, we are not privy to the deliberations of
the two commissaries through 1574, but there can be no doubt that
the task laid before them was immense.[102] Circumstances required
the commissaries not only to overcome the inherent differences
between the Aragonese and their Castilian brethren, but also to reconcile the demands of royal and papal authority with the realities of
Mercedarian life in later sixteenth-century Spain. Moreover, they
were expected to do this quickly and within the parameters of a single
document. Ultimately, the task entrusted them was no less than the
creation of a new congregation: one loyal, exemplary, observant, at

---

[99] On this see two letters in 4° from Tàrrega to Ormaneto, both undated but
Madrid, early 1574; IVDJ, env. 72, II, ff. 415r & 417r.

[100] *Ibid.*, ff. 337r & 312r–v. Ormaneto to Montaña and Fra Stefano di Incontra
(OP) respectively, both Madrid, 30th January 1574; citation f. 312r. On this period
see also APV, Antillón, ms. *Epitome*, I(ii), p. 1457.

[101] IVDJ, env. 72, II, f. 282v.

[102] Montaña's suggestions for the improvement of the Order at this time may be
traced in *ibid.*, ff. 275r (late 1573), 272r–273v (to Ormaneto, *c.*1573–4) & 372r (to
Philip II, *c.*1574).

peace with itself and with its tempestuous past in both the spiritual and the temporal order.

Though the details of this collaboration are lost to us, in Fra Pere Joan de Tàrrega we are lucky to have a highly acute observer of the Order and the religious life in general. Through Tàrrega's writing we can assess the practical and, most of all, the intensely personal obstacles to reform which, in Catalonia especially, made its implementation such a herculean task.

One of the effects of Montaña's visitation was to hasten the distinct process of transformation which the Aragonese brethren in general, and the Catalans in particular, had been undergoing for more than a generation. Though many of the Order's problems were of long-standing, some at least had been greatly exacerbated in the previous twenty or thirty years. The reasons for this decline have already been discussed in part, but it may be as well to reexamine this phenomenon at what is a turning point in the history of the Order and the Principality itself. The changing mentality of Mercedarians in the eastern provinces reflects not only their diminished importance in relation to the Peninsula as a whole, but also their resentment at the increasing power and independence of the Castilian brethren. As the sixteenth century drew on, successive generals came to recognize that the *Concordia* of 1467 had not only divided the Order, but seriously and permanently compromised their status as masters over it. The reconfirmation of the *Concordia* in 1532, and with it the establishment of Castile's exclusive authority in the Indies, dealt a blow to the Aragonese hierarchy from which, in a sense, it never recovered. The story of the Aragonese provinces after 1532 is one of retrenchment above reform, of declining discipline and failing spiritual vocation. Those of reformist or scholarly inclinations were gradually faced down and replaced by an altogether more pragmatic breed of religious. The concern of this new hierarchy was less for the Order as a spiritual entity than the preservation of a form of life now perceived to be under serious threat. The development of a new and highly unpalatable style of royal government during the 1560s, and the reform policy that followed on from it, therefore accelerated a process which had begun several decades earlier.

With this process, Tàrrega lamented, the incipient reformist and academic movement had ended, educated men were reviled, and a generation of religious had been received into the Order without scruple or proper formation. This assessment is supported by the fact that of the sixty-two novices who professed at the priory of Barcelona between 1551 and 1575 no less than twenty-eight were illiterate.[103] This situation, as Tàrrega continued, had had its inevitable effect on discipline:

> Because there has been no one in the provinces of the Crown of Aragon to instruct the religious either in Reform or in the Rule and constitutions of the Order [...] there are barely any religious who have not committed infractions, whether many or few...[104]

But not only had postulants received virtually no training, they now perceived their vocation less in terms of the vows they had sworn than in the circumstances under which they had taken them. Thus,

> Since the vicar general and his followers — having been brought up free to exercise their own will — give no importance to keeping our rule and constitutions (much less the ordinances of the reformers), they do only what pleases them. And when ordered to keep the rule and constitutions [...] they reply declaring this to be a question of observance, which they have neither vowed nor been taught to keep. Moreover, they maintain that if they had known that this obligation would be placed upon them, they would never have become friars, and that [consequently] they have no responsibility to observe anything other than that which they found at the time of their profession.[105]

This oft-repeated claim presented a serious obstacle not only to Mercedarian visitors, but to anyone charged with reducing an order to regular observance. Small wonder, then, that the reformers laid such emphasis on the establishment of suitable noviciates and *studia*, as much in Castile as in the Crown of Aragon. As Torres had declared in 1565, 'there is nothing so important for the perfection of the Order, nor a more effective means of reducing it to its primordial observance, than that great care be taken in the instruction of novices'.[106]

---

[103] Figures from the first book of professions of the priory of Barcelona, ACA, Mon., vol. 2710. Although the volume contains entries from 1510 to 1595, it is only reliable from 1547 when it was opened. Earlier professions of surviving religious were copied down from original *partidas* (some examples of which are unbound in this vol.).

[104] IVDJ, env. 72, II, f. 235r. The same general point is made by the Dominican M° Fray Pedro de Salamanca to Ormaneto in *ibid.*, ff. 82r–83r, Valencia, 2nd November 1575; f. 82v.

[105] *Ibid.*, f. 234v. The same point is made in a wider context in AGS, PR, 23-225, an anonymous *memorial* datable to 1566; f. 7r.

[106] Torres, *Comentario*, f. 23v. See also Montaña in IVDJ, env. 72, II, f. 39v, & Tàrrega in *ibid.*, f. 490v.

However, if this was an effect of the general relaxation of the Order, there was clearly no doubt in Tàrrega's mind who was responsible for perpetuating it. It was Duran, himself 'reared in the dissolution and abuse of the convent of Barcelona', who was intent on 'perpetuating and inflicting these ancient abuses on the whole Crown of Aragon', and who had confederated with the enemies of reform in each of its provinces.[107] The result, said Tàrrega, was that the religious were held in thrall to a dozen or so individuals — 'enemies of the reformation' in Montaña's words — who bullied them into silence or acquiescence.[108] Duran's adherents, at least half of them sons of the priory of Barcelona, were dispersed throughout the Crown of Aragon, including Castelló at Girona, Bertrán at Barbastro and Calvo at El Puig.[109] Other supporters included the Navarrese Fray Juan Luis de Echarri at Tarazona, the Aragonese Ángulo at Zaragoza, and the Valencians Murta and Lagarria at Játiva and (from 1573) Valencia respectively. It was these men who, under Duran's leadership, had monopolized most of the key offices in the Crown of Aragon and now blocked the progress of reform.[110] 'And because of this,' groaned Tàrrega of his brethren, 'it seems that they will never be reformed.'[111]

While circumstances within the Order played their part in establishing a nucleus of religious determined to obstruct its reform, this opposition reflects widespread anger at the increasingly intrusive presence of the crown in the Aragonese sphere as a whole. For the conflict that developed over the reform of the Mercedarians after 1567 was by no means confined to the Order itself. In their long struggle, the Catalan brethren would rely both on the immemorial privileges of the priory of Barcelona and on the rights and *furs* of the city and Principality; on the widely held conviction that, in attacking the Catalan Mercedarians, the crown was impugning the entire province also. Already, Montaña reported, the reform was being

---

[107] *Ibid.*, f. 235r.

[108] See *ibid.*, f. 482r and, for the citation, f. 272v.

[109] Tàrrega lists the opponents of reform in *ibid.*, ff. 409r–410r, 4°. Undated, but *c.*1574. The others listed are Fra Jaume Grauset, Fray Diego de León (both Barcelona professions) and Fra Pere Balaguer, a Valencian and future general of the Order. See also *ibid.*, f. 490r. A list of those favourable to the Reform is also provided, *ibid.*, f. 478r–v. This includes Fray Francisco de Salazar at Pamplona, the veteran redemptor Fray Jorge del Olivar, and Fray Miguel Dicastillo at Calatayud.

[110] *Ibid.*, f. 489v.

[111] *Ibid.*, f. 490v.

obstructed by religious who were whipping up the townsfolk and local gentry.[112] Thus, if the Reform were to have any chance of success, the trouble-makers would have to be dispersed throughout the province of Castile, and the arch-enemy Duran lured away from the Principality:

> For, being a Catalan, so long as the vicar general remains there he can both arm and shelter himself with the *furs* of Catalonia and the privileges of the *Diputació*, and thereby achieve his aims...[113]

Time, then, seemed at this moment to be on Duran's side. But such obstacles were by no means unprecedented in the Crown of Aragon. As a Castilian commentator had reminded the crown on the eve of the reform campaign in 1566,

> The freedom in which these orders live is of such longstanding as to have become virtually irremediable. Influenced in no small measure by the land itself, which is much inclined to liberty, this is evidently one of the corners of Christendom where conventualism and easy living have taken deepest root in the orders. It is because of this that reform has always been so difficult [to implement] in these parts, despite the efforts of various princes at one time or another [...] But these have lasted hardly at all, because the religious have been allowed to slide back into their relaxed ways through any trifling avenue left open to them.[114]

If this citation captures the arrogance of the Castilian reformers, then it may also go some way towards explaining the widespread sympathy and support for friars among ordinary people. The history of Catalonia under Philip II has yet to receive thorough treatment, but there can be no doubt that the reform of the Mercedarians, along with that of the abbey of Montserrat, represents one of the outstanding features of its experience during the later sixteenth century. And when, from the perspective of the 1630s, we consider Fray Juan de Antillón's grief and bitterness at the events of the previous sixty years, then the fate of the Catalan Mercedarians can well be seen as a microcosm of the Principality itself.[115]

---

[112] *Ibid.*, f. 272v.

[113] The opinions are those of Montaña, *ibid.*, f. 272v, and Tàrrega, f. 234v (citation) respectively.

[114] AGS, PR, 23-225, f. 1r. The *memorial* is anonymous.

[115] The motivations informing Antillón's activities as a historian of the Order are set out in a 'Proemio Apologetico' to his *Chronologicon*, ACA, Mss.Misc., vol. 103, ff. 1r–6r.

VIII. *The Chapter General of Guadalajara, 1574*

Despite Tàrrega's warnings, Duran was allowed to return to Catalonia unhindered. We have no details of the vicar general's stay in Madrid, but it is clear that while there he learnt of plans to convene an electoral chapter general in Castile. First mooted in 1563, it was not until 1569 that this prospect had been given serious consideration.[116] Though long delayed, the prospect of a reforming chapter general was made reality with the breakdown of Montaña's visitation, and by early 1574 the commissaries were discussing constitutional changes with Ormaneto and the papacy.[117] Once Castillo had concluded his visitation of Castile in June of that year the commissaries gave 'this most important matter' their undivided attention.[118]

As in 1568–9, Duran responded to the impending crisis with visitation. At the end of April 1574 the vicar general began a six-week tour of Aragon-Navarre, anxious no doubt to assess the mood of a province that had so far remained mostly loyal to Barcelona despite Alegría's depredations the previous year.[119] Inventories were taken and ordinances passed, though the vicar general largely confined himself to ratifying his decrees of 1568–9. By the end of May news that the election of a new general was imminent had become common knowledge in Catalonia, and friars once again began taking sides in the conflict.[120] However, it was only in September that Montaña and Castillo, in consultation with Ormaneto, summoned the delegates to a chapter general at Guadalajara for 14th November

---

[116] See AMAE, SS, leg. 34, f. 2r, and AGS, E°, leg. 149, no. 169, f. 1r respectively.

[117] See APV, Antillón, ms. *Epitome*, I(ii), pp. 1457–8; ASV, NS, vol. 8, ff. 147r–150v, Cardinale di Como to Ormaneto, Rome, 5th April 1574, f. 148v; IVDJ, env. 72, II, f. 320r and *ibid.*, ff. 57r–58v, a set of institutional, conventual and disciplinary guidelines from Monsignor Carniglia to Ormaneto, dated Rome, 26th November 1574 (possibly 1573); the covering letter is *ibid.*, f. 56r.

[118] ASV, NS, vol. 8, ff. 239r–240v. Ormaneto to Cardinale di Como, Madrid, 8th June 1574; f. 239r–v. Citation *ibid.*, f. 148v. Castillo visited Huete on 21st April 1574. See AHN, Clero, vol. 3320, f. 83r.

[119] The bulk of the visitation *acta* are in ACA, Mon., vol. 2671, ff. 69v–106r. Dated Barbastro, 29th April–1st May to El Olivar, 12th–14th June 1574. The inventory of Barbastro is in *ibid.*, vol. 2670, ff. 419r–422v. Supplementary inventories of Tudela (24th May), Calatayud (30th May) and Daroca (8th June) are in *ibid.*, vol. 2668, ff. 298r, 305r & 306v respectively.

[120] IVDJ, env. 72, II, f. 268r–v. Fray Antonio Álvarez to Ormaneto, Tortosa, 27th May 1574. Álvarez was a staunch supporter of Tàrrega.

[121] Regarding the selection of Guadalajara, see *ibid.*, f. 317r. The three summons for the provinces of Catalonia, Valencia and Aragon-Navarre, dated Madrid, 17th

1574.[121] The chapter, wrote Montaña elsewhere, was convened to ensure that 'the reformation may be more smoothly established and the Order better and more peacefully governed'.[122] But though the declared aim of the convocation was to restore the Order to its 'pristine peace and tranquility', no indication was given of how this was to be done, or of the plans to reunify it under the authority of a single general.

Copies of the convocation were sent to Castile and each of the provinces of the Crown of Aragon where they circulated during September and October, reaching some houses only three weeks before the chapter was due to sit. Religious beyond the Peninsula were not summoned, and the non-convocation of the French province provides the clearest indication that the crown had once more begun to assert its will in this affair. The Catalan convocation was taken from house to house by Mº Fray Juan Enríquez, procurator provincial of Castile, though to no avail since Duran's support held firm in the Principality.[123] Following the vicar general's example, the convocation was rejected by the entire province except for the final signatory, the maverick Fray Miguel Ángel Bruxola, now commendator of Tortosa. Elsewhere superiors gave nominal obedience to the procurators, with the exception of the Catalan Fra Sebastiá Bertrán at Barbastro who, like the rest of his countrymen, refused to sign without Duran's permission. Confident that the matter remained out of the royal domain and egged on by the Catalan authorities, on 5th October Duran appealed to Rome against the convocation.[124] In it he declared Meneses' commission to have lapsed with his death, and that consequently neither Castillo nor Montaña for that matter had the authority to celebrate a chapter general in Castile. However, this did not stop worried superiors

---

September 1574, are in *ibid.*, ff. 378r–v, 380r–v & 381r–v respectively. These are holograph copies; a notarial copy is in AGN, Clero, vol. 402, and the document is also reproduced in APV, Antillón, ms. *Epitome*, I(ii), pp. 1458–61.

[122] IVDJ, env. 72, II, f. 317r.

[123] Details on the Aragonese convocation can be found in an inquisitor's letter dated Zaragoza, 4th February 1574, *ibid.*, f. 297r. The convenor of Valencia was Fray Antonio de Ávila; on this convocation see *ibid.*, ff. 293r–294r, Fray Francisco de Zaragoza to Ormaneto, undated but *c.*December 1575. As for Catalonia, see *ibid.*, f. 378r–v. Enríquez' first stop was at Barcelona on 4th October. The danger of banditry prevented him reaching Berga and Prades; f. 378v.

[124] Regarding Duran, see *ibid.*, f. 293v. There are three copies of the appeal in AGN, Clero, vol. 402, dated Barcelona, 5th October 1574. Also reproduced in APV, Antillón, ms. *Epitome*, I(ii), pp. 1465–70.

stripping their houses of mules, gold, silver and other valuables for swift sale or redistribution.[125]

Later that month Duran summoned his supporters to a *junta* in Valencia to discuss the Aragonese course of action.[126] On about 6th November Lagarria and Fra Joan de Sant Joan were dispatched to Castile bearing a letter of protest against the convocation of the chapter.[127] A few days later Montaña left Madrid and reached the outskirts of Guadalajara on 12th November only to find his entry into the city blocked by the Aragonese on the Roman bridge over the Henares. Lagarria issued the protest to Montaña, who ordered him to refer it to the nuncio instead and swept on into Guadalajara. Two days later the chapter opened in the convent of San Antolín under Ormaneto's presidency, and with Lagarria and Sant Joan languishing in a penal cell.[128]

Despite claims by Lagarria that none from the Crown of Aragon would attend, the events of recent years had left their mark and Duran's injunctions were broken by ten, mainly Aragonese, religious.[129] Among these were Dicastillo, the provincial, and the commendators of all four Navarrese houses led by Fray Francisco de Salazar. Valencia had only two delegates at the chapter, including the commendator of Orihuela, Fray Francisco de Torres, and Catalonia a lone rebel, the inimitable Bruxola from Tortosa. For many others, however, it was a case of *obedezco pero no cumplo* — 'I obey but do not comply' — and for native Catalans, open defiance. Though the proceedings of the chapter have not survived, it is clear that the Castilian delegates attended almost to a man. Only the *acta*, which Montaña and Castillo laid before the brethren on the opening day of the chapter, have come down to us.[130]

---

[125] ACA, Mon., vol. 4144, f. 126v.

[126] IVDJ, env. 72, II, f. 293r–v.

[127] There is little agreement among chroniclers regarding this episode. The letter (undated) is that reproduced in APV, Antillón, ms. *Epitome*, I(ii), pp. 1471–4. Lagarria seems also to have carried a covering letter from Calvo to the commissaries, dated El Puig, 1st October 1574, in IVDJ, env. 72, II, f. 374r.

[128] For the transcript of an interrogation of Lagarria dated Guadalajara, 16th November 1574, see IVDJ, env. II, ff. 501r–502r. An apologetic biography of Lagarria of *c*.1587 is in ACA, Mon., vol. 2831, f. 83r–v.

[129] On this see IVDJ, env. 72, II, ff. 404r, 474r and particularly 274v–r (misbound).

[130] There are five extant copies of the *acta*, titled 'Haec sunt acta capituli generalis in civitate Guadalfaiare', dated Guadalajara, 14th November 1574. The *acta* were printed, but no copies appear to have survived. The surviving MSS are:

IX. *The Guadalajara Constitutions*

The Guadalajara decrees are among the most significant in the history of the Order, and their promulgation represents the central moment of Mercedarian Reform under Philip II. However, at first sight the fifty-six decrees present an interesting problem of definition, a tribute to the rhetorical expertise of those who fashioned them. Although outwardly no more than the *acta* of a chapter general, it gradually becomes apparent that these decrees are in fact statutes of revolutionary importance to the Order. Only at the end is it made clear that the annulment of all earlier legislation lies enshrined within them. If, despite their curiously provisional status, the *acta* soon became known as the 'Guadalajara constitutions', it was because religious recognized in them both a rupture with the past and a touchstone for the future. Above all, this document reflects both the commissaries' practical experience and the special concerns of those promoting the reform of the Order: the Castilian Mercedarians and the crown.

But, if anything, the decrees begin with an affirmation of the Albertine legislation. Aware that they were about to decree a serious diminution in his powers, the commissaries opened with a declaration of the primacy of the general in the spirit, if not the letter, of the Albertine constitutions. Thus, as in other reformed congregations,

> It is ordained that now and forevermore the general of the Order of Mercy shall be the universal head of all her religious, in whatever kingdom or province they may be [...] as much in the spiritual as in the temporal order.(121r)

(i) IVDJ, env. 72, II, ff. 1r–12v. The earliest extant copy, undated but contemporaneous with the chapter.

(ii) ACA, Mon., vol. 2832, pp. 365–402. An undated copy of *c.*1576 prepared for circulation through the Crown of Aragon, and now lacking the first and last folios.

(iii) *Ibid.*, vol. 4144 (ex-vol. 3004 *bis.*), ff. 121r–132v. A notarial copy of (ii) (taken after the loss of the final folio) dated Barcelona, 27th July 1583. Though incomplete, this copy has been reproduced with a brief commentary by Vázquez Núñez as one of his 'Fuentes para la Historia de la Merced' in *BOM*, 20 (1932), pp. 22–47. Except for the contents of the missing final folio, citations in the text are henceforth given from the MS of this copy.

(iv) BNM, ms. 2284, ff. 76v–102v. A late 16th-century copy, lacking the final paragraph.

(v) APV, ms. Cavero, 'Varia', II, ff. 170r–189v. A complete 18th-century copy by Fray José Nicolás Cavero. References to the important final paragraph (ff. 188v–189r) are given from this copy.

[131] For Tàrrega's view on this, see IVDJ, env. 72, II, f. 489r.

In line with this, the commissaries went on to revoke the *Concordia* that since 1467 had exempted the Castilians from the authority of the general, along with that of 1532 which had extended this exemption to the Indies.(121r,131v) This was no doubt welcomed by those from Castile and elsewhere, including Peñaranda and Tàrrega, who had long been pressing for its annulment as a thorn in the Order's side.[131] But if the Mercedarians were to be reunited, it was only within the context of an unprecedented administrative settlement.

Moving on to the heart of the legislation, the commissaries reduced the tenure of the general from perpetuity to six years. As first put forward in 1563 and then in 1569, the generals were to be elected in strict rotation, being drawn from the Aragonese, French and Italian sphere on the one hand, and that of Castile and the Indies on the other.(121v)[132] To avoid the coercion and violence of earlier years, a general from one provincial bloc had to be elected at a chapter general held in the other, while precise arrangements were made to ensure that chapters met regularly. Existing provisions for an electoral college of seventeen diffinitors (including five Catalans) were adapted at Guadalajara to reflect the new provincial structure. The entire Aragonese patrimony from Navarre to Sicily was joined into a single province and placed under the authority of one provincial.(123v) For the purposes of electing a general this composite 'Province of Aragon' was given a total of seven votes as against three for France and six for Castile, though in the latter case more were promised upon the establishment of fully independent provinces in the Indies.(122v)[133]

---

[132] See AMAE, SS, leg. 34, f. 2r and AGS, E°, leg. 149, no. 169, f. 1r respectively.

[133] The total of diffinitors was therefore reduced by one to sixteen. The seven Aragonese electors were to include the provincial and his two diffinitors, the prior of Barcelona and the commendators of Valencia, Zaragoza and Girona. Castile was to be represented by the provincial and five diffinitors. France was entitled to the three votes (provincial and two diffinitors) to be granted to all future provinces. Though they had their own provincials, the four American entities (Lima, Cuzco, Chile and Guatemala) remained subject to Castile, which was to govern them through a vicar general. The incumbent was to be appointed by the general in consultation with the diffinitors, though the choice had to fall on a Castilian; f. 131v. The final constitutions paid close attention to the relationship of the American provinces to the metropolis. Henceforth, the annual tribute of 100 ducats to Castile was to be paid by the province of Cuzco alone, while the other three were to submit unspecified sums of *vestuario* to the general in recognition of his nominal authority over them; see ff. 131v–132v. These are the earliest statutes of their type in any missionary order and represent a unique bond between the Spanish Mercedarians and their American brethren.

Such reforms were nothing if not controversial, and their effect in Catalonia can be imagined, particularly since Ormaneto appears to have promised Duran that the constitutions would not be tampered with.[134] Although the commissaries recognized Barcelona's status as the mother house — 'the foundation and origin of this Order' — the constitutions seriously undermined the basis of her authority as such.(124r) The appointment of the priors remained a matter for the conventuals of Barcelona, but any religious from the massive province of Aragon could now be elected to the office, which was itself reduced from life tenure to three years.(124v) While the prior's right to the office of vicar general was endorsed, the alternation of the electoral chapters (formerly celebrated only at Barcelona) and the special provisions in the decrees regarding the convocation of these emptied the conjoined title of its ancient power.[135]

However, Catalan anger was not restricted to the institutional changes laid down at Guadalajara, but also to the convulsion of the whole religious life that this implied. The new Order envisaged in the Guadalajara constitutions was not the one they had joined as novices. Particularly in its approach to discipline, punishment and personal responsibility, the new legislation rode roughshod over the cherished 'pratiga y antic costum' of the Order.[136] The general's powers of dispensation were curtailed and sentences of excommunication now carried with them a degree of spiritual rigour unknown in the 1327 constitutions.[137] 'This,' as the Barcelona fathers later wrote to the king, 'is one of the great injustices that has been done to us.' The violence and recrimination that eventually shrouded the Catalan cause and the ruinous condition of the Order in these parts must not obscure the genuine concern of religious to maintain an established pattern of life in a period of rapid change. It was on such points that the acceptance of the reform in Catalonia would ultimately depend and this which, during the 1580s, brought the Order to its knees.

---

[134] See IVDJ, env. 72, II, f. 293v.

[135] Catalan grievances against the decrees can be followed in the *marginalia* of the ACA, Mon., vol. 2832 MS (ii), pp. 365–9, and in a detailed rebuttal in AGN, Clero, vol. 416, entitled 'Repugnantias contra las antigas constitutions fetas per las actas de guadalaiara a 14 de noembre [*sic*] 1574'; undated but 1575. For a more considered refutation by Fra Francesc Cardá, see ACA, Mon., vol. 4144, ff. 19r–21r, undated but early 1583; another copy *ibid.*, ff. 36r–38r.

[136] AGN, Clero, vol. 416. Undated but *c*.1579.

[137] ASV, NS, vol. 22, ff. 40r–43v, a *memorial* by Maldonado, undated but late 1578; f. 41v.

However, these were not the only reforms legislated at Guadala-jara. Against the revocation of the two *Concordiae*, the generals would have to weigh the limitation of their tenure and a serious curtailment of what were once massive powers. Intermediary chapters general were to be held every three years in what was implicitly an assess-ment of the general's tenure.(121v) The office of provincial was final-ly removed from his gift, having to be elected in chapter every three years.(122v) A general could not replace a commendator in a foreign province without first consulting the provincial, a measure confirm-ing the largely regional dimension of his executive authority.(123r) For, in accordance with the Rule of St Augustine, the general was not so much to rule his Order, but lead it by example. Measures were taken to prevent the notorious accumulation of wealth and the other blatantly secular accoutrements that had come to be associated with the high office. Page-boys, servants, fine rooms and furnishings were to be abandoned. In Barcelona particularly, generals were to sleep in the priory and join their brethren for meals in the refectory. More-over, the general was prevented from acquiring property or private income beyond that of the barony of Algar and the *vestuario* tradition-ally given him by the provinces, for all of which he was to present account at the chapters general. Neither was he to allow any to call him 'Lord', but ensure that 'at all times he be addressed without vain and worldly titles, like the generals of reformed orders', and equally see that all religious be treated with 'justice and equality'.(123r) If the Order were to look up to a patriarchal figure, it would not be the master general, for patronage over it had implicitly devolved on the king himself.

Next the commissaries turned to what had been one of Montaña's chief concerns in the months leading up to the chapter general, the suppression of impoverished houses in the Crown of Aragon.[138] Though this matter was probably given more importance than it deserved, the reformers, and evidently the crown also, saw in these a root cause of the decline of the Order.[139] Where communities could sustain only one or two religious, conventual life and spiritual obser-vance soon collapsed into relaxation. In all no less than eleven con-

---

[138] See IVDJ, env. 72, II, ff. 272v–273r & 372r. Duran had apparently approached the crown in 1569–70 with proposals to reduce the number of Catalan houses; see APV, Antillón, ms. *Epitome*, I(ii), pp. 1443–5, and Vázquez Núñez, *Manual*, II, p. 12.
[139] See especially IVDJ, env. 72, II, f. 372r.

vents were earmarked for reduction into larger entities, and it was on
the basis of this diminution of its numerical strength that the Order's
Aragonese patrimony was to be gathered into one province.(123v)[140]

For the rest, the constitutions largely followed Castilian practice.
The decrees on novices, vows, commendators, property and conventual deposits, the preaching, collection and care of redemption
limosna, on ordination, degrees and *studia* all reflect those passed at the
chapters provincial of Guadalajara and Toledo. In line with developments in Castile, the constitutions regularized both the admission and
promotion of religious, underlining the importance of study and of
scholarly attainment as the basic criterion for advancement within
the Order. Tridentine practice was adopted where convenient — in
elections for instance — but not otherwise, as Catalan protests make
clear. Above all, the Guadalajara decrees viewed institutional change
as the basis for spiritual reform, which is alluded to only briefly. The
provisions for the spiritual life of the religious set down in the 1327
constitutions and elaborated later were implicitly allowed to stand
until they too could be adapted to suit current needs. It was this selec-
tive approach to the reform of the Order, as well as the serious
canonical problems involved, that governed the commissaries' attitude to the old constitutions, and which, ultimately, spelt their
demise. As they declared,

> Since several of these reform statutes derogate, change, alter, contra-
> dict or limit some of the Order's old constitutions […] we appeal to
> His Holiness that he confirm them *cum clausulis necessariis et opportunis*,
> and grant a licence for them to be published together as a book with
> constitutional authority.[141]

Or, as Mº Fray Juan de Montoro put it in a passage recalling Torres,
lex antiqua nova lege dissolvitur — old laws dissolved by new laws —
something of a legal cliché, but eloquent testimony to the spirit in
which the Castilians addressed the matter of reforming the Order.[142]

Though the decrees reflect a predominantly Castilian view of the

---

[140] The houses were, in Catalonia, Santa Coloma de Queralt, Sant Ramon Nonat,
Tàrrega, Prades, Montblanc and Agramunt; in Aragon, San Pedro de los Griegos,
Uncastillo and Monflorite; in Valencia, Arguines and San Ginés. Of these only San
Pedro de los Griegos and Monflorite were suppressed in the 1570s, with Prades and
San Ginés following later.

[141] APV, ms. Cavero, 'Varia', II, ff. 188v–189r.

[142] ACA, Mon., vol. 4144, ff. 45r–46v. *Memorial* from Montoro to Dom Benet Tocco, bishop of Lleida, Barcelona, 8th August 1583; f. 45v.

Order, the condition of the Crown of Aragon called for specific measures which lend the Guadalajara constitutions an air of emergency legislation. In the first place it was made clear that the new general was to remain in the eastern provinces until such time as the reform were established.(121r) Once there he was to conduct a visitation with the express aim of taking an inventory of all houses and rooting out those guilty of a range of moral abuses, from private ownership of property to the swindling of redemption alms.(125r) Alienated property was to be returned to the Order, knick-knacks confiscated and further information gathered on the whereabouts of two decades of lost *limosna*.(126v,128r) Above all, the general was charged with the establishment of noviciates at Barcelona, Zaragoza and Valencia where a new generation of reform-minded religious could be nurtured.(129v) Most controversially, however, he was to be assisted by reformed brethren from the province of Castile for an initial period of three years.(128r–v)[143] Though standard practice in other orders, this, as so much else, was quite unprecedented among the Mercedarians.[144]

The question only remained as to who the new general was to be. Practical considerations dictated that he should be selected from the handful of Aragonese religious who had attended the chapter, and on 18th November 1574 the Valencian M° Fray Francisco de Torres, commendator of Orihuela, was elected to the high office.[145] His secretary was to be P° Fray Francisco Maldonado, the former Castilian procurator in Rome, an appointment which reflects both his rehabilitation as a leading member of the province and, like the statutes themselves, the triumph of Peñaranda's more pragmatic interpretation of reform.

---

[143] For a preliminary list of fifteen Castilian reformers, see IVDJ, env. 72, II, f. 480r–v. Tàrrega had in 1573 suggested an exchange of religious between Castilian and Aragonese convents; see *ibid.*, ff. 490v–491r. *Ibid.*, ff. 475r–477r (no f. 476) provides a list of 30 disruptive elements to be removed from the eastern provinces, including nine suspected of defrauding *limosna*, and a further 22 Aragonese reckoned to be favourable to the Reform; see *ibid.*, f. 46r regarding provision to commanderies in the Crown of Aragon.

[144] In the Crown of Aragon Benedictine and particularly Augustinian houses were being reformed by Castilian religious.

[145] Torres was a native of Elche.

CHAPTER SEVEN

THE CRISIS OF REFORM (1575–93)

*Your Lordship should be aware that this [reform] is not a matter of
eight or even ten years, but of thirty or forty…*[1]

Though the chapter general of Guadalajara was over, the battle to
reform the Order was in a sense only just beginning. Since this battle
centred almost entirely on the priory of Barcelona, and lest we lose
sight of the broader context in which Mercedarian Reform was
played out, it seems appropriate to begin by briefly taking the pulse of
monastic life not only in the city and Principality, but in the Crown of
Aragon as a whole.

I. *The Reform of the Religious Orders in the Crown of Aragon*

In common with the rest of the Peninsula, the history of the religious
orders in the Crown of Aragon under Philip II has received no systematic treatment. However, already at the start of the reign the
impulse to reform was again stirring the eastern congregations into
life. Almost without exception, this impulse emanated from Castile,
where Philip had been taking an interest in monastic reform since the
early 1550s. Among the Augustinians, the pattern of whose reform
most resembles that of the Mercedarian Order, the process began in
earnest in 1555 under the sponsorship of a former provincial of
Castile, Fray Tomás de Villanueva, archbishop of Valencia.[2] However, it was only after the onset of the royal reform campaign in the
1560s that any significant progress could be made in a congregation
with no core of Observant religious.[3] Through the intervention of the

---

[1] IVDJ, env. 72, II, ff. 82r–83r. Mº Fray Pedro de Salamanca (OP) to Ormaneto,
Valencia, 2nd November 1575; f. 82r.
[2] P.Fr. Carlos Alonso, *La reforma tridentina en la provincia Agustiniana de la Corona de
Aragón (1568–1586)* (Valladolid, 1984), pp. 18–20.
[3] *Ibid.*, pp. 59–70.

crown, this shortage was made good between 1568–9 with the arrival of fifty reformed Castilian brethren in the Crown of Aragon under the Andalusian reformer general, Fray Rodrigo de Solís.[4] Even so, the frustrations and reverses that attended this campaign are exceded only by the experience of Mercedarian and Benedictine Reform in the same period.

A similar case is that of the Aragonese Dominicans.[5] Though it had largely ground to a halt by the mid sixteenth century, the reform of the Order in these parts continued to rely on Castilian assistance. Progress was resumed after 1556 under the reformist provincial Fray Pedro Mártir Coma, again with Philip's support. However, much remained to be done at the time of general Fra Vincenzo Giustiniani's Spanish visitation in 1566. The Aragonese Reform did not become fully independent until the generation of young religious formed under Fray Luis Beltrán (1526–80) in Valencia had reached maturity. The issue that dominated Dominican reform politics in Aragon during the 1560s — Philip's desire to place that province's Navarrese patrimony under Castilian authority — was shared by several other orders, particularly the Cistercians.[6] The king's concern to align ecclesiastical boundaries with political ones was, as we have seen, a basic tenet of his early monastic policy, and affected the Aragonese congregations in particular. Though influenced by religious and political considerations, Philip was also anxious that Aragonese religious should enjoy closer supervision from reformist superiors than had hitherto been possible. However, the logical extension of this policy, the establishment of independent Peninsular congregations of Augustinians, Trinitarians, Carmelites and Cistercians, could not be implemented in the 1560s, even with the support of the religious concerned.[7] As with so many other aspects of monastic reform, this matter would have to be addressed later in less strident terms.

The work of reform therefore progressed with rather mixed for-

---

[4] *Ibid.*, pp. 71–84.

[5] Beltrán de Heredia, *Historia de la reforma de la Provincia de España*, pp. 212–17.

[6] The Mercedarian province of Aragon, with its four Navarrese houses, remained unaffected by this policy.

[7] See Alonso, *La reforma tridentina en la provincia Agustiniana*, pp. 80–3 for the Augustinians and *CDEESS*, IV, xxx–xxxii, xxxvi & xlvi for the others. The Spanish Trinitarians liberated themselves from the regional particularism of the Picardy brethren later in the century; see García Oro, 'Conventualismo y observancia', pp. 339–40.

[8] See Bada, *Situació religiosa*, pp. 60 & 235–6.

tune, where it progressed at all. Visitations by Carmelite and Trinitarian superiors, recorded in the Crown of Aragon during the 1560s,
reveal a picture of neglect and degradation comparable to that of the
Mercedarians.[8] An attempted visitation of the Cistercians of
Calatayud in 1564 provoked a revolt and appeals to Rome.[9] Elsewhere in the Cistercian congregation of Navarre and the Crown of
Aragon, the *encomienda* had left indigent monks to 'live as they can
and as they will'.[10] Philip's interest in the reform of the Tarraconensian Benedictine congregation was also aroused as early as 1556, but
constitutional difficulties and the sheer scale of the enterprise prevented any serious royal intervention until towards the end of the century.[11] At Montserrat — the centrepiece of the Valladolid Congregation's presence in the Crown of Aragon since its incorporation in
1493 — decades of conflict and hatred between Castilian and Catalan monks erupted into a titanic struggle in the 1580s.[12] The years
after 1580 therefore represent a critical period for monastic reform in
the Crown of Aragon, and Barcelona in particular, on which more
later.

So much for the wider background of Mercedarian Reform in the
years before and after 1567, but what of the urban setting of monastic Barcelona in which this was played out? Here the regulars
amounted to 3 or perhaps 4% of the total population, a figure comparable with any other city in Spain.[13] Of the thirty-five or so religious houses in and around Barcelona at Philip's accession, the Mer-

---

[9] *CDEESS*, IV, xxxi.

[10] 'Viuen com poden i com volen'; cited in Sales, *Els segles de la decadència*, p. 451.

[11] See Dom Antoni Maria Tobella, 'La Congregació Claustral Tarraconense i les diverses recapitulacions de les seves Constitucions provincials' in *Catalonia Monastica: Recull de documents i estudis referents a monestirs catalans* (2 vols., Montserrat, 1927–9), II, pp. 111–251, Dom Ernesto Zaragoza Pascual, 'Documentos inéditos referentes a la reforma monástica de Cataluña durante la segunda mitad del siglo XVI (1555–1600)' in *Studia Monastica*, 19 (1977), pp. 93–203, *id.*, 'Reforma de los Bene-dictinos y de los Canónigos Regulares en Cataluña: Documentos inéditos (1588–1616)' in *Studia Monastica*, 23 (1981), pp. 71–148, *id.*, 'Documentos inéditos referentes a la reforma de los Canónigos Regulares y Benedictinos de Aragón, Cataluña, Rosellón y Cerdaña (1581–1618)' in *Studia Monastica*, 31 (1989), pp. 89–147, & Bada, *Situació religiosa*, p. 199.

[12] See Dom Ernesto Zaragoza Pascual, *Los generales de la congregación de San Benito de Valladolid* (6 vols., Santo Domingo de Silos, 1973–87); III, pp. 114–20, & Ignasi Fer-nández Terricabras, 'Refoma i obediència: Actituds institucionals durant la visita del monestir de Montserrat (1583–1586)' in *Actes del Tercer Congrés d'Història Moderna de Catalunya* [=*Pedralbes*] (2 vols., Barcelona, 1993); II, pp. 171–80.

[13] See Bada, *Situació religiosa*, pp. 55–6.

cedarian priory was among the most significant, partly because of its status and wealth as the mother house of an order, and partly because of the major shrine it housed. The city already lay under the advocation of 'Nostra Senyora de la Mercè' who was eventually confirmed as its sole patroness in 1688.[14] The priory church contained the fifth of the city's seven chapels celebrating the *goigs* ('joys') *de Maria*, the processional life of the Virgin.[15] With a community of perhaps thirty-five conventuals, its own confraternities and ransoming vocation, the priory played a significant part in the social, economic and religious life of Barcelona. After 1567 it would also acquire a major political role.[16]

Barcelona saw a dramatic readjustment in its monastic Order during the second half of the sixteenth century. The series of religious foundations which stretches from the Benedictine priory of Sant Pau del Camp (by 911) through the Dominican priory of Santa Caterina (1219) — the senior mendicant foundation — the Clares at Pedralbes (1326), and, some distance from the city, the Charterhouse of Montalegre (1433), is completed with the establishment of the Jesuits in 1545, the Minims and the first Capuchin house in Spain (both 1578), the first permanent convent of Servite friars in the Peninsula (by 1580), and the first Discalced Carmelite convent outside Castile in 1586.[17]

---

[14] See Gazulla, *La Patrona de Barcelona*, pp. 270–2. This favour owed much to the support of the *Consell de Cent* and, no doubt, to the influence of M° Fray Antonio de Sotomayor, the Andalusian general (1652–7) and bishop of Barcelona (1663–82).

[15] See Bada, *Situació religiosa*, pp. 67–8.

[16] The two medieval guild-confraternities associated with the priory were those of the *escudellers* (potters) — see *infra*, n. 132 — and the *platers* (silversmiths), the latter founded in the late 13th or early 14th century under the patronage of Sant Eloi. Its statutes were approved in 1371; see Gazulla, *La Patrona de Barcelona*, pp. 270–2.

[17] Bada, *Situació religiosa*, pp. 47–53. On the Jesuits, see *ibid.*, pp. 121–8, & Antoni Borràs i Feliu, 'La fundacío del Col·legi de Betlem de la Companyia de Jesús de Barcelona' in *Actes del Tercer Congrés d'Història Moderna de Catalunya* [=*Pedralbes*] (2 vols., Barcelona, 1993); II, pp. 203–11; on the Capuchins see P.Fr. Basili de Rubí, *Un segle de vida caputxina a Catalunya, 1564–1664: Aproximació històrico-bibliogràfica* (Barcelona, 1977), pp. 67–8; on the Servites, Fr Damian M. Charboneau, 'The Servites of Barcelona' in *Studi storici dell' Ordine dei Servi di Maria*, 30 (1980), pp. 5–85, esp. 5–12. The Servites provide another example of patronage of a religious order by the *Consell de Cent* during this period. For the Discalced Carmelite friars, see Gabriel Beltrán, 'Juan de Jesús Roca (1544–1614): Primer Carmelita Descalzo Catalán' in *El Carmelo Teresiano en Cataluña 1586–1986* [=*Revista Monte Carmelo*] (Burgos, 1986); pp. 7–54, esp. 25.

The Barcelona of Philip II therefore presents a varied monastic panorama, yet one bound together by the climate of reform. Beginning in the late fifteenth century, persistent attempts were made to reform the convents of the city, particularly the nunneries, though with little more success here than among their male counterparts.[18] The reforming efforts of Ignatius of Loyola during his stay in Catalonia between 1524–6 were rebuffed by both the Jeronymite and Dominican nuns, and a campaign against the four main city nunneries began in the 1560s only after a delay of twenty years.[19] Lack of leadership and direction certainly played its part, but if the efforts of several generations of prelates and princes went largely unrewarded it was because the city itself was from the outset divided over the question of reform. Although the religious houses were generally considered an unedifying spectacle, the urban élite found in the nunneries a useful repository for their women, who in turn resented the limitations on their personal freedom implied by reformed life. Moreover, the involvement of the crown in monastic reform had always been viewed as a challenge to the rights of patronage traditionally exercised by the *Consell de Cent* over the religious houses of the city. The overbearing tone and conduct of the campaign waged by the Catholic Kings against the nunneries of Barcelona from 1493 remained etched into the consciousness of civic and monastic authority alike. By the mid sixteenth century reform was therefore opposed as much for reasons of jurisdiction as for its disruption of an agreeable pattern of urban living.

The onset of the royal reform programme in the 1560s predicably aroused much hostility in the city. The adoption by the Franciscan *beaterio* of Santa Isabel of the Clare observance in 1564 was followed two years later by the suppression of the Benedictine priory of Sant Pau del Camp by bishop Guillem Cassador.[20] From 1566 Cassador began to move against the recalcitrant nunneries of the city, including the Benedictine abbey of Sant Pere de les Puel·les, and the convents of Mont Sió (Dominicans) and Santa Maria de

---

[18] Bada, *Situació religiosa*, pp. 129–47.

[19] *Ibid.*, pp. 122–3 & 227–35.

[20] See, respectively, Carmen Soriano Triguero, 'La reforma de las Clarisas en la Corona de Aragón (ss.XV–XVI)' in *Revista de historia moderna*, 13–14 (1995), pp. 185–98, esp. 194–5, & Bada, *Situació religiosa*, p. 239. In 1583 the Barcelona Inquisition was granted an annual subsidy of 800 ducats from the revenues of Sant Pau and other suppressed houses in the city; see Boyd, *Cardinal Quiroga*, p. 78.

Jerusalem (Franciscan Tertiaries).[21] Then, in May 1567, the crown began the final extinction of the Conventual Franciscans in Catalonia with the imposition of the Observant rule on the community of Sant Francesc in Barcelona.[22] Though this process was accepted with some resignation, the Observant provincial was soon reporting that many brethren had fled the Order, some joining the bandits in threatening the lives of reformed religious.[23] Recalcitrants were sent to Italy, from where several returned to Catalonia with the first Capuchins ten years later.[24] In this climate resistance to change became steadily more widespread, more easily condoned and more vigorously abetted. Monastic reform had always provoked conflict among religious, but under Philip II the wider social and political conjuncture imbued this process with an unexpectedly violent character, one that focused the grievances and frustrations of a broad sector of Catalan society.[25] As the *conseller en cap*, Dr. Thomàs Pujades, declared of the Mercedarian question in 1584, 'these are matters that touch on the honour of my *patria*, and therefore mine too'.[26]

If such sentiments produced life-long opponents of state-led reform, like canon Guerau Vilana, vicar general of Barcelona, and leading members of the *Consell* such as Pujades, then it reminds us also of the persistence of those committed to the realization of this grand design.[27] The names of reformers, many of them Castilians, recur time and again in the documentation. The Dominican Fray Juan Izquierdo is a case in point. In January 1549 Izquierdo, then provincial of Aragon, was visitor of the Dominican nunnery of Mont Sió; by June 1565 he was reformer of the Augustinian nuns in the Crown of Aragon, and June 1572 found him assisting Montaña with

---

[21] Bada, *Situació religiosa*, pp. 227–33. For the development of the reform of Catalonia's three Benedictine nunneries from mid century, see Dom Ernesto Zaragoza Pascual, 'Reforma de los Benedictinas de Cataluña en el siglo XVI (1589–1603)' in *Analecta Sacra Tarraconensia*, 49–50 (1976–7), pp. 177–204.

[22] See P.Fr. José García Oro, *Francisco de Asís en la España Medieval* (Santiago de Compostela, 1988), pp. 532–5.

[23] *Ibid.*, p. 535.

[24] See Basili de Rubí, *Un segle de vida caputxina a Catalunya*, pp. 20 & 35.

[25] For a comparative view of such tensions, see René Pillorget, 'Réforme monastique et conflits de rupture dans quelques localités de la France méridionale au XVIIᵉ siècle' in *Revue historique*, 253 (1975), pp. 77–106.

[26] Cited in Fernández Terricabras, 'Reforma i obediència', p. 177.

[27] On Vilana, see, for example, Zaragoza Pascual, 'Reforma de los Benedictinas de Cataluña en el siglo XVI', p. 180.

the Mercedarians of Tortosa.[28] These references remind us also that in Catalonia, as in Spain generally, the endeavour of reform was the work of a very reduced community of men and women; through them, and through the idea of reform, the Spanish religious Order was bound, in its diversity, into one entity.

II. *Resistance in the Crown of Aragon, 1574–6*

The chapter over, Francisco de Torres quit Guadalajara at the end of November 1574 and made for Madrid to give his obedience to the king.[29] Having made arrangements for Torres' confirmation, the commissaries turned their attention to the former vicar general, Fra Bernat Duran, and his fellow dissidents in the Crown of Aragon.[30] The election of Torres seems to have been received with some surprise in Valencia, where Calvo was soon writing emolliently to Montaña condemning the 'tyranny' of the old constitutions and lauding the new with citations from Aristotle and the Bible.[31] For his part, Duran greeted the constitutions with a torrent of protests to Rome, where he had no less than three procurators installed by the spring of 1575.[32] Denying the right of the commissaries either to convene a

---

[28] Bada, *Situació religiosa*, pp. 144–5, 228–9, & IVDJ, env. 72, II, ff. 306r–v & 278r. See also Zaragoza Pascual, 'Reforma de los Benedictinas de Cataluña en el siglo XVI', pp. 177–8. Izquierdo was appointed bishop of Tortosa in 1574.

[29] AHCB, ms. A-266. Mº Fray Juan de Antillón, *Memorias Chronologicas de la Religion de Nuestra Señora de la Merced Redempcion de Captivos Christianos en la Provincia y Corona de Aragon*, vol. II (1574–c.1625), ff. 3v–4r. The original MS, completed in 1643, is lost; the present vol. is a late 18th-century copy by the Valencian Mº Fray Agustín Arqués y Jover. Vol. I of this work is not known to exist, and this MS may in fact be the concluding part of a history of the Order for which the *Epitome de los Generales de la Merced* (in its two parts) is the first section; see ch. 2, n. 145. References to this work are henceforth given in the text.

[30] See AMAE, SS, leg. 34, f. 12r, Philip II to his ambassador in Rome, Juan de Zúñiga, Príncipe de Piedraprecia, 21st January 1575; another copy f. 17r. See also IVDJ, env. 72, II, f. 322v, a letter from Montaña, undated but late 1574, and particularly *ibid.*, ff. 54r–55r (4º), anonymous *memorial*, undated but early 1575. On 9th February 1575 the commissaries apparently passed a *sentencia* against those who had failed to present themselves at Guadalajara; see ACA, Mss.Misc., vol. 49, p. 30.

[31] IVDJ, env. 72, II, f. 335r–v. El Puig, 4th December 1574.

[32] Appeals to Rome survive against the convocation of the chapter (AGN, Clero, vol. 402, Barcelona, 3rd December 1574) and the treatment meted out to Lagarria (*ibid.*, Barcelona, 13th December 1574). There are reports of more on 6th, 9th, 21st & 27th December 1574, and from the *Consellers*, Barcelona, 20th January 1575. Duran's procurators were Lagarria, Alegría (since 1572) and Mº Fray Pascual del

chapter without his authority or to elect a general without prior warning, Duran steadfastly refused to recognize Torres.[33] All the while desperate attempts were being made in the Crown of Aragon to raise funds for the *pleitos* being brought in Rome. In Valencia Lagarria, newly returned from Castile, looted conventual funds and pawned a gold chain stripped from an image of the Virgin before leaving for Italy.[34] Money was donated for Duran's expenses by a number of houses — including El Puig — and extorted from others leaving several completely ruined, while property was sold and *censales* (mortgages) charged on remaining assets.[35] Furious at the exclusion of his countrymen from the chapter, the French provincial Mͤ Frey Antoine de Tremollières headed for Rome to block Torres' confirmation with support from Henry III.[36]

As appeal followed appeal, arrangements were made in Madrid for the election of a new prior of Barcelona and provincial of Aragon, while Torres made his way to the eastern kingdoms in fulfilment of the constitutions.[37] By February Ormaneto and the commissaries had lost patience with the Catalans and took direct action. Without waiting for the outcome of Duran's appeals in Rome, Montaña and Castillo passed a *sentencia* declaring the vicar general excommunicated and his office forfeit, and made arrangements to have him arrested.(4v)[38] Along with Ángulo and Murta, Duran was to be held until he had given account of his administration of the property of the Order. Finally, they ordered twenty-one recalcitrant religious to be removed from their houses and dispersed throughout Castile at Torres' discretion. To facilitate this, Ormaneto prepared commissions for

---

Molinar, who was arrested on Ormaneto's orders. For details of this embassy, see ACA, Mon., vol. 2831, f. 83r, and for Torres' revocation of the remaining procurators' licences, IVDJ, env. 72, II, f. 472v, Madrid, 27th June 1575. The Castilian procurator, appointed at Guadalajara, was M° Fray Juan Enríquez.

[33] AGN, Clero, vol. 416. *Consellers* to Ormaneto, Barcelona, 26th April 1575. The Catalan grievances are well summarized in a major *memorial* by Maldonado, ASV, NS, vol. 22, ff. 40r–43v, undated but late 1578; ff. 40v–42r.

[34] IVDJ, env. 72, II, f. 54r. For his activities in Italy, see ACA, Mon., vol. 2831, f. 83r.

[35] IVDJ, env. 72, II, ff. 54r & 294r.

[36] AMAE, SS, leg. 34, f. 13r–v. Philip II to Juan de Zúñiga, Madrid, 22nd February, 1575; f. 13r.

[37] Details in IVDJ, env. 72, II, ff. 318r, 321r–v (misbound) & 322v, Montaña's notes and letters in draft, undated but early 1575. See also *ibid.*, f. 469r, Torres to Ormaneto, undated.

[38] Dated Madrid, 9th February 1575.

the archbishops of Zaragoza and Valencia and the Castilian bishop of Barcelona, Martín Martínez del Villar.(5r) The reincorporation of the secular clergy in the reform of the Mercedarians reflects both the renewed influence of the crown and the determination of Ormaneto and the commissaries to bring this matter to a speedy conclusion, and it was Villar who detained Duran in Barcelona during March 1575.[39] By June Aragonese Mercedarians were under arrest throughout the eastern provinces and in Madrid.

The arrest of Duran in particular represents an important turning point in the reform process, because henceforth the cathedral chapter and the *consellers* of Barcelona openly championed the cause of the priory in their role as 'protectors and defenders' of the city's monasteries.(5v,28r–v)[40] The electoral chapters general, they claimed, had been held at Barcelona since the foundation of the Order, and the derogation of this right was clearly interpreted as a threat to the privileges of the city itself. For its part, the cathedral chapter issued a *requerimiento* (protest) to the nuncio condemning both the election and the persecution that had followed it.(5r)[41] However, Duran was not destined to remain in Villar's gaol for very long. Sometime towards the end of April a file was passed to him through the grille of his cell with which he broke out of a window and escaped down a rope-ladder.(6r) Provided with money and horses, the former prior fled to France.

In Rome, meanwhile, Gregory had delegated the Mercedarian

---

[39] For protests against this, see the following (all Barcelona, 1575 unless otherwise stated): AGN, Clero, vol. 402: (i) Priory of Barcelona to Gregory XIII, 20th April; (ii) *Consellers* to Gregory XIII, 22nd April; (iii) Canons of Barcelona to Gregory XIII, 24th April (two copies). (iv) IVDJ, env. 72, II, f. 467r, Fra Jeroni de Almenara, sub-prior of Barcelona, to Ormaneto, 3rd May. (v) ACA, Mon., vol. 2677, f. 128r, Priory to ? (discarded copy), 7th June. In AGN, Clero, vol. 416: (vi) *Consellers* to Ormaneto, 12th June; (vii) Canons of Barcelona to Ormaneto, 12th June. Ángulo and Murta were arrested by the archbishops of Zaragoza and Valencia respectively, and Fra Benet Camps by the bishop of Urgell, Joan Dimas Loris; see Tirso, *Historia*, II, p. 25, &, for Camps, AGN, Clero, vol. 402, Pere Ayllá(?) to Ormaneto(?), undated but mid 1576. Murta's abjuration, made shortly before his death, is in IVDJ, env. 72, II, ff. 144r–146r, Valencia, 14th June. After periods in Madrid and Valencia, Ángulo was eventually banished to Córdoba. For the general picture, see *ibid.*, f. 457r–v, ? to Ormaneto(?), same place and date, and ACA, Mon., vol. 2831, f. 83r–v.

[40] Citation from AGN, Clero, vol. 402. *Consellers* to Gregory XIII, Barcelona, 22nd April 1575. The conventuals' debt to the city and the *Consell* in particular for its support is recorded in a *memorial*, apparently by the *conseller* Dr. Joan Rafael Masnovell, in ACA, Mon., vol. 4144, ff. 29r–33r, probably dated Barcelona, 3rd August 1583.

[41] AGN, Clero, vol. 416, Barcelona, 12th June 1575.

question to two of the four cardinals of the *Comisione di Riforma* who in March issued a brief which confirmed Torres as general, but significantly left the Guadalajara constitutions unratified.(6r)[42] The brief reached Torres — now back in Madrid — in mid May from where it was dispatched to Barcelona.(6v)[43] After much discussion and disagreement, the brethren — who remained in touch with Duran throughout — finally withdrew the appeal and gave their obedience to Torres in August 1575.(7r)[44] The *Generalitat* explained that the religious had appealed not to escape the reform but in defence of their constitutional privileges.[45] Seeking a pardon, Duran now returned to Spain and, full of contrition, made his way to Madrid where he was detained along with Lagarria under new powers obtained by the nuncio.(7v,12v–13r)[46] Their enemies imprisoned and in hiding, the reformers seemed at this moment to be in the ascendant, but their cause ground to a halt at a crucial moment. In August Montaña died leaving Ormaneto with the urgent task of finding a replacement. A former Mercedarian commissary, the Dominican M° Fray Pedro de Salamanca, declined the offer on the grounds of age and infirmity.[47] The task fell instead to the Neapolitan Benedictine Dom Benet Tocco, bishop of Girona, who was accorded a perpetual commission to reform the Order.[48] Tocco, abbot of Montserrat between 1556–9 and 1562–4, was among the most important ecclesiastics in the Crown of Aragon during the reign of Philip II, and his appointment united in one person the two great monastic endeavours of Philippine Catalonia: the reform of the priory of Barcelona and the abbey of Montserrat. However, until the early 1580s it was the latter that absorbed most of his time and energy.

---

[42] Dated Rome, 28th March 1575.

[43] The authenticated briefs were dated Madrid, 18th May 1575.

[44] The act of obedience is in AGN, Clero, vol. 402. Dated Barcelona, 13th August 1575.

[45] *Ibid. Diputació* to Ormaneto, undated but *c.*August 1575.

[46] A self-justifying letter from Duran, still under arrest, to Philip II survives in *ibid.*, undated but Madrid, *c.*December 1575. The brief extending Ormaneto's powers was issued on 1st June 1575; see Torres, 'Pedro de Salamanca, O.P.', pp. 94–5. The troublesome Lagarria was shunted from Huesca to Barbastro before being banished to Murcia in *c.*1577; see ACA, Mon., vol. 2831, f. 83r–v.

[47] Salamanca's letter of appointment from Ormaneto, dated Madrid, 9th September 1575, is reproduced in Torres, 'Pedro de Salamanca, O.P.', pp. 95–6. His reply declining the offer is in IVDJ, env. 72, II, ff. 82r–83r. Salamanca had been involved in the Carmelite reform.

[48] For more on Tocco's appointment, see ACA, Mon., vol. 2831, f. 83r. A biography of Tocco is provided in Zaragoza Pascual, *Los generales de la congregación de San Benito de Valladolid*, III, pp. 364–7.

Among the Mercedarians the reformers' trials were far from over. That August Torres and Maldonado left Madrid intending to conduct a visitation of the Crown of Aragon.(8r) By the time the pair reached Zaragoza Torres was ill, and he died here, like Papiol before him, on 31st August 1575. The deaths within a few weeks of Torres and Fray Guillermo Montaña, and then that of Tárrega in Zaragoza on 9th November, left an irreplaceable void in the reformist leadership of the Aragonese provinces.[49] Matters were further complicated by the death in July of the moderate sub-prior of Barcelona, Fra Jeroni de Almenara. Under these hammer blows the reform campaign once again fell into disarray in Catalonia and the settlement briefly promised by Torres' election at Guadalajara dissolved for ten long years.

The Catalans naturally took immediate advantage of this unexpected turn of events. With Duran languishing in Madrid, on 12th September the president of Barcelona Fra Lluís Valls assumed the office of vicar general and summoned an electoral chapter general for November in clear contravention of the Guadalajara statutes.[50] Ormaneto soon learnt to his dismay that the Catalans had enrolled the support of Cardinal de Sans in Rome, and warned Philip of the possibility that a Frenchman might be elected and confirmed through the offices of Henry III.[51] Entrusted at first with the completion of Torres' visitation, Maldonado was now made visitor apostolic and ordered to Barcelona to put an end to the chapter.[52] However, the nuncio's choice was an unfortunate one since Maldonado, apart from his notorious tenure as procurator in Rome between 1567 and 1569, had in recent months been heavily involved in the disciplining of Aragonese dissenters.

The appointment of a hard-liner therefore confirmed Catalan fears that the Reform was less a sincere desire to improve the Order than a Castilian design to strip them of their immemorial rights. Quite to what degree they were justified in holding this view cannot

---

[49] On the death of Tárrega, then president of Zaragoza, see IVDJ, env. 72, II, f. 454r, an anonymous note to Ormaneto, undated but late 1575, and *ibid.*, f. 498r, Conventuals of San Lázaro to Ormaneto, Zaragoza, 16th November 1575.

[50] The summons was for 6th November 1575. For Valls' declaration of his rights as vicar general, see ACA, Mon., vol. 2832, pp. 329–30, undated and incomplete.

[51] IVDJ, env. 72, II, f. 52r–v. Undated but September or October 1575.

[52] Maldonado is recorded as having visited the house at Tarragona before heading for Barcelona; Tirso, *Historia*, II, p. 42.

easily be measured, but the religious and spiritual elements of Mercedarian Reform in Catalonia now fell away and the hard kernel of this phase in the process stood revealed. As battle was joined, it became increasingly clear that the reform of this Order, like that of so many others, was as much about power and authority as the ultimate endeavour of reform itself: the pursuit of spiritual perfection. Moreover, because the fate of the Mercedarians was seen by many in Catalonia as analogous with that of the Principality itself, the cause of the priory became, in the hands of the *Consell* and the *Generalitat*, a discourse on the wider relationship between an increasingly Castilianized crown and a steadily more marginalized territory of the monarchy.

Maldonado reached Barcelona on 4th November, the eve of the election, and presented his letters of accreditation to the viceroy, Hernando de Toledo, upon whom he was relying for succour and protection.(8v) That afternoon Maldonado made his way under armed escort to the priory, now full of delegates, and demanded entry. The events of the next few hours are vividly portrayed by Tirso.[53] Piqued no doubt by threats to raze the priory to the ground, Valls steadfastly refused to grant him entry until the viceregal soldiery had been dismissed.(9r)[54] For the rest of the afternoon Maldonado unavailingly remonstrated with the brethren through the grille of the priory door while a large crowd gathered to watch the spectacle.[55] Furious beyond description, the visitor apostolic was eventually admitted at nightfall along with three lawyers.[56] Inside, Maldonado read his commission out to the assembled priory and, buoyed up by the support of some religious, excommunicated Valls and all others who refused to give him their obedience.(9v) However, Maldonado's arrogance now got the better of him, and the few who had come out on his side withdrew their support when he started browbeating the religious with threats and punishments.(10r) By close of day he found himself alone

---

[53] *Ibid.*, pp. 42 & 47. This episode is also related in *Dietari*, V, pp. 154–5, and in Ramon Bruniquer, *Ceremonial dels Magnifichs Consellers y Regiment de la Ciutat de Barcelona* (known as *Rubriques de Bruniquer*) (5 vols., Barcelona, 1912–16), III, pp. 89–91.

[54] IVDJ, env. 89, caja 126, no. 344. Loris to Zúñiga, Barcelona, 21st February 1579.

[55] Tirso, *Historia*, II, p. 47.

[56] A report of the ensuing events by one of these, probably Dr. Ferreras, a judge of the *Audiència*, is in ASV, Inst.Misc., vol. 4497, ff. 30r–37v, undated but Barcelona, *c*.10th November 1575.

in a hostile priory. Attempts by the viceroy to spring Maldonado by force of hand during the night were repelled with a mixture of violence and ingenuity. *In extremis* the conventuals apparently resorted to marching the Holy Sacrament to the cathedral and back. Returning to the priory with a party of royal halberdiers in tow, the friars filed into the church and slammed the doors closed behind them while others pelted the soldiers with brickbats from the roof of the priory.[57] Maldonado was released through the mediation of the *Consell* the following morning.(10v–11r)

With Maldonado back in the viceregal palace, the chapter opened to the ancient ritual on 5th November. The province of Castile was not of course represented, but the absence of both Aragonese and Valencian delegates is a significant indicator of the faltering allegiances of these provinces.[58] Repeated summons had been ignored and convenors sent by Valls to Aragon and Valencia were arrested while trying to drum up support for the chapter.[59] Several Valencians, including Fra Pere Balaguer, the new commendator of El Puig, Fra Joan de Sant Joan and Fray Francisco de Zaragoza had defected to the reform party, while Murta and Fray Juan Luis de Echarri were cooperating with the authorities while under arrest.[60] The French, on the other hand, were at Barcelona in force and Ormaneto's worst fears were realized when the provincial, Mᵉ Frey Antoine de Tremollières, was unanimously elected to the high office on 6th November.[61]

Tremollières, commendator and regent of theology at the university of Toulouse, was certainly a worthy choice as general, but his election was both canonically and politically unacceptable.[62] In Madrid a

---

[57] Bada, *Situació religiosa*, p. 240.

[58] For Valls' account of the two months following the convocation, including his censure of the Castilians for their non-attendance, see ACA, Mon., vol. 2832, pp. 333–9, Valls to Covarrubias, Barcelona, 8th November 1575.

[59] *Ibid.*, pp. 336 & 338.

[60] *Ibid.*, p. 337.

[61] The election *acta* are in *ibid.*, pp. 323–6, dated Barcelona, 6th November 1575.

[62] The appeal for papal confirmation and an accompanying letter from Valls to Gregory XIII were taken to Rome by Alegría and Mᵉ Fray Pierre Masson, prior of Paris; for draft copies of the former, see ACA, Mon., vol. 2832, pp. 341–2 & 347–8, and for the latter *ibid.*, pp. 343–5, both Barcelona, 6th November 1575. For Tremollières' own appeal to the pope, see ASV, NS, vol. 14, f. 210r, Barcelona, 7th November 1575. A further appeal, from Valls' procurator general, is AMAE, SS, leg. 34, f. 162r, Rome, 18th November 1575. On Tremollières, see *Biographie Toulousaine, ou dictionnaire historique des personnages [...] célèbres dans la ville de Toulouse* (2 vols., Paris, 1823), II, pp. 451–2.

virtuous Duran was quick to play on the king's fears at the election of a foreigner, and a Frenchman to boot, as general of a Spanish religious order.[63] Proceedings were immediately set in train against the delegates by Tocco, to which the priory and the cathedral chapter responded with a succession of withering denunciations of Maldonado.[64] The conventuals, meanwhile, began to take in arms and provisions and incastellate the priory against further assault by the viceroy.[65] The nuncio, for his part, strengthened Maldonado's powers of visitation, giving him the authority to detain and transfer all rebels to Madrid.(13r)[66] On the basis of this and through the mediation of the city council, the Catalans stood down and Maldonado was able to resume his visitation of the priory in February.[67] However, he was admitted only on the condition that he refrain from draconian punishment and refer back to the *consellers* at all times. While the religious expertly drew Maldonado's teeth, the viceroy could only look on, unable to enforce the will of the crown for fear of provoking further unrest in the city.[68] In Rome, meanwhile, matters turned out differently. Despite the support of the *Consell*, Valls' attempts to have Tremollières confirmed by the papacy were thwarted by letters from Philip and Ormaneto.(12r)[69] On 20th February 1576 a brief was issued that not only annulled the election, but at last ratified the Guadalajara decrees and ordered the celebration of a chapter general in the summer.[70] With this Tremollières quit Barcelona for Toulouse, where he continued to fulminate against Maldonado and incite the

[63] AGN, Clero, vol. 402. Duran to Philip II, undated but Madrid *c*.December 1575.

[64] For a resumé of Tocco's *proceso* dated Barcelona, 4th–10th November 1575, see Manuel Milian Boix, ed., *El Fondo «Instrumenta Miscellanea» del Archivo Vaticano: Documentos referentes a España (853–1782)* (Rome, 1967), p. 383. See also ASV, NS, vol. 14, ff. 205v–206r, Canons of Barcelona to Gregory XIII, Barcelona 7th November 1575, and for the friars' declaration, IVDJ, env. 72, II, ff. 460r–464r, Barcelona, 21st December 1575.

[65] AMAE, SS, leg. 34, ff. 71r–72v. Hernando de Toledo, viceroy of Catalonia, to Zúñiga, Barcelona, 7th February 1576.

[66] For Maldonado's *poder*, see AMAE, SS, leg. 34, ff. 159r–160r. Dated Madrid, 12th January 1576. Another copy AGN, Clero, vol. 402.

[67] AGN, Clero, vol. 402, *Consellers* to Maldonado, Barcelona, 27th January 1576. The *consellers'* involvement is related in *Dietari*, V, pp. 156–8.

[68] AMAE, SS, leg. 34, f. 71r.

[69] ASV, NS, vol. 8, f. 546r–v, Ormaneto to Cardinale di Como, Madrid, 2nd December 1575; *ibid.*, ff. 556r–557v, Philip II to Gregory XIII, El Pardo, 6th December 1575; ff. 556v–557r; AGN, Clero, vol. 402, *Consellers* to Gregory XIII, Barcelona, 26th December 1575.

[70] AMAE, SS, leg. 34, ff. 158r–v, & Linás, *Bullarium*, pp. 154–5.

religious to violence in defence of their constitutions.[71] He died, still styling himself 'magister generalis', apparently at the hands of the Huguenots in August 1577.(12v)[72]

Having completed his visitation, Maldonado returned to Madrid where he was made commissary apostolic of the Order in lieu of Tocco. In line with this, he was given the presidency of a chapter provincial of Aragon to be celebrated prior to the election of a new general at Zaragoza in June. The chapter was called to El Olivar in Aragon and opened on 20th May 1576 before a sizable congregation which included a delegate from the priory of Barcelona.[73] After a reading of the Guadalajara constitutions, the chapter went on to elect the reformist Pº Fray Francisco de Salazar, scion of a great Zaragoza family, first provincial of the Crown of Aragon. No ordinances were passed, but Maldonado laid before the chapter the provisions through which a new generation of reformed religious would be nurtured. Provincial noviciates were to be established at Barcelona, El Puig and Zaragoza and 'estudios de gramatica' at Girona, Valencia and El Olivar itself, while two 'colegios de artes y teologia' were to be opened in the university towns of Lleida and Huesca that year.[74] Having stripped the 'obstinate rebel' Fra Jaume Grauset of his *magisterio* and reviewed the conventual responsions, Maldonado summoned the Aragonese electors to the chapter general of Zaragoza on 10th June and drew the proceedings to a close.[75]

Two weeks later, as Duran's life ebbed away in the priory of Barcelona, the chapter general of Zaragoza opened under the presidency of the Dominican bishop of Barbastro, Fray Felipe de Urriés.(14v–15r)[76] The French, though convened, sent no delegates,

---

[71] APV, ms. 'Varia at [*sic*] Ordinem', f. 54r–v. Tremollières to Conventuals of Barcelona, Toulouse, 1st June 1577.

[72] It should be stated that his death date is given as *c.*1589 in *Biographie Toulousaine*, II, p. 452.

[73] For the *synodalia*, see ACA, Mon., vol. 2659, ff. 1r–13r.

[74] Opposition to the *studia* among commendators had prevented any being established by 1588; *ibid.*, f. 65r–v. On the foundation of the college at Huesca in 1578, see ACA, Mss.Misc., vol. 49, p. 131, & Linás, *Bullarium*, pp. 155–8. That of Lleida, founded in a declining university, seems never to have flourished. Mercedarians were studying theology at the Dominican *studium* of Santo Domingo at Girona by 1598; see APV, (no ref. no.), book of visitations, 1589–1628, f. 41v.

[75] ACA, Mon., vol. 2659, ff. 10r–v & 12r–13r.

[76] Regarding preparations for the chapter, see AGS, Eº, leg. 158, no. 2, Ormaneto to Philip II, Madrid, 27th April 1576. An undated copy of the convocation is in AMAE, SS, leg. 34, f. 161r. Early in 1576 Duran had been deported to Valencia

while Barcelona's representative, Fra Sebastiá Bertrán, was disqualified from taking part.[77] On the eve of Pentecost Maldonado was elected to the high office, the first Castilian general since Fray Pedro de Huete in the mid fifteenth century.[78] Francisco Maldonado, a member of the great *comunero* family, was born in Salamanca in around 1535 and entered the Order in Cuzco.[79] Though he had spent most of his adult life in the Peninsula, it is unlikely that many other orders could have provided an *indiano* with the same opportunity for advancement.

The ordinances passed at Zaragoza represent not only an endorsement and extension of the 1574 constitutions, but an emendation as well.[80] Having given their obedience to the statutes for the 'reformation and the good of our Order', the delegates were enjoined to 'work towards the observance of these' by taking verbal declarations of acceptance from each of the religious.[81] Moreover, 'the reformation of this Order depends wholly on the care and zeal of the prelate, who, as a shepherd, must watch over his flock diligently and with the desire to minister, heal and improve his charges'.[82] Aware of the need to develop a climate of trust between prelates and their religious, the chapter ordered superiors to proceed with firmness but sensitivity, avoiding the stigma of public rebuke where possible. As the Dominican Fray Pedro de Salamanca had written, reform was to be mitigated by 'mixing the sweet with the bitter, with the religious partaking both of the bread and the rod [...] so that they be brought round

---

along with Ángulo, from where they sent letters of support to Barcelona in March; see ACA, Mss.Misc., vol. 49, p. 49.(7v) For a declaration regarding Duran's illness, see AGN, Clero, vol. 402, Barcelona, 28th May 1576. He died in Barcelona on 23rd June 1576, the last perpetual prior.(15r)

[77] ASV, NS, vol. 10, ff. 186r–187v; 186r–v. Ormaneto to Como, Madrid, 3rd July 1576.

[78] For Ormaneto's endorsement of the election, see *ibid.*, ff. 186r–187v and a similar letter, f. 227r, Madrid, 18th July 1576.

[79] See the two articles on Maldonado in Vázquez Núñez, *Mercedarios ilustres*, pp. 307–18 & 319–26; pp. 308–9 and the latter article present a highly questionable case for Maldonado's birth in Lima.

[80] The amended *acta*, dated 20th May 1577, survive in an 18th-century copy, APV, ms. Cavero, 'Varia', II, ff. 190r–200v. A preliminary list of suggestions for inclusion in the *acta* survives in IVDJ, env. 72, II, ff. 68r–71r (4°), Maldonado to Ormaneto, undated but spring 1576. A number of Maldonado's provisions were altered against his will by Urriés, provoking a further list of emendations to be sent to the nuncio in the summer of 1576, *ibid.*, ff. 42r–43r (4°), undated.

[81] APV, ms. Cavero, 'Varia', II, f. 191r.

[82] *Ibid.*, f. 194r–v.

through love and fear in equal measure'.[83] The new Roman breviary was accepted, but in this as in other matters the chapter underlined that customary practice was to be followed until lasting provisions could be made.[84] But if the ordinances spoke of implementation, they spoke also of uniformity, albeit one restricted to the most mundane realities of the religious life — of clothing and sustenance — diluted by the fact of provincial diversification.[85]

In the Crown of Aragon, the reform of the Order, already a distant prospect — 'humanly well nigh impossible', Salamanca had called it — was made yet more remote by Maldonado's election as general.[86] Though undoubtedly a capable and energetic man, Maldonado's overbearing manner and the bitter memories of 1567–9 and 1575–6 caused the Catalans to hold him as the incarnation of all their anger and frustration. The business of Mercedarian Reform, as Antillón put it, therefore turned on the general's 'determination to reduce the convent of Barcelona by his own hand, and the convent's determination to resist him'.(15v) In lieu of spiritual or even institutional reform, the best the authorities could hope for at present, groaned Salamanca, was to curb some of the 'licentious and relaxed living' of the religious, for, as he continued to the nuncio, 'I'm not sure that you have been fully apprised of the peculiarities of these kingdoms'.[87]

III. *Castile: Reform and Redemption, 1575–93*

Though the tensions of recent times remained in evidence in Castile, the Reform appears to have made perceptible if unspectacular progress in the years following the chapter general of Guadalajara.[88] This process can be followed in the visitation *acta* of the convent of Huete, which represents the most significant extant source for the religious life of the province in the late sixteenth and early seventeenth centuries. Here are reflected the efforts to enforce the

---

[83] IVDJ, env. 72, II, f. 82r.

[84] APV, ms. Cavero, 'Varia', II, f. 191v.

[85] *Ibid.*, ff. 196v & 197r.

[86] IVDJ, env. 72, II, f. 82r.

[87] *Ibid.*, ff. 82v & 83r.

[88] A flavour of these tensions is provided in an anonymous letter to Ormaneto of *c.*1576–7, *ibid.*, f. 115r.

reformist provisions passed first by Carrillo at Guadalajara in 1569 and then by Castillo at Toledo in 1572, which the commendator was required to read out at least once a week in the chapter of faults, 'so that they be brought to the attention of all and none can feign ignorance'.[89] The first major visitation of Castile following the Guadalajara constitutions is absent from the Huete volume, and it is not until that of October 1577 that their impact can be traced here. The visitation was conducted by the provincial Mᵒ Fray Rodrigo de Arce who had been elected at the chapter celebrated in Valladolid under Castillo's presidency in May 1576.[90] Arce's approach to the implementation of reform follows that laid down at the chapter general of Zaragoza, and his provisions underline the complementary nature of the 1574 and '76 legislation where this was concerned. The Guadalajara constitutions, he told the conventuals of Huete, 'are our Reformation', and were therefore to be engraved indelibly on the memory of each and every religious.[91] However, Arce was concerned not only with the disciplinary and material aspects of reform, but its spiritual dimension as well. A friar was obliged, he reminded them, not only to keep the basic vows of the Order, but also those religious ordinances and ceremonies 'that together constitute the true and substantial observance of religion' — 'la verdadera guarda de la substançial Religion' — an observance greater than the sum of its parts.[92] Having revised the structure of the province, a new Castilian hierarchy had therefore begun to look to the spiritual reform of the brethren as the obvious complement to their disciplinary improvement. Yet it remains to be seen how willingly and with what understanding the religious received these injunctions for their future.

In the 1577 *acta* Arce demonstrates his awareness of how difficult it was for older friars to break the habits of a lifetime, and the transcripts of succeeding visitations bear out his misgivings amply.[93] For some visitors the annoyance of seeing ordinances continually ignored and even ridiculed gave way to ill-concealed rage. In 1590 the

---

[89] See AHN, Clero, vol. 3320, ff. 11v (November–December 1571) & 13v (June 1573) respectively.

[90] AGS, Eᵒ, leg. 158, no. 2, f. 1r. The convocation of the chapter had been put back a year at Guadalajara.

[91] AHN, Clero, vol. 3320, f. 27v. Dated 9th–10th October 1577.

[92] *Ibid.*, f. 29r.

[93] *Ibid.*, f. 29v; '…por quanto despues de antiguos los Religosos se les haze mas de mal mudar costumbre si acaso la ubiese no tan a proposito…'.

provincial Fray Francisco de Medina threatened the commendator with six months' privation of office if he did not take steps to prepare an inventory of the landed property owned by the house, many of the original deeds and donations of which had been lost for over twenty years — to the great detriment of conventual revenue.[94] Issues of conventual property and income, of religious observance and above all personal conduct recur time and again in visitation *acta*, and the reformers evidently encountered a degree of passive resistance which it took their fleeting presence decades to curb. Religious were still consorting with seculars in the convent and absenting themselves from choir in 1604 as they had been thirty years earlier, and this in what the visiting provincial M° Fray Matías de Cuéllar considered should have been among the more exemplary houses.[95] On the other hand, there can be no doubt that continued adherence to the 1327 constitutions in matters of spiritual and domestic observance added to the confusion of what was a period of sustained crisis and upheaval for the Order.[96] Inconsistency therefore played its part as much as obstinacy, and it was the early seventeenth century before the mentality underlying the new legislative framework began to impress itself lastingly on the brethren at conventual level.

However, in other respects the early Reform in Castile produced more tangible results. In 1575 the province conducted its first ransoming expedition for thirteen years, embarking for Algiers under a new and richly woven banner of the Order.[97] The extent of Castile's achievement in funding and realizing this enterprise should not be underestimated, and the redemptors returned to Valencia in triumph with 139 captives.[98] From this time on the Order's traditional vocation assumes a more prominent position in its affairs, and the first problem confronting Maldonado after his election was a renewal of the ancient feud between the Mercedarians and the Trinitarians over rights to collect alms in the Crown of Aragon.(16r–v)[99] Taking advantage of the

---

[94] *Ibid.*, f. 75v, and for cases of lost documents, ff. 39v–40r & 71v. For a similar case in Catalonia in this period, see APV, ms. Girona, ff. 10v, 36r, 42r, 50v, 52r & 59v (1589–1604).

[95] AHN, Clero, vol. 3320, f. 165v. Dated 26th November 1604.

[96] See, for instance, *ibid.*, ff. 44r (1582), 52v (1585), & 56v (1585).

[97] See Vázquez Núñez, *Manual*, II, pp. 26–7.

[98] The accounts for this redemption are in BNM, ms. 2963.

[99] For details of disturbances between Mercedarians and Trinitarians over alms collection in Barcelona in 1564–5, see Bada, *Situació religiosa*, p. 61, and several documents in ACA, Mon., leg. 341, (unftd.) & ARM, Clero, no. 956 (unftd. at

weakened state of the Order, in June 1576 the Trinitarians succeeded in obtaining a royal *cédula* reversing the traditional Mercedarian *privativa* over redemption *limosna* in these parts. It took a journey to the Escorial on the part of Maldonado to restore the situation, though the clause conferring the right to bear arms was notably omitted and the Trinitarians were able to expand their Catalan patrimony from eight houses to twelve over the next few years.[100] Even so, in 1577 the Aragonese province followed the Castilians in undertaking its first ransoming expedition since 1561–2, though Catalan participation was minimal.(17r–v) Led by Fray Jorge del Olivar, the Aragonese commendator of Valencia, the redemptors made for Algiers where, along with Arce, their association with the captive Cervantes is recorded in two of his plays, *El trato de Argel* and *Los baños de Argel*.[101] Though Cervantes was eventually ransomed by the Trinitarians in 1580, Olivar's unavailing attempts to secure his release while himself a hostage earned him a lasting place both in Mercedarian tradition and in the affections of the author.

IV. *Failure in the Crown of Aragon, 1576–7*

Having arranged for a visitation of Peru, Maldonado returned to the Crown of Aragon in November 1576 to begin his winter campaign in Valencia.[102] Here he found support for the Reform wavering with

---

rear). Further trouble is reported at Balaguer in Catalonia in 1570 in APV, Antillón, ms. *Epitome*, I(ii), pp. 1442–3. The Order's rights in the Crown of Aragon were periodically reconfirmed; see ACA, Mon., vol. 2660, the 'llibre de privilegis'.

[100] The royal *cédula* and its revocation were dated 28th June and 26th September 1576; see, respectively, ACA, Mon., leg. 341, (unftd.) & *ibid.*, vol. 2661, pp. 181–97. The Trinitarians launched further attacks on the Mercedarian *privativa* in Rome the following year, in Madrid in 1578, and in Valencia during 1579–80. On the first see AMAE, SS, leg. 34, ff. 18r & 19r, Philip II to Gregory XIII and Zúñiga respectively, both El Escorial, 10th June 1577 (copies in ACA, Mon., leg. 341, unftd.), and for the last two, AHCB, ms. A-266, Antillón, *Memorias*, II, ff. 21r–v & 30r–v. Regarding Trinitarian expansion, see Joana Xandri, 'Els orígens de l'orde trinitari a Catalunya: El monestir d'Aviganya (Serós)' in *Actes del Primer Congrés d'Història de l'Església Catalana* (2 vols., Solsona, 1993); I, pp. 615–24; 618. The most significant foundation was that made at Tarragona in 1579. The Mercedarians' dominant position vis-à-vis the Trinitarians in Catalonia, as in the rest of the Crown of Aragon, had delayed their establishment in Barcelona until 1529.

[101] See P.Fr. Luis Vázquez Fernández, ed., 'Cervantes y la Merced (Documentos)' in *BPCONSM*, 24 (1986), no. 83, pp. 64–80.

[102] Regarding Peru, see Vázquez Fernández, 'Cedulario Mercedario', pp. 629–30. For the campaign, see IVDJ, env. 72, II, ff. 127r–v & 125r–v, Maldonado to Ormaneto, respectively Cuenca, 4th & Valencia, 13th November 1576.

residual allegiance to Tremollières, friars roving uncloistered and the province prey to gossip and rumour of every kind.[103] However, the general set to with his customary energy and by the time he left the province the following year many Valencians clearly saw greater advantage in acquiescence with the Reform than resistance to it, a view increasingly shared by their Aragonese brethren. The impetus for change in the Aragonese provinces was due in no small measure to the gradual infiltration of reformed Castilian religious from 1574 onwards. The chapter general of Guadalajara had banned those sent to the Crown of Aragon from returning to Castile before three years had elapsed, and though it was clearly not an attractive posting many chose to remain here for good.[104] Apart from the major houses at Zaragoza, Valencia, Pamplona and El Olivar, the centrepiece of reform in the eastern provinces, and no doubt of the Castilian presence here, was the college of Huesca, which eventually became the forcing ground for a new Aragonese élite.[105] Meanwhile, the chronic shortage of trained friars and facilities for study remained as major obstacles to reform, and it would be some time before the Aragonese began competing for university chairs like their Castilian brethren.[106] Indeed, the few details we have for Aragon and Navarre in this period indicate that, as in Valencia, success was for the time being limited to bringing brethren within the pale of reform rather than actually reforming them.

In Catalonia, however, the situation was becoming increasingly grave. Episcopal censure and the punitive measures carried out through 1576 in accordance with the February brief by canon Jerònim Manegat as judge apostolic had the effect of driving religious into the bandit country of upland Catalonia and over the bor-

---

[103] *Ibid.*, f. 125r.

[104] See ACA, Mon., vol. 4144, f. 128v. A typical case is Fray Francisco Polayno. A son of the convent of Seville and student at the Vera Cruz of Salamanca, Polayno was brought to the Crown of Aragon by Maldonado in about 1576, and became affiliated to that province in 1585. Sent to Italy, he made an unsuccessful attempt to found a house in Milan; see *ibid.*, vol. 2659, f. 54v, & Vázquez Núñez, *Manual*, II, p. 36.

[105] Vázquez Núñez, *Manual*, II, p. 38. The foundation was confirmed at the chapter provincial of Valencia in 1582, which arranged for all houses to contribute to its maintenance according to their means; ACA, Mon., vol. 2659, f. 42r–v. Disagreement over the college constitutions between students and superiors was reported at the chapter of Zaragoza in 1585; see *ibid.*, f. 54r.

[106] On this see the *acta* of the chapters of 1582, 1585 & 1588, ACA, Mon., vol. 2659, ff. 42r–v, 54r & 65r–v respectively.

der to France.[107] Maldonado, for his part, responded by vowing to reduce apostate religious to their convents by force if necessary.[108] The conflict was intensified by the death of Fra Antoni Garrole, commendator of Berga, in the nuncio's gaol in Madrid.(17r) Where conciliation was called for, the authorities therefore pursued an aggressive policy which propelled the Catalans into a dogged defence of their ancient privileges. As local and provincial institutions came out in active support of the priory, so the resolve of the brethren hardened into open opposition. By the time Maldonado took over full responsibility for implementing the brief in late 1576, irreparable damage had been done to the cause of reform.

Although it was almost certainly too late, news of his confirmation as general in Rome at the end of December encouraged Maldonado to change tack.(16r)[109] Aware of the vital importance of bringing the reform statutes to the attention of the religious at large, the general now made arrangements to circulate the Guadalajara constitutions — along with the Zaragoza statutes — throughout the Crown of Aragon.[110] The logistical obstacles to this were, as Maldonado recognized, very considerable, but on 8th January 1577 a copy of the statutes was sent by Salazar to Tudela on the first leg of a journey through fourteen houses across Navarre, Upper Aragon and into northern Catalonia. As before, commendators were required to sign their obedience, take a conventual copy and send the originals on to the next house in a pre-arranged itinerary.[111] There is no evidence

---

[107] *Ibid.*, vol. 2679, f. 257r–v, Philip II to Hernando de Toledo, 20th September 1576. See also Tirso, *Historia*, II, p. 54.

[108] IVDJ, env. 72, II, f. 125v.

[109] On Maldonado's confirmation, granted 27th October 1576 and issued 12th November, see Linás, *Bullarium*, p. 155 & AMAE, SS, leg. 34, f. 14r, Philip II to Zúñiga, El Bosque de Segovia, 12th July 1576; ASV, NS, vol. 9, ff. 167r–177v (171v–172r) & 211r–213v (213r), *Segreteria* to Ormaneto, Rome, 24th August & 12th November 1576 respectively, and *ibid.*, vol. 10, ff. 405r–408v (405r) & 411r–414v (413r), Ormaneto to Como, Madrid, 20th & 24th December 1576 respectively. The procurator of the priory of Barcelona, Fra Francesc Cardá, appealed to Rome against the confirmation; see AGN, Clero, vol. 402, Barcelona 4th January 1577. This was backed up by a letter from the *Consellers* to Gregory XIII condemning Maldonado's excesses (*ibid.*, undated but early 1577), and a vituperative memorial (*ibid.*, vol. 416, (4°), anonymous and undated but *c.*1577) with biographical details on the general's youth in Peru.

[110] IVDJ, env. 72, II, f. 127r.

[111] The copy is that in ACA, Mon., vol. 2832; see ch. 6, n. 130. This MS had lost its final folio by the time a notarial copy of it was taken in July 1583. For the commendators' signatures, etc., see pp. 400–2. An accompanying letter from Salazar is

that this first fleeting encounter with the constitutions made any but
the most superficial impression on the brethren, and the document
reached Barcelona somewhat battered on 30th March, where it has
since remained. Maldonado, for his part, continued unrecognized in
Catalonia.[112]

V. *Violence and Banditry*

As the Reform gradually fell into chaos in Catalonia, the priory of
Barcelona came under the influence of a desperate and ruthless core
of friars drawn in from across the Order. Among these was the extraordinary Fray Vicente Mendía, the archetypal 'religioso inquieto' in
whom the Mercedarian Reform has surely its most colourful and
roguish character.[113] If Mendía's experience is in some ways a
metaphor for Mercedarian life in the late sixteenth century, it serves
also as a reminder that the increasing lawlessness of the Crown of
Aragon was felt as much in ecclesiastical as in secular society.

Vicente Mendía was born in Zaragoza in about 1545 and entered
the Dominican priory there in the mid 1560s, the first stage in a
unique and extended tour through the religious life of the Crown of
Aragon and Italy.[114] A large mustachioed man with ginger hair and
a ruddy complexion, Mendía cuts an unforgettable figure with his
foul mouth and swaggering bravura.[115] If Tirso based his Don Juan
on any Mercedarian character, it could well be Vicente Mendía
whose exploits were notorious in the Order for at least a genera-

now lost. All superiors save the president of Barcelona, Fra Lluís Valls, gave their
obedience. It seems likely that a second copy, dispatched by Maldonado, passed
simultaneously through Valencia and Lower Aragon as far as Zaragoza.

[112] On the priory's refusal to recognize Maldonado, see *ibid.*, vol. 2677, ff.
135r–141r, draft documents dated Barcelona, 9th March–9th May 1577.

[113] Compare with the Montserrat Benedictine Dom Mateu Lloret, and another
Benedictine, Dom Narcís Terrades of Sant Pere de Galligans outside Girona; see,
respectively, Fernández Terricabras, 'Reforma i obediència', p. 175, & Galinier-
Pallerola, 'La Délinquance des eccélesiastiques catalans', pp. 56 & 58. For a case of a
Mercedarian bandit in Castile, that of Fray Maldonado in 1627, see José Deleito y
Piñuela, *La vida religiosa española bajo el cuarto Felipe: Santos y pecadores* (Madrid, 1952),
p. 103.

[114] Details from AMAE, SS, leg. 34, ff. 103r–112v & 204r–220r, signed affidavits
against Mendía, dated Zaragoza, 27th February to 4th March 1579, &
Barcelona/Zaragoza, 22nd October 1588 to 26th May 1589 respectively.

[115] For physical descriptions of Mendía, see *ibid.*, ff. 148r (undated note), 214v &
215r.

tion.[116] After repeated misconduct at the priory of Zaragoza in the early 1570s he was ordered to the *studium sollemne* of Luchente outside Valencia. However, he apostatized *en route*, and after a period with the Minims of Valencia was received into the Mercedarian Order at Daroca, from where he was sent as a conventual to Barbastro. It was here in Upper Aragon that Mendía first became seriously involved with banditry, and it was as an armed brigand rather than as a friar that he first appeared at the priory of Barcelona in about 1572. This did not prevent Mendía making his profession during a period of feverish recruitment, but he was soon stripped of his habit by Montaña and flung out of the priory.

Undeterred, Mendía drifted from order to order in Catalonia leaving a trail of scandal and recrimination in his wake. A period in a Servite community in Barcelona was followed by some time with the Carmelites of Girona. With his entry into the Premonstratensian house of Bellpuig de les Avellanes, Mendía's interest in the religious life developed from the parasitic into one of open revolt against reformist authority. Provided with funds to plead the abbey's case against reform, Mendía left for Italy — where, incidentally, he entered his seventh monastic incarnation as a Trinitarian in Genoa — and at length joined the legion of disaffected friars in Rome.[117] However, after a while Mendía seems to have experienced a change of heart and returned to his *alma mater* — Santo Domingo de Zaragoza — where he remained for some time, first under lock and key and then incapacitated through illness. But with health came renewed vigour, and Mendía had soon scaled the convent wall and broken free once again. Declared a 'ruin Religiosso y obstinado e incorregible', Mendía eventually found his way back to the priory of Barcelona where he made a second profession to Valls in October

---

[116] The suggestion that Mendía was a prototype for Don Juan Tenorio in Tirso's *El burlador de Sevilla* is made *en passant* by Dom Luciano Serrano in *Archivo de la Embajada de España cerca de la Santa Sede*. I: *Índice analítico de los documentos del siglo XVI* (Rome, 1915), p. 97. In a letter written in Italian, Mº Fray Francisco de Salazar informs an unnamed cardinal that, among other names, Mendía used the alias 'Don Giovanni': AMAE, SS, leg. 34, ff. 221r–222v, undated but *c*.1589; f. 222v. For Tirso on Mendía, see *Historia*, II, pp. 95–7. Clearly, I discount the theory that Tirso was not in fact the author of *El Burlador*.

[117] See AMAE, SS, leg. 34, f. 217v. For more on inter-order cooperation of this sort in Rome, where huge amounts of money were being spent to impede the various reforms, see IVDJ, env. 89, caja 125, no. 61, Cristóbal de Rojas y Sandoval, archbishop of Seville to Philip II, Seville, 7th April 1576.

1577.[118] Though soon dispatched to represent the priory in Rome, Mendía's reappearance in Barcelona at this moment reflects his past attraction to orders weakened by internal conflict. But, even so, Fray Vicente made his own special contribution, for through him the brethren cemented a nexus with that sector of society which felt driven to resist authority by means of violence.

VI. *Escalation, 1577–8*

When Maldonado — the Catalans' 'inimich mortal' — eventually returned to Barcelona in the summer of 1577, he therefore found the priory in even less conciliatory mood than he had left it a year earlier.[119] His intention was to receive the obedience due to the general of the Order, visit the priory under royal authority and proceed to reform the house with the fifteen friars he had brought from Castile. However, the campaign was marked by conflict and violence from beginning to end. Maldonado's first attempt to visit the priory in early September ended in a near riot, with the general driven off by an angry crowd of friars and townsfolk.[120] The house, he later reported, was packed with religious and rag-tag from throughout the province and had been fortified 'like La Goleta invested by the Turk'.[121] However, resistance did not end here. Mobilizing the support of the Order's protector in Rome — Íñigo Dávalos, Cardinal of Aragon — and with the *consellers* and the *Generalitat* behind them, the religious contested Maldonado's right to enter the priory in the company of royal officials.(16Ar)[122] Maldonado appealed for assistance to the new nuncio, Filippo Sega, who refused to intervene in what ostensibly remained a matter for the

---

[118] For the citation, see AMAE, SS, leg. 34, f. 110r. The profession, dated 24th October 1577, is in ACA, Mon., vol. 2710, f. 73r, while f. 73v contains a biographical résumé.

[119] *Dietari*, V, p. 157.

[120] See AMAE, SS, leg. 34, ff. 98r–99v, Maldonado to Zúñiga, Barcelona, 1st October 1577; *ibid.*, f. 15r–v, Philip II to Zúñiga, 3rd November 1577.

[121] *Ibid.*, f. 99r. The *presidio* (fortress) of La Goleta overlooking Tunis had fallen to the Turks in September 1574.

[122] See *ibid.*, f. 16r–v, Philip II to Zúñiga, Madrid, 15th September 1577, and AGN, Clero, vol. 402, Ayllá to Toledo, undated but Barcelona, *c.*September 1579. Dávalos had been appointed by Gregory XIII in 1572. For the support of the *Generalitat* at this time, see Josep Maria Sans i Travé, (gral. ed.), *Dietaris de la Generalitat de Catalunya, 1411–1714* (3 vols. +, Barcelona, 1994–), II, pp. 541–2.

crown.[123] The question was eventually put to the royal *Audiència*, which predictably enough found in favour of Maldonado on 29th September.(16Av)

However, when the conventuals persisted in their rejection of Maldonado and it became clear that the viceroy could not enforce the royal will, the nuncio delegated bishop Joan Dimas Loris to intervene in the affair.[124] Over the next few weeks Loris issued a string of censures culminating in a sentence of interdict on the priory.[125] But these were simply ignored by the brethren, who sallied forth in armed bands to rip down the episcopal placards and continued celebrating the divine office behind closed doors.[126] Maldonado found himself insulted and threatened to the extent that he dared not venture out onto the street.[127] A spate of incidents culminated in the small hours of 9th November with an attempt to set fire to Maldonado's lodgings in the precinct of the viceregal palace with burning pitch, forcing the general and his companions to flee for their lives.[128] As the viceroy issued warnings to the crown of the possibility of a rising in the city, a couple who had been unwise enough to provide Maldonado with some food were stabbed by a gang from the priory.[129]

Clerical violence and deliquency were by no means unprecedented

---

[123] On this episode, see Ángel Fernández Collado, *Gregorio XIII y Felipe II en la nunciatura de Felipe Sega (1577–1581): Aspectos político, jurisdiccional y de reforma* (Toledo, 1991), pp. 312–13. See also ASV, NS, vol. 14, f. 39r–v, Sega to Como, Madrid, 28th September 1577.

[124] See ASV, NS, vol. 14, f. 44r–v, Sega to Como, Madrid, 12th October 1577; BL, Add., vol. 28,340, ff. 324r–325r, Maldonado to Philip II, Barcelona, 1st November 1577 & *Dietari*, V, pp. 165–6.

[125] For correspondence to and from the priory at this time, see ACA, Mon., vol. 2677, ff. 148r–155v, mid October–11th December 1577.

[126] AMAE, SS, leg. 34, ff. 80r–83r. Toledo to Zúñiga, Barcelona, 8th November 1577; f. 81r. Another copy ff. 73r–75v.

[127] *Ibid.*, ff. 98v–99r.

[128] *Ibid.*, ff. 82v. See also f. 100r–v, Maldonado to Zúñiga, Barcelona, 9th November 1577, and 89r–v, Loris to Zúñiga, Barcelona, 11th November 1577. For details of similar incidents in 1604, 1623 & 1624, see James S. Amelang, 'People of the Ribera: Popular Politics and Neighborhood Identity in Early Modern Barcelona' in Barbara B. Diefendorf & Carla Hesse, eds., *Culture and Identity in Early Modern Europe (1500–1800): Essays in Honor of Natalie Zemon Davis* (Ann Arbor, 1994), pp. 119–37, esp. 127–8.

[129] See AMAE, SS, leg. 34, f. 80v, & particularly f. 77r, Toledo to Zúñiga, Barcelona, 21st December 1577 (another copy f. 76r) and especially *Dietari*, V, pp. 169–72. The danger was, however, played down in Madrid; see BL, Add., vol. 28,263, f. 179r–v, Mateo Vázquez to Philip II, Madrid, 2nd March 1578.

in Barcelona. In the 1520s Ignatius' attempted reform of the Dominican nuns of Mont Sió had ended with his being savagely beaten and
left for dead, while the Trinitarians had in 1568 greeted their provincial with blunderbusses.[130] However, the Mercedarian case was
exceptional both in its gravity and in the degree and extent of secular
support enjoyed by the brethren. 'I understand,' Philip noted, 'that
there is no shortage of seculars to incite and counsel the friars in
secret', while Toledo remarked on the 'help and favour they receive
throughout the land'.[131] Beyond the *Consell* and the *Generalitat*, the
root of the friars' support lay in the Mercedarian quarter of the city,
and particularly in the Order's *cofraria de les escudellers*, the potter's
guild or brotherhood which resided there.[132] Like that of the
brethren, the allegiance of these people was to an established way of
life, and their anger was therefore directed at those whose intrusion
threatened to destroy it. If the parish and neighbourhood as geo-
graphic spaces played little part in the political organization of the
city, there is no doubt that their population wielded much informal
power through direct attachment to the religious institutions enclosed
within them.[133] The guild-confraternity of the *escudellers* may have
provided a key to involvement in the corporate life of Barcelona, but
during the 1570s and '80s it was the Mercedarian crisis that defined
this association and the area from which both it and the priory drew
their support and membership.

The *Generalitat* had looked on at the suppression of the Conventual
Franciscans in 1567, but there would be no such passivity in the case
of the priory of Barcelona.[134] The *diputats* were particularly angered
by the arrest of a young nobleman caught raising money for the priory in September 1577, regarding it as an attack on the *privilegi militar*
enjoyed by a man of his status.[135] The *Consell*, which had always
viewed the Mercedarian case as its own, again came out openly in

---

[130] Bada, *Situació religiosa*, pp. 122–3, & 60 & 123 respectively.

[131] AMAE, SS, leg. 34, ff. 15r & 77r respectively.

[132] The foundation date of the *cofraria* is unknown, but a chapel dedicated to its
patron, Sant Hipòlit, was constructed in the conventual church by Fra Jaume
Aymerich during his priorate (1408–19); see Gazulla, *La Patrona de Barcelona*, pp. 26 &
272–3.

[133] See Amelang, 'People of the Ribera', pp. 125–7.

[134] Bada, *Situació religiosa*, p. 239.

[135] The *donzell* in question was Guerau de Sayol; see Sans i Travé, (gral. ed.),
Dietaris de la Generalitat, II, pp. 542–3. The *Generalitat*, though, left the conduct of the
Mercedarian question largely to the *Consell de Cent*.

favour of the priory.[136] On 12th October the *consellers* made a plea for clemency to the pope on behalf of the friars, citing the outrageous derogation both of their professed observance and the institutional basis of the Order implied by the Guadalajara decrees.[137] As the strength of feeling and solidarity of a wide sector of Barcelona society became apparent, Toledo retreated to a safe distance. The viceroy's earlier claim that 'it was not worth risking reputation against such obstinate and shameless people' cannot hide the fact that he was, and remained, powerless to take any concerted action against the religious.[138] In Barcelona, as Tremollières had reminded the conventuals the year before, *ius est civitas, et unius iniuria iniuria est totius civitatis.*[139]

Maldonado, meanwhile, found himself abandoned in the morass of Catalan social and political resistance:

> No bishop can stand up to such insolence. The viceroy and the Council [of Aragon] *timentes plebem* are deferring the execution of the help they have promised me. Although His Majesty had ordered them to assist me and to pacify the monastery, the *consellers* do nothing but urge me to leave and postpone the disciplining of these friars. The *diputats* likewise. The whole of Barcelona is screaming 'Death to the Castilian traitor!'.[140]

As he concluded, 'unless this matter be punished it will be impossible to reform the Crown of Aragon, neither is it in my power to carry this out'.

By the time Maldonado left for Madrid at the end of 1577, it was clear that the meagre fruit of ten years' labour was in danger of being lost. However, the papacy responded in the new year with a reaffirmation of Maldonado's authority and a conciliatory brief appointing Loris commissary and executor apostolic.[141] Loris was given the authority to absolve the religious on the condition that they accept

---

[136] Recognition of this support is made in M° Fray Juan de Antillón's fragmentary *Chronologicon Generalicio del Orden de Nuestra Señora de la Merced y Redemptores*, ACA, Mss.Misc., vol. 39, pp. 259–62. This is a draft copy of 1618; a later version, dated 1636, is *ibid.*, vol. 103; see ch. 6, n. 68.

[137] ASV, NS, vol. 14, ff. 513r–514v.

[138] AMAE, SS, leg. 34, f. 80v.

[139] APV, ms. 'Varia at [*sic*] Ordinem', f. 54v.

[140] AMAE, SS, leg. 34, f. 99r.

[141] A partial copy of this brief is in *ibid.*, f. 35r. Undated, but Rome, 7th January 1578. The brief was backed up by a letter in recommendation of Maldonado from one of the papal secretaries, Antonio Buccapadulius, to the *Consellers*, AGN, Clero, vol. 402, Rome, 10th January 1578. See also Fernández Collado, *Gregorio XIII y Felipe II*, pp. 314–16.

Maldonado as general and admit him as visitor. Drained of money by episcopal censure and diplomatic manoeuvring in Rome, the religious at last gave Maldonado their obedience — though under protest — and the interdict was duly lifted on 23rd February 1578.[142] Unwilling to expose himself any further to the ire of the Catalans, Maldonado again quit Barcelona leaving Salazar, the provincial of Aragon, with powers to visit the priory and bring the religious into the fold under a general amnesty.(20r–v) But, as the government predicted, the matter did not end here.[143] Though Salazar was admitted in April and his commission accepted, the conventuals refused to allow him to conduct his visitation under the authority of the Guadalajara statutes, for which the brief had somehow failed to make specific provision.[144] The brethren had, through artful prevarication, again stalled the progress of reform in Catalonia and won for themselves another precious year.

VII. *Over the Brink, 1578–9*

In Catalonia the events of 1577–8 established a pattern of behaviour in which the process of reform was reduced to its most basic elements and overtaken by the wider forces at work in its make-up. As the Mercedarian question became subsumed into the broader context of Catalan events, so the Order drifted into a cycle of violence, litigation and counter-litigation which must be summarized from the massive documentation that has come down to us.

Although there had been some notable defections to the reform party, including the Valencian Lagarria and Fra Jeroni Antich, commendator of Mallorca, the mass of Catalan religious remained in

---

[142] The apostolic letters were presented on 7th February; see ACA, Mon., vol. 2677, ff. 157r–v. The declaration of obedience (undated but 17th February) and Loris' absolution are in AGN, Clero, vol. 402. For details of this and the *Consell*'s mediation, see *Dietari*, V, pp. 173–6.

[143] See BL, Add., vol. 28,381, ff. 62v–63r, conde de Chinchón to Philip II, Madrid(?), 19th February 1578, and *ibid.*, f. 66r, Diego Hurtado de Mendoza, Príncipe de Melito to Philip II, Madrid(?), undated but late February 1578.

[144] The priory voiced its opposition to Salazar in an undated letter from the *procurador*, Fra Francesc Cardá, to Gregory XIII in AGN, Clero, vol. 402. For the opening of the visitation see ACA, Mon., vol. 2677, f. 161r–v, 25th April 1578, and *ibid.*, f. 163r for Salazar's suspension of it on 28th April. See also two letters from Loris to Zúñiga in AMAE, SS, leg. 34, ff. 88r–v & 87r–v, Barcelona 4th & 26th April respectively.

opposition and had either gone underground or made for the strong-
holds of Barcelona, Girona, Perpignan and Castelló d'Empuries.(30r)[145] As resistance became polarized in Catalonia, so Maldonado had to abandon plans for a healing chapter general under Sega's
presidency in 1579.[146] With the Catalan cause reviving in Rome,
Salazar was sent back to the Principality as vicar general in May
1579 with wide powers to enter and reform the centres of resistance,
beginning with Barcelona.(20v,21v)[147] Though the *consellers* remained
undecided as to whether their concerns lay in fact with the visitation
or the matter of the *locus* of elections, it was their mediation that
again secured Salazar's entry to the priory on 2nd June.(21v–22r)[148]
Escorted by Loris and representatives from the *Audiència* and the city
monasteries, Salazar convened a chapter during which the nineteen
surviving conventuals renewed their vow of obedience and for the
first time swore to observe the Guadalajara constitutions.(22v–23r)
This over, he began his visitation with the assistance of a dozen
reformist brethren.[149]

---

[145] After a succession of commanderies in the late 1570s, Lagarria was appointed
visitor of Sicily by Maldonado; see ACA, Mon., vol. 2831, f. 83v.

[146] See ASV, NS, vol. 22, f. 42r, and AHCB, Consellers, ms. XVIII–3 (Mercedaris)
(unftd.), *Consell* to Gregory XIII, Barcelona, 29th January 1579.

[147] A brief to this effect was dispatched on 16th December 1578, reaching
Barcelona in February; see ASZ, carp. 165, no. 133, Loris to Philip II, Barcelona,
18th February 1579, f. 1r, & IVDJ, env. 89, caja 126, no. 344, Loris to Zúñiga,
Barcelona, 21st February. Loris' endorsement of the December brief is in ACA,
Mon., vol. 2677, ff. 17r–20v, Barcelona, 27th March 1579, while Salazar's letters
patent from Maldonado were dated Seville, 27th April; see Fernández Collado, *Gregorio XIII y Felipe II*, pp. 316–17.

[148] Salazar's admission to the priory is witnessed in AGN, Clero, vol. 402. The period around the beginning of the visitation is covered in the *Dietari*, V, pp. 191–204, proceedings reproduced in ACA, Mon., vol. 2677, ff. 2r–11r; see also IVDJ, env. 91, caja
131, no. 561, *Consell* to Philip II, Barcelona, 1st April 1579. The *Consell* had sent Fray
Luis de Dusayel (Fra Lluís Durall?) as an ambassador to Philip II in 1578 to discuss the
Mercedarian question, providing him with an 'authentic' copy of the Order's spurious
foundation charter. This was intended to demonstrate to the king both the royal origins
of the Order and the traditional association of the generalate with Barcelona; the *Consell's* instructions to Dusayel are cited in ACA, Mon., leg. 293, (unftd.), an early-17th
century discussion of the alleged foundation charter, of which only the first 2 ff. survive.
The question of the *Consell's* interests in the Mercedarian affair is discussed in a lengthy
memorial from Loris to the king, IVDJ, env. 89, caja 126, no. 351, Barcelona, 3rd July
1579, esp. ff. 1v & 2v. While recognizing its wider importance to the crown, Loris himself questioned both the wisdom and the legality of making a stand over the *locus* issue
given the traditional rights of the priory; *ibid.*, ff. 2v–3r.

[149] Salazar's report of the entire visitation is in AMAE, SS, leg. 34, ff. 229D–378,
dated 2nd June–19th July 1579. The remains of an inventory, dated 26th June, are
in ACA, Mon., vol. 2670, ff. 395r–412r.

But once again, where conciliation was called for, the authorities attempted to browbeat the religious into acquiescence. The vicar general began by suspending all conventual officers except for the president, Fra Lluís Valls, and by mid July had confined no less than ten of the leading religious.(23v–24v) Though Salazar reluctantly heeded warnings against transferring malefactors to other houses and provinces, his decision to call in a further twenty brethren from Valencia to help administer the priory soon cost him the *Consell*'s fragile cooperation.[150] Indeed, once the *consellers* recognized that Salazar's agenda was no different from that of his Castilian general, they began to question the entire basis of his commission and the royal authority upon which it was founded. Moreover, it became increasingly clear that the conventuals' acceptance of Guadalajara did not imply a renunciation of their ongoing resistance to the work of the reformers in Rome, particularly where the *locus* question was concerned.(24r,v) As the summer wore on and the visitation showed no sign of coming to an end, tempers in both city and priory reached boiling point, and Salazar finally lost the mediation of the *Consell* that was essential to the success of his mission.

The rubicon was apparently crossed in early July when Salazar prepared to turn a number of religious over to the secular arm prior to issuing a set of thirty-two reform ordinances that faithfully transposed the new Castilian observance to Barcelona.[151] Salazar laid special emphasis on uniformity of religious observance and the restoration of conventual life as key elements of a wider organization to which every individual was to be held accountable. The instruction of religious, and particularly that of novices, Salazar considered 'the greatest and principal means to the Reformation of our Order', for it was neglect of this that had led it astray in the first place.[152] Above all, Salazar reminded the brethren of 'the quietude of the monastic life they have professed', but such quietude as there was soon to be broken.[153] The brethren were not about to suffer the dismemberment of their community and the suffocation of their cause, and though

---

[150] *Dietari*, V, pp. 203 & 199 respectively.

[151] The situation up to early July is reported in IVDJ, env. 89, caja 126, no. 351, Barcelona, 3rd July 1579. For the criminal charges against the religious, see AGN, Clero, vol. 402, Barcelona, 7th July 1579. For the ordinances, see ACA, Mon., vol. 2670, ff. 413r–418r. Copy dated 17th July 1579.

[152] Citation ACA, Mon., vol. 2670, f. 416r.

[153] *Ibid.*, f. 414v.

Salazar had actually resigned himself to the use of force against the conventuals nothing can have prepared him for what followed.[154] Rumours of impending violence were confirmed on the evening of 16th July with the discovery of two conventuals fencing on the roof of the priory church.[155] That night an armed band of over 200 men, including a number of apostate religious and members of the Order's *cofraria dels escudellers*, scattered the viceregal militia, surrounded and then entered the building.[156] Led by Mendía — recently escaped from the priory — and a masked *conseller*, the crowd freed the prisoners, broke into Salazar's rooms and flung the vicar general and his cohorts into the conventual gaol. Next morning Salazar was forced to close the visitation and absolve the rebels before being turned out onto the street with his party.[157] The reformers, who, as one declared, had had only breviaries with which to defend themselves, received a torrent of abuse from the townspeople as they made their way to the viceregal palace.[158] By noon on the 17th the Reform had effectively collapsed in Barcelona.

Loris and Toledo responded with a succession of orders and denunciations, culminating on 27th July with a failed attempt to enter the priory by force.(25v–27v)[159] The building was again incastellated and remained in a state of virtual siege until mid November.(27v) However, help was at hand for the conventuals, for beyond its immediate effect on the Order this incident provoked a major row between the viceroy and the *consellers*.[160] Outraged at their

---

[154] IVDJ, env. 89, caja 126, no. 351, f. 2r.

[155] For details of this incident, see ACA, Mon., vol. 2677, ff. 20v–58v, depositions of Salazar's religious, Barcelona, 18th July 1579. Salazar's own testimony, of the same date, is in AMAE, SS, leg. 34, ff. 201r–203v; a further statement is *ibid.*, ff. 227r–229v. See also those from the criminal tribunal of the *Audiència*, ACA, Mon., vol. 2677, ff. 73r–104v, 18th August 1579. The entire *proceso* is in AMAE, SS, leg. 34, ff. 379r–539v.

[156] For more on the *escudellers*, see ACA, Mon., vol. 2834, pp. 249, 251 & 453–4.

[157] Salazar's closure of the visitation is in AGN, Clero, vol. 402.

[158] ACA, Mon., vol. 2677, f. 33v.

[159] Measures taken against the priory between 18th & 31st July are in *ibid.*, ff. 62r–72v, while a riposte from the religious condemning Salazar's behaviour is in AGN, Clero, vol. 402 (two copies), dated 21st July 1579. For a résumé of the situation, see IVDJ, env. 89, caja 126, no. 352, Loris to Zúñiga, Barcelona, 23rd July 1579. A report to the crown from the *Consell Criminal* of the *Audiència* implicating the *consellers* in this incident and revealing the unrest in the city, along with its covering letter, is in *ibid.*, env. 91, caja 131, nos. 796 & 800 respectively, Barcelona, 4th August 1579.

[160] The period after the revolt is covered in the *Dietari*, V, pp. 204–16, proceedings reproduced in part in ACA, Mon., vol. 2677, ff. 11v–16v.

support for the rebels and refusal to cooperate with the authorities, Toledo not for the first time accused them of reneging on their declared responsibility for the priory.[161] But the *Consell* rejected this, stating that its obligation was confined to upholding the 'preeminen-ties' accorded the Order by the papacy and the traditional founder, Jaume I.[162] Neither was there any precedent for the type of 'assis-tance' being demanded of the *consellers* by the crown in its hour of need; as they told the viceroy, 'we are not saying that we do not want to assist the King, only that it does not suit the city of Barcelona to assist the officials of Your Excellency or the Lord Bishop'.[163] Support-ed by a large *junta* of theologians, the *consellers* concluded that the Guadalajara constitutions were, as the religious had been contesting here and in Rome for over a year, an affront to the privileges of both the priory and the city of Barcelona.[164] In particular, the priory's ancient and incontestable right — fixed in 'the first institution of the Order [...] and confirmed in all its ancient ordinances' — to host the electoral chapters general had been derogated by a set of constitu-tions formulated for the sole benefit of Castile.[165] Moreover, the unique status of the priory as the mother house supposedly gave its community a right of 'possession' or self-determination with respect to the rest of the Order that had been enshrined in the 1327 constitu-tions.[166] Or, as Sega facetiously put it, the right of the friars 'to live in their pristine liberty, without rule or reform'.[167] While the appeal on the *locus* of the chapters remained in progress, the *Consell* would not only refuse to recognize the royal and episcopal censure laid against the rebels, but absolved itself of all liability in respect of this. Bereft of

---

[161] *Dietari*, V, p. 206.

[162] *Ibid.*, pp. 206 & esp. 214–16.

[163] *Ibid.*, pp. 209 & 226–7, summary of a *memorial*, undated but *c.*July 1579.

[164] On this see *ibid.*, p. 200 and Fernández Collado, *Gregorio XIII y Felipe II*, pp. 313–14; also ASV, NS, vol. 14, ff. 590r–591r, Maldonado to Sega, *c.*May 1578; *ibid.*, vol. 20, ff. 102r–103v (102r–v), *Segreteria* to Sega, Rome, 17th January 1579; *ibid.*, vol. 22, ff. 40r–43v, with f. 39r–v, a covering letter from Sega to Como, dated Madrid, 11th February 1579, and *ibid.*, vol. 20, ff. 362r–364v (362v–363r), the *Segreteria's* reply to Sega, Rome, 4th May 1579.

[165] ACA, Mon., vol. 2677, f. 8r.

[166] See AMAE, SS, leg. 34, ff. 21r–22v, Philip II to Zúñiga, Bosque de Segovia, 5th June 1578, f. 21r, and AGN, Clero, vol. 402, Cardá to Gregory XIII, undated but Barcelona, early 1578.

[167] ASV, NS, vol. 11, ff. 300r–303v, Sega to Como, Madrid, 5th June 1578, f. 302v. For further correspondence from Sega to Como, see *ibid.*, vol. 22, ff. 271v–272r & 394r, Madrid, 12th August & 24th October 1579 respectively.

the *consellers*' assistance, Toledo's denunciations, like Loris' censure, fell like leaves at the priory door, while the brethren resorted in their confinement to begging for food from the conventual windows.(27r) But, as their enemies later reminded them, the broader issues of municipal and provincial freedom raised by the reform of the priory of Barcelona were being hijacked to serve interests beyond those of the Order, which was to wait an agonizingly long time for a solution to its problems.[168] Even for the crown, as Loris had earlier implied, the Mercedarian question had become more a matter of principle and reputation than one of reform in its purest sense.[169]

Of course, not all Catalans were in favour of violent resistance of this sort. For moderates like Fra Pere Pau Lleó, a procurator in Rome, mindless thuggery threatened to ruin a suit that could still succeed on its own merits.[170] Lleó was furious that a cause defended with such tenacity by the Catalans over the last ten or twelve years should now be compromised by a gang of impetuous ruffians.(223v) The view in Rome, he told the conventuals, was that the future of the Order would be decided only once the latest visitations had been completed and on the basis of a review of all relevant documentation from both sides.(224v) Moreover, it was clear to Lleó that the papacy, like the crown, not only required the religious to be reformed as a matter of principle — 'que siam reformats' — but found the 1327 constitutions upon which Barcelona's pre-eminence was based wholly unacceptable on a number of crucial points.(224v,223v) However, Lleó believed that it was still possible for the Catalans to influence the nature of this reform, and it therefore behoved them to stand united 'in one cause, one life, one being and one brotherhood' before the final reckoning.(223v–224r) As he declared, 'now is the time to demonstrate to the pope and to the whole world that we can reform ourselves far better than any sent to do it for us'.(225r)

Yet what reform was this to be? The answer, Lleó maintained, was to turn to the priory archive and, as set out in the Tridentine decrees, begin a strict observance of the earliest known constitutions of the

---

[168] See ACA, Mon., vol. 4414, ff. 155r–157v. M° Fray Pedro Carrillo & M° Fray Jorge Ongay to Tocco, undated but late 1583; f. 156v. This is tacitly admitted by Antillón in the second draft of his *Chronologicon*, ACA, Mss.Misc., vol. 103, f. 85r.

[169] IVDJ, env. 89, caja 126, no. 351, ff. 2v–3r.

[170] AMAE, SS, leg. 34, ff. 223r–226v. The transcript of what appears an intercepted letter to the priory of Barcelona, undated but Rome, *c.*August 1579. References to this document are henceforth given in the text.

Order: those introduced by Pere d'Amer in 1272.(225r–226r) The aim of the exercise, Lleó·declared, was to demonstrate 'the ancient constitutions to be of greater rigour than Maldonado's reform [...] and the latter motivated by ambition rather than a desire to reform the Order'.(225r) Or, as he added, 'better the work of our forefathers than that of our enemies'.(225v) However, Lleó was skating on decidely thin ice, for not only had the Amer constitutions accorded Barcelona no pre-eminent status, but their existence confuted the legislative framework upon which the position of the priory, and indeed the Order itself, was founded. For the Castilians as much as the Catalans, the fiction that the 1327 statutes dated in fact from the establishment of the Order a century earlier had, for now at least, to be sustained. Lleó's actions, like those of Mendía and his followers, therefore reflect the increasingly desperate measures to which Catalans felt themselves driven.[171]

Whatever its implications for the Catalan cause, the events of summer 1579 represented a severe blow to Maldonado and the reformist party as a whole. The extent of the general's misery is apparent in the piteous letter he wrote to the vice-chancellor of Aragon in the spring of 1580.[172] The Catalans, Maldonado lamented, were counting off the days to his demise while their general found himself broken in body and spirit. With the crown still largely out of the equation and the papacy holding the balance of power, Maldonado had to concede that, as things stood, the reformers were unlikely to enforce the 1574 constitutions in Catalonia. And, as Maldonado himself recognized, in its hour of need the Order found no leader equal to the gravity of the situation. The Mercedarians had no Santa Teresa to lead them to greener pastures.

VIII. *The Reform Defeated, 1579–82*

The history of the Order during the 1580s is that of the massive *pleito* which raged between the reform party and the city and priory of

---

[171] In this light the excavations conducted by the Catalans in the priory church during the early 1570s take on an added significance: a search for the primordial statutes of the Order; see ch. 6, n. 68.

[172] BNM, ms. 1761, f. 41r–v. Maldonado to (probably) Bernardo de Bolea, Zaragoza, 7th April 1580.

Barcelona. If the two sides poured their energies and money into this dispute it was not only because the survival of one or other interpretation of Mercedarian life was at stake, but because the privileges of priory and city had been made one.

Thanks to the efforts of Lleó and the *Consell* the Catalan cause began to gather pace in Rome during the latter half of 1579, despite the attentions of the ambassador, the marqués de Alcañices, and Maldonado's *procurador general*, M° Fray Juan Enríquez.[173] The Catalans managed to win a stay of execution from Dávalos and Cardinal Flavio Orsini, to whom the adjudication of the *pleito* had been entrusted by Gregory XIII, and in November the *Consell* established a permanent embassy in Rome in the person of Dr. Thomàs Pujades, a known opponent of the crown.(29r)[174] With relations worsening between Philip and the papacy and the *Consell*'s resources at his disposal, Pujades began to challenge the core of the Guadalajara reform, particularly where it affected the generalcy and the privileges traditionally enjoyed by the Catalans. But in the end Pujades pinned Catalan resistance to institutional reform on one recurrent element, the inalienable right of the priory of Barcelona to host the electoral chapters general: Mercedarian Reform reduced to an essence.

By the close of 1579 the papacy had issued the first in a succession of briefs that threatened to reverse the entire process of reform in the Principality. The archbishop of Tarragona, Antoni Agustí, was granted plenary powers over the Order in Catalonia and charged with the settlement of the ongoing dispute, a responsibility he immediately delegated to Loris.[175] However, when after nearly two years it

---

[173] Antillón's account of the *pleito*, upon which these paragraphs are in part based, was drawn from conversations with an elderly Lleó at his foundation of Rocca di Papa near Rome between 1619–22; see AHCB, ms. A-266, Antillón, *Memorias*, II, ff. 27v–28r. The *pleito*, for which massive documentation survives, may be followed in *ibid.*, ff. 28r–37v, in AMAE, SS, leg. 34, in ACA, Mon., vols. 2832 & 4144, and in *Dietari*, V, *passim*.

[174] Pujades replaced an earlier ambassador, Lluís Durall, sent out by the *Consell* to address this matter in early July; see IVDJ, env. 89, caja 126, no. 351, ff. 1v & 2v. On Pujades see, in APV, an unreferenced and unfoliated 8° vol. of notes taken by Fray José Nicolás Cavero from vol. 'III' of Antillón's *Epitome de los Generales de la Merced*, §20; on this work see ch. 2, n. 145. A rich correspondence, mainly from Pujades to the *Consell* between 1579 and 1588, survives in AHCB, CC, CCO, vols. 47–49; *ibid.*, LD, vols. 87–98; *ibid.*, RLC, vols. 61–65, & *ibid.*, RO, vols. 20–21. I am grateful to Ignasi Fernández Terricabras of the Université de Toulouse for these and other references in AHCB.

[175] ACA, Mon., vol. 2832, pp. 239–43, copy of a commission to the archbishop of Tarragona, Antoni Agustí i Albanell, dated Rome, 12th December 1579. Loris'

became clear that Loris was not going to be able to broker a solution, the curia began to consider more urgent action. In August 1581 the papacy issued a final injunction to the Catalans to give Maldonado their full obedience, and underlined its determination to resolve the *pleito* by transferring the matter to Tocco, bishop of Girona and president of Montserrat since 1581.[176] But this was to no effect, and on 28th February 1582 the papacy issued a further brief that not only suspended the election of a new general, but created Tocco commissary apostolic over the entire Order until such time as the *pleito* had been settled.[177] Though Tocco's association with the Order went back to 1575, the renewal of his appointment united the two great symbols of Catalan religious and political resistance at a crucial moment. Suggestions that Maldonado's tenure be prorogued were rejected by Philip in view of his widespread unpopularity, and the general duly relinquished his seals of office at Pentecost that year with none to replace him.[178]

This undoubtedly represented a major victory for the Catalans, who had not only reversed the process of institutional reform but successfully brought the focus of authority in the Order back to

---

powers of adjudication over the *pleito* are in a second brief of the same date, *ibid.*, pp. 353–6. See also ASV, NS, vol. 20, ff. 448r–449v, *Segreteria* to Sega, Rome, 7th September 1579; ff. 448v–449r.

[176] ACA, Mon., vol. 2832, pp. 243–53. Rome, 8th August 1581. Another copy AMAE, SS, leg. 34, ff. 165r–v.

[177] For correspondence regarding the suspension of the generalate, see the seven documents, all dating from 1582, in ACA, CA, vol. 342 (unftd.); these references I owe to the generosity of Ignasi Fernández Terricabras. The brief, drawn up by Cardinal Maffeo, is in ACA, Mon., vol. 2832, pp. 254–6, and in the *Dietari*, V, pp. 309–16. A somewhat inaccurate summary of it is given in P. Francisco J. Miquell Rosell, ed., *Regesta de letras pontificias del ACA — Cancillería Real* (Madrid, 1948), pp. 405–6. For the printed promulgation, dated Barcelona, 10th April 1582, see ACA, Mon., vol. 2658, p. 223. The commission as executor apostolic of Dr. Guerau Vilana, canon of Barcelona, is in *ibid.*, vol. 2832, pp. 236–8, dated Rome, 25th May 1582. An interesting *memorial* entitled 'Instructions pera la executio del breu apostolich dirigit al Reuerendissimo de Girona' appears to date from this time; see AGN, Clero, vol. 416. For details of the priory's acceptance of Tocco's commission, see AHCB, ms. A-266, Antillón, *Memorias*, II, ff. 29v & 33r–v.

[178] AMAE, SS, leg. 34, ff. 24r–25v, Philip II to his ambassador in Rome, Enrique de Guzmán, Count of Olivares, Setúbal, 23rd April 1582 (other copies ff. 26r–27v & 28r–30r). For further suggestions on this issue, see *ibid.*, f. 134r, an undated Castilian *memorial* in 4°. Maldonado's unpopularity evidently extended to Castile, which remained divided into rival factions, but there is evidence of support from within the priory of Barcelona itself; see the letter from Fray Jaime Ferrer, diffinitor provincial of Aragon and other reformist conventuals of Barcelona to Philip, dated Barcelona, 15th January 1582 in ACA, CA, vol. 342, unfoliated.

Barcelona. On 25th June 1582, with the Order entering its second vacancy, Fra Pere Castelló, president of Barcelona, was proclaimed vicar general by papal decree, much to Philip's annoyance.(29v,32v)[179] Apostolic letters were sent out demanding that he be obeyed not only as vicar, but as 'president general' of the Order as set out in the Albertine constitutions, though these were mostly ignored outside Catalonia.(32v)[180] The Mercedarian Reform had, for now at least, come full circle.

IX. *The Catalan Religious Order in Crisis*

The Mercedarian Order was not the only one to drift into crisis in the 1580s. Throughout the eastern provinces the reforms sponsored by the crown since the 1550s had entered a critical phase. In the case of the Augustinians, the death in January 1583 of the reformer general, Fray Rodrigo de Solís, threatened to extinguish the modest gains of fifteen years' unremitting effort.[181] The election of an anti-reformist provincial of Aragon at Barcelona in May of that year heralded the beginning of a systematic purge of Castilian and reformed religious from positions of authority. This could not be allowed to go on unchecked, and by 1585 Philip had begun to intervene in Rome on behalf of the beleaguered reformists.[182] By September of the following year the crown was able to orchestrate the election in Zaragoza of a provincial under whom the Reform could resume its laggardly progress.

Of course, what made the difference in the Augustinian case was the relative absence of local support for the opponents of reform of the kind enjoyed by the Mercedarians in Catalonia. This, however, was not true of other orders and congregations, whose claims were pressed with comparable vigour by the *Consell de Cent* and the *Generali-*

---

[179] A printed copy of the decree is in ACA, Mon., vol. 4144, between ff. 90 & 91. The documentation surrounding Castelló's appointment and the efforts to have him recognized is in *ibid.*, vol. 2832, pp. 258–316. For Philip's reaction to Olivares, see AMAE, SS, leg. 34, f. 44r–v, Lisbon, 20th August 1582. For what may be a forged brief absolving the priory of censure and interdict, see ACA, Mss.Misc., vol. 49, pp. 23–5 & 50.

[180] See AMAE, SS, leg. 34, f. 101r–v. M° Fray Jorge Ongay to Olivares, Valencia, 24th October 1582. Another copy is f. 102r–v.

[181] Alonso, *La reforma tridentina en la provincia Agustiniana*, pp. 125–9.

[182] *Ibid.*, pp. 135–47.

tat in particular. Irritated by the lack of progress towards the preparation of new constitutions, in 1582 the king began pressing for radical
measures towards the reform of the Tarraconensian Benedictines.[183]
In 1585 the *Consell* and the cathedral chapter of Barcelona reacted to
continued royal intervention by issuing a formal protest against this
and the planned secularization of the Canons Regular of St Augustine.[184] By 1587 the Tarraconensian case had reached Rome, where
the congregation's two procurators were supported by the *Consell de
Cent* and the *Generalitat*.[185] Though the crown was itself anxious 'that
the reformation should come from Rome', matters were delayed by a
succession of short pontificates until Clement VIII's major reform
bull of August 1592.[186] The Canons Regular were secularized as
expected, but it was 1618 before a mitigated implementation of the
bull could begin among the Tarraconensian *Claustrales*.[187]

Apart from the Mercedarians, the classic conflict between Castilian
and Catalan religious was that played out during the 1580s at the
great abbey of Montserrat. Claims that the Castilians were siphoning
off the abbatial income and ridiculing the Catalan language — '¡Fal-
ad en Christiano!' — served, with the support of the *Consell* and the
Generalitat, to elevate the affair into a matter of provincial importance.[188] Following a disastrous visitation by Castilian monks in 1582,
the *Consell* began a campaign to drive all 'monjos estrangers' out of
the abbey and remove it from the Valladolid Congregation.[189] The
ensuing events are intimately associated with the Mercedarian question, and it is difficult to escape the conclusion that, in Catalonia par-

---

[183] See Tobella, 'La Congregació Claustral Tarraconense', pp. 135–6.

[184] See Zaragoza Pascual, 'Documentos inéditos referentes a la reforma de los
Canónigos Regulares y Benedictinos', p. 90.

[185] *Ibid.*, p. 91. By the early 1590s the *Consell* had installed Mossèn Joan Palau in
Rome as procurator in this matter; see *id.*, 'Documentos inéditos referentes a la
reforma de los Benedictinos catalanes (1573–1596)' in *Analecta Sacra Tarraconensia*, 59
(1986), pp. 105–18; 106.

[186] See *id.*, 'Reforma de los Benedictinos y de los Canónigos Regulares en
Cataluña', pp. 75–7; citation p. 75. The struggle to implement this bull provides an
important example of the development of royal patronage over abbatial appointments at this time; see *id.*, 'Documentos inéditos referentes a la reforma de los Benedictinos catalanes', pp. 107–8.

[187] *Id.*, 'Documentos inéditos referentes a la reforma de los Canónigos Regulares y
Benedictinos', p. 95.

[188] In 1584 the *Consell* established an eight-member committee — *vuitena* — to deal
with the Montserrat affair, possibly modelled on an earlier Mercedarian committee;
see Fernández Terricabras, 'Reforma i obediència', p. 176.

[189] *Ibid.*, p. 172.

ticularly, the bitterness provoked by the reform of this order after 1567 coloured local reaction to monastic affairs as a whole. Equally, it is clear that the violence which erupted throughout the Catalan monastic Order in the 1580s represented a major source of concern to the crown in what was an extremely difficult decade in the eastern provinces. Catalonia had been ravaged by influenza during the summer of 1580, and three years later the Andalusian preacher Diego Pérez de Valdivia captured the sense of despair that hung over the Principality in a sermon delivered in the church of Santa Maria del Mar in Barcelona, describing

> the king, don Felipe, an old and sick man; the kingdom poor and worn out, for many a year nothing has gone right; the land full of thieves, murderers, idlers, the sick and the wretched; everything in ruins...[190]

X. *Litigation, 1582–4*

Developments in Catalonia were received with resolution in Castile where Mº Fray Pedro Carrillo, who had been elected to a second provincialate at Guadalajara in May 1582, began to style himself 'vicar general' of the Order as allowed for in the 1574 constitutions. In Valencia allegiances wavered, with the conventuals of El Puig refusing to obey Maldonado and, so Pujades reported to the *Consell*, eager for matters to return to their former state.[191] However, in Aragon the survival of the reformist climate established by Salazar during his long provincialate (1576–82) was ensured by the election at Valencia that year of the Navarrese Mº Fray Jorge Ongay, rector of Huesca, under the general's presidency.(31r–v)[192] Though many commendators and friars clearly remained as disobedient as their Catalan peers, the catalogue of fraud and immorality that peppers the Valencia *synodalia* also bears witness to the huge efforts being made to raise standards and punish the most flagrant abuses. The veteran Bruxola was relieved of his commandery at Calatayud for embezzling redemption *limosna*, while the Mercedarian *beaterio* at Orihuela was suppressed after repeated indiscretions on the part of the

---

[190] Cited in Kamen, *The Phoenix and the Flame*, p. 80.

[191] AHCB, CC, CCO, vol. 48, ff. 167r–168v, Rome, 5th March 1582.

[192] The proceedings of this chapter, dated 11th–16th May 1582, are in ACA, Mon., vol. 2659, ff. 16r–45r. Maldonado had been a *diputat* in Valencia that year in his capacity as general of the Order.

beatas with their brother religious.[193] The reformers were anxious above all to curb the flood of fugitives, and encourage observance of the mishmash of old and reform constitutions under which the Order was labouring.[194] However, the prevailing situation clearly made all this rather too much to expect.

Of course, this fragile continuum was overshadowed by the crisis that still hung over the Order. At year's end Philip still cherished hopes of an early election under Salazar's presidency, but it became clear that the crown and the reformers had still not regained the initiative.[195] Attempts to have the commission turned over to Sega were ignored by a papacy determined to marginalize the crown as far as possible. Reinforced by a further brief, Tocco began making preparations for the suit over the *locus* of electoral chapters general upon which the fate of Mercedarian Reform would be decided.[196] Carrillo and Ongay dispatched procurators to Barcelona where, in August 1583, the two parties began to debate the issue that lay at the heart of the reform crisis.[197] After some vacillation, Philip decided to leave the matter to papal arbitration, and restricted himself to a face-saving policy of coercion with respect to the Catalans.[198]

The Catalan case rested on the inviolability of a set of constitutions widely — though erroneously — claimed to be the primordial observance of the Order, the value of which had supposedly been endorsed by the Council of Trent.[199] Enshrined within these was the very essence of the Order, along with the vows, laws and precepts

---

[193] See *ibid.*, ff. 24v–25r & 37r–38v respectively.

[194] See *ibid.*, ff. 42r, and 41r & 42v respectively.

[195] See three letters from Philip to Olivares, AMAE, SS, leg. 34, ff. 32r–v, 31r–v & 33r–v, respectively Lisbon, 18th October, 1st November & 20th December 1582.

[196] No copy of this brief has been found, but it dates from *c.*February 1583 when Tocco had transferred from the see of Girona to that of Lleida. See *ibid.*, ff. 61r, 34r–v & 90r, royal secretary Hierónimo Gassol, Philip and then Tocco to Olivares, respectively Madrid, 9th & 24th May, & Barcelona, 6th July 1583. A reply from Olivares to Tocco is ff. 117r–118r, Rome, August 1583.

[197] Regarding the procurators, see *ibid.*, f. 91r–v, Tocco to Olivares, Barcelona, 7th August 1583, & ACA, Mon., vol. 4144, ff. 54r & 55v, Carrillo to Castelló, Valladolid, 21st July 1583, and five unnumbered 4° ff. between ff. 97 & 98, Ongay to Tocco, Zaragoza, 4th September 1583.

[198] See two letters from Philip to Olivares, AMAE, SS, leg. 34, ff. 36r (another copy f. 39r–v) & 40r–v, Aranjuez, 31st December 1583 & 14th January 1584, two more from Tocco, ff. 93r–v & 94r–v, Barcelona, 20th & 31st January 1584, and a further three from Gassol, ff. 64r, 63r–v & 66r–v, respectively Madrid, 26th September & 12th November 1583, & 1st February 1584.

[199] ACA, Mon., vol. 4144, ff. 14r–17r. *Memorial* from Fra Francesc Cardá, procurator of Barcelona, to Tocco, Barcelona, 19th July 1583; f. 14r–v.

observed by religious for generation after generation.[200] Attempting to set the reformers against the papacy, the Catalans declared the reform authorized by Pius V in 1567 to be incompatible with the wholesale revocation of the constitutions that had followed.[201] It was only the naked greed and ambition of the province of Castile that had caused this hallowed tradition to be broken at Guadalajara in 1574.[202] The Catalans could therefore accept reform, but not of this kind.[203]

The reformists, however, took a view that reflects the gulf-like difference in mentalities which divided the Order.[204] If the reform constitutions did not follow the letter then they had certainly followed the spirit of the Tridentine decrees, which, they declared, had 'included certain ordinances then felt to be necessary, but which have later proved to be impractical'.[205] By the same token, the old provisions on the *locus* of chapters general were passed at a moment when 'the Order was small and of few houses', statutes which the passage of time had implicitly served to invalidate.[206] To Carrillo, moreover, any loss incurred by the revocation of the old statutes was more than compensated for by the essential fairness of the new legislation, what he referred to as 'the equality of justice'.[207] The Albertine constitutions, he declared, were both 'contrary and pernicious to those standards of good government and religious life now being kept and observed in all other orders'.[208] By way of conclusion, Carrillo made it plain that if the Guadalajara statutes were revoked and the Order reunified under the 1327 legislation, his province would have no

---

[200] *Ibid.*, ff. 15v & 16r.

[201] *Ibid.*, ff. 94r–96r. *Memorial* from Cardá to Tocco, undated but Barcelona, *c*.August 1583; f. 94r.

[202] *Ibid.*, ff. 15r, 15v & 16r.

[203] *Ibid.*, ff. 113r–115r. *Memorial* from Cardá to Tocco, undated but Barcelona, *c*.September 1583; f. 113v.

[204] As a start, see the *memorial* sent by the Castilian procurator in Rome since *c*.1578, M° Fray Fernando Suárez, to the pope, AMAE, SS, leg. 34, ff. 129r–130v, undated but Rome, *c*.1582–3.

[205] ACA, Mon., vol. 4144, ff. 99r–101r. *Memorial* from M° Fray Jorge Ongay to Tocco, Zaragoza(?), 10th October 1583; f. 99v.

[206] *Ibid.*, f. 100r, & ff. 45r–46v, *Memorial* from Montoro to Tocco, Barcelona, 8th August 1583. An undated Castilian version of the latter *memorial* from Carrillo is in *ibid.*, ff. 48r–50r. The same point is made in a *memorial* by the Castilian *procurador* M° Fray Fernando Suárez to Gregory XIII in AMAE, SS, leg. 34, ff. 138r–139v, undated but Rome, *c*.1583–4; f. 138r.

[207] ACA, Mon., vol. 4144, f. 48r.

[208] *Ibid.*, f. 48v.

option but to secede again from the 'subieçion del general de Catalu-nia' that would inevitably follow.[209] Indeed, for the Castilian procura-tor Mº Fray Fernando Suárez, the differences between the two provinces were such that permanent division represented the only viable answer, though this was an extreme view.[210]

Mercedarian Reform therefore resolved itself into a conflict between tradition and innovation, between those intent on preserving an established order and those who would build afresh within the framework of a new religious climate. Whether in perpetuating one system or in creating another, it is clear that both sides considered their cause as one of reform, whose perspective implicitly extended to the past, to the present and to the future of the Order.

It soon became apparent that the papacy was going to judge the *pleito* on its merits, and, after the triumphs of 1582 and early 1583, the Catalan cause began to falter. The reformers' case was strength-ened by the ill-treatment meted out to Fray Juan de Montoro, the Castilian representative in Barcelona, and by Castelló's death at the height of the *pleito* in August 1583.(34r)[211] Castelló's last fateful action was to appoint the ambitious Mendía to succeed him as pres-ident of Barcelona.[212] Though Tocco refused to allow him to become prior as well, by the end of the year Mendía had succeeded in dispersing many leading conventuals to commanderies through-out the Principality, while others appear to have been driven out of the Order altogether.(34v–35r) In March of 1584, having dis-patched several more to preach a Lenten indulgence, Mendía and his cohorts bullied the remaining conventuals into electing him pri-or of Barcelona. Almost immediately he removed 500 *escudos*' worth of valuables from the priory's deposit in the *taula* of Barcelona and fled to Rome to obtain his confirmation.[213] This act lost the priory its last shred of credibility, and the Catalan suit collapsed in division and recrimination. Summer found the king crowing triumphantly and threatening to inflict exemplary punishment on the whole

[209] *Ibid.*, f. 50r.
[210] See AMAE, SS, leg. 34, ff. 140r–141v & 151r, a *memorial* and a letter to the pope, both undated but Rome, *c.*1583–4; see, in the former, f. 141r–v. Suárez also appears frequently as Hernando Juárez.
[211] Vázquez Núñez, *Manual*, II, p. 34.
[212] AMAE, SS, leg. 34, ff. 95r–v & 96r–v. Tocco to Olivares, respectively Lleida, 6th April & Montserrat, 29th July 1584.
[213] See *ibid.*, f. 95v, & f. 42r, Philip II to Olivares, El Escorial, 30th May 1584.

wretched community.[214] However, the arch scoundrel remained at large. Although assisted by Pujades in Rome, it was clear that Mendía's reputation had preceded him and he was obliged to flee the city.[215] Evading his pursuers, he returned to Spain in August with only a sheaf of forged letters to show for his efforts.[216] After some time in hiding around Perpignan, Mendía joined the *cuadrilla* of the celebrated Aragonese bandit Lupercio Latras.[217] He was eventually arrested in 1588, imprisoned at San Lázaro in Zaragoza and brought to trial at the convent of Valladolid where he was at length condemned to ten years in the galleys.[218] This ought, perhaps, to have been the last of Fray Vicente Mendía, but it proved otherwise. In May 1590 Philip reported that he had broken out of the convent with the friar supposed to be guarding him and fled, like so many before him, towards Italy.[219]

XI. *Survival and Recovery, 1584–6*

Though the organization of the *pleito* was Tocco's primary responsibility, he did not neglect the matter of reform itself. Once the *proceso* had been completed in September 1583 the commissary began a personal visitation of the priory of Barcelona which, thanks no doubt to his other commitments, he completed only in March of the following year.[220] Although Tocco's fears that 'these fathers are going to give me a lot of trouble' were realized with Mendía's election that March,

---

[214] *Ibid.*, ff 43r–v & 45r–v, El Escorial, 20th July & 22nd August 1584; see also f. 42v.

[215] See *ibid.*, ff. 121r–v & 125r–v, letters from Olivares to (probably) Juan de Zúñiga, conde de Miranda, viceroy of Catalonia, undated but Rome, *c.*April 1584, and to Gregory XIII, undated but Rome, *c.*May 1584.

[216] See *ibid.*, f. 86r–v, Cardinal Alessandrino(?) to Íñigo Dávalos, Cardinal of Aragon, Rome, 14th July 1584, & f. 97r–v, Tocco to Olivares, Montserrat, 22nd September 1584.

[217] On this see the results of an inquiry in *ibid.*, ff. 126r–127v, dated 20th September 1584; see also f. 222v.

[218] See *ibid.*, leg. 9, f. 73r, Gassol to Olivares, Madrid, 4th February 1589 (among others), & *ibid.*, leg. 34, f. 200r–v, Philip II to Olivares, El Escorial, 26th May 1589. Hoping for a sentence of capital punishment, the crown had sent the matter to Rome.

[219] *Ibid.*, leg. 34, f. 199r–v, Philip II to Olivares, Aranjuez, 16th May 1590.

[220] Tocco had been appointed visitor apostolic of Montserrat in June 1583. See *ibid.*, ff. 95r, & 92r–v, Tocco to Olivares, Barcelona, 30th September 1583. The *proceso* was not, however, sent to Rome until the end of January; see *ibid.*, f. 94r.

the prior's disappearance removed a major obstacle to the reform of what was now a thoroughly demoralized province.[221] Here was an opportunity that Tocco lost no time in exploiting, and by the beginning of April 1584 three visitors had been appointed, two for Catalonia and Fray Baltasar García, life commendator of Oran, for the subprovince of Italy and Sicily.(35v)[222] The Catalan appointments reflect Tocco's wholly practical approach to the business of reform. His choices fell on two Girona religious, the Valencian-born commendator P.ᵗ Fra Francesc Andreu, who had been declared a rebel after refusing to appear at the chapter provincial of Valencia in 1582, and a Basque conventual, Fray Severino de la Puente.[223] In Andreu particularly Tocco had appointed a visitor who could at last talk to the religious in their own language, both as a Catalan speaker and as a fellow Mercedarian, and his confidence was not misplaced.

The visitation began at Palma de Mallorca on 14th April and took the religious on a tour of Catalonia that only ended at Barcelona the following spring.(35v)[224] Needless to say, the visitors found the province ravaged by years of neglect and indiscipline, its houses filled with the sullen diaspora of the priory of Barcelona. The thrust of the visitation — the improvement of religious observance, personal morality, the noviciate, conventual organization, financial probity and accountability — was no different from any other. At Tarragona, for instance, the visitors warned the religious against sheltering fugitives, though some of these had fled Montblanc for want of anything to eat.[225] Andreu and Puente found but one religious in this house,

---

[221] *Ibid.*, f. 92r.

[222] *Ibid.*, f. 95r. García appears to have turned against the Reform in Rome; see *ibid.*, ff. 136r–137v, a *memorial* from Suárez to Olivares(?), undated but mid 1585. Carrillo was also given a commission to visit his province; see APV, Antillón, ms. *Epitome*, 'III', §21. Tocco, meanwhile, began his visitation of Montserrat in May 1584.

[223] On Andreu, see Mᵒ Fray Marcos Salmerón, *Recuerdos Historicos y Politicos de los Servicios que los Generales y Varones Illustres de la Religion de Nuestra Señora de la Merced [...] han hecho a los Reyes de España [...] desde [...] 1218 hasta el año 1640* (Valencia: Herederos de Chrysosthomo Garriz, por Bernardo Nogues, 1646); p. 365. Andreu appears as president of Valencia during Dicastillo's tenure as commendator in 1578 and '80; see ARV, Clero, lib. 1305, ff. 10r, 11r & 20r.

[224] The *acta* of this visitation campaign, except for Barcelona, are in ACA, Mon., vol. 2850. The visitors' presence at Barcelona from late 1584 is recorded in *ibid.*, vol. 2710, f. 103v; see also vol. 2670, esp. ff. 397v–398r. The visitation of Barcelona seems to have been preceded by a further commission from Tocco, dated Montserrat, 14th October 1584; on this see AHCB, ms. A-266, Antillón, *Memorias*, II, f. 35v.

[225] See ACA, Mon., vol. 2850, f. 83v.

which was roofless and abandoned when Henry Cock, an archer of the king's Flemish guard, passed through the following year.[226] Other religious had fled to the embattled abbey of Montserrat.[227] However, there was a distinctly sympathetic tone about this visitation which pointed the way ahead. Although the visitors saw fit to remove several commendators, including the new president of Barcelona, Fra Francesc Serafí, their ordinances are remarkably free of the withering threats that characterize others.(35v) 'Because part of the reformation we are trying to introduce…' reasoned one article, while others made clear that the religious would for the time being continue to live under both 'the old and new constitutions of the Order', and follow the accustomed liturgy of the Aragonese provinces.[228]

The visitation of Barcelona was still in progress when, in February 1585, news arrived of Tocco's death on Montserrat. In earlier years this would have brought matters to a halt, but now Andreu and Puente, with the support of four city lawyers, were able to go through with the removal of Serafí and draw the visitation to a close under their own authority.(35v–36r) Ignoring appeals by the *Consell* to restore the government of the Order to the priory of Barcelona, the papacy transferred Tocco's authority to the bishop of Vic, Juan Bautista de Cardona.[229] By the time Salazar was elected to a second term as provincial at Zaragoza in May it was clear that the new pope, the Franciscan Sixtus V, had resolved the *pleito* in favour of the Reform.[230] As a gesture of 'peace and fraternity', the chapter appointed nine of the Barcelona religious to commanderies throughout Catalonia and sent a conciliatory letter to the *Consell*.[231] A last-ditch attempt by the Catalans to stall the matter over the injustice done to the French province in the Guadalajara constitutions was brushed aside by Suárez and Olivares, leaving Pujades to contemplate

[226] *Ibid.*, f. 75r, and Henry Cock, *Relación del viaje hecho por Felipe II, en 1585, a Zaragoza, Barcelona y Valencia* (Madrid, 1876), p. 109.

[227] Vázquez Núñez, ed., 'Fuentes' [1574], p. 46.

[228] ACA, Mon., vol. 2850, ff. 79v ('Por quanto parte de la reformaçion que se pretende…'), 20v & 18v respectively.

[229] AMAE, SS, leg. 34, ff. 144r–v & 176r–v respectively, Pujades(?) to Gregory XIII, Rome(?), 12th March 1585, and Gregory to Cardona, Rome, 18th March 1585.

[230] The *synodalia* are in ACA, Mon., vol. 2659, ff. 46r–57v, dated 17th–24th May 1585. The nuncio, Luiggi Taberna, was present; see AMAE, SS, leg. 34, f. 70r–v, Salazar to Olivares, Zaragoza, 29th June 1585.

[231] See, respectively, AHCB, CC, CCO, vol. 49, ff. 18–26 (printed), & 29r–v, both Salazar *et al.* to *Consell*, Zaragoza, 21st & 25th May 1585.

defeat.[232] By August Philip, who had travelled to Monzón for the celebration of the Aragonese *cortes*, was congratulating the papacy on its
decision and looking to restore the crown's influence in this matter
with veiled assurances of clemency for the Catalans.[233]

The restoration of the generalcy was now a priority and in November 1585 the papacy issued a brief confirming its judgement in the
pleito, and ordering preparations to be made both for an electoral
chapter general at Zaragoza and for a revision of the Guadalajara
constitutions.[234] Perpetual silence was imposed on all dissenters, but
the Catalans had by no means emerged empty-handed. Electoral
chapters could be celebrated away from Barcelona, but in recognition
of its ancient status the priors were to be elected in community and
could retain the title of vicar general during the vacancy.[235] However,
much to their annoyance, the crown, following the Guadalajara
decrees, endorsed Salazar as vicar general and commissary apostolic
in Aragon until the forthcoming chapter, and it was he who represented the Order at the *cortes* of Monzón in 1585.(37v–38r)[236]

But for the events of previous months, the Mercedarian affair
might have occupied rather more of Philip's time at the *cortes* than
in fact proved to be the case, and it was the deepening conflict at
Montserrat that instead concerned the assembly. Even so, the
events discussed bear more than a passing resemblance to those
experienced by the Mercedarian Order. The death in February of
Tocco, the visitor apostolic, had brought on a total collapse of the
situation. Within a few days most of the remaining Catalan and
Aragonese religious had fled the mountain and taken refuge in the
suppressed priory of Sant Pau del Camp under the protection of the

[232] See AMAE, SS, leg. 34, ff. 149r, 145r & 132r, respectively Luiggi, Cardinale
d'Este to Olivares(?), Tivoli, 7th August 1585, Suárez to Martínez de Carnazedo,
Olivares' secretary, undated but Rome, *c*.August 1585 & Pujades to Cardinale di
Cesis, undated but Rome, mid 1585.

[233] See ASV, NS, vol. 1, f. 464r–v, Cardinale di Sant Marcello to Philip II, Rome,
25th July 1585, and the king's reply, AMAE, SS, leg. 34, f. 48r, undated but August
1585. See also *ibid.*, ff. 46r–v & 47r, Philip II to Olivares & Sixtus V respectively,
both Monzón, 22nd August 1585.

[234] AMAE, SS, leg. 34, ff. 181r–184v, dated Rome, 5th November 1585; ff. 182r–v
& 183r. Preliminary suggestions on this are *ibid.*, ff. 38r & 50r, the former anonymous, the latter from Taberna. For Cardona's commission to execute the brief, see
ibid., f. 179r–v, Sixtus V to Taberna, Rome, 12th January 1586.

[235] *Ibid.*, f. 183r.

[236] For details of Salazar's activities at Monzón, see an apologetic biography in
ACA, Mon., vol. 2681, ff. 107v–111r, undated but late 1591; ff. 109v–110r.

Consell.[237] Then, on 16th March, a party of forty monks and bandits returned to Montserrat and rounded up the entire Castilian community with the intention of depositing it on the Aragonese frontier. The viceroy gave chase, forcing the Catalans to abandon their charges at Cervera, and it was only after a series of similar incidents that Zúñiga and the *Consell* were able to pacify the abbey later that month. Encroaching on the *Generalitat's* traditional field of activity, the *Consell* sent a delegation to Monzón which reiterated earlier demands for the separation of Montserrat from the Valladolid Congregation, and declared that no stable remedy would be found until the Aragonese Benedictines were gathered into a single province.[238] And indeed, the matter dragged on into the seventeenth century.

But, in view of recent developments, the king could well afford a degree of indulgence to the Mercedarians, whom he honoured in Barcelona that summer by selecting the priory church for the celebration of his birthday jubilee.[239] The king offered the brethren fifty-eight *escudos* for each year of his life and declared a plenary indulgence for all those confessing their sins there during the day in question, 21st May 1585. In January of the following year Philip took the opportunity of lunching at the shrine of El Puig during his stately progress towards Valencia, and then favoured the house with the presentation of a costly gold fountain on his departure for Castile.[240]

XII. *The Reform Triumphant, 1587–9*

Even so, opposition continued in Catalonia, and it was early 1587 before Salazar felt able to issue letters of convocation for a chapter general at Pentecost that year. This opened at Zaragoza on 16th May under the presidency of the archbishop, Andrés de Bobadilla, and with the entire Order represented except for the priory of

---

[237] Fernández Terricabras, 'Reforma i obediència', p. 173.

[238] *Ibid.*, p. 177, & Zaragoza Pascual, *Los generales de la congregación de San Benito de Valladolid*, III, p. 119. The *consellers* were again able to address the king on the Mercedarian and Montserrat issues (among others) in Barcelona on 8th June 1585; Agustí Duran i Sanpere & Josep Sanabre, eds., *Llibre de les Solemnitats de Barcelona* (2 vols., Barcelona, 1930–47), I, p. 62.

[239] Duran i Sanpere & Sanabre, eds., *Llibre de les Solemnitats*, II, pp. 60–1. See also Gazulla, *La Patrona de Barcelona*, p. 60.

[240] Cock, *Relación del viaje*, pp. 209–10, 224 & 314.

Barcelona.[241] Following the procedure laid down at Guadalajara in 1574, the diffinitors elected Salazar to the high office before turning to the pressing institutional issues delayed by the crisis in the Order. In particular, the division of Castile into two provinces, first mooted in 1576, was now made reality.(3–4)[242] The Reform had no doubt impressed on the Castilian hierarchy both the difficulty of governing a provincial entity 600 miles long and 300 across, and the inappropriateness of one prelate holding authority 'a mari usque ad mare'.[243] The split was to take effect at the chapter provincial of Castile the following year, with the new province of Andalusia encompassing all houses south of the Guadiana. Though this reflects the development of a strong provincial identity among the Andalusian brethren, the division of the province was complicated by the rapid and lucrative expansion of the Order in America, to which religious from throughout the Kingdom of Castile had contributed in equal measure. The immediate solution, therefore, was the appointment by each province of vicars general who were to exercise authority in the viceroyalties of Peru and New Spain alternately.[244]

However, it was the pursuit of peace in the Crown of Aragon and the unification of the Order within a renewed legislative settlement that most exercised the delegates at Zaragoza. From the beginning the chapter was conducted in a spirit of reconciliation with the Catalans. Allowances were made for the thirty or more houses in the Crown of Aragon, France and Italy qualified by the chapter as 'impoverished', while a number of Aragonese were accepted as *presentados* without the requisite degrees in theology.(5,10)[245] Finally, several of the penalties ordained by the 'constituciones de la nueva reformacion' in 1574, including that of excommunication, were explicitly

[241] A résumé of the *synodalia* is in ACA, Mon., vol. 2683, pp. 2–18. References to this document are henceforth given in the text. See also ACA, Mss.Misc., vol. 49, pp. 148–9 & Vázquez Núñez, *Manual*, II, p. 42.

[242] For the relevant *acta* from the chapter general of Zaragoza in 1576, see APV, ms. Cavero, 'Varia', II, ff. 193v & 199r.

[243] IVDJ, env. 72, II, ff. 141r–142r. *Memorial* from an Andalusian Mercedarian to Ormaneto, undated but *c.*1576; citation f. 141v.

[244] APV, Antillón, ms. *Epitome*, 'III', §22. For Salazar's *poder*, dated Madrid, 5th June 1589, see M° Fray Bernardo de Vargas, *Chronica Sacri et Militaris Ordinis Beatae Mariae de Mercede Redemptionis Captivorum* (2 vols., Palermo: Ioannes Baptista Maringum, 1619–22); II, pp. 200–7.

[245] Ten of the impoverished houses were in Catalonia and six in Aragon. It should be noted that many of the Aragonese *presentados* were stripped of their degrees by Zumel at the chapter general of Calatayud in 1593.

moderated at Zaragoza.(5) There was, however, to be no remission for the violent criminal, the unlicensed priest or the persistent rebel or apostate, for whom the galleys or the death penalty awaited.(5–6) Nevertheless, the congregation was determined to draw a veil over the excesses of the past, and Maldonado was therefore ordered to surrender the *acta* of his visitations as general.(7–8)[246] These, together with the *procesos* against the Catalans and all the documentary detritus of twenty years of conflict, were to be committed to the flames before the assembled chapter, 'because they are now felt to be things of the past'.(8) Finally, the chapter issued an amnesty to the rebels, offering a pardon to all who came and gave the general their obedience.(8)[247]

So much for the capitular ordinances, but the basis of the continued reform and revival of the Order lay in the creation of a new set of constitutions that would incorporate the religious provisions of the old and the institutional reforms of the new. To this task the chapter commissioned the leading Mercedarian mind of the later sixteenth century, Mº Fray Francisco Zumel.[248] Born in Palencia in about 1540, Zumel entered the Order at Salamanca in 1555 where he pursued studies in theology under Gaspar de Torres.[249] After two years at the college of La Concepción in Alcalá, Zumel returned to Salamanca in 1570 where, as rector, he resumed Torres' work in establishing the Vera Cruz as the centrepiece of reform in the province of Castile.[250] A string of minor chairs through the 1570s culminated in 1580 with the Durandus *cathedra* of moral philosophy, vacated by Fray Luis de León the previous year.[251] In 1585, the year of his election as provincial, Zumel published the first of two commentaries on Aquinas' *Summa* which reflect the middle course he steered in the *De Auxiliis* debate that raged at Salamanca at the end of the century.[252]

Zumel, who apparently had an audience with the king in the

---

[246] Salazar's own visitation *acta* and *procesos* have, of course, survived in ACA, Mon., vol. 2677 & AMAE, SS, leg. 34.

[247] See AHCB, CC, CCO, vol. 49, f. 174r–v, Bobadilla to *Consellers*, Zaragoza, 22nd May 1587, in which the priory of Barcelona was given three months to organize a delegation from the whole province to render obedience to Salazar.

[248] See Vázquez Núñez, *El Padre Francisco Zumel*, *passim*, and two articles in *id.*, *Mercedarios ilustres*, pp. 350–68.

[249] *Id.*, *Mercedarios ilustres*, p. 357.

[250] *Ibid.*, pp. 357–8.

[251] *Ibid.*, pp. 358–9.

[252] *De Deo, eiusque operibus [...] Commentaria in Primam Partem Sancti Thomae Aquinatis* (2 vols., Salamanca: Petrus Lassus, 1585–7), & *In Primam Secundae Sancti Thomae Commentaria* (2 vols., Salamanca: Joannes Ferdinandus, 1593–4).

spring of 1586, was therefore the obvious choice to redraft the Mercedarian constitutions.[253] What emerged in 1588 was a compromise between old and new, between the established spiritual and religious life of the Order and the institutional provisions set down at Guadalajara fourteen years before.[254] Torres' profession formula of 1565 became standard, mental prayer was made obligatory and, in line with current developments, daily communion was advocated for all religious.[255] The result, said Salazar at the chapter provincial of Valencia that year, was a unified corpus of legislation 'which enshrines all the substance and ceremony of our Order'.[256] However, in the tradition of Gaver, Zorita and Torres, Zumel's *Regula et Constitutiones* is somewhat more than a set of statutes; it is, rather, a conspectus of the past and present of the Order that spans the hopes and ideals of a new generation of Mercedarians.[257] In his *De Initio* and *De Vitis Patrum*, Zumel follows Torres' interpretation of the establishment of the Order closely, but by no means slavishly.[258] Though Nolasch is now recognized as the 'first master' and indeed the 'Patriarch', the impression of him remains that of a tool of divine and royal will rather than the sole founder of the Order.[259] Even so, Nolasch now shares the king's vision of the Virgin and replaces Penyafort as the first Mercedarian legislator, the author, we are told, of those statutes that Amer later collated and modified into the 1272 constitutions.[260] These, as the Dominican Montaña had already made clear, were to be regarded as the primordial Mercedarian observance, since, as Fray Felipe de Guimerán explained in his *Breve Historia* of 1591, 'at

---

[253] Vázquez Núñez, *El Padre Francisco Zumel*, p. 34.

[254] For a brief comparative discussion, see González Castro, 'Las constituciones del P. Raimundo Albert', pp. 126–8. It should be noted that a number of important amendments were made to the constitutions at the chapter general of Calatayud in 1593, and in the *acta* confirmed by Clement VIII the following year.

[255] Vázquez Núñez, *Manual*, II, p. 44. On the reception and training of novices, see Vázquez Fernández, 'La formación en las diversas constituciones', pp. 335–8.

[256] ACA, Mon., vol. 2659, f. 64r.

[257] *Regula et Constitutiones Fratrum Sacri Ordinis Beatae Mariae de Mercede Redemptionis Captivorum* (Salamanca: Cornelius Bonardus, 1588, 4°). The contents of this volume are as follows: (i) Zumel's *De Initio ac Fundatione sacri ordinis...*, pp. 1–23; (ii) the Rule of St Augustine, pp. 23–52 and (iii) the constitutions, pp. 53–190. Bound into the same vol. is (iv) the *Instructio Officiorum Ordinis...*, the new office, pp. 1–57, and finally (v) Zumel's *De Vitis Patrum et Magistrorum Generalium Ordinis [...] Brevis historia*, pp. 59–135.

[258] See Zumel, *De Initio*, pp. 2–9, and *De Vitis Patrum*, pp. 61–71, where Nolasch's role is more firmly expressed.

[259] *Id.*, *De Initio*, p. 4, and *De Vitis Patrum*, p. 61.

[260] *Id.*, *De Initio*, p. 4, and *De Vitis Patrum*, p. 85.

this time the Order, being still in its infancy, adhered closely to the rigour of its foundation'.[261]

With the Amer statutes reckoned to be the last tangible connection with the Patriarch and his supposedly military brotherhood, the Albertine constitutions, revoked in 1574 and now superseded by Zumel's new legislation, gradually receded in importance. This did not, however, prevent Zumel saluting Albert as a fellow reformer and administrator, or lauding the provisions he set out in them for the redemption of captives, *Christo Iesu Salvatori assimilatur*.[262] But, beyond what the Catalans had been able to salvage for themselves during the 1580s, the institutional core of the past had been swept away and on this basis Mercedarians looked to the creation of a new religious life, a new spirituality, and a new Order.

Not surprisingly, the optimism of the chapter general of Zaragoza was not shared in Catalonia.[263] Angry at the continued abuse of its traditional privileges, the priory launched itself into a final campaign to prevent Salazar's confirmation in Rome.[264] By August 1587 Fra Pere

---

[261] Guimerán, *Breve historia*, p. 201; see also p. 196.

[262] Zumel, *De Initio*, p. 13, and *De Vitis Patrum*, p. 98. His contemporary Guimerán is much less restrained, tacitly associating the 1588 constitutions with Albert's legislative framework; see *Breve historia*, pp. 219–20, esp. 220. However, the concern to associate the origins of the Mercedarian constitution with the primordial Order caused Albert's role to be marginalized in the early 17th century. This endeavour was founded on the assumption among Mercedarian chroniclers of the essential continuity of the 1588 constitutions with respect to the medieval legislation of the Order; discussed in González Castro, 'Las constituciones del P. Raimundo Albert', pp. 139–46. Already by 1618 Remón was minimizing the differences between the Amer and Albertine legislation; *Historia*, I, f. 228r. In his *Chronica* published the following year Vargas portrayed Albert as having merely gathered all earlier statutes into one corpus of legislation and translated them into Latin; *Chronica*, I, p. 149. Tirso, writing, in the mid 1630s, implies likewise; *Historia*, I, p. 250. In 1646 Salmerón claimed that Albert was responsible only for obtaining the confirmation of a set of statutes already drafted by Amer in the 13th century; *Recuerdos Historicos*, p. 151. It is unconvincing to attribute this progression entirely to confusion among chroniclers. The promulgation of a totally new set of constitutions in eight distinctions in 1692 may well have provided the basis for a restoration of Albert's role during the following century; see Estevan, *Symbolo de la Concepción de María*, p. 286.

[263] See ASV, NS, vol. 33, ff. 342r–343v, & vol. 34, ff. 28r–31v, Nuncio Cesare Spacciani to Cardinal Rusticucci, Sixtus V's secretary, Madrid, 4th August & 12th November 1587 respectively.

[264] See AHCB, ms. A-266, Antillón, *Memorias*, II, ff. 39v–43r. Requests to Sixtus V for Salazar's confirmation survive from Bobadilla and Philip in AMAE, leg. 34, f. 68r & 49r, Zaragoza, 23rd May & Madrid, 27th June 1587 respectively. See also ASV, NS, vol. 33, f. 351r, Spacciani to Rusticucci, Madrid, 17th August 1587, & AMAE, leg. 34, f. 64r, conde de Chinchón, president of the Council of Aragon, to Olivares, Madrid, 2nd February 1588.

Pau Lleó had returned to Italy and the *Consell* was again appealing to the papacy on the priory's behalf.[265] However, it was soon apparent that the Catalan cause could not be revived in Rome, particularly since the departure of Pujades the year before.[266] Salazar was confirmed in October, but matters dragged on until the following April when the papacy issued a brief underlining its judgement on the *locus* question.[267] With reconciliation in the air, the *Consell* finally withdrew its support having spent a reputed 70,000 *escudos* on the Mercedarian cause, and in July 1588 Salazar celebrated a chapter provincial in Valencia attended by representatives of almost every house in Catalonia.(2v,47r)[268] Among a range of familiar ordinances, the delegates were enjoined to observe Zumel's newly printed constitutions and destroy all earlier legislation.[269] Only Barcelona held out. Resistance finally collapsed after attempts to elect a prior provoked a second brief in which the main offenders were singled out for severe punishment.(43r–v)[270] In March 1589, two conventuals made their way to Zaragoza to give their unconditional obedience to the general in a ceremony witnessed by representatives of the *Consell*.(47r–v) The institutional reform of the Mercedarian Order was, for now at least, complete.

Though the Catalans had been defeated, the travails of the Order were not over. Already in December 1588 Salazar had secretly obtained from the papacy a brief dispensing him from calling the obligatory mid-term chapter general at Calatayud in 1590.(59v–64r)

---

[265] See AHCB, CC, CCO, vol. 49, f. 184r, Barcelona, 10th August 1587, & ACA, Mon., vol. 2837, p. 87, Barcelona, 30th October 1587. An appeal from the *Consell* to the crown is in *ibid.*, vol. 2832, p. 207, Barcelona, 28th October 1587.

[266] AHCB, CC, CCO, vol. 49, f. 188r–v. Lleó to *Consell*, Rome, 20th September 1587.

[267] On the confirmation, see APV, Antillón, ms. *Epitome*, 'III', §22. A further appeal from the *Consell* is ASV, NS, vol. 38, ff. 84v–85r, Barcelona, 30th January 1588. The brief, dated 26th April 1588, also confirmed the new constitutions: see BNM, ms. 6140, ff. 115r–116v, and a printed version, AGN, Clero, vol. 402. The date of this brief is sometimes incorrectly given as 26th April 1589; see Linás, *Bullarium*, pp. 164–5.

[268] The *synodalia* are in ACA, Mon., vol. 2659, ff. 58r–67v, Valencia, 1st–7th July 1588. See also a letter from Salazar in ASZ, carp. 165, no. 135, Valencia, 6th June 1588.

[269] ACA, Mon., vol. 2659, f. 64r. The constitutions were confirmed that year.

[270] For details of a reconciliation in Girona, see ASV, NS, vol. 37, f. 272r, Cardona to Spacciani, Girona, 7th October 1587. The brief, which appears to date from October 1588, was sent to Juan Teres, archbishop of Tarragona, for execution. See ASZ, carp. 165, no. 134, Teres to Philip II, Tarragona(?), 26th June 1588, & ASV, NS, vol. 34, ff. 593r–598v, Spacciani to Cardinal Montalto, Madrid, 17th November 1588; f. 594v.

Aiming no doubt to secure re-election as general in 1593, Salazar set about weakening the provinces of Andalusia and Castile through a policy of divide and rule. Naturally enough, this provoked a furious reaction throughout Castile, not least from the king who despaired of ever reducing this order to obedience.[271] Though evidently relieved at the election of his favoured candidate for the generalcy — Fray Francisco Zumel — in 1593, Philip ordered his ambassador in Rome to prevent the issue of any papal decrees

> without my intercession as patron of the Order […] so that with this they may attend to the government and observance of their Order without dabbling in those stratagems that have brought it such harm.[272]

The Mercedarian prelacy had finally been made aware of the higher authority to which it had become directly responsible; reminded, as Philip thundered, that they could no longer treat their Order 'as if it were their own patrimony'.[273]

XIII. *A Last Throw of the Dice*

The coda to this chapter lies, perhaps, in Italy. The process of Mercedarian Reform, as we have seen, was shaped as much by the involvement of the papacy as the sponsorship of the crown and the support of the Catalan institutions. Equally, the eventual victory of the reformist party owed much to the establishment of a permanent presence in both Madrid and Rome from the 1560s. Though the generals had periodically maintained *procuradores* in Rome since the mid fifteenth century, it was during the reform period that the need for constant representation became a priority for both sides in the conflict. Where the reformers were concerned, this development coincides with the expansion and renewal of the Order in Italy through the efforts of Castilian religious after 1569.[274] In that year the

---

[271] See IVDJ, env. 43, caja 56, f. 405r–v, *Memorial* of the *Junta de Noche* to Philip II, Madrid, 27th March 1593; AMAE, SS, leg. 34, ff. 51r–v (another copy 52r–v) & 53r–v, Philip II to duque de Sessa, El Escorial, 10th July & El Pardo, 13th November 1593 respectively.

[272] AMAE, SS, leg. 34, f. 51v.

[273] *Ibid.*, f. 53r.

[274] Though officially part of the Order's Aragonese patrimony, the Italian houses had traditionally been subject to the direct authority of the general and were governed by his vicar. Foundations made in Italy from the 1570s onwards were added to

chapter provincial of Castile dispatched Fray Juan Ordóñez to reform the convent at Naples, and it was he who, in the early 1570s, founded the first Mercedarian house in Rome at Santa Ruffina in Trastevere.[275] Beyond providing its *procuradores* with a base for their activities, this foundation, which purported to represent the Order as a whole, afforded the reformist cause a patina of legitimacy denied its Catalan opponents. However, by the time Salazar dispatched the Valencian Mº Fray Francisco de Torres to Rome as his *procurador general* and vicar general in Italy in 1587, it was clear that existing facilities were no longer adequate.(41v) Under Torres' influence, Santa Ruffina was abandoned in 1589 for the ancient basilica of San Adriano in the Forum, which remained in the custody of the Order until the early part of this century.[276]

However, these were not the only houses founded in Italy during the reign of Philip II, and neither were reformists the only religious to settle there. Frightened and disaffected Catalan friars had been appearing here since the Mercedarian conflict had intensified in the 1570s. By 1579 Maldonado was complaining to the papacy at the number of dispensations being granted to Catalans to leave the Order.[277] A few years later Suárez reported that half a dozen conventuals of Barcelona had arrived in Rome seeking permission to change orders to escape the retribution of their enemies.[278] However, Italy also offered sanctuary for those who wished to remain as Mercedarians after the defeat of the priory of Barcelona, yet refused to live under the 1588 settlement. Fearing the wrath of the authorities, in that year the veteran Catalan procurator Fra Pere Pau Lleó left Barcelona never to return.(44r–v,46v) Within a few years he had founded a small house at Rocca di Papa outside Rome over which he presided as superior until his death in 1626. Details of this movement survive in the *Lignum Vitae* of the Flemish Benedictine Arnold Wion, a description of the orders and congregations derived from the tradition of St Benedict.[279] According to Wion,

the Aragonese province, except in the case of Rome which remained a dependency of the generals even after the foundation of the province of Italy first in 1606 and then in 1619.

[275] See ACA, Mon., vol. 2836, f. 195v. There had, however, been hostels here at different times.
[276] *Ibid.*, ff. 195v–197r. See also Linás, *Bullarium*, pp. 162–4 & 165.
[277] ASV, NS, vol. 22, f. 42r.
[278] AMAE, SS, leg. 34, f. 143r, Suárez to Olivares, undated but Rome, *c.*1584.
[279] Two vols. (Venice: Georgium Angelerium, 1595, 4°), I, ch. 86, pp. 120–2.

in 1593 two disaffected Catalan Mercedarians had taken lodging in the abbey of San Giorgio Maggiore not far from Rome. These declared the Mercedarians to have been founded as a military order under the Rule of St Benedict until this was replaced in 1230 by that of St Augustine.[280] As against their 'clerical' brethren in Spain who allegedly followed the latter, the Catalans described themselves as the only Mercedarians still living under the Benedictine observance of the military fathers of the Order, and gave a spurious profession formula as proof of this.[281]

The tendency to view the origins of the Order as part military was, as we have seen, shared by Zumel in Castile.[282] The notion was further developed by Guimerán in his highly tendentious *Breve Historia*: 'la orden de nuestra Señora de la Merced es orden militar, y de caballeria'.[283] The basis for this interpretation would seem to rest partly in tradition, partly in a wilful misreading of the 1272 statutes, combined with a desire to appeal to the militant spirituality of the age. However, this outward stress on the laic origins of the Order ran counter to the markedly clericalizing aims of the Mercedarian hierarchy at the close of the sixteenth century. The increased proportion of ordained religious during the reform period had gone hand in hand with a steady erosion of the rights of their lay brethren in conventual life.[284] At the chapters general of 1596 and 1599 *hermanos legos* were not only denied their traditional vote and status in conventual affairs, but barred from entering the Order in the future. It is a further testament to the strength of the Mercedarian laic tradition that the brethren were able to establish an organized opposition to this policy not only at the convent-college of Huesca in Aragon, but throughout the province of Andalusia.[285] In 1602 the Aragonese leader of the brethren, Fray Gaspar Amade, appeared in Rome protesting against the ordinances and claiming, like the Catalans in 1593, that they

---

[280] *Ibid.*, p. 121. A precedent for this may be the adoption by the Clare house of Sant Antoni in Barcelona of the Benedictine rule in 1512 after attempts to reduce it to the Franciscan Observance. See P.Fr. Tarsicio de Azcona, 'Paso del monasterio de Santa Clara de Barcelona a la Regla Benedictina (1512–1518)' in *Collectanea Franciscana*, 38 (1968), pp. 68–134.

[281] Wion, *Lignum Vitae*, I, p. 122.

[282] See Zumel, *De Initio*, p. 20, and *De Vitis Patrum*, p. 68.

[283] *Op. cit.*, p. 47.

[284] See P.Fr. Ramón Serratosa Queralt, 'La leyenda del sacerdocio de San Pedro Nolasco' in *BOM*, 14 (1926), pp. 69–73, 101–2, 134–6 & 165–6; esp. 69–71.

[285] *Ibid.*, p. 73.

alone were the rightful successors of the lay fathers of the Order.[286] Although the capitular decrees were upheld by Clement VIII, recognition of the traditional role of the brethren caused many of them to be revoked soon after and *hermanos legos* have continued to play their part in Mercedarian conventual life.[287]

In Catalonia the threat presented by a Castilian-led campaign of reform had afforded this laic tradition an added dimension. In 1579 Lleó had written urging the conventuals of Barcelona to search the priory archive for a primordial observance that would efface all others. Lack of Mercedarian sources clearly obliged the religious to look further afield, as the copy of the 'constituziones del orden de santiago' found by Andreu and Puerta at Castelló d'Empuries in 1584, and the Benedictine expedient resorted to in Italy would perhaps indicate.[288] Here, then, is a last throw of the dice for the conventuals of Barcelona. The outcome of this chimerical venture, if Wion's account is to be trusted, reflects the efforts of Catalans to assert *their* interpretation of reform above all others.

---

[286] AHCB, ms. A-266, Antillón, *Memorias*, II, ff. 127r–128r.

[287] For successive ordinances passed on this issue at the chapters provincial of Valencia from 1603 onwards, see ARV, Clero, lib. 1705, esp. f. 8r–v (1603).

[288] ACA, Mon., vol. 2850, f. 52v. The copy in question could well have been *La regla de la orden de Santiago* (Alcalá de Henares: A. de Ángulo, 1565). It should be made clear that the military Order of Santiago observed the Rule of St Augustine and permitted its members to marry. In connection with this, see IVDJ, env. 17, ms. 26-II-21, ff. 18v–22v, 'De como fue instituida la Orden de Santiago con los maestros que ha habido, de la Orden de la Merced y de la orden de los caballeros de Cristo en Portugal'; undated but late 16th century.

CHAPTER EIGHT

A NEW ORDER (1593–1648)

Envied now rather than envious, with this our Order acquired the sta-
tus of the most eminent congregations [...] and after more than four
hundred years our glorious virgin patrons were reborn in the knowledge
of the faithful, and the veneration of the Church militant.[1]

In the half century or so following the accession of Fray Francisco
Zumel as general (1593–9) the Mercedarian Order developed into
one of the leading Spanish religious congregations. The reasons for
this lie as much in its past as in the unique circumstances that made
the later Habsburg period a golden age for the Spanish religious
Order as a whole. After centuries on the fringes of ecclesiastical life
and the prostration of the 1570s and '80s the Mercedarians now succeeded in carving a lasting niche for themselves in the spiritual, material, cultural and academic fabric of Spanish and colonial society. For
the first time the Order began to make its presence felt not only in
popular devotion and spirituality, but simultaneously in episcopal
candidature, in theological debate, in the highest literary, artistic and
intellectual circles, and finally in politics and government. In many
respects, however, the period remained one of painful adjustment for
an order completing the final phases of a process already at least thirty years in the making. It served to underline many of the enduring
problems of Mercedarian life: the conflict between the lay and clerical tendency in the Order, the spiritual disjuncture enshrined within
this, and the fact of provincial diversity and national allegiance. Carried over from the reign of Philip II, these and other elements were
resolved, confirmed or amplified in the decades that followed as the
Order took its place as a major public institution. However neglected
or disregarded the field as a whole, the scope of these issues — shared
by any one of seventy religious congregations — reminds us not only
of the complexity of the orders concerned but of the central role

---

[1] Tirso, *Historia*, II, p. 547, commenting on the beatification of San Pedro Nolasco
and San Ramón Nonato in 1628.

played by them in Spanish Habsburg society. It is this diversity that the following pages shall seek to explore.

I. *Jurisdiction and Realignment*

The seventeenth century, the greatest in its history, began inauspiciously for the Mercedarian Order. Following the stability of Zumel's generalate the Order again found itself plunged into crisis with the premature death of his successor, the Valencian Mc Fra Pere Balaguer, in December 1599. This was a serious setback for the united Aragonese province which already felt itself to be at a disadvantage with respect to the Castilian bloc and now faced the prospect of a further generalate from that congregation after only a year. The events surrounding the chapter general of Valencia called to elect Balaguer's successor the following May provide the clearest example yet of the bitter inter-provincial rivalry that continued to afflict the Order after its reunification under the 1588 constitutions. It also reflects the serious dysfunction in government that the Mercedarians had inherited from the past and to which they had as yet found no satisfactory answer.

Shortly before the chapter the prior of Barcelona and vicar general Mc Fra Bernat Papiol, a veteran of the troubles of the previous century, made his way to Zaragoza to confer with the influential former master, Fray Francisco de Salazar, now vicar provincial of the Crown of Aragon.[2] Here they agreed that the votes of their province be cast in favour of the Castilian M° Fray Francisco de Medina.[3] Medina was not only an ally of Salazar, who had appointed him his vicar general in Castile in 1588 in deliberate obstruction of Zumel's provincialcy; he had the virtue of being both old and infirm and was not reckoned to have much longer to live.(61v) With an early death the alternation of the generalcy would return to the eastern bloc and so redress the balance of power which the Aragonese rightly felt was being prised from their grasp. Of this there had already been warning signals. Basking in its huge revenues from the Indies, in 1593 the new province of Andalusia had attempted to gain precedence over that of

---

[2] See AHCB, ms. A-266, Antillón, *Memorias*, II, f. 93v. Where convenient, references to this MS will henceforth be made in the text.
[3] *Ibid.*, ff. 93v & 103v–104r. Antillón was a witness to this agreement.

France on the basis of Castile's own superiority.(75Av–75Br) The bid was rejected unanimously, but the die was cast and in 1599 a group of religious responded to the election of the Valencian Fra Pere Balaguer by petitioning the crown for the appointment of a commissary general to represent the American provinces in Spain exempt from his jurisdiction.[4] The office, which was to be modelled on that established by the Franciscans of Castile as a measure against foreign intervention, received the support of the Council of the Indies but was rejected in Rome as grossly prejudicial of the masters' authority.[5] There can be no doubt that during his tenure as general (1587–93) the Aragonese Salazar had deeply antagonized the Andalusian province in particular, which withdrew its obedience in 1590 and made strenuous efforts to have him removed from office.[6] Balaguer, for his part, had moved against his enemies 'with implacable severity, aiming to crush them with a single blow'.[7] Even so, these initiatives reflect the increasingly aggressive stance taken by elements in the Kingdom of Castile against the privileges traditionally enjoyed by the oldest provinces in the Order and the authority of their generals. Henceforth, says Antillón, the Aragonese bloc undertook never to support an Andalusian for the generalcy, preferring Castilian candidates instead; and indeed it was 1632 before the Order elected its first Andalusian to the high office.(104r)

By the time the chapter general of Valencia opened under the presidency of Patriarch Ribera in May 1600, the ambitious provincial of Castile, M° Fray Pedro de Oña, and his Andalusian counterpart, M° Fray Luis de Heredia, had taken steps to forward their candidature in Rome and Madrid.[8] Heredia, alive to the mood of the curia, had attempted to garner support by portraying himself as a committed reformer.(94r–v) Oña, for his part, arrived at the chapter laden

---

[4] See ACA, Mon., vol. 2683, pp. 47–8. At Valladolid in 1599 M° Fray Pedro de Oña, provincial of Castile, attempted unsuccessfully to secure precedence for his province at chapters general held in Castile; see Tirso, *Historia*, II, p. 216. On the commissary issue, see *ibid.*, p. 218.

[5] See Salmerón, *Recuerdos Historicos*, pp. 286–7.

[6] AHCB, ms. A-266, Antillón, *Memorias*, II, ff. 60r–68r. The root of this opposition appears to have been Salazar's appointment of P° Fray Francisco de Vera as visitor general of Andalusia, in deliberate obstruction of M° Fray Juan de Ribas' authority as provincial; Tirso, *Historia*, II, p. 144.

[7] Tirso, *Historia*, II, p. 218.

[8] See AHCB, ms. A-266, Antillón, *Memorias*, II, f. 94r–v, and, for the chapter, ff. 101r–104v & Tirso, *Historia*, II, pp. 247–9.

with 'cartas de Principes y Titulados', though his suit was soon dashed in a welter of calumny from his own province.[9] Ribera, with thirty years' experience of the Order behind him, watched with disgust as his own candidate, the saintly Mº Fray Juan Bernal of Seville, was rejected by the delegates 'because it seemed to them that his would be a very rigid government'.[10] With the Castilian bloc riven by strife and faction, Francisco de Medina, the new provincial of Castile, was elected to the high office with the weight of Aragonese support behind him. Incensed at this, Oña and others left for Madrid before the proceedings were over and there presented Philip III with a *memorial* declaring Medina to have been simoniacally elected. The king transferred the matter to the new nuncio, Domenico Ginnasio, and before Medina had concluded his business in Valencia a brief was issued suspending him from office. An unsuspecting Medina left for Madrid on 5th June, and it was in the middle of a field not far from Guadalajara that he finally received news of his deposition.[11] From here he made his way as ordered to Huete to await developments while the nuncio carried out a full investigation of the circumstances surrounding the election. One of Oña's supporters, the distinguished Andalusian preacher Mº Fray Hernando de Santiago, was sent to Zaragoza as commissary apostolic with orders to search the convent of San Lázaro for evidence incriminating Salazar and others in complicity to elect Medina.(105r) By the time Medina was permitted to resume his journey after three weeks' confinement, a full *proceso* had been brought against him in Madrid.(104v) Salazar, Papiol and others were summoned to answer a series of accusations, but against them no action appears to have been taken.(105v)

Although exonerated of complicity in the scandal, Ginnasio refused to reinstate Medina and turned instead to the appointment of a vicar general to govern during the interregnum. The matter was complicated by the fact that the rightful incumbent, the newly elected prior of Barcelona, Mᵉ Fra Montserrat Ausias, had yet to receive his

---

[9] AHCB, ms. A-266, Antillón, *Memorias*, II, ff. 101v–102r; the citation is at f. 101v.

[10] *Ibid.*, f. 101v & Tirso, *Historia*, II, p. 248. Bernal is among those depicted in Francisco Pacheco's *Libro de descripcion de verdaderos retratos, de ilustres y memorables varones* completed in Seville in 1599; facs. edn. by Pedro M. Piñero Ramírez & Rogelio Reyes Cano (Seville, 1985), f. 1r.

[11] Tirso, *Historia*, II, p. 249. For a somewhat different version of events, see P. Quintín Pérez, *Fr. Hernando de Santiago, predicador del Siglo de Oro (1575–1639)* (Madrid, 1949), p. 41.

confirmation. However, on 1st August Ginnasio went ahead on his own authority and appointed the provincial of Andalusia, M° Fray Luis de Heredia, vicar general apostolic of the Order, removing Medina definitively in the process.(106r) In Rome, meanwhile, Cardinal Aldobrandino, the papal secretary, saw to the issue of a brief confirming Medina's deposition and affording Ginnasio wide powers to resolve the matter.[12] Heredia's appointment was confirmed in October in a brief issued by Ginnasio himself, with which all provinces granted the vicar general their obedience.[13] Protests continued against the background of feverish diplomacy among the various *procuradores* in Rome, but the curia was not to be swayed and by the end of 1601 Ginnasio was contemplating the selection of a new general.(108r–109r) Interest once again centred on Fray Juan Bernal, whose candidature was pressed by Clement VIII and Philip III's confessor, the Dominican M° Fray Gaspar de Córdoba.(119v–121r) The pope eventually left the matter in Ginnasio's hands with the sole proviso that he make his choice with Córdoba's agreement. In November 1601, however, Bernal's death removed the leading candidate, and tempers began to fray in the Order as it became obvious that the next general would not be elected but appointed. As interest began to centre on the new provincial of Andalusia, P° Fray Alonso de Monroy, in August 1602 a number of senior religious appealed to the king as patron of the Order to uphold its constitutional right to elect its own general.[14] Philip duly wrote to the pope, but it was clearly far too late and on 26th August Ginnasio secretly appointed Monroy master general of the Order.[15] A torrent of protests followed both in Rome and at court, where Heredia complained bitterly to the Royal Council of Castile. However, there was nothing to be done and on 14th October 1602 Monroy was confirmed in the high office until Pentecost 1609 with full powers to punish all dissenters.

The reasons for Monroy's appointment are far from clear, but it is hard to attribute the marked rise in his standing at court to merit

---

[12] AHCB, ms. A-266, Antillón, *Memorias*, II, f. 107r. The brief was dated 21st August 1600.

[13] *Ibid.*, f. 107v; dated Madrid, 29th October 1600.

[14] *Ibid.*, f. 122r–v. The protest was dated Madrid, 7th August 1602. Plague caused the transfer of the chapter provincial of Andalusia from Seville to Monroy's own estate at Ginés outside the city. Monroy was elected here on 4th May 1602; *ibid.*, f. 119r.

[15] *Ibid.*, f. 123r–v. His appointment as general was made public in Valladolid on 23rd September 1602.

alone.[16] During the 1590s he had served as Zumel's vicar general in Peru and returned to his native Seville having amassed a vast fortune in bullion.[17] From this time on Monroy undertook the lavish reconstruction and decoration of the Seville convent, and there can be no doubt that he was extremely well placed to advance his candidature in Madrid. The preference for an Andalusian, no doubt to counterbalance the overbearing influence of Castilians at court, is apparent from the beginning, with the interest in Bernal being followed by the appointment of Heredia as vicar general. Whatever the case may be, it seems that the nuncio saw in Monroy a tractable and reform-minded figure who would govern the Order in a style amenable both to the papacy and the crown. As the general apparently promised Clement VIII shortly after his appointment, once the Order had been reformed under his leadership it would embark on a rigorous observance of its rule and constitutions.[18] For the time being, however, the Mercedarians had much to ponder where their status and position was concerned.

The nature of Monroy's accession represents a further milestone in the evolving relationship of the Order with higher authority. The appointment was, in its way, quite unprecedented, even during the crises of recent decades.[19] After the severe disturbances of Salazar's tenure, for instance, Philip II had informed the chapter general of Calatayud in 1593 that the election of Zumel alone was acceptable to the crown. The king's wishes were met, but the increased influence of the nuncios after his death in 1598 is apparent in the appointment by Ginnasio's predecessor, Camillo Caetani, of the bishop of Valladolid as president of the chapter general celebrated there in May of the following year.[20] Although this appears to have been at the request of a number of the delegates, impositions of this sort were widely regarded as intrusions from which reformed orders could expect themselves to be exempt.[21] In light of this, Ginnasio's appointment of an Andalusian *presentado*, Fray Juan de Santofimia, as president of the Castilian

---

[16] For the circumstances under which Monroy came to Ginnasio's notice, see *ibid.*, ff. 120v–121v, & Tirso, *Historia*, II, pp. 266–77.

[17] Tirso, *Historia*, II, p. 265.

[18] *Ibid.*, p. 270.

[19] The high office had, however, been subject first to episcopal and then papal jurisdiction throughout much of the 14th century, and as late as 1441 the Castilian Fray Pedro de Huete was appointed general under the authority of a bishop.

[20] Tirso, *Historia*, II, p. 215. The bishop in question was Bartolomé de la Plaza.

[21] See the *synodalia* of the chapter in ACA, Mon., vol. 2683, pp. 37–8.

assembly at Burgos in April 1600, and then of Ribera at Valencia in May, no doubt came as particularly unwelcome developments.[22] But never before had a nuncio imposed a general on the Order on his own authority, not least because of the serious infringement of royal jurisdiction that this implied. The fact that he could do so reflects the changed approach of the Lerma regime to religious affairs within Spain, for in this respect Philip II was destined to have no successor as an ecclesiastical meddler. Where such blatant intrusion on the part of a papal representative would have been unthinkable during the previous reign, the government was now satisfied to leave matters of this sort to the nuncio in consultation with a royal agent.[23] However, this state of affairs is itself a legacy of Philip's reign, during which the crown reluctantly admitted the need for direct apostolic assistance if it was to fulfil its programme of ecclesiastical reform. From the 1570s onwards the nunciature therefore established an indispensable mediating and then executive role for itself as Philip's unwieldy reform policies began to break down through mismanagement and appeal to Rome.[24] In Rome, too, the king's death allowed the *Congregazione di Vescovi i Regolari*, which had played an increasingly significant part in Mercedarian reform since the 1580s, to establish itself as the ultimate arbiter of Spanish monastic affairs.[25]

However, the measures taken against the Mercedarian Order following the chapter general of Valencia in 1600 also reflect profound irritation in both royal and papal circles at the parade of scandal and conflict that had marked its progress for thirty years. After Salazar's refusal to celebrate an intermediary chapter general in 1590, the dishonesty surrounding Medina's election at Valencia clearly brought the authorities to the end of their tether where the Order was concerned. Found incapable of managing its affairs in a respectable manner, the Order now forfeited the right to elect its general and had to suffer the humiliation of having one foisted upon it. As Antillón explained,

---

[22] Tirso, *Historia*, II, pp. 234–5 & 248.

[23] The increased influence of the nuncios is reflected in the attempt by Giovanni Garzia Millino (1605–7) while presiding over the chapter general of Madrid in 1606 to have the next chapter celebrated in Rome; see Vázquez Núñez, *Manual*, II, p. 92.

[24] I am grateful to Ignasi Fernández Terricabras for generously sharing the fruit of his researches with me on this matter.

[25] The *Congregazione* was established through a brief of Sixtus V on 17th May 1586. Its influence owes much to its first prefect, the Dominican Fra Michele Bonelli, Cardinal Alessandrino, a nephew of Pius V.

the pope upheld the nuncio's decision, declaring that in electing badly the Order had lost the right to elect at all, and that this right had
thereby devolved on him [i.e. the nuncio], who was fully aware of the
action to be taken in this matter — that is, that a religious be
appointed from the Order itself to see to its reformation and good
government.[26]

The effect in the Order was a reassessment of the ties that bound it to
the poles of patronage and authority in Rome and Madrid, and a
belated recognition of the fundamental duty of outward dignity and
probity required of a major religious institution. In this respect the
Order would never be the same again.

II. *Patronage and Advancement*

The rise of the Order in the seventeenth century cannot be understood without reference to its increasing involvement in patronage
networks at court, among the provincial aristocracy and urban élites
of Andalusia in particular, and in Rome where a permanent presence
was established in 1587. In this light, the foundation of the convent of
Madrid in 1564 represents not only a key moment in the fortunes of
the province of Castile, but of the Order as a whole, though it was
one not destined to come to fruition for many years. Except in
Barcelona and Valencia, the stench of scandal and corruption that
permeated the farthest reaches of the Order during the 1570s and
'80s prevented the development of any lasting ties of patronage, and
it was not until the 1590s that the Mercedarians began to restore and
extend the contacts lost and discouraged in former years.[27] However,
once the brethren began to get their house in order, particularly in
the matter of the redemption of captives, recovery and then expan-

---

[26] AHCB, ms. A-266, Antillón, *Memorias*, II, f. 120r. The citation is a paraphrase of
a letter from Clement VIII to an unnamed Mercedarian — possibly Heredia. See
also Tirso, *Historia*, II, p. 266.
[27] In Barcelona the Cofraria de Nostra Senyora de la Soletat, which included
nobles among its members, had been founded by 1606; see Gazulla, *La Patrona de
Barcelona*, pp. 265–6, & especially AUB, ms. 753, no. 28, ff. 103r–106r: 'Informacion
abierta en la curia episcopal de Barcelona acerca de la cofradia B. M. de la Soletat
de la Merce', dated Barcelona, 18th July 1606. In Valencia, meanwhile, the period
1566–1600 saw a significant increase in donations and bequests before dropping off
markedly in the first decade of the 17th century; see ARV, Clero, lib. 2147, ff.
64r–78v.

sion came extraordinarily quickly. Until the seventeenth century Mercedarians had only exceptionally found themselves at the centre of government, and very few can be reckoned to have wielded significant influence beyond the Order itself.[28] Though royal and noble patronage was hardly unknown, the brethren had traditionally found their staunchest supporters in the mercantile classes and among the ordinary people in town and country from whom the majority of their alms and personnel were drawn. By the 1590s, however, the wealth, position and expertise of a hitherto untapped resource in the Spanish Church had come to notice, and in this way Mercedarians began to gain access to the circles of power and influence that had formerly been closed to them.

One of the first signs of a revival in patronage comes in 1594 with the foundation of a house in the Extremaduran town of Trujillo by Francisca Pizarro, marquesa de Charcas. The donation was made in recognition of the important services rendered by the Mercedarians in Peru to her father the *conquistador* Francisco Pizarro, 'que tan devoto fue siempre desta Orden'.[29] The Order's distinctive vocation and long involvement in the colonization of America made it a popular choice for the new Andalusian nobility enriched by the Indies trade. In the early 1590s the house at Écija was granted an endowment of 100 *escudos* per year by Luis de Aguilar in return for the *patronazgo* of the province of Andalusia and the undertaking that henceforth all its chapters be celebrated there.[30] In Seville, the convent of La Asunción received the profession of Doña Felipa Enríquez, duquesa de Arcos,

---

[28] Among these were the Catalan general Fra Antoní Caixal, ambassador of Ferran I of Aragon (1412–16) at the Council of Constance; the Galician Fray Diego de Muros, chaplain of Henry IV and envoy of Isabella the Catholic, and a lesser-known figure, the Catalan Fra Antoni Blasi, a trusted confidant of Juan I of Aragon (1379–90) and archbishop of Athens and bishop of Cagliari. For Caixal, see Fr Conrad Eubel, *Die Avignonesische Obedienz der Mendikanten-Orden, sowie der Orden der Mercedarier und Trinitarier zur Zeit des grossen Schismus: Beleuchtet durch die von Clemens VII. und Benedict XIII. an dieselben gerichteten Schreiben* (Paderborn, 1900), and for Blasi, or Blas, Vázquez Núñez, *Mercedarios ilustres*, pp. 71–5, Kenneth M. Setton, *The Papacy and the Levant (1204–1571)* (4 vols., Philadelphia, 1976–84), I, p. 464, & Brodman, 'Ransomers or Royal Agents', p. 249.

[29] On this house, of which Tirso de Molina was commendator between 1626–9, see P.Fr. Luis Vázquez Fernández, 'Los Pizarros, la Merced, el convento de Trujillo (Cáceres) y Tirso' in *Estudios*, 40 (1984), pp. 203–427, & Vázquez Núñez, 'Conventos de la Orden', pp. 156–7; citation p. 156.

[30] Tirso, *Historia*, II, p. 201. The agreement was the cause of a serious dispute in the province in 1598, but appears to have been resolved with alternate chapters being celebrated here from 1594 onwards; see *ibid.*, p. 540.

and within a few years the Order had attracted the patronage of the flower of the Andalusian nobility, including the dukes of Medina Sidonia and the condesa de Castellar.[31] However, it was at court that the improved standing of the Order bore the most significant fruit. By 1600 the provincial of Castile, M° Fray Pedro de Oña, had established contacts high in the Lerma government, including with the principal secretary Pedro Franqueza, subsequently conde de Villalonga.[32] These did not avail Oña in his attempt to become general at Valencia that year, but they provided him with the means to destroy Medina and then secure the episcopate that would deliver him from the wrath of his enemies.[33] Through the offices of Franqueza Oña obtained the bishopric of Venezuela in 1601, though he turned it down two years later in favour of Gaeta in the Kingdom of Naples, this 'so as to spare himself the perils of the Ocean' snorted Tirso, himself a veteran of the Atlantic crossing.[34]

Despite the increasing profile of the Order at court, voices had for some time been raised against the prevalence and worldly entanglements of senior religious in Madrid.[35] In 1600 the Castilian M° Fray Juan de Peñacerrada appealed to the *Congregazione di Vescovi i Regolari* in Rome to limit the amount of time spent by the generals in Madrid to twenty days per year.[36] However, this was rejected after vehement protests by the Andalusian *procurador general*, M° Fray Bernardo de Vargas, who condemned it as a blatant attempt to obstruct the free access of non-Castilian generals to the court. A few months later the chapter general of Valencia turned instead on the provincials of Castile and Andalusia, restricting their presence in Madrid and Seville respectively to two months per year.[37] But this was never observed, and Oña's favoured position at court appears to have been taken by his ally, the Andalusian preacher Fray Hernando de Santiago. When the court transferred to Valladolid in 1601 Monroy saw to the appointment of Santiago as commendator of the Mercedarian house there the following year, a move which infuriated the Castil-

---

[31] *Ibid.*, p. 213.
[32] *Ibid.*, pp. 229 & 247.
[33] *Ibid.*, pp. 248 & 250. See also Vázquez Núñez, *Mercedarios ilustres*, pp. 402–6.
[34] Tirso, *Historia*, II, p. 251.
[35] See, for example, AHN, Clero, vol. 3320, f. 51r–v (1584), *ibid.*, f. 73v (1588), AHCB, ms. A-266, Antillón, *Memorias*, II, f. 65r (1590), & ACA, Mon., vol. 2683, p. 23 (1593).
[36] Tirso, *Historia*, II, pp. 230–1.
[37] ACA, Mon., vol. 2683, p. 54.

ians.[38] In 1603 Santiago dedicated his *Santoral* to Lerma and two years later was dispatched to Rome on confidential royal business with a stipend of 400 *reales* per annum.[39] At court, meanwhile, Monroy retained the unswerving support of Ginnasio, his successors, and the royal confessor Fray Gaspar de Córdoba against all attempts to unseat him. The Mercedarians had finally 'arrived' in Habsburg court society.[40]

In the decades that followed the Mercedarian generalate greatly extended its patronage connections and therefore its usefulness to the crown. By 1620 the Sardinian general M° Fray Ambrosio Machín (1618–22) had established himself as an important preacher at court enjoying close relations with the royal family, which he once hosted at a *merienda* in the convent of Madrid.[41] His successor, the Castilian M° Fray Gaspar Prieto (1622–7), cultivated links with the Olivares regime which he supported as a delegate at the *cortes* of Monzón and Valencia in 1626.[42] Despite his differences with the Count-Duke, Prieto was appointed bishop of Alghero in 1627 and then captain-general of Sardinia in 1631, the highest royal office gained by a Mercedarian since the fifteenth century.[43]

For senior members of the Mercedarian hierarchy the connections established at court and in Rome from the 1590s onwards now offered the opportunity of an episcopal career after the conclusion of their prelacy in the Order, one that, at the very least, might allow them to escape the vengeance of their enemies in old age. As Tirso wrote of Fray Pedro de Oña, and no doubt from bitter experience himself, 'victorious over his enemies and unwilling to tempt fate a second time in conventual society, which is an even trickier environment, he negotiated for himself the bishopric of Venezuela, in the Indies...'.[44] If Oña was the first to benefit in this way from the

---

[38] Pérez, *Fr. Hernando de Santiago*, p. 42.

[39] *Ibid.*, pp. 42 & 45. The full title of the *Santoral* is *Consideraciones sobre los Evangelios de los Santos* (Madrid: Pedro Madrigal, 1603).

[40] Tirso, *Historia*, II, pp. 297–8.

[41] Vázquez Núñez, *Manual*, II, p. 120.

[42] *Id., Mercedarios ilustres*, pp. 436–7 & Tirso, *Historia*, II, pp. 492–3. Prieto published two *memoriales* supporting Olivares' 'Union of Arms': *Allegationes duae in materia celebrationis comitiorum quae Cortes Generales audiunt pro Philipo Rege Quarto* (Madrid: ?, 1626); see Placer López, *Bibliografía mercedaria*, II, p. 551.

[43] Vázquez Núñez, *Manual*, II, p. 126.

[44] Tirso, *Historia*, II, p. 251. He was not, of course, the first Mercedarian bishop; this honour falls to Fra Antoni Blasi, archbishop of Athens (1388–92) and bishop of Cagliari (1403–14).

improved standing of the Order at court then he was by no means the last, and from now on Mercedarians began to gain episcopal appointments with a regularity unprecedented in its history. In 1610, after a succession of suffragan and titular appointments, the *indiano* M° Fray Alonso Enríquez de Armendáriz, a former vicar general of Peru, obtained the bishopric of Santiago de Cuba through the patronage of the conde de Lemos.[45] He was followed by the Andalusian redemptor M° Fray Francisco de Vera who was appointed to the diocese of Elna in 1613.[46]

However, it was through the generalate that the Order was most affected by the episcopal opportunities now open to its hierarchy. Each of the six Mercedarian generals from Monroy's successor, the Valencian M° Fray Felipe de Guimerán (1609–15), to the Andalusian M° Fray Diego Serrano (1632–5) succeeded to an episcopal appointment. Monroy himself turned down the archbishopric of Puerto Rico and retired to his private estate at Ginés near Seville.[47] Impressive though this sequence is, the impact on the Order as a whole was very severe, for of the generals involved between 1615 and 1635 only one — Guimerán — completed his tenure before taking up the appointment. This circumstance not only disrupted the synchronized pattern of chapters general and provincial, it exposed the Order to what had consistently been the most volatile period in its cycle of government: the vacancy of the generalate.[48] In 1617, for instance, the Order was again thrown into a serious conflict over the traditional right of the priors of Barcelona to the office of vicar general during the vacancy following the presentation of the Castilian M° Fray Francisco de Ribera to the Mexican diocese of Guadalajara. The ongoing dispute, which had narrowly been avoided after the death of Balaguer in 1599, now reopened and was sustained through 1618 with a bitterness reminiscent of the previous century.[49] The rights of the priory of Barcelona were upheld, but much damage had been done between

---

[45] *Ibid.*, p. 280 & Vázquez Núñez, *Mercedarios ilustres*, pp. 411–12.

[46] Vázquez Núñez, *Manual*, II, p. 92.

[47] *Ibid.*

[48] As a measure against the savage infighting which characterized them, in 1621 the general M° Fray Ambrosio Machín secured an amendment to the constitutions whereby chapters provincial would be celebrated after the electoral chapter general rather than before it in the event of a vacancy; see AHCB, ms. A-266, Antillón, *Memorias*, II, ff. 421v–427v.

[49] On this episode, see *infra*. For the events following Balaguer's death, see AHCB, ms. A-266, Antillón, *Memorias*, II, ff. 92v–93r.

Ribera's acceptance of the bishopric in April 1617 and his abdication as general in January of the following year. To remedy this, in 1622 the chapter general of Zaragoza required generals to surrender the seals of office within eight days of their appointment as bishop, though the statute was rejected in Rome.[50] As a result, the delegates at Toledo in 1627 appealed that incumbents refrain from presenting their candidacy until the end of the tenure for which they had been elected.[51] Even so, the Order could not prevent a general accepting a bishopric if this were offered to him, and abdication of office continued to be a cause of serious disruption and inter-provincial strife.

Whatever its consequences for the Order, the reality of episcopal appointment owes much to the general increase in the number of mitred friars and monks in Spain from the late sixteenth century, and especially during the *privanza* of the duque de Lerma (1599–1618).[52] By the reign of Charles II (1665–1700) the proportion of Castilian episcopal sees held by religious had risen to 36% of the total, up threefold from the 1570s and with the Mercedarian representation exceeded only by that of the Franciscans and Dominicans.[53] However, it is equally the case that a university formation, and particularly training in theology, had become essential for preferment, and in this respect also the development of a major academic vocation in the Order during the sixteenth century proved the key to its success in the seventeenth.

III. *The Apogee of Mercedarian Scholarship*

It was against this background of expansion and readjustment that Gabriel Téllez — 'Tirso de Molina' — was recruited into the Order in Madrid in January 1600, at the age of nearly twenty-one.[54] Sent to

---

[50] Tirso, *Historia*, II, p. 484.

[51] Vázquez Núñez, *Manual*, II, p. 133.

[52] See Helen E. Rawlings, 'The Secularisation of Castilian Episcopal Office Under the Habsburgs, c.1516–1700' in *Journal of Ecclesiastical History*, 38 (1987), pp. 53–79, esp. 64 & 71.

[53] *Ibid.*, p. 78.

[54] Tirso, *Historia*, I, xli–xlii. The date of reception is conjectural, but the profession was made after the statutory year on 21st January 1601. For the latest appraisal, see P.Fr. Luis Vázquez Fernández, 'Apuntes para una nueva biografía de Tirso' in *Tirso de Molina: Vida y Obra. Actas del Primer Simposio Internacional sobre Tirso* [=*Estudios*] (Madrid, 1987); pp. 9–50.

the provincial noviciate at Guadalajara, Fray Gabriel professed a year later and went on to the college of the Vera Cruz at Salamanca, the centrepiece of Mercedarian involvement in academic life. Whatever the problems besetting its government and organization, in this area at least the Order, and Castile above all, could look with intense pride at the achievements of the last fifty years.

The academic vocation which had been developing in the Order since the fifteenth century, and especially from the 1550s, received a major impulse with the election of M° Fray Francisco Zumel as general in 1593. It was Zumel who had consolidated the position of the Vera Cruz as the forcing ground of the Mercedarian élite in both Spain and America, and by his own hand established the Order as a player in the theological debates that erupted at the university of Salamanca towards the end of the sixteenth century. Through his appointments and scholastic writing Zumel was the first Mercedarian to wield significant influence in university life, and his successes had a profound impact on the Order as a centre of culture and learning for generations after his death. As Tirso put it in the 1630s, 'there is not one *maestro* in our Order, of whatever province he may be, who does not consider himself a disciple of his, or of those who were so'.[55]

For the Vera Cruz, over which Zumel assumed the rectorship in 1570, the turning point with respect to its academic standing came in 1585 when the Order successfully petitioned the crown to concede the college one of the eight *actos mayores de teología* celebrated annually in the university.[56] This honour, gained in the teeth of resistance from the secular clergy, was the forum through which many of the newer orders including the Jesuits and the Cistercians made their mark in the university. The Mercedarians appear to have been no exception, and this, together with the publication of Zumel's commentary on the *Prima Pars* of the *Summa Theologica* between 1585–7, effectively set the seal on an expansion that can be dated to the arrival of San Juan from Paris seventy years before. Business in the Order kept Zumel away from Salamanca for extended periods until 1599, but he was eventually able to marry the duties of general, professor and vice-chancellor of the university through a grueling schedule of summer chapters and visitations

---

[55] Tirso, *Historia*, II, p. 204. For discussions of Zumel's influence on Tirso himself, see P. Rafael María de Hornedo, 'La teología zumeliana de Tirso de Molina' in *Estudios eclesiásticos*, 24 (1950), pp. 217–36, and Sullivan, *Tirso de Molina*, pp. 34–6.

[56] Vázquez Núñez, *El Padre Francisco Zumel*, p. 33.

that took him back and forth across the Peninsula. During his absence the former general, Mº Fray Francisco Maldonado, saw to the reconstruction of the Vera Cruz in the Plateresque style with which it took its place among the leading religious colleges in the university.[57]

Following Salamanca's lead, the 1580s and '90s saw an unprecedented growth in education and learning in the Order across its range, with the encouragement of noviciates and provincial *studia*, the foundation of several colleges, and a greater number of religious entering the universities than ever before. In Castile especially, the effort to raise intellectual standards was rooted in the development of a conventual dimension to study which mirrors that in other orders. By the 1580s the increasing demands on the colleges at Salamanca, Alcalá and Valladolid had caused the establishment of a number of conventual *studia* to carry the burden of preliminary teaching in Latin and the arts which these establishments had previously shouldered.[58] While teaching in the arts continued, the colleges were given greater freedom to devote themselves to study and the training of religious for university degrees, as well as the competition for chairs upon which the Order's academic prestige depended. We have few details on the *studia* themselves until 1600, when the administration and Aristotelian curriculum of that of Huete was the subject of a number of ordinances which were presumably shared by the others as well.[59]

---

[57] On the reconstruction, see the *acta* of the chapter general of Valladolid in 1596, ACA, Mon., vol. 2683, p. 34. The same reference relates the ruinous condition of the Colegio de la Concepción at Alcalá, with orders that it be rebuilt. In 1593 the university officially suppressed the office of *juez conservador* granted to the college in 1518 and absorbed it into that of the rector of the *colegio mayor* of San Ildefonso. Protests by the Order were upheld by the Royal Council of Castile, but the college was still in litigation with San Ildefonso in 1606; see the *acta* of the chapter general of Madrid that year, *ibid.*, p. 81. Successive chapters provincial of Castile attempted to placate the university *claustro* by offering a choice of two candidates of verified *limpieza de sangre*, as at Guadalajara in 1608; BNM, ms. 2684, f. 43r. This appears to have been central to the issue, which provoked severe disturbances in the university. The Order emerged victorious in 1651, but the office was greatly reduced in importance; see Vázquez Núñez, *Manual*, II, p. 92, & esp. García Oro, *La Universidad de Alcalá*, pp. 243–4.

[58] Conventual *studia* were founded at Toledo (arts, *c.*1569–72), Segovia (theology, ?; moved to Valladolid when this acquired full collegial status in 1594, but had been reestablished here by 1618), Guadalajara (arts, 1578) and Huete (arts, 1578; not fully established until 1588); see respectively BNM, ms. 2684, ff. 37r, 27r, 118v, & AHN, Clero, vol. 3320, f. 66v. Another arts *studium* had appeared at El Puig in Valencia by 1617; ARV, Clero, lib. 1705, f. 149r.

[59] AHN, Clero, vol. 3320, ff. 160r–161r: 'Lo que se a de Guardar para el estudio de esta cassa'. Dated 23rd November 1600. It is to be assumed that these provisions were laid down at the chapter provincial of Burgos in April and May of that year.

In 1603 the chapter provincial of Castile restricted the number of arts courses to four and ordered that these be kept to 'the quietest and best equipped houses'.[60] Admission to the courses, which were usually of three years' duration, was made dependent on proficiency in Latin and on the merits of individual candidates: 'on no account should the incompetent or ill-disciplined be permitted to study, but only the brightest and most worthy students'.[61] The teaching was to be carried out by *lectores de artes*, who were to compete for their posts like their senior counterparts in theology. These developments *extra collegium* were capped at the chapter general of Zaragoza in 1622 with instructions that a chair of scripture be established at the leading house of every province.[62]

This expansion was reflected in the Crown of Aragon, where in 1588 the chapter provincial of Valencia reiterated the need for 'estudios de gramatica', and ordered the establishment of noviciates in university towns as a means of improving the quality of vocations.[63] The delegates also expressed the wish that Mercedarians should now aspire to university professorships,

> for it does little to enhance the reputation of our Institute that there be no religious to compete for university chairs like other orders, with all the honour there is to be accrued from this.[64]

Within a few years the brethren had gained several chairs at Huesca, the proceeds of which were to be put towards the maintenance of the college founded here in 1578.[65] However, these funds were clearly insufficient, and in 1593 the newly elected Zumel ordered that two houses in Aragon and four in Catalonia be suppressed and their revenues applied to the colleges at Huesca and Lleida respectively, though this was never fully carried out.[66]

---

[60] Tirso, *Historia*, II, p. 274.

[61] Cited in *ibid.*

[62] Vázquez Núñez, *Manual*, II, p. 121.

[63] See, respectively, ACA, Mon., vol. 2659, ff. 65r–v & 65v.

[64] *Ibid.*, f. 65r.

[65] Vázquez Núñez, *Manual*, II, p. 50. The first Mercedarian professor at Huesca appears to have been M° Fray Jerónimo Boneta who held the Prime chair of theology in the 1580s; Tirso, *Historia*, II, p. 101. P° Fray Nicolás Valero was professor here in 1597; Vázquez Núñez, *Manual*, II, p. 60.

[66] See AMAE, SS, leg. 12, f. 145r, Philip II to duque de Sessa, El Escorial, 10th July 1593, & AHCB, ms. A-266, Antillón, *Memorias*, II, f. 76r–v. The houses were, in Aragon, Uncastillo and Sarrión, and in Catalonia Berga, Tàrrega, Prades and Mont-

In Andalusia, meanwhile, the restrictions and increased expense of maintaining religious at the colleges in Salamanca and Alcalá following its separation from Castile made the foundation of a provincial *studium* a matter of some urgency.[67] In 1593 an offer was made by two brothers, the Salamanca-trained Mº Fray Francisco de Veamonte and the vicar general of Peru Pº Fray Alonso Enríquez de Armendáriz, for the endowment of the Colegio de San Laureano in Seville from private funds.[68] The foundation was made on the condition that their brother, Don Juan de Castellanos, be granted the *patronazgo* of the college. This was accepted by Zumel at the chapter general of Calatayud and Veamonte was appointed rector *ad vitam*. However, progress was painfully slow. Limited at first to the study of arts, the building still lay unfinished in the 1630s and it was the second half of the seventeenth century before the college developed a significant role in the formation of religious.[69] Meanwhile, the Order was making its mark at Valladolid, where in 1590 Mº Fray Juan Negrón became the first in a long line of Mercedarians to hold professorships in the university, taking the Scripture and then the Durandus chair in 1597 and 1600 respectively.[70] That standards were high is indicated by the decision of the chapter provincial of Castile in 1606 to vacate the arts chairs held by its religious at the universities of Valladolid and Toledo, believing these to 'add little prestige to the Order and less benefit to those holding them'.[71]

This expansion was not, however, confined to the Peninsula. From the 1570s an increasing proportion of those embarking for America were graduates of the colleges of Salamanca and Alcalá, which had its inevitable effect on the character of the Mercedarian missions. By 1581 the Order had established a full *studium* in Lima and two years later one of its *lectores*, Fray Nicolás de Ovalle, gained the Prime chair

---

blanc. With the exception of Berga and Sarrión these houses had all been slated for closure since 1574. The decree was moderated at Valladolid in 1596 and in the end only Prades was closed; see *ibid.*, f. 82r–v.

[67] In 1587 the chapter general of Zaragoza limited the province to five collegials at the Vera Cruz and three at Alcalá, though any self-supporting religious could be admitted with a licence from his provincial; Vázquez Núñez, *Manual*, II, p. 44.

[68] *Ibid.*, p. 58. Attempts to oblige those holding rents in the province to apply them towards the foundation appear largely to have failed; see the *acta* of the chapters general of Calatayud and Valladolid in 1593 and 1596 respectively, ACA, Mon., vol. 2683, pp. 22, & 31–2.

[69] Tirso, *Historia*, II, pp. 185–6 & 280.

[70] See Muñoz Delgado, 'El convento de Valladolid', pp. 56–8.

[71] Tirso, *Historia*, II, p. 289, & BNM, ms. 2684, f. 32v.

of theology at the university of San Marcos.[72] In 1594 Zumel made good the licence long held by the Order to found a college in Mexico City for the training of religious from across the viceroyalty of New Spain.[73] The delay owed much to the poor reputation acquired by the brethren in Mexico in particular during the 1530s, and in this respect the foundation provides tangible evidence of the rehabilitation of the Order in the upper reaches of colonial society. Armed with letters of support from Philip II and the nuncio, Camillo Caetani, in April 1594 Zumel dispatched eight Andalusian religious to Mexico under M° Fray Francisco de Vera to effect the foundation.[74] It was on this basis that Fray Alonso Enríquez de Armendáriz, probably a former student of the Vera Cruz, established the Colegio de San Ramón Nonato as a constituent part of the University of Mexico between 1624–8.[75] The college, which Enríquez placed under Mercedarian control, was founded for the training of clergy in canon law from the dioceses of Santiago de Cuba and Michoacán held by him after his final departure from Spain in 1610.

The Salamanca which Tirso reached in 1601 was therefore at the height of its influence both as a centre for the formation of the Mercedarian élite and as the basis of its academic expansion. The previous year Zumel had been appointed dean of the faculty of theology in succession to the Augustinian Fray Juan de Guevara, and he remained a leading figure in the university and in the theological debates sustained there until his death in 1607.[76] Although nothing survives to record Tirso's sojourn in Salamanca there can be little doubt that the arts course he took at the Vera Cruz between 1601–3 corresponded to that

---

[72] See Pérez, *Religiosos de la Merced*, pp. 212–19, & Vázquez Núñez, *Manual*, I, p. 540, & II, pp. 25 & 47–8. Orders for the establishment of a *studium* of 'grammar, arts and theology' in Lima were issued by Maldonado as general in 1576, though the house had a *lector de artes* as early as 1574. The foundation was effected by M° Fray Juan Bernal as vicar general of Peru some time between 1578–81; *id., Mercedarios ilustres*, p. 336. By 1579 *studia* had been opened in the houses at Cuzco and Quito also; Pérez, *Religiosos de la Merced*, p. 215.

[73] Vázquez Núñez, *Manual*, II, pp. 60–1. For attempts to establish the college in the 1560s, see Pérez, *Religiosos de la Merced*, pp. 120–1.

[74] Pérez, *Religiosos de la Merced*, p. 131, and for events surrounding the foundation, *ibid.*, pp. 122–9.

[75] Vázquez Núñez, *Mercedarios ilustres*, pp. 412–13.

[76] See *ibid.*, p. 366, and, for a flavour of the Vera Cruz in this period, P.Fr. Vicente Muñoz Delgado, 'Los Mercedarios de la Vera Cruz en el «Diario de un estudiante» (1603–1607) de Salamanca' in *BPCONSM*, 16 (1978), no. 50, pp. 49–54. The diary in question is George Haley, ed., *El diario de un estudiante de Salamanca: La cronica inédita de Girolamo da Sommaia (1603–1607)* (Salamanca, 1977).

taught throughout the province of Castile. In 1603 the chapter provincial of Guadalajara, no doubt under Zumel's influence, described the curriculum as consisting of three year-long courses in logic, philosophy and metaphysics.[77] These were to be made up of two lectures daily, *conferencias* every evening and *conclusiones* on Sundays, as well as participation in an *acto público* once a year.[78] In line with the requirements for the degree of *presentado*, Tirso went on to take four theological courses (including scripture, patristics and Church and conciliar history) at Toledo and Guadalajara between 1603–7 and finally at Alcalá between 1608–10.[79] From at least 1603 onwards the conferral of the degree was made conditional on the completion of a further five years of teaching as a *lector*, first in the three-year arts course and then in theology. These requirements Tirso fulfilled as a coadjutor *lector de artes* in Toledo between 1611–15, as a *lector de teología* in Santo Domingo on the island of Hispaniola in 1616–18 and at Segovia from 1618 to 1620, when he was finally awarded his *presentatura*.[80]

The ordinances passed with respect to curricula and the granting of degrees at Guadalajara in 1603 provide an important insight into the steps being taken towards the establishment of a culture of learning in the Order in Castile. Not only had the standard and duration of training been increased since 1574, but aspirants were required to serve long periods teaching in the conventual *studia* in which they themselves had been nurtured. The *magisterio*, which had formerly required three extra years of training in theology, was now made contingent on six or seven years of unbroken study.[81] In line with this, the minimum age for consideration as a *presentado* in Castile was set at thirty-three, and no less than forty for the degree of *maestro*. This, however, appears to have been regarded as excessive, and in 1609 — two years after Zumel's death — the chapter general of Guadalajara lowered the minimum ages to thirty and thirty-five respectively.[82]

---

[77] Tirso, *Historia*, II, pp. 274–5. Since Tirso moved directly to Salamanca after his profession it can be assumed that he was competent in Latin, as might be expected of a student of the Jesuit college in Madrid; *ibid.*, I, xl.

[78] Tirso, *Historia*, II, p. 275. The duration of the «liciones», stipulated as of an hour here, was raised to an hour and a half at the chapter general of Guadalajara in 1609; Vázquez Núñez, *Manual*, II, p. 97.

[79] Tirso, *Historia*, I, xlv & xlvii.

[80] *Ibid.*, li, lx, lxviii & lxxiii.

[81] *Ibid.*, II, p. 275. See also Tirso's comments with respect to the *acta* of the chapter general of Calatayud in 1593 as confirmed the following year; *ibid.*, p. 187.

[82] ACA, Mon., vol. 2863, p. 60.

As a measure against indiscriminate conferment of degrees, the Guadalajara constitutions of 1574 had limited the number of *maestros* and *presentados* in each province to twelve and twenty-four respectively.[83] These, the *maestros* or *presentados de número*, were accorded a vote in the chapters provincial. At Zaragoza in 1587 an additional two *presentaturas de púlpito* were established in each province for preachers of at least ten years' standing, though on condition that they have some training in philosophy and a minimum of four years' university study in theology behind them.[84] These and other ordinances established degrees as the *sine qua non* for office and privilege, and their attainment remained a significant element in the internal politics of the Order. Ever since the Mercedarians had acquired the faculty of awarding degrees during the fifteenth century, superiors had used the authority and privilege increasingly attached to them to extend their patronage networks through liberal conferment. Despite efforts to control this with the establishment of *studia* and specific curricula, religious continued to receive degrees with inadequate training and so acquire the commanderies and other offices through which their voices could be heard in the Order. Unsurprisingly, not least of the charges levelled against the Order in the 1560s was the freedom with which it graduated its members and the poor formation received by them.[85] Despite efforts to repair this circumstance, the Salazar generalate (1587–93) in particular was notorious for a mass of grace and favour appointments and dispensations among his clients and supporters.[86] By 1589 resentment was growing throughout the Kingdom of Castile at what was regarded as a gross abuse of the degree system, and on his election in 1593 Zumel set about stripping unworthy recipients of their titles, particularly where deserving candidates had been passed over.[87] By the time he had finished, the twenty or so *maestros* in the Crown of Aragon had been cut to eight, and the *presentados* reduced from twenty-six to a mere seven.[88] Castile and Andalusia, meanwhile, boasted a total of twenty-one *maestros* and forty-five *presen-*

---

[83] These were increased to fourteen and twenty-six respectively in 1605; *ibid.*, p. 80.

[84] *Ibid.*, p. 9.

[85] See AGS, PR, 23-212, f. 5r–v.

[86] Tirso, *Historia*, II, p. 137.

[87] *Ibid.*, pp. 143 & 183–5.

[88] The chapter general of 1587 had recorded ten Aragonese, seven Castilian, eleven Andalusian and four French *maestros*; Vázquez Núñez, *Manual*, II, p. 45.

tados, a testament to the advantage in learning and academic involvement held by these provinces. Only with the French province was Zumel moved to leniency, and then solely in view of the destruction of its houses and scattering of its religious over the previous thirty years.[89] The chapter agreed that any friar holding a bachelor's or doctoral degree could assume the title of *présenté* or *maître*, giving a total of three and six respectively for this province.[90]

Despite Zumel's measures, appointment to degrees and then admission to the fixed number of holders with electoral powers in the chapters provincial remained a source of constant friction in the Order. Oña, for instance, though granted the degree and privileges of *maestro* at Calatayud in 1593 and later elected provincial, had to wait until the death of the former general Fray Francisco Maldonado in 1598 before he could take his place among the twelve *maestros de número* of the province of Castile.[91] It need hardly be said how soughtafter these degrees and the privileges associated with them were, and how bitter was the wrangling over appointment and succession. At Valencia in 1600, for example, the newly elected general, Fray Francisco de Medina, refused to ratify the *presentatura* of one of his rival Oña's creatures, Fray Juan de Bustos. Though the judgement was eventually upheld in Rome it is hard to believe that a rigorous application of standards was solely to blame for Bustos' non-admission.[92] The generalate of Fray Alonso de Monroy — himself only a *presentado* on appointment — was notorious for what Tirso called 'the aggrandizement of his favourites and supporters'.[93] As a measure against this, in 1609 the chapter general of Guadalajara ordered the establishment of provincial commissions to examine the merits of degree candidates, but abuse continued on a grand scale as Tirso's fulminations in the 1630s bear witness.[94] Elsewhere, the tendency of religious to abandon their studies for vacant offices came as a source of concern to an Order trying to raise its intellectual profile, and a ban was issued in 1600 on the movement of any student reli-

---

[89] Tirso, *Historia*, II, p. 185.

[90] Vázquez Núñez, *Manual*, II, p. 56. The same privileges were granted to the provinces of Guatemala and Tucumán at Valencia in 1600, where the quota of *maestros* and *presentados* was set at four and six respectively in each case; *ibid.*, p. 75.

[91] *Ibid.*, p. 73.

[92] Tirso, *Historia*, II, pp. 251–2. The delegates at Guadalajara in 1603 imposed perpetual silence on Bustos where this was concerned; see BNM, ms. 2684, f. 31r.

[93] *Ibid.*, p. 288.

[94] See AHCB, ms. A-266, Antillón, *Memorias*, II, f. 208r–v, & Tirso, *Historia*, I, clxi.

gious to America until they had completed their courses of study.[95] But the dangers of over-exposure to learning were also recognized, and in 1603 the chapter provincial of Catalonia-Aragon felt the need to prohibit study among novices in the interests of a proper religious formation.[96]

However, with Zumel at the height of his influence and religious acquiring chairs and degrees as never before, the early seventeenth century represents a golden age for the Mercedarians as an academic order.[97] By the 1630s the brethren held chairs at Salamanca, Valladolid, Huesca, Zaragoza, Santiago de Compostela and Mexico City and the Order had a total of nine colleges in Europe and the Indies.[98] There was never a Mercedarian school of theology, but Zumel's contribution to the great disputations of the age was recognized by the Order which in 1609 asserted its adherence to Thomist doctrine as expounded in the *Commentaria* of 1585–7 and 1593–4.[99] Already in 1593 Pedro de Oña's Aristotelian works had been given to Zumel for approval as standard texts for the Order, and in this way the Mercedarians began to acquire a corpus of theological, exegetical and philosophical authority where previously they had had to look to the masters of other congregations.[100] Even so, the attachment to the Dominicans remained strong, and in 1596, at the height of the *De Auxiliis* debate, Zumel exhorted the commendator and *lectores* of the *studium* at Huete to ensure that

> the doctrine read in these faculties [of arts and theology] be always pure and as endorsed by the school of St Thomas, and that it be in accordance with the writings of the Angelic Doctor, master and pre-

---

[95] AHCB, ms. A-266, Antillón, *Memorias*, II, f. 98r, & ACA, Mon., vol. 2683, p. 60.

[96] Vázquez Núñez, *Manual*, II, p. 84. In 1612 the chapter general of Murcia approved the constitutions prepared by the provincial M° Fray José de Aguayo for the noviciates of Castile, and later adopted by the rest of the Order; *ibid.*, pp. 98–9.

[97] *Ibid.*, p. 91.

[98] On this see *ibid.*, p. 138. For Mexico, see *ibid.*, p. 123, and for Santiago, P.Fr. Vicente Muñoz Delgado, 'Fray Martín de Acevedo (†1658), comendador de Conjo, profesor y obispo; otros Mercedarios catedráticos de la universidad compostelana' in *BPCONSM*, 22 (1984), no. 77, pp. 56–66.

[99] AHCB, ms. A-266, Antillón, *Memorias*, II, f. 197v. The ordinance was repeated at Murcia in 1612; *ibid.*, f. 208r. For a summary of Zumel's theological place and contribution, see Melquiades Andrés Martín *et al.*, ed., *Historia de la teología española* (2 vols., Madrid, 1983–7), II, pp. 32–4.

[100] Vázquez Núñez, *Manual*, II, pp. 58–60. For some notes on Mercedarian exegetes in this period, see Andrés Martín *et al.*, ed., *Historia de la teología española*, II, pp. 80–109, esp. 102–9.

ceptor of the Church. Further, we hereby prohibit by virtue of holy obedience the study of the new doctrines, paradoxes and opinions which have lately been invented and which represent such a danger to sacred doctrine, and so distance ourselves from those modern authors who have recently attempted to sully the purity of philosophical and theological doctrine.[101]

At the chapter general of Murcia in 1612 the Order once again made manifest its adherence to Zumel's own reading of the Thomist canon, declaring that

> as for the *lectores*, in arts as much as in theology, [...] let none expound or teach except through the doctrine of the Angelic Doctor St Thomas, and, where his commentators are concerned, following the Most Reverend *Maestro* Fray Francisco Zumel of blessed memory, teaching and defending him in public disputation, naming him and taking him as the head of our studies and schools [...] And in matters not treated by him, they should expound and teach St Thomas in line with Dominican authors and commentators.(218v–219r)

Though the Mercedarians remained close allies of the Dominicans, their particular Marian advocation forced them to part company where the dogma of the Immaculate Conception was concerned, and the Friars Preachers were left completely isolated in this issue. Thus, at Calatayud three years later the delegates reaffirmed the Order's attachment to Aquinas and his Dominican commentators,

> except in the matter of the clean and immaculate Conception of the Virgin Our Lady, whose exceeding purity and cleanliness must always and inviolably be defended throughout the Order, as much in the pulpit as in the schools.(219r)

Accordingly, among the most important tasks entrusted to Tirso and his companions on their mission to Santo Domingo in 1616 was the introduction of the Immaculist dogma to an island that had hitherto been closed it.[102]

Having consolidated its theological and institutional position as an academic entity, the Order went on in the seventeenth century to extend these developments and the values enshrined within them to

---

[101] AHN, Clero, vol. 3320, f. 148r. For Zumel's stance against Molina in particular, see P.Fr. Vicente Muñoz Delgado, ed., *Zumel y el molinismo: Informe del P. Francisco Zumel, Mercedario, sobre las doctrinas del P. Luis Molina, S.J., presentado en julio de 1595* (Madrid, 1953).

[102] Tirso, *Historia*, II, p. 357.

the area that had traditionally proved most resistant to change: the
Crown of Aragon. As at the end of the previous century, it was the
college at Huesca which remained the focus of academic life here
after that of Lleida had dwindled into insignificance. By mid century
the Colegio de la Merced had developed an important presence in a
university in which the religious orders played a preponderant role.
Elsewhere, the Mercedarians shared in the marked expansion of the
regulars in academic life which mirrors that in the episcopate. The
first chair to be held beyond Huesca was gained by Mº Fray Juan
Pérez de Munébrega at the university of Zaragoza in the 1630s.[103]
The Order provided at least five professors to the university of Tarragona over the course of the century, and in the person of Mᵉ Fra
Thomàs de Tàrrega regained the Prime chair of theology at Valencia
once held by Fray Jerónimo Pérez.[104] Despite these advances, no
steps were taken toward a second foundation in these parts until 1630
with the opening of the Colegio de San Pedro Nolasco in Valencia to
serve as the *studium* of that province.[105] It was followed in 1647 by a
second college under this advocation, founded in Zaragoza by the
archbishop and former general, Mº Fray Juan Cebrián (1627–32),
and then a third in Barcelona established by the nobleman Agustí
Mercader in 1668.[106]

*

The great convent rebuilt and refurbished by Monroy and his successors in Seville is in many ways an apotheosis of Mercedarian Reform
after the terrible trials of the sixteenth century. Here, and at Madrid
also, the brethren set out to celebrate the achievements of the past
and the promise of the future, of which their academic vocation was
clearly a major element. At Seville in particular the Order had the
luck and the perspicacity to engage the artist Francisco de Zurbarán
when he was at the height of his powers. Some time around 1630
Zurbarán produced eleven canvases for the conventual library, of

---

[103] Vázquez Núñez, *Manual*, II, p. 138.
[104] BUV, ms. 884, pp. 59–60.
[105] For the foundation and endowment, see ARV, Clero, lib. 1249, and the *acta* of
the chapters provincial of Valencia from 1631 onwards in *ibid.*, lib. 1705.
[106] Vázquez Núñez, 'Conventos de la Orden', pp. 142 & 136 respectively.

which ten were full-length portraits of the great scholars and writers of the Order.[107] Of these, six, or perhaps seven, survive, though only five can be identified with certainty.[108] The group is led by Zumel, seen composing one of his commentaries on Aquinas, and includes the Extremaduran theologian and professor at Salamanca Mº Fray Pedro Machado (†1609), Fray Pedro de Oña as bishop of Gaeta, the preacher Fray Hernando de Santiago (a life portrait this), and the Valencian Mº Fray Jerónimo Pérez (†1549). A sixth canvas, traditionally held to depict Fray Alonso de Sotomayor, would be more consistent with Mº Fray Melchor Rodríguez de Torres, titular bishop of Ross in Ireland and author of the *Agricultura del alma* printed in 1603, or even Monroy himself.[109] It is possible to speculate on the subjects of the three or four canvases from this series which appear not to have survived: Gaspar de Torres, professor at Salamanca and bishop of Medauro (†1584); Fray Juan Negrón, professor of moral philosophy at Valladolid (†1603), and the Portuguese jurist Mº Fray Serafín de Freitas (†1633), holder of the Vespers chair of canon law at Valladolid (1605–26) and author of an attack on Grotius, the *De Iusto Imperio Lusitanorum Asiatico* of 1625.[110] The series could well have been completed with the Navarrese Fray Domingo de San Juan de Pie del Puerto (†1540), the Order's first major academic figure in Spain. Whatever the case may be, the five paintings whose subject is certain underline a newfound pride in the development of a culture of learning over the previous hundred years, one to which religious from across the Order had made their contribution.

Despite Tirso's evident distaste for the political involvement that

---

[107] See Paul Guinard, *Zurbarán et les peintres espagnols de la vie monastique* (Paris, 1960), pp. 95–6. Two canvases sometimes reckoned to be part of this series, those depicting San Pedro Pascual and San Carmelo, were in fact produced for the 'sala de láminas'; *ibid.*, p. 95. See also P.Fr. Luis Vázquez Fernández, 'Pintura y escultura del Convento Grande de la Merced de Sevilla en 1730' in *Estudios*, 54 (1998), pp. 191–208.

[108] The possible seventh, a lesser-known canvas in the Musée des Beaux-Arts in Pau, depicts an unknown bishop, perhaps Mº Fray Alonso Enríquez de Armendáriz, founder of the colleges of San Laureano in Seville and San Ramón Nonato in Mexico City; see Guinard, *Zurbarán*, pp. 96 & 261.

[109] *Agricultura del Alma y Exercicios de la Vida Religiosa, con varias cosas para pulpito y espiritu* (Burgos: Juan Baptista Varesio, 1603, 4º). Sotomayor (*c*.1607–82) was an undistinguished religious in his early 20s at the time this painting was executed.

[110] Valladolid: Ex Officina Hieronymi Morillo, 1625, 4º. On Freitas, who joined the Order only in 1609, see Vázquez Núñez, *Mercedarios ilustres*, pp. 425–9, & P.Fr. Gumersindo Placer López, *Fray Serafín de Freitas, mercedario, jurisconsulto portugués: Estudio bio-bibliográfico (1577–1633)* (Madrid, 1956).

had brought him such harm, and his conviction that the qualities required of it were anathema to study — 'there are those who claim that distinction in politics requires only prudence, and that this is wholly at odds with the pursuit of knowledge' — there can be no doubt that the improved standing and influence of the Order in wider society had gone hand in hand with a continued emphasis on the education of its members.[111] That this should come to fruition after the advances of the sixteenth century owes much to Zumel, whose generalcy and career provided leadership and example at a critical time in the fortunes of the Order. In reiterating the importance of learning as the basis for advancement in the Order, Zumel, more than any other general, established the primacy of the academic vocation as the key to Mercedarian Reform, success and expansion.

IV. *Redemption: Challenge, Probity and Expansion*

The area in which the reformers found the Order to be most lacking in the 1560s was perhaps that of its principle vocation, the redemption of captives. Even the most superficial examination revealed a history of neglect and corruption stretching back decades, and the restoration of this activity was therefore among the more pressing responsibilities urged on the Order by the crown. In the thirty years since the Aragonese visited Algiers in 1537 the brethren appear to have mustered funds for only three ransoming expeditions as the Muslim onslaught broke against the shores of the Peninsula.[112] The lamentable condition of both the Mercedarians and the Trinitarians in this matter and the urgent need for their services caused the crown to institute a series of measures to regulate the preparation and conduct of redemptions.[113] In the early 1570s the licencing of these was entrusted to the Council of Aragon and the Royal Council of Castile, to which the general of each order was to apply for authorization

---

[111] Tirso, *Historia*, II, p. 264.

[112] These were the joint Aragonese-French expedition of 1545–6, that of the Crown of Aragon in 1555, and the Castilian-Aragonese effort in 1561–2; all took place in Algiers. The French province's participation in 1545–6 appears to have been its last until the 1630 ransoming in Morocco; see Vázquez Núñez, *Manual*, I, pp. 465–6, 477 & 480–1, & *DHEE*, suppl. I, pp. 636 & 639.

[113] Friedman, *Spanish Captives*, pp. 107–8.

once sufficient funds had been gathered. In the case of Castile the approval consisted of a licence to effect the redemption as well as to collect alms and publicize it throughout the Kingdom.[114] In the Crown of Aragon, meanwhile, the disputed Mercedarian *privativa* over the collection of *limosna* required the issue of a separate document, but in both instances the main licence stated the purpose and itinerary of the expedition and the names of the redemptors involved. Above all, the ransomers were, in the Castilian case at least, to be accompanied by a notary appointed by the Council who was to keep close account of all transactions and submit a final report to the crown on the conclusion of the expedition. These impositions therefore served both the interests of reform and of the crown, which had much to gain from the smooth functioning of the two main ransoming agencies at its disposal. The provisions were accepted at the chapter general of Guadalajara in 1574, which abolished the traditional procession of ransomed captives in Castile, though not in Aragon.[115] The first redemption to be conducted under these guidelines was that of 1575 by Mº Fray Rodrigo de Arce and Fray Antonio de Valdepeñas of the province of Castile, for which meticulous accounts survive.[116]

As in the 1520s, the emphasis on education in the Order brought renewed calls that those involved in this vocation be men of learning. In 1585 the Aragonese redemptor Fray Jorge del Olivar presented a *memorial* at the chapter provincial of Zaragoza in which he made clear that the ignorance of those assigned to preach the redemption was contributing to a decline in donations.[117] To remedy this he suggested that all qualified *predicadores de la redención* and redemptors be made eligible for the degrees enjoyed by their *letrado* brethren with university training. This was accepted by the delegates and Olivar was himself confirmed as *maestro* by the chapter general in 1587, but it was not until the generalate of Fray Francisco Zumel that degrees were created specifically for redemption purposes.[118] During his tenure Zumel

---

[114] The Castilian expedition to Tétouan in 1579 required the issue of a Portuguese passport as well; see *CODOIN*, VI, pp. 162–4, esp. 164, Philip II to Cristóbal de Moura, El Pardo, 19th February 1579.

[115] Vázquez Núñez, *Manual*, II, pp. 13–14.

[116] *Ibid.*, pp. 26–7. The accounts for this redemption are in BNM, ms. 2963; for a detailed summary, see *DHEE*, suppl. I, pp. 636–9.

[117] Vázquez Núñez, *Manual*, II, p. 36. Complaints to this effect had been made since at least 1571.

[118] *Ibid.*, pp. 45 & 58.

increased the number of *presentaturas de púlpito* from two to eight in each province, with the requirement that those selected be no younger than fifty and preach the redemption for eight years continuously as *comisarios generales de la Santa Redención* to earn their degree.[119] However, voices were soon heard against this, and in 1600 the Castilian M° Fray Juan de Peñacerrada protested in Rome against the *presentaturas* on the grounds that recipients 'tend usually to be illiterate, ignorant and unworthy of the said degree'.(97r) This view seems to have been widely held, and the *Congregazione di Vescovi i Regolari* ordered them to be abolished soon after.[120] Although the work of redemption remained mostly the preserve of men with little interest or aptitude for study, from the end of the sixteenth century several of the Order's most distinguished scholars appeared as redemptors in Africa: witness M° Fray Juan Negrón at Algiers in 1597–8 and his fellow Castilian M° Fray Isidro de Valcázar, holder of the *Súmulas* chair at Valladolid (1594–*c*.1600), in Tétouan in 1615.[121] Even so, the developments outlined here reflect the largely subordinated role of the redemptive vocation as a conduit to power and influence in the Order over the course of the sixteenth century. The days when redemptors could aspire to high office by dint of this service alone were over.[122]

Whatever the relative position of redemptors and *predicadores* in the Mercedarian hierarchy, the work to which they were entrusted was of immeasurable importance where the image and position of the Order was concerned. The recovery and expansion of this *métier* is one of the most signal achievements of Mercedarian Reform after decades of gross peculation, and at a time when thousands of Spaniards were languishing in captivity on the Barbary Coast.[123] Although occasional questions were raised as to the probity of the Order following the resumption of ransoming activity in the 1570s, there can be little

---

[119] See Tirso, *Historia*, II, pp. 191–2, & AHCB, ms. A-266, Antillón, *Memorias*, II, ff. 85v–86r.

[120] Tirso, *Historia*, II, pp. 231–2. The judgement was successfully challenged by the *procurador general*, M° Fray Bernardo de Vargas, but no further *comisarios* were appointed.

[121] Vázquez Núñez, *Mercedarios ilustres*, pp. 366 & 420–2 respectively.

[122] The last redemptor to be elected general was the Catalan Mᶜ Fra Miquel Puig (1546–67), who participated in the joint Aragonese-French expedition to Algiers in 1545–6; see *DHEE*, suppl. I, p. 636.

[123] Redemption expeditions per decade: 1530s – 3; 1540s – 1; 1550s – 1; 1560s — 1; 1570s – 3; 1580s – 3; 1590s – 3; 1600s – 4; 1610s – 4; 1620s – 4; 1630s – 6; 1640s – 8.

doubt that the most heinous abuses had been extirpated by the end of the century.[124] In 1593, for instance, the newly elected Zumel had his predecessor Fray Francisco de Salazar brought to Almazán under arrest in order to demand the return of 3000 ducats which he had removed from Castile to Aragon for redemption purposes.[125] That the Order had begun to police itself is confirmed by the case of the Castilian P° Fray Francisco Galindo, who was imprisoned on suspicion of defrauding *limosna* during the Algiers redemption of 1627, though he was eventually absolved by the papacy for lack of evidence.[126] For the most part, though, the Mercedarians cultivated an image of unity and integrity in the face of the Muslim threat. Although the majority of expeditions continued to be organized by provincial blocs, the great joint redemption of 1561–2 appears to have set an important precedent and enterprises of this sort occurred periodically after that of 1597–8 to Algiers.[127] The first independent redemption conducted by the province of Andalusia took place in Morocco in 1601 under M° Fray Juan Bernal, while the earliest American representation in a joint Castilian ransoming came at Tétouan in 1609.[128] The other significant advance in this field during the latter part of the sixteenth century is the development of Morocco as a significant ransoming destination, for which the house opened in Gibraltar in 1582 served as a forward base.[129]

The upsurge in Muslim captive-taking following the 'clash of empires' between Spain and the Turks during the sixteenth century and the expulsion of the *moriscos* in 1609–14 brought a huge increase in ransoming funds into the hands of the Order.[130] From the begin-

---

[124] See IVDJ, env. 43, f. 213r. *Memorial* of Licenciado Boorques to *Junta de Noche*, 29th May 1591. The *memorial*, 'sobre las diferencias entre los frailes trinitarios', suggests that the Mercedarians of the Kingdom of Castile could be as guilty as the Trinitarians in mismanaging redemption funds. I am grateful to Dr I.A.A. Thompson of the University of Keele for this reference.

[125] Tirso, *Historia*, II, pp. 186–7. The Aragonese expedition to Algiers in 1589 appears to have been based on these funds.

[126] See *ibid.*, pp. 495, 549 & 592, & Vázquez Núñez, *Manual*, II, p. 130.

[127] Other joint expeditions between the Aragonese and Castilian blocs took place in 1615 and 1627, the first to Tétouan, the second to Algiers.

[128] Vázquez Núñez, *Manual*, II, pp. 78 & 104.

[129] For Gibraltar, see *id.*, 'Conventos de la Orden', p. 168, and for Morocco, P.Fr. Faustino D. Gazulla, 'Noticias sobre la acción de los religiosos de la Orden de Nuestra Señora de la Merced en Marruecos' in *Boletín de la Orden de la Merced*, 16 (1928), pp. 148–52.

[130] See Andrew C. Hess, *The Forgotten Frontier: A History of the Sixteenth-Century Ibero-African Frontier* (Chicago, 1978).

ning the Mercedarians found the willing support of the crown where the funding of their expeditions was concerned. The 1575 redemption, for instance, was supported by donations of 159,240 *maravedís* confiscated from fleeing Valencian *moriscos* and a further 628,000 from the *Consejo de Órdenes* for the ransom of captives from lands belonging to the military order of Santiago, or failing this from those of Alcántara and Calatrava.[131] Redemption funds were usually bolstered by the *Consejo de la Cruzada* which often disposed of *abintestato* and *mostrenco* revenue in the Mercedarians' favour.[132] The 1575 expedition appears to have received 529,744 *maravedís* from this source.[133] The Council also made grants to the Order, usually of around 500 ducats and often for specific captives, while entrusting it with the administration of sundry endowments and bequests made for redemption purposes. In this respect the Mercedarians' status as a Spanish congregation gave them a distinct advantage over the Trinitarians, whose ministers general continued to be drawn from the French provinces of the Order.[134]

However, it was from individual donors large and small that the Order and its *opus* benefited most, and this which represents the heart of Mercedarian patronage as a whole in this period. Between 1660 and 1678, for instance, a substantial endowment fund established by Elvira Manrique de Lara, the foundress of the Discalced house of Santa Bárbara in Madrid, yielded over 77,000 *reales* for five redemptions in Africa.[135] However, many smaller trusts were supervised by the Order during the seventeenth century; in 1648, for example, a clutch of these in Andalusia afforded that province 35,205 *reales* in redemption *limosna*, while a group of sixteen trusts held at Seville pro-

---

[131] See Friedman, *Spanish Captives*, pp. 117 & 114 respectively. No more than 52,500 *maravedís* was to be spent on any one captive. The last recorded donation from this source was a mere 49,844 *maravedís* in 1654.

[132] That is, the estate of those dying heirless and intestate, and proceeds from the sale of abandoned property; *ibid.*, p. 111.

[133] See *DHEE*, suppl. I, p. 636. These figures, which come to 1.31 million *maravedís*, compare with a total of 1.33 million gathered by the province of Castile for this expedition. This suggests that, where Castile was concerned, the crown agreed to match any sum gathered by the province itself.

[134] Between 1580 and 1700 the Calced and Discalced Trinitarians conducted 45 expeditions against the Mercedarians' 75, though it must be borne in mind that the former devoted part of their funds to the maintenance of a network of hospitals for captives in Algiers; see, respectively, *ibid.*, pp. 630, 631 & 639–40, & Friedman, *Spanish Captives*, p. 91.

[135] Friedman, *Spanish Captives*, p. 117.

vided 42,787 more in 1678.[136] Over the course of the seventeenth century these funds increasingly consisted of *adjutorios* provided for specific captives, but for the most part their use was unrestricted.[137] Such revenues were of course in addition to the proceeds of the Order's alms-collecting activity, which continued to be gathered by the *procuradores de la redención* at chapters provincial. The abolition of the system of conventual responsions in 1588 perhaps contributed to a relative decline in the proportion of these monies with respect to ransoming funds as a whole, but they still provided 30% of the total treasure carried by the Castilian-Andalusian expedition in 1651.[138]

It is unclear to what extent the huge rise in donations during the seventeenth century caused the Order to reserve the income acquired from its properties in Spain and America for its own ends, but the number of redemptions and captives ransomed increased markedly during this period. In 1612 the chapter general of Murcia produced a list calculating the number ransomed in the sixteen redemptions since 1562 at 2,710.[139] Three years later the delegates at Calatayud claimed that the Order had redeemed the somewhat less plausible figure of 21,632 Christians from Muslim captivity since its foundation 400 years earlier.[140] Whatever the true figure, counting the redemption conducted by the Kingdom of Castile in 1612, the Order, including France, ransomed a further 3,451 captives in twenty-two expeditions up to 1648.[141] Between 1650 and 1698 the figures are 6,143 in thirty redemptions.

Until the seventeenth century it was obligatory for the Order to transport two thirds of its ransoming funds to Africa in the form of merchandise rather than bullion, thereby limiting the egress of money to the Infidel.[142] In 1575, for instance, the Castilians made a profit

---

[136] *Ibid.*, p. 118.

[137] See *ibid.*, pp. 118–20.

[138] *Ibid.*, pp. 118–19. The figures given are 141,821 *reales* out of a total of 478,858. This compares with 50% in the Castilian redemption of 1575. See also Fray Melchor García Navarro, *Redenciones de cautivos en África (1723–1725)*, ed. P.Fr. Manuel Vázquez Pájaro (Madrid, 1956), p. 17.

[139] Vázquez Núñez, *Manual*, II, p. 104. The figure given for the number of redemptions is based on my own research. It should be noted that P.Fr. José Antonio Gari y Siumell, *La Orden Redentora de la Merced [...] Historia de las redenciones de cautivos cristianos realizadas por [...] la Orden de la Merced* (Barcelona, 1873) is statistically completely unreliable.

[140] Vázquez Núñez, *Manual*, II, pp. 104–5.

[141] See *DHEE*, suppl. I, pp. 639–40.

[142] Friedman, *Spanish Captives*, p. 121.

of nearly 40% on the sale of pearls and cloth in Algiers, the proceeds of which were put towards the redemption itself. However, successive expeditions saw diminishing returns were this was concerned, with only 23% earned for similar goods at Tétouan in 1583. The risk and effort involved in turning *limosna* into marketable goods in Spain and then selling them on the Barbary Coast began to outweigh the profits earned, and it seems that by the early seventeenth century the Order was petitioning the crown for an easing of its restrictions on the transport of bullion.[143] In 1609 the Council of Castile responded by permitting the provinces of Castile and Andalusia to carry the bulk of their resources in specie, leaving the sale of merchandise at the friars' discretion.[144] The practice continued for some time on a diminished scale — Spanish hats, for instance, were clearly much in demand on the Barbary Coast — before petering out altogether towards the end of the century.

The concession of 1609 no doubt fuelled growing opposition in Spain to the organized redemption of captives by the Mercedarians and other ransoming agencies. With some justification is was argued that their activities not only encouraged the taking of more and more captives, but represented an intolerable drain of money to Spain's enemies. At the *cortes* of Monzón in 1626 the Valencian *arbitrista* Guillermo Garret held that redemption funds would be better employed towards the maintenance of a fleet to guard the coast and act as a deterrent to corsair activity.[145] The suggestion provoked a furious reply from both orders, who defended their vocation by making clear that even if the littoral were so protected captives would continue to be taken on the high seas and in Africa itself.[146] Neither,

---

[143] García Navarro, *Redenciones de cautivos*, pp. 17–19.

[144] A somewhat different interpretation of this decision is given in Friedman, *Spanish Captives*, p. 122. The attitude of the Council of Castile contrasts with that of the Council of Aragon which apparently attempted to refuse the brethren a redemption licence in 1602, 'donant per rahó de estat que convenia no aportar diners als enemichs'; see Jeroni Pujades, *Dietari*, ed. Josep Maria Casas Homs (4 vols., Barcelona, 1975–6), I, pp. 371–2; citation p. 372.

[145] See Friedman, *Spanish Captives*, p. 31, & Placer López, *Bibliografía mercedaria*, II, p. 307. The suggestion was directly opposed by the Castilian general M° Fray Gaspar Prieto, who was present at the *cortes*; Tirso, *Historia*, II, pp. 493–4.

[146] For the Mercedarian reply, see M° Fray Pedro Merino, *Memorial en defensa de la Redencion de cautivos segun la forma en que oy la exerce el sagrado Orden de nuestra Señora de la Merced* (Madrid: ?, 1627), and M° Fray Serafin de Freitas, *Por la Redempcion de cautivos. Sobre que no se deve impedir por la redempcion que llaman preservativa* (?: ?, 1631) in BNM, ms. 3536, ff. 10r–13v; apparently there is a MS copy in BNM, ms. 3572, ff. 326r–334r.

they said, was it acceptable that the many thousands already in captivity should be abandoned to their fate. Whatever the case may be, there can be little doubt that a loss of financial incentive would have lessened the intensity of captive taking, but the work of redemption carried a spiritual imperative which overrode all criticism.

Although severe restrictions on the export of money were eventually imposed, there was continual opposition to the drain of funds, particularly those from America.[147] In 1658 a *consulta* of the Council of the Indies to Philip IV lamented the tolerance shown to 'so many millions in silver which comes unregistered to Spain [from America] under the control of the religious, to the total ruin of the balance of Your Majesty's treasury'.[148] In this the Mercedarians were clearly the main offenders, but if the crown was prepared to tolerate such a haemorrhage of revenue it was because the Order rendered important services in return. The great redemption expeditions of the second half of the century were financed to a considerable degree by American *limosna*, which the crown permitted the Order to transport tax free on the condition that it give priority to the ransom of specified captives.[149] These were usually either creoles or seamen from the *Carrera de Indias* captured when their ships were snapped up by the corsairs off Gibraltar.[150] The *limosna* in question was supervised by the Council of the Indies, which, much to the Order's disgust, reserved the right of auditing its accounts. However, the monies gathered in America increasingly became the lifeblood of Mercedarian redemption, rising from 28.8% of the total *limosna* in 1648 to no less than 72.2% in 1668, a level maintained into the eighteenth century. The Mercedarian Indies had at last repaid their debt to the mother provinces.

V. *America: A Debt Repaid*

Towards the end of the sixteenth century the Mercedarians began to recover the status they had briefly held in the 1520s and 1530s as

---

[147] Friedman, *Spanish Captives*, pp. 109–10.

[148] Cited in Antonio Domínguez Ortiz, *The Golden Age of Spain, 1516–1659* (London, 1971), p. 301.

[149] Friedman, *Spanish Captives*, pp. 114–15. This requirement obviously caused significant problems where donations had themselves been given as *adjutorios* for individuals.

[150] *Ibid.*, p. 115.

a serious missionary order in America. This recovery owed much to
a tightening of discipline from the 1550s and then a formal adjustment of the relationship between the Order and its overseas patrimony in the following decade. The Mercedarians' status as a predominantly Spanish order lends a particular interest to this relationship, whose evolution into the seventeenth century provides an eloquent and unnoticed comment on the ties between America and the
metropolis.

The period immediately following the establishment of the four
sub-provinces of Lima, Cuzco, Chile and Guatemala in 1563 saw a
modest expansion and consolidation of the Order's position in America after the trials of recent years.[151] Three houses were founded in
Tucumán under the aegis of the province of Cuzco, while the
brethren distinguished themselves in the Araucanian rebellion that
shook the captain-generalcy of Chile during the 1570s.[152] The
Guadalajara constitutions of 1574 recognized the status of the Indies
within the greater Castilian entity and endorsed the right of that
province to maintain a vicar there, though the appointment had
nominally to be made by the general.[153] By the end of the decade the
American provincial system was operating smoothly, its hierarchy
bolstered periodically by the arrival of religious such as Pº Fray Diego
de Ángulo, the Salamanca-trained visitor general and twice provincial of Lima (1574–9, 1586–90?) who no doubt laid his bones in *ultra-
mar*.[154] However, the crisis of reform and its attendant shortage of
funds caused American affairs to be neglected in Spain, and it was
not until the Zumel provincialate (1585–8) that Castile felt able to
reassert its *superintendencia* over the Indies.[155]

In 1586 Zumel dispatched Fray Alonso Enríquez de Armendáriz
to Peru as visitor general at the head of a party of eighteen religious.
Enríquez, who was born in the Indies in about 1550, was instrumental in asserting a strong metropolitan presence in the American
provinces, where he remained an influential figure until his death as

---

[151] For more detail, see the relevant chs. of Pérez, *Historia de las misiones mercedarias*.

[152] Vázquez Núñez, *Manual*, I, pp. 540–1.

[153] ACA, Mon., vol. 4144, f. 131v.

[154] Pérez, *Religiosos de la Merced*, pp. 207–10, & Vázquez Núñez, *Manual*, II, pp. 30
& 39. Ángulo reached Peru in 1570 or '71. After some disparity, the duration of the
provincials' tenure was fixed at four years in 1593 given the huge territories over
which their authority extended; *ibid.*, p. 72.

[155] Vázquez Núñez, *Manual*, II, p. 39.

bishop of Michoacán in 1628.[156] Though accepted only reluctantly at first, his position was strengthened by the newly elected general, Fray Francisco de Salazar, who endorsed the appointment in 1587. At Zaragoza that year the chapter general agreed to the appointment of two vicars general for the Indies, as they are henceforth known: one for the viceroyalty of Peru and the other for the Order's holdings in Guatemala and Santo Domingo.[157] These offices were to be held in alternation by the provinces of Castile and Andalusia, the first vicar of Guatemala being another graduate of the Vera Cruz, the Castilian P° Fray Baltasar Camacho.[158] At Salazar's behest Enríquez returned to Spain in 1589–90 to familiarize himself with the new constitutions before heading back to the Indies with increased powers as vicar general of Peru.[159] In 1592 Enríquez summoned the three provinces of the viceroyalty to a major chapter in Lima at which the reform constitutions were promulgated and steps taken towards the creation of the province of Tucumán out of that of Cuzco.[160] The following year the delegates at Calatayud approved the concession of full electoral rights to the American provinces, by which the Castilian bloc gained a preeminent voice in the chapters general.[161]

As in Spain, the turn of the seventeenth century saw a marked expansion in the Mercedarian presence in America, with the establishment of numerous houses and *doctrinas* and an influx of new religious from the metropolis. Convents were founded at Asunción in 1593 and then at Puebla and Oaxaca in Mexico in 1599, along with several missions in Esmeraldas province in the presidency of Quito.[162] In 1608 Monroy saw to the erection of a sixth province in the Indies, that of Santo Domingo with a mere five houses and fifty religious, followed in 1615 by those of Quito and Mexico out of Lima and Guatemala respectively.[163] In Chile, however, the Araucanian insurrection of 1597 destroyed seven houses and accounted for much of

---

[156] *Id., Mercedarios ilustres*, pp. 407–13.

[157] *Id., Manual*, II, p. 44. The latter was eventually responsible for the entire viceroyalty of New Spain.

[158] *Ibid.*, p. 46.

[159] Enríquez's *patente* granted by Salazar in 1589 is reproduced in Vargas, *Chronica*, II, pp. 200–7.

[160] Pérez, *Religiosos de la Merced*, p. 233, & Vázquez Núñez, *Manual*, II, p. 63. The separation was ratified at Valladolid in 1599.

[161] Tirso, *Historia*, II, pp. 187–8.

[162] Vázquez Núñez, *Manual*, II, pp. 64, 86, & 62 respectively.

[163] *Ibid.*, pp. 85 & 110.

the province's personnel, but once again it was in adversity that the Mercedarians showed their mettle and the brethren distinguished themselves defending the beleaguered towns of the captain-general-cy.[164] Among these was Fray Alonso de Traña who entered the Order after a notable career in the royal cavalry and served as advi-sor to the governor García de Loyola on fortifications before his death in 1598. Another cavalryman, Francisco Ponce de León, a sur-vivor of the English attack on Cadiz in 1596, joined the Order in America early the following century and made his mark as a mission-ary among the Mayna indians of the Amazon basin.[165] In 1622 the viceroy of Peru, the marqués de Guadalcázar, appointed him *capellán mayor* of the army and navy at a time when the colonists were threat-ened by Dutch piracy and a further Araucanian rebellion. He spent five years with the army in Chile, of which he became provincial in 1628, and returned to Spain definitively in 1639 where the crown granted him an annual pension of 300 ducats in recognition of his services.

However, the most distinctive figure is Fray Diego de Porres, the apostle of Charcas, who joined the Mercedarians in Cuzco after par-ticipating in the conquest of Peru and gave nearly fifty years' service to the Order.[166] As we have seen, the brethren were not above taking up arms when circumstances required it, and the following incident, reported years later by Porres himself, provides an unusually vivid impression of the type of men who formed the Mercedarian mission-ary corps. Infuriated at the outrages committed against indians and colonists by Diego de Mendoza, the rebel governor of Santa Cruz de la Sierra, in June or July of 1576 Porres rode against him at the head of a party of thirty armed men, obliging him to negotiate after a series of running battles lasting two days.[167] These details and others like them remind us of the reputation that the Mercedarians carved out for themselves as military chaplains and frontiersmen *par excellence* in the harsh reality of American colonial life, for which their charac-ter and *métier* proved so eminently suited. They also explain the strong attraction of Mercedarian life for former soldiers, and the

---

[164] *Ibid.*, p. 68.

[165] *Ibid.*, pp. 140–2, & *id.*, *Mercedarios ilustres*, pp. 521–6.

[166] See Pérez, *Religiosos de la Merced*, pp. 236–46, and for an account of Porres' life and work see the *memorial* he presented to Philip II in 1585, reproduced in Vázquez Núñez, *Manual*, I, pp. 514–19.

[167] Pérez, *Religiosos de la Merced*, pp. 240–3.

favoured status of the Order and its brethren among the *conquistadores* themselves during the early colonial period.

Whatever the achievements of individual Mercedarians, the key to the Order's affairs in America in this period was personnel, jurisdiction, and above all money. As early as 1560 the American brethren had accused the Castilian hierarchy of having no interest in the development of the missions, but only in the lucre to be extracted from its subject provinces.[168] Whatever the truth of this allegation, there can be little doubt that the question of money, and particularly redemption *limosna*, was central to the agreement by which the American provinces were established in 1563, and to their relations with the metropolis thereafter. At Calatayud in 1593 the chapter general confirmed the exclusive right of the provinces of Castile and Andalusia to American *limosna*, which henceforth played an increasingly significant part in the funding of redemption expeditions.[169] Nevertheless, this was hardly the only revenue to reach Spain from America, and it is clear that religious had for some time been returning from the Indies with immense private fortunes. In 1596 the chapter general of Valladolid ordered five of these to be entailed as *rentas* devolving on specific houses, on which their erstwhile holders could hold usufructuary rights.[170] However, this privilege was only available to those with apostolic permission to possess money, and the rest were liable to have their lucre confiscated and applied to the colleges at Salamanca, Alcalá and Seville.[171]

With regard to the vexed issue of *espolio* — the money and property of deceased religious in the Indies — the delegates ruled that these should be granted to poor convents and *studia* in America in view of the 'discord, greed, scandal and disturbance which this matter has caused, and so that there be some restitution for the neediest and most pitiable houses'.[172] This was at odds with the 1588 constitutions

---

[168] Vázquez Núñez, *Manual*, I, p. 508.

[169] Tirso, *Historia*, II, pp. 188–9.

[170] The chapter imposed perpetual silence on these resolutions; ACA, Mon., vol. 2683, pp. 31–2. Fray Pedro de Curiel received a similar settlement at Zaragoza in 1587; see *ibid.*, pp. 17–18.

[171] *Ibid.*, p. 32. For an exception see the case of Monroy's successor as vicar general of Peru, the Castilian M° Fray Juan López Salmerón, whose 2500 ducats were first embargoed and then divided by the chapter general of Madrid (1606) between his mother house and himself; Vázquez Núñez, *Manual*, II, p. 95.

[172] ACA, Mon., vol. 2683, p. 31. The poverty of many Mercedarian houses in the viceroyalty of Peru was reported by the missionary Fray Diego de Porres in a *memorial* to the crown of *c*.1585; see Vázquez Núñez, *Manual*, II, p. 48.

which had required all *espolio* to be applied to the convent of profession, and from now on any property returned to Spain illicitly was to be put towards the maintenance of the colleges in Castile and Andalusia.[173] Even so, concern for the impoverishment of many houses in the Indies did not prevent the chapter general of Madrid in 1606 apportioning 3300 *escudos* of American provincial funds for the maintenance of San Adriano in Rome.[174] The view, rehearsed by Tirso himself in the 1630s, that in the five provinces of the viceroyalty of Peru 'there is greater wealth in one house than the Order in Europe put together' continued to prevail.[175] But clearly, as in Spain itself, the wealth of the Order in America rested in the hands of a few senior religious whose paths, at least until the 1620s, often led them back to the Peninsula.

While most friars tolerated the imposition of visitors and vicars general, the rapacity of some provoked deep resentment in the Indies. At Calatayud in 1593 the chapter general made provision for reports to be prepared on the vicar general's tenure and set his *vestuario* in Peru at 400 *pesos* annually for the province of Lima, and 300 each for those of Cuzco and Chile, but abuses continued on a grand scale.[176] During his tenure as vicar general of Peru in 1597–*c*.1599, the future master Fray Alonso de Monroy was claimed to have stripped the provinces of much of their wealth which he spirited back to Seville under an assumed name.[177] In 1599 the scandals of recent years prompted the crown to insist that henceforth the vicars for the Indies be elected by secret ballot at the chapters general, and the following year the *Congregazione* ordered the implementation of a brief issued to this effect by Gregory XIII.[178] Nevertheless, the Indies remained easy prey for abuse by Peninsular superiors who extorted revenue and shared the leading offices in its provinces between them. A slew of decrees passed at the chapter general of Guadalajara in 1609 had little effect, and from 1621 the provinces of Lima and Cuzco began petitioning the Council of the Indies for the office of vicar

---

[173] Vázquez Núñez, *Manual*, II, p. 72. This provision was, however, altered frequently, notably in 1615 when the *espolio* was reserved for the convents of Rome, Madrid, Barcelona and Alcalá; *ibid.*, p. 111.

[174] ACA, Mon., vol. 2683, p. 72.

[175] Tirso, *Historia*, II, p. 570.

[176] *Ibid.*, p. 190, & Vázquez Núñez, *Manual*, II, p. 72.

[177] Tirso, *Historia*, II, p. 283.

[178] Pérez, *Religiosos de la Merced*, p. 256, & Tirso, *Historia*, II, pp. 231 & 234.

general to be suppressed.[179] This was granted by Philip IV in May of the following year 'in view of the great disruption that has resulted from the frequency with which vicars general have been dispatched to the Indies'.[180] The delegates of the chapter general of Zaragoza appealed successfully against the *cédula*, but the 1620s saw considerable disruption in America, particularly in Lima, Mexico, and Tucumán, and it was not until the promulgation of a series of ordinances regulating the conduct of the vicars in 1639 that matters settled.[181] Even so, the issue dragged on until 1740 when Philip V passed a *sentencia definitiva* upholding the generals' right to send vicars to America.[182]

Set against the lucre received by the brethren from the Indies were the huge inroads made into the financial and above all human resources of the province of Castile in the development of the American missions during the sixteenth and early seventeenth centuries. From the time of the Order's slow recovery in America in the 1550s to the last major convoys of religious in the second decade of the seventeenth century, at least 295 friars left Spain for the Indies, most of them never to return.[183] This gives an average loss of five religious per year to America over the sixty years in question, and a mean of over eight friars in each of the thirty-six expeditions that took them there. Though initially drawn from throughout the Kingdom of Castile, the burden of providing religious increasingly fell on Andalusia which as a result saw a significant decline in its numbers in the last quarter of the sixteenth century.[184] Nevertheless, the convent of Seville established itself as the basis of Mercedarian expansion in America, where volunteers from all over the kingdom mustered to await the officials of the *Casa de la Con-*

---

[179] Pérez, *Religiosos de la Merced*, p. 422.
[180] Cited in *ibid.*, p. 423.
[181] See Vázquez Núñez, *Manual*, II, pp. 116, 123–4, & 133 respectively, & Pérez, *Religiosos de la Merced*, p. 423. Despite the appeal, the *cédula* found its way into the *Recopilación de las leyes de Indias* of 1628, though in modified form. For a contemporaneous view of this issue, see Salmerón, *Recuerdos Historicos*, pp. 307–19. The matter surfaced again in Peru at the end of the century; see Bernard Lavallé, *Las promesas ambiguas: Ensayos sobre el criollismo colonial en los Andes* (Lima, 1993), pp. 211–24.
[182] Pérez, *Religiosos de la Merced*, p. 424.
[183] This figure is extrapolated from *ibid.*, *passim*. I have tried not to include visitors and others who I know to have returned to the Peninsula in due course. Even given the greater reliability of figures from the *Casa de la Contratación* in Seville after 1552, these statistics must be seen as a low estimate; the true figure may well have been as much as 25% higher or more.
[184] See Appendix III. Castile was also affected, but both quickly recovered their numbers in the early 17th century.

tratación and the preparation of the transoceanic convoys that would
take them to the Indies.[185] Having journeyed down the Guadalquivir,
the brethren — most of them in their early thirties — embarked with
their food and possessions at Cadiz or Sanlúcar de Barrameda in readiness for a voyage that could last four months. Mortality rates were not
high *en route* — perhaps one in a hundred[186] — but religious were often
ill on arrival and the rigours of missionary life brought many to a premature end. However, during the period as a whole the Mercedarian
population in America rose from 154 in twenty-one houses in 1553 to
no less than 800 in eighty around 1615, while its mother provinces
increased from 330 to nearly 1000 over the same period.[187] No other
missionary order in Castile came near to matching this ratio of American to Peninsular religious over the period in question. These statistics
also serve to underline the importance of including missionary personnel in any assessment of the strength of the religious orders in the
metropolis, and of the Spanish Church in general.

The first sign of a significant resumption in the dispatch of Mercedarians to America after the crises of the 1530s and '40s comes in
1559, when six were sent to Santo Domingo and six more to
Guatemala.[188] Following the establishment of the four American
provinces in 1563, the crown sponsored the passage of twenty-one
religious to Peru under Fray Juan de Vargas, who travelled there in
two groups between 1563–5.[189] The onset of the Reform in Spain and
the ensuing shortage of money curtailed any significant dispatch of
religious until 1577, when Maldonado sent thirteen to Peru and seven
to Santo Domingo.[190] Seventeen more left in 1580, but this was not
enough to support the rapid expansion of the Order in the Indies. The
extent and growth of local recruitment is difficult to judge on this evidence, but clearly it was rather a long time coming for an order whose
missions often lay on the frontiers of Spanish settlement.[191] In 1581

---

[185] Pérez, *Religiosos de la Merced*, pp. 11–13.
[186] This figure compares with a mortality rate of 34% for Jesuit missionaries sent
from Portugal to China via Goa between 1581–1712 — that is, 127 out 376; C.R.
Boxer, *The Church Militant and Iberian Expansion, 1440–1770* (Baltimore, 1978), p. 82.
[187] Statistics from Vázquez Fernández, 'Cedulario mercedario', p. 619, & Vázquez
Núñez, *Manual*, II, pp. 88–9 respectively; see Appendix III.
[188] Pérez, *Religiosos de la Merced*, pp. 55–6 & 101 respectively.
[189] *Ibid.*, pp. 204–7.
[190] *Ibid.*, pp. 211–12 & 59–61.
[191] Evidence for local recruitment can no doubt be found in the rich conventual
archives of Lima, Cuzco and Quito.

the provincial of Lima, M° Fray Mateo de la Cuadra, informed the king that

> The greatest need that the Order now has in this kingdom is for religious to assist us, because at our present strength we can neither attend to the sustenance of our convents nor to the *studia* and Indian missions, and are often obliged to withdraw students prematurely so that they can fill in where they are needed.[192]

The crown responded by financing expeditions to Peru in 1588, to Guatemala in 1593 and to the new province of Tucumán in 1600, but it was the provincialate and then the generalate of Fray Francisco Zumel that afforded the Order's overseas expansion its greatest impulse.[193] During the former (1585–8) Zumel sent no less than five expeditions to the Indies, three to the viceroyalty of Peru and one each to Guatemala and Santo Domingo with a total of sixty-nine religious, perhaps six or eight per cent of the strength of the united province of Castile.[194] As general (1593–9), Zumel sent out a further fifty-two in seven expeditions, three to Peru, two to Santo Domingo, and one each to Mexico City and the viceroyalty of New Spain.[195] The pace of emigration was maintained into the early years of the seventeenth century, but the rate soon slackened and the expedition that took Tirso to Santo Domingo in 1616 was among the last of any size to reach the Indies.[196] The final major exodus — of twenty-one religious — was dispatched to Guatemala in 1617 by the Castilian general, M° Fray Francisco de Ribera.[197] The decline no doubt reflects the establishment of the Order as a significant ecclesiastical and academic presence in many of the leading cities of the empire — Mexico City, Lima, Cuzco and Quito in particular — and the increasing number of American-born religious that it attracted thereby. It reflects also the disillusionment of the brethren over the apti-

---

[192] Cited in Vázquez Núñez, *Manual*, II, pp. 30–1.

[193] For the expeditions paid for out of the *Real Hacienda*, see Pérez, *Religiosos de la Merced*, pp. 246–7, 116–17, & 473–4 respectively, and for some general remarks, pp. 11–13 & 15–16. The 21-strong party to Guatemala in 1617 cost the crown over 600,000 *maravedís*; *ibid.*, p. 385. The 1588 expedition was dispatched by Zumel as provincial.

[194] *Ibid.*, pp. 220–1, 236–7, 246–7, 112–13, & 64–5 respectively.

[195] *Ibid.*, pp. 249–50, 250–1, 253–4, 65–8, 68–9, 131–2, & 132–3 respectively.

[196] *Ibid.*, pp. 326–7. The register of the eight-strong party, made by the *Casa de la Contratación* on 23rd January 1616, describes Tirso as of 33 years of age (he appears in fact to have been just short of his 37th birthday), with a black beard and high forehead — 'frente [e]lebada, barbinegro'; *ibid.*, p. 326, & Tirso, *Historia*, I, xxvii.

[197] Pérez, *Religiosos de la Merced*, pp. 381–5.

tude of the Indians for Christian civility, in which they mirror the views expressed earlier by the three mendicant orders in America.[198] With the decline in Peninsular influence came the development of a *criollo* sentiment, of which the first expression is the protest of 1621 against the imposition of metropolitan vicars general. However, it was *limosna* that remained the key element, and the great *arcas de la redención* (redemption chests) that survive in Mercedarian houses throughout America bear witness to the immense contribution made by its provinces to the wealth and vocation of the Order in Castile during the seventeenth and eighteenth centuries.

VI. *The Mercedarian Discalced Movement*

When, in the 1630s, Tirso turned in his *Historia* to the spiritual obser-vance of the Order at the time of his profession in 1600, his comments are redolent of the frankness which prevented it being published for over three centuries. 'We lived,' he said, 'if not in relaxation then cer-tainly with a degree of indulgence which weakness and lack of fervour had sown among us, as it had done in other orders.'[199] Though this state of affairs remained the choice of the majority, by the close of the sixteenth century the discalced movement that had made such an impression on the Spanish religious Order was attracting the interest of many Mercedarians for whom the Reform had clearly not delivered its desired emphasis on spiritual renewal. Though the Order had no notable contemplative tradition, a number of recollect brethren had begun to appear in its ranks in mid-century and it was on this basis that the Discalced Mercedarian congregation was established in the years after 1600.[200] In Aragon the isolated convent of El Olivar had managed to retain its status as a house of retreat, earning it one of the few compliments the Dominican visitor Fray Guillermo Montaña felt able to pay the Order in these parts in the early 1570s.[201] At Alcalá,

---

[198] Vázquez Núñez, *Manual*, II, p. 108.

[199] *Op. cit.*, II, p. 276. The original reads: 'Viviásse no relajado pero con algunas permisiones que la flaqueça y poco ferbor avía, como acontece a los demás, intro-ducido entre los nuestros'.

[200] The main source is Fray Pedro de San Cecilio, *Annales del Orden de Descalzos de Nuestra Señora de la Merced Redempcion de Cautivos Christianos* (2 vols., Barcelona: Dionisio Hidalgo, 1669; facs. Madrid, 1985).

[201] IVDJ, env. 72, II, f. 35Av. The house, said Montaña in 1573 or '74, 'es de mucha devoçion'.

meanwhile, a small group gathered around the rector of the college of La Concepción, the mystic Agustín de Revenga (†1569), which included the Protestant Fray Rodrigo Guerrero.[202] Like Jerónimo Pérez and Pere Joan de Tàrrega at Gandía, this circle was attracted to the Jesuits with its stress on mental prayer and frequent reception of the sacraments, and Revenga and two others took the spiritual exercises at Alcalá in 1551. Revenga was also the author of a short spiritual tract — *Avisos para la vida espiritual de los Religiosos* — apparently the first work of its type by a Mercedarian.[203] The yearning for spiritual reform was therefore making a significant impression, and by 1556 Pº Fray Baltasar de Torres — Gaspar's brother — was commendator of an isolated hermitage at Fuensanta, not far from Albacete in La Mancha.[204]

However, the principal figure was Fray Juan Bautista González (1553–1616) who professed at Olmedo in Castile in 1573.[205] The severe asceticism practised by González provoked concern among Castilian superiors anxious to avoid a repetition of the Carmelite Reform in their own province, and for several years he led the life of an itinerant, visiting Rome in 1575 and moving from convent to convent throughout the Order. By the time of his ordination in 1579 Fray Juan Bautista seems to have been ready to establish a recollect branch, but continued opposition in Castile and the air of crisis that hung over the Order appears to have dissuaded him. Instead he accompanied the vicar general Fray Alonso Enríquez de Armendáriz to Peru in 1586 and, quite uniquely, it is here that the origins of the Discalced movement must be seen to lie.[206] Under the aegis of archbishop Toribio de Mogrovejo, González gathered a number of like-minded religious from the Mercedarian convent in Lima and retreated to a mission in the hinterland where he established a community whose reform lay in apostolic activity. However, attempts to found a

---

[202] See Vázquez Núñez, *Mercedarios ilustres*, p. 268.

[203] On this see Fray Melchor Rodríguez de Torres, *Agricultura del Alma*, ff. 125r–127r.

[204] See Vázquez Núñez, 'Conventos de la Orden', p. 147. The house, Nuestra Señora de los Remedios in the Desierto de Roda, had by 1558 been taken over by the Trinitarians. Recollect houses were later established at Moratalla in the Kingdom of Murcia (1590s) and Burriana in Valencia (1594); see *ibid.*, pp. 170 & 158 respectively.

[205] See P.Fr. Francisco Cano Manrique, 'Los Mercedarios Descalzos y América' in P.Fr. Luis Vázquez Fernández, ed., *Presencia de la Merced en América* [=*Estudios*] (2 vols., Madrid, 1991); II, pp. 845–7, esp. 850–60.

[206] Pérez, *Religiosos de la Merced*, pp. 221–2.

recollect convent in Lima and then Quito were blocked by Enríquez, and Fray Juan Bautista returned to Spain in 1591.

Though opposition and ridicule continued to mark his progress, the Order to which he returned was in a period of rapid evolution.[207] During the 1590s pressure mounted for the provision of facilities to satisfy the needs of such religious, several of whom sought refuge in more austere orders. This urge no doubt intensified as the Order deepened its involvement in wider society, and in 1593 the future general Fray Felipe de Guimerán obtained a brief permitting him to enter the Carthusians, though he appears not to have availed himself of it.[208] During his generalate Zumel responded to these demands by designating the convents of Segovia and Cazorla as houses of recollection for the provinces of Castile and Andalusia respectively.[209] However, the hierarchy persisted in regarding asceticism as a punishment rather than a vocation, and the use of these convents as penitenciaries for rebels made it impossible for religious to sustain a genuinely recollect life within them. The attitude of the Order at large is neatly encapsulated in the reaction of the chapter general of 1600 to the candidature of the ascetic Fray Juan Bernal. The delegates, said Tirso,

> shrank from the austerity and mortification of his life, declaring that since such rigour was his own perfection, the misery and difficulty of communicating it to others, along with the problems of imposing long-forgotten observances at a stroke, would bring despair to the faint-hearted and dejection to those unaccustomed to such measures.[210]

Even so, the failure of Zumel's initiative was clearly a turning point, and henceforth González found growing support for the establishment of a congregation that would allow Mercedarians to pursue an ascetic spirituality 'withdrawn from the clamour of this age' yet without leaving the Order.[211] At this moment, too, the brethren found the patronage not only of Monroy but of an influential Andalusian noblewoman, Beatriz Ramírez de Mendoza, condesa de

---

[207] P.Fr. Francisco Cano Manrique, 'Desarrollo histórico de la Orden Mercedaria Descalza' in *Analecta Mercedaria*, 7 (1988), pp. 129–50, esp. 131–7.

[208] Vázquez Núñez, *Manual*, II, pp. 80 & 98.

[209] *Ibid.*, p. 80. On Segovia, selected in 1594, see Tirso, *Historia*, II, p. 190, BNM, ms. 2684, f. 27r & v, & AHN, Clero, vol. 3320, f. 156v, where the house was described as being 'for the strict observance of our constitutions' — 'para que en el se guardase puntualmente nuestra constituçion'.

[210] Cited in Tirso, *Historia*, II, p. 248.

[211] Cited in *ibid.*, p. 276.

Castellar, who in 1603 proposed the foundation of two recollect houses on her immense Andalusian estates: one at El Viso near Seville and the other at Almoraima in the diocese of Cadiz.(135Bv) Until such time as the two Andalusian houses and a third endowed by her at Ribas de Jarama were ready, the brethren were permitted to take up lodging under Fray Juan Bautista in the countess' palace in Madrid.[212]

At his appointment in October 1602 Monroy, influenced perhaps by Castellar and the increasing strength of the recollect movement, had promised the papacy that he would take steps to further the reform of the Order.[213] True to his word, at the chapter provincial of Castile celebrated in May of the following year Monroy accepted the foundation of the two houses and, among a number of ordinances touching on religious observance, made provision for the drafting of a set of statutes by which these might be administered.[214] Rather than the establishment of a new congregation, the ostensible aim of the recollect foundations was to allow religious to pass back and forth from them with the permission of their superiors as and when they felt the need.[215] However, succeeding events demonstrate that rather more than this was intended. Immediately after the chapter, on 8th May 1603, the four founders of the Mercedarian recollect movement led by Fray Juan Bautista ceremonially discalced in the convent of Madrid.[216] The movement which had touched the Franciscans (1559), Carmelites (1562), Augustinians (1588), Benedictines (1588), and Trinitarians (1599) finally reached the Mercedarian Order, the last in Spain to give institutional expression to a discalced tendency within its ranks.[217]

---

[212] *Ibid.*

[213] *Ibid.*

[214] AHCB, ms. A-266, Antillón, *Memorias*, II, f. 135Bv. The *acta* of the chapter, which was held at Guadalajara, are reproduced in Tirso, *Historia*, II, pp. 273–5.

[215] AHCB, ms. A-266, Antillón, *Memorias*, II, ff. 135Av–135Br & 135Bv.

[216] The four were González — henceforth Fray Juan Bautista del Santísimo Sacramento — Fray Luis de Escobar (de Jesús María), Fray Miguel de Arribas (de las Llagas), and Fray Juan Maroto (de San José), along with two others who quickly abandoned the movement; Vázquez Núñez, *Manual*, II, p. 80. The ceremony was attended by Monroy and presumably by Fray Juan Bautista's distinguished brother, Mº Fray Cristóbal González, then commendator of Madrid.

[217] The Discalced or Recollect Franciscans, founded by Fray Pedro de Alcántara, are also known as the Alcantarines. The Recollect Benedictine congregation of Dom Sebastián de Villoslada (or de Nájera) provoked fierce opposition and was suppressed in 1609.

To the observance of the Recollect Franciscans adopted by the congregation was added a set of ten statutes providing for a stricter adherence to the 1588 constitutions as well as the use of the simpler habit traditionally worn by discalced friars.[218] Almost immediately, however, the Discalced found themselves at the centre of a major controversy, for Monroy had not only brooched this most delicate issue without consulting the rest of the Order, he had failed to reveal the involvement of a lay patron, Doña Beatriz herself.(135Br,135Bv) When he attempted to have the Discalced constitutions confirmed in Rome the following year, the proposal was turned down by the *Congregazione di Regolari* in view of the 'confusion and discord usually provoked by such foundations'.[219] Clearly, the papacy found the degree of separation envisaged by Monroy to be unacceptable, and the Recollection was limited to two or three designated convents in each province where strict observance — 'esta mayor reformaçion' — could be followed perpetually and without hindrance.[220] This observance, it was said rather pointedly, was to take 'the form first disposed by the Founders [of the Order] and followed by many of their successors', though as Tirso made clear this was effectively a reformed version of the existing constitutions.[221] The unsatisfactory constitutional history of the Mercedarians remained as serious an obstacle for the Discalced in 1603 as it had been for the Order at large in 1574.

Undaunted, Monroy persisted in Rome and on 23rd August 1606 his envoy Fray Hernando de Santiago obtained from Paul V the confirmation which Clement VIII had previously denied.(158v) In the early years the congregation provided a place of sanctuary for Mercedarians seeking spiritual refreshment, but it was soon attracting members in its own right. Thanks to the patronage of the condesa de Castellar and the example of the *beata* Mariana de Jesús

---

[218] AHCB, ms. A-266, Antillón, *Memorias*, II, f. 135Av. Though published by Monroy, the statutes or *Decalogo* were in fact prepared by M° Fray Hernando de Santiago; *Constituciones de los religiosos de la Recoleccion de la Orden de nuestra Señora de la Merced, Redencion de cautivos [...] para la fundacion y dotacion que haze la señora doña Beatriz Ramirez de Mendoza, Condesa de Castellar, de los primeros conventos de Recoleccion que instituye* (Madrid: Pedro Madrigal, 1603). These are reprinted in San Cecilio, *Anales*, I, pp. 291–9.

[219] The judgement of the *Congregazione*, made on 25th January 1604, is translated in Tirso, *Historia*, II, pp. 277–8; 277.

[220] Cited in *ibid.*, p. 278.

[221] Cited in *ibid.*, p. 277.

(1565–1624), the congregation expanded rapidly and began to acquire a character and momentum of its own.[222] Drawing on prevailing spiritual currents, the Discalced exchanged the scholasticism and Marian devotion of the parent order for the christocentric mysticism of the Franciscan and Carmelite reforms. More so than in the past, the brethren began to develop a spirituality focused first on the captive as worthy of charity and thence on the redemptive mystery of Christ. In doing so they significantly broadened the appeal of the congregation, particularly among the Andalusian aristocracy, which apart from the condesa endowed five houses in these parts between 1605 and 1624.[223] The modest needs of the religious were no doubt a further incentive, and their greatest patrons, the eighth duke and duchess of Medina Sidonia, established two convents at Sanlúcar de Barrameda and Vejer de la Frontera in 1615 and 1620 respectively.[224] Houses abandoned by the Calced or by other friars were snapped up by the brethren: three of the Order's convents in Sicily were transferred to them by Guimerán in 1612 while that of Valdunquillo near Valladolid was taken over after an abortive foundation by the Discalced Trinitarians.[225] By 1617 there were seven houses in Castile, ten in Andalusia, and six in Sicily, where the Discalced to a large extent took over from the Order itself.[226] The surge of novice vocations came after 1610 and by 1617 the total of affiliated religious appears to have reached 100. Support was particularly marked in Andalusia and among lay brothers who may have seen the congregation as means of gaining the representation which had earlier been denied them. Despite initial interest, this expansion did not extend to the Crown of Aragon proper where the provincial hierarchy banned the Discalced from making foundations, a move

---

[222] On Mariana, see P.Fr. Elías Gómez Domínguez, *Beata Mariana de Jesús: Mercedaria madrileña* (Rome, 1991), & Jodi Bilinkoff, 'A Saint for a City: Mariana de Jesús and Madrid, 1565–1624' in *Archiv für Reformationsgeschichte*, 88 (1997), pp. 322–7. For an impression of the life and spirituality of a Discalced community, see the visitation and profession book of the house of Argamasilla de Alba in La Mancha; BNM, ms. 6908. The volume stretches from its foundation in 1608 to 1656.

[223] See Vázquez Núñez, 'Conventos de la Orden', pp. 91–3.

[224] *Ibid.*, pp. 92–3. The others were Huelva, by the conde de Niebla (1605); Osuna, by the duke thereof (1609), and Cartaya by the duque de Béjar (1624).

[225] *Ibid.*, pp. 95 & 90.

[226] See Appendix III. Several of the Sicilian houses were apparently appropriated from the Order, having to be restored by Antillón in 1620; see AHCB, ms. A-266, Antillón, *Memorias*, II, ff. 411r & 412v.

supported by the Council of Aragon and the Valencian general Fray Felipe de Guimerán.[227]

Within a few years of the foundation the strain was beginning to tell on the Order itself. In 1608 the chapter provincial of Castile emphasized that passage to the Discalced was solely for those in search of greater austerity and contemplation, and ordered that henceforth *maestros* and *presentados* be prohibited from exercising their electoral rights while in seclusion.[228] Clearly, the aim of this legislation was not only to curb the exodus of religious to the Discalced, but to limit its capacity for representation in the chapters provincial. In this respect it also reflects increasing concern for the unity of the Order faced by the growing success and distinctiveness of the Discalced, which contributed to a wave of unrest and recrimination against Monroy. As the chronicler Vargas said, the Mercedarians could hardly expect their Discalced to be different from those of any other order, and so it turned out.[229]

Almost from its inception a series of important recruits into the Discalced began to fuel a desire for independence within the congregation. At Murcia in 1612 one of the founders, Fray Luis de Jesús María, successfully petitioned the Order not only to concede the Discalced a place in the four-member diffinitories of Castile and Andalusia, but also to grant the congregation a vote at the electoral chapters general.[230] The new Discalced constitutions were approved at Calatayud three years later, but in 1617 the brethren expressed the desire to elect their own provincials in Castile and Andalusia which the Order could not accept.[231] The battle for separation which followed was no simple conflict between the Calced and the Recollect congregation. Like the Carmelite Reform fifty years earlier, the matter was complicated by shifting allegiances and vicious in-fighting

---

[227] See *ibid.*, f. 135Br. Though the chapter provincial of El Olivar in 1603 seriously considered the transfer of the Valencian houses of Burriana or Sollana, nothing ever came of this; ARV, Clero, lib. 1705, f. 8r–v. With the partial exception of that founded by 1700 in the town of Utiel, then in the Kingdom of Castile and later annexed to that of Valencia, there has never been a Discalced Mercedarian house in the Peninsular Crown of Aragon. At the request of the provincial of France, Mᵉ Frey Jean Dubuc, the house at Bordeaux was declared one of 'recolección' by the chapter general of Murcia in 1612, though local opposition caused this project to be abandoned; Vázquez Núñez, *Manual*, II, p. 100.

[228] BNM, ms. 2684, f. 34r–v.

[229] Vázquez Núñez, *Manual*, II, pp. 80–1.

[230] *Ibid.*, p. 100.

[231] *Ibid.*, p. 111, & AHCB, ms. A-266, Antillón, *Memorias*, II, f. 136r respectively.

among the Calced brethren in particular, and by patronage, steady diplomacy and artful propaganda from their Discalced counterparts. In the Mercedarian case the *pleito* was to a large extent played out in Italy, and in the context of the troubled accession and tenure of the Sardinian general, M° Fray Ambrosio Machín (1618–22).

Beyond the establishment of the Discalced congregation itself, the origins of the *pleito* can be traced back to 1605 with the dispatch of M° Fray Hernando de Santiago to Rome as vicar general of Italy, Sicily, Sardinia and France.[232] Among other things, Santiago was able to expedite the establishment of a province of Italy, first tabled at the chapter provincial of the Crown of Aragon in 1603.[233] Although Sardinia seceded from the arrangement, preferring to remain part of the Aragonese province, in May 1606 Santiago managed to convene the Italian and Sicilian commendators to a chapter in Rome which elected him first provincial of Italy.(156r–v) From the outset the province was designed as a Spanish enclave in Italy — 'which is and always will be composed of Spanish religious' Santiago optimistically wrote in June of that year.[234] In token of this, the royal arms were affixed to the convent doors of San Adriano in Rome and Spaniards selected to fill the four-member diffinitory and all the leading commanderies. Santiago was confirmed in November, but the province very soon began to encounter stern opposition not only from Italian religious, who resented the overtly Spanish character of the new hierarchy, but from the many fugitives who had fled Monroy's regime in Spain and feared the establishment of a scion in Italy.[235] The turning point appears to have come with a royal directive originating from Monroy to the effect that the eight Italian and Sicilian houses were to be suppressed, probably as a measure against the large number of fugitives residing within them.(165v) The ensuing outcry almost forced the Spanish brethren out of Italy altogether, but in the end it was Santiago who paid the price and in November 1607 the province was suppressed and its erstwhile provincial ordered back to Spain in disgrace.[236]

---

[232] Pérez, *Fr. Hernando de Santiago*, p. 46.
[233] See Vázquez Núñez, *Manual*, II, p. 84, and for a full coverage of this episode, AHCB, ms. A-266, Antillón, *Memorias*, II, ff. 154r–177r, & Pérez, *Fr. Hernando de Santiago*, pp. 45–57.
[234] Pérez, *Fr. Hernando de Santiago*, pp. 47–8; citation p. 48.
[235] Vázquez Núñez, *Manual*, II, p. 84, & AHCB, ms. A-266, Antillón, *Memorias*, II, f. 159r.
[236] Vázquez Núñez, *Manual*, II, p. 85.

The events of 1606–7 confirmed Italy as a centre of opposition to the Monroy regime, and it was here that the disgruntled M° Fray Juan Teodoro de Monlluna made his stand against the general after his removal as provincial of Valencia in 1608.[237] By the time the re-establishment of the Italian province came under discussion at the chapter general of Murcia in 1612 the Discalced had begun to develop an important presence in Sicily, with no less than five communities established that year and a sixth following in 1614.[238] The settlement of these houses was supervised by the vicar general of Sicily, the Castilian-born member of the province of Andalusia, M° Fray Esteban de Muniera.[239] It was Muniera who, between 1618–19, unsuccessfully challenged the right of the prior of Barcelona, the Sardinian Fray Ambrosio Machín, to the vicar generalcy of the Order after Ribera's abdication from the high office.[240] The minutiae of this episode are beyond the scope of the present work, but it is important to place it in the context of the secession of the Discalced brethren from the main order, in which Muniera played a significant role.

The matter began with the appointment by Paul V of Muniera — then *procurador general* — as vicar general of the Order in February 1618, a month after the outgoing master, Fray Francisco de Ribera, finally gave up the seals of office. When Machín protested his ancient right as prior of Barcelona to the office of vicar general during the vacancy, a major crisis developed in both Spain and Italy. Though Discalced allegiances appear to have been as divided as those of the rest of the Order, it is clear that Muniera's support for the Recollect brethren in Sicily and the general antipathy felt by Andalusian brethren in particular towards the Aragonese gave him a consider-

---

[237] Also called Fray Juan Tadeo de Moluna. See AHCB, ms. A-266, Antillón, *Memorias*, II, ff. 177r–179v, & Tirso, *Historia*, II, pp. 294–8. The province of Valencia had been established out of that of the Crown of Aragon at El Olivar in 1603; see AHCB, ms. A-266, Antillón, *Memorias*, II, ff. 129r–131v.

[238] AHCB, ms. A-266, Antillón, *Memorias*, II, ff. 207v–208r, & Vázquez Núñez, 'Conventos de la Orden', pp. 94–6.

[239] Vázquez Núñez, *Manual*, II, p. 102. Muniera served as confessor both of the conde de Lemos during his tenure as viceroy of Sicily, and then of his successor the conde de Castro; *ibid.*, p. 81 & AHCB, ms. A-266, Antillón, *Memorias*, II, f. 411r respectively. There is a biography in Tirso, *Historia*, II, pp. 429–39.

[240] This episode is treated in great detail in AHCB, ms. A-266, Antillón, *Memorias*, II, ff. 224r–366r & Tirso, *Historia*, II, pp. 381–428. See also ACA, Mon., vol. 2837, pp. 61–2. For a brief discussion and some documents, see Vázquez Núñez, *Mercedarios ilustres*, pp. 454–69. Machín's election as general was not declared canonical until April 1619; see AHCB, ms. A-266, Antillón, *Memorias*, II, f. 391r.

able body of support in this quarter. However, the issue also came at a time of increasing tension between the Order and its Discalced congregation, which was to take the fullest possible advantage of the opportunities presented by it.

The Discalced question appears to have been set in train by the death of the founder, Fray Juan Bautista, in the new convent of Santa Bárbara in Madrid on 5th October 1616.[241] In early 1617 an inept attempt by the Andalusian brethren to gain independence from the provincial was foiled in Rome, resulting in a humiliating climbdown for the congregation at large.[242] Within a few months, however, the Discalced were demanding the right at the chapter provincial of Guadalajara to elect their own provincials in Castile and Andalusia.(136r) When this was turned down the Discalced electors flatly refused to have any further part in the proceedings and lodged a furious protest in Rome which it took a letter from Philip III to quash.[243] The stormy chapter general at which Machín was elected in June of the following year appears to have provided them with little satisfaction, and in September 1618, with the dispute over the vicar generalcy at its height, the Andalusian Discalced dispatched two religious to Rome in order to endorse Muniera's claim and obtain permission for the erection of their two provinces.[244]

However, once the brethren — Fray Juan Bautista de la Madre de Dios and Fray Diego de San Pablo — reached Rome, it became clear that their intention was to procure the separation of the Discalced from the main order.[245] In this endeavour they had the support of the

---

[241] Vázquez Núñez, *Manual*, II, p. 111.

[242] See Tirso, *Historia*, II, pp. 360–3, & particularly pp. 361–3 for the *poder* sent to Ribera and the *procurador general* in Rome by the Andalusian Discalced, dated Seville, 27th February 1617.

[243] See Vázquez Núñez, *Manual*, II, p. 111, & AHCB, ms. A-266, Antillón, *Memorias*, II, f. 383r–v for a partial reproduction of Philip's letter to his ambassador, Cardinal Gaspar de Borja, dated Madrid, 10th July 1617; see also *ibid.*, f. 398v.

[244] AHCB, ms. A-266, Antillón, *Memorias*, II, ff. 260v–267r. The chapter was attended by Tirso as diffinitor of Santo Domingo; *ibid.*, ff. 263v & 265r–v. On the Discalced religious, see *ibid.*, ff. 341r–342v. Whereas Tirso pays it scant attention, Antillón treats the separation of the Discalced at great length, as one would expect given the depth of his involvement in the affair; *ibid.*, ff. 341r–348r & 373v–436r. His account is to a large extent a defence of his record as *procurador general* in Rome between 1619–22; see *ibid.*, ff. 136v & 374v.

[245] *Ibid.*, ff. 373v–374r. This was the pair involved in the attempted separation of the Andalusian brethren in late 1616 or early 1617. Fray Diego de San Pablo, a distinguished preacher, was known as Pº Fray Diego de Sotomayor before his passage to the Discalced; Tirso, *Historia*, II, p. 301.

duke and particularly the duchess of Medina Sidonia, who recognized the opportunity both of seeing her Discalced confessor elected
first provincial of Andalusia and of holding the patronage of a new
religious order. 'Loaded with money and favours', as Antillón ruefully
put it, the brethren enlisted the support of Philip III's ambassador in
Rome, Cardinal Gaspar de Borja, vice-Protector of the Order, who
agreed to advance the matter without recourse to the chapter general.[246] Although apparently endorsed by Machín as *procurador general* in
a gesture of goodwill, Muniera clearly harboured a deep grudge
toward the new regime against which he exacted full revenge. Until
such time as the chronicler Mº Fray Juan de Antillón, Machín's personal *procurador*, was able to make his presence felt in the summer of
1619, the Discalced were free to pursue their interests in Rome without effective opposition.(375r–v) In this climate the Discalced were
able to recruit Muniera to the cause with plans to re-establish the
Italian province as a joint concern with the Calced, and the promise
to see him elected general of the Order in succession to
Machín.(375v–376r) As an Aragonese, Antillón was deeply concerned by the prospect of a further diminution in his province's status
through the re-establishment of a largely Castilian-based entity in
Italy, but there was little he could do to prevent it.(367v) In May of
that year the Discalced obtained a brief approving the foundation of
the Italian province and granting them the right to erect two more in
Castile and Andalusia.(377v–378r) Although Machín regarded the
province of Italy as a wholly impractical affair, he was prepared to
accept its establishment and Muniera duly convened a chapter at
Naples for 29th June 1619.[247] However, when news of further developments reached the general in June he adopted a much less conciliatory tone. From Seville he wrote to Antillón ordering him to do all
in his power to block the separation of the Discalced, but otherwise to
ensure that any rupture be final,

> so that they leave us and have their own general since we can no
> longer tolerate them and their disruption, and the day we forsake them
> the Recollection will itself be abandoned, and they will be burned alive
> for their ambition…[248]

---

[246] AHCB, ms. A-266, Antillón, *Memorias*, II, f. 374r; citation f. 373v.

[247] *Ibid.*, ff. 377v, 384r–v, & 393v–395v.

[248] The letter, dated Seville, 11th June 1619, is reproduced in part in *ibid.*, f.
377r–v; citation f. 377v.

Time would show this to be a serious miscalculation on his part, and it is clear that circumstances in Spain and disinformation from Muniera together caused the general to form an inaccurate picture of the mood in Italy. Elements of the Discalced were uneasy at the steps taken by Madre de Dios and San Pablo in Rome, while Machín evidently believed that no major decision could or would be made without his consent.[249] However, once details of the affair and the scurrilous manner in which it was being prosecuted became known to him, Machín fairly exploded with rage in a series of letters to Antillón. His comments provide an unusual exposé of the bitterness generated by the development of recollect movements within the religious orders during this period:

> The matter which concerns me most at present is this unjust separation contrived by the Discalced fathers. These, in their little nests and unendowed huts, are so few and so bereft of learned men that when I turned to the appointment of new commendators at this past chapter of Andalusia [at Seville] I found none suitable for the task. Their leaders, as few in number now as they have been since the Recollection was founded, have completely tyrannized the rest. It is therefore quite disgraceful that they should aspire to this, being as there is not one among them who by our standards would have reached beyond the rank of *presentado* at most — and even then there cannot be more than one or two of them […] such is their surpassing ignorance. Moreover, both experience and the actions of their leaders have demonstrated that they are driven by naked ambition, by the desire to rule and be lords over those whom they have oppressed and tyrannized. Fearful of being deprived of this lordship, they have interposed the duchess of Medina [Sidonia] in this matter, who has endorsed and supported their passion and vanity in return for the election of her confessor as provincial.[250]

But Machín's opposition was of course based on practical as well as emotional considerations. As he made clear in the *memorial* that accompanied this letter, the ten electoral votes that the Discalced would acquire through the creation of their two provinces would give them the balance of power at the chapters general and so disrupt the

---

[249] See *ibid.*, ff. 387v & 384v–385r respectively.

[250] The letter, which includes a seven-point *memorial*, is dated Seville, 9th July 1619 and is cited *in extenso* in *ibid.*, ff. 385v–387v; passage cited ff. 385v–386r. Despite Machín's references to the ignorance of the Discalced, *studia* in theology had been founded at Salamanca and Alcalá in 1608 and 1612 respectively, and in arts at Valladolid (after 1606) and Ribas de Jarama (after 1603); see Cano Manrique, 'Desarrollo histórico de la Orden Mercedaria Descalza', p. 137.

fragile settlement laid down in the 1588 constitutions.[251] It would be only a matter of time before they demanded a share in the alternation of the generalate itself, while the creation of further provinces would be followed by requests to conduct redemptions in their own right, along with efforts to assume the mantle of 'visitors and reformers of the Order' as a whole.(386v) The Recollects, in short, threatened to usurp the position of the 'primitive Order' by taking the spiritual high ground as the Discalced Carmelites had done the previous century — if, that is, they did not first secede altogether.[252]

As might be expected, Machín reacted angrily to what he regarded as a gross act of betrayal on the part of a handful of Discalced who did not represent the views of the majority of the congregation. (386v–387v) While he set about informing the king in Lisbon and preparing the despatch of a delegation to Rome, he urged Antillón to approach Paul V and attempt to bring round Cardinal Borja and his *letrado de cámara*, Diego de Saavedra y Fajardo.(387v) In Spain Machín published a tract against the separation of the Discalced while Antillón — now *procurador general* — presented Paul V with a long *memorial* in September 1619.[253] Despite his bluster, when it became clear that opinions were not to be swayed in Rome Machín ceded ground to the extent of offering the Discalced a commissary general in return for the withdrawal of the planned provinces.[254] As Machín told Antillón, he had no expectation of this being sufficient to put an end to the matter, but in mid-September he travelled to Sanlúcar de Barrameda to discuss the proposal with the duke and duchess of Medina Sidonia.(401r) After negotiations here an agreement was reached whereby the Discalced renounced the brief of May

---

[251] See AHCB, ms. A-266, Antillón, *Memorias*, II, f. 386r, and a further letter to Antillón, dated Seville, 16th July 1619, reproduced in part in *ibid.*, ff. 388r–389r; 388v.

[252] The comparison between the Mercedarians and the Calced and Discalced Carmelites is specifically made by Machín in *ibid.*, ff. 387r & 388r–v.

[253] *Ibid.*, ff. 398r & 400v. A copy of the tract, *Informacion o Apologia contra la separacion que de los Padres Calzados pretenden algunos Recoletos de la Merced*, in 22 ff. and printed in August or September 1619, apparently survives in the Biblioteca Universitaria de Sevilla, vol. 112/22. For another printed tract, by M° Fray Gerónimo de Bustamante & M° Fray Serafin de Freitas, *Discurso contra el progresso y separacion que pretenden los padres Recoletos de la Orden de nuestra señora de la Merced*, undated but *c*.1621, see Bod.L., Arch. Seld. A Subt. 21(32). On Antillón's *memorial*, see AHCB, ms. A-266, Antillón, *Memorias*, II, ff. 398v–400r.

[254] See Machín's letter to Antillón dated Seville, 3rd September 1619, reproduced in part in AHCB, ms. A-266, Antillón, *Memorias*, II, ff. 400v–401r.

1619 in favour of the provision of commissaries for Castile and Andalusia.

The *concordiae* which followed in Andalusia and Castile during September 1619 and January 1620 resemble those signed between orders and congregations in Spain since the fifteenth century.[255] Through these the Discalced remained part of the Order, but they were afforded a considerable degree of independence within it. Though responsible to the general, the commissaries were to hold jurisdiction over the Discalced houses in the area concerned with the same authority as the Calced provincial himself.(401v) These were to be elected at the chapter provincial by the general, the capitular president, the outgoing commissary, the provincial-elect and the Discalced commendators, and were to hold office for three years.(402v) However, though the commissary was granted wide powers, in practice his authority remained tied to that of the provincial, and like other arrangements of this sort it was not destined to last.

By the time Fray Juan de San José, one of the four founders of the congregation, was appointed *Comisario general de la Recolección de Castilla* in December 1619, both Madre de Dios and San Pablo had made their way back to Rome.[256] Here Borja again placed them under his protection and ordered Antillón to leave them undisturbed as they began pressing first for the enactment of the May brief and then for complete independence.(405r) In February 1620 Antillón succeeded in having the ongoing dispute placed under the nuncio's jurisdiction in Madrid, but as the year wore on it became obvious that, once again, the Order had little means of controlling the Discalced in Italy.(405r–406r) Attempts by the nuncio, Francesco Cennini, and Philip III himself to block any future separation were ignored in Rome where the Discalced had mobilized powerful support in the *Congregazione di Regolari*.[257] Despite Antillón's attentions the brethren succeeded in purchasing a hospice in Rome with Borja's support, and it is clear that they were in receipt of money from Spain and highly

---

[255] The text of the Castilian *concordia* is reproduced in *ibid.*, ff. 401v–403r. See also *ibid.*, f. 430r.

[256] *Ibid.*, ff. 403r–404r. His appointment was not confirmed by the nuncio until 25th June 1620.

[257] Philip's letter to his ambassador in Rome, the duque de Alburquerque, dated Madrid, 8th July 1620, is reproduced in *ibid.*, ff. 409v–410r. For an impression of the support enjoyed by the Discalced, which included the former nuncio to Spain Cardinal Ginnasio, see *ibid.*, f. 425r.

sensitive information from within the convent of San Adriano itself.[258] During a visitation of Sicily that summer Antillón found the Discalced as truculent as their fellows in Rome, and Muniera orchestrating their resistance from the viceregal court in Palermo.(410v–413r) Back in Rome, Fray Esteban de la Concepción, a Discalced commissary general sent by Machín to oppose the separation, promptly defected to the rebels leaving the hapless Antillón more isolated than ever.(413r–414r) In the hospice, meanwhile, San Pablo adopted the title of *procurador apostólico de la Recolección* and with Antillón's agreement departed for Madrid ostensibly to negotiate a solution to the crisis with the general.(414r–416r) This, however, was clearly no more than a ploy to return to Spain under safeconduct so as to gauge opinion in Andalusia and replenish funds for the final push in Rome.[259]

Machín, for his part, was by now at least as concerned with his imminent preconization as bishop of Alghero and the election of his successor as in the Discalced question.[260] A Calced commissary dispatched by him to address the matter in Rome, P° Fray Pedro Franco de Guzmán, turned out in fact to be on a mission to secure the Italian votes for the election of M° Fray Gaspar Prieto, provincial of Castile, at the forthcoming chapter general.[261] Within a few months, however, Guzmán had fallen out with Machín and Prieto and began to support the candidature of another Castilian, the former provincial M° Fray Juan de Peñacerrada (1617–20).(424r–v) Not only that, but Guzmán followed Concepción in defecting to the Discalced hospice and began to mount a campaign of disruption against Antillón in Rome.[262] By the time Guzmán's commission was revoked in August 1621 a great deal of damage had been done to the Order's credibility, and San Pablo's return that April found Antillón in an extremely poor position to defend its interests.(426r–427r)

Negotiations had been held between San Pablo and Machín in Madrid during January in which the general had offered the Dis-

---

[258] *Ibid.*, ff. 408r–409r. The hospice neighboured that established by the Discalced Trinitarians in 1619; *ibid.*, f. 409r.

[259] *Ibid.*, ff. 415v–416r & 428r–v.

[260] See his letter to Antillón dated Madrid, 2nd November 1620, reproduced in part in *ibid.*, ff. 414v–415r.

[261] *Ibid.*, ff. 419v–420r. Machín was also manoeuvering for the chapter general of Zaragoza, scheduled for Pentecost 1622, to be brought forward to March of that year in order to improve Prieto's chances of election; *ibid.*, ff. 420v–421v.

[262] *Ibid.*, ff. 420r, 423r, & 424v.

calced fully independent provinces and even a vicar general, but nothing came of them.[263] Machín's proposal that the congregation enjoy autonomy in all but name — even to the extent of celebrating their own chapters in isolation from those of the Calced — clearly failed to satisfy the underlying desire of significant power in the Order as a whole or else complete independence. Having consulted with the Andalusian Discalced and the duchess of Medina Sidonia in Sanlúcar de Barrameda, San Pablo made his way back to Rome to prepare the final assault.[264] However, the general's resolve was now broken and voices were being raised throughout the Order for an end to this matter.(430v) Machín had already sanctioned a complete severance with the Discalced, and having secured a renunciation of all rights to collect *limosna* and conduct redemptions, Antillón signed the act of separation on 26th May 1621.[265]

The *Concordia* provided for the appointment by the papacy of a vicar general who would govern the Discalced congregation with full powers until the next electoral chapter.[266] Here a successor would be elected by the Recollect commendators for a period of six years and henceforth the Calced and Discalced were to celebrate their chapters and conduct their affairs independently.(431v) Both parties surrendered all rights to intervene in the capitular or conventual affairs of the other, while the general and provincials of the Calced relinquished their authority and jurisdiction over the Recollects.[267] The Discalced, on the other hand, recognized the work of redemption as a preserve of the parent order, and undertook neither to collect alms nor to disrupt the transfer of the bequests and legacies donated to them for this purpose.(432v) Despite the opening words of the *Concordia* — 'Capitula separationis ac totalis dismembrationis inita inter partes' — the Recollects retained nominal ties with the Calced,

---

[263] See *ibid.*, f. 414v & Machín's letter to Antillón dated Madrid, 22nd January 1621, reproduced in part in *ibid.*, ff. 427v–428r.

[264] See Machín's letter to Antillón dated Madrid, 18th March 1621, reproduced in part in *ibid.*, f. 428r–v.

[265] *Ibid.*, f. 428v. The *Concordia*, signed under Borja's authority as cardinal protector of the Order, is reproduced in part in *ibid.*, ff. 431r–433r. It was confirmed by the *Congregazione di Regolari* on 20th July 1621 and by Gregory XV in a brief on 4th September, though Antillón questions whether this document was in fact the one to which he had earlier given his signature; see *ibid.*, ff. 433r–436r.

[266] *Ibid.*, f. 431r–v. The *comisario general* Fray Juan de San José was appointed.

[267] *Ibid.*, ff. 431v–432r. The only exception was the Discalced nunnery of Madrid, founded by the secular priest P. Juan Pacheco de Alarcón in 1609, which remained under the authority of the generals; *ibid.*, f. 432r.

whose master was afforded the right of confirming the vicars general.[268] However, the separation was to all intents and purposes final. A first redemption was undertaken in 1633, and in 1640 twenty-five years of litigation in Rome were brought to an end with the establishment of a new Discalced Mercedarian Order.

*

The Mercedarian hierarchy had clearly been outmanoeuvered by the Discalced, but it is hard to avoid the conclusion that its diplomacy was increasingly marked by an attitude of resignation where this matter was concerned. As Machín wrote to Antillón in November 1620,

> I've done what I can, but my good intentions have not borne fruit. This grieves me, for I cherish the peace and tranquility of the Order, but I am shortly to be leaving her [...] and although the creation of these Discalced provinces now seems likely I no longer have the money to grease as many palms as are required. I trust that Your Reverence will always do everything possible for the Order...(414v–415r)

However, from the beginning the Order had effectively restricted the Discalced to the choice of subservient union or complete separation, and there can be no doubt that the experience of the Carmelite and particularly the Trinitarian Reform had a significant bearing on the evolution of this issue.[269] Equally, the Mercedarian Discalced community had almost from its inception predicated its development on an ever-greater degree of independence within the Order, in which the aims and achievements of their brother and sister congregations provided the obvious model. The manner in which this separation was prosecuted by a minority of its members, through patronage, diplomacy and deception, provides a further example of the importance of institutional change to the survival of a spiritual reform. Machín, certainly, was under no illusions: 'they are,' he wrote in June 1620, 'a base and ignorant rabble, immature, puffed up, disobedient, without virtue or recollection, who have deceived everyone with a

---

[268] *Ibid.*, ff. 431r (citation) & 432v.

[269] For an overview of the contemporaneous Discalced Trinitarian movement, see *DHEE*, IV, p. 2595, and for a summary of the development of the Carmelite reform, see Allison Peers, *Handbook to the Life and Times*, pp. 3–104.

façade of coarse cloth and bare feet, and there will be no pacifying them until they are expelled altogether'.[270] Here, then, is the other side of the coin of Discalced reform in early modern Spain, a reminder that such congregations were neither universally popular nor necessarily free of the ambition and worldliness which they excoriated in their parent orders.[271]

The departure and indeed the formation of the Discalced by no means stripped the Order proper of its spiritual core. The ambient in which the congregation was founded is remarkable for the impulse to spiritual reform that had developed across the Order, however reticent the majority of religious were to such currents. The Mercedarians, it was felt around 1600, 'had cooled somewhat [in their spiritual fervour], and threatened to lapse once more into relaxation', and the support enjoyed by Fray Juan Bernal and others at this time bears witness to the efforts made to correct this state of affairs.[272] To this end Monroy accompanied the foundation of the Discalced at the chapter provincial of Castile in 1603 with a series of ordinances aimed at tightening the observance of the religious at large, and the chapters and visitations of succeeding years bear witness to the efforts made to implement them.[273] At Huete in 1604 the visitor M° Fray Matías de Cuéllar urged the religious to fulfil their duty of contemplation 'since this is of an essence to spiritual union and the consolation of the soul'.[274] The importance of mental prayer was underlined by Guimerán at the chapter general of Murcia in 1612, and the following year the Calced established a recollect house in Lima — over twenty years after Fray Juan Bautista had first attempted to do so.[275] But this was not all. If the physical work of redemption had failed as the Mercedarian 'observance', the spiritual significance of this activity represented a vast field which Mercedarian mystics and theolo-

---

[270] The letter to Antillón, dated Valladolid, 3rd June 1620, is reproduced in part in AHCB, ms. A-266, Antillón, *Memorias*, II, f. 430v.

[271] For an attack on the discalced movement as a whole, see the *Historia de Monte Celia de Nuestra Señora de la Salceda* (Granada: Juan Muñoz, 1616) of the Franciscan archbishop of Zaragoza, Fray Pedro González de Mendoza.

[272] Tirso, *Historia*, II, p. 267. See also the short biography by M° Fray Bernardo de Vargas, *Breve Relacion de la vida y muerte del [...] Maestro Fray Iuan Bernal...* (Naples: Iuan Iacomo Carlino, 1602).

[273] Tirso, *Historia*, II, pp. 273–4. In 1604 Monroy had printed in Seville a number of *Cartas pastorales a sus subditos exhortandolos a la mas extricta observancia*; see Placer López, *Bibliografía mercedaria*, II, p. 340.

[274] AHN, Clero, vol. 3320, f. 166v.

[275] Vázquez Núñez, *Manual*, II, pp. 98 & 117.

gians were only beginning to explore. The convent of Madrid developed an important school of spiritual writers during this period and in Fray Juan Falconi (1596–1638) the Order provided one of the leading mystical figures of the Spanish Baroque.[276] Yet the bitterness remained, and in one of the more truculent moments of the *Historia* Tirso scoffs at the Discalced, affirming that 'we do not miss them but take their separation as good riddance, and rejoice that their success [...] should come in exchange for the uniformity which we now enjoy'.[277]

VII. *Politics and Opposition*

The Discalced issue was hardly the first in which patronage and political intrigue had been brought to bear on the affairs of the Order, but none had had so considerable an effect on it. Shaken by the events of recent years and the growing unrest in the Indies, the premature death of Philip III in March 1621 came as a severe blow to the Mercedarians of Castile who had assiduously cultivated his patronage. As Tirso, mindful no doubt of the reversal of his own fortunes, lamented fifteen years later,

> With him died and died again the peace of his realm, the fecundity of his subjects, and the golden age itself. Just as the ruin of a great structure brings down all that is sumptuous, rich and learned, so our happiness perished with him, leaving us with but memories of so much good that had been lost.[278]

The onset of the Olivares regime with its strong Andalusian character soon alienated much of the Castilian hierarchy, accustomed as it was to having its voice heard at court. The patronage of the ill-fated

---

[276] For the Mercedarian Madrid school, see Gómez Domínguez, *Primer convento*, pp. 55–67. A follower of Santa Teresa, Falconi was the author of a pair of important mystical works, firstly the two *Cartillas para saber leer en Cristo*, and then *El pan nuestro de cada día* in which he advocated frequent communion. The earliest surviving editions of the two *Cartillas* are Antwerp: Jean Cnobbaert, 1637, 18°, and Zaragoza: Hospital Real, 1651, 4°. *El pan nuestro de cada día, esto es del SS. Sacramento del Altar...* (2nd edn., Madrid: Diego Díaz, 1661, 16°; 1st edn. Madrid, 1656), & ed. P.Fr. Elías Gómez Domínguez (Madrid, 1961); see Edgar Allison Peers, *Studies of the Spanish Mystics* (2 vols., London, 1927–30), II, pp. 345–92, and for M° Fray Mateo de Villaroel, another advocate of frequent reception of the sacraments, Vázquez Núñez, *Mercedarios ilustres*, pp. 430–2.
[277] Tirso, *Historia*, II, p. 278.
[278] *Ibid.*, p. 445.

Rodrigo Calderón, marqués de Siete Iglesias, over the convent of Madrid from 1618 provides an indication of the allegiances of its leading inmates.[279] The downfall of Philip III's influential confessor, the Dominican inquisitor general Fray Luis de Aliaga, inflicted further damage and hastened Machín's departure to the dismal Sardinian diocese of Alghero.[280] Despite a series of measures, Olivares failed in his attempt to have one of his creatures, the provincial of Andalusia Mº Fray Hernando de Rivera, elected at the chapter general of Zaragoza in May 1622.[281] The *Conde Duque* certainly had his supporters in the Order — the chronicler and playwright Mº Fray Alonso Remón for one — but this episode appears to have been a turning point, and in Tirso de Molina Olivares made a vulnerable but articulate enemy who was then at the height of his powers as a dramatist.[282] Frustrated by his failure to receive the recognition he felt was his due, by 1623 Tirso had begun to sharpen his pen against Olivares and his *privanza*. The government was not long in replying. In March 1624 the *Junta de Reformación*, a committee established to uphold public morality, recommended that friars be prohibited from attending plays or bullfights.[283] However, Fray Gabriel's barbs evidently continued to find their mark, and on 6th March 1625 the *Junta* issued a decree banning him from writing any profane literature and ordering him to be expelled from Madrid and sent 'to one of the most distant houses in his Order'.[284] Tirso duly fled to Andalusia, but returned to

---

[279] Gómez Domínguez, *Primer convento*, p. 99.

[280] Tirso, *Historia*, II, p. 475.

[281] *Ibid.*, I, lxxvi–lxxvii & cxli.

[282] For Tirso and the change of regime, see Ruth Lee Kennedy, '*La prudencia en la mujer* and the Ambient that Brought it Forth' in *Proceedings of the Modern Languages Association*, 63 (1948), pp. 1131–90, & J.C.J. Metford, 'Tirso de Molina and the Conde-Duque de Olivares' in *Bulletin of Hispanic Studies*, 36 (1959), pp. 15–27. On Remón, see P.Fr. Gumersindo Placer López, 'Biografia del Padre Alonso Remón, clásico español' in *Estudios*, 1 (1945), no. 2, pp. 99–127, & no. 3, pp. 59–90, and *id.*, 'Bibliografia del maestro Alonso Remón: Siglos XVI–XVII' in *Analecta Mercedaria*, 3 (1984), pp. 109–211.

[283] *Ibid.*, p. 15. In 1615 the chapter general of Calatayud had passed an ordinance banning the staging of plays in convents and otherwise prohibiting religious from attending them; Vázquez Núñez, *Manual*, II, p. 110. This, unsurprisingly, does not appear in Tirso's redaction of the synodalia in question (*Historia*, II, pp. 352–4). The first surviving ordinance on this question comes at Huete in 1596 when Zumel issued a ban against all religious from attending 'comedias farsas ni Representaçiones a la ciudad ni fuera de ella'; AHN, Clero, vol. 3320, f. 147r.

[284] On this see Ángel González Palencia, 'Quevedo y Tirso ante la Junta de Reformación' in *Boletín de la Real Academia Española*, 25 (1946), pp. 43–84, esp. 77–8. The decree is reproduced in Tirso, *Historia*, I, cxliii. The other Mercedarian dramatist, the chronicler Mº Fray Alonso Remón, was not implicated in this affair.

Castile the following year where the chapter provincial of Guadalajara elected him commendator of Trujillo in Extremadura, some 200
miles south-west of Madrid.[285]

There can be little doubt that Olivares was behind the dire warning issued to Tirso, but this was not the only way in which he made
his influence felt on the Order.[286] At the same chapter provincial the
notorious Fray Pedro Franco de Guzmán, a *pariente* of the Count-
Duke, acquired the commandery of Madrid through the offices of
Olivares' son-in-law, the marqués de Heliche.[287] Tempers were still
running high over the fiasco of the Discalced secession in which
Guzmán's negligence and obstruction in Rome was reckoned to have
contributed significantly to the outcome.[288] His appointment to one
of the most influential posts in the Order therefore served at once to
galvanize an incipient opposition and encourage Olivares to extend
his patronage network further. In 1627 the Count-Duke deprived the
outgoing master, the Castilian Mº Fray Gaspar Prieto, of the presidency of the chapter general of Toledo when he learnt that Prieto
intended to oppose the government's choice as successor, the
Aragonese Mº Fray Juan Cebrián.[289] This time Olivares did not fail
and Cebrián was duly elected to the high office, but the Mercedarian
opposition party now came out into the open. Led by Prieto, in May
1628 a group of religious turned on Guzmán and denounced him to
the Inquisition as a blasphemous and unashamed *converso*.[290] In his
defence Guzmán maintained that revenge was being taken on him
both for a number of serious accusations he had made against the
former general, and his having been instrumental in obliging Prieto's
brother Melchor to renounce the bishopric of Asunción in
Paraguay.[291] The issue had abated by the end of 1628 with Gaspar
Prieto's enforced departure for his diocese in Sardinia and the disper-
sal of other members of the Castilian opposition. Guzmán was
acquitted the following year, but the affair provides evidence of a
deep fissure within the province of Castile and the convent of Madrid

---

[285] Tirso, *Historia*, I, lxxx–lxxxii.
[286] See Metford, 'Tirso de Molina and the Conde-Duque de Olivares', *passim*.
[287] Tirso, *Historia*, I, cxli & cxliii. For Guzmán's kinship, see *ibid.*, cxxix.
[288] *Ibid.*, II, p. 488. It should be stated that the lengthy case made by Penedo Rey
for the enmity between Guzmán and Tirso has no direct evidence to support it; *ibid.*,
I, cxxvii–cxlv.
[289] *Ibid.*, cxl.
[290] *Ibid.*, xc–xci & cxxix–cxlv.
[291] *Ibid.*, cxl–cxli.

in particular with respect to Olivares which did not subside while the regime lasted.

Although the Church largely retained its close attachment to the crown during the reign of Philip IV, the *privanza* of the Count-Duke of Olivares provided the regulars at least with a less hospitable environment at court than had been the case during the previous reign.[292] The impression of a court 'waylaid by religious' lessened during the 1620s as the new regime adopted a less indulgent attitude to the increasing wealth and recruitment of the orders.[293] By the accession of Philip IV the intense opposition faced by the Discalced congregations over the proliferation of houses, land and personnel was beginning to spread to the entire Spanish religious Order. Although estimates of the size of the ecclesiastical estate were often grossly exaggerated, this would appear to have been over 100,000 by this time with the regular clergy numbering at least 60,000 and rising fast.[294] As the chronicler Gil González Dávila put it in 1623, 'I am a priest, but I must confess that there are more of us than are needed'.[295] With the *cortes* of Castile urging a firm stance to be taken in this matter, the Cistercian Fray Ángel Manrique added to the chorus of clerical *arbitristas* arguing for a drastic reduction in the size of the orders.[296] As he declared in 1624 with respect to the twofold increase in the number of religious houses over the previous fifty years,

> it is not that it would be impious to suppress large numbers of monasteries, but that piety itself demands that this be done […] for there are those who say that the orders have become a livelihood and that religious enter them as they might a business…[297]

While Mercedarians might pay lip-service to this general view, little was done to bring it to fruition.[298] Among the issues raised by the Order in its attack on the Discalced was the proliferation of houses

---

[292] See J.H. Elliott, *The Count-Duke of Olivares: The Statesman in an Age of Decline* (New Haven, 1986), pp. 182–4.

[293] Cited in Deleito y Piñuela, *La vida religiosa española*, p. 47.

[294] These rough estimates are based on the figures for the Kingdom of Castile in 1591 given in Ruiz Martín, 'Demografía religiosa' in *DHEE*, II, p. 685. See also Molinié-Bertrand, 'Le Clergé dans le royaume de Castille à la fin du XVIᵉ siècle', *passim*.

[295] Cited in Deleito y Piñuela, *La vida religiosa española*, p. 76.

[296] On the *cortes*, see *ibid.*, pp. 56–7 & 83–4.

[297] Cited in *ibid.*, p. 79.

[298] See, for example, the ordinance passed at Guadalajara in 1609, cited in Vázquez Núñez, *Manual*, II, p. 95.

implied by a full separation, but Mercedarian convents continued to be founded in Spain and elsewhere.[299] At the chapter general of Seville in 1625 the delegates ordered that henceforth none be admitted without a licence from the general or provincial, in view 'of the excessive number of religious that there are at present in the Order, to the extent that the convents can barely give them sustenance'.[300] However, the view expressed at the chapter provincial of Aragon in 1597 that no able young man be turned away for want of money or the lack of an old habit continued to prevail, and between 1619 and 1629 the number of conventuals at Madrid rose from seventy-eight to 126.[301]

Nevertheless, such criticisms were widely shared and despite their deep piety Spaniards began increasingly to draw distinctions between the spiritual and the economic and social order.[302] In 1626, for instance, the *cortes* warned that the kingdom was slowly falling under ecclesiastical control not only in terms of numbers, but in the acquisition of land in mortmain which threatened to suffocate lay society.[303] Towards the end of the reign Gaspar de Criales, bishop of Reggio di Calabria, informed the king that 'the great number of friars, priests and nuns has undoubtedly [...] served to limit procreation, to which the great shortage of people in the kingdom is principally due'.[304] These considerations were no doubt in Olivares' mind as he grappled with the commanding issues of foreign and domestic policy, but the services rendered by senior prelates in both Church and state were too significant and relations with the papacy too delicate for such issues to be pressed with any conviction.[305] The idea of the Church and its clergy as the bulwark of the faith was reinforced in many works during this period, not least the *Conservacion de monarquias religiosa y politica* (Madrid: D. García y Moras, 1648) of the Mercedarian Fray Francisco Henríquez, who rejoiced in the legions of religious interceding for Spain with the Almighty. It was this view which con-

---

[299] Bod.L., Arch. Seld. A Subt. 21(32), *Discurso*, pp. 2–4.

[300] Cited in Vázquez Núñez, *Manual*, II, p. 122.

[301] See *ibid.*, p. 60 and, for Madrid, Gómez Domínguez, *Primer convento*, p. 70. A further forty or fifty *criados* must be added to the latter figure. Numbers fell during the 1630s and remained static at around 110 religious until the mid-1660s when the figure rose to 128.

[302] Deleito y Piñuela, *La vida religiosa española*, p. 53.

[303] *Ibid.*, pp. 53 & 56.

[304] Cited in *ibid.*, p. 79.

[305] Elliott, *The Count-Duke of Olivares*, pp. 183–4.

tinued to prevail, and the Church was therefore able to escape the worst of the fiscal and other exactions planned for it by the *arbitristas* and the *cortes*. The regulars, meanwhile, continued to accumulate personnel, houses, and land until the eighteenth century, and by 1700 the Mercedarians — not including the Discalced — had reached a total of perhaps 4800 religious in 217 houses, statistics which place it among the half dozen or so largest orders in Spain.[306]

Despite continued opposition of this sort, matters settled after the Guzmán affair of 1628–9 and during the Cebrián and Serrano generalates the Order entered a period of acquiescence or cooperation with the regime. Tirso, who returned from exile in Trujillo in 1629, began a slow rehabilitation during the provincialate of his friend M° Fray Pedro Merino (1629–32), being appointed diffinitor provincial of Castile and chronicler general in succession to Fray Alonso Remón in 1632.[307] Henceforth he was deeply engaged in the preparation of the *Historia*, but as the decade drew on Fray Gabriel fell out rather badly with the influential M° Fray Marcos Salmerón who guided the fortunes of Castile as provincial and then vicar provincial between 1632 and 1639. The long duration of his tenure, caused by the death of the recently elected provincial M° Fray Juan de Peñacerrada in 1636, provoked much anger in Castile, not least in M° Fray Gabriel Téllez.[308] Never a man to hold his tongue, in 1639 Tirso issued the following opinion on the end of Salmerón's tenure in the closing chapters of the *Historia*:

> I'm not sure if [he] hadn't exhausted himself with so much governing, for, to be sure, a seven-year provincialate is neither bearable for the incumbent nor tolerable for his subjects since even the six of the general tends to be more than enough — and that that we don't see him too often. With this, however, the former found himself unburdened and the rest of us unvexed.[309]

But Salmerón was not the only object of Fray Gabriel's spleen, for as the fortunes of the monarchy began to wane in the late 1630s so elements of the province of Castile resumed their opposition to Oli-

---

[306] See Appendix III. The figures, which cover the entire Order, represent a more than fivefold increase in religious and twofold increase in houses on 1550.

[307] See Tirso, *Historia*, I, xc–xci, xcv–xcvi, & clii.

[308] Conceded the title of *maestro* by dint of his services as *cronista general* in 1636, the appointment was confirmed in Rome the following year and executed on the completion of the *Historia* in January 1639; *ibid.*, cvi & clxv.

[309] *Ibid.*, II, p. 602.

vares.[310] While on a trip to the Crown of Aragon to conduct his researches, Tirso had witnessed the humiliating defeat of the Spanish army outside Leucatte in Languedoc in September 1637, an experience which left him deeply embittered against the regime.[311] However, worse was in store both for Tirso and the government. The Revolt of the Catalans which broke out in earnest in May 1640 found the general Me Fra Dalmau Serra, a native of Olot, stranded in Barcelona.[312] At court the commendator of Madrid, Pº Fray Juan de Fonseca, was faced with the unenviable task of defending Serra against claims that he had left for Barcelona with the intention of fomenting sedition against the crown and that he had previously supported the Catalan embassy in Castile. The evidence for this is unclear and Serra was later acquitted by Philip IV, but the interim was to have serious consequences for Tirso once Salmerón assumed the vicar-generalcy in the master's absence.[313] As in 1625, Tirso's subversive literary activity had crossed the bounds of acceptability for someone in his position and this time it was Salmerón who moved against him. During a visitation of the convent of Madrid in September 1640 Salmerón passed a series of ordinances designed to silence Fray Gabriel's insolence once and for all.[314] Not only were the religious banned from attending theatres and from keeping dramatical works and other profane literature in their cells, but the following ordinance was issued under pain of excommunication:

> I order each and every religious in this convent to desist from writing satirical verse in couplets or letters in prose against the government or individuals of whatsoever condition or degree they may be, desiring as I do to avoid any inconvenience which malice or carelessness in this matter may cause. This, as befits their estate, the religious will observe as much in word and deed as in their writings.[315]

---

[310] *Ibid.*, I, cx.

[311] See *ibid.*, I, cv, & II, pp. 609–11, and, for the background, Elliott, *The Revolt of the Catalans*, pp. 325–6.

[312] Tirso, *Historia*, I, cx–cxii. Usually called Dalmacio Sierra.

[313] The body of the murdered viceroy, the count de Santa Coloma, was recovered by the Mercedarians and laid out in the priory church on 7th June 1640, presumably at Serra's instigation; Gazulla, *La Patrona de Barcelona*, p. 44. Three years later Serra is recorded among the many religious in Barcelona to have observed the funeral exequies of Louis XIII; Duran i Sanpere & Sanabre, eds., *Llibre de les Solemnitats*, II, pp. 257–8.

[314] See P.Fr. Manuel Penedo Rey, 'Tirso de Molina: Aportaciones biográficas' in *Estudios*, 5 (1949), pp. 19–122, esp. 86–7.

[315] Cited in *ibid.*, pp. 86–7 & Tirso, *Historia*, I, cxi.

The justification for the ordinance is ostensibly that of preserving the Order against potential detractors, but there can be little doubt as to who the object of this drubbing was. To reinforce his point, Salmerón demoted Tirso from the office of *cronista general* to that of a mere *cronista de anillo*, and exiled him to Cuenca from where he issued a futile protest in October 1640.[316] Though he is recorded as vice-commendator of Toledo in December 1643 and became commendator of Soria in 1645, this episode effectively destroyed Fray Gabriel's career in the Order, and the twilight of his life was spent chafing under Salmerón's generalcy (1642–8) as the *Historia General de la Orden de Nuestra Señora de las Mercedes* fell into oblivion in the conventual archive of Madrid.[317] His dramatic output continued, but as for Maldonado in 1582 and for many others who fill the pages of his chronicle, time had measured 'the intolerable distance that there is between ruling and being ruled'.[318] Salmerón's death in January 1648 briefly promised a restoration of Tirso's fortunes, but it was on his way back to Madrid, the scene of his greatest achievements, that he died at the convent of Almazán on about the 20th February 1648.[319]

VIII. *The Politics of Canonization*

The canonizations and beatifications achieved by the Order from the 1620s onwards represent the apogee of Mercedarian Reform. Through them the Order completed its lengthy evolution from lay brotherhood to religious institute and was granted access to the stellar heights of Spanish Baroque orthodoxy. Yet the canonizations are nothing if not the product of Mercedarian Reform itself, and on close observation bear witness not only to the tortuousness of that process as it had unfolded over the previous sixty years, but to a broader legacy stretching back four centuries.

One of the features which distinguishes the Mercedarian Order from its monastic and mendicant counterparts until the seventeenth century is the absence of a body of canonized and beatified saints. In

---

[316] For this and Tirso's reaction, see Penedo Rey, 'Tirso de Molina: Aportaciones biográficas', pp. 80–92, & Tirso, *Historia*, I, cx & cxii–cxiii.

[317] Tirso, *Historia*, I, cxv–cxix.

[318] *Ibid.*, II, p. 45.

[319] *Ibid.*, I, cxix–cxxii.

its earliest days the Order had taken the advocation of the mother house, the convent of Santa Eulàlia in Barcelona, but by 1250 this was being supplanted by that of *Nostra Senyora de la Mercè*. This advocation was strengthened in succeeding decades by the establishment of Marian shrines at El Olivar, El Puig and at Barcelona itself where the conventual church was rededicated to Our Lady of Mercy in the 1270s. By the 1380s the Virgin was established as the patroness of the Order which henceforth fixed on her name as its official title. This allegiance remained strong, particularly in the Crown of Aragon where Our Lady of Mercy gradually replaced the original dedications in most houses.[320] By the end of the fifteenth century the Mercedarian liturgy was — as it has remained — predominantly Marian in character, with precise dispositions for the recitation of the prayers associated with the four main feasts of the Virgin; in 1487, for instance, the ordinances of the chapter general of Pamplona required the Mercedarian day to be punctuated with the refrain *In omni tribulatione et angustia subveniat nobis Virgo Maria* uttered on the stroke of every hour.[321]

However, it is in this period also that the increasing concern among Mercedarians for the spirituality of the earliest members of the Order becomes apparent. In 1499 the Catalan general M⁰ Fra Joan Urgell endowed the priory church of Barcelona with a costly altarpiece adorned, among other things, with statues of Ramon Nonat and Pere Armengol.[322] Of these only the former can be identified with any documented figure, though even here confusion reigns with three or four different candidates spanning the thirteenth and fourteenth centuries.[323] As for Armengol, the Catalan nobleman and

---

[320] Vázquez Núñez, *Manual*, I, p. 344.

[321] *Ibid.*, p. 386.

[322] Gazulla, *La Patrona de Barcelona*, p. 38.

[323] In 1239 one Raimundus Nonnatus was raised to the purple by Gregory IX, though he died the following year; see Fr Conrad Eubel, *Hierachia Catholica Medii Aevi*, vol. I (Münster, 1913), p. 6. In 1338 a second Mercedarian, Raimundus Montfort, was created cardinal by Benedict XII, but he too died almost immediately; *ibid.*, p. 17. For the latest interpretation, see Antoni Llorens i Solé, 'Sant Ramon Nonat: Un nou camí que mena al coneixement del sant. Era el cinqué i darrer fill del cavaller, Arnau de Cardona' in *Analecta Sacra Tarraconensia*, 59 (1986), pp. 223–57. On the other hand the bones venerated at the convent of Sant Ramon Nonat at El Portell near Lleida appear to have belonged to a religious of the mid-14th century, Fra Ramon Saló; Vázquez Núñez, *Mercedarios ilustres*, p. 40. This house, acquired by the Order as the hermitage of Sant Nicolau in 1245, was renamed in the second half of the 15th century and, with some lacunae, remained a lucrative dependency of the priory of Barcelona until the 19th century. It is also known as Bell-Lloch and La Manresana; see *id.*, 'Conventos de la Orden', p. 140.

Mercedarian redemptor who purportedly died in 1300, virtually nothing is known prior to the Urgell commission. Even so, within a few years both Nonat and Armengol had appeared in that scrapbook of Renaissance piety, the *Commentaria urbana* of Raffaello Maffei (Volaterrano), tangible evidence of the spread of their cult.[324] In 1496 a confraternity was established at the Mercedarian house in Perpignan under the advocation of (the uncanonized) Sant Serapi, the English or Scottish crusader who, as one of Nolasco's earliest followers, was supposedly disembowelled in North Africa for attempting to proselytize during a redemption.[325] By the 1520s Mº Fray Domingo de Clavería had raised an altar to Serapi (Serapio) at his convent of Girona, with a second dedicated at Barcelona at about this time.[326] While there is as little reliable evidence for his existence as for Armengol's, Serapi seems to have been the only 'primitive' figure to have found liturgical representation in the Mercedarian breviaries printed in the first half of the sixteenth century.[327] In 1575 one of Serapio's ribs is recorded as having been brought from Rome to Tarragona, but by this time the spiritual condition of the Order was demanding the canonization not so much of the founder's followers as of the Patriarch himself.[328]

The peculiar status of the Mercedarian constitution and the issue of royal patronage had prevented the founding role of Pere Nolasch being developed until the 1560s, and it was not until the following decade that the Dominican visitor Fray Guillermo Montaña identified him as the spiritual guide of the Order. Even so, matters progressed slowly, and only after the Reform crisis had passed could steps be taken to procure his canonization. Meanwhile, the cult of Ramon Nonat continued to gain in popularity, especially at El Portell near Lleida where his bones had been venerated since the mid fifteenth century.[329] In 1584 the visitors felt obliged to prohibit the removal of any more relics from his tomb, and his image is recorded

---

[324] First edn. Rome: J. Besicken, 1506; see Vázquez Núñez, *Mercedarios ilustres*, pp. 37–8 & 40.

[325] See P.Fr. Ernesto González Castro, 'Iter canónico y estado actual del santoral Mercedario' in *La Orden de la Merced* [=*Estudios*] (Madrid, 1970); pp. 273–328; 293–4.

[326] Tirso, *Historia*, I, p. 453. The claims made for the age of these shrines during the beatification inquiries in 1717 would appear to be exaggerated; González Castro, 'Iter canónico', p. 294.

[327] Vázquez Núñez, 'La antigua liturgia mercedaria', p. 17.

[328] On the relic of Serapio, see ACA, Mon., vol. 2676, f. 468r.

[329] González Castro, 'Iter canónico', p. 291.

as having performed miracles at Perpignan fourteen years later.[330] Evidence that the Order was making efforts to promote his cult comes in 1592 when the vicar general of Peru, Fray Alonso Enríquez de Armendáriz, ordered that all communities in the viceroyalty erect a chapel and altar to San Ramón in the conventual church.[331] However, it was Zumel's *De Vitis Patrum* of 1588 and Guimerán's *Breve historia* published three years later which provided the historical background of this and future canonizations, and the period is characterized by a growing interest in reclaiming the thirteenth century as the primordial age of the Order. At the chapter general of Valladolid in 1596 the delegates ordered that henceforth the feast of St Laurence — 10th August — was to be celebrated as the anniversary of the legendary foundation in 1218.[332] This was reiterated three years later, and the anniversary of the Order's confirmation — 17th January 1235, the feast of St Antony Abbot — along with the Nativity of the Virgin (8th September) were added as days of solemn observance.[333] The delegates also ordered that a *ceremonial* be compiled by a religious from each of the Crowns of Aragon and Castile, while the 'Rezos de los santos' (sanctorale), apparently approved by Sixtus V in 1587, was to be published forthwith.[334]

In this environment the canonization of the Dominican Ramon de Penyafort (Raymond of Pennafort) in 1601 represented an important fillip for Mercedarian efforts to achieve similar status for their own patriarchs. Penyafort's supposed role in the foundation of the Order as Jaume I's confessor for the first time brought Pere Nolasch into the spotlight of popular spirituality. As the diarist Jeroni Pujades reported of the celebrations held to mark the event in Barcelona in May of that year, the Mercedarian *escudellers* confraternity bore on their *carro triomphal* a tableau showing the Virgin appearing to Penyafort, Jaume

---

[330] See ACA, Mon., vol. 2850, f. 60r, & Tirso, *Historia*, II, pp. 201–2.

[331] Pérez, *Religiosos de la Merced*, pp. 235–6.

[332] ACA, Mon., vol. 2683, p. 28; see also Vázquez Núñez, *Mercedarios ilustres*, p. 364.

[333] ACA, Mon., vol. 2683, p. 41, & Tirso, *Historia*, II, pp. 233 & 234. The latter date, chosen as the anniversary of the apparation of the Virgin to Nolasco, Jaume I and Ramon de Penyafort in 1218, was transferred in 1616 to the last Sunday in August; AHCB, ms. A-266, Antillón, *Memorias*, II, f. 223v.

[334] ACA, Mon., vol. 2683, p. 41, and, for Sixtus' approval, AHCB, ms. A-266, Antillón, *Memorias*, II, f. 223v. The office did not, however, appear until Ribera had the *Officia Propria Festorum* printed along with the *Missae propriae festorum* in Madrid in 1617; see Placer López, *Bibliografía mercedaria*, II, p. 616.

I and 'Pere Nolasc, the first master general and founder of the Order'.[335] Although Dominican claims that Penyafort was in fact the founder of the Mercedarians soon dampened their enthusiasm, the canonization provided a significant platform for the Order's own campaign in Spain and Rome. As a result of assertions made in the *proceso* and the canonization bull, in 1602 the Mercedarians were for the first time able to obtain papal confirmation for the triple apparition of the Virgin at the founding of the Order, and matters progressed steadily from now on.[336] At the chapter general of Madrid in 1606 the delegates ordered proceedings to be initiated towards the beatification of Ramon Nonat and entrusted the matter to two Castilian religious, M° Fray Cristóbal González and M° Fray Jerónimo de Bustamante.[337] At Guadalajara in 1609 the chapter ordered that his feast day (30th August) be celebrated and alms gathered throughout the Order towards the cost of beatification.[338] At Murcia three years later González and Bustamante were replaced by the Sardinian Fray Ambrosio Machín, who immediately began gathering testimonies in the Crown of Aragon. In 1615 the campaign received a major boost with the donation by the bishop of Santiago de Cuba, Fray Alonso Enríquez de Armendáriz, of some 5000 *escudos* to defray the rising expenses of the *proceso*.[339] By now, moreover, the Order was turning its attention to the quatercentenary of the foundation in 1218. After some difficulty the new Mercedarian office was confirmed by Paul V between 1615–16, but the celebrations were overshadowed by the Discalced crisis and the dispute over the vicar generalcy which raged throughout 1618.[340] After the settlement of the Discalced matter in 1621 the Order turned to the formation of a corpus of saints as a salve not only for the wounds of recent years but for the disasters and humiliation that had befallen it over the previous three or four generations. In this way the canonization issue developed into the great

---

[335] Cited in Pujades, *Dietari*, IV, p. 112. The friars themselves carried a tabernacle depicting the same scene; *ibid.*, p. 115. For more on the canonization and festivities in Barcelona, see *Dietari [del Antich Consell]*, VII, pp. 306–64.

[336] See González Castro, 'Las constituciones del P. Raimundo Albert', pp. 143–4. The bull of confirmation was issued by Clement VIII on 9th July 1602; see Linás, *Bullarium*, p. 176.

[337] ACA, Mon., vol. 2683, p. 74.

[338] González Castro, 'Iter canónico', p. 291.

[339] Vázquez Núñez, *Manual*, II, p. 108.

[340] The office particularly concerned the vigil of 10th August, the anniversary of the foundation of the Order; see AHCB, ms. A-266, Antillón, *Memorias*, II, f. 223r–v.

endeavour of the 1620s and '30s, in which the Order strained every sinew to ensure its realization, and from which it emerged utterly transfigured.

In view of the increasing attention being paid to it as the mother house of the Order, the priory of Barcelona underwent a gradual rehabilitation from the end of the sixteenth century. At Valladolid in 1599 the delegates extended the voting powers of the prior in view of the status of his convent, and three years later the Aragonese redemptors chose Barcelona as their point of embarkation for North Africa, the first time in many decades that the city had played host to this spectacle.[341] As Pujades pointed out, the Catalans deeply resented the way in which Valencia had consistently been favoured in this matter despite the number of Mercedarian *baciners* operating in the Principality, and the return of the expedition to Barcelona in August 1604 was celebrated with a lengthy procession through the city.[342] Ever since the Reform crisis of the 1570s and '80s, both the finances and the fabric of the priory had been in a distinctly parlous state — 'aquella tan pobre quanto antigua cassa' as Tirso said of it in the 1630s.[343] However, help was at hand and in 1599 Philip III voted the priory 1000 ducats from the sale of old galleys in order to rebuild a part of the convent which had just collapsed.[344] This largesse was followed in 1612 with the grant of the royal rents of Agramunt for a period of six years in order to effect the repairs, but it was soon made clear that this could not yield the 50,000 *escudos* needed to make good the reconstruction.[345] Further royal subsidies followed in 1613 and 1619, and in 1627 the delegates at Toledo agreed to apply the *espolios* of all Peninsular religious deceased in the Indies to the priory for five years, this in view of 'the great poverty and lack of buildings of this, our mother house'.[346] But although the reconstruction did not come in time for the great events that followed, the priory of Barcelona had already played her essential part in their elaboration.

*

---

[341] See, respectively, ACA, Mon., vol. 2683, p. 42, & Pujades, *Dietari*, I, p. 240.
[342] Pujades, *Dietari*, I, pp. 370–2.
[343] Tirso, *Historia*, II, p. 279.
[344] ACA, Mon., vol. 2661, pp. 241–2.
[345] *Ibid.*, pp. 295 & 305.
[346] *Ibid.*, pp. 315 & 357, & Tirso, *Historia*, II, p. 540.

However tenuous the evidence for his life and sanctity, the emphasis on Nonat in the years after 1600 reflects both the survival of his body at El Portell and the development of a significant cult over the previous century and a half. Neither of these basic preconditions existed for Pere Nolasch, whose beatification *proceso* presented the Order with major problems of authentication.[347] Nevertheless, in 1622 — the year of four canonizations in Spain — the chapter general of Zaragoza charged the new master Fray Gaspar Prieto with the weighty responsibility of obtaining recognition of the cult of both Nonato and the Patriarch.[348] The matter was pursued in Rome by a succession of *procuradores generales* and from now on the two *procesos* are intimately associated. That of Nonato, however, proved considerably more straightforward and he was beatified with the assistance of the Discalced *procurador* Fray Diego de San Ramón in November 1625, a rare case of cooperation between the two congregations.[349]

Beyond the absence of a body, the greatest difficulty faced by the Mercedarians in obtaining similar status for Nolasco was the lack of genuine information regarding his nationality and date of birth, or even the precise circumstances of his establishment of the Order.[350] These issues were consistently raised during the *proceso* which by the mid-1620s was evidently in serious difficulties. The impasse was to some extent broken late in 1626 by the 'discovery' in the priory of Barcelona of the *Documento de los sellos*, a forgery of the *acta* of the chapter general of 1260 purporting to furnish details of the life of the Patriarch.[351] However, this clearly failed to sway every opinion in Rome, not least because the ambitious prior of Barcelona, Fra Josep

---

[347] On this see P.Fr. José María Delgado Varela, 'Sobre la canonización de San Pedro Nolasco' in *Estudios*, 12 (1956), pp. 265–95, & González Castro, 'Iter canónico', pp. 276–89.

[348] Tirso, *Historia*, II, pp. 483–4.

[349] González Castro, 'Iter canónico', p. 292. The Calced version of the beatification was granted in May of the following year.

[350] *Ibid.*, p. 278.

[351] See *ibid.*, p. 277, & Delgado Varela, 'Sobre la canonización', pp. 266–8. The *Documento de los sellos* is reproduced in M° Fray Felipe Colombo, *Vida de Nuestro Gloriosissimo Patriarca y Padre S. Pedro Nolasco...* (Madrid: Imprenta Real, 1674), pp. 441–6. The extent to which credence is still given to the apocryphal stories and writings produced by the Order in this period is as disappointing as it is surprising; for some particularly flagrant examples, see Francisco Javier Fernández Conde & Antonio Oliver Montserrat, 'Cultura y pensamiento religioso en la baja Edad Media' in *HIE*, II(ii), pp. 175–253, esp. 205, 211 *et seq.*, & 250.

Soler, openly declared the *acta* to be apocryphal.[352] Despite continued support from Diego de San Ramón and the 2000 *escudos* voted by the delegates at Toledo, the *procurador general* M° Fray Luis de Aparicio suffered an important setback in December 1627 when the *Congregazione di Riti* rejected Nolasco's candidature for lack of evidence.[353] However, the Discalced still wielded much influence in Rome, and with the help of a substantial financial inducement San Ramón was able to persuade Cardinal Antonio Barberini to grant the *proceso* a second hearing before the *Congregazione*. This, after sitting in July and August, accepted Pedro Nolasco as an immemorial cult in view of his status as the founder of an Order and duly beatified him on 11th October 1628.[354]

The news was naturally received with great rejoicing in the Order, where costly festivities and *certámenes literarios* (literary tourneys) were held in Madrid, Toledo, Segovia, Seville, Granada, Barcelona, Cuzco and Lima from 1628 onwards.[355] Those at Salamanca were organized by Tirso himself in October 1629 while Lope de Vega's play *La vida de San Pedro Nolasco* was performed at court before the royal family.[356] In Rome, however, the effort to obtain the canonization of a representative group of Mercedarian saints was far from over. Between 1626 and 1630 the *procesos* of a further four saints from the Mercedarian *centuria primera* were initiated in Rome. The first was that of Pedro Pascual, the supposedly Mercedarian bishop of Jaén who died in Granada in 1300.[357] In 1627 it was the turn of Maria de Cervelló (or de Socós) of Barcelona, the noblewoman reckoned by the Order to have been its first nun.[358] Those of Pedro Armengol and Serapio followed in 1627 and 1630 respectively, and that of the Discalced tertiary Mariana de Jesús was tabled by Diego de San Ramón

---

[352] See Delgado Varela, 'Sobre la canonización', p. 273, & Tirso, *Historia*, II, p. 545.

[353] González Castro, 'Iter canónico', p. 283. For the Toledo subsidy, see Tirso, *Historia*, II, pp. 540–1.

[354] González Castro, 'Iter canónico', pp. 284 & 289. The full canonization did not come until 1664 for Pedro Nolasco and 1669 for Ramón Nonato.

[355] See *ibid.*, pp. 284–5, & Tirso, *Historia*, II, p. 547. Others are known to have been celebrated at Guadalajara, Cuenca and Palma.

[356] See Tirso, *Historia*, I, xci & clxvii, & Vázquez Núñez, *Manual*, II, p. 134. The play is published in vol. V of the Biblioteca de Autores Españoles (Madrid, 1895).

[357] See González Castro, 'Iter canónico', pp. 299–301.

[358] *Ibid.*, pp. 302–5. Her cult appears to date from the late 14th century; see Gazulla, *La Patrona de Barcelona*, p. 18. On the reaction in Barcelona between 1627–9, see Pujades, *Dietari*, IV, pp. 118, 128–9, & 214–15.

in 1628, only four years after her death.[359] Despite — or perhaps because of — the elaborate forgeries prepared in support of their canonizations, none of these progressed beyond beatification and that of Mariana de Jesús had to wait until 1783 for acceptance in Rome.[360]

Whatever the case may be, the canonizations and beatifications represented a major triumph for the Order which for more than a century dedicated the talents of its most gifted members to their realization. Beyond the pioneering work of Zumel and Guimerán in the 1580s and '90s, a succession of religious turned their hands to the hagiographies upon which the cult and tradition of most of their subjects depended. The appearance of Fray Bernardo de Vargas' brief *Vita et Martyrium Sancti Serapionis Martyris* in 1619 heralded the beginning of a flood of hagiographical works, penned both independently and as part of the new chronicles then being written.[361] Between 1628 and 1629 no less than six biographies of San Pedro Nolasco were published by some of the most distinguished members of the Order.[362] At least one life of San Ramón Nonato appeared in the Crown of Aragon in the early 1630s, while Antillón completed a double biography of Nolasco and Nonato which, like so much else in these parts, was never printed.[363] 1629 saw the publication of the first biographies of Pedro

---

[359] See, respectively, González Castro, 'Iter canónico', pp. 296–9, 293–6, and, for Mariana, 305–9 & Gómez Domínguez, *Beata Mariana de Jesús, passim.*

[360] For some of the forgeries used, see Vázquez Núñez, *Manual*, I, ix. Pedro Pascual was granted *culto inmemorial* in 1655 and beatified in 1670; Pedro Armengol in 1686 and 1688 respectively; Maria de Cervelló 1692 and 1729; Serapio 1728 and 1743. Mariana de Jesús has yet to receive *culto inmemorial.* Though only beatified, these with the exception of Mariana customarily carry the title of 'saint'. To this roll must of course be added the Virgen de la Merced herself, whose feast, 24th September, was placed on the Latin calendar in 1696.

[361] On the *Vita*, a pamphlet in 4 ff., see Placer López, *Bibliografía mercedaria*, II, p. 995.

[362] These were, in 1628, M° Fray Pedro Merino and M° Fray Alonso Remón, and in 1629 M° Fray Francisco Boyl (or Boil), Fray Esteban Morales, M° Fray Melchor Prieto and M° Fray Bernardo de Vargas; see the relevant entries in Placer López, *Bibliografía mercedaria*, I & II, & *id.*, 'Libros y escritos mercedarios en torno a San Pedro Nolasco' in *Estudios*, 12 (1956), pp. 585–620. It should be noted that M° Fray Melchor Rodríguez de Torres claimed to have completed a life of Nolasco in 1603; see *ibid.*, p. 611.

[363] A biography by Fray Esteban Morales was apparently published in Valencia in 1632; see Placer López, *Bibliografía mercedaria*, II, p. 358. For Nolasco and Nonato, see M° Fray Juan de Antillón's *Chronologicon Generalicio, o Memorias Chronologicas. Contienen las Vidas de Nuestro Padre y Patriarca San Pedro Nolasco, y San Ramon Nonat* completed in 1633. The original MS is lost and the work survives in a late 18th-century copy by the Valencian M° Fray Agustín Arqués y Jover in BUV, ms. 1106.

Pascual and of Maria de Cervelló, to which Tirso added a second in around 1640.[364] Neither were the Order's shrines forgotten. The *Nuestra Señora del Puche* (1631) of the Valencian Mº Fray Francisco Boyl — another victim of the Olivares regime — provided the basis for a similar work by Tirso which he included in the first volume of the *Historia*.[365] One of Tirso's best-known *autos sacramentales*, *La dama del Olivar*, was first published in the *Quinta Parte* of his *Comedias* in 1636.[366] These details bear witness not only to Tirso's personal interest in the Marian shrines of the Order, but to his deep involvement in the elaboration of a new Mercedarian image and spirituality, of which his *Historia* was intended to be a major component.[367] Its rejection in 1640 deprived the Mercedarians of the complete printed vernacular chronicle that had so long been awaited and it was 1646 before Salmerón's *Recuerdos Historicos* was able to provide the Order with a substitute.[368]

The importance given to chronicles and hagiographies in emphasizing the antiquity of the Order was matched by the efforts to give iconographical form to the saints and miracles by which it was reckoned to have been created and afforded its distinctive character. In 1626 the Mercedarians ordered a set of twenty-five engravings depicting the life of the as yet unbeatified Pedro Nolasco from Jusepe Martínez, an Aragonese artist resident in Rome.[369] These appeared

---

[364] These are, respectively, Fray Pedro de San Cecilio (OMD), *Vida y martirio de san Pedro Pascual obispo de Jaen de la Orden de la Merced* (Granada: Bartolomé de Lorenzana, 1629); Fray Esteban de Corbera, *Vida y echos maravillosos de doña Maria de Cervellon llamada Maria Socos* (Barcelona: Pedro Lacaualleria, 1629), & Tirso's *Vida de la Santa Madre Doña Maria de Cervellón*, ed. Marcelino Menéndez Pelayo (Madrid, 1908). On the latter, see Tirso, *Historia*, I, cix.

[365] *Nuestra Señora del Puche, Camara Angelical de Maria Santissima...* (Valencia: Silvestre Esparsa, 1631). On Boyl, who was exiled to El Puig by the government in 1629, see Tirso, *Historia*, I, cclxix. Tirso's version is in *ibid.*, pp. 81–97, published as *El monasterio de el Puig y su Virgen*, ed. P.Fr. Juan Devesa Blanco (Valencia, 1968).

[366] See *La Dama del Olivar*, ed. Juan A. Hormigón (Madrid, 1970).

[367] On Tirso's Marian interest, see *id.*, *Historia*, I, xcii & cix.

[368] The first complete history of the Order, Vargas' *Chronica*, appeared in two volumes between 1619–22. The first vernacular chronicle, Remón's *Historia*, was conceived in three volumes, but the author completed only the first two, these being published between 1618–33. It was this work which Tirso was commissioned to complete as chronicler general in 1632, his remit being the period from 1574 to the present. Having done so in 1636 Tirso apparently decided that Remón's work was unworthy of his third volume and that he would go on to produce a complete history of the Order. This he concluded in 1639. The resulting *Historia* was apparently rejected as unsuitable and at times irreverent; see *ibid.*, I, clii–clxxiv.

[369] These are discussed and illustrated in Delgado Varela, 'Sobre la canonización', pp. 273–89.

the following year in time to assist the ongoing *proceso* with an illustrated description of Nolasco's cult. In August 1628, shortly before the official announcement of Nolasco's beatification in Rome, the artist Francisco de Zurbarán was commissioned by the Mercedarians of Seville to produce a cycle of twenty-two canvases illustrating the life of the Patriarch.[370] When Zurbarán turned to the fulfilment of this commission it was on the basis of Martínez' work that many of the paintings were conceived and executed, though it seems likely from the contract that the artist was specifically required to adhere to the engravings in question. Of this cycle, which was hung along the 'Claustro de los bojes', only twelve or fifteen paintings were executed, of which but six are known to have been carried out by Zurbarán himself.[371] Though there is no evidence to support it, the contract may well have been satisfied with other paintings, including the ten *doctores* discussed above and several more of the friars whose beatification the Order was pursuing in Rome. Indeed, it may be that events caused the Nolasco cycle to be delayed somewhat, for the only dated canvas to survive from 1628 is that of the crucified San Serapio, whose *proceso* had begun in Rome the previous year.[372] A companion portrait, perhaps that of San Pedro Armengol (*proceso* 1630), also hung in the 'Sala de profundis', while two more depicting the similarly uncanonized San Carmelo and San Pedro Pascual (*proceso* 1626) were produced for the 'Sala de láminas'.[373] At Madrid, meanwhile, the Order commissioned the talents of Eugenio Cajés, Gregorio Hernández, Francisco Herrera the elder and Vicente Carducho in the lavish decoration of the convent of Nuestra Señora de los Remedios, though its destruction in 1835 prevents us recreating this scheme to the same degree.[374] Here, too, the Order enjoyed significant patronage from the early seventeenth century, including Pedro Franqueza, the ill-fated conde de Villalonga, and Mencía de la Cerda, marquesa del Valle, who was buried in the sumptuous *capilla may-*

---

[370] On this see Guinard, *Zurbarán*, pp. 88–94, esp. 88–9. It should be noted that a nephew of the artist, Fray Sebastián de Zurbarán, was a member of the Seville community at this time; see P.Fr. Luis Vázquez Fernández, 'Zurbarán: Escultor para la Merced de Azuaga' in *BPCONSM*, 36 (1998), no. 131, pp. 75–9.

[371] See *Zurbarán* [Museo del Prado] (Madrid, 1988), pp. 16–17.

[372] Guinard, *Zurbarán*, p. 94.

[373] *Ibid.*, p. 95.

[374] See Gómez Domínguez, *Primer convento*, pp. 95–116, & P.Fr. Eliseo Tourón del Pie, 'Pintores y escultores que trabajaron para la Merced en el siglo XVII, que figuran en A. Palomino' in *Analecta Mercedaria*, 3 (1984), pp. 61–82.

or along with her husband in 1637.[375] These observations remind us
not only how intimate was the association between art and religious
politics in the seventeenth century, but how far the Mercedarian
Order had come in the previous fifty or sixty years of its history.

IX. *Epilogue*

Whatever the achievements of recent decades, the problems faced by
the Order from the 1560s reflect not only the unsatisfactory spiritual
and constitutional legacy inherited by Mercedarians from their
medieval past, but also the heightened standards of a new age in religious society. Of those whose canonization the Mercedarians pursued
from 1600 onwards, one, San Pedro Pascual, the spurious bishop of
Jaén, is palpably an invention of the early seventeenth century.[376]
Yet, fabricated though he is, in Pedro Pascual's character we can
detect the aspirations of leading Mercedarians as much for the past as
for the present and future of their Order.[377] Thus, the scholarly
Pedro, a companion of Aquinas and Bonaventure at the university of
Paris, is first raised to the episcopate and then hideously martyred in
Granada in 1300 after confounding a group of Muslim and Jewish
theologians. The impression of the Order as ancient, steeped in
learning, passionate in the defence of Christianity against the Infidel,
and above all worthy of comparison with any other, was one that the
Mercedarian élite was anxious to convey to the faithful. These preoc-
cupations can also be detected in the identities of the other figures
promoted by the Order at this time: Nonato, the redemptor and Cardinal, evidence of its power within the Church; Serapio, the crusad-
ing Briton who had joined Nolasco's company, proof of its interna-

---

[375] Gómez Domínguez, *Primer convento*, pp. 99–100.

[376] A Pedro Pascual is recorded as bishop of Jaén between 1296–1300, but there is
no evidence that he was a Mercedarian; see Eubel, *Hierarchia Catholica*, I, p. 262. All
points to his adoption as such in the early 17th century. For the array of spiritual
writings attributed to the Pseudo-Pedro Pascual (Pere Pasqual) from this time, consult Vicenç Beltran, Gemma Avenoza, & B.J. Concheff, eds., *Bibliografia de textos catalans antichs* on CD-ROM of ADMYTE (Madrid: Micronet, Fundación V Centenario,
Biblioteca Nacional, 1994). For one particular measure resorted to by the Order in
this area, see Jaume Riera i Sans, 'La doble falsificació de la portadella d'un incunable (Hain 12433)' in *Revista de llibreria antiquària*, 10 (1985), pp. 1–13. I am grateful to
Dra. Gemma Avenoza of the Universitat de Barcelona for her assistance on this
subject.

[377] For a standard biography, see Tirso, *Historia*, I, pp. 177–84.

tional appeal; Cervelló, the noble foundress of an ancient congregation of nuns, and finally and most pointedly, Armengol, the Catalan bandit turned ransomer.[378] The elaboration of San Pedro Pascual and his like, of a past and tradition that had never belonged to the Mercedarians, is therefore bound up with the creation of a new observance and what is ultimately a new religious order. Or, as Tirso put it,

> Envied now rather than envious, with this our Order acquired the status of the most eminent congregations [...] and after more than four hundred years our glorious virgin patrons were reborn in the knowledge of the faithful, and the veneration of the Church militant.[379]

---

[378] Armengol was the subject of a novela by Tirso in the *Deleitar aprovechando* cycle, *El bandolero*; see André Nougué, *L'Œuvre en prose de Tirso de Molina: «Los Cigarrales de Toledo» et «Deleytar Aprovechando»* (Toulouse, 1962), pp. 241–51, and for the anonymous play, *El honor en el suplicio y prodigio de Cataluña San Pedro Armengol, ibid.*, pp. 307–9.

[379] Tirso, *Historia*, II, p. 547.

CONCLUSION

STRUCTURES OF REFORM

Victorious we shall emerge [...] from all our shipwrecks.[1]

It is apparent to anyone studying the history of the Mercedarian Order *in toto* that its reform cannot be confined solely to the eighty years around the turn of the seventeenth century which make up the core of this work. Since reform is indivisible from the religious life itself it cannot therefore be abstracted from any part or period of it. In this sense, reform represents a continuing dialogue between the spiritual and institutional elements through which each order is moulded. But a religious order is not an isolated entity. Religious may withdraw from the world but they cannot leave it, and their orders are in turn shaped and modified by the external realities they were founded to complement. The reform of a religious order is therefore a reassertion of its spiritual and corporeal significance for the reform of *Christianitas*. As Fray Gabriel Téllez declared in his secular incognito, 'it is through the spiritual recollection of their lives that religious communities shore up that which vice is ever on the point of bringing to ruination'.[2] It is in this cast of mind, in respect of the wider relationship of the monastic order in society, that the problem of Mercedarian Reform has here been addressed.

By the end of the thirteenth century the conflict between the lay and clerical elements in the Order's make-up had come to the surface. Though Ramon Albert's reform in the years after 1317 was broadly a clericalizing one, his legislation could not expunge the lay characteristics which Fra Pere Nolasch and his successors had enshrined in the vocation, structure and outlook of the Order. That these characteristics survived into the late sixteenth century is apparent not only from the events discussed in the closing paragraphs of

---

[1] Tirso, *Historia*, II, p. 9.

[2] *Id.*, *Les trois maris mystifiés (Los tres maridos burlados)*, ed. André Nougué (Paris, 1966), p. 118. A novela, part of the *Cigarrales de Toledo* cycle, composed *c.*1611; see Nougué, *L'Œuvre en prose de Tirso de Molina*, pp. 117–32.

Chapter Seven, but in the measures taken to curb them during the period as a whole. Many of the most significant priorities of reformist Mercedarians under Philip II — restructuring, uniformity and the development of a more organized spiritual life — are in the same vein as Albert's clericalizing reform of 250 years before. In 1699, only nine years after Alexander VIII had extended to the Mercedarians the privileges enjoyed by the mendicant orders, Charles II accorded the masters general the status of grandees in Spain.[3] It is this essential continuity of Mercedarian life and reform, and the contradictions underpinning it, that I wish to draw attention to here.

By the 1560s, however, Albert's compromise solution was on the verge of collapse. This was due not only to the rise of the province of Castile within the Order, but to Philip's enhanced perception of his duties as king in the feverish climate of Post-Tridentine Spain. It was the development of the *Patronato Real* as a tool of royal administration and the religious concerns and standards of the crown that provided the immediate basis for Mercedarian Reform. While the imposition of these criteria provided a platform for change, the deeper reform of the Order could come only from a degree of consensus among Mercedarians themselves. But it was over the question of reform itself that the tensions inherent in the Order were set into greatest relief. As we have seen, though there were individuals who recognized the need for change, there was little agreement on the form this should take. Some, like Gaspar de Torres, viewed reform as a gradual and above all internal process of spiritual and disciplinary change or *mudanza*. Others, like Pedro Carrillo, recognized the opportunity for Castile to assert herself as the dominant province in the Order through the influence of the crown. Then there were those, like Juan de Peñaranda, who saw in reform the subjection of the Order to royal patronage and the end of its independence from higher authority.

Thus, while most prelates recognized spiritual improvement as the necessary end of Mercedarian Reform, few saw this as the driving force behind the process itself. The structural and disciplinary problems besetting the Order were all too severe for religious suddenly to adopt the strict spiritual observance that had never been an outstanding feature of Mercedarian life. Indeed, the direction that any spiritual reform must take — implicitly a reclericalization of the

---

[3] For the title of *grande*, see ACA, Mon., vol. 2829, f. 491r. The Order's mendicant status was confirmed by Benedict XIII in 1725; *ibid.*, vol. 2836, pp. 40–4.

Order and a deepening of its religious vocation — militated against the active lives traditionally pursued by the brethren. Though the establishment of a reformed observance is unquestionably one of the greatest achievements of Zumel and his successors, the basis of this reform lies in the institutional and disciplinary changes legislated at Guadalajara in 1574. The Mercedarian case and the others discussed in previous chapters lead us to a fundamental conclusion about the reform of the old orders in this period: that, depending on the extent of a congregation's decline, spiritual reform could survive and prosper only on the basis of institutional change. There can be no question that the motivation behind Santa Teresa's Carmelite reform was spiritual, but this could thrive and be perpetuated only through institutional adjustment; through the series of measures that led to the establishment of a new community, a new congregation and finally a new order.

Equally, there were Mercedarians for whom the spiritual reform of the Order had not gone far enough, and it was from this group that the Discalced movement emerged towards the end of the sixteenth century. The establishment of the Discalced congregation is a watershed in Mercedarian history, one which for various reasons focused the ideas and aspirations of a significant element within the Order while confirming the tastes and convictions of a majority of religious. Finding the Order uncongenial to their outlook, within a generation the Discalced fathers had severed their ties with the parent body and struck out on a different road. The almost inevitable separation of the Discalced brethren may be interpreted as a final rupture between the lay and clerical traditions in the Order; ultimately between those who interpreted the Mercedarian vocation as an active apostolate, and those who viewed it in predominantly spiritual terms. But damaging as the secession was, it came at a time of unprecedented growth and fecundity within the Order, one which owes much to the fostering of study and the development of a strong academic vocation over the previous century. In politics, scholarship, patronage, spirituality and culture, the first half of the seventeenth century brought to a culmination the reformist ideals towards which Mercedarians had been moving, at times imperceptibly slowly, for more than 150 years. In Fray Juan Falconi, for instance, the Castilians had one of the major mystical writers of the seventeenth century in Spain; in Fray Francisco Zumel one of its leading theologians. Yet in Tirso de Molina the Order also possessed an artist of universal importance, one who, for a time at least, was able to marry his religious vocation to a successful career as a dramatist.

*

Of the great literary figures of the Spanish Golden Age, Tirso de Molina is in many ways the least accessible and the least understood.[4] This status rests partly in the apparent dichotomy between his activities as a playwright and the religious vocation that sustained him as a Mercedarian friar. However, it is perfectly clear that Fray Gabriel's life as a religious served not as an obstacle to his dramatic output, but as an essential complement to it, and *vice versa*.[5] In his profane as much as in his religious works, Tirso attempted to explore the uneasy commingling of the divine and the earthly in human psyche, for which his own experience as a friar served as the obvious model. This element — though evidently in different ways — is as apparent in the fates of Paulo and Enrico in *El condenado por desconfiado* as it is in the *Historia General*, in which Fray Gabriel conducts a recurrent dialogue between his duties as hagiographer and historian, between the rival claims of faith and reason, aspiration and credibility.[6] In the latter case this feature can be related to the conflict of interest that rested at the heart of his Order of ransoming friars, between the clerical and lay elements which perhaps he had attempted to resolve in his own being as friar-dramatist, and to the peculiar construct of seventeenth-century Mercedarian spirituality. But above all both can be tied to the central and recurring theme in the monastic life: how are individuals to reconcile the apparent contradiction of seeking the Kingdom of Heaven while at the same time working for the kingdom of this world?

---

[4] See, however, Henry W. Sullivan, *Tirso de Molina and the Drama of the Counter-Reformation* (Amsterdam, 1976). Critics have continually pointed out the need for a study of Fray Gabriel the Mercedarian as a basis for understanding Tirso the dramatist; see Margaret Wilson, 'Tirso's Texts, and More on *El condenado por desconfiado*' in *Bulletin of Hispanic Studies*, 70 (1993), pp. 97–104; 102, & especially Alan K.G. Paterson, 'Tirso de Molina and the Androgyne: *El Áquiles* and *La dama del Olivar*' in *ibid.*, pp. 105–14; esp. 108 & 112–13.

[5] See Vázquez Fernández, 'Apuntes para una nueva biografía de Tirso', p. 50.

[6] Evidently, I accept Tirso's authorship of *El condenado por desconfiado*. Regarding the *Historia*, see Michael Zappala, 'History and Hagiography in Tirso de Molina's *Historia General de la Orden de Nuestra Señora de las Mercedes*' in *Tirso de Molina: Vida y Obra. Actas del Primer Simposio Internacional sobre Tirso* [=*Estudios*, 43] (Madrid, 1987); pp. 67–77.

If Tirso embodies many of the conflicts and characteristics of the old institution, he is also a symbol of the new Order that rose afresh in the seventeenth century and to which he was himself a contributor. Before the institutional reform of the Order had been fully accepted Mercedarians had begun to draw on prevailing spiritual currents and develop a distinctive charism adapted to their perception of the Order and its place in society. The battle for constitutional change and improved discipline fought out during the reign of Philip II therefore culminated in the seventeenth century with the elaboration of a complex spirituality and iconography. Although it was never published, the *Historia General de la Orden de Nuestra Señora de las Mercedes* is one of the most signal achievements of this endeavour. The circumstances under which it was written, its distinctive character and ultimately the reasons for its non-publication provide a forceful reminder of the intimate ties between reform and history in the monastic culture of Catholic Europe.[7] The reform of a religious order implied a detailed assessment of its past, particularly of the primordial observance in which it had been founded, and in this the Mercedarians were no exception. The intense scrutiny to which the Order was subjected during the 1560s and '70s revealed its early history to be a fractured and nebulous void, one which appeared to bear little relation to the reality of Mercedarian life at the close of the sixteenth century. The elaboration of a new *centuria primera* therefore became an urgent priority of the reformed Mercedarian Order, to which many of its finest minds bent their talents over the course of the next 150 years.

Among the earliest signs of this enhanced concern for the history and tradition of the Order can be found at the chapter provincial of Toledo in 1588, where 'chroniclers' were appointed for Castile and Andalusia with responsibility for the collection of all relevant bulls and privileges.[8] The primary aim was clearly the preparation of a *bullarium* through which the licenses and concessions of the Order might be made known and its rights upheld, particularly with respect to the gathering of redemption *limosna*.[9] But in reality the chroniclers'

---

[7] For some notes on the origins of this, see Kristeller, 'The Contribution of Religious Orders', p. 18. See also Simon Ditchfield, *Liturgy, Sanctity and History in Tridentine Italy: Pietro Maria Campi and the Preservation of the Particular* (Cambridge, 1995).

[8] BNM, ms. 2684, f. 37r. The 'coronistas' were M° Fray Melchor Rodríguez de Torres for Castile and M° Fray Luis de Heredia for Andalusia.

[9] Though unfinished, the first Mercedarian *bullarium* was that of M° Fray Serafín de Freitas, *Bullae et Privilegia Sacri ac Regalis Ordinis Redemptorum Beatae Mariae de Mercede*

duties were to extend far beyond this, for it fell to them and their successors to people the void of Mercedarian history with the saints and traditions upon which the Order's spirituality and reputation would in future be based. That the means now existed to make good this endeavour is beyond doubt. It was in this period that the genre of the *crónica de la orden* reached its apogee through the histories of Castillo, Sigüenza, Yepes and of course Tirso himself, so that by the end of the seventeenth century virtually every religious congregation in Spain was represented and edified by at least one such monument to its status and vocation.[10] The emphasis on the early history of the religious orders throughout the Catholic Reformation itself reflects a wider concern with the Early Church and patristic theology, an interest which translates into a profound nostalgia for the purity and simplicity of Christian antiquity.[11] For the Mercedarian Order, whose primordial observance had been largely expunged in the schism of an earlier age, this movement *ad fontes* took the form of creation and imagination on a scale unmatched by any of its contemporaries. The nature and magnitude of this achievement is one of the most distinctive features of Mercedarian Reform.

*

The marked impact of the Reform on Mercedarian image and spirituality raises the question of the extent of change not only in observance and discipline, but within the social structure and mores of the

---

(Madrid: Typographia Regni, 1636). See also M° Fray José Linás, *Bullarium Cælestis ac Regalis Ordinis Beatae Mariae Virginis de Mercede Redemptionis Captivorum* (Barcelona: Raphaëlis Figueró, 1696).

[10] M° Fray Fernando (or Hernando) del Castillo, *Historia General de Santo Domingo y su Orden de Predicadores* (5 vols., Madrid: Francisco Sanchez, 1584, Valladolid: Diego Fernandez de Cordova, 1592–1615, & Valladolid: Juan de la Rueda, 1621); Fray José de Sigüenza, *Historia de la Orden de San Geronimo* (2 vols., Madrid: Iuan Flamenco, 1600–5); Dom Antonio de Yepes, *Coronica General de la Orden de San Benito* (7 vols., Irache: Matias Mares, 1609; Irache: Nicolas Assiayn, 1610, & Valladolid: Francisco Fernandez de Cordova, 1613–21).

[11] On this see two articles by Bruno Neveu, 'L'Erudition ecclésiastique du XVIIe siècle et la nostalgie de l'antiquité chrétienne' in Keith G. Robbins, ed., *Religion and Humanism* [*Studies in Church History*, vol. XVIII] (Oxford, 1981); pp. 195–225, & 'Archéolatrie et modernité dans le savoir ecclésiastique au XVIIe siècle' in *XVIIe Siècle*, 33 (1981), pp. 169–84. In a similar vein see Alain Saint-Saëns, *La Nostalgie du désert: L'Ideal érémitique en Castille au Siècle d'Or* (San Francisco, 1993).

Order itself. Although the generals were stripped of immense powers at Guadalajara in 1574, the extension of the Order into new fields gave the masters a range of influence they had never previously enjoyed, though by the 1630s Tirso was recognizing a number of serious constraints on their authority.[12] Otherwise the distance between prelates and religious in the Order remained very great, with provincials retaining much of their power and the wealth of commendators and officers standing in stark contrast to the poverty and misery of many conventuals. At Huete in 1590 the visitor and provincial M° Fray Francisco de Medina ordered that henceforth sick novices be provided with any food and remedies prescribed for them by a doctor, whatever the expense, 'since we have been informed that they are very badly treated when sick, and some have been obliged to purchase themselves the chickens they have been told to eat'.[13] Ten years later, with Castile in the grip of famine and pestilence, the visitor M° Fray Diego Coronel ordered the friars' rations to be improved with the addition of an extra three *reales* to the daily expenditure on food, this so as to 'allow them to get by with greater ease', and so that the wine 'be drinkable rather than vinegar'.[14] For, as Coronel reminded the commendator, 'there can be no doubt that by not providing the religious with what they so obviously need, like food and drink, the prelate commits a mortal sin'.

In other respects, also, the Reform saw relatively little improvement where the attitude of many superiors to government and administration was concerned. The vicars general in the Indies in particular were felt to secure their appointment through means rather than merit, and then serve out their tenure in an orgy of greed and corruption heedless of the effect on the Order.[15] But for most Mercedarians, unconscious of the greater forces at work in a period of rapid change, the imposition of reform was a cause of dislocation and uncertainty. Throughout the Order, religious were increasingly expected to obey regulations that had not been enforced at the time of their profession, and which many will have hoped never to observe at all. Moreover, they were being checked on their adherence to these more rigorously and more often than any could have thought

---

[12] Tirso, *Historia*, II, pp. 442 & 570.
[13] AHN, Clero, vol. 3320, f. 75v; reiterated in 1600, *ibid.*, f. 158v.
[14] *Ibid.*, f. 159r.
[15] Tirso, *Historia*, II, p. 443.

possible in, say, 1550. The visitation book for the Castilian house of
Huete, about 100 miles east of Madrid, begins in 1569, the year the
reform process began in earnest.[16] From 1569 on Huete was subjected to a barrage of visitations and ordinances, sometimes two or three
a year, promulgating an increasing number of regulations. It was only
in the 1590s that periods of two or more years were allowed to pass
between visitations by the prelates of the Order. Although the house
had reached a modicum of discipline and observance by this time,
many of the ordinances set down in the book year after year were as
persistently ignored. The brethren were still committing the same
infractions in 1630 that they had in 1569: women in the cloister, friars playing cards and dodging choir, along with the countless trans-
gressions of which religious had always been guilty. There was no
concerted opposition to reform in Castile, only the same intransi-
gence and inertia shared by the rest of the Order, but which circumstances in Catalonia transformed into dissent and violence.

The visitation book of Girona in north-eastern Catalonia opens in
1589, the year in which resistance finally collapsed in Barcelona.[17]
Girona, which had been a bastion of Catalan resistance, gives all the
impression in the 1590s of needing a complete reconstruction of its
religious life and observance. In 1594 the visitor, Mº Fray Miguel
Perlas, provincial of the Crown of Aragon, remarked on the unwill-
ingness of the religious to observe the constitutions of the Order and
the ordinances passed both in chapter and in the visitations themselves.[18] Two years later Perlas commanded the visitation *acta* to be
read out to the community over and over again in the weekly chapter
of faults, this so that 'the religious know what is required of them and
cannot plead ignorance during the visitations'.[19] In 1598 his successor
Mͤ Fra Pere Balaguer found it necessary to lay before the brethren
the basic tenets of the religious life and the role of their community in
Christian society. The brethren, he said, were to aspire to 'live the
obedient and exemplary lives to which they are obliged, and as befits
those who profess an evangelical vocation'.[20] In this respect, friars
had to accept once and for all that misdemeanours were to be pun-

---

[16] AHN, Clero. vol. 3320, book of professions and visitations, 1569–1638.
[17] APV, (no ref. no.), book of visitations, 1589–1628.
[18] *Ibid.*, f. 32r–v.
[19] *Ibid.*, f. 36v.
[20] *Ibid.*, f. 41v.

ished rigorously and to the letter of the ordinances and constitutions. The importance of observing the divine office, he declared, lay both in the service of God and 'because through it the faithful are moved not only to attend church, but to benefit convents with their alms, all of which redounds greatly to both corporeal and spiritual health'.[21] Yet negligence and disobedience continued, albeit on a diminished scale, and it is the second decade of the seventeenth century before any marked improvement is discernible at Girona. Evidently, though a community might be rescued from complete apathy and dissolution, the progression to a strict religious life was clearly one which it remained beyond the means of the hierarchy to encourage or cajole to any significant degree.

*

For Philip II, meanwhile, the insolence of the Catalan Mercedarians was consistent with the continual impugning of his right to govern in the Crown of Aragon. Events were to prove that all too often the opposition of even one of the local institutions falling back on claims of violated privileges was sufficient to render royal policy unworkable. The field of sixteenth-century Catalonia has yet to receive the treatment it deserves, but it was during the reign of Philip II that Catalans first awakened to the steadily more marginalized position of the Principality within the *Monarquía Española*, and to the increasingly intrusive attitude of the crown where its affairs were concerned. The onset of the reform programme in the 1560s therefore contributed to the embittering of Catalan society toward royal authority, and made a deep impression on local attitudes which lasted into the eighteenth century.[22] Equally, the reform of the orders served to remind the crown that religious issues could not be resolved without the coopera-

---

[21] *Ibid.*, f. 42r.

[22] To cite two Mercedarian examples, see AHCB, ms. A–266, Antillón, *Memorias*, II, ff. 247r–249r (1618), and ACA, Mon., vol. 2676, f. 538r–v (1632–4), in both of which cases the *Consell de Cent* specifically reminded the priory of Barcelona of its defence of its privileges against the reformers during the 1570s and '80s. See also Henry Kamen, 'The Catalan Phoenix: Narcís Feliu de la Penya and the Programme for Industrial Renewal in Catalonia' in *id.*, *Crisis and Change in Early Modern Spain* (Aldershot, 1993), essay XI, p. 12, for the prior of Barcelona and brother of the above, Mᶜ Fra Salvador Feliu de la Penya, a vociferous critic of Charles II's government and supporter of the Habsburg cause in the War of Succession.

tion of local authorities, or for that matter independently of Rome. In the 1560s Philip had blithely embarked on this course of action believing that he had both enough power and enough jurisdiction to carry it through. But as the process broke down in Spain and religious took their grievances to Rome the king had increasingly to rely on the nuncios and his ambassadors to deliver him from situations that had escaped his grasp. Indeed, Philip had to learn that, by its very nature, monastic reform all too often lay beyond the range of his authority, and by the end of the century the papacy had largely recovered the arbitrating role in Spanish monastic affairs that it had first ceded during the reign of the Catholic Kings.

That this should have been the case is in part a reflection of the scale of Philip's aims where monastic reform was concerned. The absence of any detailed study on the reform of the religious orders from the reign of the Catholic Kings onwards makes it difficult to assess the development of royal policy in this area. However, it is clear that the early part of Philip's reign followed a traditional pattern, not least because the relatively low emphasis placed on active sponsorship of reform by Charles V resulted in a loss of competence and practical experience in this field. Both under the Catholic Kings and Philip II the business of reform was conducted by a small steering committee drawn from the inner circle of court and government. In both cases, too, matters were approached from an authoritarian perspective and the onset of reform was marked by some exceptionally inept and insensitive measures with respect to the task at hand. The policies of the Catholic Kings in Barcelona in 1493 and those of Philip II toward the Isidrites and Alcantarine Franciscans in 1567 bear witness to this. Such circumstances can be attributed to inexperience on the part of those entrusted with this most delicate of tasks, but even so it is clear that the crown often had a very limited sense of the dynamics of monastic life and organization. Attempts to organize reform along diocesan lines rather than the territorial delineations of the orders themselves enjoyed uniformly poor success, of which the visitations of 1567–9 provide the clearest example. The crown, for instance, laid disproportionate emphasis on the suppression of houses and distribution of their miserable revenues to other communities — often, one suspects, in lieu of any more resolute action. Above all, Philip persistently underestimated the extent to which local and provincial rights and culture had become invested in those of the orders in their midst. In the case of the Mercedarians as of other orders, the effects of this miscalculation were to prove very costly indeed, and it was not until the 1580s that the crown acquired a grasp of the mechanics of monastic reform.

Whatever the changes in policy over the period concerned, it is clear that the premise underpinning royal support for monastic reform remained largely unaltered. In the Augustinian tradition, the crown accepted monasticism as the purest form of religious life and the basis through prayer, learning and example of the renewal of Christian society towards God. In a practical sense the crown regarded the monastic Order as its natural ally and a bulwark of the Faith, and the monarch as its patron and protector. With the accession of Philip II prevailing circumstances and the king's style of government transformed this notion into a formidable ideal of state. Apart from the king's own convictions, in which he showed none of the vacillation characteristic of other areas of government, three elements contributed to the formation of this ideal. Firstly, the expansion of royal bureaucracy; secondly, the increased reservoir of reformist prelates with university training available to the crown; and thirdly the development of a nationalist mentality among the Castilian clergy with respect to the rest of the Peninsula during the sixteenth century. Philip therefore found himself better prepared to address the question of monastic reform than any of his predecessors, and perhaps because of this the king set his aims impossibly high. For the first time the reform of entire congregations in Spain was contemplated and initiated, often with insufficient authority and on the basis of almost complete ignorance of local conditions. The effort to bring these plans to fruition, the problems encountered and the resulting modification of reform policy with respect to the peculiar characteristics of each congregation has provided one of the themes of this study. The effect of this process in the context of Post-Tridentine Catholicism was a major adjustment in Spanish religious life and culture, one which had far-reaching effects throughout society. Seen from the perspective of the early seventeenth century, the impact of this policy was the extension of reform from local or regional level to national level as a major development in the history of the religious orders in Spain over the period in question. The Mercedarian Order is the classic expression of this model.

*

By 1650 the reform of the Mercedarians had long since fulfilled the guiding aims of its sponsors, not least those of the crown. The institutional reform begun in 1574 was largely complete, and the crown had established its patronage over an order that now played its full part in Spanish Catholic-Reformation orthodoxy. Though it remained for the deeper implications of this reform to filter down from the hierarchy to the rank and file, no religious can have been unaware of a new and powerful authority in the Order, one to which all were considered responsible. Neither can he have felt abstracted from the new identity forged by chroniclers and hagiographers as a common bond for all members of the Order, and upon which its success and unity depended. Despite the separation of the Discalced and the provincial and personal disputes that continued to cloud relations within the Order, it is the creation of this identity which must stand as the crowning achievement of Mercedarian Reform.

Yet, as we have seen, this identity was founded on a basic compromise of history and tradition, for, as Châtellier has written, 'to reform the world it was necessary to adapt to it'.[23] What this book has attempted to do is suggest the complexity and diversity of interpretation to which the abused concept of reform lends itself, not only in the monastic field, but implicitly elsewhere also. As the Mercedarians found, the road to reform had no sure beginning, no certain trajectory, and no absolute end.

---

[23] Louis Châtellier, *The Europe of the Devout: The Catholic Reformation and the Formation of a New Society* (Cambridge, 1989), p. 253. See also John Bossy, 'The Counter-Reformation and the People of Catholic Europe' in *Past and Present*, 47 (1970), pp. 51–70, esp. 67, & Anne J. Cruz & Mary Elizabeth Perry, eds., *Culture and Control in Counter-Reformation Spain* (Minneapolis, 1992), xiv.

APPENDIX I

PROVINCES, CHAPTERS AND OFFICERS (1420–1648) *

I. *Chapters and Generals (1419–1648)*

The title of master gained currency as the supreme office of the Order in the 1250s, and that of general became established after 1317 to denote the conjoined spiritual and temporal authority of the holder. The office was of life tenure until 1574 and sexennial thereafter. Where vicars general are concerned, only those who held prolonged tenure in exceptional circumstances are listed; all other vacancies in the generalate can be assumed to have been presided over by the priors of Barcelona. Confirmed generals and electoral chapters are in **bold** type.

Barcelona-Tarragona	1401	**Fra Jaume Taust** (Cat; †1405)
Lleida	1402	–
Tarragona	1405	–
Barcelona	1405	**Me Fra Antoni Caixal** (Cat; †1417)
Tarragona	1406	–
Valladolid	1407	–
Vic	1411	–
Estella	1414	–
Barcelona	1417	**Frey Bernard de la Plaigne** (Fr; †1419)
Berga	1418	–
Barcelona	1419	**Fra Jaume Aymerich** (Cat; †1428)
Játiva	1419	–
Córdoba	1421	–
Lleida	1426	–
Valencia	1427	–
Barcelona	1429	**Fra Antoni Dullan** (Cat; deposed 1441)
Montblanc	1430	–

---

* Death dates (†) are given where an individual died in office. Equally, where a term of office was prematurely curtailed — through removal or presentation to a bishopric for instance — the reason is given. Where an individual held the same office more than once, this is indicated as follows: (i), (ii), etc.

Abbreviations: Anda – Andalusian; apptd – appointed; Arag – Aragonese; b. – place or region of birth where different from provincial affiliation; Barc. – Barcelona; bp – bishop; Cast – Castilian; Cat – Catalan; Disc – Discalced; Fr – French; gral – general; im – intermediary chapter general; nc – not confirmed; PofB – Prior of Barcelona; provl – provincial; Sard – Sardinian; Val – Valencian; vg – vicar general; vp – vicar provincial.

Valladolid	1431	–
Teruel	1432	–
Calatayud	1434	–
Almazán	1435	–
?	1437	–
–	1441	**Fray Pedro de Huete** (Cast, apptd; †1452)
–	1442	**Fra Nadal Gaver** (Cat, apptd; †1474)
Barcelona	1442	–
Huesca	1443	–
Girona	1444	–
El Puig	1446	–
Valladolid	1455	–
Barcelona	1456	–
Castelló d'Empuries	1458	–
Játiva	1460	–
Sarrión	1464	–
Toledo	1466	–
Guadalajara	1467	–
Maleville	1468	–
Daroca	1469	–
Barcelona	1474	**Fra Llorens Company** (Val; †1479)
Calatayud	1475	–
Valencia	1478	–
Barcelona	1480	**Mᵉ Frey Antoine Maurel** (Fr; †1492)
Girona	1481	–
Toulouse	1485	–
Pamplona	1487	–
Valencia	1489	–
Barcelona	1492	**Fra Joan Urgell** (Cat; †1513)
Huesca	1493	–
Perpignan	1499	–
Girona	1503	–
Girona	1506	–
Barcelona	1513	**Mᵉ Fray Jaime Lorenzo de la Mata** (Arag; †1522)
Játiva	1514	–
Zaragoza	1517	–
Lleida	1519	–
Barcelona	1522	**Mᵉ Fra Benet Zafont** (Cat, b.Val; †1535)
Barcelona	1523	–
Barcelona	1535	**Fra Pere Sorell** (Cat; †1546)
Zaragoza	1536	–
Valencia	1544	–
Montblanc	1545	–
Barcelona	1546	**Mᵉ Fra Miquel Puig** (Cat; †1567)
Girona	1546	–
Girona	1547	–

Zaragoza	1554	–
Zaragoza	1555	–
Barcelona	1561	–
Barcelona	1567	–
Barcelona	1568	Me Fra Maties Papiol (Cat; nc)
Vacant	*1568–74*	
Vicar general		Me Fra Bernat Duran (Cat; 1568–74)
Commissaries apostolic:		
Crown of Aragon		Mr Fray Guillermo Montaña (OP), 1569–74
Castile		Mr Fray Felipe de Meneses (OP), 1569–71†
		Mr Fray Hernando del Castillo (OP), 1572–4
Guadalajara	1574	**Mr Fray Francisco de Torres** (Val; †1575)
Vicar general (nc)	*1575–6*	Fra Lluís Valls (Cat)
Barcelona	1575	Me Frey Antoine de Tremollières (Fr; nc)
Zaragoza	1576	**Mr Fray Francisco Maldonado** (Cast)
Vacant	*1582–7*	
Vicar general		Fra Pere Castelló (Cat; 1582–3†)
Commissaries apostolic		Dom Benet Tocco (OSB) (1582–5†)
		Juan Bautista de Cardona (bp Vic) (1585–7)
Zaragoza	1587	**Mr Fray Francisco de Salazar** (Arag)
Calatayud	1593	**Mr Fray Francisco Zumel** (Cast)
Valladolid (im)	1596	–
Valladolid	1599	**Me Fra Pere Balaguer** (Val; †1599)
Valencia	1600	Mr Fray Francisco de Medina (Cast, nc)
Vacant	*1600–2*	
Vicar general		Mr Fray Luis de Heredia (Anda; 1600–2)
–	1602	**Pr Fray Alonso de Monroy** (Anda; apptd)
Madrid (im)	1606	–
Guadalajara	1609	**Mr Fray Felipe de Guimerán** (Val)
Murcia (im)	1612	–
Calatayud	1615	**Mr Fray Francisco de Ribera** (Cast; apptd bp 1617)
Guadalajara	1618	**Mr Fray Ambrosio Machín** (Sard; apptd bp 1622)
Zaragoza	1622	**Mr Fray Gaspar Prieto** (Cast; apptd bp 1627)
Seville	1625	–
Toledo	1627	**Mr Fray Juan Cebrián** (Arag; apptd bp 1632)
Barcelona	1632	**Mr Fray Diego Serrano** (Anda; apptd bp 1635)
Murcia	1636	**Me Fra Dalmau Serra** (Cat; stranded in Barc. 1640)
Vicar general		Mr Fray Marcos Salmerón (Cast; 1640–2)
Calatayud	1642	**Mr Fray Marcos Salmerón** (†1648)

II. *Priors of Barcelona (1419–1625)*

The office developed out of that of master's chaplain and by the 1270s had become the second dignity in the Order. The 1327 constitutions afforded the priors the vicar generalcy of the Order during the vacancy of the mastership, with which their leading position in Mercedarian affairs was assured. Until 1574 the priors also held the *de facto* provincialcy of Catalonia. The priorship was of life tenure until 1574 and triennial thereafter. Elections were held in Barcelona and all incumbents listed are Catalans or sons of the priory except where otherwise indicated.

Fra Jaume Aymerich	1417–19 (elected gral)
Fra Antoni Dullan	1419–29 (elected gral)
Fra Nadal Gaver	1429–42 (elected gral)
Fra Joan de Segalars (i)	1442–64 (resigned)
Fra Damia Quart	1464–66 (resigned)
Fra Joan de Segalars (ii)	1466 (resigned?)
Mᵉ Fra Pascuet	1466–73?
Mᵉ Fra Joan Urgell	1473–92 (elected gral)
Fra Nicolau Borrassá	1492–1502†
Fra Esteve Sebastiá	1502–15†
Mᵉ Fra Benet Zafont	1515–22 (elected gral)
Fra Pere Sorell	1522–35 (elected gral)
Mᵉ Fra Miquel Puig	1535–46 (elected gral)
Mᵉ Fra Joan de Mata	1546–66†
Mᵉ Fra Maties Papiol	1566–8 (elected gral)
Mᵉ Fra Bernat Duran	1568–75
Under presidency	*1575–88*
Fra Lluís Valls	1575–9 (removed)
Fra Pere Castelló	1579–83†
Fray Vicente Mendía	1583–4 (elected prior 1584; disappeared)
Fra Francesc Serafi	1584–5 (removed)
Fra Antoni Joan Barray	1585†
Fra Francesc Esteve	1585–90
Fra Jaume Grauset	1588–9 (nc)
Mᵉ Fra Bernat Papiol (i)	1590–3
Mº Fray Antonio Simón (i)	1593–6
Mº Fray Francisco Salazar	1596–7 (Arag; resigned)
Mᵉ Fra Bernat Papiol (ii)	1597–1600
Mᵉ Fra Montserrat Ausias	1600–2†
Mº Fray Antonio Simón (ii)	1602–3 (elected provl of Cat & Arag-Nav)
Mº Fray Domingo Pérez	1603–6 (Arag)
Mᵉ Fra Bernat Papiol (iii)	1606–9
Mᵉ Fra Llorens Altava	1609–11
Pᵗ Fra Jaume Pinell (i)	1611–14 (resigned)
Mᵉ Fra Bernat Papiol (iv)	1615–17 (resigned)

Mᵒ Fray Ambrosio Machín	1617–18 (elected gral)
Mᵉ Fra Jaume Pinell (ii)	1618–22
Mᵒ Fray Juan Cebrián	1622–5 (Arag; elected provl of Cat & Arag-Nav)

III. *Provincials of Aragon-Navarre (1443–1576)*

The province of Aragon, the heartland of the Order, was effectively created by the erection of that of Castile in the early 14th century, after which those of Valencia and Provence (France) followed at the chapter general of Lleida in 1320. A province of Catalonia was also established in 1320 over which the priors of Barcelona held authority, but this area together with Aragon-Navarre remained the centre of the master's patrimony and was for some time under his direct control. The first *comendador mayor* of Aragon-Navarre itself appears in 1375, and its provincials, enjoying life tenure, continued to be appointed by the generals until 1574. In that year Aragon-Navarre became the centre of an amalgamated province of the Crown of Aragon under the authority of a single provincial.

Mᵉ Fra Bernat de Tàrrega	1443–62 (Cat?)
Fray Miguel de Gaviría	1462–74 (vg)
Fray Jorge de la Puerta	1474–86†
Fray Pedro de la Puerta	1486–94
Fra Esteve Sebastiá	1494–1515† (Cat; PofB also from 1502)
Mᵉ Fra Benet Zafont	1515–22 (Cat; also PofB until elected gral)
Fray Martín de Labayán	*c.*1524–39†
Fray Juan López *or* Lupi	1539–44†
Mᵉ Fra Climent Ginebrosa	1544–51 (b.Cat)
Mᵒ Fray Agustín de Molinar	1551–64†
Mᵒ Fray Miguel Dicastillo	1565–76

IV. *Provincials of Valencia (1446–1574)*

The origins of the province of Valencia can be traced back to the early 14th century: its first *comendador mayor* appears in 1317 and its existence was confirmed at the chapter general of Lleida in 1320. The *comendadores mayores* and provincials were appointed by the generals and enjoyed life tenure until 1574, when the province was subsumed into that of the Crown of Aragon, though it recovered its independence in 1603. The borders of this province changed more than any other. The houses of Murcia and Lorca were lost to Castile in 1467, but the province received that of Oran on the Barbary Coast in return in 1532.

Fra Antoni de Agramunt	1446–56 (b.Cat)
Mᶜ Fra Valentí Rovira	1456–78
Fra Joan Ferrandis de Tuesta	*c.*1478–*c.*1481
Fra Nicolau Borrassá	*c.*1482–92 (b.Cat)
Fra Pere Lluís Sans	1492–after 1506
Mᶜ Fra Lluís Boyl	by 1516–*c.*1536
Mᶜ Fra Vicent Martí	*c.*1536–44
Mᵒ Fray Jerónimo Pérez	1544–7
Mᵒ Fray Juan Calvo	1547–74† (b.Anda)

V. *Chapters and Provincials — Crown of Aragon (1576–1640)*

The province was created in 1574 through the amalgamation of those of Catalonia, Aragon-Navarre and Valencia, and included all the Italian and Sardinian houses of the Order. The provincials were elected in triennial tenure. Valencia regained its independence in 1603, and the Italian province, first created in 1606, separated definitively in 1619.

El Olivar	1576	Mᵒ Fray Francisco de Salazar (i; Arag)
Valencia	1582	Mᵒ Fray Jorge Ongay (Nav)
Zaragoza	1585	Mᵒ Fray Francisco de Salazar (ii; elected gral 1587)
Valencia	1588	Mᶜ Fra Pere Balaguer (i; Val)
Barcelona	1591	Mᵒ Fray Asencio Lagarria (Val; removed 1592)
Vicars provincial		Mᵒ Fray Nadal Silvestre (Arag; †1592)
		Mᶜ Fra Miquel Perlas (Val; 1592–4)
Calatayud	1594	Mᶜ Fra Miquel Perlas (†1596)
Vicar provincial		Mᶜ Fra Pere Balaguer (1596–7)
Zaragoza	1597	Mᶜ Fra Pere Balaguer (ii; elected gral 1599)
Vicar provincial		Mᵒ Fray Francisco de Salazar (1599–1600)
El Puig	1600	Mᵒ Fray Domingo Pérez (Arag)
El Olivar	1603	Mᵒ Fray Antonio Simón (Cat; †1605)

Daroca	1606	Pᵛ Fray Domingo Usabiaga (Arag; b.Guipúzcoa)
Calatayud	1609	Mᶜ Fra Bernat Papiol (i; Cat)
Barcelona	1612	Mᵒ Fray Pedro Visiedo (Arag)
Zaragoza	1615	Mᵒ Fray Ambrosio Machín (Sard; elected PofB 1617)
Daroca	1619	Pᵛ Fray Juan Cavero (Arag)
Zaragoza	1622	Mᶜ Fra Jaume Pinell (Cat)
Barcelona	1625	Mᵒ Fray Juan Cebrián (Arag; elected gral 1627)
El Olivar	1628	Mᵒ Fray Juan Ferrero (Arag)
Huesca	1631	Mᶜ Fra Bernat Papiol (ii)
Barbastro	1634	Mᶜ Fra Dalmau Serra (Cat)
Barcelona	1637	Mᵒ Fray Juan de Molina y Entrena (Arag)
Barcelona	1640	Mᶜ Fra Miquel Cors (Cat)

VI. *Chapters and Provincials — Valencia (1603–40)*

The province was re-established out of that of the Crown of Aragon in 1603, and included the houses of Palma de Mallorca, Tarragona and Tortosa in Catalonia, Sarrión and Teruel in Aragon, and that of Oran in North Africa. The office of provincial was of triennial tenure.

[El Olivar]	1603	Mᵒ Fray Felipe de Guimerán
Valencia	1606	Mᵒ Fray Juan Teodoro de Monlluna (removed 1608)
Valencia	1609	Mᶜ Fra Francesc Alemany
?	1612	Mᵒ Fray Nicolás Valero
?	1615	Mᶜ Fra Francesc Andreu
Teruel	1619	Mᵒ Fray Gaspar Fito
El Puig	1622	Mᶜ Fra Thomàs Sans
Orihuela	1625	Mᶜ Fra Jaume Torner
El Puig	1628	Mᶜ Fra Antoni Gralla i Gombau
El Puig	1631	Mᶜ Fra Vicent Felici
Valencia	1634	Mᵒ Fray Fulgencio Tormo
El Puig	1637	Mᶜ Fra Vicent Serra
?	1640	Mᶜ Fra Francesc Ballester

VII. *Chapters and Provincials — Castile (c.1436–1639)*

The province of Castile dates from *c.*1311, the first major territorial division of the Order. Already by 1327 it was governed by the master's lieutenant, and its *comendadores mayores* or provincials continued to be appointed by the generals until 1467. Henceforth the Castilians had the right to elect their provincials in chapter (a distinction reflected in the listing below), though internal problems prevented this being exercised for some time. The office was of life tenure until 1542, henceforth sexennial (to 1550), triennial (to 1556), sexennial again (to 1565), quadrennial (to 1569) and finally triennial thereafter. In line with territorial divisions, the houses of Burceña (Vizcaya) and Logroño (La Rioja) and the two Murcian convents of Lorca and Murcia itself were to transferred to Castile in 1467. The province of Andalusia was created through the partition of Castile in 1588, though one or other region had been under the authority of a vicar provincial since the beginning of the century.

Mᵒ Fray Pedro de Valencia	by 1436–*c.*1441	
Mᵒ Fray Pedro de Huete	1441–52 (governed in Cast as gral)	
Mᵒ Fray Macías de Monterrey	1452–65†	
Mᵒ Fray Diego de Muros	1465–72 (apptd bp 1472; Muros was removed from office by Gaver in favour of Pᵛ Fray Hernando de Córdoba during 1466, though reinstated later that year)	

Almazán	1469	–
–	1472	Pᵛ Fray Hernando de Córdoba (apptd 1471); provincialcy contested by Mᵒ Fray Francisco de Mondragón from 1471
?	1482	Mᵒ Fray Pedro de Logroño
?	*c.*1490	Mᵒ Fray Antonio de Valladolid
Olmedo	1494	–
?	1508	Mᵒ Fray Jorge de Sevilla
?	by 1512	Mᵒ Fray Juan de Baena
Seville	1515	–
Segovia	1523	Mᵒ Fray Alonso de Zorita (†1542)
Burgos	1526	–
Guadalajara	1532	–
Guadalajara	1539	–
Seville	1542	Fray Diego Enríquez (†1544)
Seville	1544	Mᵒ Fray Pedro de Oriona
Segovia	1550	Fray Juan de Somorrostro
Toledo	1553	Mᵒ Fray Pedro de Salazar
Toledo	1556	–

Toledo	1559	Mº Fray Gaspar de Torres
Toledo	1565	Mº Fray Juan de Peñaranda
Guadalajara	1569	Mº Fray Pedro Carrillo (i)
Toledo	1572	Mº Fray Juan de Covarrubias
Valladolid	1576	Mº Fray Rodrigo de Arce
Guadalajara	1579	Mº Fray Alonso Muñoz
Guadalajara	1582	Mº Fray Pedro Carrillo (ii)
Toledo	1585	Mº Fray Francisco Zumel
Toledo	1588	Mº Fray Francisco de Medina (i)
Guadalajara	1591	Mº Fray Pedro Machado
Segovia	1594	Mº Fray Juan Negrón
Guadalajara	1597	Mº Fray Pedro de Oña
Burgos	1600	Mº Fray Francisco de Medina (ii; elected gral 1600; nc)
Vicar provincial		Mº Fray Diego Coronel (1600–3)
Guadalajara	1603	Mº Fray Matías de Cuéllar
Madrid	1606	Mº Fray Juan de Temporal (†1606)
Vicar provincial		Mº Fray Cristóbal González (1606–8)
Guadalajara	1608	Mº Fray Jerónimo de Bustamante
Huete	1611	Mº Fray José de Aguayo (†1612)
Vicar provincial		Mº Fray Francisco de Ribera (1612–14)
Huete	1614	Mº Fray Francisco de Ribera (elected gral 1615)
Vicar provincial		Mº Fray Matías de Cuéllar (1615–17)
Guadalajara	1617	Mº Fray Juan de Peñacerrada (i)
Valladolid	1620	Mº Fray Gaspar Prieto (elected gral 1622)
Vicar provincial		Mº Fray Juan de Peñacerrada (1622–3)
Burgos	1623	Mº Fray Melchor Prieto
Guadalajara	1626	Mº Fray Blas de Tineo
Guadalajara	1629	Mº Fray Pedro Merino
Guadalajara	1632	Mº Fray Marcos Salmerón
Guadalajara	1636	Mº Fray Juan de Peñacerrada (ii; †1636)
Vicar provincial		Mº Fray Marcos Salmerón (1636–9)
Guadalajara	1639	Mº Fray Jerónimo de Valderas

VIII. *Chapters and Provincials — Andalusia (1588–1637)*

The province was founded in 1588 through the division of Castile on a line following the course of the river Guadiana. The office of provincial was held in triennial tenure.

[Toledo]	1588	Mᵒ Fray Juan de Ribas
Úbeda	1591	Mᵒ Fray Rodrigo de Arce
Écija	1594	Mᵒ Fray Juan Bernal
Écija?	1597	Mᵒ Fray Francisco de Móstoles (†1598)
Vicar provincial		Mᵒ Fray Andrés de Aguilar (1598–9)
Córdoba	1599	Mᵒ Fray Luis de Heredia (apptd vg 1600)
Vicar provincial		Mᵒ Fray Alonso Enríquez de Armendáriz (1600–2)
Ginés (Seville)	1602	Pᵒ Fray Alonso de Monroy (apptd gral 1602)
Vicar provincial		Mᵒ Fray Francisco de Prado (1602–4)
Écija	1604	Mᵒ Fray Pedro de Medina
Cazorla	1607	Mᵒ Fray Hernando de Rivera (i)
Écija	1610	Mᵒ Fray Melchor Guerrero
Úbeda	1613	Mᵒ Fray Jerónimo de Orellana
Écija	1616	Mᵒ Fray Andrés de Portes
Seville	1619	Mᵒ Fray Hernando de Rivera (ii)
Écija	1622	Mᵒ Fray Jorge de Arriola
Seville	1625	Mᵒ Fray Juan de Herrera
Écija	1628	Mᵒ Fray Luis de Vilches
Granada	1631	Mᵒ Fray Diego Serrano (elected gral 1632)
Vicars provincial		Mᵒ Fray Hernando de Rivera (†)
		Mᵒ Fray Luis de Vilches (?–1634)
Écija	1634	Mᵒ Fray Francisco de Torres (†1635)
Vicar provincial		Mᵒ Fray Pedro Álvarez (1635–7)
Granada	1637	Mᵒ Fray Tomás de Baena y Castillo

IX. *Chapters and Provincials — France (c.1523–1612)*

The Provençal houses were among the oldest in the Order and their union as a province was recognized in 1319. It is unclear when the French acquired the right to elect their own provincials, but the office remained of life tenure until the 1590s, becoming triennial thereafter. Dispersed by the Wars of Religion, the French brethren appear to have been governed by vicars provincial between 1579–99. The Paris Congregation was elevated to the status of vice province in 1672.

–	by 1523	Pᶜ Frey Jean de Potja *or* Potia
–	1540s	Mᶜ Frey Jean Gallofy
–	by 1567–*c.*1574	Mᶜ Frey Pierre Penchenat
–	*c.*1575–7†	Mᶜ Frey Antoine de Tremollières (elected gral 1575; nc)
–	in 1587	Mᶜ Frey Bernard (vp?)
–	1587–93	Mᶜ Frey Pierre Masson (vp?)
Toulouse	1599	Mᶜ Frey Jean Castet
?	1602?	?
?	1605?	?
Aurignac	1608	Mᶜ Frey Jean Castet (†1608)
Vicar provincial		Frey Jean Fillolet (1608–10)
Vicar general		*id.* (1610–12)
?	1612	Mᶜ Frey Jean Dubuc

X. *Chapters and Provincials — Italy (1606–22)*

Though officially part of the Order's Aragonese patrimony, the Italian houses had traditionally been subject to the direct authority of the general and were governed by his vicar. The province was founded out of that of the Crown of Aragon in 1606 but suppressed the following year. It was re-established in 1619 largely through the influence of the Sicilian Discalced and with the provincials holding triennial tenure, though the house at Rome remained a dependency of the masters with the *procuradores* holding the post of vicar general in Italy. The Sardinian congregation had excluded itself from this arrangement in 1606 and remained part of the province of Catalonia and Aragon-Navarre until it acquired vice-provincial status in 1750.

Rome	1606	Mʳ Fray Hernando de Santiago (Anda; removed 1607)
Naples	1619	Fray Juan Hurtado (Disc)
?	1622	Fray Alonso de Molina (Disc)

XI. *Procurators in Rome (1530–1642)*

Though the generals had periodically maintained *procuradores* in Rome since the mid fifteenth century, and particularly from the 1530s, it was only in 1587 that the office acquired permanent status and two years later an official residence in the convent of San Adriano. Successive crises from the 1560s onwards required the presence in Rome of important procurators from the province of Castile and later from the Discalced congregation; these are listed where appropriate and the appointing officer and province indicated in brackets; otherwise all *procuradores generales* are in **bold** type with the appointing general similarly included in brackets. It should be noted that beside their diplomatic duties the *procuradores* invariably held the post of vicar general in Italy as well.

Mᵉ Fra Miquel Puig	1530–5 (Zafont)
Mᵉ Fray Domingo de Clavería	*c.*1530–*c.*1532 (Zafont)
Fray Pedro de Miño	*c.*1530–*c.*1532 (Cast; Zorita)
Mᵒ Fray Andrés de Hermosilla	*c.*1535–8† (Sorell)
Fray Luis de Narváez	*c.*1538–46 (Sorell)
Fray Pedro Sagren	1546–50 (Puig)
Fray Amador de Medrano	1550–*c.*1558 (Puig)
Mᵉ Fra Maties Papiol	1558–66 (Puig)
Fra Thomàs Serralta	*c.*1565–8† (Puig)
Pᵉ Fray Francisco Maldonado	1567–9 (Cast; Peñaranda)
Fra Jeroni Antich	1568 (Cat; Papiol)
Fray Juan Ordóñez	1569–*c.*1574 (Cast; Carrillo)
Fray Pedro Alegría	1572–*c.*1575 (Cat; Duran)
Mᵉ Fray Asencio Lagarria	*c.*1575 (Val; Duran)
Mᵉ Fray Pascual del Molinar	*c.*1575 (Arag; Duran)
Mᵉ Fray Juan Enríquez	1574–5 (Cast; Covarrubias)
Mᵒ Fray Juan Enríquez	1575–82 (Maldonado)
Mᵉ Fray Fernando Suárez *or* Juárez	*c.*1578–*c.*1585 (Cast; Arce, Muñoz, Carrillo)
Fra Pere Pau Lleó	*c.*1579–*c.*1585 (Cat; priory of Barcelona)
Mᵒ Fray Juan Ordóñez	1582–7 *generalate vacant*
Mᵒ Fray Francisco de Torres	1587–90† (Salazar)
Mᵒ Fray Mateo Benedicto	1591–3 (Salazar)
Mᵒ Fray Fernando Suárez *or* Juárez	1593–7† (Zumel)
Pᵒ Fray Nicolás Malla	1597–8† (Zumel)
Mᵒ Fray Bernardo de Vargas	1598–1606 (Zumel, Monroy)
Fray Juan de Proano	1601–2 (Heredia, vg)
Mᵒ Fray Hernando de Santiago	1606–7 (Monroy)
Fray Francisco de Escobar	1607–9 (Monroy)
Mᵒ Fray Esteban de Muniera	1609–12 (Guimerán)
Pᵒ Fray Juan de Bustos	1612–15 (Guimerán)

Mᵒ Fray Esteban de Muniera	1615–19 (Ribera, Machín)
Fray Juan Bautista de la Madre de Dios/	
Fray Diego de San Pablo	1618–19; 1619–20; 1621
	(both Disc)
Mᵒ Fray Juan de Antillón	1619–22 (Machín)
Mᵒ Fray Juan de Quintanilla	1623–7 (Prieto)
Fray Diego de San Ramón	*c.*1625–*c.*1628 (Disc)
Mᵒ Fray Luis de Aparicio	1627–9 (Cebrián)
Mᵒ Fray Juan Pérez de Rojas	1629–32 (Cebrián)
Mᵒ Fray Tomás del Castillo y Baena	1632–6 (Serrano)
Mᵒ Fray Juan Pérez de Munébrega	1636–42? (Serra)

XII. *Foundation of American Provinces*

The first American entities (Lima, Cuzco, Chile and Guatemala) were founded as sub-provinces in 1563 and placed under Castilian control, though nominally under the authority of the generals. The 1574 constitutions included the American sub-provinces in the Castilian electoral bloc, but it was not until 1593 that these were raised to full provincial and therefore full electoral status. To the following list the vice-province of Maranhão (Brazil), founded in 1662, must be added.

Lima	1563
Cuzco	1563
Chile	1563
Guatemala	1563
Tucumán	1592 (out of Cuzco)
Santo Domingo	1608 (out of Guatemala)
Quito	1615 (out of Lima)
Mexico	1615 (out of Guatemala)

APPENDIX II

MAJOR VISITATION CAMPAIGNS (1567–85)

Date	Area of Visitation	Visitors

ORDER-WIDE

10/1567–early 1569 (varies)	Royal visitation arranged by diocese with Dominican support	

CASTILE

mid-1567	New Castile, Andalusia	Peñaranda
mid-1567	Old Castile, León	Maldonado
06/1569–mid-1570	Castile & Andalusia	Carrillo
10/1570–09/1571	La Mancha & Northern Castile	Meneses (OP) with Carrillo
*c.*10/1571–early 1572	Castile	Carrillo
*c.*Summer 1572–06/1574	Castile & Andalusia	Castillo (OP) (with Covarrubias?)
*c.*Summer/Autumn 1573	Castile & Andalusia?	Covarrubias
*c.*Summer/Autumn 1575	Castile & Andalusia?	Peñaranda
*c.*Summer/Autumn 1577	Castile & Andalusia?	Arce
*c.*Spring 1578–Spring 1579	Castile (including Basque *beaterios*)	Maldonado
*c.*Autumn/Winter 1580	Castile & Andalusia?	Muñoz
*c.*Autumn/Winter 1582	Castile & Andalusia?	Carrillo
*c.*Summer/Autumn 1585	Castile & Andalusia?	Zumel

CROWN OF ARAGON

11/1568–02/1569	Aragon-Navarre	Duran with Antich
07–12/1569	Aragon-Navarre, Valencia & Catalonia	Antich with Bertrán
12/1570–early 1571	Catalonia; Aragon-Navarre; Valencia	Montaña (OP)
Summer 1571	Aragon	Dicastillo

Date	*Area of Visitation*	*Visitors*

CROWN OF ARAGON

Date	Area of Visitation	Visitors
09/1571–05/1572	Aragon	Alegría
04–06/1572	Catalonia; Valencia; Aragon-Navarre?	Montaña (OP)
04/1573	Convent of Valencia	Duran
04–06/1574	Aragon-Navarre	Duran
08/1575–early 1576	Aragon, Tarragona, Barcelona	Maldonado after d. of Torres
11/1576–Summer 1577	Valencia, Aragon?	Maldonado
09–12/1577	Barcelona	Maldonado
*c.*1577–*c.*1580	Sicily	Lagarria
05–07/1579	Barcelona	Salazar
*c.*09/1583–03/1584	Barcelona	Tocco (OSB)
04–*c.*10/1584	Catalonia & Mallorca	Andreu with Puente
1584	Italy & Sicily	García

MERCEDARIAN DEMOGRAPHY:
NUMBERS OF RELIGIOUS AND (HOUSES)[1]

Aragonese Grouping

	c.1450[2]	1500	1547[3]	c.1573[4]	c.1584[5]	c.1603	1620	1650	1700
Catalonia	(14)	(14)	87(14)	92(16)	85(16)	(13)	(13)	(12)	(13)
Aragon-Navarre	(19)	(17)	123(16)	123(16)	(14)	(12)	(12)	(14)	(15)
Valencia	(9)	(7)	78(8)	82(8)	(8)	(13)	(14)	(15)	(15)
France	(13)	(14)	137(15)	(c.7)	40(4/5)	(c.11)	(c.13)	(c.18)	(c.20)
Others	(3)	(3)	25(3)	(3)	(5)	(8)	(11)	(11)	(12)
Peninsula	300(42)	(38)	288(38)	297(40)	c.280(38)	(38)	(39)	(41)	(43)
Total	**400(58)**	**(55)**	**450(56)**	**c.390(50)**	**c.350(48)**	**(c.57)**	**(c.63)**	**(c.70)**	**(c.75)**

[1] Statistics are for personnel, and for houses in brackets. Instances where no data is available are marked '?'; a figure prefaced '*circa*' should be understood as a reasoned estimate rather than the product of direct evidence. Where possible, statistics have been calculated from manuscript sources in conjunction with Vázquez Núñez, 'Conventos de la Orden' in particular. With regard to house statistics, the results are presented with some confidence as to their accuracy, with the exception of those for the Indies which (1553 and c.1620 apart) are largely conjectural. As for personnel, it has often not been possible to give an accurate breakdown of figures for each province, but the data nonetheless represents a significant addition and correction to existing estimates.

[2] *Id.*, ed., *La Merced a mediados*, pp. 31–3.

[3] *Ibid.*, pp. 89–92.

[4] Figures extrapolated from **IVDJ**, env. 72, **II**, ff. 34r–40r.

[5] The Catalan figures, dating from 1584, are from ACA, Mon., vol. 2850; the French ones, an estimate from 1585, are contained in AMAE, SS, leg. 34, f. 145r.

Castilian Grouping

		1467[6]	1500	1553[7]	c.1576[8]	c.1584	1591[9]	c.1620[10]	1650	1700
Castile		(17)	(18)	(18)	420(19)	(19)	c.400(19)	(20)	(20)	(21)
		200		**330**						
Andalusia		(11)	(12)	(16)	408(16)	(17)	c.335(18)	(20)	(21)	(21)
Indies	Peru			100(14)	?	?	?	541(50)	?	?
	New Spain/			54(7)	?	?	?	250(30)	?	?
	New Granada									
Discalced	Castile							(8)	(8)	(10)
	Andalusia							c.**150**(11)	(18)	(19)
	Sicily							(7)	(10)	(11)
Peninsula		200(28)	(30)	330(34)	828(35)	(36)	c.735(37)	(40)	(41)	(42)
Indies				154(21)	c.330(c.40)	(c.50)	(c.60)	800(80)	(c.90)	(c.100)
Discalced								150(26)	(36)	(40)
Total		**200(28)**	**(30)**	**484(55)**	c.**1160**(c.**75**)	(c.**86**)	(c.**97**)	(**146**)	(c.**167**)	(c.**182**)

Aggregate Totals[11]

	c.1467	1500	c.1550	c.1574	c.1584	c.1600	c.1620	1650	1700
Religious	**600**	–	**934**	c.**1550**	–	c.**2500**	–	c.**4000**	c.**5200**
Houses	**(85)**	**(85)**	**(111)**	(c.**125**)	(c.**135**)	(c.**165**)	(c.**209**)	(c.**237**)	(c.**257**)

[6] Vázquez Núñez, ed., *La Merced a mediados*, pp. 31–3. The figure in **bold** type is that for both Castile and Andalusia, which remained part of the same province until 1588.

[7] The joint Castilian figure (given in **bold**) is from *ibid*., pp. 95–7, the American ones from Vázquez Fernández, 'Cedulario mercedario', p. 619.

[8] IVDJ, env. 72, II, ff. 139r & 140r. The figures represent a staggering growth of 150% in a little over twenty years.

[9] Figures extrapolated from Ruiz Martín, 'Demografía eclesiástica' in *DHEE*, II, pp. 718–19. The decline in numbers on 1576, particularly in Andalusia, is explained by loss of personnel to the Indies rather than the wider demographic conjuncture. These statistics correct those given in *ibid*. and in Molinié-Bertrand, 'Le Clergé dans le royaume de Castille à la fin du XVIᵉ siècle', p. 29, where the personnel and, in the latter case, the houses of the Order in Castile have been significantly underestimated.

[10] The American figures are from Vázquez Núñez, *Manual*, II, pp. 88–9, the Peruvian ones from 1612, and those of New Spain from 1619. The estimate of the number of Discalced religious (given in **bold** type) refers to the entire congregation; see *ibid*., p. 83, & Cano Manrique, 'Desarrollo histórico de la Orden Mercedaria Descalza', pp. 136–7.

[11] The figures in this table are based in part on those given in the *Dizionario degli Istituti di Perfezioni*, V, p. 1223. Note that, where relevant, the totals include the Discalced statistics even after their separation from the main order in 1621.

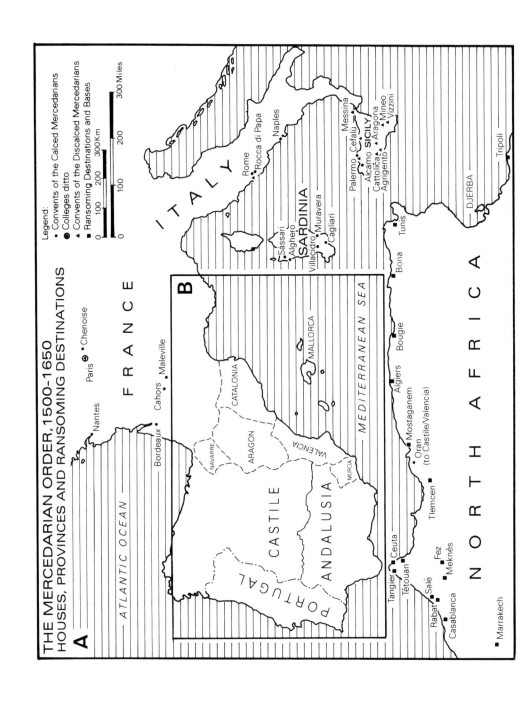

THE MERCEDARIAN ORDER, 1500–1650
HOUSES, PROVINCES AND RANSOMING DESTINATIONS

Legend:
- Convents of the Calced Mercedarians
- Colleges ditto
- Convents of the Discalced Mercedarians
- Ransoming Destinations and Bases

A

B

FRANCE

ATLANTIC OCEAN

Nantes

Bordeaux

Cahors • Maleville

Paris ● •Chenoise

PORTUGAL

CASTILE

ANDALUSIA

NAVARRE

ARAGON

CATALONIA

VALENCIA

MURCIA

MALLORCA

MEDITERRANEAN SEA

ITALY

Rome
Rocca di Papa

Naples

SARDINIA

Sássari
Alghero
Villacidro •Muravera
Cagliari

SICILY
Palermo• Cefalù
Alcamo Messina
Cattolica▲ ▲Aragona
Agrigento •Mineo
•Vizzini

Tunis

Bona

Algiers

Bougie

Mostaganem

Oran
(to Castile/Valencia)

Tlemcen

Ceuta

Tangier
Tétouan
Salé
Rabat
Casablanca

Fez
Meknès

Marrakech

DJERBA

Tripoli

NORTH AFRICA

0 100 200 300 Km
0   100   200   300 Miles

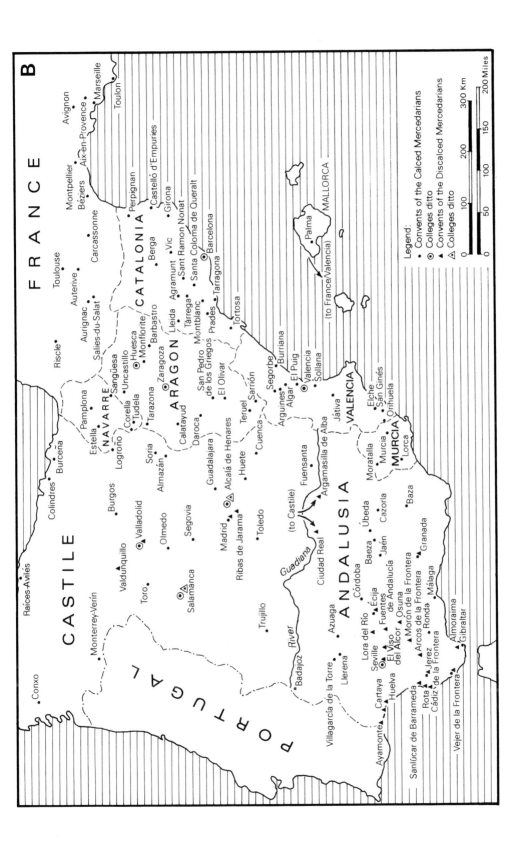

B

FRANCE

CASTILE

PORTUGAL

NAVARRE

ARAGON

CATALONIA

VALENCIA

ANDALUSIA

MURCIA

MALLORCA

• Conxo

Raíces·Avilés

Colindres•
•Burceña

Monterrey·Verín•

•Burgos

Valdunquillo▲

Toro•
•Olmedo

Segovia•

⊙▲Valladolid

Salamanca
⊙△

•Trujillo

•Badajoz

Guadiana River

Riscle•

Auterive•

Aurignac•
Salies-du-Salat•

Toulouse•

Carcassonne•

Montpellier•
Béziers•
Aix-en-Provence•

Avignon•

Toulon•
•Marseille

Perpignan•

Castelló d'Empuries•
•Girona

Berga•
Vic•

Santa Coloma de Queralt
Sant Ramon Nonat•
Barcelona
⊙•

Tarragona•

Tortosa•

Pamplona•
Estella•
Logroño•
Soria•
Almazán•

Sangüesa•
•Uncastillo
•Huesca
Corella•
Tudela•
Monflorite
Barbastro•
Tarazona•
Zaragoza•

Calatayud•
Daroca•

Guadalajara•

Alcalá de Henares
⊙△▲

Madrid▲

Ribas de Jarama▲

Huete•

Toledo•

(to Castile)

Ciudad Real•

Teruel•

Lleida•
Tàrrega•
Agramunt•
Prades•
Montblanc•
San Pedro
de los Griegos•
El Olivar•
Sarrión•

Cuenca•

Segorbe•
Burriana•
El Puig•
Valencia
⊙
Sollana•

Arguines•
Algar•

Játiva•

Elche•
San Ginés•
Orihuela•

Murcia
⊙▲
Lorca•

Moratalla▲

Fuensanta•

Argamasilla de Alba•

Baza•

Cazorla•

Úbeda•
Baeza•
Jaén•

Granada•

Córdoba•

Écija▲
Fuentes
de Andalucía•
Osuna▲

Morón de la Frontera▲

Ronda▲
Málaga•

Arcos de la Frontera▲

Almorama▲

Gibraltar▲

Lora del Río•

Azuaga•

Llerena•

El Viso
del Alcor▲

Seville
⊙▲

Huelva•

Cartaya▲

Ayamonte▲

Villagarcía de la Torre▲

Sanlúcar de Barrameda▲

Rota▲
Cádiz de la Frontera▲
Jerez▲

Vejer de la Frontera▲

(to France/Valencia)

Palma•

Legend:
• Convents of the Calced Mercedarians
⊙ Colleges ditto
▲ Convents of the Discalced Mercedarians
△ Colleges ditto

0   100   200   300 Km

0   50   100   150   200 Miles

GLOSSARY

Beaterio. A house of holy women — *beatas* — living in community and often to no specific rule, though usually in close association with a religious house.

Chapter (capítulo/capitol). A gathering of religious for the purpose of discussing and legislating the business of a convent, province or the Order itself, and of electing the high officers. The Guadalajara constitutions of 1574 required chapters provincial and general to be celebrated on a triennial basis at a pre-ordained location. Except for Castile, chapters had previously been called either on the death of a *provincial* or *master general*, or at their discretion. Where houses were concerned, the weekly conventual chapter or chapter of faults was instituted in the late 16th century as a means of improving local administration and encouraging the religious to greater spiritual and disciplinary observance. With the exception of the priory of Barcelona, the practice of electing *commendators* in conventual chapters was abandoned in 1574. For more on the evolution of the chapters provincial in particular, see Appendix I.

Clavari/Depositario. In a convent, the religious entrusted with the maintenance of house accounts and alms collected for the redemption of captives, as well as the safekeeping of the deposit box. The Guadalajara constitutions of 1574 required each house to have three *clavaris* with separate keys to the deposit box, and a separate safe for redemption *limosna*. Larger convents appear to have appointed a *procurador* who was charged with overseeing the wider financial affairs of the house and the management of its estates. In the ransoming field, the *depositario* was an alternative name for the *procurador de la redención* whose duty it was to gather and distribute the *limosna* and organize the logistics of the expedition itself.

Commendator (comendador). The superior of a Mercedarian house. The title is taken from the usage of the military orders and reflects the territorial dimension of the commendator's authority where the collection of alms for the ransom of captives was concerned.

Commissary (comisario). An individual appointed externally and usually with apostolic authority to whom the government of an order would be temporarily entrusted for the purposes of reform and visitation. The Mercedarians were placed under the authority of commissaries apostolic between 1569–74 and 1582–7; see Appendix I.

Conventualism. In the language of reform, and particularly of the early Franciscan Order, a mitigated interpretation of the religious life in which adherents attempted to square the spirit of a rule or observance with the reality of an active vocation. In practice this was often used as an excuse for relaxation, a feature which contributed to the gradual extinction of Conventual life in Spain in favour of the *Observant* tendency from the end of the 15th century.

Diffinitor (definidor). The diffinitors were those officials delegated to vote and conduct the business of chapters general and provincial. Where chapters general were concerned, attendance was limited to the 'diffinitory' — *definitorio* — which until 1574 consisted of seventeen members, including two elected representatives from each of the chapters provincial and a total of five Catalans. At the electoral chapters general the diffinitory was restricted to seven members with each of the five provinces represented by a single diffinitor. The remaining places in the electoral college were filled by the vicar general and the ordained conventual of longest profession in the priory of Barcelona. After 1574 the composition of the chapters general, electoral or otherwise, was fixed at sixteen delegates: seven Aragonese, six Castilians and three French, with all future provinces permitted the votes of three diffinitors general. As for chapters provincial, business was conducted by a four-member diffinitory which was drawn from the assembled delegates at the start of proceedings. Here, though, the election of the provincial was a matter for the entire chapter, not just the diffinitors.

Discalced (Descalzo). The Discalced movement developed in 16th-century Spain among religious anxious for greater asceticism and a stricter spiritual observance of their rule and constitutions than was available to them in their parent orders. The result was a string of reformed congregations beginning with the Discalced Franciscans under Fray Pedro de Alcántara in 1559, and concluding with that founded among the Mercedarians in 1603. Although the Discalced went unshod for ceremonial purposes, religious usually wore sandals in favour of the boots and shoes worn by their 'Calced' counterparts.

Espolio. The money and property of a deceased religious, whose distribution remained a matter of some controversy in the Order.

Lay Brothers (hermanos legos). The unordained majority of Mercedarians who played an essential role in the domestic life of the Order and whose influence was felt mainly at conventual level.

Lector. The origin of this office among the Mercedarians can be traced to 1523 with the appointment by the general, Mᶜ Fra Benet Zafont, of three provincial *lectores* for the teaching of philosophy and theology for the Crown of Aragon. The intention was clearly to provide a conventual dimension to study, but the office did not acquire real importance until the establishment of *studia* for this purpose in the late 16th century. The responsibility of initiating the religious in arts and theology was borne by *lectores* who thereby played a crucial role in the raising of intellectual standards in the Order. In 1603 the attainment of the degree of *Presentado* was made conditional on the completion of an additional three years as a *lector de artes* and a further two as a *lector de teología* in the conventual *studia*.

Limosna. The alms raised by the brethren specifically for the ransom of captives. As a non-mendicant order the Mercedarians were forbidden from begging alms to support themselves, but a bull of Leo X in 1516 permitted the Order to retain a third of all redemption *limosna* for its own purposes.

Maestro/Maestre/Maître. During the 15th century the Order began to confer the title of *Maestro* (M°/M^e) on bachelors in theology and on those with long and distinguished service in the Order. Following university norms, in 1475 the requirement for bachelors was set at four years of theology at an approved *studium generale*, followed by a public defence at a chapter general or provincial. The title was extended to graduates in canon law in the first half of the 16th century and from 1574 was confirmed as being dependent on the completion of a further three years of study, bringing the requisite total to seven. From this time also the number of *maestros* per province was limited to twelve as a measure against indiscriminate conferment, and there can be no doubt that the conferral of this degree and the privileges associated with it provided a key incentive to the development of an academic vocation in the Order; see also *Presentado*.

Master General (maestro/maestre general). The high office of the Order, of life tenure until 1574 and sexennial thereafter; for details of its development, see Appendix I.

Observant/Observantine. The opposite of *Conventualism*, the Observant movement owes its origins to the dispute which permanently divided the Franciscan Order in the years following the founder's death in 1226. The allegiance of the Observant congregation was to a strict obedience of the Rule of St Francis and a close adherence to the spirit of his life and teaching. During the 15th century the Observant congregations of many orders in Spain, and especially the Franciscans, gained the spiritual high ground over their Conventual brethren, eventually replacing them as the sole viable expression of the religious life in the Peninsula.

Presentado/Presentat/Présenté. During the 16th century the Order began to confer its own title of *presentado* on bachelors as the essential precondition for those wishing to attain the degree of *maestro*. In line with efforts to promote learning in the Order, the 1574 constitutions endorsed the right of *presentados* to vote in the chapters provincial and limited the number of these to 24 per province to avoid indiscriminate conferment. In addition to a bachelor's degree, from 1603 the attainment of the title of *Presentado* was made conditional on the completion of three years as a *lector de artes* and a further two as a *lector de teología* in the newly founded conventual *studia*. Through these and other measures the Mercedarians established learning as the *sine qua non* for advancement and privilege in the Order and provided the means for a

marked improvement in the education of its members; see also *Maestro* &
Lector.

Prior. The title held by the superior of three important houses in the
Aragonese provinces of the Order: Barcelona (Nostra Senyora de la Mercè),
Sant Ramon Nonat (a dependency of Barcelona), and Palermo (Santa
Anna). On the priors of Barcelona, see Appendix I.

Privativa. The privilege, granted by Pere IV of Aragon in 1366, by which the
Order enjoyed a monopoly over the collection of redemption *limosna* in the
Crown of Aragon.

Procurator (procurador). Title given to several Mercedarian offices whose common feature is the representation of the Order, its members and affairs in
wider society. The most important figure bearing this title was the *procurador
general* who was appointed by the master to represent the Order before the
papacy. Though the generals had periodically maintained *procuradores* in
Rome since the mid fifteenth century, it was only in 1587 that the office
acquired permanent status; see Appendix I. The name *procurador* was also
given to those representatives of prelates or provinces who habitually
thronged the court and curia on private or official business. For the *procurador de la redención* and the conventual *procurador*, see under *Clavari/Depositario*.

Provincial. The senior prelate of any of the main territorial divisions of the
Order. On the development of this office among the Mercedarians, see
Appendix I.

Rector. The superior of any of the Order's twelve university colleges, *viz.*
Salamanca (Vera Cruz, founded *c.*1411), Paris (La Merci, 1515), Alcalá (La
Concepción, 1518), Huesca (Nuestra Señora de la Merced, 1578), Lima
(Nuestra Señora de la Merced?, *c.*1581), Seville (San Laureano, 1593), Val-
ladolid (Nuestra Señora de la Merced, 1594), Mexico City (Nuestra Señora
de la Merced?, 1594; San Ramón Nonato, *c.*1624–8), Valencia (San Pedro
Nolasco, 1630), Zaragoza (San Pedro Nolasco, 1647), Barcelona (San Pedro
Nolasco, 1668).

Redemptor (redentor). The individual charged with leading the ransoming
expeditions to North Africa which constituted the principal vocation of the
Order. Redemptors usually worked in pairs and were responsible for con-
veying the Order's money and goods to the Barbary Coast, for ransoming
the captives themselves and seeing to their safe return to Spain. Once
returned they were required to present account of their expenditure and
lead the procession of ransomed captives through town and country.

Responsion. The remittance of monies collected for the ransom of captives in
a given area by a commendator at the chapter provincial. This system was
abolished in 1588.

Vestuario. The tribute paid annually by a subject province to the general or provincial for his official expenses. The *Concordia* of 1467, for example, set the Castilian *vestuario* to the generals at 40 *doblas* in gold per year. In 1563 the four sub-provinces in the Indies agreed to send the provincial of Castile an annual tribute of 100 ducats, though this had risen to over 1000 by 1593.

Vicar (vicario/vicari). A prelate holding authority delegated by a senior officer in the Order, usually a general or provincial. The priors of Barcelona held the *de facto* office of vicar general of the Order from the death of the master to the confirmation of his successor. The other vicars general were those appointed by the provinces of Castile and Andalusia in token of their authority over the American provinces. In 1587 the chapter general of Zaragoza legislated for the appointment of two such officers, one for the viceroyalty of Peru and the other for the Order's holdings in Guatemala and Santo Domingo. Until its partition in 1588 the government of one or other half of the province of Castile was habitually delegated to a vicar provincial.

Visitor (visitador). Any individual charged with visiting a house or houses of the Order with a view to gathering information as to its condition or promoting improved standards of discipline and religious observance. The office was often delegated by the general or provincial.

SOURCES AND BIBLIOGRAPHY

I. *Manuscript Sources*

Words and letters in **bold** correspond to their abbreviations in the footnotes.

Main Collections

ACA: Archivo de la Corona de Aragón, Barcelona.
CA: Consejo de Aragón; vol. no. 342.
LT: Generalitat, Lletres Trameses; vol. no. 785.
Mon.: Monacales de Hacienda; vol. nos.
   2655, 2658, 2659, 2660, 2661, 2662, 2665, 2658, 2663, 2665, 2667, 2668, 2669,
   2670, 2671, 2673, 2676, 2677, 2678, 2679, 2680, 2681, 2683, 2691, 2703, 2710,
   2730, 2829, 2830, 2831, 2832, 2833, 2834, 2835, 2836, 2837, 2848, 2850, 2851,
   4144.
Ibid., leg. nos. 293, 298, 306, 323, 341, 348.
Mss.Misc.: Manuscritos Miscelánea; vol. nos. 39, 44, 49, 55, 58, 62, 93, 103.
   Vols. 39 & 103 contain sections of Mº Fray Juan de **Antillón**, *Chronologicon
   Generalicio del Orden de Nuestra Señora de la Merced y Redemptores* (1618 & 1636
   respectively).
Mss.Varia: Manuscritos Varia; vol. no. II.
RC: Registros de Cancillería; vol. nos. 3899, 3900, 4351, 4352.

AGN: Archivo General de Navarra; Pamplona.
Clero: vol. nos. 306, 402, 416, 417.

AGS: Archivo General de Simancas; Valladolid.
Eº: Estado; leg. nos. 140, 149, 150, 151, 158, 161, 162, 164, 333, 897, 910, 911.
PR: Patronato Real:
   leg. 10, doc. no.23.
   leg. 15, doc. no. 4.
   leg. 23, doc. nos. 47, 48, 49, 50(i–v), 51(i–ii), 52(i–ii), 53(i–xxvii), 68, 69, 85, 179,
   188, 198, 207, 208, 212, 225, 227.

AHCB: Arxiu Històric de la Ciutat de Barcelona.
CC: Consell de Cent:
CCO: Cartes Comunes Originals; vol. nos. 47, 48, 49.
   LDCC: Llibre de Deliberacions del Consell de Cent; vol. nos. 87, 88, 89, 90, 91,
      92, 93, 94, 95, 96, 97, 98.
   RLC: Registre de Lletres Closes; vol. nos. 61, 62, 63, 64, 65.
   RO: Registre d'Ordinacions; vol. nos. 20, 21.
Cons.: Consellers Mss.; secció XVIII-3 (Mercedaris).
Ms. A-266. Mº Fray Juan de **Antillón**, *Memorias Chronologicas de la
   Religion de Nuestra Señora de la Merced Redempcion de Captivos Christianos en la Provincia y
   Corona de Aragon*, vol. II (1643).

AHN: Archivo Histórico Nacional, Madrid.
Clero: carp. nos. 125, 126, 198, 558, 617, 1380–1383, 1425–1428, 1981, 2904,
   2905, 2920, 2921, 3132, 3133, 3199–3207, 3345–3354, 3520, 3660–3662.
      vol. nos. 3320, 7737, 13,410, 16,046.

AMAE: Archivo del Ministerio de Asuntos Exteriores, Madrid.
SS: Santa Sede; leg. nos. 9, 12, 34, 142.

APV: Archivo Privado, Valencia [Name withheld at owners' request].
Archive not catalogued.
Ms. M° Fray Juan de **Antillón, *Epitome*** de los Generales de la Merced, vol. I(ii) (*c.*1640).
Ms. M° Fray José Nicolás Cavero, with notes from **Antillón, *Epitome***, vol. 'III' (*c.*1640).
Mss. Fray José Nicolás **Cavero, 'Varia'**, 2 vols.; 18th c., 4°.
Mss. Fray Anselmo **Dempere, *Necrologio*** Mercedario, 8 vols; 18th c.
Ms. **Girona** (Visitation book of Girona, 1589–1628).
Ms. **Varia at** [*sic*] **Ordinem**; mostly 18th c.

ARV: Archivo del Reino de Valencia, Valencia.
Clero: lib. nos. 1249, 1305, 1705, 1720, 1776, 2147, 2266, 2958.

ASV: Archivio Segretto Vaticano, Rome.
NS: Nunziatura di Spagna; vol. nos. 1, 2, 4, 5, 6(i), 6(ii), 8, 9, 10, 11, 13, 14, 18, 20, 22, 30, 31, 33, 34, 37, 38, 43, 44, 319, 320, 440.
Inst.Misc.: Instrumenta Miscellanea; vol. no. 4497.

ASZ: Archivo Santiago Zabálburu, Madrid.
Carp. nos. 163, 165, 227.

BL: British Library, London.
Add.: Additional; vol. nos. 28,263, 28,340, 28,342, 28,381, 28,404, 28,489, 28,708.

BNM: Biblioteca Nacional, Madrid.
Sección de Manuscritos: ms. vols. 1761, 2284, 2448, 2684, 2718, 2906, 2963, 3530, 3536, 3588, 6134, 6140, 6184, 6569, 6908, 7327, 12,337, 13,337.

BPC: Biblioteca Pública de Cádiz.
Mss. 94-108 & 109: M° Fray Juan de **Antillón,**
Epitome de los Generales de la Merced, vols. I(i) & I(ii) (*c.*1640).

IVDJ: Instituto de Valencia de Don Juan, Madrid.
Envío nos. 17(ms. 26), 43, 72(II), 89, 91.

Other Collections

ACPMC: Archivo de la Curia Provincial de la Merced de Castilla, Madrid.
Vol. nos. 567, 584, 720, 824.

ADH: Archives Départementales de l'Hérault, Montpellier.
Série **H**: Sous-série 50; liasse nos. 1, 2, 25, 26, 33, 51, 50, 66.

ADHG: Archives Départementales de Haute-Garonne, Toulouse.
Série **H**: Sous-série 130; liasse nos. 1, 12, 15, 37.

APCC: Arxiu Provincial dels Caputxins de Catalunya, Barcelona.
Secció: A-2-28.

ARM: Archivo del Reino de Mallorca, Palma.
AH: Arxiu Històric; no. 4334.
Clero: nos. 956, 1740, 4178.

AUB: Arxiu de l'Universitat de Barcelona.
Mss. 353, 753, 779, 1500.

Bod.L.: Bodleian Library, Oxford.
Arch. A b. 8 (4), (20*) & (20**): 3 printed indulgences of *c*.1510 (4), & 1532 (20* & 20**).
Arch. Seld. A Subt. 11(15): printed *relación* by M° Fray Alonso Remón of 1624; see in section IV below.
Arch. Seld. A Subt. 21(32): printed *discurso* by M° Fray Gerónimo de Bustamante & M° Fray Serafin de Freitas of *c*.1621; see in section IV below.

BUV: Biblioteca Universitaria de Valencia.
Mss. 884, 1106.
Ms. 1106 contains M° Fray Juan de Antillón's *Chronologicon Generalicio, o Memorias Chronologicas. Contienen las Vidas de Nuestro Padre y Patriarca San Pedro Nolasco, y San Ramon Nonat* (1633).

II. *Printed Sources*

Anon., ed., 'Reducción y conversión de los Indios en Nicaragua (1607–1612)' in *Boletín de la Orden de la Merced*, 5 (1917), pp. 92–6, 127–31,163–70, 193–4 & 205–7.
Barriga, P.Fr. Manuel Victor, OdeM, ed., 'Los Mercedarios en la provincia de Lima: Memorial del P.M.Fr. Luis de Vera' in *Boletín de la Orden de la Merced*, 19 (1931), pp. 16–22, 75–85, 104–12, 188–91 & 222–30.
—, ed., 'Establecimiento de los Mercedarios en Cuzco; información al Real Consejo de Indias' in *Boletín de la Orden de la Merced*, 20 (1932), pp. 29–47.
—, ed., 'Información de servicios de la Orden de la Merced en el Perú hecha en 1570' in *Boletín de la Orden de la Merced*, 21–2 (1933–4).
Beltrán de Heredia, P.Fr. Vicente, OP, ed., *Cartulario de la Universidad de Salamanca (1218–1600)* (6 vols., Salamanca, 1969–73).
Bruniquer, Ramon, *Ceremonial dels Magnifichs Consellers y Regiment de la Ciutat de Barcelona* (known as *Rubriques de Bruniquer*) (5 vols., Barcelona, 1912–16).
Calendar of Letters and State Papers Relating to English Affairs, Preserved Principally in the Archives of Simancas, vol. I: *Elizabeth, 1558–1567* (London, 1892).
Colección de documentos inéditos para la historia de España [CODOIN], ed. Martín Fernández de Navarrete, Miguel Salvá, & Pedro Sainz de Baranda (112 vols., Madrid, 1842–96).
Comes, [Pere] Joan, *Libre de algunes coses asanyalades succehides en Barcelona y en altres parts* (Barcelona, 1878).
Dietari del Antich Consell Barceloní (28 vols., Barcelona, 1892–1975).
Duran i Sanpere, Agustí, & Josep Sanabre, eds., *Llibre de les Solemnitats de Barcelona* (2 vols., Barcelona, 1930–47).
'F.J.C.', ed., 'Notas y textos: Privilegios imperiales y reales de la religión […] de la Merced […], los cuales mandó imprimir […] Fray Alonso de Zorita' in *Estudios*, 19 (1963), pp. 139–43.
García Navarro, Fray Melchor, OdeM, *Redenciones de cautivos en África (1723–1725)*, ed. P.Fr. Manuel Vázquez Pájaro, OdeM (Madrid, 1956).
Milian Boix, Manuel, ed., *El Fondo «Instrumenta Miscellanea» del Archivo Vaticano: Docu-*

mentos referentes a España (853–1782) (Rome, 1967); also in *Anthologica Annua*, 15 (1967), pp. 489–1014.

Miquell Rosell, P. Francisco J., ed., *Regesta de letras pontificias del ACA — Cancillería Real* (Madrid, 1948).

Olarra y Garmendía, José de, 'Catálogo de los códices 418–498 de la Biblioteca de la Embajada de España cerca de la Santa Sede' in *Anthologica Annua*, 2 (1954), pp. 457–691.

Olarra y Garmendía, José de, & María Luisa de Larramendi, *Índices de la correspondencia entre la Nunciatura de España y la Santa Sede durante el reinado de Felipe II (1556–1598)* (2 vols., Madrid, 1948–9).

Olarra y Garmendía(†), José de, & María Luisa de Larramendi, viuda de Olarra, *Índices de la correspondencia entre la Nunciatura de España y la Santa Sede durante el reinado de Felipe III (1598–1621)* (7 vols., Rome, 1960–6), and serialized in *Anthologica Annua*, 7 & 9–14 (1959 & 1961–6).

Sans i Travé, Josep Maria, gral. ed., *Dietaris de la Generalitat de Catalunya, 1411–1714* (3 vols. of 10 pubd. thus far, Barcelona, 1994–).

Serrano, Dom Luciano, OSB, *Correspondencia diplomática entre España y la Santa Sede durante el pontificado de S. Pío V (1565–72)* (4 vols., Madrid, 1914).

Torre y del Cerro, Antonio de la, ed., *Documentos sobre relaciones internacionales de los Reyes Católicos* (5 vols., Barcelona, 1949–66).

Vázquez Núñez, P.Fr. Guillermo, OdeM, ed., 'Los Mercedarios en la Universidad Complutense' in *Boletín de la Orden de la Merced*, 1 (1913), pp. 193–6 & 252–8; 2 (1914), pp. 317–22 & 413–19.

—, ed., *Monumenta ad historiam Ordinis de Mercede Reverendissimi Patris Natalis Gaver. Cathalogus Magistrorum Generalium et Priorum Conventus Barchinonae anno 1445* (Toledo, 1928), and in *Boletín de la Orden de la Merced*, 14 (1926).

—, ed., *Actas del Capítulo General de 1317...* (Rome, 1930), and serialized in *Boletín de la Orden de la Merced*, 17 & 18 (1929 & 1930).

—, ed., *La Merced a mediados de los siglos XV y XVI: Documentos inéditos y observaciones* (Rome, 1931).

—, ed., 'Memorial del Maestro Fray Pedro de Logroño a Calixto III' in *Boletín de la Orden de la Merced*, 19 (1931), pp. 1–7.

—, ed., 'Fuentes para la historia de la Merced' [The Guadalajara Constitutions of 1574] in *Boletín de la Orden de la Merced*, 20 (1932), pp. 22–47.

—, ed., 'Un parecer inédito del Maestro Fray Hernando de Santiago' in *Boletín de la Orden de la Merced*, 21 (1933), pp. 48–59.

Zurita, Jerónimo de, *Anales de Aragón*, vols. V & VII (Zaragoza, 1974 & 1977).

III. *Secondary Sources*

Anon., 'Del Archivo Vaticano' [catalogues] serialized in *Boletín de la Orden de la Merced*, 9–17 (1921–9).

—, *La Vie de Lazarillo de Tormès (La vida de Lazarillo de Tormes)*, ed. Marcel Bataillon (Paris, 1958).

—, *Lazarillo de Tormes*, ed. R.O. Jones (Manchester, 1963).

—, *Lazarillo de Tormes*, ed. Francisco Rico (Madrid, 1996).

—, 'Lista de los documentos referentes à la Orden de la Merced existentes en la R. Biblioteca Nacional de Madrid, en la sección de Manuscritos' in *Boletín de la Orden de la Merced*, 16 (1928), pp. 297–304.

—, 'Los Mercedarios en la Universidad de San Marcos de Lima' in *Boletín de la Orden de la Merced*, 11 (1923), pp. 81–8.

In collab., *El convent, 1562–1994* [Sollana, Valencia] (Sollana, 1994).

—, *Evolución histórico-arquitectónica del Palacio de la Capitanía General de Cataluña* (Barcelona, 1981).

Alarcón Bejarano, P.Fr. Eleuterio, OdeM, 'Las constituciones de 1691: Estudio críti-co-canónico' in *Analecta Mercedaria*, 2 (1983), pp. 209–79.

Alberigo, Giuseppe, 'Du Concile de Trente au tridentinisme' in *Irenikon*, 54 (1981), pp. 194–210.

—, 'Méthodologie de l'histoire de l'Église en Europe' in *Revue d'histoire ecclèsiastique*, 81 (1986), pp. 401–20.

Alcina, L., 'Fray Lope de Olmedo y su discutida obra monástica' in *Yermo*, 2 (1964), pp. 29–57.

Alcolea, Santiago, *Zurbarán* (English trans., Barcelona, 1989).

Aldana, Fray Cristóbal de, *Crónica de la Merced de México*, ed. Jorge Gurría Lacroix (Mexico City, 1953).

Aldea Vaquero, P. Quintín, SI, *Iglesia y estado en la España del siglo XVII* (Comillas, 1961).

—, *et al.*, ed., *Diccionario de Historia Eclesiástica de España* (5 vols., Madrid, 1972–87).

Allison Peers, Edgar, *Studies of the Spanish Mystics* (2 vols., London, 1927–30).

—, *Saint Teresa of Jesus* (London, 1953).

—, *Handbook to the Life and Times of St Teresa and St John of the Cross* (London, 1954).

Alonso, P.Fr. Carlos, OSA, *La reforma tridentina en la provincia Agustiniana de la Corona de Aragón (1568–1586)* (Valladolid, 1984).

Altman, Ida, *Emigrants and Society. Extremadura and America in the Sixteenth Century* (Berkeley, 1989).

Álvarez, L., 'Contribución a la reforma religiosa en el reinado de los Reyes Católicos' in *Revista agustiniana de espiritualidad*, 5 (1964), pp. 145–212.

Amelang, James S., *Honored Citizens of Barcelona: Patrician Culture and Class Relations, 1490–1714* (Princeton, 1986).

—, 'Public Ceremonies and Private Fetes: Social Segregation and Aristocratic Culture in Barcelona, 1500–1800' in Gary W. McDonogh, ed., *Conflict in Catalonia: Images of an Urban Society* (Gainesville, Fla., 1986), pp. 17–32.

—, 'People of the Ribera: Popular Politics and Neighborhood Identity in Early Modern Barcelona' in Barbara B. Diefendorf & Carla Hesse, eds., *Culture and Identity in Early Modern Europe (1500–1800): Essays in Honor of Natalie Zemon Davis* (Ann Arbor, Mich., 1994), pp. 119–37.

d'Amer, Fra Pere, *Constitucions dels Pares antichs del Orde de la Verge Maria de la Mercé*, ed. 'J.M.F.' in *Recull de textes catalanes antichs*, vol. VII (Barcelona, 1907).

—, *Constitucions dels Pares antichs de l'Orde de la Verge Maria de la Mercé* [anon. ed.] (Rome, 1922) and in *Boletín de la Orden de la Merced*, 10 (1922), pp. 203–9 & 242–5.

Andrés Martín, Melquiades, 'Reforma y estudio de teología entre los Agustinos reformados españoles (1431–1550)' in *Anthologica Annua*, 4 (1956), pp. 439–62.

—, 'Reforma y estudio de teología en los Franciscanos españoles' in *Anthologica Annua*, 8 (1960), pp. 43–82.

—, *Historia de la teología en España (1470–1570): Instituciones teológicas* (Rome, 1962).

—, 'Evangelismo, humanismo, reforma y observancias en España' in *Missionalia Hispanica*, 63 (1966), pp. 5–24.

—, 'Pensamiento teológico y vivencia religiosa en la reforma española' in García Villoslada, gral. ed., *Historia de la Iglesia en España*, III(ii) (1980), pp. 269–361.

—, *et al.*, ed., *Historia de la teología española* (2 vols., Madrid, 1983–7).

Aparicio, P.Fr. Severo, OdeM, 'Los Mercedarios de América y la redención de cautivos, siglos XVI–XIX' in *Analecta Mercedaria*, 1 (1982), pp. 1–56.

Arce, P. Rafael, *San Juan de Ávila y la reforma de la Iglesia en España* (Madrid, 1970).

Arriaga, José de, 'Los Mercedarios de Burceña' in *Estudios*, 11 (1955), pp. 121–4.

Augé, Dom Ramir, OSB, 'La Butlle de Clement VIIIè per a la reforma de la Congregació Claustral Tarraconense' in *Catalonia Monastica: Recull de documents i estudis referents a monestirs catalans* (2 vols., Montserrat, 1927–9); II, pp. 259–383.

Augustine of Hippo, St, (attributed), *Regula ad Servos Dei* in J.-P. Migne, ed., *Patrologia Cursus Completus [...] Series Latina*, vol. XXXII (Paris, 1877); cols. 1377–452.

Bada [Elias], P. Joan, 'El Concilio de Trento y Barcelona' in *Miscellanea Barcinonensia*, 4 (1965), pp. 97–111, & 5 (1966), pp. 109–22 & 131–50.

—, *Situació religiosa de Barcelona en el segle XVI* (Barcelona, 1970).

Bada, P. Joan, & Genís Samper, eds., *Catalonia Religiosa. Atlas Històric: Dels orígens als nostres dies* (Barcelona, 1991).

Bakhtin, Mikhail, *Rabelais and His World*, trans. H. Iswolsky (Cambridge, Mass., 1968).

Barraquer i Roviralta, P.Fr. Cayetano, OSST, *Las casas de religiosos en Cataluña durante el primer tercio del siglo XIX* (2 vols., Barcelona, 1906).

—, *Los religiosos en Cataluña durante la primera mitad del siglo XIX* (4 vols., Barcelona, 1915–17).

Barriga, P.Fr. Victor Manuel, OdeM, *Mercedarios ilustres en el Perú* (2 vols., Arequipa, 1943–9).

Basili de Rubí, P.Fr., OFMCap, *Un segle de vida caputxina a Catalunya, 1564–1664: Aproximació històrico-bibliogràfica* (Barcelona, 1977).

Bataillon, Marcel, *El sentido del «Lazarillo de Tormes»* (Paris-Toulouse, 1954).

—, *Erasmo y España: Estudios sobre la historia espiritual del siglo XVI*, trans. Antonio Alatorre, 2nd Spanish edn. (Mexico City, 1966); also *Erasme et l'Espagne*, 2nd French edn. (3 vols., Geneva, 1991).

Batllori, P. Miquel, SI, *Catalunya a l'època moderna: Recerques d'història cultural i religiosa* (Barcelona, 1971).

—, 'Temes i problemes de la història religiosa de Catalunya' in *Actes del Primer Congrés d'Història Moderna de Catalunya* [=*Pedralbes*] (2 vols., Barcelona, 1984); II, pp. 371–9.

—, *Humanismo y Renacimiento: Estudios hispano-europeos* (Barcelona, 1987).

Belenguer Cebrià, Ernest, *La Corona de Aragón en la época de Felipe II* (Valladolid, 1986).

Beltrán, Gabriel, 'Juan de Jesús Roca (1544–1614): Primer Carmelita Descalzo Catalán' in *El Carmelo Teresiano en Cataluña 1586–1986* [=*Revista Monte Carmelo*] (Burgos, 1986); pp. 7–54.

Beltran, Vicenç, Gemma Avenoza, & B.J. Concheff, eds., *Bibliografia de textos catalans antichs* on CD-ROM of ADMYTE (Madrid: Micronet, Fundación V Centenario, Biblioteca Nacional, 1994).

Beltrán de Heredia, P.Fr. Vicente, OP, *Historia de la reforma de la Provincia de España (1450–1550)* (Rome, 1939).

—, *Las corrientes de espiritualidad entre los dominicos de Castilla durante la primera mitad del siglo XVI* (Salamanca, 1941).

—, 'Noticias sobre la familia del teólogo mercedario Francisco Zumel' in *La ciencia tomista*, 89 (1962), pp. 309–13.

—, 'The Beginnings of Dominican Reform in Castile' in J.R.L. Highfield, ed., *Spain in the Fifteenth Century* (London, 1972); pp. 226–47.

Bennassar, Bartolomé, *Valladolid en el siglo de oro: Una ciudad de Castilla y su entorno agrario en el siglo XVI* (Valladolid, 1983).

Bennassar, Bartolomé & Lucile, *Los cristianos de Alá: La fascinante aventura de los renegados* (Madrid, 1989).

Bergin, Joseph A., 'The Crown, the Papacy and the Reform of the Old Orders in Early Seventeenth-Century France' in *Journal of Ecclesiastical History*, 33 (1982), pp. 234–55.

—, 'Ways and Means of Monastic Reform in Seventeenth-Century France: Saint-Denis de Reims, 1630–1633' in *Catholic Historical Review*, 72 (1986), pp. 14–32.

—, *Cardinal de La Rochefoucauld: Leadership and Reform in the French Church* (New Haven, 1987).

Bernhard, Jean, Charles Lefebvre, & Francis Rapp, *L'Époque de la Réforme et du Concile de Trente* (Paris, 1990).

Bilinkoff, Jodi, *The Ávila of Saint Teresa: Religious Reform in a Sixteenth-Century City* (Ithaca, 1989).

—, 'A Saint for a City: Mariana de Jesús and Madrid, 1565–1624' in *Archiv für Reformationsgeschichte*, 88 (1997), pp. 322–37.

Biographie Toulousaine, ou dictionnaire historique des personnages [...] célèbres dans la ville de Toulouse (2 vols., Paris, 1823).

Bireley, Fr Robert, SI, *Religion and Politics in the Age of the Counter Reformation. Emperor Ferdinand II, William Lamormaini, S.J., and the Formation of Imperial Policy* (Chapel Hill, 1981).

Bisson, Thomas N., *The Medieval Crown of Aragon: A Short History* (Oxford, 1986).

Biver, Paul & Marie-Louise, *Abbayes, monastères et couvents de Paris des origines à la fin du XVIIIᵉ siècle* (Paris, 1970).

Black, Christopher, 'Perugia and Post-Tridentine Church Reform' in *Journal of Ecclesiastical History*, 35 (1984), pp. 429–51.

Blasco Martínez, Rosa María, *Sociología de una comunidad religiosa* (Zaragoza, 1974).

Borràs i Feliu, Antoni, 'La fundació del Col·legi de Betlem de la Companyia de Jesús de Barcelona' in *Actes del Tercer Congrés d'Història Moderna de Catalunya* [=*Pedralbes*] (2 vols., Barcelona, 1993); II, pp. 203–11.

Bossy, John, 'The Counter-Reformation and the People of Catholic Europe' in *Past and Present*, 47 (1970), pp. 51–70.

—, *Christianity in the West, 1400–1700* (Oxford, 1985).

Bouza Álvarez, José Luis, *Religiosidad contrarreformista y cultura simbólica del Barroco* (Madrid, 1990).

Boxer, C.R., *The Church Militant and Iberian Expansion, 1440–1770* (Baltimore, 1978).

Boyd, Maurice, *Cardinal Quiroga, Inquisitor General of Spain* (Dubuque, Iowa, 1954).

Brann, Noel L., *The Abbot Trithemius (1462–1516): The Renaissance of Monastic Humanism* (Leiden, 1981).

Braudel, Fernand, 'Les Espagnols et l'Afrique du Nord de 1492 à 1577' in *Revue africaine*, 69 (1928), pp. 184–233 & 351–428.

—, *The Mediterranean and the Mediterranean World in the Age of Philip II*, trans. Siân Reynolds (2 vols., London, 1972–3).

Braunfels, Wolfgang, *Monasteries of Western Europe* (London, 1972).

Briggs, Robin, *Communities of Belief: Cultural and Social Tensions in Early Modern France* (Oxford, 1989).

Brodman, James William, 'The Origins of the Mercedarian Order: A Reassessment' in *Studia Monastica*, 19 (1977), pp. 353–60.

—, 'The Mercedarian Order: The Problem of Royal Patronage during the Reign of James I' in *Jaime I y su época, X Congreso de Historia de la Corona de Aragón* (5 vols. in two tomes, Zaragoza, 1982), II, pp. 71–6.

—, *Ransoming Captives in Crusader Spain: The Order of Merced on the Christian-Islamic Frontier* (Philadelphia, 1986; Catalan trans. *L'Orde de la Mercè*, Barcelona, 1990).

—, 'Ransomers or Royal Agents: The Mercedarians and the Aragonese Crown in the Fourteenth Century' in *Iberia and the Mediterranean World of the Middle Ages: Essays in Honor of Robert I. Burns S.J.*, vol. II, ed. P.E. Chevedden, D.J. Kagay, & P.G. Padilla (Leiden, 1996), pp. 239–51.

Brooke, Christopher, *The Monastic World, 1000–1300* (New York, 1974).

Brown, Jonathan, *Zurbarán* (New York, 1975).

—, *Images and Ideas in Seventeenth-Century Spanish Painting* (Princeton, 1978).

Brown, Judith C., *Immodest Acts: The Life of a Lesbian Nun in Renaissance Italy* (New York, 1986).

Brown, P.R.L., *The Cult of Saints: Its Rise and Function in Latin Christianity* (London, 1981).

Burke, Peter, *Popular Culture in Early Modern Europe* (London, 1978).

—, 'How to Become a Counter-Reformation Saint' in Kaspar von Greyerz, ed., *Religion and Society in Early Modern Europe, 1500–1800* (London, 1984), pp. 45–55.

Burns, Fr Robert Ignatius, SI, *The Crusader Kingdom of Valencia: Reconstruction on a Thirteenth-Century Frontier* (2 vols., Cambridge, Mass., 1967).

Cabanes Pecourt, María Desamparados, *Los monasterios valencianos: Su economía en el siglo XV* (2 vols., Valencia, 1974).

Caille, Jacqueline, 'Hospices et assistance à Narbonne (XIIIe–XIVe siècles)' in *Assistance et charité* [*Cahiers de Fanjeaux*, vol. XIII] (Toulouse, 1978), pp. 261–80.

Cano Manrique, P.Fr. Francisco, OMD, 'Desarrollo histórico de la Orden Mercedaria Descalza' in *Analecta Mercedaria*, 7 (1988), pp. 129–50.

—, 'Los Mercedarios Descalzos y América' in Vázquez Fernández, ed., *Presencia de la Merced en América*, II, pp. 845–67.

The Canons and Decrees of the [...] Council of Trent, trans. J. Waterworth, 2nd edn. (London, 1888).

Canons and Decrees of the Council of Trent, trans. Fr H.J. Schroeder, OP (St. Louis, Mo., 1941).

Carini, P. Francesco Maria, SI, *Monsignor Niccolò Ormaneto veronese, vescovo di Padova, nunzio apostolico della corte di Filippo II re di Spagna (1572–1577)* (Rome, 1894).

Caro Baroja, Julio, *Las formas complejas de la vida religiosa. (Religión, sociedad y carácter en la España de los siglos XVI y XVII)* (Madrid, 1978).

Carreras y Candi, Francesc, *Geografía General de Catalunya* (6 vols., Barcelona, 1913–18).

Casadeviega, J., 'El mercedario Fray Luis Gil de Xátiva, calígrafo y miniaturista, que pasó a Iberoamérica en el siglo XVI' in *Obra Mercedaria*, no. 203 (1991), pp. 60–3.

Casey, James, *The Kingdom of Valencia in the Seventeenth Century* (Cambridge, 1979).

Castro, Manuel de, 'Supresión de Franciscanos Conventuales en la España de Felipe II' in *Archivo ibero-americano*, 42 (1982), pp. 185–265.

—, 'Desamortización de terciarios regulares franciscanos en el reinado de Felipe II' in *Boletín de la Real Academia de la Historia*, no. 180 (1983), pp. 21–148.

Castro Seoane, P.Fr. José, OdeM, 'La expansión de la Merced en la América Colonial' in *Missionalia Hispanica*, 1 (1944), pp. 73–108; repr. in *Analecta Mercedaria*, 9 (1990), pp. 5–42.

—, 'Aviamiento y catálogo de misiones de la Merced de Castilla a las Indias durante el siglo XVI, según los libros de contratación de pasajeros de Indias' in *Missionalia Hispanica*, 19 (1962), pp. 35–101, & 20 (1963), pp. 257–318.

Catalano, Gaetano, *Controversie giurisdizionale tra chiesa e stato nell'età di Gregorio XIII e Filippo II* (Palermo, 1955).

Catalogue des manuscrits des Bibliothèques Publiques de France. Départements, vol. VII: *Manuscrits de la Bibliothèque de Toulouse* (Paris, 1883).

Caturla, María Luisa, & Odile Delenda, *Francisco de Zurbarán* (Paris, 1994).

Cazenave, Annie, 'Les Ordres mendiants dans l'Aude et l'Ariège' in *Les Mendiants en pays d'Oc au XIIIe siècle* [*Cahiers de Fanjeaux*, vol. VIII] (Toulouse, 1973), pp. 143–76.

—, 'Les Origines catalanes de l'Ordre de la Merci pour la rédemption des captifs' in *Actes du 97e Congrès National des Sociétés Savantes (Section de philologie et d'histoire jusqu'a 1610; Nantes, 1972)* (Paris, 1979), pp. 277–86.

Cervantes Saavedra, Miguel de, *Los baños de Argel*, ed. Jean Canavaggio (Madrid, 1992).

—, *El trato de Argel*, ed. Florencio Sevilla Arroyo & Antonio Rey Hazas (Madrid, 1996).

Charboneau, Fr Damian M., OSM, 'The Servites of Barcelona' in *Studi storici dell' Ordine dei Servi di Maria*, 30 (1980), pp. 5–85.

Châtellier, Louis, *The Europe of the Devout: The Catholic Reformation and the Formation of a New Society* (Cambridge, 1989).

Chaunu, Pierre, *Les Temps des Réformes. Histoire religieuse et système de civilisation. La Crise de la chrétienté: L'Éclatement (1250–1550)* (Paris, 1975).

—, *Église, culture et société: Essais sur Réforme et Contre-Réforme, 1517–1620* (Paris, 1981).

Christian, William A., *Local Religion in Sixteenth-Century Spain* (Princeton, 1981).

—, *Apparitions in Late Medieval and Renaissance Spain* (Princeton, 1981).

Clissold, Stephen, *The Barbary Slaves* (New York, 1992).

Cock, Henry, *Relación del viaje hecho por Felipe II, en 1585, a Zaragoza, Barcelona y Valencia* (Madrid, 1876).

Colás Latorre, Gregorio, & José Antonio Salas Ausens, *Aragón en el siglo XVI: Alteraciones sociales y conflictos políticos* (Zaragoza, 1982).

Collett, Barry, *Italian Benedictine Scholars and The Reformation: The Congregation of Santa Giustina of Padua* (Oxford, 1985).

Colombás, Dom García M., OSB, *Un reformador benedictino en tiempos de los Reyes Católicos: García Jiménez de Cisneros, abad de Montserrat* (Montserrat, 1955).

Corteguera, Luis R., 'El motín: ¿Una institución de la política popular en la Barcelona del XVI y XVII?' in *Actes del Tercer Congrés d'Història Moderna de Catalunya* [=*Pedralbes*] (2 vols., Barcelona, 1993); II, pp. 235–41.

Cruz, Anne J., & Mary Elizabeth Perry, *Culture and Control in Counter-Reformation Spain* (Minneapolis, 1992).

Cueto, Ronald, 'On the Significance of the Reform of the Religious Orders in the Catholic Monarchy in the 15th, 16th and 17th Centuries: Teresa de Jesús, the Foundress, in Historical Perspective' in Margaret A. Rees, ed., *Teresa de Jesús and her World* (Leeds, 1981), pp. 19–50.

Dacosta Kaufman, Thomas, *Court, Cloister and City: The Art and Culture of Central Europe, 1450–1800* (London, 1995).

Defourneaux, Marcelin, *Daily Life in Spain in the Golden Age* (London, 1970).

Deleito y Piñuela, José, *La vida religiosa española bajo el cuarto Felipe: Santos y pecadores* (Madrid, 1952; 2nd edn., Madrid, 1963).

Delgado Capeans, P.Fr. Ricardo, OdeM, 'La Orden de la Merced en Lima' serialized in *Boletín de la Orden de la Merced*, 14–15 (1926–7).

Delgado Varela, P.Fr. José María, OdeM, 'Sobre la canonización de San Pedro Nolasco' in *Estudios*, 12 (1956), pp. 265–95.

Delumeau, Jean, *Catholicism between Luther and Voltaire: A New View of the Counter-Reformation* (London, 1977).

De Maio, Romeo, *Riforme [...] e miti nella Chiesa del Cinquecento* (Naples, 1973).

DeMolen, Richard L., *Religious Orders of the Catholic Reformation, in Honor of John C. Olin on his Seventy-Fifth Birthday* (New York, 1994).

Denifle, Fr Heinrich, OP, 'Die Constitutionen des Predigerordens' in *Archiv für Litteratur- und Kirchengeschichte des Mittelalters*, 5 (1889), pp. 530–64.

Deslandres, Paul, *L'Ordre des Trinitaires pour le rachat des captifs* (2 vols., Toulouse-Paris, 1903).

Despuig, Cristòfor, *Los col·loquis de la insigne ciutat de Tortosa*, ed. Eulàlia Duran (Barcelona, 1981).

Devesa Blanco, P.Fr. Juan, OdeM, 'Las primitivas constituciones de la Orden de la Merced o «Constituciones Amerianas»: Códice del P. Nadal Gaver' in *Analecta Mercedaria*, 2 (1983), pp. 5–119.

—, 'La verdadera fecha de la muerte de San Pedro Nolasco' in *Analecta Mercedaria*, 4 (1985), pp. 5–72.

—, 'Los orígenes de la Orden de Nuestra Señora de la Merced' in *Analecta Mercedaria*, 7 (1988), pp. 37–52.

Dickens, A.G., *The Counter Reformation* (London, 1968).

Dictionnaire d'histoire et de géographie ecclésiastiques (26 vols.+, Paris, 1912–).

Dictionnaire de spiritualité ascétique et mystique, doctrine et histoire (16 vols. in twenty-one tomes, Paris, 1937–94).

Dictionnaire de théologie catholique, ed. A. Vacant, E. Mangenot, & E. Amann (15 vols., Paris, 1903–50).

Ditchfield, Simon, *Liturgy, Sanctity and History in Tridentine Italy: Pietro Maria Campi and the Preservation of the Particular* (Cambridge, 1995).

Dizionario degli Istituti di Perfezione, ed. Guerrino Pelliccia & Giancarlo Roca (8 vols.+, Rome, 1974–).

Domínguez Ortiz, Antonio, *La sociedad española en el siglo XVII* (2 vols., Madrid, 1963–70).

—, *The Golden Age of Spain, 1516–1659* (London, 1971).

—, 'Aspectos sociales de la vida eclesiástica en los siglos XVII y XVIII' in García Villoslada, gral. ed., *Historia de la Iglesia en España*, IV (1979), pp. 5–72.

—, *Instituciones y sociedad en la España de los Austrias* (Barcelona, 1985).

Dompnier, Bernard, *Enquête au pays des frères des anges: Les Capucins de la province de Lyon aux XVIIᵉ et XVIIIᵉ siècles* (Sainte-Etienne, 1993).

Dossat, Yves, 'Les Ordres de rachat, Les Mercédaires' in *Assistance et charité* [*Cahiers de Fanjeaux*, vol. XIII] (Toulouse, 1978), pp. 365–87.

Dufourcq, Charles-Emmanuel, *L'Espagne catalane et le Maghrib aux XIIIᵉ et XIVᵉ siècles* (Paris, 1966).

Du Mège, A., *Histoire des institutions religieuses, politiques, judiciaires et littéraires de la ville de Toulouse* (4 vols., Toulouse, 1844–6).

Durán Gudiol, Antonio, 'Notas para la historia de la Universidad de Huesca en el siglo XVI' in *Hispania Sacra*, 21 (1968), pp. 87–154.

Duran i Sanpere, Agustí, *Barcelona i la seva història: La formació d'una gran ciutat* (3 vols., Barcelona, 1973–5).

Efrén de la Madre de Dios, P.Fr., OCD, & P.Fr. Otger Steggink, OCD, *Tiempo y vida de Santa Teresa* (Madrid, 1968).

—, *Tiempo y vida de Santa Teresa* (2 vols. in three tomes, Salamanca, 1982–4).

Eire, Carlos M.N., *From Madrid to Purgatory. The Art and Conflict of Dying in Sixteenth-Century Spain* (Cambridge, 1995).

Elliott, J.H., *The Revolt of the Catalans: A Study in the Decline of Spain (1598–1640)* (Cambridge, 1963).

—, *Imperial Spain (1469–1716)*, 2nd edn. (Harmondsworth, 1970).

—, *The Count-Duke of Olivares: The Statesman in an Age of Decline* (New Haven, 1986).

—, *Spain and its World, 1500–1700* (New Haven, 1989).

—, 'A Europe of Composite Monarchies' in *Past and Present*, no. 137 (1992), pp. 48–71.

Emery, Richard W., *The Friars in Medieval France: A Catalogue of French Mendicant Convents, 1200–1550* (New York, 1962).

Escobar, M., *Ordini e congregazione religiosi* (2 vols., Rome, 1951, & Turin, 1953).

Eslava Galán, Juan, *Historias de la Inquisición* (Barcelona, 1992).

Esteban Mateo, León, 'Catedráticos eclesiásticos de la Universidad Valenciana del siglo XVI' in *Repertorio de Historia de las Ciencias Eclesiásticas en España*, 6 (1977), pp. 349–439.

Eubel, Fr Conrad, *Die avignonesische Obedienz der Mendikanten-Orden, sowie der Orden der Mercedarier und Trinitarier zur Zeit des grossen Schismus: Beleuchtet durch die von Clemens VII. und Benedikt XIII. an dieselben gerichteten Schreiben* (Paderborn, 1900).

—, *Hierarchia Catholica Medii Aevi...*, vols. I–IV (Münster, 1913–35; repr. Padua, 1960).

Evans, R.J.W., *The Making of the Habsburg Monarchy, 1550–1700* (Oxford, 1979).

Evennett, H. Outram, *The Spirit of the Counter-Reformation*, ed. with a 'Postscript' by John Bossy (Cambridge, 1968).

Febvre, Lucien, *Au cœur religieux du XVIᵉ siècle*, 2nd edn. (Paris, 1968).

Fernández Álvarez, Manuel, *La sociedad española en el siglo de oro* (2 vols., Madrid, 1983).

Fernández Collado, Ángel, 'Intervención del Nuncio Felipe Sega en la reforma de la Iglesia en España (1577–1581)' in *Anthologica Annua*, 37 (1990), pp. 57–129.

—, *Gregorio XIII y Felipe II en la nunciatura de Felipe Sega (1577–1581): Aspectos político, jurisdiccional y de reforma* (Toledo, 1991).

Fernández Conde, Francisco Javier, *Gutierre de Toledo, Obispo de Oviedo (1377–89). Reforma eclesiástica en la Asturias bajomedieval* (Oviedo, 1978).

Fernández Conde, Francisco Javier, & Antonio Oliver Montserrat, 'Cultura y pensamiento religioso en la baja Edad Media' in García Villoslada, gral. ed., *Historia de la Iglesia en España*, II(ii) (1982), pp. 175–253.

Fernández y Fernández de Retana, Luis, *España en tiempos de Felipe II (1556–1598)* (Madrid, 1958), vol. XIX (in two tomes) of Ramón Menéndez Pidal, ed., *Historia de España*.

Fernández Martín, Luis, 'La provisión de diocésis y abadías en la Corona de Aragón (1557–64)' in *Hispania Sacra*, 33 (1981), pp. 549–62.

Fernández Martínez, Rvda.M. Ángeles, OdeM, 'Breve historia del Convento-Colegio de Madre de Dios de la Consolación, de la Celestial, Real y Militar Orden de la Merced, Redención de Cautivos, de la ciudad de Lorca, Provincia de Murcia' in *Boletín de la Orden de la Merced*, 12 (1924), pp. 171–6, 199–204, 248–53, & 13 (1925), pp. 283–90, 347–51, & 392–5.

Fernández-Santamaría, J.A., *The State, War and Peace: Spanish Political Thought in the Renaissance, 1516–1559* (Cambridge, 1977).

Fernández Terricabras, Ignacio [Ignasi], 'Refoma i obediència: Actituds institucionals durant la visita del monestir de Montserrat (1583–1586)' in *Actes del Tercer Congrés d'Història Moderna de Catalunya [=Pedralbes]* (2 vols., Barcelona, 1993); II, pp. 171–80.

—, 'Un ejemplo de la política religiosa de Felipe II: El intento de reforma de las monjas de la Tercera Orden de San Francisco (1567–1571)' in *Primer Congreso Internacional del Monacato Femenino en España, Portugal y América (1492–1992)* (2 vols., León, 1993); II, pp. 159–71.

—, 'Els bisbes de Catalunya, Felip II i l'execució del Concili de Trento' in *Actes del Primer Congrés d'Història de l'Església Catalana* (2 vols., Solsona, 1993; also *Analecta Sacra Tarraconensia*, 67, nos. 1–2 (1994)); II, pp. 321–32.

—, 'Por una geografía del Patronazgo Real: Teólogos y juristas en las presentaciones episcopales de Felipe II' in Enrique Martínez Ruíz & Vicente Suárez Grimón, eds., *Iglesia y sociedad en el Antiguo Régimen: III reunión científica de la Asociación Española de Historia Moderna* (Las Palmas, 1994); pp. 601–9.

—, 'Au carrefour de l'historiographie espagnole sur la Contre-Réforme: Entre préjugés du passé et choix du futur' in Michael Weinzierl, ed., *Individualisierung, Rationalisierung, Säkularisierung: Neue Wege der Religionsgeschichte* (Munich, 1997); pp. 112–29.

—, 'El episcopado hispano y el Patronato Real: Reflexión sobre algunas discrepancias entre Clemente VIII y Felipe II' in José Martínez Millán, ed., *Europa y la Monarquía Católica* (4 vols. in 5 tomes, Madrid, 1998); III, pp. 209–23.

—, 'Visites ecclésiastiques et résistances aux réformes au XVIᵉ siècle: Le cas de Roncevaux' in Michel Brunet, Serge Brunet & Claudine Pailhes, eds., *Pays Pyrénéens. Pouvoirs Centraux. XVIᵉ–XXᵉ siècles* (Toulouse, 1995); pp. 437–50.

—, 'La reforma de las órdenes religiosas en tiempos de Felipe II: Aproximación cronológica' in Ernest Belenguer Cebrià, ed., *Felipe II y el Mediterráneo* (4 vols., Madrid, 1999); II, pp. 181–204.

—, *Philippe II et la Contre-Réforme: L'Église espagnole à l'heure du Concile de Trente* (Ph.D. thesis, Université de Toulouse-Le Mirail, 1999).

Ferrando Roig, P. J., *La Basílica de la Merced* (Barcelona, 1941).

Ferrer i Mallol, Maria Teresa, 'La redempció de captius a la corona catalano-aragonesa (segle XIV)' in *Anuario de estudios medievales*, 15 (1985), pp. 237–98.

Ferro, Víctor, *El dret públic català: Les institucions a Catalunya fins al Decret de Nova Planta* (Vic, 1987).

Flórez, Fray Enrique, *et al.*, *España sagrada. Teatro geográfico-histórico de la iglesia de España* (58 vols., Madrid, 1747–1918).

Flynn, Maureen, *Sacred Charity: Confraternities and Social Welfare in Spain, 1400–1700* (London, 1989).

Forey, Alan, *The Military Orders from the Twelfth to the Early Fourteenth Centuries* (London, 1992).

Friedman, Ellen G., 'Trinitarian Hospitals in Algiers: An Early Example of Health-care for Prisoners of War' in *Catholic Historical Review*, 66 (1980), pp. 551–64.

—, *Spanish Captives in North Africa in the Early Modern Age* (Madison, 1983).

Fuentes, P.Fr. Manuel, O.SS.T., 'La Orden Trinitaria: Ocho siglos al sevicio de la liberación' in *Analecta Mercedaria*, 7 (1988), pp. 53–68.

Fuster i Ortells, Joan, *El bandolerisme catalá*, [vol.] II: *La llegenda* (Barcelona, 1963). *For* vol. I *see* Reglà, *El bandolerisme*.

—, *Heretgies, revoltes i sermones* (Barcelona, 1968).

—, *Poetas, moriscos y curas* (Madrid, 1969).

Galbraith, G.K., ed., *The Constitution of the Dominican Order, 1216–1360* (Manchester, 1925).

Galinier-Pallerola, Jean-François, *La Religion populare en Andorre, XVIᵉ–XIXᵉ siècles* (Paris-Toulouse, 1990).

—, 'La Délinquance des ecclésiastiques catalans á l'époque moderne d'après les archives du tribunal du Bref' in *Annals du Midi*, no. 104 (1992), pp. 43–67.

Gállego, Julián, & José Gudiol, *Zurbarán* (Barcelona, 1976).

Gams, Pius Bonifatius, *Die Kirchengeschichte von Spanien* (3 vols. in five tomes, Graz, 1956).

García Cárcel, Ricardo, *Historia de Cataluña: Siglos XVI–XVII* (2 vols., Barcelona, 1985).

—, *Las culturas del Siglo de Oro* (Madrid, 1989).

—, *Felipe II y Cataluña* (Valladolid, 1997).

García Cuéllar, Fidel, 'Política de Felipe II en torno a la convocación de la tercera etapa del Concilio Tridentino' in *Hispania Sacra*, 16 (1963), pp. 25–60.

García Gutiérrez, Pedro Francisco, *Iconografia mercedaria: Nolasco y su obra* (Madrid, 1985).

García Oro, P.Fr. José, OFM, *La reforma de los religiosos españoles en tiempo de los Reyes Católicos* (Valladolid, 1969).

—, *Cisneros y la reforma del clero español en tiempo de los Reyes Católicos* (Madrid, 1971).

—, 'Conventualismo y observancia: La reforma de las órdenes religiosas en los siglos XV y XVI' in García Villoslada, gral. ed., *Historia de la Iglesia en España*, III(i) (1980), pp. 211–349.

—, *Francisco de Asís en la España medieval* (Santiago de Compostela, 1988).

—, *La Universidad de Alcalá en la etapa fundacional (1458–1578)* (Santiago, 1992).

García Oro, P.Fr. José, & María José Portela Silva, 'Felipe II y las iglesias de Castilla a la hora de la Reforma Tridentina. (Preguntas y respuestas sobre la vida religiosa castellana)' in *Cuadernos de historia moderna*, 20 (1998), pp. 9–32.

—, 'Felipe II y la reforma de las órdenes redentoras' in *Estudios*, 54 (1998), pp. 5–155.

García Suárez, P.Fr. Germán, OdeM, 'El Maestro Gaspar de Torres y su obra «Comentario a las Constituciones»' in *Analecta Mercedaria*, 3 (1984), pp. 5–60.

—, 'La teología espiritual en el Maestro Cristóbal González, O. de M. († 1612)' in *Boletín de la Provincia de Castilla de la Orden de Nuestra Señora de la Merced*, 27 (1989), no. 96, pp. 46–51.

García Villoslada, P. Ricardo, SI, *La Universidad de Paris durante los estudios de Francisco de Vitoria O.P. (1507–1522)* (Rome, 1938).

—, gral. ed., *Historia de la Iglesia en España* (5 vols. in seven tomes, Madrid, 1980–1).

—, 'Felipe II y la Contrarreforma Católica' in *id.*, ed., *Historia de la Iglesia en España*, III(ii) (1980), pp. 3–106.

Gari y Siumell, P.Fr. José Antonio, OdeM, *La Orden Redentora de la Merced […] Historia de las redenciones de cautivos cristianos realizadas por los hijos de la Orden de la Merced* (Barcelona, 1873).

—, *Biblioteca Mercedaria, o sea escritores de la Celeste, Real y Militar Orden Merced…* (Barcelona, 1875).

Gaussin, Pierre Roger, *L'Europe des ordres et des congrégations: Des Bénédictins aux mendiants, VIᵉ–XVIᵉ siècle* (Sainte-Etienne, 1984).

Gaver, Fra Nadal, *Speculum fratrum*, see Vázquez Núñez, ed., *Monumenta*.

Gazulla, P.Fr. Faustino Decoroso, OdeM, 'Don Jaime de Aragón y la Orden de la Nuestra Señora de la Merced' in *Congrés d'història de la Corona de Aragó, dedicat al rey En Jaume I i la sua época* (2 vols., Barcelona 1909–13), I, pp. 327–88.

—, *¿La Orden de la Merced se fundó en 1218?* (Barcelona, 1914); also serialized in *Boletín de la Orden de la Merced*, 1–2 (1913–14).

—, *La Patrona de Barcelona y su santuario* (Barcelona, 1918).

—, *Refutación de un libro titulado «San Raimundo de Peñafort, Fundador de la Orden de la Merced»* (Barcelona, 1920).

—, 'Noticias sobre la acción de los religiosos de la Orden de Nuestra Señora de la Merced en Marruecos' in *Boletín de la Orden de la Merced*, 16 (1928), pp. 148–52.

—, 'El convento de la Merced de Barcelona' in *Boletín de la Orden de la Merced*, 20 (1932), pp. 119–27.

—, *La Orden de Nuestra Señora de la Merced: Estudios historicocríticos (1218–1317)* (vol. I Barcelona, 1934; vols. I & II collected and amended by P.Fr. Juan Devesa Blanco, OdeM, Valencia, 1985).

Gazulla, P.Fr. Policarpo, OdeM, 'Los primeros apóstoles de América y la primera misa en el Tucumán' in *Boletín de la Orden de la Merced*, 22 (1934), pp. 229–53.

Geertz, Clifford, *The Interpretation of Cultures: Selected Essays* (New York, 1973).

Genet, Jean-Philippe, & Bernard Vincent, eds., *État et Église dans la genèse de l'état moderne* (Madrid, 1986).

Germain, Alexandre Charles, *Histoire de la commune de Montpellier* (3 vols., Montpellier, 1851).

Gil, P. Pere, *Geografia de Catalunya […]*, ed. Josep Iglésies (Barcelona, 1949).

Gil, Xavier, 'Crown and Cortes in Early Modern Aragon: Reassessing Revisionisms' in *Parliaments, Estates and Representation*, 13, ii (1993), pp. 109–22.

Ginzburg, Carlo, *The Cheese and the Worms: The Cosmos of a Sixteenth-Century Miller* (London, 1980).

Gleason, Elisabeth G., ed., *Reform Thought in Sixteenth-Century Italy* (Chico, Calif., 1981).

Gómez Domínguez, P.Fr. Elías, OdeM, 'Sobre espiritualidad mercedaria' in *La Orden de la Merced* [=*Estudios*] (Madrid, 1970); pp. 133–94.

—, *Primer convento mercedario en Madrid: Monasterio de Tirso de Molina* (Madrid, 1986); also in *Estudios*, 42 (1986), pp. 5–128.

—, *Beata Mariana de Jesús: Mercedaria madrileña* (Rome, 1991).

Gómez y Gómez, Ildefonso María, 'La Cartuja en España' in *Studia Monastica*, 4 (1962), pp. 139–76.

González Castro, P.Fr. Ernesto, OdeM, 'Iter canónico y estado actual del santoral Mercedario' in *La Orden de la Merced* [=*Estudios*] (Madrid, 1970); pp. 273–328.

—, 'Las constituciones del P. Raimundo Albert (1327), segundo texto constitucional de la Orden de la Merced: Presentación y análisis' in *Analecta Mercedaria*, 2 (1983), pp. 121–207.

González Novalín, P. José Luis, 'Religiosidad y reforma del pueblo cristiano' in García Villoslada, gral. ed., *Historia de la Iglesia en España*, vol. III(i) (1980), pp. 351–84.

—, 'La Inquisición Española' in García Villoslada, gral. ed., *Historia de la Iglesia en España*, vol. III(ii) (1980), pp. 107–268.

González Palencia, Ángel, 'Quevedo y Tirso ante la Junta de Reformación' in *Boletín de la Real Academia Española*, 25 (1946), pp. 43–84.

Goñi Gaztambide, P. José, 'La reforma de los Premonstratenses españoles del siglo XVI' in *Hispania Sacra*, 13 (1960), pp. 5–96.
—, 'La reforma tridentina en la diócesis de Pamplona: Notas complementarias' in *Hispania Sacra*, 16 (1963), pp. 265–322.
Goodman, Anthony, & Angus MacKay, eds., *The Impact of Humanism on Western Europe* (London, 1990).
Gran Enciclopèdia Catalana, 2nd edn. (24 vols., Barcelona, 1986–9).
Greengrass, Mark, 'The Anatomy of a Religious Riot in Toulouse in May 1562' in *Journal of Ecclesiastical History*, 34 (1983), pp. 367–91.
Guinard, Paul, *Zurbarán et les peintres espagnols de la vie monastique* (Paris, 1960).
Gutiérrez, P. Constancio, SI, *Españoles en Trento* (Valladolid, 1951).
Haley, George, ed., *El diario de un estudiante de Salamanca: La cronica inédita de Girolamo da Sommaia (1603–1607)* (Salamanca, 1977).
Haskell, Francis, *Patrons and Painters* (New Haven, 1980).
Hay, Denys, *The Church in Italy in the Fifteenth Century* (Cambridge, 1977).
—, 'Scholarship, Religion and the Church' in Keith G. Robbins, ed., *Religion and Humanism* [*Studies in Church History*, vol. 18] (Oxford, 1981); pp. 1–18.
Headley, John M., & John B. Tomaro, eds., *San Carlo Borromeo: Catholic Reform and Ecclesiastical Politics in the Second Half of the Sixteenth Century* (Washington, D.C., 1988).
Heimbucher, Fr Max, *Die Orden und Kongregationen der katholischen Kirche*, 3rd edn. (2 vols., Paderborn, 1933–4).
Hermann, Christian, *L'Église d'Espagne sous le patronage royal (1476–1834)* (Madrid, 1988).
—, ed., *Le Premier âge de l'état en Espagne (1450–1700)* (Paris, 1989).
'Hermanu' [pseud.], 'La teología espiritual en el Mtro. Fr. Pedro de Medina, O. de M.' in *Boletín de la Provincia de Castilla de la Orden de Nuestra Señora de la Merced*, 27 (1989), no. 95, pp. 31–9.
Hernández Carretero, P.Fr. Secundino, OdeM, 'Literatos Mercedarios' in *La Orden de la Merced* [=*Estudios*] (Madrid, 1970); pp. 195–222.
Hess, Andrew C., *The Forgotten Frontier: A History of the Sixteenth-Century Ibero-African Frontier* (Chicago, 1978).
Highfield, J.R.L., 'The Jeronimites in Spain, their Patrons and Success, 1373–1516' in *Journal of Ecclesiastical History*, 34 (1983), pp. 513–33.
—, 'How Much did it Cost to Found a Jeronimite Monastery in late Medieval Spain?' in Henry Mayr-Harting & R.I. Moore eds., *Studies in Medieval History presented to R.H.C. Davis* (London, 1985); pp. 271–81.
Hillgarth, J.N., *The Spanish Kingdoms, 1250–1516* (2 vols., Oxford, 1976–8).
Hinnebusch, Fr William A., OP, *The History of the Dominican Order* (2 vols., New York, 1966–73).
Hinojosa, Ricardo de, ed., *Estudios sobre Felipe II* (Madrid, 1887).
—, *Los despachos de la diplomacia pontificia en España* (Madrid, 1896).
Homenaje a Tirso de Molina [=*Estudios*, 37] (Madrid, 1981).
Hornedo, P. Rafael María de, SI, 'La teología zumeliana de Tirso de Molina' in *Estudios eclesiásticos*, 24 (1950), pp. 217–36.
—, 'Teatro e Iglesia en los siglos XVII y XVIII' in García Villoslada, gral. ed., *Historia de la Iglesia en España*, IV (1979), pp. 309–58.
Janelle, Pierre, *The Catholic Reformation* (London, 1971).
Jedin, Fr Hubert, 'Zur Vorgeschichte der Regularenreform Trid. Sess. XXV' in *Römische Quartalschrift*, 44 (1936), pp. 231–81.
—, 'Catholic Reformation or Counter-Reformation?' in David M. Luebke, ed., *The Counter-Reformation* (Oxford, 1999).
—, *Crisis and Closure of the Council of Trent* (London, 1967).
—, *Historia del Concilio de Trento* (4 vols. in six tomes, Pamplona, 1972–81).

—, ed., *History of the Church*; vol. V: *Reformation and Counter Reformation* (London, 1980).

Kagan, Richard L., *Students and Society in Early Modern Spain* (Baltimore, 1974)

—, *Spanish Cities of the Golden Age: The Views of Anton van den Wyngaerde* (Berkeley, 1989).

—, *Lucretia's Dreams* (Berkelcy, 1990).

Kamen, Henry, 'Clerical Violence in a Catholic Society: The Hispanic World, 1450–1720' in W.J. Shiels, ed., *The Church and War* [*Studies in Church History*, vol. XX] (Oxford, 1983); pp. 201–16.

—, 'La contrarreforma en Cataluña' in *Historia 16*, 9, no. 98 (June 1984), pp. 57–62.

—, *Inquisition and Society in Spain in the Sixteenth and Seventeenth Centuries* (London, 1985).

—, *Spain 1469–1714: A Society of Conflict*, 2nd edn. (London, 1991).

—, *The Phoenix and the Flame: Catalonia and the Counter-Reformation* (New Haven, 1993).

—, 'The Catalan Phoenix: Narcís Feliu de la Penya and the Programme for Industrial Renewal in Catalonia' in *id., Crisis and Change in Early Modern Spain* (Aldershot, 1993), essay XI.

—, *Philip of Spain* (New Haven, 1997).

Kennedy, Ruth Lee, '*La prudencia en la mujer* and the Ambient that Brought it Forth' in *Proceedings of the Modern Languages Association*, 63 (1948), pp. 1131–90; Spanish trans. '«La prudencia en la mujer» y el ambiente en que se concebió' in *Estudios*, 5 (1949), pp. 223–93.

—, *Studies in Tirso*, vol. I: *The Dramatist and his Competitors, 1620–26* (Chapel Hill, NC, 1974); Spanish trans. *Estudios sobre Tirso* [=*Estudios*, 39] (Madrid, 1983).

Kinder, A. Gordon, *Casiodoro de Reina: Spanish Reformer of the Sixteenth Century* (London, 1975).

Knowles, Dom David, OSB, *The Religious Orders in England* (3 vols., Cambridge, 1948–59).

—, *From Pachomius to Ignatius: A Study in the Constitutional History of the Religious Orders* (Oxford, 1966).

—, *Christian Monasticism* (London, 1969).

Knox, Dilwyn, '*Disciplina*: The Monastic and Clerical Origins of European Civility' in John Monfasani & Ronald G. Musto, eds., *Renaissance Society and Culture: Essays in Honor of Eugene F. Rice, Jr.* (New York, 1991), pp. 107–35.

Koenigsberger, H.G., *The Practice of Empire* (Ithaca, 1969).

—, 'The Statecraft of Philip II' in *European Studies Review*, 1 (1971), pp. 1–21.

Krailsheimer, Alban J., *Rabelais and the Franciscans* (Oxford, 1963).

Kristeller, Paul Oskar, 'The Contribution of Religious Orders to Renaissance Thought and Learning' in *American Benedictine Review*, 21 (1970), pp. 1–55.

Ladner, Gerhart B., *The Idea of Reform: Its Impact on Christian Thought and Action in the Age of the Fathers* (Cambridge, Mass., 1959).

Lahoz, P.Fr. Bienvenido, OdeM, 'La Merced en Barcelona' in *Boletín de la Orden de la Merced*, 23 (1951), pp. 15–29, & 24 (1952), pp. 9–18 & 75–82.

Laka Kortabitarte, P.Fr. Juan, OdeM, 'Zurbarán y la Merced' in *Boletín de la Provincia de Castilla de la Orden de Nuestra Señora de la Merced*, 19 (1981), no. 62, pp. 80–7.

Lalinde Abadía, Jesús, *La gobernación general en la Corona de Aragón* (Madrid, 1963).

—, *La institución virreinal en Cataluña (1471–1716)* (Barcelona, 1964).

—, *Los Fueros de Aragón* (Zaragoza, 1975).

Lavallé, Bernard, *Las promesas ambiguas: Ensayos sobre el criollismo colonial en los Andes* (Lima, 1993).

Lawrance, J.N.H., 'The Spread of Lay Literacy in Late Medieval Castile' in *Bulletin of Hispanic Studies*, 62 (1985), pp. 79–94.

—, 'Humanism in the Iberian Peninsula' in Anthony Goodman & Angus MacKay, eds., *The Impact of Humanism on Western Europe* (London, 1990), pp. 220–58.

Lawrence, C.H., *Medieval Monasticism: Forms of Religious Life in Western Europe in the Middle Ages*, 2nd edn. (London, 1989).

—, *The Friars: The Impact of the Early Mendicant Movement on Western Society* (London, 1994).

Layna Serrano, Francisco, *Los conventos antiguos de Guadalajara* (Madrid, 1943).

Leclercq, Dom Jean, OSB, *The Love of Learning and the Desire for God: A Study of Monastic Culture*, trans. Catharine Misrahi, 3rd English edn. (New York, 1982).

Lejarza, P.Fr. Fidel de, & P.Fr. Ángel Uribe, OFM, eds., *Introducción a los orígenes de la Observancia en España: Las reformas en los siglos XIV y XV* [=*Archivo ibero-americano*] (Madrid, 1958).

—, '¿Cuándo y dónde comenzó Villacreces su reforma?' in *Archivo ibero-americano*, 20 (1960), pp. 79–94.

Lekai, Fr Louis J., OCist, *The Rise of the Cistercian Strict Observance in Seventeenth-Century France* (Washington, D.C., 1968).

Lemoine, Dom Robert, OSB, *Le Monde des religieux: L'Époque moderne (1563–1789)* (Paris, 1976).

Linage Conde, Antonio, 'El monacato español hasta el Concilio de Trento' in *Repertorio de Historia de las Ciencias Eclesiásticas en España*, 5 (1976), pp. 403–506.

—, *El monacato en España e Hispanoamérica* (Salamanca, 1977).

Linage Conde, Antonio, & Antonio Oliver Monserrat, 'Las órdenes religiosas en la Baja Edad Media: Los mendicantes' in García Villoslada, gral. ed., *Historia de la Iglesia en España*, II(ii) (1982), pp. 117–74.

Linehan, Peter, *The Ladies of Zamora* (University Park, Pa., 1997).

Lladonosa i Pujol, Josep, *Història de Lleida* (2 vols., Tàrrega, 1972–4).

Llorca, P. Bernardino, SI, 'Participación de España en el Concilio de Trento' in García Villoslada, gral. ed., *Historia de la Iglesia en España*, III(i) (1980), pp. 385–503.

Llorens i Solé, Antoni, 'Sant Ramon Nonat: Un nou camí que mena al coneixement del sant. Era el cinqué i darrer fill del cavaller, Arnau de Cardona' in *Analecta Sacra Tarraconensia*, 59 (1986), pp. 223–57.

Lomax, Derek W., 'Las órdenes militares en la Península Ibérica durante la Edad Media' in *Repertorio de Historia de las Ciencias Eclesiásticas en España*, 6 (1976), pp. 9–110.

Lope de Vega, *La vida de San Pedro Nolasco*, Biblioteca de Autores Españoles, vol. V (Madrid, 1895).

Lopetegui, León, 'La Iglesia española y la hispanoamericana de 1493 a 1810' in García Villoslada, gral. ed., *Historia de la Iglesia en España*, III(ii) (1980), pp. 363–441.

Lorenzo, P.Fr. Jesús, OdeM, 'Noticias para la historia del culto y convento de San Ramón Nonato' in *Boletín de la Orden de la Merced*, 25 (1953), pp. 62–9.

Lovett, Albert W., *Philip II and Mateo Vázquez de Leca: The Government of Spain (1572–1592)* (Geneva, 1977).

—, *Early Habsburg Spain, 1517–1598* (Oxford, 1986).

Luebke, David M., ed., *The Counter-Reformation* (Oxford, 1999).

Lynch, John, 'Philip II and the Papacy' in *Transactions of the Royal Historical Society*, 5th Series, 11 (1961), pp. 23–42.

—, *Spain under the Habsburgs*, vol. I: *Empire and Absolutism, 1516–1598*, & vol. II: *Spain and America, 1598–1700*, 2nd edns. (Oxford, 1981).

—, *Spain, 1516–1598: From Nation State to World Empire* (Oxford, 1991), & *The Hispanic World in Crisis and Change, 1598-1700* (Oxford, 1992).

Madurell Marimón, José María, 'La capilla de San Ramón Nonato del Castillo de Cardona y el retablo mayor del Santuario del Portell' in *Analecta Sacra Tarraconensia*, 38 (1965), pp. 281–308.

Madurell Marimón, José María, & Jorge Rubió y Balaguer, *Documentos para la historia de la imprenta y librería en Barcelona (1474–1553)* (Barcelona, 1955).

Mañaricúa, A.E., *El convento mercedario de Burceña* (San Sebastián, 1956).

Maravall, José Antonio, 'La oposición político-religiosa del siglo XVI: El erasmismo tardío de Felipe de la Torre' in *id.*, *La oposición política bajo los Austrias* (Barcelona, 1972), pp. 53–92.

—, *Utopía y reformismo en la España de los Austrias* (Madrid, 1982).

—, *Culture of the Baroque: Analysis of a Historical Structure* (Minneapolis, 1986).

March, José María, *Niñez y juventud de Felipe II* (2 vols., Madrid, 1941–2).

Marcos, Balbino, 'Literatura religiosa en el Siglo de Oro español' in García Villoslada, gral. ed., *Historia de la Iglesia en España*, III(ii) (1980), pp. 443–552.

Marquès, Josep M., 'La investigació de la història religiosa de Catalunya als arxius' in *Actes del Primer Congrés d'Història de l'Església Catalana* (2 vols., Solsona, 1993; also *Analecta Sacra Tarraconensia*, 67, nos. 1–2 (1994)); I, pp. 9–28.

Martín Hernández, Francisco, *La formación clerical en los colegios universitarios españoles (1371–1563)* (Vitoria, 1961).

—, 'La formación del clero en los siglos XVII y XVIII' in García Villoslada, gral. ed., *Historia de la Iglesia en España*, IV (1979), pp. 523–82.

Martínez Escalada, Jesús, *Historia de las calles de Tudela* (Tudela, 1974).

Martínez Millán, José, ed., *La corte de Felipe II* (Madrid, 1994).

—, 'En busca de la ortodoxia: El inquisidor general Diego de Espinosa' in *id.*, ed., *La corte de Felipe II*, pp. 189–228.

Martyr D'Anghera, Peter, *De Orbe Novo: The Eight Decades…*, trans. & ed. Francis Augustus MacNutt (2 vols., New York, 1912).

Martz, Linda, *Poverty and Welfare in Habsburg Spain: The Example of Toledo* (Cambridge, 1983).

Mas, J., *Notícies Històriques del Bisbat de Barcelona* (14 vols., Barcelona, 1906).

Masoliver, Alexandre, 'El monaquisme a Catalunya en els segles XVI i XVII' in *Studia Monastica*, 20 (1978), pp. 345–96.

—, 'Els religiosos a Catalunya: 1600 anys de història' in *Actes del Primer Congrés d'Història de l'Església Catalana* (2 vols., Solsona, 1993; also *Analecta Sacra Tarraconensia*, 67, nos. 1–2 (1994)); I, pp. 435–97.

Massaut, Jean-Pierre, *Josse Clichtove, l'humanisme et la réforme du clergé* (2 vols., Paris, 1968).

Matheson, Peter, 'Humanism and Reform Movements' in Anthony Goodman & Angus MacKay, eds., *The Impact of Humanism on Western Europe* (London, 1990), pp. 23–42.

Los Mercedarios en Bolivia (La Paz, 1977).

Metford, J.C.J., 'Tirso de Molina and the Conde-Duque de Olivares' in *Bulletin of Hispanic Studies*, 36 (1959), pp. 15–27.

Meyerson, Mark D., *The Muslims of Valencia in the Age of Fernando and Isabel: Between Coexistence and Crusade* (Berkeley, 1991).

Milis, Ludo J.R., *Angelic Monks and Earthly Men: Monasticism and its Meaning to Medieval Society* (Woodbridge, 1992).

Millan, Émile, 'Investigaciones sobre el convento de Nuestra Señora del Olivar en conexión con la obra de Tirso de Molina: Contribución a la historia de Aragón' in *Estudios*, 37 (1981), pp. 37–118.

Millán Rubio, P.Fr. Joaquín, OdeM, 'Fray Pedro de Amer, Maestre de la Merced (1271–1301). Treinta años de historia mercedaria' in *Estudios*, 29 (1973), pp. 3–63.

—, 'El voto Mercedario de dar la vida por los cautivos cristianos' in *Studia Silensia*, 1 (1975), pp. 113–41.

—, 'El padre Jaime Lorenzo de La Mata y su convento de Santa María de El Olivar' in *Analecta Mercedaria*, 8 (1989), pp. 5–83.

—, *La Orden de Nuestra Señora de la Merced (1301–1400)* (Rome, 1992).

Miquell Rosell, P. Francisco J., 'Inventario de manuscritos de la Biblioteca Universitaria de Barcelona, referentes a órdenes religiosas' in *Hispania Sacra*, 2 (1949), pp. 209–20.

Mitjá, Marina, 'L'Orde de la Mercè en crisi en el regnat de Joan I' in *Cuaderns de Arqueologia e Història de la Ciutat*, 9 (1969), pp. 62–89.

Miura Andrades, José María, *Fundaciones religiosas y milagros en la Écija de fines de la edad media* (Écija, 1992).

Molas Ribalta, Pere, *Consejos y audiencias durante el reinado de Felipe II* (Valladolid, 1984).

——, *Família i política al segle XVI català* (Barcelona, 1990).

Molina Meliá, Antonio, *Iglesia y estado en el Siglo de Oro español: El pensamiento de Francisco Suárez* (Valencia, 1977).

Molinié-Bertrand, Annie, 'Le Clergé dans le royaume de Castille à la fin du XVIᵉ siècle: Approche cartografique' in *Revue d'histoire economique et sociale*, 51 (1973), pp. 5–53.

Monroy, P.Fr. Joel Leónidas, OdeM, 'Don Fray Alonso Enríquez de Almendáriz, obispo mercedario. (Apuntes para su biografía)' in *Boletín de la Orden de la Merced*, 9 (1921), pp. 106–23.

——, *El convento de la Merced de Quito de 1534–1617* (Quito, 1937).

Monter, William, *Frontiers of Heresy: The Inquisition from the Basque Lands to Sicily* (Cambridge, 1990).

Mora Cañada, Adela, *Monjes y campesinos: El señorío de la Valldigna en los siglos XVII y XVIII* (Alicante, 1986).

Morales Ramírez, P.Fr. Alfonso, OdeM, *Historia general de la Orden de la Merced en Chile (1535–1831)* (Santiago de Chile, 1983).

——, *La Orden de la Merced en la evangelización de América, siglos XVI–XVII* (Bogotá, 1986).

Mullett, Michael, *The Counter-Reformation and the Catholic Reformation in Early Modern Europe* (London, 1984).

Muñoz Delgado, P.Fr. Vicente, OdeM, ed., *Zumel y el molinismo: Informe del P. Francisco Zumel, Mercedario, sobre las doctrinas del P. Luis Molina, S.J., presentado en julio de 1595* (Madrid, 1953).

——, ed., *Obras teológicas del P. Jerónimo Pérez (†1549), Mercedario* (Pontevedra, 1962).

——, 'La exposición sumulista de la doctrina silogística de Fr. Domingo de San Juan de Pie del Puerto (†1540)' in *Estudios*, 19 (1963), pp. 3–50.

——, *La lógica nominalista en la universidad de Salamanca (1510–1530)* (Madrid, 1964).

——, 'Domingo Báñez y las súmulas en Salamanca a fines del siglo XVI' in *Estudios*, 21 (1965), pp. 3–20.

——, 'La teología entre los Mercedarios españoles hasta 1600' in *Repertorio de Historia de las Ciencias Eclesiásticas en España*, 3 (1971), pp. 395–405.

——, 'El convento de Valladolid y el apostolado mercedario' in *Boletín de la Provincia de Castilla de la Orden de Nuestra Señora de la Merced*, 16 (1978), no. 53, pp. 45–60.

——, 'Los Mercedarios de la Vera Cruz en el «Diario de un estudiante» (1603–1607) de Salamanca' in *Boletín de la Provincia de Castilla de la Orden de Nuestra Señora de la Merced*, 16 (1978), no. 50, pp. 49–54.

——, 'El maestro Fray Martín de Samunde († ca. 1539) y su defensa de Erasmo en 1527' in *Revista española de teología*, 44 (1984), pp. 441–64.

——, 'La Veracruz de Salamanca y sus dos primeros profesores de la universidad en la investigación de Guillermo Vázquez' in *Boletín de la Provincia de Castilla de la Orden de Nuestra Señora de la Merced*, 22 (1984), no. 75, pp. 27–42.

——, 'El general Fr. Francisco Maldonado y la Veracruz de Salamanca: Un documento para nuestra historia' in *Boletín de la Provincia de Castilla de la Orden de Nuestra Señora de la Merced*, 22 (1984), no. 76, pp. 36–8.

——, 'Fray Martín de Acevedo (†1658), comendador de Conjo, profesor y obispo; otros Mercedarios catedráticos de la universidad compostelana' in *Boletín de la Provincia de Castilla de la Orden de Nuestra Señora de la Merced*, 22 (1984), no. 77, pp. 56–66.

——, 'Los Mercedarios en el Perú durante el período español: Colaboración hispano-peruana en estudios, profesores, colegios, universidades y escritos' in Antonio Heredia Soriano, ed., *Actas del IV Seminario de Historia de la Filosofía Española* (Salamanca, 1986); pp. 77–173.

Murúa, Fray Martín de, *Historia general del Perú*, ed. Manuel Ballesteros Gaibrois (Madrid, 1987).

Mutgé, Josefina, 'Algunes notes sobre Alfons el Benigne i l'Orde de la Mercè de Barcelona' in *Anuario de estudios medievales*, 11 (1981), pp. 853–8.

Nadal i Farreras, Joaquim, *Dos segles d'obscuritat (XVI i XVII)* (Barcelona, 1979).

Nadal Oller, Jordi, *La población española. (Siglos XVI a XX)*, 2nd edn. (Barcelona, 1984).

Nadal Oller, Jordi, & E. Giralt, *La Population catalane de 1553 à 1717: L'Immigration française* (Paris, 1960).

Nalle, Sara T., 'Literacy and Culture in Early Modern Castile' in *Past and Present*, no. 125 (1989), pp. 65–96.

—, *God in La Mancha: Religious Reform and the People of Cuenca, 1500–1650* (Baltimore, 1992).

Neveu, Bruno, 'Archéolatrie et modernité dans le savoir ecclésiastique au XVIIᵉ siècle' in *XVIIᵉ Siècle*, 33 (1981), pp. 169–84.

—, 'L'Erudition ecclésiastique du XVIIᵉ siècle et la nostalgie de l'antiquité chrétienne' in Keith G. Robbins, ed., *Religion and Humanism* [Studies in Church History, vol. XVIII] (Oxford, 1981); pp. 195–225.

New Catholic Encyclopedia (18 vols., Washington, D.C., & New York, 1967–88).

Nieto, José C., *Juan de Valdés y los orígenes de la reforma en España y Italia*, 2nd [Spanish] edn. (Mexico City, 1979).

Nieto Soria, José Manuel, *Iglesia y génesis del estado moderno en Castilla (1369–1480)* (Madrid, 1993).

Norton, F.J., *Printing in Spain, 1501–1520* (Cambridge, 1966).

—, *A Descriptive Catalogue of Printing in Spain and Portugal, 1501–1520* (Cambridge, 1978).

Nougué, André, *L'Œuvre en prose de Tirso de Molina: Los Cigarrales de Toledo et Deleytar Aprovechando* (Toulouse, 1962).

Olin, John C., *The Catholic Reformation: Savonarola to Ignatius of Loyola: Reform in the Church, 1495–1540* (New York, 1969).

—, *Catholic Reform from Cardinal Ximenes to the Council of Trent, 1495–1563* (New York, 1990).

O'Malley, Fr John W., SI, *Giles of Viterbo on Church and Reform: A Study in Renaissance Thought* (Leiden, 1968).

—, ed., *Catholicism in Early Modern History: A Guide to Research* (St. Louis, 1988).

—, 'Was Ignatius Loyola a Church Reformer? How to Look at Early Modern Catholicism' in *Catholic Historical Review*, 77 (1991), pp. 177–93.

—, *The First Jesuits* (Cambridge, Mass., 1993).

La Orden de la Merced [=*Estudios*] (Madrid, 1970).

La Orden de la Merced en Centroamérica (Rome, 1989).

La Orden de Santa María de la Merced, 1218–1992: Síntesis histórica (Rome, 1997).

Oss, Adriaan C. van, *Catholic Colonialism: A Parish History of Guatemala, 1524–1821* (Cambridge, 1986).

Oviedo Cavada, P.Fr. Carlos, OdeM, *Los obispos mercedarios* (Santiago de Chile, 1981).

Ozment, Steven, *The Age of Reform, 1250–1550: An Intellectual and Religious History of Late Medieval and Reformation Europe* (New Haven, 1980).

Pacheco, Francisco, *Libro de descripcion de verdaderos retratos, de ilustres y memorables varones*, ed. Pedro M. Piñero Ramírez & Rogelio Reyes Cano (Seville, 1985).

Palacio, P.Fr. Eudoxio de Jesús, OdeM, *Los Mercedarios en Bolivia: Documentos para su historia, 1535–1975*, ed. P.Fr. José Brunet, OdeM (La Paz, 1975).

Palos, Joan Lluís, *Catalunya a l'imperi dels Àustria: La pràctica de govern (segles XVI i XVII)* (Lleida, 1994).

Parker, Geoffrey, *Philip II*, 3rd edn. (Chicago, 1995).

Parker, T.M., 'The Papacy, Catholic Reform and Christian Missions' in R.B. Wernham, ed., *New Cambridge Modern History*; vol. III: *The Counter Reformation and the Price Revolution* (Cambridge, 1968).

Parra, P.Fr. Juan, OdeM, 'El Puig de Sta. María, su iglesia y monasterio' in *Boletín de la Orden de la Merced*, 23 (1951), pp. 30–9.

Pastor, Ludwig von, *The History of the Popes from the close of the Middle Ages*, vols. 15–24 (London, 1928–33; repr. 1951–2).

Paterson, Alan K.G., 'Tirso de Molina: Two Bibliographical Studies' in *Hispanic Review*, 35 (1967), pp. 43–68.

—, 'Tirso de Molina and the Androgyne: *El Áquiles* and *La dama del Olivar*' in *Bulletin of Hispanic Studies*,70 (1993), pp. 105–14.

Payne, Stanley G., *Spanish Catholicism: An Historical Overview* (Madison, 1984).

Penedo Rey, P.Fr. Manuel, OdeM, 'Tirso de Molina: Aportaciones biográficas' in *Estudios*, 5 (1949), pp. 19–122.

Peña, Manuel, *Cataluña en el Renacimiento: Libros y lenguas* (Lleida, 1996).

Pérez, Joseph, 'Moines frondeurs et sermons subversifs en Castille pendant le premier séjour de Charles-Quint en Espagne' in *Bulletin hispanique*, 67 (1965), pp. 5–25.

Pérez, P.Fr. Pedro Nolasco, OdeM, *Religiosos de la Merced que pasaron a la América española (1514–1777), con documentos del Archivo General de Indias* (Seville, 1924).

—, 'Grados Universitarios obtenidos por algunos religiosos de la Merced en la Universidad de Sevilla, 1564–1727' in *Boletín de la Orden de la Merced*, 13 (1925), pp. 280–3.

—, *Los obispos de la Merced que pasaron a América (1601–1926): Documentos del Archivo General de Indias* (Santiago de Chile, 1927).

—, 'Apostolado de los Mercedarios entre los indios de América' in *Boletín de la Orden de la Merced*, 20 (1932), pp. 91–9 & 250–9.

—, *Historia de las misiones mercedarias en América* [=*Estudios*, 22] (Madrid, 1966).

Pérez, P. Quintín, SI, *Fr. Hernando de Santiago, predicador del Siglo de Oro (1575–1639)* (Madrid, 1949).

Pérez Goyena, P. Antonio, SI, 'Los grandes teólogos mercedarios' in *Estudios eclesiásticos*, 4 (1919), pp. 29–41.

—, 'La teología entre los Mercedarios españoles' in *Boletín de la Orden de la Merced*, 20 (1932), pp. 225–49 & 318–41.

Pérez Martínez, Lorenzo, 'Diego de Arnedo, obispo de Mallorca, reformador tridentino. (Datos para una biografía)' in *Anthologica Annua*, 6 (1958), pp. 123–82.

Philippson, Martin, 'Felipe II y el Pontificado' in Ricardo de Hinojosa, ed., *Estudios sobre Felipe II* (Madrid, 1887), pp. 87–192.

Phelan, John Leddy, *The Millenial Kingdom of the Franciscans in the New World* (Berkeley, 1956).

Pi Corrales, Magdalena de Pazzis, Dolores Pérez Baltasar, Virginia León Sanz, & David García Hernán, 'Las órdenes religiosas en la España moderna: Dimensiones de la investigación histórica' in Enrique Martínez Ruíz & Vicente Suárez Grimón, eds., *Iglesia y sociedad en el Antiguo Régimen: III reunión científica de la Asociación Española de Historia Moderna* (Las Palmas, 1994); pp. 205–51.

Pikaza, P.Fr. Javier, OdeM, 'Notas para un estudio de los filósofos y teólogos de la Merced en España' in *La Orden de la Merced* [=*Estudios*] (Madrid, 1970); pp. 83–131.

Pike, Ruth, *Aristocrats and Traders: Sevillian Society in the Sixteenth Century* (Ithaca, 1972).

Pillorget, René, 'Réforme monastique et conflits de rupture dans quelques localités de la France méridionale au XVIIᵉ siècle' in *Revue historique*, no. 253 (1975), pp. 77–106.

Pizarro Llorente, Henar, 'El control de la conciencia regia: El confesor real Fray Bernardo de Fresneda' in José Martínez Millán, ed., *La corte de Felipe II* (Madrid, 1994). pp. 149–88.

Placer López, P.Fr. Gumersindo, OdeM, 'Biografía del Padre Alonso Remón, clásico español' in *Estudios*, 1 (1945), no. 2, pp. 99–127, & no. 3, pp. 59–90.

—, 'La Virgen de la Merced, patrona de Jerez de la Frontera' in *Boletín de la Orden de la Merced*, 26 (1954), pp. 1–6.

—, 'Bibliografías mercedarias' in *Estudios*, 11 (1955), pp. 303–36.

—, *Fray Serafín de Freitas, mercedario, jurisconsulto portugués: Estudio bio-bibliográfico (1577–1633)* (Madrid, 1956).

—, 'Libros y escritos mercedarios en torno a San Pedro Nolasco' in *Estudios*, 12 (1956), pp. 585–620.

—, 'Manuscritos mercedarios de la Biblioteca Nacional de Madrid' in *Estudios*, 15 (1959), pp. 197–250; 17 (1961), pp. 497–502; 18 (1962), pp. 345–52 & 517–35; & 23 (1967), pp. 271–9.

—, *Bibliografía mercedaria* (3 vols., Madrid, 1968–83).

—, 'Oratoria mercedaria' in *La Orden de la Merced* [=*Estudios*] (Madrid, 1970); pp. 223–72.

—, 'Mercedarios en Valladolid' in *Boletín de la Provincia de Castilla de la Orden de Nuestra Señora de la Merced*, 16 (1978), no. 53, pp. 37–44.

—, 'Bibliografía del maestro Alonso Remón: Siglos XVI–XVII' in *Analecta Mercedaria*, 3 (1984), pp. 109–211.

—, 'Fuentes y bibliografía de la presencia de la Merced en el Nuevo Mundo' in Vázquez Fernández, ed., *Presencia de la Merced en América*, I, pp. 57–66.

Pladevall, Antoni, *Els monestirs Catalans* (Barcelona, 1968).

—, *Història de l'Església a Catalunya* (Barcelona, 1989).

Pons, Guillermo, 'La reforma eclesiástica en Mallorca durante el pontificado de D. Juan Vich y Manrique de Lara (1573–1604)' in *Anthologica Annua*, 16 (1968), pp. 175–325.

Poole, Fr Stafford, SI, *Pedro Moya de Contreras: Catholic Reform and Royal Power in New Spain, 1571–1591* (Berkeley, 1987).

Pou i Marti, P.Fr. José M., OFM, *Archivo de la Embajada de España cerca de la Santa Sede*, vol. II: *Índice analítico de los documentos del siglo XVII* (Rome, 1917); *for* vol. I *see* Dom Luciano Serrano, *Archivo*.

—, 'Fray Bernardo de Fresneda, confesor de Felipe II, obispo de Cuenca y Córdoba y arzobispo de Zaragoza' in *Archivo ibero-americano*, 33 (1930), pp. 582–603.

Puig, Carole, 'La Merci de Perpignan et le rachat des captifs chrétiens au XIIIᵉ siècle' in *Études roussillonnaises*, 14 (1995–6), pp. 31–8.

Pujades, Gerónimo, *Crónica universal del Principado de Cataluña* (8 vols., Barcelona, 1829–32).

—, [Jeroni], *Dietari*, ed. Josep Maria Casas Homs (4 vols., Barcelona, 1975–6).

Raitt, Jill, ed., *Christian Spirituality: High Middle Ages and Reformation* (London, 1987).

Ramos Folqués, Alejandro, *Historia de Elche* (Elche, 1970).

Rapp, Francis, *L'Église et la vie religieuse en Occident a la fin du moyen âge* (Paris, 1971).

—, *Réformes et Réformation à Strasbourg. Église et société dans la diocèse de Strasbourg (1450–1525)* (Paris, 1974).

Rawlings, Helen E., 'The Secularisation of Castilian Episcopal Office Under the Habsburgs, c.1516–1700' in *Journal of Ecclesiastical History*, 38 (1987), pp. 53–79.

Reglà Campistol, Joan, *Felip II i Catalunya* (Barcelona, 1955).

—, *Els segles XVI i XVII* (Barcelona, 1956).

—, *Els virreis de Catalunya* (Barcelona, 1956).

—, *El bandolerisme català del barroc* (Barcelona, 1966). *For* vol. I *see* Fuster i Ortells, *El bandolerisme*.

—, *Estudios sobre los moriscos*, 3rd edn. (Barcelona, 1974).

Reinhard, Wolfgang, 'Reformation, Counter-Reformation and the Early Modern State: A Reassessment' in *Catholic Historical Review*, 75 (1989), pp. 383–405.

Remesal, Fray Antonio de, OP, *Historia General de las Indias Occidentales y Particular de la Gobernación de Chiapa y Guatemala*, ed. P. Carmelo Sáenz de Santa María (2 vols., Madrid, 1964).

Riba y García, Carlos, *El consejo supremo de Aragón en el reinado de Felipe II* (Madrid, 1915).

Ricard, Robert, *The Spiritual Conquest of Mexico*, trans. Lesley Byrd Simpson (Berkeley, 1966).

Rice, Eugene F., 'The Humanist Idea of Christian Antiquity: Lefèvre d'Étaples and his Circle' in *Studies in the Renaissance*, 9 (1962), pp. 126–60.

—, *Saint Jerome in the Renaissance* (Baltimore, 1985).

Riera i Sans, Jaume, 'La doble falsificació de la portadella d'un incunable (Hain 12433)' in *Revista de llibreria antiquària*, 10 (1985), pp. 1–13.

Robinson, Revd. Cuthbert, *Nicolo Ormaneto: A Papal Envoy in the Sixteenth Century* (London, 1920).

Roda Peña, José, 'La Virgen de la Merced: Iconografía escultórica en los conventos sevillanos de Mercedarias' in *Archivo hispalense*, 2a. época, 75 (1993), no. 232, pp. 109–20 + 5 plates.

Rodríguez Carrajo, P.Fr. Manuel, OdeM, 'Ramas femeninas Mercedarias' in *La Orden de la Merced* [=*Estudios*] (Madrid, 1970); pp. 329–56.

—, 'La redención de cautivos. (Aspectos sociológicos)' in *La Orden de la Merced* [=*Estudios*] (Madrid, 1970); pp. 361–400.

Rodríguez Carrajo, P.Fr. Manuel, OdeM, & P.Fr. Bonifacio Porres, OSST, 'Redención de cautivos' in Aldea *et al.*, ed., *Diccionario de Historia Eclesiástica de España*, suppl. I, pp. 625–42.

Rodríguez Cruz, Rvda.M. Águeda María, OP, *Historia de la Universidad de Salamanca* (Salamanca, 1990).

Rodríguez-Moñino Soriano, Rafael, *Razón de Estado y dogmatismo religioso en la España del siglo XVII* (Barcelona, 1976).

Rodríguez-Salgado, M.J., *The Changing Face of Empire: Charles V, Philip II and Habsburg Authority, 1551–1559* (Cambridge, 1988).

—, 'The Court of Philip II of Spain' in Ronald G. Asch & Adolf M. Birke, eds., *Princes, Patronage, and the Nobility: The Court at the Beginning of the Modern Age c.1450–1650* (Oxford, 1991).

Rosenwein, Barbara, & Lester Little, 'Social Meaning in the Monastic and Mendicant Spiritualities' in *Past and Present*, 63 (1974), pp. 4–32.

Rouco Varela, Antonio María, *Staat und Kirche im Spanien des 16. Jahrhunderts* (Münich, 1965).

Rubió, Jordi, 'Carta de privilegis de Juli II als confrares de la Mercè' in *Analecta Sacra Tarraconensia*, 28 (1955), pp. 425–41.

Ruiz Martín, Felipe, 'Demografía religiosa' in Aldea *et al.*, ed., *Diccionario de Historia Eclesiástica de España*, II, pp. 682–733.

Sahlins, Peter, *Boundaries: The Making of France and Spain in the Pyrenees* (Berkeley, 1989).

Saint-Saëns, Alain, *La Nostalgie du désert: L'Ideal érémitique en Castille au Siècle d'Or* (San Francisco, 1993).

—, *Art and Faith in Tridentine Spain (1545–1690)* (New York, 1995).

Sáinz de la Maza Lasoli, Regina, 'Los Mercedarios en la Corona de Aragón durante la segunda mitad del siglo XIV' in *Miscel·lània de textos medievales*, 4 (1988), pp. 221–99.

Sales, Núria, *Els segles de la decadència: Segles XVI–XVIII*, vol. IV (1989) of Pierre Vilar, gral. ed., *Història de Catalunya* (8 vols., Barcelona, 1987–90).

Saló, P. Miguel, *La imagen de Nuestra Señora de la Merced: Algunas noticias acerca de su orígen y belleza artística* (Barcelona, 1881).

Salomon, Nöel, *La Campagne de Nouvelle Castille à la fin du XVI⁰ siècle* (Paris, 1964); Spanish trans., *La vida rural castellana en tiempos de Felipe II* (Barcelona, 1973).

Salrach, Josep M., 'Els orígens de l'Orde de la Mercè i el rescat de captius. Les Croades i l'exercici de la caritat a l'edat mitjana' in *Acta Medievalia*, 9 (1988), pp. 89–101.

Salrach, Josep M., & Eulàlia Duran, *Història dels Països Catalans: Dels orígens a 1714* (2 vols., Barcelona, 1981).

Salvan, Abbé, OSB, *Histoire générale de l'église de Toulouse* (4 vols., Toulouse, 1856–60).

Sánchez, Dolores M., *El deber de consejo en el estado moderno. Las juntas 'ad hoc' en España (1471–1665)* (Madrid, 1993).

Sanchis Guarner, Manuel, ed., *La processó valenciana del Corpus en l'any 1800* (Valencia 1978).

Sancho Blanco, P.Fr. Amerio, OdeM, *Catalogus Documentorum Ordinis Beatae Mariae Virginis de Mercede quae in Archivo Coronae Aragoniae asservatur* (Rome, 1922).

—, 'Los Procuradores Generales de nuestra Celeste, Real y Militar Orden' serialized in *Boletín de la Orden de la Merced*, 16–18 (1928–30).

—, *Provinciales de la Merced de Valencia* (Rome, 1933), and *Boletín de la Orden de la Merced*, 21 (1933), pp. 60–86.

—, *Provinciales de la Merced de Aragón* (Rome, 1933), and *Boletín de la Orden de la Merced*, 21 (1933), pp. 209–66.

Sanlés Martínez, P.Fr. Ricardo, OdeM, 'Trayectoria de la Merced en la conquista de América' in *La Orden de la Merced* [=*Estudios*] (Madrid, 1970); pp. 49–82.

Santos Díez, José Luis, *La encomienda de monasterios en la Corona de Castilla. Siglos X–XV* (Rome, 1961).

—, *Política conciliar postridentina en España. El Concilio provincial de Toledo de 1565: Planteamiento jurídico canónico* (Rome, 1969), and in *Anthologica Annua*, 15 (1967), pp. 309–461.

Sauzet, Robert, *Mendiants et Réformes: Les réguliers mendiants acteurs du changement religieux dans le royaume de France (1480–1560)* (Tours, 1994).

Savage, Roland Burke, *Catherine McAuley: The First Sister of Mercy* (Dublin, 1955).

Schäfer, Ernst, *Beiträge zur Geschichte des spanischen Protestantismus und der Inquisition im 16. Jahrhundert, nach den Original-Akten in Madrid und Simancas* (3 vols., Gütersloh, 1902).

Seguí Cantos, José, 'Poder político, iglesia y cultura en Valencia (1545–1611)' in *Estudis. Revista d'Història Moderna*, 17 (1991), pp. 199–211.

Serrano, Dom Luciano, OSB, *Pío IV y Felipe II: Primeros diez meses de la embajada de Don Luis de Requeséns en Roma* (Rome, 1891).

—, *Archivo de la Embajada de España cerca de la Santa Sede*, vol. I: *Índice analítico de los documentos del siglo XVI* (Rome, 1915); *for* vol. II *see* P.Fr. José M. Pou y Marti, *Archivo*.

—, 'Primeras negociaciones de Felipe II con San Pío V' in *Hispania: Revista española de historia*, 1 (1940), pp. 83–124.

—, 'Un legado pontificio en la corte de Felipe II' in *Hispania: Revista española de historia*, 2 (1942), pp. 64–91.

Serratosa Queralt, P.Fr. Ramón, OdeM, *Santos de la Merced que gozan de culto inmemorial* (Rome, 1912).

—, 'Las misiones entre los Mercedarios' in *Boletín de la Orden de la Merced*, 5 (1917), pp. 97–108, 132–44 & 171–2.

—, 'La leyenda del sacerdocio de San Pedro Nolasco' in *Boletín de la Orden de la Merced*, 14 (1926), pp. 69–73, 101–2, 134–6 & 165–6.

—, 'El P. Maestro Fr. Gabriel Téllez, como religioso' in *Estudios*, 5 (1949), pp. 687–97.

—, 'Las constituciones primitivas de la Merced comparadas con la legislación militar religiosa: Estudio crítico, histórico y canónico' in *Estudios*, 12 (1956), pp. 413–583.

Setton, Kenneth M., *The Papacy and the Levant (1204–1571)* (4 vols., Philadelphia, 1976–84).

Seward, Desmond, *The Monks of War: The Military Religious Orders* (London, 1972).

Shiels, Fr W.E., SI, *King and Church: The Rise and Fall of the Patronato Real* (Chicago, 1961).

Skinner, Quentin, *The Foundations of Modern Political Thought* (2 vols., Cambridge, 1978).

Smith, Hilary Dansey, *Preaching in the Spanish Golden Age: A Study of Some of the Preachers of the Reign of Philip III* (Oxford, 1978).

Soldevila, Ferran, 'Un indici favorable a l'incunable Barceloní de 1468' in *Germinabit: Circular de la Unió Escolania de Montserrat*, 61 (April 1959), pp. 8–9.

—, *Història de Catalunya*, 2nd edn. (Barcelona, 1963).

Soldevila, Ferran, & Ferran Valls i Taberner, *Historia de Cataluña* (Madrid, 1982).

Soriano Triguero, Carmen, 'La reforma de las Clarisas en la Corona de Aragón (ss.XV–XVI)' in *Revista de historia moderna*, 13–14 (1995), pp. 185–98.

Southern, R.W., *Western Society and the Church in the Middle Ages* (Harmondsworth, 1970).

Speiss, Lincoln Bunce, *A Mercedarian Antiphonary*, with notes on painted ornaments by E. Boyd (Santa Fe, NM, 1965).

Steggink, P.Fr. Otger, OCD, *La reforma del Carmelo español: La visita canónica del general Rubeo y su encuentro con Santa Teresa (1566–1567)*, 2nd edn. (Ávila, 1993).

Stinger, Charles L., *Humanism and the Church Fathers: Ambrogio Traversari (1386–1439) and Christian Antiquity in the Italian Renaissance* (Albany, NY, 1977).

Stoichita, Victor I., *Visionary Experience in the Golden Age of Spanish Art* (London, 1995).

Stratton, Suzanne L., *The Immaculate Conception in Spanish Art* (Cambridge, 1994).

Sullivan, Henry W., *Tirso de Molina and the Drama of the Counter-Reformation* (Amsterdam, 1976).

Surtz, Ronald E., *The Guitar of God. Gender, Power, and Authority in the Visionary World of Mother Juana de la Cruz (1481–1534)* (Philadelphia, 1990).

Tarsicio de Azcona, P.Fr., OFMCap, *La elección y reforma del episcopado español en tiempo de los Reyes Católicos* (Madrid, 1960).

—, 'Reforma de religiosas benedictinas y cistercienses de Cataluña en tiempo de los Reyes Católicos' in *Studia Monastica*, 9 (1967), pp. 75–166.

—, 'Paso del monasterio de Santa Clara de Barcelona a la Regla Benedictina (1512–1518)' in *Collectanea Franciscana*, 38 (1968), pp. 68–134.

—, 'Reforma del episcopado y del clero en España en tiempo de los Reyes Católicos y de Carlos V (1475–1558)' in García Villoslada, gral. ed., *Historia de la Iglesia en España*, III(i) (1980), pp. 115–210.

—, 'Reforma de la Tercera Orden Regular de San Francisco en España en tiempos de Felipe II' in *Estudios franciscanos*, 83 (1982), pp. 311–78.

—, *Isabel la Católica: Estudio crítico de su vida y su reinado*, 3rd edn. (Madrid, 1993).

Taylor, Bruce, 'La Orden Mercedaria: Política, sociedad y reforma religiosa bajo Felipe II' in *Actes del Tercer Congrés d'Història Moderna de Catalunya* [=*Pedralbes*] (2 vols., Barcelona, 1993); II, pp. 191–201.

Tellechea Idígoras, José Ignacio, *El Obispo ideal en el siglo de la Reforma* (Rome, 1963).

—, *El arzobispo Carranza y su tiempo* (2 vols., Madrid, 1968).

—, *Tiempos recios: Inquisición y heterodoxias* (Salamanca, 1977).

Téllez, Fray Gabriel, *see* Tirso de Molina.

Teresa of Ávila, *The Complete Works of St Teresa of Jesus*, trans. & ed. Edgar Allison Peers (3 vols, London, 1946).

—, *The Life of Saint Teresa of Ávila by Herself*, trans. J.M. Cohen (Harmondsworth, 1957).

Thompson, Colin P., *The Poet and the Mystic: A Study of the* Cántico espiritual *of San Juan de la Cruz* (Oxford, 1977).

—, *The Strife of Tongues: Fray Luis de León and the Golden Age of Spain* (Cambridge, 1988).

Thompson, I.A.A., *War and Government in Habsburg Spain, 1560–1620* (London, 1976).

Tiron, Dom René, OSB, *Historia y trajes de las órdenes religiosas* (2 vols., Barcelona, 1851).

Tirso de Molina (pseud. of Fray Gabriel Téllez), *Comedias*, ed. Emilio Cotarelo y Mori (2 vols., Madrid, 1906–7).

—, *Los tres maridos burlados*, ed. María Clara Rocchi Barbotta, 2nd edn. (Rome, 1962).

—, *Les trois maris mystifiés (Los tres maridos burlados)*, ed. André Nougué (Paris, 1966).

—, *El monasterio de el Puig y su Virgen*, ed. P.Fr. Juan Devesa Blanco, OdeM (Valencia, 1968).

—, *La Dama del Olivar*, ed. Juan A. Hormigón (Madrid, 1970).

—, *Historia General de la Orden de Nuestra Señora de las Mercedes*, ed. P.Fr. Manuel Penedo Rey, OdeM (2 vols., Madrid, 1973–4).

—, *Cigarrales de Toledo*, ed. P.Fr. Luis Vázquez Fernández, OdeM (Madrid, 1996).

Tirso de Molina: Ensayos sobre la biografía y la obra del Padre Maestro Fray Gabriel Téllez [=*Estudios*, 5] (Madrid, 1949).

Tobar Díez, P.Fr. Félix, OdeM, *Palma de Mallorca: Historia del Convento de Nuestra Señora de la Merced* (Mallorca, 1968).

Tobella, Dom Antoni Maria, OSB, 'La Congregació Claustral Tarraconense i les diverses recapitulacions de les seves Constitucions provincials' in *Catalonia Monastica: Recull de documents i estudis referents a monestirs catalans* (2 vols., Montserrat, 1927–9); II, pp. 111–251.

Torra Pérez, Alberto, 'Los antiguos archivos de los conventos de Trinitarios y Mercedarios de Barcelona' in *Memoria Ecclesiae*, 11 (1997), pp. 337–53.

Torràs i Ribé, Josep Maria, *Els municipis catalans de l'antic règim (1453–1808). (Procediments electorals, organs de poder i grups dominants)* (Barcelona, 1983).

Torres, P.Fr. Laureano, OP, 'Pedro de Salamanca, O.P., reformador de la Merced' in *Estudios*, 38 (1982), pp. 85–96.

Torres i Sans, Xavier, *Els bandolers (s. XVI–XVII)* (Vic, 1991).

Tourón del Pie, P.Fr. Eliseo, OdeM, 'Pintores y escultores que trabajaron para la Merced en el siglo XVII, que figuran en A. Palomino' in *Analecta Mercedaria*, 3 (1984), pp. 61–82.

—, 'Desarrollo histórico de la Merced (siglos XIV–XX)' in *Analecta Mercedaria*, 7 (1988), pp. 69–128.

Traversari, Ambrogio, *Hodoeporicon*, ed. Vittorio Tamburini & Eugenio Garin (Florence, 1985).

Ultee, Maarten, *The Abbey of St Germain des Prés in the Seventeenth Century* (New Haven, 1981).

Vacas Galindo, P.Fr. Enrique, OP, *San Raimundo de Peñafort, fundador de la Orden de la Merced* (Rome, 1919).

Varela, Julia, *Modos de educación en la España de la Contrarreforma* (Madrid, 1983).

Vassberg, David E., *Land and Society in Golden Age Castile* (Cambridge, 1984).

Vázquez Fernández, P.Fr. Antonio, OdeM, 'La formación en las diversas constituciones de la Orden' in *Analecta Mercedaria*, 2 (1983), pp. 317–62.

Vázquez Fernández, P.Fr. Luis, OdeM, 'La Historia de la Merced, de Tirso (1639), y la de los Mercedarios de la Congregación de Paris (1685)' in *Estudios*, 37 (1981), pp. 575–604.

—, 'Mercedarios en las Universidades de Sigüenza y Alcalá (1500–1625)' in *Estudios*, 39 (1983), pp. 605–23.

—, 'Los Pizarros, la Merced, el convento de Trujillo (Cáceres) y Tirso' in *Estudios*, 40 (1984), pp. 203–427.

—, ed., 'Cervantes y la Merced (Documentos)' in *Boletín de la Provincia de Castilla de la Orden de Nuestra Señora de la Merced*, 24 (1986), no. 83, pp. 64–80.

—, 'Apuntes para una nueva biografía de Tirso' in *Tirso de Molina: Vida y Obra. Actas del Primer Simposio Internacional sobre Tirso* [=*Estudios*, 43] (Madrid, 1987); pp. 9–50.

—, ed., 'Dos Mercedarios de Toledo — Fray Domingo Lozano y Fray Blas de Villagarcía — jueces defensores de los derechos de la viuda e hijos de Garcilaso de la Vega (1547)' in *Boletín de la Provincia de Castilla de la Orden de Nuestra Señora de la Merced*, 25 (1987), no. 89, pp. 23–41.

—, 'Encuentros Trinidad-Merced a través de los siglos' in *Analecta Mercedaria*, 7 (1988), pp. 231–94.

—, ed., *Presencia de la Merced en América* [=*Estudios*, 47] (2 vols., Madrid, 1991).

—, 'Cedulario Mercedario en su relación con el Nuevo Mundo: 1518–1599' in *id.*, ed., *Presencia de la Merced en América*, II, pp. 597–659.

—, 'Pintura y escultura del Convento Grande de la Merced de Sevilla en 1730' in *Estudios*, 54 (1998), pp. 191–208.

—, 'Zurbarán: Escultor para la Merced de Azuaga' in *Boletín de la Provincia de Castilla de la Orden de Nuestra Señora de la Merced*, 36 (1998), no. 131, pp. 75–9.

Vázquez Núñez, P.Fr. Guillermo, OdeM, 'Terciarios y cofrades de la Merced' in *Boletín de la Orden de la Merced*, 5 (1917), pp. 66–71.

—, *Don Diego de Muros, Obispo de Tuy y de Ciudad-Rodrigo de la Orden de la Merced (1405?–1492)* (Madrid, 1919).

—, *El Padre Francisco Zumel: General de la Merced y catedrático de Salamanca (1540–1607)* (Madrid, 1920).

—, 'El convento de Mercedarias de Bilbao' in *Boletín de la Orden de la Merced*, 8 (1920), pp. 340–8.

—, 'Los provinciales de la Merced de Castilla' in *Boletín de la Orden de la Merced*, 11 (1923), pp. 111–17, & 12 (1924), pp. 133–8.

—, *La Universidad de Salamanca en los años 1548 a 1568: Biografía del Maestro Fray Gaspar de Torres…*, 2nd edn. (Madrid, 1927); 1st edn. in *Boletín de la Orden de la Merced*, 12 (1924), pp. 228–47, & 13 (1925), pp. 272–80 & 317–35.

—, 'Origen de las misiones mercedarias en el continente americano' in *Boletín de la Orden de la Merced*, 17 (1929), pp. 142–8, 164–71 & 219–23; also in *La Merced en Hispanoamérica*, pp. 63–87.

—, 'Los conventos de Mercedarias de Marquina y Escoriaza' in *Boletín de la Orden de la Merced*, 18 (1930), pp. 12–26.

—, 'Los provinciales de la Merced de Andalucía desde su separación de Castilla en 1588' in *Boletín de la Orden de la Merced*, 18 (1930), pp. 166–71.

—, 'El convento de MM. Mercedarias de la Vera Cruz de Bérriz' in *Boletín de la Orden de la Merced*, 18 (1930), pp. 210–13.

—, *Manual de historia de la Orden de Nuestra Señora de la Merced* (2 vols., Toledo, 1931 & Madrid, 1936; vol. II fragmentary); other fragments of vol. II are collected in *Estudios*, 12 (1956), pp. 79–114, ed. P.Fr. Alfredo Pérez, OdeM.

—, 'La conquista de los indios americanos por los primeros misioneros' in *Boletín de la Orden de la Merced*, 19 (1931), pp. 239–57; also in *La Merced en Hispanoamérica*, pp. 39–62.

—, 'Los grados académicos entre los Mercedarios' in *Boletín de la Orden de la Merced*, 19 (1931), pp. 283–7.

—, *Breve reseña de los conventos de la Orden de la Merced* (Rome, 1932), as 'Conventos de la Orden de la Merced' in *Boletín de la Orden de la Merced*, 20 (1932), pp. 135–72, 289–303 & 353–94, & 21 (1933), pp. 87–96.

—, 'Misiones primitivas de los Mercedarios en Quito y Popayán' in *Boletín de la Orden de la Merced*, 20 (1932), pp. 99–118; also in *id.*, *La Merced en Hispanoamérica*, pp. 115–41.

—, 'La erección de las provincias de América' in *Boletín de la Orden de la Merced*, 21 (1933), pp. 125–36; also in *id.*, *La Merced en Hispanoamérica*, pp. 181–95.

—, 'La antigua liturgia mercedaria' in *Boletín de la Orden de la Merced*, 22 (1934), pp. 12–20.

—, 'Más sobre la erección de las provincias de América' in *Boletín de la Orden de la Merced*, 22 (1934), pp. 162–76; also in *id.*, *La Merced en Hispanoamérica*, pp. 197–216.

—, 'Vida literaria y científica de la Provincia Mercedaria de Castilla' in *Estudios*, 12 (1956), pp. 401–11.

—, *Mercedarios ilustres* [collected articles], ed. P.Fr. Ricardo Sanlés Martínez, OdeM (Madrid, 1966).

—, *La Merced en Hispanoamérica* [collected articles], ed. P.Fr. Ricardo Sanlés Martínez, OdeM (Madrid, 1968).

—, 'Comentando un refrán antiguo: «Los frailes de la Merced son pocos, mas hácenlo bien»' in *Boletín de la Provincia de Castilla de la Orden de Nuestra Señora de la Merced*, 22 (1984), no. 75, pp. 52–6.

Vénard, Marc, *L'Église d'Avignon au XVIème siècle* (5 vols., Lille, 1980).

Verlinden, Charles, *L'Ésclavage dans l'Europe médiévale*, vol. I: *Péninsule ibérique, France* (Bruges, 1955).

Vicens i Vives, Jaume, *Ferran II i la ciutat de Barcelona, 1479–1516* (3 vols., Barcelona, 1936–7).

—, 'The Administrative Structure of the State in the Sixteenth and Seventeenth Centuries' in Henry J. Cohn, ed., *Government in Reformation Europe, 1520–1560* (London, 1971); pp. 58–87.

Vilar, Pierre, *Catalunya dins l'Espanya moderna* (3 vols., Barcelona, 1964).

—, gral. ed., *Història de Catalunya* (8 vols., Barcelona, 1987–90).

Villanueva, Joaquín Lorenzo, *Viage literario a las iglesias de España* (5 vols., Madrid, 1803–6, & Valencia, 1821) [This is in fact the work of Joaquín Lorenzo's brother P.Fr. Jaime Villanueva, OP].

Vizcargüenaga, P.Fr. Ignacio, OSST, 'Los orígenes de la Orden Trinitaria' in *Analecta Mercedaria*, 7 (1988), pp. 9–35.

Vossler, Karl, *Lecciones sobre Tirso de Molina* (Madrid, 1965).

Whitmore, P.J.S., *The Order of Minims in Seventeenth-Century France* (The Hague, 1967).

Wilson, Margaret, *Spanish Drama of the Golden Age* (Oxford, 1989).

—, 'Tirso's Texts, and More on *El condenado por desconfiado*' in *Bulletin of Hispanic Studies*, 70 (1993), pp. 97–104.

Wilson, Stephen, ed., *Saints and their Cults: Studies in Religious Sociology, Folklore and History* (Cambridge, 1983).

Wolf, John B., *The Barbary Coast: Algiers under the Turks, 1500–1830* (New York, 1979).

Wright, A.D., 'The Significance of the Council of Trent' in *Journal of Ecclesiastical History*, 26 (1975), pp. 353–62.

—, *The Counter-Reformation: Catholic Europe and the Non-Christian World* (London, 1982).

—, 'The Religious Life in the Spain of Philip II and Philip III' in W.J. Shiels, ed., *Monks, Hermits and the Ascetic Tradition* [*Studies in Church History*, vol. XXII] (Oxford, 1985); pp. 251–74.

—, 'Church and State in Post-Tridentine Spain' in Margaret A. Rees, ed., *Catholic Tastes and Times: Essays in Honour of Michael E. Williams* (Leeds, 1987); pp. 303–62.

—, *Catholicism and Spanish Society under the Reign of Philip II, 1555–1598, and Philip III, 1598–1621* (Lampeter, 1991).

—, '"A Race to the Altar": Philip Neri and Ignatius Loyola' in *Leeds Papers on Symbol and Image in Iberian Arts* (Leeds, 1994), pp. 151–60.

Wright, L.P., 'The Military Orders in Sixteenth- and Seventeenth-Century Spanish Society: The Institutional Embodiment of a Historical Tradition' in *Past and Present*, 43 (1969), pp. 34–70.

Xamena, Pere, & Francesc Riera, *Història de l'església a Mallorca* (Palma, 1993).

Xandri, Joana, 'Els orígens de l'orde trinitari a Catalunya: El monestir d'Aviganya (Seròs)' in *Actes del Primer Congrés d'Història de l'Església Catalana* (2 vols., Solsona, 1993; also *Analecta Sacra Tarraconensia*, 67, nos. 1–2 (1994)); I, pp. 615–24.

Zakar, Fr Polycarpe, OCist, *Histoire de la stricte observance de l'Ordre Cistercien depuis ses débuts jusqu'au généralat du Cardinal de Richelieu (1606–1635)* (Rome, 1966).

Zaporta Pallarés, P.Fr. Juan [should read 'José'], OdeM, *Religiosos Mercedarios en Panamá (1519–1992), con testimonios históricos de Tirso de Molina* (Madrid, 1996).

Zappala, Michael, 'History and Hagiography in Tirso de Molina's *Historia General de la Orden de Nuestra Señora de las Mercedes*' in *Tirso de Molina: Vida y Obra. Actas del Primer Simposio Internacional sobre Tirso* [=*Estudios*, 43] (Madrid, 1987); pp. 67–77.

Zaragoza Pascual, Dom Ernesto, OSB, *Los generales de la congregación de San Benito de Valladolid* (6 vols., Santo Domingo de Silos, 1973–87).

—, 'Reforma de los Benedictinas de Cataluña en el siglo XVI (1589–1603)' in *Analecta Sacra Tarraconensia*, 49–50 (1976–7), pp. 177–204.

—, 'Documentos inéditos referentes a la reforma monástica de Cataluña durante la segunda mitad del siglo XVI (1555–1600)' in *Studia Monastica*, 19 (1977), pp. 93–203.

—, 'Reforma de los Benedictinas de Cataluña en el siglo XVII (1601–1616)' in *Analecta Sacra Tarraconensia*, 51–2 (1978–9), pp. 171–90.

—, 'Reforma de los Benedictinos y de los Canónigos Regulares en Cataluña: Documentos inéditos (1588–1616)' in *Studia Monastica*, 23 (1981), pp. 71–148.

—, 'Documentos inéditos sobre la visita apostólica de Montserrat (1584–1613)' in *Studia Monastica*, 26 (1984), pp. 91–114.

—, 'Documentos inéditos referentes a la reforma de los Benedictinos catalanes (1573–1596)' in *Analecta Sacra Tarraconensia*, 59 (1986), pp. 105–18.

—, 'Documentos inéditos referentes a la reforma de los Canónigos Regulares y Benedictinos de Aragón, Cataluña, Rosellón y Cerdaña (1581–1618)' in *Studia Monastica*, 31 (1989), pp. 89–147.

Zurbarán [Museo del Prado] (Madrid, 1988).

IV. *Early Printed Books*

Nicolás Antonio, *Biblioteca hispana vetus*, 2nd edn. by Francisco Pérez Bayer (2 vols., Madrid: Ibarra, 1788).

—, *Biblioteca hispana nova*, ed. Tomás Antonio Sánchez, Juan Antonio Pellicer, & Rafael Casalbón (2 vols., Madrid: Ibarra, 1783–8; both vols. in fact 1788).

Fr Jean Bolland, SI, *et al.*, *Acta sanctorum* (60 vols., Antwerp: various printers, 1643–1883).

M° Fray Gerónimo de Bustamante & M° Fray Serafín de Freitas, OdeM, *Discurso contra el progresso y separacion que pretenden los padres Recoletos de la Orden de nuestra señora de la Merced* (?: ?, *c.*1621) [Bod.L., Arch. Seld. A Subt. 21(32)].

Fray Pedro de Cijar (or Citjar, Sitjar), OdeM, *Opusculum tantum quinque editus per frate Petrum Cüarii super conmutatione votorum in redemptionem captiuorum* (Zaragoza: ?, 1491; Barcelona: Pere Posa, 1491, 4°; & Paris: ?, 1506) [BNM, R.2-101585].

M° Fray Felipe Colombo, OdeM, *Vida de Nuestro Gloriosissimo Patriarca y Padre S. Pedro Nolasco…* (Madrid: Imprenta Real, 1674) [BNM, 3-36862].

Fray Francisco Diago, OP, *Historia de la provincia de Aragon de la Orden de Predicadores, desde su origen y principio hasta el año de mil y seyscientos* (Barcelona: Sebastian de Cormellas, 1599).

Bernal Díaz del Castillo, *Historia Verdadera de la Conquista de la Nueva España*, ed. M° Fray Alonso Remón, OdeM (Madrid: Emprenta del Reyno, 1632).

M° Fray Damián Estevan, OdeM, *Symbolo de la Concepción de María sellado en la caridad y Religión Mercedaria* (Madrid: Imprenta del Convento de la Merced, 1728).

P° Fray Juan Falconi, OdeM, *El pan nuestro de cada dia, esto es del SS. Sacramento del Altar…*, 2nd edn. (Madrid: Diego Diaz, 1661, 16°); ed. P.Fr. Elias Gómez Domínguez, OdeM (Madrid, 1961).

M° Fray Serafín de Freitas, OdeM, *Por la Redempcion de cautivos. Sobre que no se deve impedir por la redempcion que llaman preservativa* (?: ?, 1631).

—, *Bullae et Privilegia Sacri ac Regalis Ordinis Redemptorum Beatae Mariae de Mercede* (Madrid: Typographia Regni, 1636).

M° Fray Felipe de Guimerán, OdeM, *Breve historia de la orden de nuestra Señora de la Merced de redempcion de cautivos* (Valencia: Herederos de Juan Navarro, 1591, 4°).

Dom Diego de Haëdo, OSB, *Topographia e historia general de Argel* (Valladolid: Diego Fernandez de Cordova y Oviedo, 1612; 3 vols., Madrid, 1929).

Pierre Hélyot, *Dictionnaire des ordres monastiques, religieux et militaires, et des congregations seculieres* (8 vols., Paris: Nicolas Gosselin, 1714–19).

Histoire de l'ordre sacre, royal et militaire de Notre-Dame de la Mercy, Redemption des Captifs [...] composée par les reverends Péres de la Mercy de la congregation de Paris (Amiens: Guislain Le Bel, 1685).

Frey Jean Latomy, OdeM, *Histoire de la fondation de l'Ordre de Notre Dame de la Mercy* (Paris: Sebastian Huré, 1685, 12°).

M° Fray José Linás, OdeM, *Bullarium Cælestis ac Regalis Ordinis Beatae Mariae Virginis de Mercede Redemptionis Captivorum* (Barcelona: Raphaëlis Figueró, 1696).

M° Fray Pedro Merino, OdeM, *Memorial en defensa de la Redencion de cautivos segun la forma en que oy la exerce el sagrado Orden de nuestra Señora de la Merced* (Madrid: ?, 1627).

M° Fray Francisco de Neyla, OdeM, *Gloriosa Fecundidad de Maria en el Campo de la Catolica Iglesia. Descripcion de las excelencias, e Ilustres hijos del Real Convento de San Lazaro de la Ciudad de Zaragoça del Real, y Militar Orden de nuestra Señora de la Merced Redencion de Cautivos* (Barcelona: Rafael Figueró, 1698, 4°) [BNM, R.2-46374; Biblioteca del Monasterio del Poio].

M° Fray Jerónimo Pérez, OdeM, *Commentaria Expositio [...] super primam partem Summae S. Thomae Aquinatis, quantum ad ea quae concernunt primum librum Sententiarum* (Valencia: Typis Ioannis Mey Flandri, 1548) [BUV, Z-7-59; Biblioteca de la Universidad de Salamanca, 1/21192].

Jerónimo de Quintana, *La muy antigua, noble y coronada villa de Madrid. Historia de su antigüedad, nobleza y grandeza* (Madrid: Imprenta del Reyno, 1629; Madrid, 1954).

M° Fray Alonso Remón, OdeM, *Historia General de la Orden de Nuestra Señora de la Merced, Redempcion de Cautivos* (2 vols., Madrid: Luis Sánchez, 1618–33).

——, *Relacion de como martirizaron los hereges Olandeses, Gelandeses y Pechiligues [...] al religioso y observante varon, el Padre Presentado fray Alonso Gomez de Enzinas...* (?: ?, 1624).

M° Fray Manuel Mariano Ribera, OdeM, *Real Patronato de los Serenissimos Señores Reyes de España en la Real y Militar Orden de Nuestra Señora de la Merced, Redención de cautivos* (Barcelona: Raphaëlis Figueró, 1725).

——, *Centuria Primera de la Real, y Militar Instituto de la ínclita Religión de Nuestra Señora de la Merced Redempción de cautivos Christianos* (Barcelona: Raphaëlis Figueró, 1726).

M° Fray Melchor Rodríguez de Torres, OdeM, *Agricultura del Alma y Exercicios de la Vida Religiosa, con varias cosas para pulpito y espiritu* (Burgos: Juan Baptista Varesio, 1603, 4°) [ACPMC; BNM, R.25024].

M° Fray Marcos Salmerón, OdeM, *Recuerdos Historicos y Politicos de los Servicios que los Generales y Varones Illustres de la Religion de Nuestra Señora de la Merced [...] han hecho a los Reyes de España [...] desde [...] 1218 hasta el año 1640* (Valencia: Herederos de Chrysosthomo Garriz, por Bernardo Nogues, 1646).

Fray Pedro de San Cecilio, OMD, *Annales del Orden de Descalzos de Nuestra Señora de la Merced Redempcion de Cautivos Christianos* (2 vols., Barcelona: Dionisio Hidalgo, 1669; facs. Madrid, 1985).

Fray Pedro de Sitjar, *see* Cijar.

M° Fray Gaspar de Torres, OdeM, *Regula et Constitutiones sacri ordinis beatae Mariae de mercedis redemptionis captivorum* (Salamanca: Mathius Gastius, 1565, 4°) [ACA, XXV-4-17].

M° Fray Bernardo de Vargas, OdeM, *Chronica Sacri et Militaris Ordinis Beatae Mariae de Mercede Redemptionis Captivorum* (2 vols., Palermo: Ioannes Baptista Maringum, 1619–22).

Dom Arnaldus Wion, OSB, *Lignum Vitae, ornamentum, et decus Ecclesiae* (2 vols., Venice: Georgium Angelerium, 1595, 4°).

M° Fray Alonso de Zorita, OdeM, *Speculum fratrum sacri ordinis sancte Maria de mercede redemptionis captivorum* (Valladolid: Nicolás Thierry, 1533, 4°) [ACA, XXVI-4-3, APV, & sections in BNM, R.2364 & R.9651].

M° Fray Francisco Zumel, OdeM, *De Deo, eiusque operibus […] Commentaria in Primam Partem Sancti Thomae Aquinatis* (2 vols., Salamanca: Petrus Lassus, 1585–7).

—, *Regula et Constitutiones Fratrum Sacri Ordinis Beatae Mariae de Mercede Redemptionis Captivorum* (Salamanca: Cornelius Bonardus, 1588, 4°).

—, *De initio ac fundatione sacri Ordinis Beatae Mariae de Mercede Redemptionis Captivorum* (Salamanca: Cornelius Bonardus, 1588, 4°); ed. P.Fr. Guillermo Vázquez Núñez, OdeM (Rome, 1932) & in *Boletín de la Orden de la Merced*, 20 (1932); pp. 57–77.

—, *De Vitis Patrum et Magistrorum Generalium Ordinis Redemptorum Beatae Mariae de Mercede, Brevis Historia* (Salamanca: Cornelius Bonardus, 1588, 4°); ed. P.Fr. Guillermo Vázquez Núñez, OdeM (Rome, 1932) & in *Boletín de la Orden de la Merced*, 20 (1932), pp. 178–201, 21 (1933), pp. 321–40, & 22 (1934), pp. 21–39.

—, *In Primam Secundae Sancti Thomae Commentaria* (2 vols., Salamanca: Joannes Ferdinandus, 1593–4).

INDEX

Abbreviations

abp — archbishop; amb. — ambassador; bp — bishop;
ch — chapter; gral — general; hse — house; M. — Mercedarian;
monas. — monastery; nun. — nuncio; prov. — province; provl — provincial;
O. — [Mercedarian] Order; ref. — reform;
Ref. — [Mercedarian] Reform

For other abbreviations, see xviii

All religious are Calced Mercedarians unless otherwise stated.
The dates of Mercedarian and Discalced foundations are given in brackets as
appropriate.

CULTURES, BELIEFS AND TRADITIONS

MEDIEVAL AND EARLY MODERN PEOPLES

Cultures, Beliefs and Traditions *is a forum for an interdisciplinary sharing of insights into past popular experience in the European and European-related world, from late antiquity to the modern era. The series covers studies in a wide range of phenomena, among them popular rituals and religion, art, music, material culture and domestic space, and it favors a variety of approaches: historical anthropology, folklore and gender studies, art- and literary analysis, and integrative approaches employing a combination of disciplines. It contains monographs, text editions (with translation and commentary), collections of essays on defined themes, acta of conferences and works of reference.*

1. HEN, Y. *Culture and Religion in Merovingian Gaul*, A.D. *481-751*. 1995. ISBN 90 04 10347 3
2. MEGGED, A. *Exporting the Catholic Reformation*. Local Religion in Early-Colonial Mexico. 1996. ISBN 90 04 10400 3
3. SLUHOVSKY, M. *Patroness of Paris*. Rituals of Devotion in Early Modern France. 1998. ISBN 90 04 10851 3
4. ZIOLKOWSKI, J.M. *Obscenity*. Social Control and Artistic Creation in the European Middle Ages. 1998. ISBN 90 04 10928 5
5. POSKA, A.M. *Regulating the People*. The Catholic Reformation in Seventeenth-Century Spain. 1998. ISBN 90 04 11036 4
6. FERREIRO, A. (ed.). *The Devil, Heresy and Witchcraft in the Middle Ages*. Essays in Honor of Jeffrey B. Russell. 1998. ISBN 90 04 10610 3
7. SÖRLIN, P. *'Wicked Arts'*. Witchcraft and Magic Trials in Southern Sweden, 1635-1754. 1999. ISBN 90 04 11183 2
8. MITCHELL, K. & I. WOOD (eds.). *The World of Gregory of Tours*. 2001. ISBN 90 04 11034 8
9. FRIEDLANDER, A. *The Hammer of the Inquisitors*. Brother Bernard Délicieux and the Struggle Against the Inquisition in Fourteenth-Century France. 2000. ISBN 90 04 11519 6

ISSN 1382-5364